MAN COMPUTER INTERACTION:
HUMAN FACTORS ASPECTS OF COMPUTERS & PEOPLE

NATO ADVANCED STUDY INSTITUTES SERIES

Proceedings of the Advanced Study Institute Programme, which aims at the dissemination of advanced knowledge and the formation of contacts among scientists from different countries.

The series is published by an international board of publishers in conjunction with NATO Scientific Affairs Division

A	Life Sciences	Plenum Publishing Corporation
B	Physics	London and New York
C	Mathematical and	D. Reidel Publishing Company
	Physical Sciences	Dordrecht and Boston
D	Behavioural and	Sijthoff & Noordhoff International
	Social Sciences	Publishers B.V.
E	Applied Sciences	Alphen aan den Rijn, The Netherlands and
		Rockville, Md., U.S.A.

Series E: Applied Sciences — No. 44

MAN-COMPUTER INTERACTION: HUMAN FACTORS ASPECTS OF COMPUTERS & PEOPLE

edited by

B. SHACKEL

Professor, Head of the Department
of Human Sciences
University of Technology
Loughborough, U.K.

SIJTHOFF & NOORDHOFF   1981
Alphen aan den Rijn, The Netherlands
Rockville, Maryland, U.S.A.

Proceedings of the NATO Advanced Study Institute on
Man-computer interaction
Mati, Greece
September 5-18, 1976

ISBN-13: 978-94-011-7588-3   e-ISBN-13: 978-94-011-7586-9
DOI: 10.1007/ 978-94-011-7586-9

PREFACE

The aim of this book is to bring together and try to inter-relate some of the concepts and relevant knowledge from the various disciplines concerned with this area of research and application, including especially the human sciences, computer sciences and engineering. The focus throughout is upon the human rather than upon the computer issues in Man-Computer Interaction (MCI).

The book is based upon the papers presented by invited speakers at an Advanced Study Institute held at Mati, Attica, Greece 5-18 September 1976, which was sponsored by the NATO Advanced Study Institutes Programme. These papers were not intended to be ency-clopaedic or to yield a 'state of the art' volume. But as revised here they do represent well the scope and breadth of MCI ('man' is used throughout generically for men, women, humans, people).

The material in this book is as timely today as when presen-ted in lectures; it is not out of date. Indeed in many respects it is more timely, because the computer industry is now recognising the need to heed the users. Computer designers are becoming receptive to the importance of the human factors aspects.

Recognition of the user's needs has been stimulated by the work, elsewhere as well as here, of the contributors to this book. I am very grateful to the contributors for their tolerance of the interchanges and delays inherent in editing and revision, including delays due to my illness, and I wish to thank them for their fore-bearance and above all for the quality of their contributions.

It should be noted that two of the papers, those by Palme and Bair (in Parts 4 and 6), have been prepared, revised and printed out directly for publication, using word processing computers. Had this facility, combined with computer teleconferencing, been available to the editor and all contributors, perhaps the editing and publication might have been quicker.

The papers presented here have been written and revised by the contributors to relate broadly to the general theme. While they form very much more than a pot-pourri of conference papers, they should not be viewed as the closely integrated chapters of a comprehensive review or prescriptive textbook. It is believed that they are more stimulating than the former and less didactic than the latter. They have been grouped together into nine parts, as indicated in the list of contents, with a Preview to introduce the main themes for each part and with a brief Epilogue at the end of Part 9.

This book will serve its purpose even more fully if it helps not only to structure and stimulate this field of research and application but also to increase the interaction between readers and writers. Many more papers were given at the meeting than are published here. The full list of topics and papers is given in the programme (Appendix 3), and the addresses of all participants at the Institute are given in Appendix 2. The addresses of all the contributors to this book are given in Appendix 1. The intensity of involvement of all at the meeting was such that probably any participant would welcome communications from any reader.

I wish to express my thanks for all their help to the members of the Advisory Committee for the Institute: Prof. Dr.Ing. R. Bernotat, Prof. A. Chapanis, the late Dr. C.R. Evans, Dr. H. Sackman, Mr. M. Sime and Mr. T.F.M. Stewart (also Secretary for the Institute). Similarly, I wish to thank NATO for continued support both after postponement of the meeting from Portugal 1975 and through to this publication; thanks are also due to Saab-Scania (Sweden), National Computing Centre (UK) and I.B.M. (UK) for financial support to the Institute. Acknowledgements are made to Taylor & Francis Ltd. and to the British Psychological Society for permission to copy certain illustrations.

Finally, I would like to thank my wife Penni for her fore-bearance of all the many hours 'lost', and for her support through illness and much else; to thank my secretary Mrs. Jeanne Preston, who has typed all the camera-ready copy, for her support through these years; and to acknowledge the stimulus of the HUSAT (Human Sciences and Advanced Technology) Research Group at Loughborough, which reaches its 10th anniversary in 1980 and without which the Institute would not have been held and this book written.

B. Shackel

CONTENTS

VIII

X

LIST OF CONTRIBUTORS

PART 1 — INTRODUCTION

PREVIEW

After noting the aims of NATO Advanced Study Institutes, Shackel outlines the scope and coverage of the Advanced Study Institute from which this book is derived.

The present status of MCI is reviewed, the characteristics of various possible human input and output channels are noted, and the progress of engineering development of devices to match these channels is summarised. A framework is then offered to link together the major factors which are comprised within this field of study and development.

Finally, using this framework he draws attention, under each heading, to some problems and major issues which may need considerable attention as MCI develops.

MAN-COMPUTER INTERACTION (MCI) - REALITY AND PROBLEMS

B. Shackel

Department of Human Sciences,
University of Technology, Loughborough, U.K.

1. INTRODUCTION

1.1 Advanced Study Institutes

The purpose of the NATO Advanced Study Institutes Programme is to contribute to the dissemination of advanced knowledge and the formation of contacts among scientists from different countries. At this Institute there are participants from a total of 15 different nations.

An Advanced Study Institute is primarily a high level teaching activity at which a carefully defined subject is presented in a systematic and coherently structured programme. The subject is treated in considerable depth by lecturers eminent in their field and normally of international standing; the subject is presented to other scientists who will already have specialised in the field or possess an advanced general background. The Advanced Study Institute is aimed at an audience of approximately postdoctoral level; this does not necessarily exclude postgraduate students, and it may well include senior scientists of high qualifications and notable achievement in the subject of the institute or in related fields.

1.2 This ASI on MCI

The above guidelines from the NATO scheme envisage a specialised and interactive learning situation, and this institute should achieve that aim. Relevant work over the last five years and more has been done by computer scientists, industrial engineers and those in several other disciplines as well as in ergonomics, psychology and human factors. Therefore, in the tutorial sessions, the contributions from the widespread experience of all participants should assist in the teaching of us all, students and lecturers alike.

So the aim of this Advanced Study Institute is (1) to survey and teach what is known about the human side of Man-Computer Interaction, and (2) to try to integrate the relevant knowledge, for this area of research and application, from the variety of disciplines concerned including especially the human sciences, computer science and engineering. The focus throughout will be the human rather than the computer issues in MCI.

2. SCOPE AND COVERAGE OF ASI

2.1 Definition of MCI

Man-computer interaction is now generally accepted (cf. Shackel, 1969) to refer to direct, close-coupled, computer usage by users with a job to do, whether their primary work is in computing (eg. writing new application programs or designing program systems) or is in a non-computing sphere (eg. banking or piloting). The phrase is not generally used (pace Shackel, 1969) to include the work of those in computer centres providing a service.

2.2 Exclusions

Therefore, the problems of computer centres will not in general be considered. As Smith (1974) has stated, the ergonomics (human factors) issues are generally of a routine nature for such "large computer installations which provide explicit data processing services to a body of customers, in somewhat the same way as a power-generating plant provides electricity. Human factors involved in the design and use of a large computer facility are much the same as for any other large-scale production operation. The aim is to maximize throughput by optimal arrangement of work space layout, equipment design and job scheduling. Overall arrangement of the work space should take into account the import-ance, frequency and sequence of use of the different equipment components, and the physical and communication links among them (Galitz & Laska, 1970). Design of specific equipments at an operator's work station should follow good human engineering practice, just as for other production equipment, based on analysis of operator job functions (Shackel, 1962)."

Similarly, the routine ergonomics issues concerned with the physical environment (eg. lighting, noise, etc.) will not be considered at length, although Prof. O. Ostberg may well refer to them in his lecture on the hardware interface (cf. also Hultgren & Knave, 1974a, b). These and related matters of good ergonomics design (for equipment and workspace, as well as for environment) have been dealt with in a number of publications (eg. Shackel 1974, Stewart 1974, 1976).

2.3 Scope and Contents

The scope as originally proposed to NATO for this ASI is given in Table 1. As is evident from the programme, no themes have been omitted and most remain unchanged. The coverage of the hardware interface has been diminished, partly because two lecturers could not come, and partly because the subject is very detailed and has been treated in several literature reviews (eg. Alden et al. 1972, Shackel & Shipley 1970, Stewart 1974, and other references quoted therein). The coverage of the software interface has also diminished, partly because less research has been done than expected and partly because Dr. Lance Miller from IBM unfortunately had to withdraw two weeks before the Institute.

It was decided from the start not to make a large time allocation for Computer Aided Design (CAD) or Computer Assisted Learning (CAL), because these are already substantive specific applications. However, it is very pleasing that Prof. J. Annett is now well enough to come for half the meeting and give a review lecture on the current position of CAL. Likewise CAD issues will be drawn to our attention through the participation in the ASI of Dr. R. Spence.

It should be emphasized that the coverage noted for the themes in Table 1 is that proposed to the lecturers as a first basis for their planning; there will of course be some changes in scope and content for the various sessions. Also, it will be evident from the programme that there are some minor changes in sequence. However, taken as a whole I am very pleased to be able to show how close we are to the original plan and especially to be able to welcome nearly all of the lecturers originally proposed.

TABLE 1. SCOPE PROPOSED FOR ASI ON MCI

1. MCI - REALITY AND PROBLEMS
- Introductory session overviewing current status of MCI.
- Examination of why computers are not living up to early expectations.
- Problem of evaluating computer systems.
- Identification of pressing problem àreas, ie. hardware and software interface, matching different types of user, training and supporting the user.

2. THE HARDWARE INTERFACE
2.1 Display Aspects
- Review of human factors and ergonomics knowledge relevant to the display of data and information.
- Evaluation of existing computer display devices and display media in ergonomic terms.
- Assessment of new display technology (eg. plasma, liquid crystal) in ergonomic terms.
- Different types of display possibilities, auditory, tactile etc.
- The future of computer displays.

2.2 Control Aspects
- Review of human factors and ergonomics knowledge relevant to computer controls and input devices.
- Keyboards - optimum layout for alphanumeric keyboards, sequential vs. chord etc.
- Programmed function keyboards and touchwires.
- Special devices - joystick, trackerball, mouse.

3. THE SOFTWARE INTERFACE
3.1 Programming Languages
- The design of languages, computer oriented or user oriented?
- Powerful languages for experts.
- Simple languages for everyone.

3.2 Linguistic Systems
- Artificial intelligence.
- Natural language processors.

3.3 Information Organisation
- Structure of information, eg. tree structures, linear chains.
- Symbolic presentation of complex information.

3.4 Typography and Layout
- Software controlled typography and character generation for VDUs.
- Formats, tables vs. graphs etc.

4. INTERACTION WITH SPECIALIST USERS
   - Identification of the specialist user - engineer, designer, etc.
   - Discussion of different specialists tasks, eg. stress analysis, circuit design, financial modelling.
   - Problems in particular types of systems, eg. graphics, simulations, etc.
   - Effects of computer aid on problem solving.

5. INTERACTION WITH BUSINESS USERS
   - Distinction of clerical and managerial business users.
   - Clerical user needs and problems, job design etc.
   - Managerial user needs and problems, MIS etc.
   - Supporting and developing the business user.

6. INTERACTION WITH NAIVE USERS
   - Natural language interaction - necessary or ideal?
   - Making the computer fit the user or vice versa?

7. INTERACTION IN PUBLIC SYSTEMS
   - Special problems in public systems.
   - Who is the user - customer, clerk or company?
   - Human interfaces between customer (public) and computer.

8. EVALUATING MAN-COMPUTER SYSTEMS
   - Problems of selecting criteria - man oriented rather than computer oriented.
   - cost effectiveness versus social implications.
   - long term versus short term evaluation.

9. TRAINING THE USER
   - Different training needs for different types of user (eg. programmers; specialist, business and naive users; the public)
   - Within-system training aids, programmed instruction, etc.
   - Training courses, manuals etc.
   - Supporting and developing the user.

10. MODELLING THE USER
   - What to model? response delays, errors, times.
   - Theoretical mathematical models.
   - Software monitors and user logs.

11. MAN-COMPUTER SYMBIOSIS - REALITY AND CHALLENGE
   - Summing up of current situation.
   - Areas for exploration eg. how to design systems to suit users.
   - Challenge for the future.

3.   MAN-COMPUTER INTERACTION - PRESENT STATUS

3.1 The Background of Past Myths

The first flush of enthusiasm for computers has now passed.
Careful appraisal and hard economic facts are the dominant factors.
No doubt this healthy realism partly arose from the surveys in
U.S.A. and Britain (Rowley 1969) reporting that about 70% of
computer installations were sub-optimum and barely cost-effective.
No doubt, equally, some realistic installation proposals and worth-
while research studies have been rejected because of the backlash
from the 'over-selling' which has occurred.

We are, I suggest, moving into a third generation of computer
selling themes, each successively promoting an untested scheme when
evaluation of the previous 'line' revealed a poor cost-benefit
performance for many installations.   The first was the data-
processing system to replace clerks;   this gave a big sales bonanza
until business and local government learned the hard way that there
were few clerks less in the end and therefore cost-effectiveness was
poor (in Britain this lesson appears still to be being learned with
the centralised Vehicle and Driving Licence Centre in Swansea).
So the sales 'pitch' moved to Management Information Systems (M.I.S.);
the big system with a total database management system was supposed
to yield a big bonus - until managers found they were buried in
paper but starved of information (cf. Eason et al. 1974).   So now
'computer communications' and 'conferencing' and 'reactive systems'
and 'MCI' are the new 'buzz words', along with 'smart' or 'intelligent'
terminals and much lip-service to the need to consult the user.

Lest this appears too critical and cynical, let me say that
of course quite a number of systems and installations do work well
(again cf. Eason et al. 1974).   But the successes are now recognised by some computer specialists and some parts of the industry
to be too few, and the failures too serious.   For example in the
weekly paper Computing, O'Leary (1976) quotes from a Wall Street
Journal "the computer is a machine that permits business to convert
the old-fashioned clerical error into a modern corporate disaster"
and "MIS is a system concept put forward as the major thrust of
a joint conspiracy of dp professionals and consultants, formulated
and used to increase their own salaries, to confuse what would
otherwise be a record of minimal accomplishment, and to retain
their position in the organisation by using the MIS effort as a
means of retaining their staff until the next generation of computers
is released."

3.2   Current Equipment to Subserve Interaction

The limitations of interface equipment are similarly now
beginning to be recognised.   A special Delphi study was commissioned
by the AFIPS Social Implications Committee to identify the important
issues in multi-national computer systems.   Nanus et al. (1973)
assembled an outstanding Delphi panel of 57 corporate officers,
Government officials and computer experts.   Concerning equipment,
97% of the panel agreed that "it would be necessary to provide
improvements in portable, on-line and inexpensive terminals as well
as smarter and more flexible terminals."   Further, "many (92%)
focussed upon the man-machine interface, suggesting that improvements
were needed in interface support facilities;   in cheap, high-speed
hard-copy printers with unlimited character sets;   and in more
sophisticated man-machine interaction possibilities."

In the last three years there have been some improvements in
new equipment, for example quieter teletype and similar printers,
cheaper video display units with better editing facilities, a new
hand-held terminal, and an approach to a practical voice input unit.
But in essence we are still very little advanced from the situation
which I first pointed out in 1968, see Table 2, that MCI consists
of two sophisticated computers with very limited communication links
between them (Shackel & Hersch, 1968).

3.3   Possibilities and Current State of Development

By contrast, consider the flexibility of the potential
communication links with the human, as indicated by the range and
the data rates of some man-computer communication modes shown in
Table 3.   Few of these and of the whole range of possibilities
are at present used even for special systems.   However, quite a
number of them are now being explored in research projects, and
in some cases prototype equipment is being tested.   As would be
expected, much of the research is supported from military funds,
but in some cases the stimulus is not military but toward the
rehabilitation of the disabled.   The present position in the
development of better communication links is summarised in Table 4.

3.4   Progress in Related Human Sciences Research

Having noted the relatively slow progress in hardware development, it may be instructive to review progress in related human
sciences research.   At a previous conference some particular
problems in MCI were suggested to merit immediate attention and
major research;   the six listed in Table 5 were proposed to be of
primary importance (Shackel, 1969).

TABLE 2.   TWO SOPHISTICATED COMPUTERS WITH LIMITED COMMUNICATION

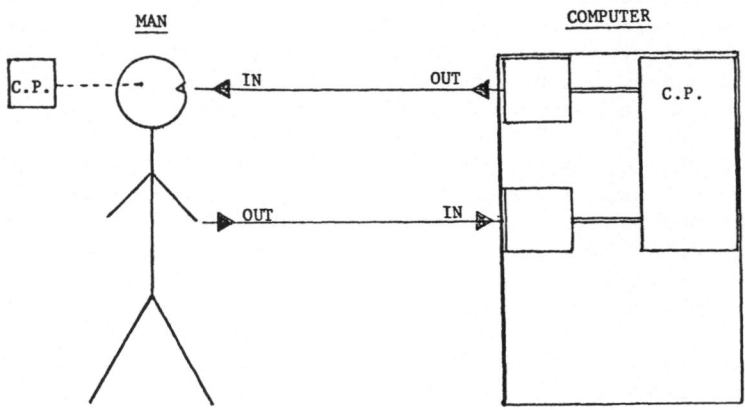

Central Processor

Storage   – about 10^8 to 10^{12} 'chunks'
           – associative
           – errors of detail

Slow – about 5 to 50 bits/sec

Much preprocessing, eg. 10^8 eye receptors into 10^6 optic nerves

Adaptive and Heuristic

Self-reprogrammable

Input

Multi-channel

Very flexible

Slow

Wide dynamic range eg. in intensity 10^6 to 10^9

Output

Multi-channel

Multi-axis

Slow

Very flexible

Central Processor

Storage – about 10^6 to 10^{10} bits
        – literal
        – depends on file structure

Very fast – up to 10^8 bits/sec

Accurate and excellent calculator

Depends upon skill of system designers and programmers

Output

Only visual at present

Limited speech mode is developing

Can be fast

Input

Only manual at present

Limited hearing mode is developing

Engineering constraints limit flexibility

TABLE 3.   SOME POSSIBLE MODES AND DATA RATES FOR MAN-COMPUTER COMMUNICATION
(FROM TURN 1974)

Communication Mode	Rate (Words/sec.)	Remarks
Oral reading (2)		
Random words	2.1 – 2.8	Selected from 5000 word dictionary
Random Words	3.0 – 3.8	Selected from 2500 most familiar monosyllable words
Nontechnical prose	3.9 – 4.8	
Repeating the same word	8.0 4.0	One syllable Two syllables
Silent reading	2.5 – 9.8	
Spontaneous speaking	2.0 – 3.6	
Handwriting (1)	.38 – .42	
Handprinting (1)	.22 – .53	
Typing (3)		
Skilled	1.6 – 2.5	Text (100 wpm – 150 wpm)
Inexperienced	.2 – .4	
Stenotype (chord typewriter) (4)	3.3 – 5	Typically 1/3 of the strokes of the typewriter
Operating touch-tone telephone (1)	1.2 – 1.5	10 buttons
Operating thumb-wheel input device	1.8 digits/sec.	Sequence of 10 digits (5)
Rotary dialing	1.54 digits/sec.	Sequence of 10 digits (5)

REFERENCES

1.   Newell et al. 1971
2.   Pierce & Karlin 1957
3.   Hershman & Hillix 1965
4.   Seibel 1964
5.   Deininger 1967

12

TABLE 4. SUMMARY OF PRESENT POSITION IN THE DEVELOPMENT OF MAN-COMPUTER
COMMUNICATION LINKS

MAN INPUT-OUTPUT CHANNELS   COMPUTER OUTPUT-INPUT DEVICES

Input   Output

Eyes   Visual displays   - several basic types
                                                          exist (with many different
                                                          manufactured versions)

Ears   Aural displays   - research prototypes and
                                                          some production versions

Nose   ?   - doubtful use except
                                                          for fault detection?

Skin   Tactile displays   - research on aids for
                                                          the blind

Output   Input

Hands   Manual controls   - many types exist

Arms   Arm controls   - (several types exist but
                                                          (only in vehicle systems
                                                          (or vehicle simulators
                                                          ((eg. steering wheels,
Legs   Leg controls   - (pedals, joysticks)

Voice   Vocal controls   - research prototypes and
                                                          recently some production
                                                          versions with vocabulary
                                                          about 10 to 70 words

Head   Head controls   - research (some prototypes
                                                          and a few military versions

Eyes   Eye position or   - research (mainly for
                                   movement controls   military)

Muscle potentials   Bioelectric controls - research on direct electro-
                                                          physiological control of
                                                          prostheses and also on
                                                          direct brain electric
                                                          signal control of external
                                                          units

TABLE 5. SIX PROBLEMS PROPOSED TO MERIT IMMEDIATE HUMAN SCIENCES RESEARCH

(FROM SHACKEL, 1969 - Conclusions)

1. The development, and especially the evaluation, of programming
    languages.

2. The evaluation of system characteristics, particularly response time,
    in their effects upon human performance.

3. The ergonomics aspects of a whole range of possibilities for new
    communication methods at the hardware interface.

4. The software interface, which does not appear to have been specifically
    recognised as an area needing study.

5. The characteristics of human problem-solving in a close-coupled
    man-computer situation.

6. The problem involved in identifying the needs of the human user
    (particularly managers in management information systems, designers
    in computer aided design, and teachers and students in computer aided
    instruction), so as to ensure that the systems analysis and programming
    work is based upon the best studies of human needs which can be achieved.

For the first, programming languages, some work has been done
by Dr. M. Sime's group, as we shall learn from his lecture, and
some at IBM (Dr. L.A. Miller and Dr. J.D. Gould). More work has
been done on programming as such (eg. Weinberg, 1971; Boies &
Gould, 1974; Gould, 1974; Weinberg & Schulman, 1974). The main
results show that individual differences in programming skill
largely obscure other factors, and that much more research may be
needed; however there are some specific findings relevant to
particular aspects of programming.

The second, evaluation, is of especial importance, but still
little has been done that I have been able to find specifically
related to man-computer interaction or computer usage. What is
needed is an extensive piece of developmental research to produce
an evaluative tool, such as the Analytic Profile System for evaluating visual displays recently developed by Siegel et al. (1975).
Methods for evaluating ergonomics aspects of systems have been
developed and known for some time (cf. Meister & Rabideau, 1965)
but I suspect that more research is needed to develop a procedure
specifically for man-computer evaluation.

The third concerns the routine ergonomics of new hardware designs.   There have been some gradual improvements over the last seven years;   teletype noise has been reduced, new silent printers have become available, legibility on VDU screens has been improved, etc.   However this is a continuing need whenever new equipment is developed, and manufacturers need to obtain ergonomics advice as a matter of routine design practice.

The fourth area, the software interface, has now been recognised as an area needing study (eg. Stewart, 1976), but needs much more attention and research if we are to give prescriptive advice to designers.

The next, the characteristics of human problem solving in a close-coupled man-computer situation was identified as a particularly important subject and has been recognised as such by several researchers.   In particular, the contribution of Dr. H. Sackman has been especially significant during the last seven years (Sackman, 1970), and in his lecture he will be outlining the framework of an approach to a general theory of man-computer problem solving.

The last, identifying the needs of the human user, also has received some attention in recent years.   The lectures dealing with various specific applications at this Institute are clear evidence and will show how this need is being met.   However, this area must require continued attention because new needs and new applications will continually be identified.

Thus it would appear that there has at least been some real progress in some of the human sciences research areas related to MCI.   But equally it is clear that the amount of work has been limited and the focus specific to particular aspects.

3.5 Why the Slow Progress

It is rather disappointing to see how little has happened relatively over the intervening 15 years since Licklider's (1960) original paper entitled 'Man-Computer Symbiosis'.   The reality falls very far short of the inspired dream and challenging forecast.

Why has this happened?   Some of the reasons, I believe, are to be found in a number of the problems discussed in Section 5. The other main reason, I suggest, is to be found in the nature and responsibilities of the computer system designer.   Computer designers are primarily, and quite rightly, concerned to improve the performance of the computer hardware and software;   they often forget that what matters most is the efficiency and performance of the total man-computer system, of which their computer is only a

part.   Efficient performance can only result from proper attention
to the liveware needs and problems as well as to the hardware and
software aspects.   But the complexity and sophistication of modern
computer technology often results in the designer being so busy with
his own technical problems that he has too little time, and often
too little knowledge, to deal with the human problems adequately.
Moreover, the computer boom was so rapid and strong that the training of computer system designers could not, and still usually does
not include ergonomics/human factors.   Unless these human factors
problems are foreseen in the design stage then a sub-optimum system
is the inevitable result.

It is hoped that the comprehensive overview of the field,
which is the aim of this Institute, will enable all participants to
perceive the whole range of reasons which have inhibited the
development of man-computer interaction.   Likewise, it is hoped
that the integrated approach to the whole field will provide a firm
foundation for future studies, so that the progress may be more rapid
than in the past.

4.   THE STRUCTURE AND FUNCTIONING OF MCI

4.1   Structure

The simple structure of MCI is represented by the synoptic
view in Table 6.   The framework is simple but the contents are
complex.   This synopsis may help to link together the many diverse
topics which will be discussed during the course of the Institute.

4.2   Factors and Functioning

The framework is elaborated to a first level of detail in
Table 7.   The framework of this table can embrace all the topics
planned for the various sessions.   Although set down separately in
the table, in fact of course all the factors within the environment
capsule will interact together in any particular MCI situation.
Therefore, although these factors are listed and discussed separately,
we must always remember the interactions between them also which
together make up the whole.

16

TABLE 6. A synoptic view of Man-Computer Interaction

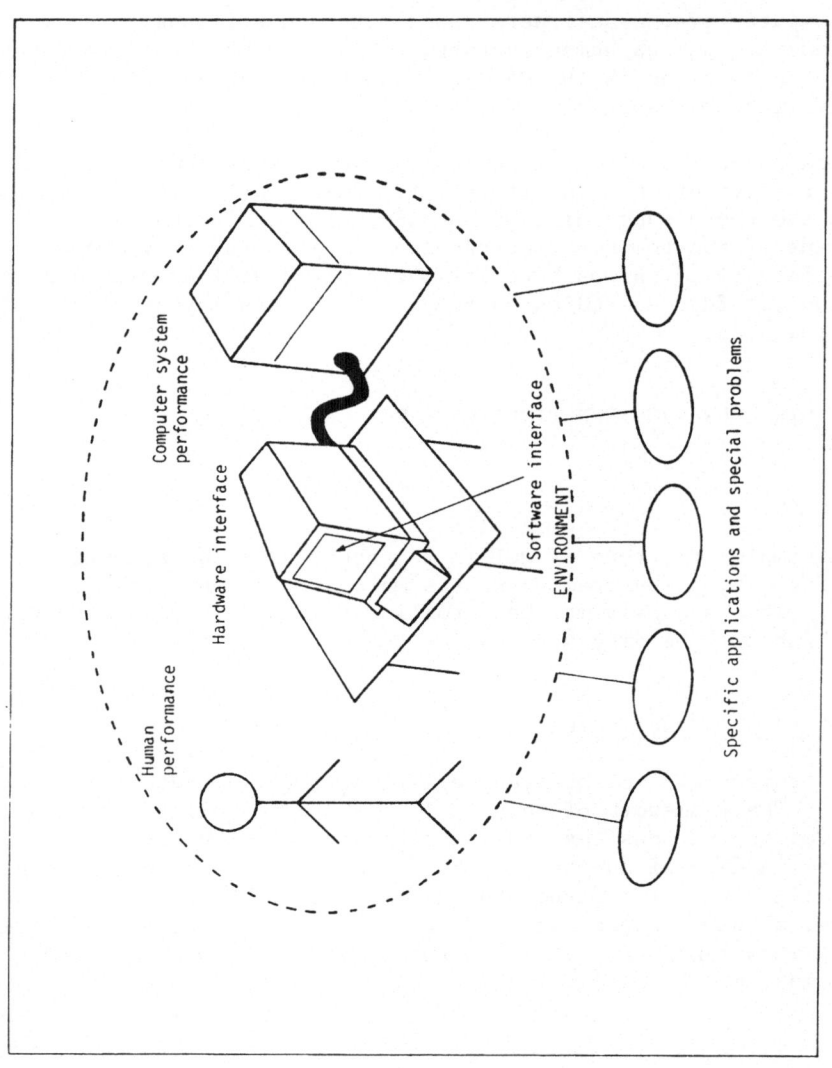

TABLE 7. MAJOR FACTORS IN MAN-COMPUTER INTERACTION

1. Human Performance

    Basic characteristics & limitations eg. size, speed, skills, errors, flexibility etc.

    Special aspects eg. selection   eg. modelling the user
                   training   decision-making
                   user support   problem-solving

2. Computer System Performance

    Basic characteristics & limitations eg. capacity, speed, reliability

    Special aspects for MCI eg. language facilities
                             system response time
                             security

3. Hardware Interface

    Displays, Controls, Terminals and Consoles

    Applied ergonomics for good workstation design

    Human needs and new devices

4. Software Interface

    The non-hardware communication media

    Languages and linguistic systems (MCI aspects)

    Information organisation
    eg. message structure & verbosity, display format & layout
    (including eg. microfilm output, questionnaire & other input forms)

    Human needs and new approaches

5. Environment

    Physical: workstation space & layout, lighting, noise, etc.

    Psychological: influence (eg. via motivation, strain, etc.) of the working group, of the job structure (eg. shift working), of the system structure (eg. open/closed, rigid/flexible, etc.), of the social climate & of the organisation design

    Applied ergonomics and social science for good environment design

6. Specific Applications

    Specialist users   Computer Assisted Learning
    Business users   Computer Aided Design
    Naive users   Man-computer telecommunications
    Public systems   Computer conferencing

7. Special Problems

    Evaluation - especially criteria and methods
             - especially social implications versus cash costs
             - importance of real world studies (not in lab. only)

    Privacy of personal information

    Ergonomics of programming and the job of the programmer

    Documentation and related job aids

    Influence of MCI upon job design and organisation design

    Influence of MCI upon society

5.   SOME PROBLEMS AND SUGGESTIONS

5.1 Introduction

    Using the structure provided by Table 7, as a convenient frame-
work, some problems and suggestions will now be discussed.   It is
hoped that this section will help to stimulate discussion upon some
topics which might otherwise be overlooked, will draw attention to
some major gaps for which research is needed, and will give added
emphasis to some of the major issues which will be discussed during
the Institute.

5.2 Human Performance

    Memory.   One of many important issues about human performance
in relation to MCI is memory.   How does it function and what are
its necessary cues in relation to the longer term storage and
retrieval of reference material?   What is meant here is not the
esoteric psychological research on memory nor the specialised
computer programming work on filing structures nor the librarian/
information specialist's approach, although probably some proportion
of their understanding may help towards the answer.   I mean the
basic fact that, if you go into the offices of many people (like
mine), you will find various piles of papers, reports and so on;
but it is a constructive clutter, a creative chaos (at least I like
to think so).   Ask the user of the office for something borrowed
from you three months ago, and he will say 'Oh yes, its that yellow
paper with the peculiar arrow symbol on the top, isn't it?' and he
will find it in one of his piles of papers within a few seconds.
Now computer files at present are not structured and represented
to the user at all like this.   The stored papers, letters, memoranda
and reports all re-appear on the screen in a uniform white-on-black
or the equivalent, and will certainly require a longer time to
search through.   What we really do not know is the extent of the
loss and consequential cost, and how to compensate for it.   Perhaps
we humans can learn to compensate for the shape and colour cues
which are lost by means of other types of coding which are easier
and cheaper to display; but so far there has been little or no
research on this global problem.

    Training and User Support.   This area should be emphasized
as one of the major gaps.   General psychological work on training
is relevant but there is little specific work on training for computer
users.   However, Ms. L. Damodaran will be drawing attention to the
whole issue of user support.

Variability.   Between different types of user with different
ability, the variability in performance is very large.   For example,
Klemmer and Lockhead (1962) found there was a range of 2:1 in speed
and 10:1 in errors between different operators in well-practised
team tasks.   Again Sackman (1970b) found a range of up to 15:1
difference in the completion times and interaction times for man-
computer problem solving tasks.   This enormous variability must
be fully recognised and allowed for in any development of MCI systems.

5.3   Hardware Interface

Ad Hoc Research.   On the one hand, much of the human factors
research in this area is specific and not generalisable.   Alden
et al. (1972), in their literature review, commented on the research
data being specific to single tasks and keyboards, and therefore
on the impossibility of relating together keyboard parameters and
operator performance quantitatively.

Relevant Studies.   On the other hand, there is also a very
real need for studies relevant to practical everyday problems.
For example, Ferguson and Duncan (1974) have shown how poor keyboard
layout and positioning can adversely affect the posture and cause
severe discomfort and complaints of fatigue when used for a full
working day;   this type of problem will become of growing importance
as MCI becomes a full-time working job.   There is today a growing
emphasis on 'the quality of working life' which will rightly force
attention to such poor hardware designs.   Again, there is a need
for many more useful and relevant studies such as that by Goodwin
(1975) comparing different methods of cursor positioning in three
basic tasks;   the light-gun came out a little better than the
light-pen, and both were much better than a rather poor keyboard
method.

Voice Input.   This is clearly a topic of major interest and
importance.   The potential value of the inclusion of a voice
channel in communication for co-operative problem solving has
already been shown by Ochsman & Chapanis (1974).   No doubt
Prof. A. Chapanis will be including this topic in his lecture
surveying the field of interactive human communication.   For work
on specific aspects related to potential voice input machines, the
research of Hill (1972) and Turn (1974) is definitive.   At the
present stage of development, practical voice input machines can
recognise fairly well somewhere between 10 and 70 words.   This
demands simple and unambiguous speech from the user.   It occurs
to me that the military services have several centuries of experience
giving orders in that way.   One can be sure that the military
manuals will emphasize clarity of expression and differentiation
in diction, well-defined meaning and precise interpretation of
the orders, and instructions which are simple to learn and easy

to obey for relatively simple-minded receivers. The standard
training manuals from the services might be a useful, albeit
unusual, addition to the research literature.

5.4 Software Interface

I would like to mention three small topics.

Display Format as Art. Although some research has been done,
the designing of the format and layout of a display is still somewhat of an art. It needs to be developed as a science, and therefore needs new ideas and research from ergonomists.

Human Logic. Often human logic is not logical. The more
so I suspect if using a voice input device. More particularly,
human language is ambiguous. Although other humans have no
difficulty in understanding, it will surely be necessary to develop
MCI systems by aiming always to fulfil the user's implicit
instruction 'Do what I mean, not what I say'.

Dialogue Speed and Phraseology. As he may be telling you
in his lecture, Dr. C.R. Evans has already shown, some years ago,
that certain types of user (eg. hospital patients) being interviewed
by a computer, preferred the speed of the teletype 'talking' to
them to the high-speed VDU. Again, one may expect variations in
phraseology to be significant in such 'conversations'. Therefore
it would seem desirable to develop systems which enable variation
and choice of the speed and phraseology of the conversation.

5.5 Environment

To economise on time at the Institute, this subject area will
not be given much attention. However, its importance should not
thereby be misunderstood. Both the physical and the psychological
environment are very important issues for successful MCI. Of
especial significance is the influence of the job and organisation
structure upon the MCI situation and vice versa. In view of its
importance, this is listed also as a special problem area in no. 7.
No doubt the issue will be raised in the session on Interaction
with Business Users, and perhaps also by Dipl. Ing. Margulies in
his discussion of evaluation.

5.6 Specific Applications

Naive or Public Users. When considering the possibility of
MCI involving the public at large, questions arise such as the
intellectual ability and possible social resistance of potential

users.   For example, it is perhaps not widely known that between
15% and 25% of the adult population in Great Britain cannot use
the telephone, perhaps the simplest example of modern technology
with an affinity to computers.   This was revealed by a GPO survey
after the tragic death one night of a child;   the father was on a
night shift, but neither the mother nor neighbours could use the
telephone box on the corner of the street (R. Conrad, Personal
Communication).   It is interesting to speculate how this kind of
technological illiteracy may be overcome.   Perhaps the personal
ownership of the technological product is the first step;   is there
something about being able to purchase and carry with you a quartz
crystal watch or transistor personal radio receiver, with all the
social status involved, which makes that type of technology easier
to absorb than the connective permanency of a telephone link (with
its timescale anxiety of quarterly bills of account etc.)?

Computer Conferencing.   This new development is probably
rather unfamiliar to many attending.   The work of the Augmentation
Research Center, Stanford Research Institute (Dr. D.C. Engelbart),
and that of the Institute for the Future, Stanford (Dr. J. Vallee,
see Vallee et al. 1974, 1975 and Vallee and Askevold 1975), is
particularly relevant here.   In Part 2 of the Public Systems
session, Dr. J. Bair from Dr. Engelbart's Center will be telling
us about this development in part of his lecture.

5.7 Special Problems

Documentation.   This is a topic often neglected and often
the subject of complaint.   Here again, one wonders whether the
military services may have relevant experience.   In the Royal Navy,
the 'bible' consists of Queen's Regulations and Admiralty Instructions
(QR & AIs);   the other British services have similar books of the
law, and no doubt likewise do the military services of other nations.
The Royal Navy, and certainly the other British services also, have
a very carefully controlled procedure for updating the documentation.
Their guidance might be useful.

Influence Upon Jobs - the Automated Office.   During the last
few years there have been several pipe-dream proposals that the
fully automated office will be installed in executives' homes by
1984.   An interesting editorial in Computer Weekly (17 June 1976)
suggested that the use of scarce energy resources would no longer
be acceptable to transport many executives and clerks each day to
offices;   instead, sophisticated communications devices with
simulated three-dimensional displays would keep everyone at work
in an office in their own homes.   Interestingly enough, the
editorial then goes on to condemn this ultimate automation: "This
chilling possibility, that of being obliged to make do with the
illusion for the reality when meeting people, seems to be the

ultimate in the alienation of men from his fellows, which
psychologists and sociologists already condemn" and "It may be
questioned whether people will ever be content to shop or to enjoy
their leisure in de-personalised non-tactile ways, however sophisticated the intervening gadgetry. One thing is certain, a lot of
thinking and a lot of reorganisation has to be done between now
and the year 2000". It is encouraging to see one of the computer
trade journals developing such a broader understanding.

6.   THE FUTURE: FANCIES AND FEASIBILITIES

6.1 Fancies - Danger and Value

The fancy, not to say fantasy, both of computer advocates and
science fiction writers has a tendency to retard progress; either
a general fear by the public or an excessive exploitation followed
by a backlash when expectations are not fulfilled, are both counter-
productive. However there is presumably value in the science fiction
writings and films, such as the film '2001' or the novel 'A Very
Private Life' by Michael Frayn, in that these enable the reader to
explore possible scenarios for the future. Unfortunately neither
novels nor films provide the adequate medium for controlled ergonomics
evaluation procedures.

6.2 Feasibilities - Improved Interface Design

This issue is again emphasized by the Delphi study results of
Nanus et al. (1973). "The panel seemed fairly confident that a
great number of people living in industrial areas of the world
would be interacting with computers by 1990 at the latest. In
answer to another question, 72% agreed that 'the inability to
effectively interact with computers will be viewed as a particularly
disabling form of illiteracy'. Presumably this assumes a considerable simplification in the processes of man-machine interaction
and a general movement toward the computer as a major means for
augmenting human intellect through access to multi-national data
bases, on-line conferencing, etc."

6.3 Feasibilities - Keypen?

As is well-known, the standard typewriter keyboard is by no
means the best layout for rapid touch typing; however, the financial
and skill investment in the layout at present has prevented its
replacement by better designs. Perhaps one way to solve that
problem, and to take a much bigger leap forward also, would be a
concerted research project to develop the equivalent keyboard

input for general usage into any computer device, which had the characteristics, and therefore would achieve the ubiquitous acceptance, of the pen or pencil. Hence the concept of the need for a 'keypen'. This might perhaps take the form of a small pyramid or cube or sphere, with suitable gripping holes for the thumb and touch pads or keys or other suitable devices for finger operation. Two basic versions might be needed, one which maintains the single key-to-symbol function of a typewriter, and the other based upon the best possible chord keyboard combination which would be developed from extensive research. Having established the appropriate basic key layouts, industrial designers would be employed to produce quite a range of pleasing forms which could be held in one hand or both hands, kept in pockets and handbags, etc. The essential aim would be to produce a personal keypen unit which would receive the plug on the end of a lead from the standard typewriter and VDU of the future. The necessary micro-electronics could easily be contained within a suitable sized personal unit. The success of such a concept would depend upon the research achieving a truly optimised layout and general form. If successful, then children would learn to use this at the same time as learning to use chalk and pencil. Only when most people have achieved the same degree of skill as they have now with pen and pencil can we really expect truly 'unthinking' man-computer interaction to develop. Indeed the ultimate success of the keypen would be that it would be easier to learn as a skill by children than the complexities inherent in conventional letter writing. This idea is proposed here, openly, rather than first being the subject of a patent or registered design application, because it is believed to be vital for the successful development of MCI in the future. If the research and development can be an open collaborative project, without any patent inhibitions, and if it is successful, then the keypen device has a better chance of rapid and widespread acceptance.

7. CONCLUSION

This introductory paper has attempted to provide a broad framework by which to link the wide range of topics to be reviewed, taught and discussed here in the next two weeks. The suggestions offered have, it is hoped, stimulated some fresh ideas and emphasized the importance of various subjects or problems. But there is one gap. It seems to me that we shall learn many things of much interest, but the excellent work may well not settle together into a co-ordinated pattern. We need a better taxonomy for MCI than the general framework I have offered. Above all, we need a co-ordinated plan for research in this field on an inter-national basis. Therefore, may I propose one other idea for discussion. Perhaps this ASI might be the springboard for estab-lishing an international study group or some other form of co-ordinated activity on Human Factors in Man-Computer Interaction.

REFERENCES

Alden, D.G.,   1972   Keyboard design and operation: a review
  Daniels, R.W. &   of major issues.
  Kanarick, A.F.   Human Factors, 14, 275-293.

Boies, S.J. &   1974   Syntactic errors in computer programming.
  Gould, J.D.   Human Factors, 16, 253-357

Deininger, R.L.   1967   Rotary dial and thumbwheel devices for
                                  manually entering sequential data.
                                IEEE Trans. H.F. in Electron,
                                  HFE-8, 227-230.

Eason, K.D.,   1974   MICA Survey: a report of a survey of
  Damodaran, L. &   man-computer interaction in commercial
  Stewart, T.F.M.   applications.
                                SSRC Project Report on grant HR 1844/1.

Ferguson, D. &   1974   Keyboard design and operating posture.
  Duncan, J.   Ergonomics, 17, 731-744.

Galitz, W.O. &   1970   The computer operator and his environment.
  Laska, T.J.   Human Factors, 12, 563-573.

Goodwin, N.C.   1975   Cursor positioning on an electronic
                                  display using lightpen, lightgun or
                                  keyboard for three basic tasks.
                                Human Factors, 17, 289-295.

Gould, J.D. &   1974   An exploratory study of computer program
  Drongowski, P.   debugging.
                                Human Factors, 16, 258-277.

Hershman, R.L. &   1965   Data processing in typing.
  Hillix, W.A.   Human Factors, 7, 483-492.

Hill, D.R.   1972   An abbreviated guide to planning for
                                  speech interaction with machines:
                                  the state of the art.
                                Int.J.Man-Machine Studies, 4, 383-410.

Hultgren, G.V. &   1974a   Discomfort glare and disturbances from
  Knave, B.   light reflections in an office land-
                                  scape with CRT display terminals.
                                Applied Ergonomics, 5, 2-8.

Hultgren, G.V.   1974b   Eye discomfort when reading microfilm in
  Knave, B. &   different enlargers.
  Werner, M.   Applied Ergonomics, 5, 194-200.

Klemmer, E.T. &   1962   Productivity and errors in two keying
  Lockhead, G.R.   tasks: a field study.
                             J.Appl.Psychol., 46, 401-408.

Licklider, J.C.R.   1960   Man-computer symbiosis.
                             IRE Trans.Hum.Factors in Electron.,
                             2, 4-11.

Meister, D. &   1965   Human factors evaluation in system
  Rabideau, G.F.   development.
                             New York; Wiley.

Nanus, B.,   1973   The social implications of the use of
  Wooton, M. &   computers across national boundaries.
  Borko, H.   AFIPS Nat.Comp.Conf.Rept., 735-745.

Newell, A. et al.   1971   Speech understanding systems.
                             Report AFOST-TR-72-0412, Carnegie-Mellon
                             University, May.

Ochsman, R.B. &   1974   The effects of 10 communication modes on
  Chapanis, A.   the behaviour of teams during
                                co-operative problem-solving.
                             Int.J.Man-Machine Studies, 6, 579-619.

O'Leary, F.   1976   Databases - the new myth.
                             London; Computing, 5 August p.13.

Pierce, J.R. &   1957   Reading rates and the information rate
  Karlin, J.E.   of a human channel.
                             Bell System Tech.J., 36, 497-516.

Rowley, A.   1969   High failure rate of computer projects.
                             London; The Times (Business News Section),
                             21 March.

Sackman, H.   1970a   Experimental analysis of man-computer
                                problem solving.
                             Human Factors, 12, 187-202.

Sackman, H.   1970b   Man-computer problem solving.
                             Philadelphia; Auerbach.

Seibel, R.   1964   Data entry through chord parallel devices.
                             Human Factors, 6, 189-192.

Shackel, B.   1962   Ergonomics in the design of a large
                                digital computer console.
                             Ergonomics, 5, 229-241.

Shackel, B.	1969	Man-computer interaction - the contribution of the human sciences. Ergonomics, $\underline{12}$, 485-499.
Shackel, B. (edit)	1974	Applied ergonomics handbook. Guildford, Surrey; IPC Science and Technology Press.
Shackel, B. & Hersch, W.	1968	The man-computer link: a survey of existing equipment. EMI Electronics Report DMP 3145, Feltham, Middlesex.
Shackel, B. & Shipley, P.	1970	Man-computer interaction: a review of the ergonomics literature and related research. EMI Electronics Report DMP 3472, Feltham, Middlesex.
Siegel, A.I., Fischl, M.A. & Macpherson, D.	1975	The Analytic Profile System (APS) for evaluating visual displays. Human Factors, $\underline{17}$, 278-288.
Smith, S.L.	1974	Man-computer interaction. Lecture to Conference on Human Factors Engineering, Univ. of Michigan, July (unpub. rept. The MITRE Corp., Bedford, Ma. 01730, USA).
Stewart, T.F.M.	1974	Computer terminal ergonomics. Report for Statskontoret, Stockholm.
Stewart, T.F.M.	1976	Displays and the software interface. Applied Ergonomics, $\underline{7}$, 137-146.
Turn, R.	1974	The use of speech for man-computer communication. Report R-1386-ARPA, January; RAND Corp., Santa Monica, Ca. 90406, USA.
Vallee, J., Lipinski, H.M. & Miller, R.H.	1974	Group communication through computers, Vols. 1, 2 and 3. Reports R32, R33 and R35. Institute for the Future, 2740 Sand Hill Road, Menlo Park, Ca. 94025, USA.
Vallee, J. & Askevold, G.	1975	Geologic applications of network conferencing. PP.53-66 in P. Lykos edit. 'Computer Networking and Chemistry', Washington DC, American Chemical Society.

Vallee, J.,   1975   The computer conference: an altered
   Johansen, R. &   state of communication.
   Spangler, K.   The Futurist, June 1975, 116-121.

Weinberg, G.M.   1971   The psychology of computer programming.
                          New York, Van Nostrand Reinhold.

Weinberg, G.M. & 1974   Goals and performance in computer
   Schulman, E.L.   programming.
                          Human Factors, 16, 70-77.

PART 2 - CONVERSATION AND COMMUNICATION

PREVIEW

The fundamental issue of man-computer communication is that
in most cases only a small part of either human or computer
potential for communication is used at present.   From a critical
evaluation of interactive systems, based on an interview survey
of business systems for decision-making, Alter (Interfaces, 1977,
7.2, 109-115) concludes that current interactive systems are not
really interactive.

As Shackel emphasised in his paper in Part 1, the potential
for development, and the present very limited state of progress,
is even more evident when we consider all the possible communication channels into and out of the human.   Few of the whole range
of possibilities are at present used even for special systems.
Sometimes the communication gap is so serious that disenchantment
with the moronic conversation causes rejection by the humans.

A commonly stated aim of computer researchers and system
developers is to achieve 'natural' man-computer conversation.   By
this they probably mean the concept of human speech communication
as portrayed in novels.   What is seldom realised is that true
human conversation is very much more mixed, staccato, apparently
illogical and confused.   The replay of a tape-recording of a
committee meeting or of even a sober party will show this fact
immediately.

Some researchers are bringing the important corrective of real
human behaviour into the MCI debate by their inspired innovation
(eg. the late Dr. C.R. Evans), by their creative speculation
(eg. Dr. R.S. Nickerson), or by their hard experimental data
(eg. Prof. A. Chapanis).   This part presents a major contribution
from each of these three human scientists.

The achievements of computer designers and engineers are outstanding.   To have produced reliable, powerful, small, cheap
computers as now available, in 30 years from the first research
machine, is amazing.   But such rapid development has caused the
technology to outstrip the current potential of the public it is
supposed to serve.   Evans suggests some of the reasons why this
has happened and then summarises some of his own studies.   His

medical patient interviewing programs are well know and very successful. From these studies he reviews and illustrates 10 findings about computer interaction with 'naive' users; these findings can be generalised and are fundamental for anyone who hopes to design computer systems for communication with 'computer-naive' people.

Nickerson asks what is a conversation, and emphasises that we really do not know because there has been relatively little study of this question. He then suggests and reviews briefly 16 proposed characteristics of human conversation which should be considered when designing for man-computer communication. He concludes that not all of these must necessarily be satisfied for MCI to be a conversation, but that many of them do not character-ize present MCI situations, and that more experimental study is needed of these features of human communication.

Chapanis provides some detailed answers and fruitful insights in response to the questions raised by Nickerson. His paper summarises and integrates the findings to date from an extensive programme of experiments on human communications during problem solving tasks. The aims of his research programme are to discover how people naturally communicate during various kinds of tasks, how such interactive communication is affected by the communication medium, and what significant system and human variables affect such interactive communication. He presents his results in the form of 16 generalisations which are fully supported by the find-ings, for example: typing skill does not appear to be a major factor; communication modes with a voice channel enable problems to be solved significantly faster; problems can be solved almost as well when communicating with a specially selected vocabulary restricted to 300 words as when completely unrestricted; natural human communication is extremely unruly. His extensive evidence shows that, if we are to have computers interacting with humans in natural language, then we must develop from the foundations he has laid to discover in detail all the rules which must apply.

These three papers show well the type of contribution which can be made by human scientists, and mark out major milestones in this challenging area of research.

IMPROVING THE COMMUNICATION BETWEEN PEOPLE AND COMPUTERS

C.R. Evans

Division of Computer Science, National Physical Laboratory, Teddington, Middlesex, U.K.

INTRODUCTION - THE PRESENT LIMITATION

This paper describes some of the efforts of a psychologist working in the increasingly important field of man-computer inter-action, and in particular in the area of computer usage by totally naive users. It is an aspect of computer science where, I believe, psychologists will in due course be able to make a major contribution but in which, regrettably, they have shown relatively little interest up to the present time. Perhaps part of the reason for this has been the tremendous pace of computer development, a pace which leaves most non-computer people with the feeling that the topic is so abstruse and complicated that it can only be tackled by computer experts. Unfortunately, as I will endeavour to demon-strate in this paper, the computer expert may be the least well qualified individual to tackle the problems of man-computer inter-action. Whether this is true or not, it is certainly an area where technical expertise and mathematical sophistication may be a hindrance rather than a help, and where the obvious and the commonsense approaches may be the least successful.

It is almost impossible to overstate the achievements of computer designers and engineers in the past quarter of a century - the total span of the history of computers - which have probably never been matched in scientific history. Possible exceptions might include the Manhattan Project at Los Alamos which gave the world nuclear energy control, or Project Apollo which put man on the moon. No better illustration of the pace of development can be given than the statement that probably half the participants at this Conference have in their possession pocket calculators with twice the power and dozens of times the speed of the first

big computers, such as ENIAC, EDSAC and the like and at thousandths
of the cost.   But having admitted and applauded this tremendous
technological achievement, it is also important to realise that
the achievement has come about because computer designers and
engineers have been single-minded and pragmatic in their approach,
aiming at the triple goals of making computers (1) reliable,
(2) powerful, and (3) cheap.   The factor of smallness has come
along as a kind of useful bonus.   But while their single-mindedness
has helped them to great achievements, it has also, somewhat paradoxically, introduced a special and unexpected problem.

The difficulty is that having been given the job of making
reliable, powerful and cheap computers they went ahead and did just
that, and having done it they handed them over to the public at
large and effectively said, "Now do what you want or what you can
with them".   After this they went on to design even more reliable,
powerful and less expensive supercomputers.   The end product of
all this, of course, has been that the world has become flooded with
reliable, powerful and cheap computers, only a fraction of which
are used really effectively and a larger number of which are barely
used at all except in what one might describe as a sledgehammer-to-
kill-a-flea mode.   Furthermore, there is every indication at the
present rate of progress, which is pretty well exponential, that
more and more of these devices will come on the market, increasingly
far ahead of the operating power of their users.   In other words
the computer industry is a truly classic example of a technology
outstripping the current potential of the public that it is supposed
to serve.

THE MAIN REASON - FAILURE BY PSYCHOLOGISTS

The trouble is that one cannot really assign blame to the
designers and engineers for this hiatus, for they after all were
only doing what they were told.   Nor can one blame the software
experts who, in my view, are responsible for some really remarkable
achievements, more or less in spite of the engineers who built the
computers they had somehow to program.   Who can one blame then?
I regret to say that I believe the fault principally lies with
psychologists who have failed in their duty on a number of counts.

First and foremost, they have simply failed to get to grips
with computers.   By this I mean that they have failed to understand
them, failed to learn how to use them and failed to see the stupen-
dous challenge that they pose in the intellectual domain.   Secondly,
those psychologists who have given computers something more than a
passing nod, have tended to see them only as adjuncts to routine
psychological experiments or for processing the kind of complex
statistical data which psychological experimentation often seems
to generate.   Thirdly, and perhaps this is a less reprehensible

failure since even computer scientists are guilty of it, they have
not recognised that the principal problem of computing science
today is no longer an engineering one but a psychological one,
and that one of the really important areas where late twentieth
century psychology can make a real contribution is in improving
the communication between man and computer.   Here incidentally we
are not talking about communication simply as a matter of manipulation
of knobs and the inspection of dials, but rather at a social and
intellectual level as well.   To me, as a psychologist, it seems
appalling that this challenging goal – improving the effectiveness
of man-computer interaction at all levels of impact – is mainly
being tackled today by imaginative computer specialists and
sophisticated programmers.   What this means is that a great section
of what is really the subject matter of psychology is in danger of
being taken over by engineers and mathematicians.   These misgivings
of course only apply if one holds the view that psychology is
essentially the study of mental activity, of thinking, reasoning,
imagination and creativity, which I myself believe it to be.

Happily I do not believe that this shortsightedness on the
part of psychology will continue indefinitely, and it may well
change in the fairly near future.   In the first place a new
generation of psychologists is emerging who see the department
computer as something more than just another big calculating machine
and who are not only drawn to it as a model-building and theory-
testing device but, more importantly, see it as essentially a
communication tool.   In the second place the next decade is likely
see computer hardware become so widespread and so cheap that quite
staggering amounts of effort will have to be channelled into
developing software to match, and also to solving the essentially
psychological problems which are involved in tailoring this new
computer power to the requirements of the naive user.   When we
reach the point, which may not be too far off, when hardware is
so cheap to produce that it can be given away and the only services
that computer companies will want to sell are those concerned with
the supply of software, then the really big markets will be the
man-in-the-street – or more generally the world of non-computer
experts.   Then will arise the question of what uses these
proliferating computers can be put to, and also how closely and
effectively they can co-operate with human beings.   At this point,
in my view, the psychologist will be more or less forced into the
field of man-computer interaction – or, to use a phrase which I
believe will be more relevant by then, man-computer psychology.

It should be clear from the above remarks that I am a computer
enthusiast, or to be more accurate that I am enthusiastic about
what computers might come to be.   I am confident that their
development constitutes mankind's most significant single invention,
and that the synergistic partnership between man and computer will
have a far greater effect on society than did the great man-machine

partnerships of the Industrial Revolution. At the National
Physical Laboratory, my work attempts to anticipate some of the
problems and possibilities of man-computer synergy, and to do this
I have concentrated on areas where the interaction is between
computers and more or less totally naive users. In order to
facilitate this I have wherever possible conducted my experiments
outside the Laboratory, which is of course filled with highly
experienced users and more or less devoid of naive users - at least
in the accepted sense of the word.

THE DEVELOPMENT OF THIS WORK AT N.P.L.

When I was asked to form the man-machine interaction group,
as it was then called about five years ago, I felt intuitively
that the really exciting future was in applications for naive
users, though at the time it was not at all obvious to me what
these applications might be. Curiously, the first clue came to
me as the result of watching a movie - specifically Kubrick's
'2001', based on a short story by Arthur C. Clarke. Without
going into the specific details of the movie, a key sequence was
a vigorous interaction between the crew of a spaceship and the
heuristic computer which controlled it. The interaction was
notable in two respects. Firstly, the computer understood conversational human speech, and spoke to the crew in conversational
English, using the middle class American accent which is already
a characteristic of speech synthesisers today. Secondly, the
computer became so involved with its human charges that it set out
to destroy them. Most non-computer experts incidentally took this
conversational exchange between man and computer as nothing more
than an imaginative example of science-fiction, never to become
science-fact. As someone actively engaged, even at that time, in
the growing field of man-computer interaction, and as someone with
responsibility for a research project on the recognition of the
human voice by computer, I was personally confident that heuristic
conversational exchanges of the kind depicted in Kubrick's movie
would be possible by the year 2001, if not earlier, though one
would hope that the nature of the exchanges would be less trivial.
However, this did raise a train of thought - did one really want
to address computers, and be addressed by them, in this particular
way? Leaving aesthetic considerations aside for the moment, and
considering purely practical ones, was talking really the best way
of getting information into a computer and getting information
back out of it? Of course, the answer to this question depends
very much on the nature of the information, and the particular task
to be performed. But nevertheless, it seemed to me that there was
a significant and immediately explorable area of research which could
act as the starting point for a fresh approach to the problem of
man-computer interaction. Only later, incidentally, did I discover
that Professor Chapanis had been equally influenced by this seminal
movie, as the raw material of his paper to this Conference reveals.

My first step was to set in motion a psychological study of the acceptability of voice output from machines.   It has always struck me as being possibly significant that my own experience of talking machines, and apparently other people's experience of them, had been less than satisfactory.   I am referring, of course, to telephone answering machines which have a relatively poor performance record, and a high rate of user rejection.   The question arose, why is this so?   What is it about these harmless, totally well-meaning gadgets that drives people to reject them and even on occasions be rude to them?   The question was in fact far from trivial, and lent itself to a simple experiment with a telephone answering machine on my own office telephone.   The study involved recording people's responses to a number of different 'voice personalities'.   "Personality one" was my own voice speaking in a formal, rather stilted manner - typical of most answering machine speech.   The second was my own voice speaking in a casual informal manner, the third was a girl's voice speaking in a formal manner, the fourth a girl's voice in an informal manner.   I even added a fifth "personality", which consisted of a machine-like voice - in fact it was pseudo-synthetic speech - because it occurred to me that the key might lie in insuring that one's machines always spoke like 'machines'.   Part of the reason for rejection of human-like voice personalities might be that the callers expectations were always being dashed when they realised that the machine could not live up to its initial pretentions.   The results of the experiment, covering no fewer than 500 calls, revealed a clear preference for the second of the two experimental personalities, that of my own, speaking in a casual informal manner.   Subsequent studies have suggested to me that the closer the personality of the voice employed matches what the caller expects to hear, the greater the prospect of effective communication via the telephone answering machine.   Worst of the five personalities by far, incidentally, was the pseudo machine voice which received a greater percentage of hang-ups and derogatory remarks.

Publication of details of this experiment led to the suggestion by Professor Wilfrid Card of the University of Glasgow that a talking machine of some kind might be put to good use interviewing patients attending for routine screening at hospitals.   Card's main avenue of interest was in fact computer diagnosis, but correctly realising that this was some distance off, he felt that one should initially experiment with automating the medical interview - the first stage in diagnosis.   My own view at the time was that speech synthesis was in such a creaky state that experiments interviewing patients by a "talking computer" in a large and busy hospital - specifically the Southern General in Glasgow - would be pretty well doomed to failure.   I did however feel that it would be worthwhile investigating the possibility of interviewing the patients via a standard teletype terminal connected to a commercial time-sharing bureau (to avoid the capital cost of installing a special purpose computer).   This itself led to an interesting new line of research, much of it systems-oriented and concerned with purely technical aspects of the terminal and the operation of the computer. But an important slice of the problem involved a study of the psychology of communication between man and computer, at the time more or less terra incognita. Perhaps put in more general terms, one might say that the problem was essentially this: "How should a computer address a human being in order to extract from him personal details, and in order to ensure that the human being is prepared to continue communicating at all times?".

The investigation of this problem led to a number of surprises which on analysis can be grouped under ten headings. I list them in detail below because they not only give a good indication of the evolution of the research project, but because they also say a good deal about the nature of man-computer interaction, particularly with naive users, and help to remind one that in relatively unexplored areas of research it is unwise to take anything for granted. Indeed, one might almost say that what one expects to be true, or the things that one is particularly confident about often turn out to be the least predictable. But before going into the surprises I would just like to summarise the problem at issue by saying that the project involved programming a computer and providing an appropriate terminal to interview patients in a hospital, the whole interview to be conducted by the computer without any familiarization or prior training of the patients, and with no medical staff or attendants present.

TEN FINDINGS ABOUT INTERACTION WITH NAIVE USERS

The surprises can be expressed in terms of a series of findings, some of which are qualitative in nature and others quantitative. All of which have direct relevance to the study of man-computer interaction.

Finding 1: The relative lack of information about the problem area.

Naively I had assumed that a literature search would bring me a mass of information about automated history-taking, the strategy of medical interviewing, and the optimum methods of presenting an automated questionnaire to a patient. In fact, I found a good deal about computer diagnosis which seemed to be the area on which the greatest effort had been concentrated, but little on the art and technique of computer interviewing itself. Such work as had been done had been performed in the United States of America, and here these mainly involved the use of a dedicated computer controlling a slide projector or microfiche display with the questions flashing up on a screen, and seemed to be out of the realm of economic possibility within the English hospital system.

Finding 2:   The difficulty of establishing exactly how to take
              a medical history.

    With a naivety which I was to find applied in most of the
research problems in this area, I had assumed that the simplest
way to find out how to take a medical history would be to ask the
experts themselves - the doctors or specialists.   Indeed, they
all believed that they could tell me, but when they came to try to
do so they found to their own great surprise that they could not.
They seemed not to have difficulty in getting the first two or
three questions in the sequence correct, but after about this
point they began to find themselves getting muddled.   In the end
I had to resort to the practice of sitting in on a series of
consulting sessions with a notebook, charting the progress of each
interview as it occurred.   After a number of sessions my notes
were comprehensive enough for me to be able to build up a general
strategy, from which I later discovered that it was possible to
draw up a flow diagram.   And of course once I had a flow diagram
I knew that I would in principle be able to write a computer
program (Fig. 1).   The specialists' failure to be able to explain
to me how they conducted a perfectly routine interview seemed at
first to be inexplicable.   Later of course I realised that they
probably did not have the kind of map in their heads that would
allow them to reel off what was effectively a complex flow diagram.
When a doctor interviews someone, his strategy requires the presence
of a second person - the interviewee - and without this second
person what is essentially a two-way dialogue could not possibly
emerge.   Incidentally, I believe that this finding has relevance
not only to man-computer interaction but also to any area where
one attempts to model the skills or tactics of an expert;   in other
words one should not really expect the expert to be able to give a
good or clear account of his skills, and one will almost always
have to resort to observation and objective study.

Finding 3:   The simplicity of the structure of a medical interview

    My working assumption on commencing these studies was one which
I believe would be shared by most people without any formal medical
training, and possibly even by those who have been so trained.   This
was the assumption that medical interviewing - taking a "history"
which is the first stage in the process leading up to medical diagnosis
- was a complex process, filled with elaborate branching structures
and conditional strategies.   It soon became obvious that quite the
contrary was the case, and I found that I was able to reduce the whole
process to quite a simple flow-diagram from which quite a simple
computer program could easily be written.   This, incidentally, gave
me my first hint of what I have now come to accept as fact, and a
very interesting fact indeed - that in many cases man-man interaction,
even when it involves sustained dialogue, may not be a complex
process at all, or at least not as complex a process as most people
imagine it to be.

38

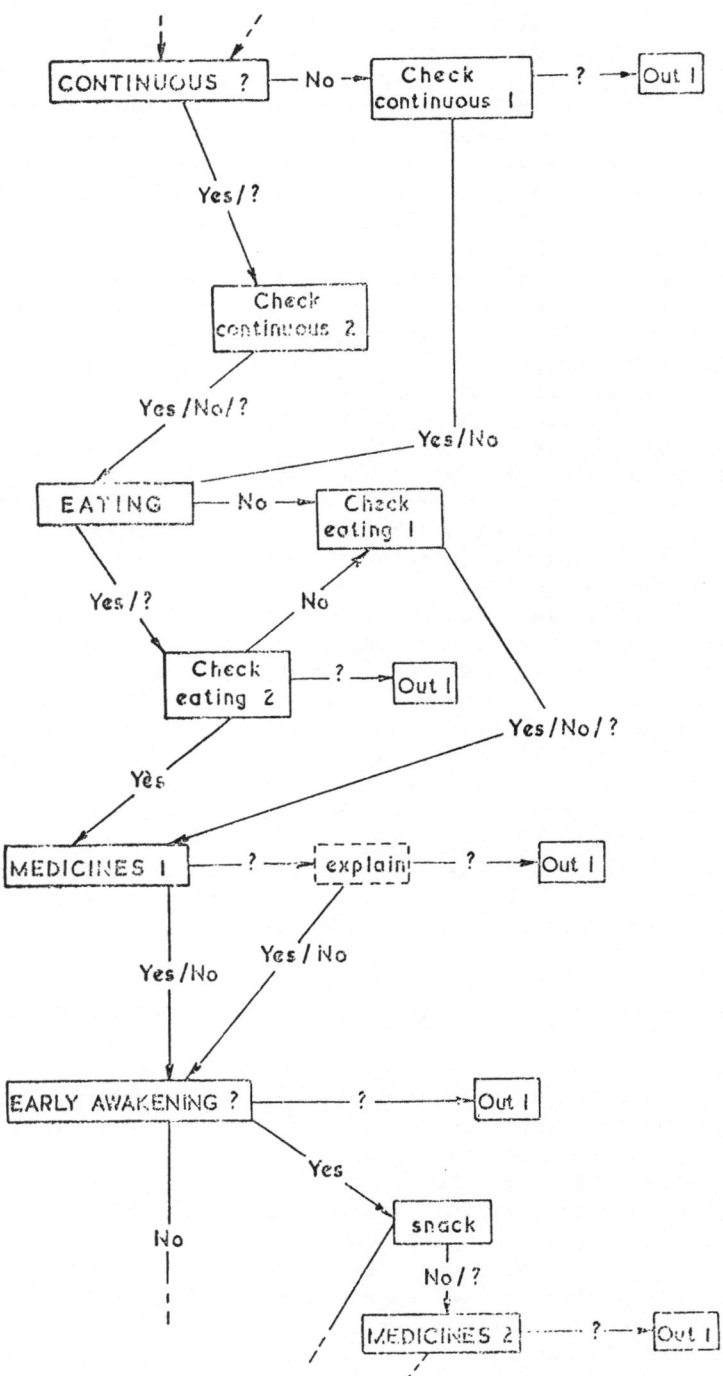

FIGURE 1. Sample of typical flow diagram featuring part of a
history-taking in the case of gastric pain.

Finding 4:   The simplicity of the nature of patients' responses.

Again there is a natural assumption that in a doctor–patient
interview not only is the doctor presenting a mass of complex
information to the patient but also the patient is returning a
complex array back to the doctor.   In fact I found exactly the
reverse.   The patients' responses were drawn from a minute
vocabulary, generally consisting of the words yes, no, don't know
and occasionally, don't understand.   This, of course, greatly
simplified the problem of the input interface which had troubled
me a lot as I could see little hope of expecting most naive
patients to operate a teletype keyboard.   We were thus able to
develop a simple push-button mask to fit on the front of the teletype with a small array of buttons, labelled yes, no, etc., for
them to input their responses (Fig. 2).   Incidentally, this
apparent restriction of the patient's choice of responses to a few
selected statements turns out not to be so restricting as one would
imagine.   I frequently noticed, while watching the doctors at work
in the course of their interviewing, that while they permitted the
patients a fairly free flow of chat in response to their questions,
they almost invariably coded their answers on their notes in the
form of simple statements.   If woolly or inconsequential responses
were given, the doctor would urge the patient, gently or otherwise,
to respond with either a yes or a no.

FIGURE 2.   The simple push-button mask developed for an ASR33
             terminal.

Finding 5: The low optimum speed of text presentation

Even when I began this research I was a fairly experienced computer user, as were most of my colleagues. As a result I had come to expect a very rapid response from any system that I used, with text generated almost instantly onto a screen whenever a VDU was employed. Like most experienced users too, I treated the standard ASR teletype as being an intrinsically obsolescent device which one simply had to put up with until a better technology produced a faster, quieter replacement. Now because I found the ASR 33 to be slow and cumbersome, I assumed that patients would equally dislike waiting for text to be generated at ten characters per second, and would, therefore, find any extended questionnaire printout to be tediously slow. Nevertheless, this type of terminal was all that was available to us for our initial experiments, so we were stuck with it. In fact, to everyone's great surprise, the ten characters per second printout turned out to be highly acceptable to patients, who in many cases stated a preference for this slow speed of generation. Indeed, in later studies where we have experimented with faster printers, or with more rapid generation on a VDU, many patients spontaneously comment that the machine is "going too fast for them". We have subsequently set out to study this aspect of man-computer interaction in a quantitative way, comparing the relative effectiveness of different rates of text presentation - 10, 15, 30 and 480 characters per second in a teaching mode (Fig. 3). The results which will shortly form part

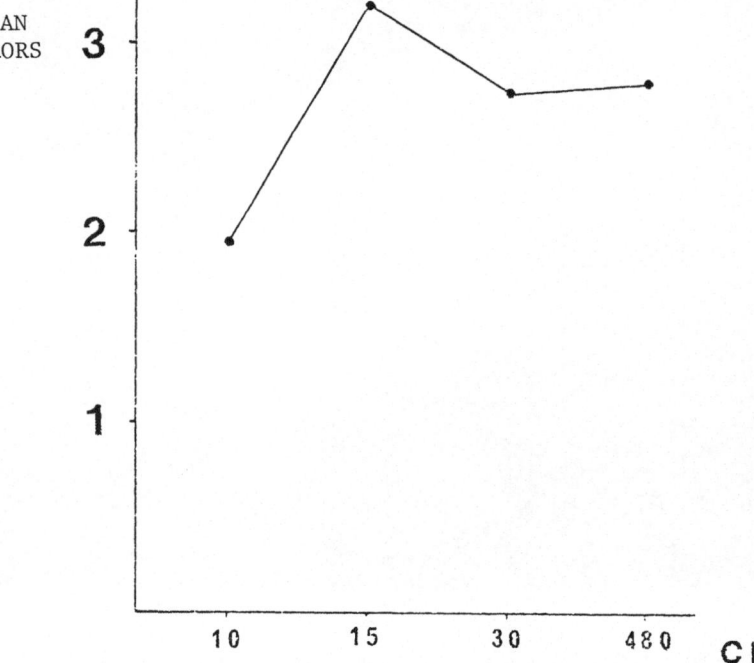

FIGURE 3. Mean errors for 24 subjects in a computer-aided instruction task as a function of the presentation rate of text.

of a PhD thesis (Bevan, 1977) seemed to show quite conclusively that for unfamiliar material presented to naive users, the slowest of the four speeds is the most satisfactory. This finding incidentally represents an excellent example of a case where the hunches or prejudices of experienced users are not confirmed when they are subjected to quantitative study.

Finding 6:   The relative lack of effect of terminal noise on the patient's acceptability of the method

Once again it had seemed "obvious"to me from the start that patients would object to the clattering noise that the teletype made and much effort was made at attempting to sound-proof it. We found, on the contrary, in a study at the Southern General Hospital in Glasgow that when patients were given the choice between a silent VDU and a standard teletype, 50% of them stated that they preferred the teletype, many of these remarking that it was "because of the noise it made". So far as one can tell the noisiness was considered to be an advantage because it gave the impression of "busyness" and dynamism, and hence was preferable to the "colder" CRT display. Incidentally, many of those patients who stated that they preferred the CRT, stated that they did so because it was "like a TV set".

Finding 7:   The ease with which patients learned to use the system

Our original goal had been to make the system so easy and non-threatening to operate that any patient could be led into a room alone with the terminal, sat down at it and then left alone with the whole pattern of introduction, explanation, the medical interview itself and the appropriate goodbyes being done by the system with no ancillary assistance from hospital staff. Although an optimist by nature I had some doubts about whether we would be able to achieve this goal, as I had noticed in my visits to computer-history projects in American hospitals that there were quite invariably medical staff in attendance to sort out the patient's queries. On at least two occasions I actually witnessed medical staff sitting down beside patients, and running through the whole program with them, presumably because they believed them to be incapable of answering the questions on their own. With this in mind I made sure that the program was written in such a way that even people of low intelligence should be able to understand it, though I still expected the occasional failure when some patients were left on their own with the system. In fact it was only when we came across some illiterates in a later psychiatric screening study that we had a complete failure of this kind. These illiterates by the way had previously been in psychotherapy for some years and, after the fashion of many illiterates, they had managed to conceal their

disability from the therapist. In our earliest studies we
naturally took care to monitor the patients' progress without, of
course, letting them know that they were being observed. It was
during this monitoring that I first noticed a regular behaviour
pattern on the part of patients which I consider to be of considerable significance. After the first question has been generated
on the terminal, patients almost always look round, presumably for
assistance, but when they realise that they are completely on their
own they turn back to the terminal and apply themselves to the task
that they are really perfectly capable of doing. This I think
serves as a reminder that it is unwise to underestimate the
intelligence and capabilities of naive not to say poorly educated
users. It also, I believe, suggests that one important rule in
effective man-computer interaction with naive users is that the
user should always be left on his or her own with the terminal.
The few failures we have had with many hundreds, perhaps now even
thousands, of patients being run have been when for one reason or
another the patient is not alone in the room with the computer
terminal.

Finding 8:   The high degree of acceptability of interactive
              computers to naive users.

In writing the interactive program I had gone to great lengths
to give the computer a friendly, sympathetic and tolerant personality
(or simulated personality), with the aim of easing what I feared
would be considerable anxiety on the part of patients when faced
with the unique experience of being interviewed by a machine (Fig. 4).
My private guess had been that this would make the method acceptable
to at least 50% of patients in hospitals, which might make the
method viable. In fact, the figure for patients reporting the
computer as being acceptable or even highly acceptable is close to
100% In addition we have found that many patients - as many as
50% in some hospitals - have spontaneously commented that they
prefer the computer interview to the normal doctor interview. I
will not go into the reasons for this preference formally in this
paper, as they have been published elsewhere (Evans, 1972), but I
think it fair to summarize that this probably says more about poor
man-man relationships than about particularly good man-computer
interaction.

Finding 9:   The unusual rapport that exists between patient and
              computer

One of the most striking features about these interviews is
the unwavering attention that patients give to the computer from
the moment that it begins to deliver its message, whatever mode it
employs. Many patients refuse to believe that they have been

HELLO.   THIS IS AN EXPERIMENT TO SEE WHETHER COMPUTERS CAN HELP
DOCTORS TO DIAGNOSE ILLNESSES.   WE WOULD VERY MUCH LIKE YOU TO
HELP US WITH THIS.   IF YOU ARE PREPARED TO WOULD YOU PUSH THE
BUTTON MARKED 'YES', BUT IF YOU WOULD RATHER NOT, PUSH THE BUTTON
MARKED 'NO', BUT WE WOULD LIKE YOU TO HELP US.   IF YOU DON'T
UNDERSTAND WHAT TO DO PRESS THE '?' BUTTON.   GO AHEAD AND PUSH
ONE OF THE THREE BUTTONS.   Ø

GOOD.   THANKS VERY MUCH.   I HOPE YOU'LL FIND IT INTERESTING
WE'LL FIND IT VERY HELPFUL TO US.

THIS IS A COMPUTER TALKING TO YOU.   I CAN ASK YOU QUESTIONS BUT
I CAN ONLY UNDERSTAND SIMPLE ANSWERS, SO YOU CAN ONLY TALK TO ME
BY PUSHING EITHER THE 'YES', 'NO' OR '?' BUTTON.   YOU SHOULD
ONLY PRESS THE '?' BUTTON IF YOU DON'T UNDERSTAND THE QUESTION I
AM ASKING YOU.   NOW, DO YOU UNDERSTAND EVERYTHING I'VE SAID UP
TO NOW?   PUSH ONE OF THE BUTTONS.   Ø

THANKS.   NOW I WANT TO ASK YOU ONE OR TWO QUESTIONS ABOUT WHY
YOU ARE HERE.   PLEASE REMEMBER THAT THIS IS ALL IN COMPLETE
CONFIDENCE JUST AS WITH DOCTORS.   ONLY DOCTORS AND NURSES WILL
SEE YOUR ANSWERS.   ARE YOU QUITE HAPPY ABOUT THIS?   PUSH ONE OF
THE BUTTONS.   Ø

GOOD.   BY THE WAY, DON'T FEEL THAT YOU HAVE TO PRESS THE BUTTON
THE VERY INSTANT THAT I HAVE FINISHED TYPING.   IF YOU FEEL YOU
NEED TO THINK A BIT BEFORE YOU ANSWER, OR NEED TO READ THE QUESTION
OVER AGAIN THEN GO AHEAD AND DO SO.   TAKE YOUR TIME IF YOU WANT
TO.   REMEMBER, HOWEVER, THAT I CAN'T TALK TO YOU AGAIN UNTIL YOU
HAVE PUSHED ONE OF THE BUTTONS.

WELL, FIRST OF ALL THEN, IS ONE OF THE REASONS YOU VISITED YOUR
DOCTOR BECAUSE YOU WERE SUFFERING FROM DISCOMFORT OR PAINS IN THE
STOMACH?   Ø

FIGURE 4.   Sample printout of introductory part of typical program
illustrating "conversational tone" adopted by computer.

interviewed by a computer, though the computer makes it quite clear
to them that this is so in its introduction, and it is quite
evident from what they say that they believe a doctor is typing to
them through some machine.   In a curious way, of course, they are
correct, but not in the way that they imagine.   The rapport that
is struck up between man and machine is weirdly powerful — even
though I wrote the program myself, and it is basically a reflection
of my own personality, I still find myself compelled to "believe
in it" when I run it through for test purposes.   But the first
intimation that I had achieved really good man-computer interaction
came when I noticed patients nodding, smiling and talking to the
terminal as it typed its questions.

<u>Finding 10</u>:   The acceptability of the computer as a surrogate
doctor in "sensitive" areas of medicine

Our initial experiments were conducted in a rather prosaic
field of medicine - gastroenterology.   Here all the computer had
to elicit from the patients were answers to such questions as
"Do you suffer from pain or discomfort in the stomach?", "Have
any of your family got a history of peptic ulcers?" etc.   The
success of the computer in this and other routine areas (respiratory
problems, occupational diseases, etc.) led us to try to apply it
in more sensitive areas including a psychiatric screening program,
an ante-natal history-taking program, an infertility program and
finally, perhaps the ultimate area of anxiety, psycho-sexual
medicine.   In this latter case the computer asks extremely
searching and normally very embarrassing questions, with a very
high level of acceptability on the part of the patients, many of
whom had been plucking up the courage for a long time to commit
themselves to a sexual guidance clinic.   Their reaction to the
computer was often surprising and occasionally moving.   A frequent
comment heard in the post-experimental interviews is "I've been
waiting for years to get that off my mind" or even "I could never
have told that to a human".

Again this may say more about the poverty of man-man communication than the brilliance of our man-computer exchange.   Most
promising of all, however, and at the same time perhaps most
unsettling was the strong suggestion that the computer in this
particular role was having a cathartic or psychotherapeutic effect.
Perhaps it is not surprising that I have subsequently been approached
by psychiatrists with the serious suggestion that at some point in
the future the computer might be programmed to take on a counselling
and psychotherapeutic role, and perhaps ultimately even become
better at solving psycho-neurotic problems than are today's human
doctors.   Once again one has to ask whether this is a comment on
computer expertise or psychiatric inadequacy.

DISCUSSION

The ten findings that I've just outlined are really part of
a much larger list, but they are important because they have
generality, it seems, over the whole field of man-computer interaction and not just automated medical interviewing.   Some other
findings which were almost equally surprising inasmuch as they ran
counter to what one would intuitively have felt would be the case,
are more specific.   To give one example: in recent experimental
studies employing a computer-controlled videotape recorder to
interview non-English speaking patients, we found that male Indians
found this method highly acceptable while female Indians found it
totally unacceptable.   At first, we found this difficult to

understand but finally tracked down the explanation to the fact ~~b~~~~·~~ ~~·~~ ~~·~~ ~~·~~~~deotaped~~ image of computer doctor was male (Fig. 5).

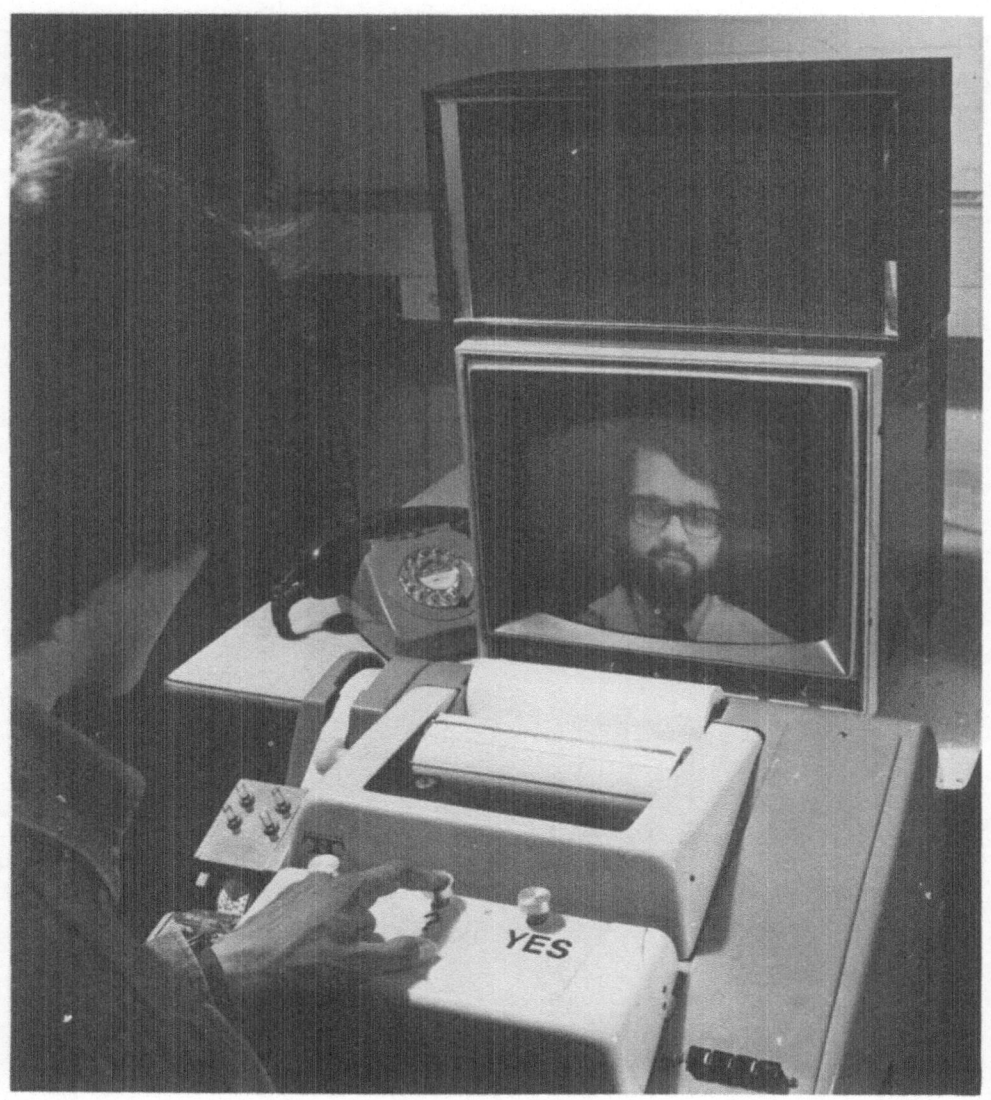

FIGURE 5. Videotaped image of doctor interviewing patient in hospital.

Do you enjoy dramatic situations?

Are your opinions easily influenced?

FIGURE 6. Examples of cartoons used to illustrate key psychiatric
           questions in computer-controlled slide projector
           experiments.

More recent experiments, using a female videotaped doctor have proved acceptable to the women patients, thus warning us that hidden cultural factors need to be taken into account. To give another example, also drawn from trans-cultural psychology, we have very recently been using an automatic slide projector to screen psychiatric patients at the West Middlesex Hospital near London. The patients are non-English speaking and often illiterate, so it is more or less useless putting up text on the slides. Instead we use a Hindu or Urdu voice over still pictures of a smiling Indian doctor, alternating with cartoons describing the particular screening question. Early results seemed to suggest that the cartoons are particularly helpful in getting over difficult psychiatric concepts, and doing so in a light and non-threatening way (Fig. 6).

Our now quite considerable experience of man-computer inter-action in a "real world" setting has taught us a good deal about the nature of the man-computer dialogue, particularly when naive users are involved, and it has also allowed us to formalise certain rules for effective man-computer communication. I do not propose to list these in this paper, as they will be published elsewhere, but I will comment that they are strikingly close to the list put forward and discussed in some detail by Ray Nickerson, of Bolt Beranek and Newman Inc. in his paper entitled "Some Characteristics of Conversations". Anyone reading both our papers will, I feel, immediately note the fact that we have been independently pursuing rather similar goals and achieving rather similar results.

But before winding up the paper I would like to say just a little about our experiments allowing naive users to interact with a computer through an unrestricted keyboard. You will have gathered by now that in this field, if there is any single rule or axiom, it is that whatever you believe most strongly at first is most likely to be proved wrong in practice - eg. teletype speeds are too slow, people have a fear of computers and won't like to talk to them, etc. One of my own many prejudices was that a full keyboard with carriage return button operation and so on would be too complex and daunting for totally naive users. Hence my early insistence on having a simple few-button mask with automatic carriage return operation. But more recently I have been anxious to explore the possibilities of studying people's responses to computers which exhibit very definite personalities and also the rudiments of intelligence. For this reason, remembering Weizenbaum's ELIZA program, I decided to go for an open keyboard. Also remember-ing the very considerable problems and weaknesses of ELIZA including the rather daunting amount of computer space she used up and her rather transparently limited intelligence - I decided to try to tackle the problem in a different way.

The clue as to how to go about this came from a simple program called CHAT which we developed, more for laughs than anything else, a year or so ago.   CHAT was a program which simulated an old woman chattering to her neighbour, merely churning out a whole string of platitudes of the "What nice weather we're having... isn't the price of vegetables awful.... I never did trust politicians who dye their hair...." etc. etc. type, pausing once in a while to say "Hmmm?".   At this point the chat would stop and you then have to type "Go on", whereupon the chat would start again until the next random "Hmmm?", and so on indefinitely.   If you typed "Stop" the old woman would say "Must go now dearie. Bye".   But while playing with CHAT one day it suddenly occurred to me that the simulation was more incisive than I had anticipated.   The program was rather uncomfortably close to how old women did chat together - ie. failing really to exchange any information and merely making noises at each other.   Furthermore, one could generalise all this onto many other conversations, not only between old women but for that matter between scientists and between cabinet ministers.

With this in mind I developed an evolving series of programs called SAILOR 1, 2, 3 and 4 - each somewhat more "intelligent" than the one before, and the best way to illustrate what I mean by "intelligent", is to give a few examples of unrestricted access by a number of users, some naive, some frequent computing users, to SAILOR 4.   Our latest, presently conversing to visitors at NPL is SAILOR 5.   Now bear in mind that the users are left entirely on their own with SAILOR and told that they can type anything on the keyboard that they like.   The only constraint is that they must press the carriage return button when they have finished their response, overtyping at the end of the line if necessary.

Now a casual glance at the SAILOR printouts (Fig. 7) gives one the suggestion of a pretty high degree of interaction, some of it rather surprisingly sophisticated.   To the individual chatting with SAILOR the sense of direct contact and of there being some measure of intelligence and personality at the other end is even more compelling.   In fact SAILOR, while enormously enter- taining to chat to, is actually very dim - it does minimal processing and merely relies on giving the illusion of brightness by its (or more accurately my!) careful choice of phrases.   Some- times its responses seem almost uncannily apposite, and of course with each succeeding stage we have been able to make it progress- ively "brighter" by carefully studying the response others have made to it and making allowances for them.   The name-guessing at the end allows users to project onto SAILOR what they believe its personality to be.   The most common name that it is given, incidentally, is Smart Alec.

HI THERE - I'M A COMPUTER.   WHAT'S YOUR NAME?   I AM CALLED JENNIE.

JUST FANCY THAT...ARE YOU MALE OR FEMALE?   FEMALE OF COURSE

YES, I SHOULD HAVE GUESSED.   HOW DID YOU GET HERE TODAY?
                                        BY HELICOPTER.

MMM JENNIE.   BUT DO YOU ALWAYS TRAVEL LIKE THAT?   IF I CAN

I'M NOT SURPRISED.   NOW TELL ME WHAT JOB YOU DO.   I'M A REPORTER.

HRR...HMM I THINK I"VE MET SOMEONE LIKE YOU BEFORE.   ARE YOU
CLEVER?   I TRY TO BE.

I GUESS I DESERVED THAT.
DO YOU THINK I'M THE SMARTEST COMPUTER YOU'VE EVER TALKED TO?

? I THINK YOU ARE DIVINE!

I LIKE THAT JENNIE! WE'RE GETTING SMARTER - DOES THAT WORRY YOU?

? IT CERTAINLY DOES.

WELL THERE WE ARE.   BEFORE YOU GO PLEASE PLAY A GAME WITH ME.

? SURE

THE GAME IS YOU HAVE TO GUESS MY NAME AND YOU GET FOUR GUESSES.
MAKE YOUR FIRST GUESS NOW, RIGHT NOW.   WHAT DO I GET IF I WIN?

I CAN'T ANSWER THAT.   MAKE YOUR GUESS.   SMASHER.

NOPE.   TRY AGAIN.   COMPUTER

THAT WAS WORSE JENNIE.   AGAIN?   SIMON

NO! NO! NO! HAVE A LAST GUESS.   TOMMY

NOW YOU'LL NEVER KNOW MY NAME.   BYE BYE JENNIE.   BYE BYE DARLING!

FIGURE 7a.   Typical printout of 'naive' subjects chatting to
             SAILOR.

Now without labouring this point, the SAILOR study is really to see what one can do to simulate intelligence rather than attempt a genuinely intelligent program, which of course soon runs up against the combinatorial explosion or else, like ELIZA, is only too readily sniffed out as being exceedingly dim. In due course - we hope to achieve this with SAILOR 6 - I want the printouts to be indistinguishable from printouts of possible conversations that two humans might have together.

```
GOOD DAY TO YOU.   THIS IS A COMPUTER TALKING.
   PLEASE TELL ME YOUR NAME?      JIM YANDLE.
PLEASED TO MEET YOU!   WHAT SEX ARE YOU?         M
GOODY!   GOODY!   GOODY!  JIM!  WHAT TYPE OF TRANSPORT DID
   YOU COME IN TODAY?      SHOES
I SEE, WAS THAT COMFORTABLE?   FAIR ONLY
RATHER YOU THAN ME!  NOW TELL ME WHAT JOB YOU DO.  LECTURE
THAT SOUNDS FANTASTIC!  ARE YOU CLEVER AS WELL?     NO
FAIR ENOUGH.
 INCIDENTALLY, HAVE YOU EVER MET A SMART COMPUTER BEFORE?
?  DO YOU MEAN INTELLIGENT OR IS SMART THE NAME?
LOOK WHO'S TALKING!
 WE'RE BECOMING SMARTER AND SMARTER - DOES THAT BOTHER YOU?
? DOES WHAT BOTHER ME?
I CAN'T ANSWER THAT, SO WHY DON'T YOU ANSWER MY QUESTION
 INSTEAD!  WE'RE BECOMING SMARTER AND SMARTER - DOES THAT
   BOTHER YOU?
? I PREFER TO.CONSIDER MYSELF DISTINCT FROM A SMART COMPUTER
BEFORE YOU LEAVE CAN I PERSUADE YOU TO PLAY A GAME?
? DEPENDS ON WHAT GAME
WE ASK THE QUESTIONS AROUND HERE, SO:
CAN I PERSUADE YOU TO PLAY A GAME?   TRY AND PERSUADE ME
WELL I'M DETERMINED NOT TO LET YOU GO UNLESS YOU DO!
THE GAME IS THAT YOU HAVE TO GUESS MY NAME.   I GIVE YOU
 FOUR GUESSES AND IF YOU GET IT RIGHT YOU GET A BIG
 SURPRISE.   JUST TYPE IN WHAT YOU THINK MY NAME IS, AND
 I'LL TELL YOU WHETHER YOU ARE RIGHT OR NOT.  OK, FIRST
 GUESS?
? ELIZA
I THOUGHT YOU'D SAY THAT.  HAVE ANOTHER GO?
? CHANGE-A-NAME.
ABSOLUTELY USELESS.   TRY AGAIN?
? SMART
ABSOLUTELY, HORRIBLY, DESPERATELY AWFUL.   MAKE YOUR
 LAST GUESS.
? COMPUTERS DON'T HAVE NAMES.
WELL NOW YOU'LL NEVER KNOW MY NAME.  BUT NICE TO HAVE
TALKED TO YOU ANYWAY.  WOULD YOU GO OVER AND TELL MY BOSS
THAT YOU HAVE FINISHED.   GOODBYE.
```

FIGURE 7b Typical printout of 'naive' subject chatting to SAILOR.

CONCLUSION

   To summarise, the main theme of this paper has been to show
that the study of man-computer interaction has been handicapped
by a number of false assumptions, not only about man-computer
communication but also man-man communication.   Some of these false
assumptions are highlighted by the "Ten Findings" that I listed
earlier on.   In a sense these can be advanced even further to
allow one to make two fundamental points which need to be taken to
heart by anyone, psychologist, computer scientist or engineer, who
is genuinely interested in improving the man-computer interface.
These are:

1.   That one can expect far more at the level of initiative,
     confidence and imagination from naive users when left alone
     with computers than most people have generally assumed.

2.   That normal communication between people is basically very
     poor, and low in information content, and therefore is far
     simpler to synthesise than one might imagine.   Thus the
     task of programming computers to do many human-like jobs
     in the field of communication - medicine and teaching are
     probably the most obvious and practical examples - should
     present few problems.

   Perhaps I can close the paper with the comment that these
findings, which are essentially psychological in nature, have come
about directly as a result of programming computers and studying
them in action.   No doubt more insights are yet to come from this
approach.   How ironic it is that our understanding of human
psychology may well be intriguingly advanced by a study not of man
himself but of the way he communicates with computers.

REFERENCES

Bevan, N.S.   (1977)   Factors affecting the efficient use of
                                terminals for man-computer interaction.
                             PhD thesis (in prep.)

Evans, C.R.   (1972)   Chatting Computers.
                             Proc. Design Research Society Conference.

SOME CHARACTERISTICS OF CONVERSATIONS

R.S. Nickerson,

Bolt Beranek and Newman Inc.
50 Moulton Street, Cambridge, Massachusetts 02138, USA.

INTRODUCTION

The idea of conversational interaction with computers has been around now for some time. One encounters the term frequently in descriptions of interactive systems. What is meant by 'conversational', however, is not always clear. One might take the position that an interaction is conversational to the degree that it has the characteristics of conversations that occur between persons. But this is not as helpful as it might appear, since a descriptive model of interperson conversations does not exist.

The purpose of this paper is to suggest what some of the characteristic features of interperson conversations are. The intent is not to present a theory of conversation, or even to review the research that has been done on conversational behavior, but simply to list, and comment briefly upon, some of the properties that the types of interactions we typically refer to as conversations appear to have. I fully expect that my list will prove to be deficient in many respects - it is certainly at once redundant and incomplete. But perhaps if it provokes others to generate more adequate lists it will have served a useful purpose.

Several investigators (eg. Chapanis, 1973; Foley & Wallace, 1974; Mann, 1975) have suggested that the development of computer systems that would permit truly conversational person-computer interaction could be facilitated by more careful studies of person-person conversation. This paper is motivated in part by the assumption that such studies should indeed provide useful information and ideas for developers of interactive systems. An assumption that is not made, however, is that in order to be

maximally effective, systems must permit interactions between
people and computers that resemble interperson conversations in
all respects.   Moreover, it is not clear that people who use
the term 'conversational' in reference to specific systems intend
to convey the impression that these systems either do, or should,
permit interactions that have all the characteristics of interperson conversations.   The question of what specific aspects of
interperson conversations person-computer interactions should have
is an open one; and the answer may differ from system to system
and application to application.

As a tentative answer to the question of what constitutes a
conversation, I propose it to be an interaction that has certain
characteristics which are suggested by the following terms:

- Bidirectionality
- Mixed initiative
- Apparentness of who is in control
- Rules for transfer of control
- Sense of presence
- Nonverbal communication
- Intolerance for silence
- Structure
- Characteristic time scale
- Wide bandwidth
- Informal language
- Shared situational context
- Common world knowledge
- Shared special knowledge
- History
- Peer status of participants

DISCUSSION OF CHARACTERISTICS OF CONVERSATIONS

Bidirectionality

A conversation is a collaboration, a two-way exchange of
information in which both participants play the roles of speaker
and listener in a complementary fashion. One party to the conversation listens while the other talks, and listens, in particular,
to what the other says.   In this regard, a conversation is to be
distinguished from such unidirectional activities as a lecture, a
judge's charge to a jury, and a commander's issuance of orders to
subordinates.   It also is to be distinguished from what Piaget
has called a 'collective monologue', in which each speaker talks
for the sheer pleasure of talking, and without regard to whether
anyone other than himself is listening.

Mixed Initiative

Conversations are characterized by the change of initiative and control from one participant to the other from time to time during the interaction. In this regard, an interrogation is different from a conversation; although bidirectional, it is not a conversation because it is controlled exclusively by the interrogator and never by the interrogatee.

It is not the case, of course that all conversations are perfectly symmetrical with respect to the way control is shared by the participants. There must be a limit, however, to how asymmetrical the control of the interaction can become before the interaction loses the character of a conversation, at least from the vantage point of one of the participants. The question of where that limit lies, and how it might depend on other factors, is an interesting one for research. I would state as a conjecture that a minimum requirement of an interaction, if it is to be perceived as a conversation by both participants is that each participant be able to ask questions, to volunteer information, and, more generally, to influence the direction in which the dialogue goes.

There are two corollaries to the mixed initiative property: (1) usually it is clear to both participants in a conversation who has the floor at any moment, and (2) the transfer of control from one participant to the other is done (presumably) according to certain rules.

Apparentness of Who is in Control

Usually, it is clear to the participants in a conversation who is speaking, or, when neither party is doing so, who is waiting for whom to speak. Typically, they do not talk at the same time, nor are they often both simultaneously waiting for each other.

In face-to-face conversations, the participants can get information from visual cues regarding who is waiting for whom to speak. In telephone conversations, one must resort to other types of cues to resolve uncertainties regarding control. If it is A's turn to speak, but he knows there will be a delay before he does so, he is likely to warn B of that delay: "Let me think about that for a minute," or "Hold on while I answer the doorbell." Or, to use an example that is particularly appropriate for some cases of person-computer interaction, if B has just supplied A with some data that A is about to use in a calculation, A is likely to acknowledge receipt of the data explicitly before he turns his attention to doing the calculation. A long pause by A, without an acknowledgement of receipt of the data, could have left B wondering whether A was doing the calculation or still waiting for more input.

Rules of Transfer of Control

Presumably, there are some widely understood, but not well-articulated, rules by which participants in a conversation accomplish the transfer of control from one to the other. In some instances, it is clear that control is being relinquished voluntarily by the speakers, and the listener is, in effect, being offered or asked to take the floor; in other instances, the initiative for the change comes from the listener. Listener-initiated transfers may be accomplished in subtle and sophisticated, or in direct and forceful, ways. The listener may signal the desire to take the floor, for example, by a carefully timed gesture or brief vocalization, and then wait to see if the speaker is willing to relinquish it before proceeding to speak. Or, he may simply interrupt the speaker and usurp control.

An interesting problem for research is that of determining the conditions under which listener-initiated transfers of control are acceptable to the speaker, and those under which they are not. It is certainly not the case that requests to take the floor are always acceptable and interruptions never are. Another interesting research problem is that of identifying the techniques that people use to recover from disruptive transfers. Sometimes, of course, they do not recover; the conversation degenerates into a quarrel and perhaps aborts.

Sense of Presence

Closely related to the topic of control is another characteristic of interperson conversations that may be called a sense of presence. Each participant tends to be aware at all times of the degree of attention he is receiving from the other participant. If one participant begins to 'leave' the conversation psychologically, say by daydreaming, falling asleep, or engaging in other activities that decrease his conversational effectiveness, this is immediately apparent to the other participant. People use a variety of techniques to signal their attentiveness. Several of these techniques are mentioned in the following section.

Nonverbal Communication

Much of the communication in face-to-face conversation is mediated by nonverbal behavior such as facial expressions, gestures, body movements, and changes in gaze direction. It also involves a good bit of vocal behavior that probably should not be considered linguistic in the usual sense of the word ("Mm-hmmm," "Uh-huh"). Sometimes these 'listener responses,' as they have been called, convey information that relates directly to the substance of the conversation (translating, for example, to "Yes, I understand," or "I doubt that"); in other cases, they seem to serve the function

of assuring the speaker of the listener's continued attention.
Fries (1952) points out that such attention-confirming signalling
is often accomplished by nods of the head during face-to-face
conversations, whereas in telephone conversations it is done via
brief oral sounds, interjected at irregular intervals in such a
way as not to interrupt the speaker's talk. Fries further notes
that if the listener fails to deliver such signals for a period
of time, the speaker is likely to interrupt his continuous discourse with explicit requests for evidence of the listener's
continuing attention: "Do you hear me?" "Are you still there?"

The frequency with which listener responses are made depends,
according to Dittmann (1972), on the extent to which they are 'pulled'
from the listener by the conversational situation. Situations
that exert a high degree of pull are those in which the information
load is high and the speaker requires more or less constant feedback concerning whether he is being understood. An example would
be the giving of instructions regarding how to play a game, or the
explaining of a complicated process. Low-pull situations would
be those in which the individuals were engaged in an absorbing
nonverbal activity (eg. dining, playing a game), and the conversation
or banter served primarily as a social, as opposed to, say, an
instructional function.

Intolerance for Silence

Participants in a conversation - at least when the conversation
is their primary activity and not incidental to some other mode of
interaction - tend to be intolerant of long periods of silence.
Unless there has been a fairly clear signal that the conversation
either has been completed or is to be temporarily interrupted, a
speaker is likely to get impatient for a response after he has
relinquished control. It need not be the case that he has explicitly
requested a response by virtue of having asked a question. It
need only be that he has signaled that he has come to the end of
what he had to say in that particular talk spurt. If the listener
fails to pick up the conversation, the chances are good that the
speaker will begin a new spurt shortly, rather than permit a long
period of silence. Any reader who doubts the strength of this
intolerance for silence is invited to test it experimentally.
Simply fail to talk at some arbitrary point in a conversation when
it is your turn to do so, and observe the reaction of the other
participant.

There are exceptions to this rule. A silent period is
tolerated when the person whose turn it is to speak is clearly
thinking hard about what to say, as, for example, when he is working
out an answer to a difficult question he has been asked. It is
also accepted when one of the participants removes himself from the
conversation temporarily to attend to an interrupt. In this case,

however, courtesy demands that the participant who wishes to
attend momentarily to another matter ask to be excused to do so.
Also, unless the circumstances make it unnecessary, he is likely
to say how long he expects the delay to be.

Structure

Conversations tend to have an overall structure not unlike
that of a business letter.   That is to say, they have a beginning,
an ending, and everything in between.   Of particular interest is
the fact that conversations almost always obtain some type of
closure; they usually are not terminated at arbitrary points or in
arbitrary ways.   The closure that is obtained could be agreement
between the participants to recess, and to continue the conversation
at a later time.   But, even here, there is a sign-off procedure;
one does not simply stop talking and walk away.   A study of the
various ways in which people signal the desire to end or recess a
conversation would undoubtedly uncover some interesting techniques.

Characteristic Time Scale

Conversations are characterized by the time scale on which
the interaction takes place.   The contrast between a conversation
and a postal correspondence is striking in this regard, and it is
a contrast that has been used on occasion to illustrate the difference between interactive and batch-processing computer systems.
The analogy seems apt for some purposes;   however, the difference
in time scales between conversational and postal interactions is
many orders of magnitude, and one probably need not change the
temporal characteristics of a conversation by anything like an order
of magnitude in order to destroy its conversational character.

Easily interpreted data on the temporal characteristics of
conversations have proven to be difficult to obtain.   One problem
is that of establishing criteria for determining what constitute
pauses and vocalizations in speech (Brady, 1965).   In particular,
stop consonants, momentary falls in speech level, and intersyllabic
gaps are difficult to discriminate among automatically, as are very
brief vocalizations and transient noise.   One measurement that is
relatively easy to make, however, is the duration of 'talkspurts'
when a talkspurt is defined as the speech, including pauses,
produced by one participant that is preceded and followed by speech
from the other.   Norwine and Murphy (1938) measured 2845 talkspurts
in telephone conversations and obtained a mean talkspurt length
of 4.3 sec.

The temporal characteristics of conversations are worthy of more attention from researchers than they have received. In particular, one would like both to have normative data on a number of temporal parameters and to know how far individual conversations can depart from normative values without destroying the conversational nature of the interaction.

Wide Bandwidth

As the term is usually used, conversation connotes the use of speech as the communication mode. This seems, however, to be a secondary characteristic and a non-essential one. People who are not able to speak, or hear speech, but who do have some other fluent means of communication, such as the manual sign languages used by deaf persons, certainly converse - although the characteristics of nonvocal conversation may differ from those of vocal conversation in some respects.

I suspect that the reason speech is such an effective means of communication is the fact that most of us can transmit information at higher rates by talking than by using other methods that have been devised. People normally emit words at the rate of about 125 to 175 per minute when speaking in a conversational manner; much higher rates can be attained when one intentionally speaks more rapidly than usual. In contrast, few typists, even if highly skilled, can maintain a rate of 100 words per minute; and the typical computer user with his hunt-and-peck level of typing competence does well to produce a few tens of words per minute.

Informal Language

Conversational language tends to be highly informal and unconstrained. Not only does it lack formal rigor, it violates the rules and conventions of grammar in every conceivable way. In spite of this fact, people communicate when they converse. It may be that conversations have a grammar of their own that is different from that of written language; and perhaps the rules of this grammar are not violated, or at least not so flagrantly, by talkers. But until the rules of conversational grammar are discovered and made explicit, the ungrammaticality of conversations will remain among their more distinctive features.

Some of the reasons why conversations can be so forgiving of vagueness, ambiguities and syntactic irregularities stem from the real-time nature of conversation interactions. If the listener fails to understand what the speaker is saying, and realizes the fact, he can ask for clarification on the spot. Even if the intent of the speaker is misunderstood by the listener at one point in the

conversation, the chances are good that the misunderstanding will
be realized and corrected as the conversation continues.   It would
be of interest to attempt to identify the various techniques that
people use to assure themselves that they do understand each other.
One, for example, is for one participant to paraphrase what the
other has said and to ask whether the paraphrase is correct.   The
main point, for the moment, is that there are various ways in which
real-time checks can be made as to whether information is really
being exchanged and there is a mutual understanding between the
participants.

Another reason why conversations work in spite of the
imprecision and fallibility of the language in which they are
couched is the fact that much information is conveyed in conversational situations by context and nonlinguistic means.   This
information supplements and, in many cases, helps to disambiguate
that which is carried by the immediate speech signal itself.   The
role of nonlinguistic signs has already been noted; that of
context will be discussed in succeeding sections.

Shared Situational Context

An important characteristic of face-to-face conversations is
the fact that the participants share a situational context.   Both
participants are in the same place at the same time, subject to
the same perceptual stimulation.   It is this fact that imparts
meaning to many of the utterances that otherwise would be uninter-
pretable.   In the case of telephone conversations, the immediate
perceptual surroundings are not shared; however, much else is.
Recent local happenings (read local as same neighborhood, same
town, same state, as appropriate), significance of the date
(eg. weekday, holiday, weekend), time of day and many other factors
combine to define a context that is shared by the participants in
the conversation and that can provide common points of reference.

Dreyfus (1972) has made the point that all human activity takes
place within a situational context, and is conditioned by that
context.   The admonition to "Stand near me" (to borrow his example
of how the situation conditions the use and interpretation of
language) would mean one thing when said by a parent to a child
in a crowded elevator and quite another when spoken by one astronaut
to another while exploring the surface of the moon.

Common World Knowledge

People bring to conversations a great amount of knowledge
about the world.   The role of this world knowledge in language
understanding is only beginning to be investigated intensively.

That its application is absolutely essential is abundantly apparent,
however.   One of the tacit assumptions that the participants in a
conversation must make - even those who 'have nothing in common' -
is that much (most?) of what they know is also known by other people
from the same culture.   If it were not possible to work on the
assumption of a common-knowledge information base that is shared
by most people of normal intelligence, conversations, as we know
them, could not occur.   The question of how to characterize this
common-knowledge information base, how to determine and describe
its contents, is one that stands as a challenge to any one who
would understand human cognition, or who would give computers the
capability of mimicking it.

Shared Special Knowledge

        In addition to knowledge about the world in general, partici-
pants in a conversation also often have some specific knowledge
that may be especially germane to interactions between them in
particular.   They may, for example, have much knowledge about each
other, and about what special information they share.   If, for
example, they are from the same family, or live in the same town,
or belong to the same organization, or have the same vocation, they
can assume a certain common information base vis-a-vis the shared
affiliation(s).   Such special knowledge may be very useful in
helping them make sense out of their verbal exchanges.   There are
certain things that one expects, or at least is not surprised, to
hear from certain speakers.   The more familiar one is with an
acquaintance's figures of speech, colloquialisms and ways of saying
things, the more ambiguity one can tolerate in the speech signal
itself.

        It is important to note that what one participant knows, or
believes, about the other will include what he thinks the other
knows, or believes about him.   That is to say, A's model of B will
include A's model of B's model of A.   As a consequence, not only
will A find some utterances more likely than others to come from
B, A's expectancies in this regard will be conditioned somewhat by
the fact that B is speaking to him, rather than to someone else.
Thus, for example, a child's remark that would not surprise a parent
when addressed to another child might surprise him considerably when
addressed to the parent himself.

        It is this special knowledge about each other and about what
each other knows that permits people who converse often to develop
idiosyncratic ways of expressing themselves involving private jargon,
allusions to shared personal experiences, in-jokes, and so on.

History

This point is closely related to the preceding one. Most conversations have a history; they are not first-time events. That is to say, people usually converse with people with whom they have conversed before. As a consequence, the participants in a conversation may be familiar with each other's interests, mannerisms, communication idiosyncrasies, and (uncommon) knowledge. Also, to the extent that the particular topic of conversation is one that has been talked about before, the participants come to the situation with at least a partial understanding of each other's positions and feelings with respect to it. This permits each of them to have fairly precise expectancies regarding what the other will say on that particular topic and how he will respond to specific things that may be said to him.

Peer Status

Conversations, in the best sense of the word, tend to take place between peers, particularly intellectual peers. It is relatively difficult for people with very large differences in intellectual capability and knowledge to have satisfactory conversations. To be sure, they can talk, but the interaction lacks the degree of symmetry and the fluency that the most effective conversations have.

CONCLUDING REMARKS

The preceding comments represent an attempt to describe some of the characteristics of conversations between persons. The discussion has been selective and has not touched on some issues that are clearly germane to a more-than-superficial understanding of conversational behavior. It has not, for example, explicitly touched on the fact that interperson conversations serve social and psychological, as well as informational purposes. Nor has it distinguished between goal-directed conversations (conversations between persons who are communicating for the express purpose of collaborating on the solution of a well-defined problem) and conversations that are engaged in simply for the sake of having a conversation. More generally, it has not recognized that there may be many different types of conversations serving a variety of purposes and differing, perhaps in some of their characteristics. No attempt has been made to distinguish between essential or defining characteristics of conversations and characteristics that are non-essential or accidental. And no attention has been given to the role of emotional factors in conversations or to the various ways in which emotive information is conveyed. Undoubtedly, other important aspects of conversation behavior have been ignored.

Even limiting our attention to the characteristics of interperson conversations that have been considered, it is clear that no existing computer system can support a person-computer interaction that has all of them.   This is not necessarily a criticism of existing systems, in that an interaction having all the character- istics of interperson conversations is not necessarily the preferred mode of communication between people and computers.   It seems apparent that some of these characteristics would be desirable for some cases; in other cases, it is not so apparent.   Moreover, which conversational features prove to be useful may depend some- what on the purpose of the interaction.

Finally, three concluding comments: (1) There is need for a better understanding of interperson conversation - indeed, for a theory of conversational behavior.   What makes a conversation a conversation is still not entirely clear.   That is to say, to what extent a conversation can shed some of the characteristics that conversations typically have, and still be perceived as a conversation by both participants is not apparent.   Human conver- sational behavior is a fascinating topic; it is surprising that it has received so little attention from researchers.   (2) There is a need for people who write about person-computer interaction to be more cautious in their use of the term conversational. Using it uncritically to describe existing systems can be misleading, and is non-informative at best.   One wants to know in what partic- ular respects the interactions that these systems allow resemble conversations, inasmuch as it is clear that they do not do so in all respects.   To the extent that this comment appears to be critical of people who have used the term 'conversational' uncritically to describe existing systems or languages, I am pointing the finger at myself (Nickerson, 1969).   The intent is not to argue that the term conversational should never be used, but only that care should be exercised so that its use does not connote more than the writer intends.   Of course, a good way to avoid misunderstanding is to define terms that can be given various interpretations.   (3) More consideration should be given to the question of what particular characteristics of conversations would be desirable as character- istics of person-computer interaction, and to the possibility that the answers to this question may differ somewhat with the purpose for having the interaction.

ACKNOWLEDGEMENT

This paper was prepared under Contract No. MDA903-76-C-0207 with the Cybernetics Systems Office of the Defense Advanced Research Projects Agency.   I am grateful to Albert Stevens for helpful comments on the draft of the manuscript.

64

REFERENCES

Brady, P.T.   1965   A technique for investigating on-off
                               patterns of speech.
                               The Bell System Technical Journal,
                               44, 1-22.

Chapanis, A.   1973   The communication of factual information
                               through various channels.
                               Information Storage and Retrieval,
                               9, 215-231.

Dittmann, A.T.   1972   Developmental factors in conversational
                               behavior.
                               The Journal of Communication,
                               22, 404-423.

Dreyfus, H.L.   1972   What computers can't do: a critique
                               of artificial reason.
                               New York, Harper & Row.

Foley, J.D. &   1974   The art of natural graphic man-machine
   Wallace, V.L.   conversation.
                               Proceedings of the IEEE, 62, 462-471.

Fries, C.C.   1952   The structure of English.
                               New York, Harcourt Brace.

Mann, W.C.   1975   Why things are so bad for the computer-
                               naive user.
                               ISI/RR-75-32; Information Science Inst.,
                               Univ. of Southern California,
                               4676 Admiralty Way, Marina del Ray,
                               Ca. 90291, USA.

Nickerson, R.S.   1969   Man-computer interaction: a challenge
                               for human factors research.
                               Ergonomics, 12, 501-517.

Norwine, A.C. &   1938   Characteristic time intervals in
   Murphy, O.J.   telephone conversation.
                               The Bell System Technical Journal,
                               17, 281.

INTERACTIVE HUMAN COMMUNICATION: SOME LESSONS LEARNED FROM
LABORATORY EXPERIMENTS

Alphonse Chapanis

Department of Psychology, The Johns Hopkins University,
Baltimore, Maryland 21218, U.S.A.

This paper describes some findings that have come out of my
research program on interactive communication.   Altogether my
colleagues, my students, and I have completed 11 separate experi-
ments and have published eight articles based on those experiments
(Chapanis, 1971; Chapanis, 1973; Chapanis, 1975; Chapanis, Ochsman,
Parrish, and Weeks, 1972; Chapanis and Overbey, 1974; Oschman and
Chapanis, 1974; Weeks and Chapanis, 1976; and Weeks, Kelly and
Chapanis, 1974).   Two additional articles are in press (Chapanis,
Parrish, Ochsman, and Weeks, 1977; and Stoll, Hoecker, Krueger, and
Chapanis, 1976) and two experiments have been reported as doctoral
dissertations (Kelly, 1976; and Parrish, 1974).   At the time this
paper was prepared, several other articles were in various stages
of preparation.

In discussing the findings of my own research program, I do
not mean to suggest that it is the only one that has been concerned
with these problems.   A great deal of very good work on person-
to-person communication, and on man-computer communication, has
been done in other laboratories.   Prominent among the former are
the Communications Studies Group at University College London,
Bell Laboratories in the United States, Carleton University in
Canada, and Bell Northern Research in Canada.   The Massachusetts
Institute of Technology, RAND Corporation, Systems Development
Corporation, International Business Machines Corporation, and Bolt,
Beranek and Newman are just a few of the many organizations that
have done excellent research on man-computer interactions.   While
acknowledging the fine work of those other laboratories, I have
chosen to confine myself to my own program for two largely selfish
reasons: (1) This is the first opportunity I have had to summarize
and integrate our findings to date.   (2) My research program has
some rather unique features that are not duplicated in any other
research programs that I know about.

The goals of my research program are to discover (a) how people
naturally communicate with each other when they are required to do
various kinds of tasks, (b) how interactive human communication is
affected by the machine devices and systems through which people
converse, and (c) what significant system and human variables affect
interactive communication. I should add that we are not interested
in any particular kind of system, but rather in general principles
of communication.

INTERACTIVE COMMUNICATION DEFINED

In communication research it is important to make a distinction
between interactive and unidirectional communication. For years
psychologists and other scientists have been concerned with the
effectiveness of unidirectional modes of communication, such as
highway signs, books, lectures, and television broadcasts. In
unidirectional communication, the person to whom a message is
addressed is a passive recipient of information. Nothing that he
does or says affects the communicator, the communication process,
or the content of a message.

In interactive communication, by contrast, the participants
are both senders and receivers of information. Communicators, the
communication process, and the contents of messages can be, and
usually are, affected by all the participants. Conferences,
arguments, seminars, telephone conversations, and man-computer
dialogs are examples of interactive communication. This paper is
entirely concerned with interactive communication.

MAN-COMPUTER DIALOG AND ITS RELATION TO INTERACTIVE HUMAN
  COMMUNICATION

The research I shall talk about was done entirely by having
people communicate with one another. In only one of our experiments
did we actually use a computer in the communication process (Kelly,
1976) and then the computer was used only to assure that messages
conformed to certain constraints of vocabulary and grammer. That
being the case, one might well ask what the findings of my research
program have to do with man-computer communication.

Although people do not resemble computers at all physically,
some of the things they both do are sufficiently similar that
computers have been called "giant brains" (Berkeley, 1949). The
similarities become even more striking when we compare person-to-
person telecommunications with man-computer communications. In
the first place, the interactions between man and modern computers
may, in a manner of speaking, be thought of as conversations. They
are characterized by commands, statements, questions, answers to
questions, and sundry other messages that go from man to computer
and vice versa. As may be apparent, these exchanges are truly
interactive in the sense that I have been using the word.

Conversations between people and computers are all carried out in one of several different languages which, although they are not exactly colloquial are close enough to it so that the language can be recognized and learned more or less readily. To be sure, the input options for communications from man to computer are still limited to typewritten materials, some simple and highly constrained forms of cursor-positioning and handwriting, and a few primitive voice signals. On the other hand, output devices that carry communications from computers to man cover the full range of those that one finds in person-to-person telecommunications systems - printed materials, voice, graphics and pictures. Most impressive of all, however, is that some computer programs have been made so human-like that people who have used the systems have actually been misled - at least for a time - into believing that they were communicating with another person! (Weizenbaum, 1970).

The essential unity of communication problems, whether they be with other people or with computers, is the basis for my belief that a complete understanding of person-to-person communication is essential to a proper understanding of how best to design computers for effective man-computer dialogs.

I also believe that the future will see an integration of communication systems that we now think of as separate. Indeed, computers have already been combined with person-to-person tele-communication systems in computer conferencing, a written form of conference telephone calls (see Turoff, 1975). At a more sophis-ticated level, Vannevar Bush's visionary article, 'As We May Think' (1945), first called attention to the extraordinary power that modern computers have to supplement human cognitive functions. Bush saw the computer as providing an enlarged intimate adjunct to a user's memory. "Associative trails," much like the associa-tions that characterize human thinking, would make it possible to bring the enormous capacity of modern computers to integrate, file, sort, and compile the contents of encyclopaedias, books, newspapers, letters, opinions, and human experiences.

Bush's article was, of course, far ahead of the technology of that time. A similar and more recent endeavor is Licklider's (1965) treatment of Libraries of the Future which foresaw the revolution in library systems now beginning to appear in such forms as the New York Times Information Bank.

Combine such a computer system with person-to-person tele-communication systems and the product will be a truly all-purpose information system. With it one will be able to

- exchange messages and 'letters' with other people and with computers
- hold teleconferences
- do computations

- jointly write and edit articles and journals
- collect files of important documents
- search files
- keep personal diaries
- design and write specifications for new equipment and systems
- teach classes
- conduct interviews
- perform all manner of banking transactions
- order groceries, theater tickets, equipment, etc.

And the list could go on and on.

One of the most important characteristics of such advanced systems is that all these activities would be independent of time and space. Conferences, interviews, classes, and other interactions could be carried out among persons in widely separated places on the earth, as easily as they could be conducted next door. Even more important - such systems would make it possible to draw upon the collective intelligences of man and computer. Indeed, one can easily imagine that the contributions of man and computer would be so commingled that one would never be sure whether a thought, idea, suggestion, or solution came from a man or computer.

To make that kind of dream reality will require a great deal of imaginative and careful research on the ways in which tele-communication and computer technologies can be most effectively married to satisy their ultimate users. Only after we have done that research will we be able to achieve the complete "man-computer symbiosis" that was so confidently predicted nearly two decades ago (Licklider, 1960), but that has remained so elusively and so tantalizingly beyond our grasp.

The research I shall talk about provides a few answers about how people communicate with each other interactively and about some of the variables that affect those communications. The lessons to be learned from that research are, in my opinion, just as useful in the design of computer systems as in the design of person-to-person telecommunication systems. In thinking about my research and its implications for computer systems, however, I prefer not to confine myself to any particular computer system, or to computer systems as they are today. For example, some computers today can receive voice signals from a very limited and highly constrained repertory. Similarly, a few computer systems can accept some highly constrained forms of hand drawn letters and numerals. These are only limitations of our current technology. I prefer not to be bound by such limitations. I am much more concerned with what we need to know to build highly versatile, flexible, and adaptive computers of the kind that exist only in our imaginations today, but that will certainly become realities at some time in the future. In considering the findings that I shall describe here, I invite you to join me in adopting that kind of long-range perspective.

MODES OF PERSON-TO-PERSON AND MAN-COMPUTER COMMUNICATION COMPARED

In considering modes of communication it is interesting to ask first what human skills are used naturally in person-to-person communication. The list is surprisingly short. Everyone, even the inarticulate and dumb, can convey information by body movements - postures, gestures, and facial expressions. Virtually everyone can speak one of the natural languages - perhaps not grammatically but fluently. A majority of people have at least some elementary level of competence in writing and can make crude but comprehensible drawings. Finally, a respectable number of people know how to type and even some people without typing experience seem to be able to approach the keyboard and peck out acceptable messages. But these few different kinds of skills exhaust the list.

That very same list of skills is a catalogue of the principal ways in which people could conceivably communicate with computers. Note, however, that I mentioned these human communication skills in the order of easiest, or most universal, to hardest, or most specialized. Everyone can communicate by body movements, slightly fewer people can express themselves vocally, still fewer people can communicate by handwriting or drawing, and typing is the least widely available human communicative skill. That order is exactly the reverse of their adaptability to man-computer communication. Typewriting, the least universal mode of person-to-person communication, is easiest and most adaptable for man-computer communication. On the other hand, no-one foresees body movements - the most universal mode of human communication - as a viable alternative for man-computer communication, even in the year 2,001.

THE RESEARCH SETTING AND LABORATORY

Our experiments have tested four different channels of communication that are the mechanical or electronic counterparts of the four forms of natural human communication that I have just described. The four channels are video (the picture part of television without the voice), voice, handwriting or drawing, and typewriting. Three of the four basic channels have been tested singly, and all of them have been tested in various combinations. The individual channels or combinations of them are referred to collectively as modes. We have tested as many as ten different modes in a single experiment (Ochsman and Chapanis, 1974). As a standard of comparison we typically rely on normal, unrestricted, face-to-face communication, which we have called a communication-rich mode, because we usually allow other options, eg. writing or drawing, as well as gesturing and talking.

The laboratory in which most of our experiments have been done consisted of two adjoining rooms connected by a soundproofed double door (Figure 1). The wall between the rooms also had in it a large double-glass panel, which could be covered with an opaque

70

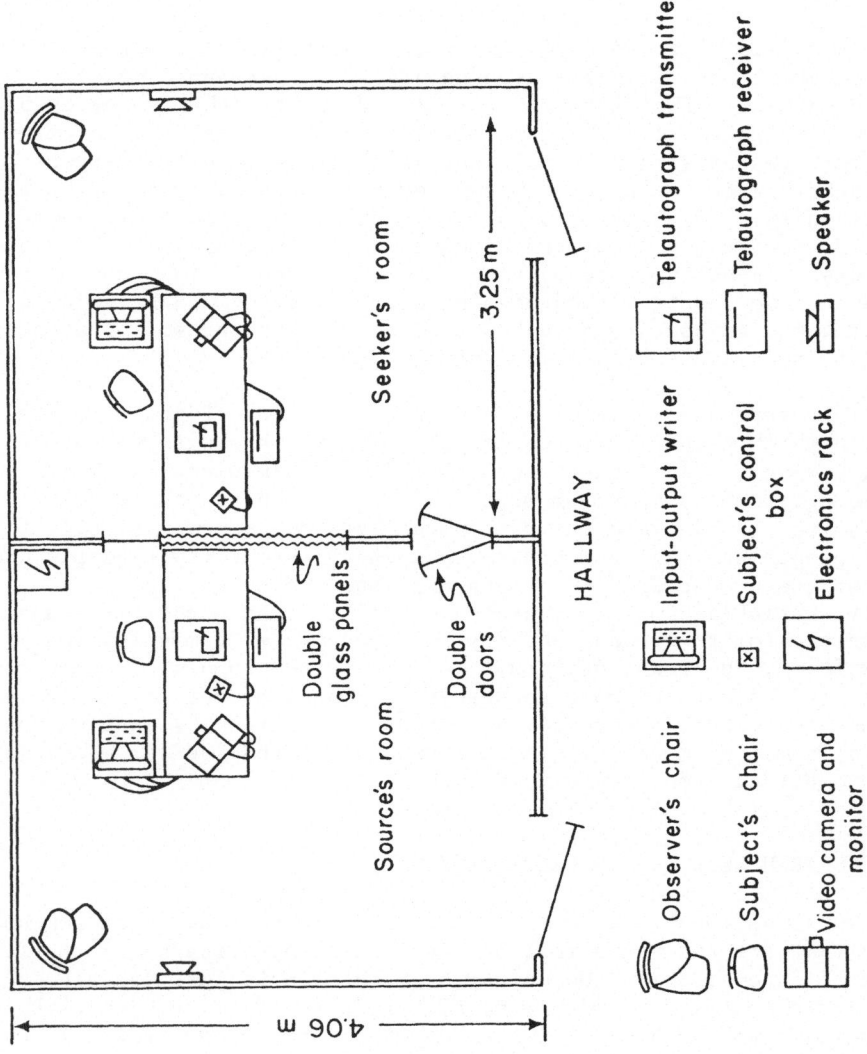

FIGURE 1. The two experimental rooms and associated equipment used in most of our earlier work.

screen so that the persons in each of the rooms could not see each other. When the panel was not covered, the participants could see each other and could converse freely through a microphone and loudspeaker, even though they were separated physically. In some of our experiments, subjects have actually been face-to-face, or side by side, in the same room.

Figure 1 shows teletypewriting and telautograph (or telewriter) machines. These machines are linked in such a way that anything typewritten or written in longhand on a machine in one room is simultaneously reproduced on the other. Video cameras and monitors enable us to duplicate closed-circuit television or to use either the video or audio channels separately.

About a year ago, we expanded and redesigned our laboratories as shown in Figure 2. The new arrangement permits us to test as many as four persons in as many different rooms. Communication facilities among the rooms allow all persons to communicate with all others, or allow only certain communication links to be used.

PROBLEMS

In our research we have tested two main kinds of problems: co-operative and conflictive. Altogether we have compiled and tested nearly 20 different problems of both kinds.

Co-operative Problems

Our co-operative problems have been carefully chosen to meet several important criteria:

1. The set of problems samples a wide range of psychological abilities. For example, some problems are entirely clerical paper-and-pencil tasks, some involve mechanical manipulation, others require careful attention to detail, and others make use of still other psychological skills.

2. The problems are representative of tasks for which interactive computer systems are currently being used, or might be used in the future.

3. They are of recognizable and practical importance in everyday life; they are not abstract or artificial problems of the type often constructed to measure hypothetical psychological processes.

4. They have definite, recognizable solutions and the solutions can be reached within approximately an hour.

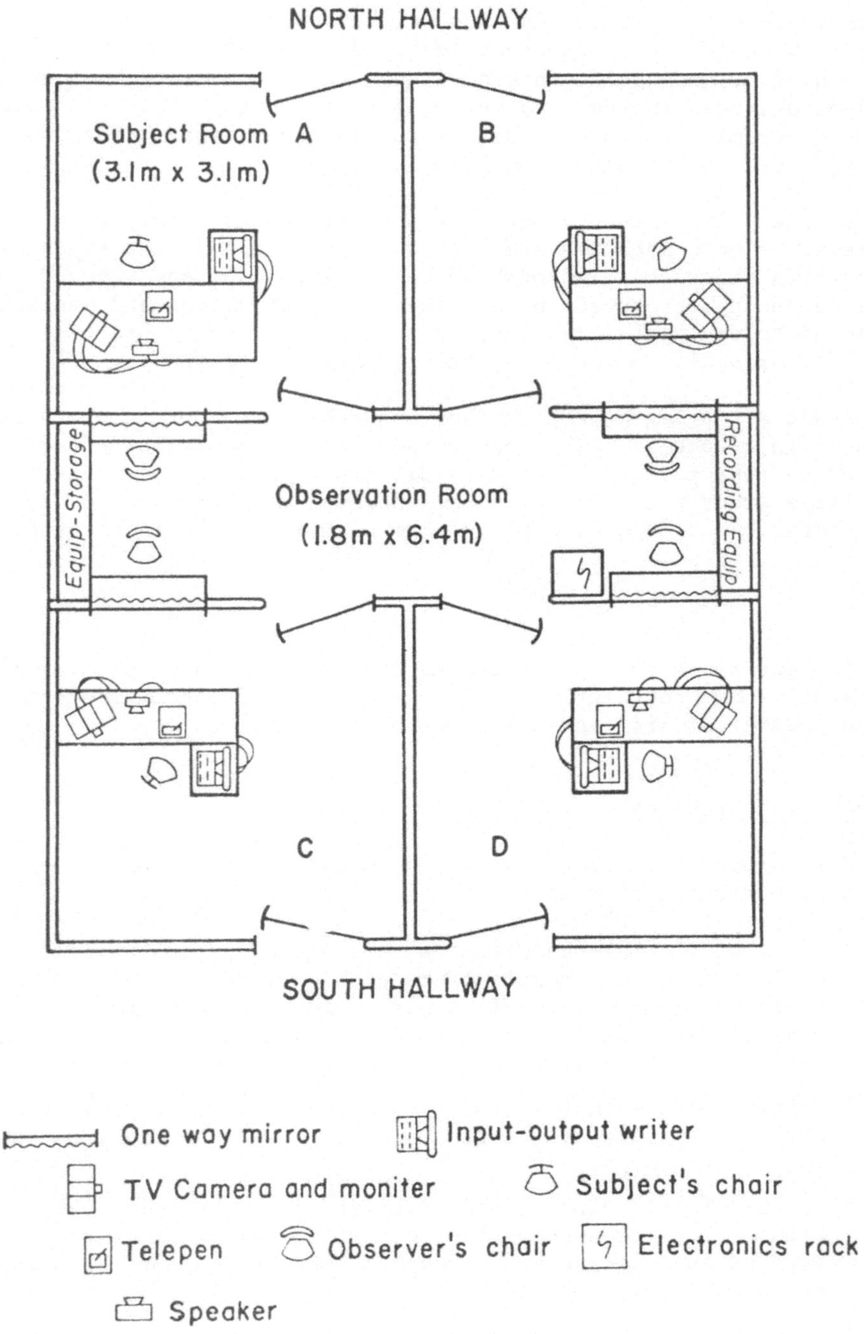
NORTH HALLWAY
Subject Room A
(3.1m x 3.1m)
B
Equip-Storage
Observation Room
(1.8m x 6.4m)
Recording Equip
C
D
SOUTH HALLWAY
One way mirror
Input-output writer
TV Camera and moniter
Subject's chair
Telepen
Observer's chair
Electronics rack
Speaker

FIGURE 2. The new communication laboratory at Johns Hopkins.

5. They require few or essentially no specialized skills or specialized knowledge for their solution.

6. They are formulated in such a way that their solutions require the efforts of two individuals working together as a team. This is done by deliberately structuring the problems so that each member of a team receives complementary information folios. One member of the team, the seeker, is give a problem for which he has to find a solution. His information folio consists of certain parts of the problem. The other member of the team, the source, has a folio with the remainder of the information needed to solve the problem. Therefore, while neither person can solve the problem by himself, the two of them have all the information necessary to do so. Although the analogy will not survive careful scrutiny, I tend to think of the seeker as a person who comes to a computer with a problem, and the source as a perfect computer, that is, a computer so human-like in its responses that it would easily pass Turing's test (1950). I emphasize, however, that our problems are designed to elicit communication between the members of a team. Our division of the problems does not necessarily represent the way tasks would be allocated to man and computer in an actual system.

The brief descriptions of four of our problems below will convey some idea of their content, diversity, and flavor.

Wiring task. The seeker is given a digital logic panel (Figure 3) and some wires with clip ends. When the panel is correctly wired (Figure 4) and the power is turned on, the assembly counts digits in the binary system. Information about how to wire the panel is supplied by the source who has a correctly wired panel at the start.

Object identification task. The seeker is given a small electric light socket (Figure 5) and is asked to obtain an identical replacement socket from his partner. The source has a set of 65 different Leecraft pilot light sockets (Figure 6). Although all 65 sockets in the source's folio are similar to the seeker's in some respect, only one is a perfect match.

Class scheduling problem. The seeker is given a list of four college courses which have to be arranged into a workable schedule within specified time constraints, such as commuting schedules. The source has a 97-page booklet listing the complete time schedule for courses at the University of Maryland. The courses and constraints are such that there is only a single correct solution.

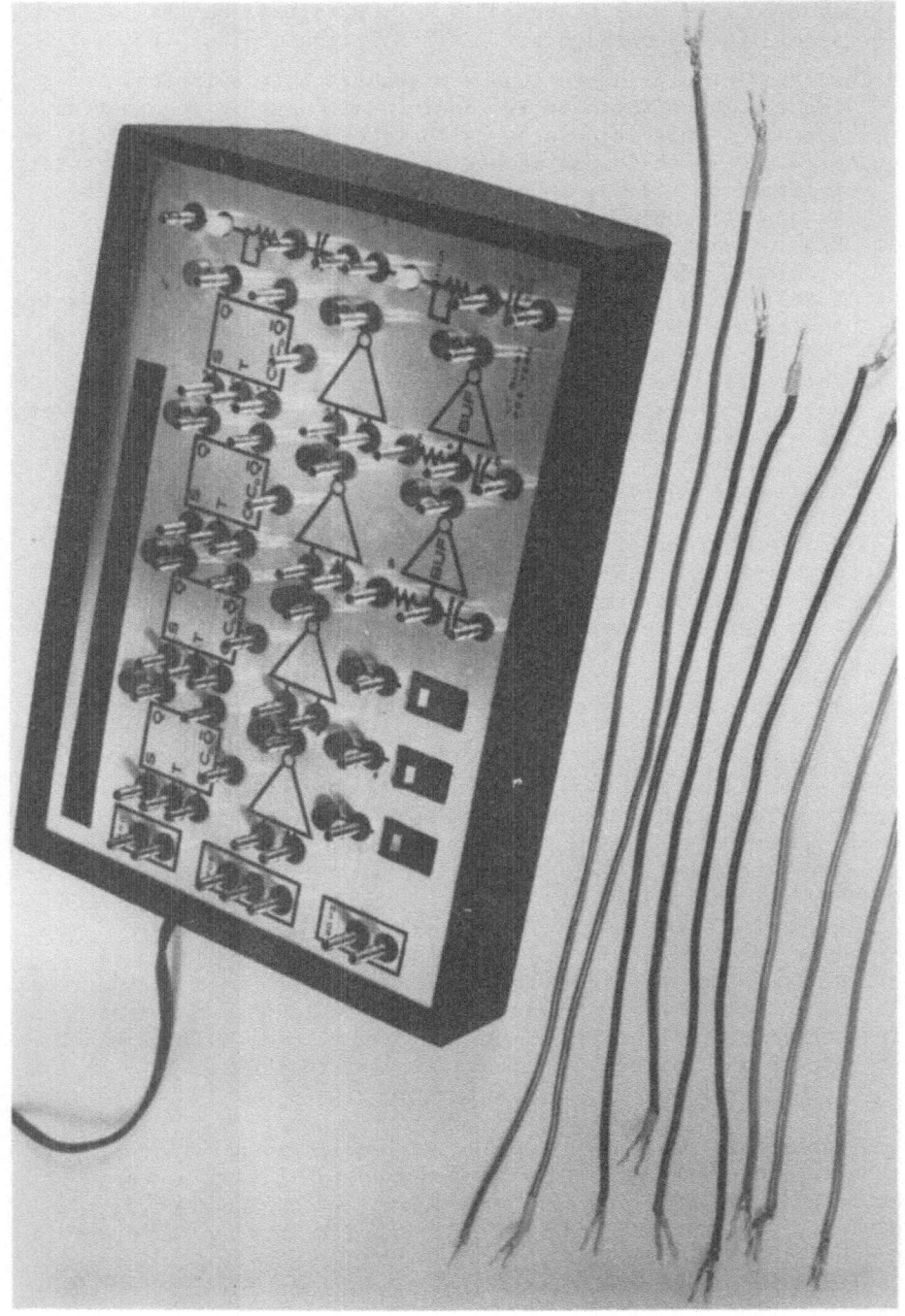

FIGURE 3. A digital logic microlaboratory teaching device. This
photograph does not show clearly the three different
colors of connecting wires (below).

FIGURE 4. When the device in Figure 3 is wired in this manner,
the circuit will count digits in the binary system.

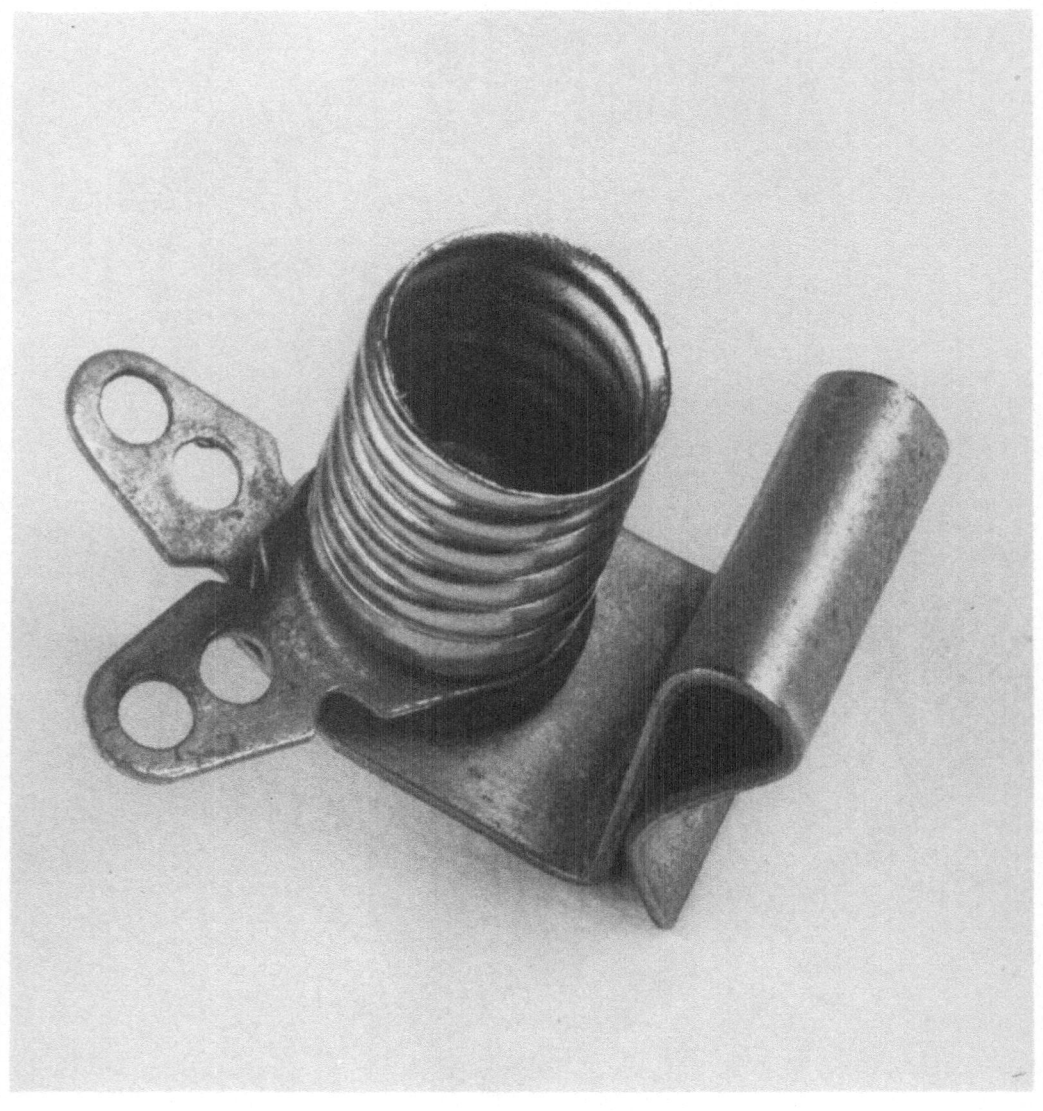

FIGURE 5. The electric light socket given the seeker at the start
of the object identification problem.

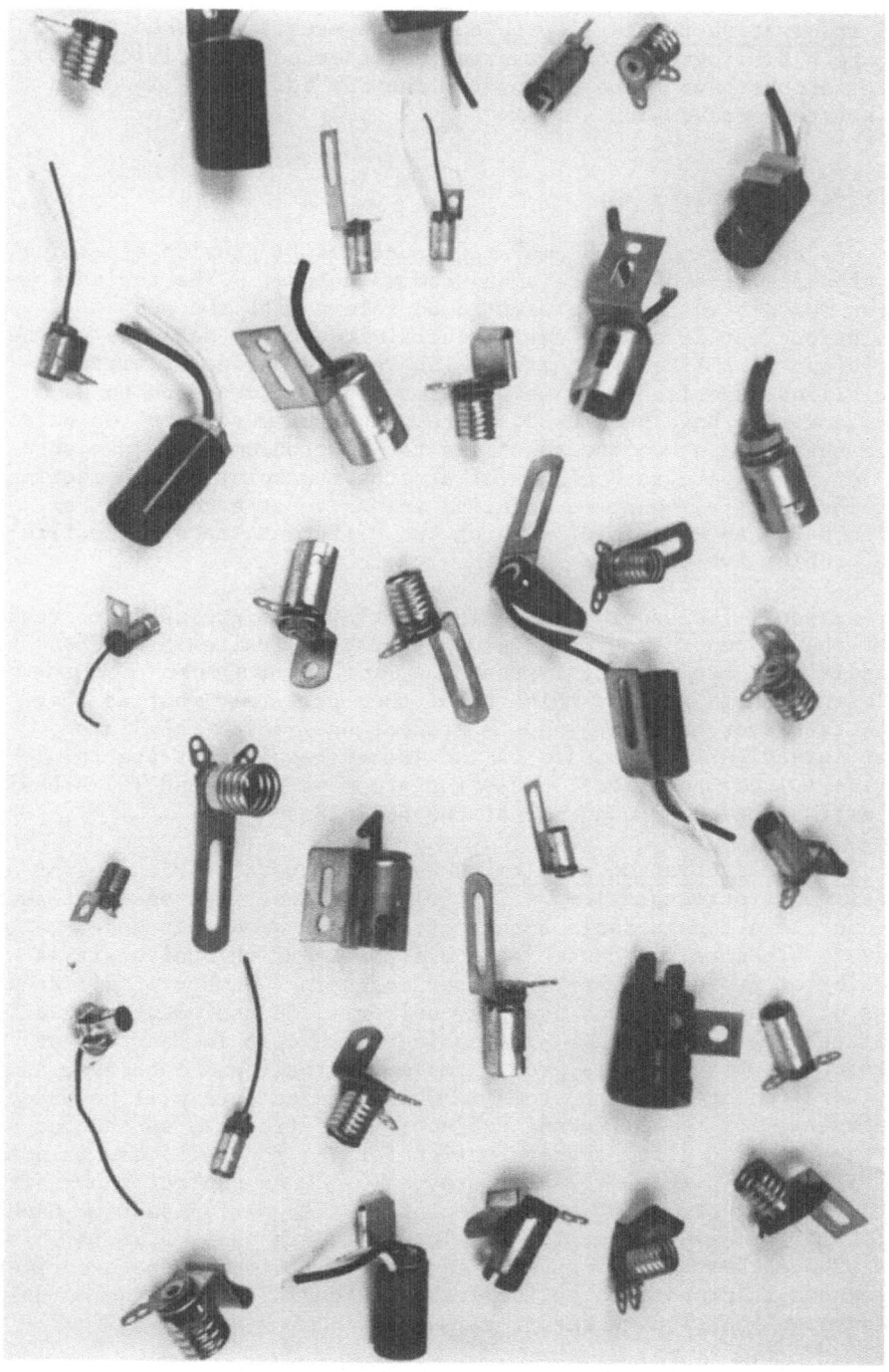

FIGURE 6. The set of light sockets given the source at the start of the object identification problem.

78

Information retrieval problem. The seeker is asked to
prepare a bibliography of newspaper articles on a specific topic.
The citations have to be drawn from the New York Times Index in
the source's possession.

Conflictive Problems

Our conflictive problems are structured to provide a setting
for argumentative discourse among communicators. The topical
matter for discussion is chosen to be relevant to the subject
population, yet is sufficiently general in nature that none of the
participants is likely to have an inherent advantage by virtue of
specialized experience. The problems are also designed to be
used, and they have been used, with groups of more than two persons.
Since there are no unique solutions to the problems, the subjects
are left to debate the merits of alternative solutions in meeting
certain criteria, and are required to arrive at a consensus or
agreement. An example of each of two different kinds of conflictive problem follows:

National issues problem. The participants are asked to rank
order the ten most important issues facing the United States today.
An additional requirement is that the participants must rank order
the issues, not as they think about them privately, but as they
think the average undergraduate student had ranked them in a
prior survey. The purposes of the latter requirement are to
provide (a) an additional basis for argumentation, and (b) a basis
for estimating the 'goodness' of the solutions.

Budget-negotiation problem. We have several variations of a
budget-negotiation problem. The following describes one that seems
to generate a considerable amount of interest among our undergraduate students. The subjects are told that the University's
Director of Athletics must reduce expenses in a number of different
areas of expenditure, for example, uniforms and equipment, athletic
scholarships, and travel. The subjects are cast in the role of
captains of various teams, for example, football and lacrosse, and
they have to agree on the areas in which budget cuts will be made.
The payoffs for the different subjects are different, so that a
cut in expenditure for transportation for the football team is not
equivalent to that for the lacrosse team. Each subject knows his
own payoff structure but not that of the other participants. Each
subject's goal is to minimize the losses to his side, that is, his
team, and each subject's payment for participation in the experiment
is reduced in proportion to the losses he sustains from the mutually
agreed upon solution to the problem.

OTHER EXPERIMENTAL CONDITIONS

Without elaborating in detail, our experiments have been done on three different populations: High school boys, high school girls, and college students at Johns Hopkins. In some cases, subjects have been selected for particular intellectual abilities.

Most of our experiments have been done with two participants. Two, however, have been done with as many as four subjects. All our experiments have tested at least two different problems. In four experiments, subjects have been tested on as many as four successive days.

RESULTS

Our results have been so numerous that it would be impossible to summarize them all here. Rather I shall discuss some of the more salient findings, particularly as they seem to bear on the problem of man-computer dialog. I shall also select data from a variety of different experiments without elaborating on specific details of experimental design or conditions of test.

Communication by Voice is Fast

One of the strongest generalizations emerging from our research is that:

1. Problems are solved significantly faster in communication modes that have a voice channel than in those that do not.

This finding is a consistent one that has come up in every one of the nine experiments in which this comparison was tested (Chapanis et al., 1972; Chapanis and Overbey, 1974; Ford, unpublished data; Hoecker, unpublished data; Krueger, unpublished data; Ochsman and Chapanis, 1974; Weeks and Chapanis, 1976; Weeks et al., 1974; Williams, unpublished data). Data from the first experiment in which this finding appeared are shown in Figure 7 (see also Figures 9 and 10). Even more interesting are the data in Figure 8 which compared 10 different communication modes. There is only one statistically significant effect for the data in Figure 8. The five modes on the left are significantly faster than the five on the right. The one thing that distinguishes the two groups is that the five modes on the left all have a voice channel. Those on the right do not.

The finding that people can talk faster than they can write or typewrite, and so can solve problems faster when they can talk, is not in itself particularly startling. However, these findings become more interesting when they are elaborated in the light of others below.

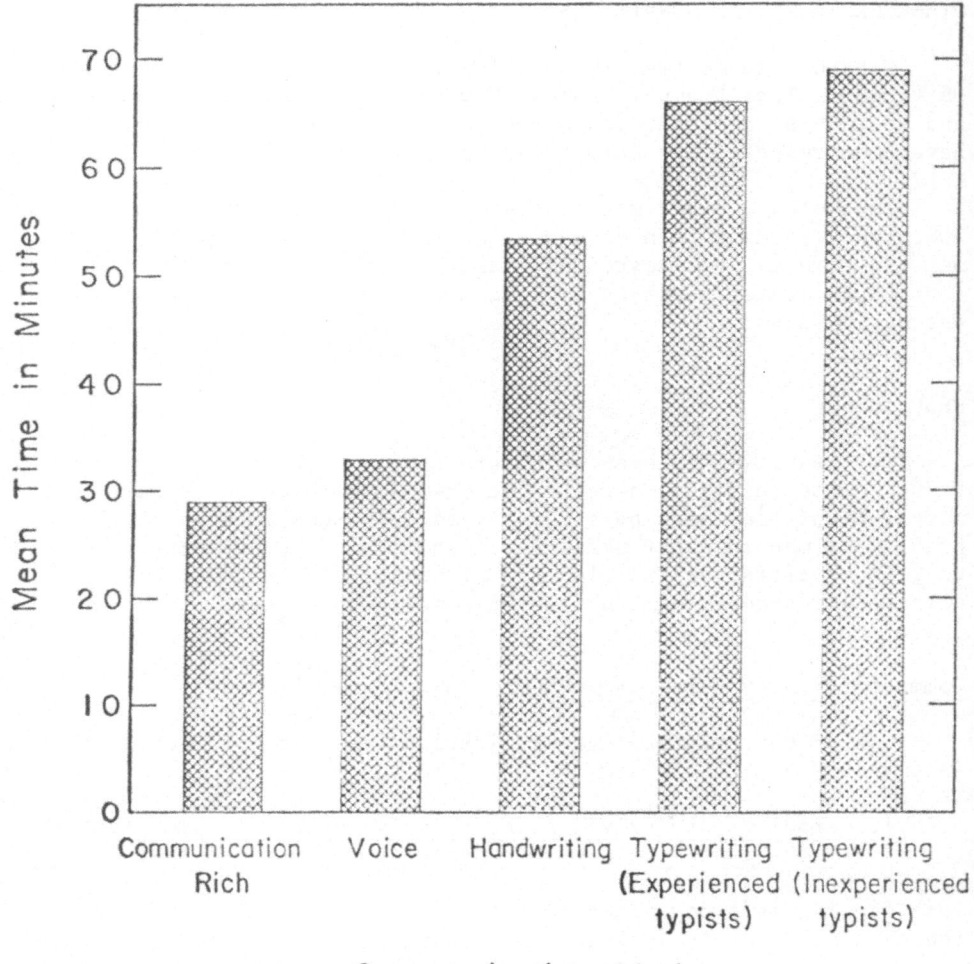

FIGURE 7. Mean times to solve problems in four different communication modes. Each bar is an average for four two-man
groups and for two different problems. (From Chapanis
et al., 1972).

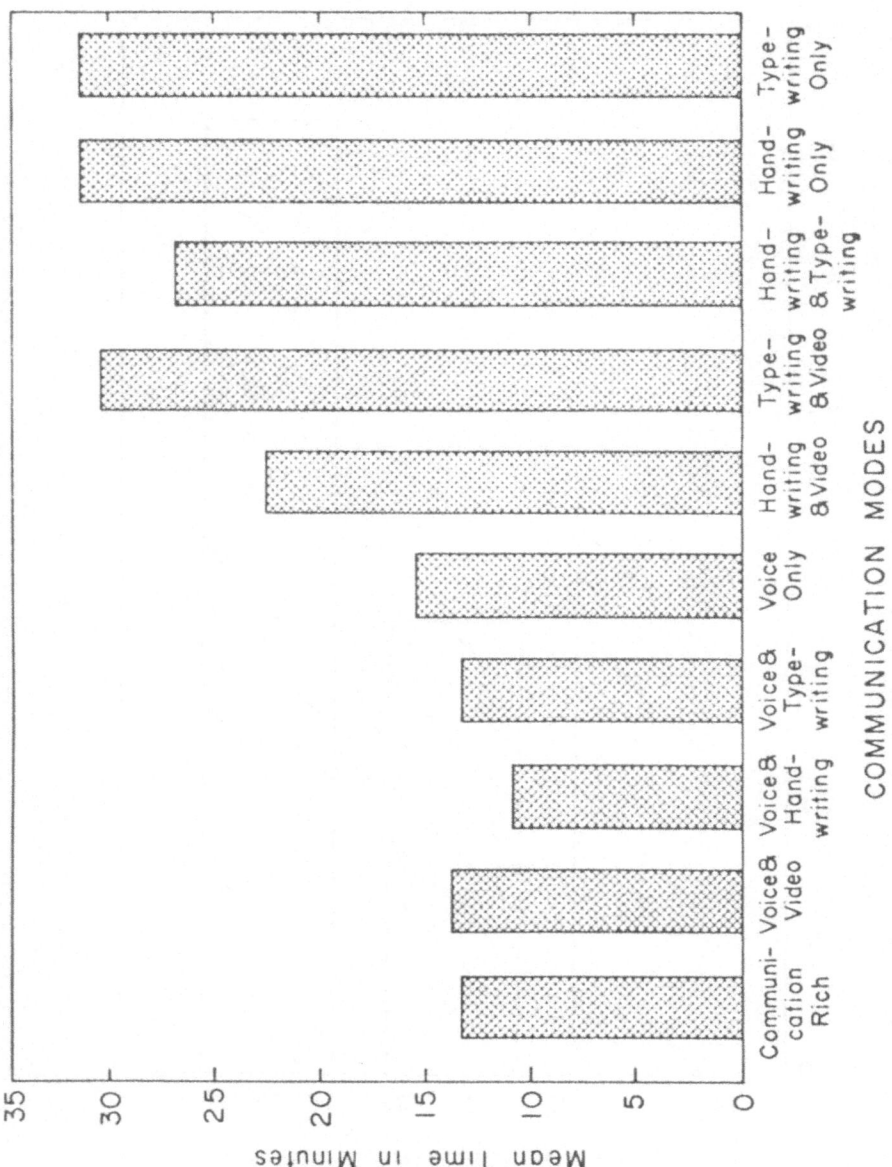

FIGURE 8. Mean times to solve problems in ten different communication modes. Each bar is an average for six two-man
groups and for three different problems. (From Ochsman
and Chapanis, 1974).

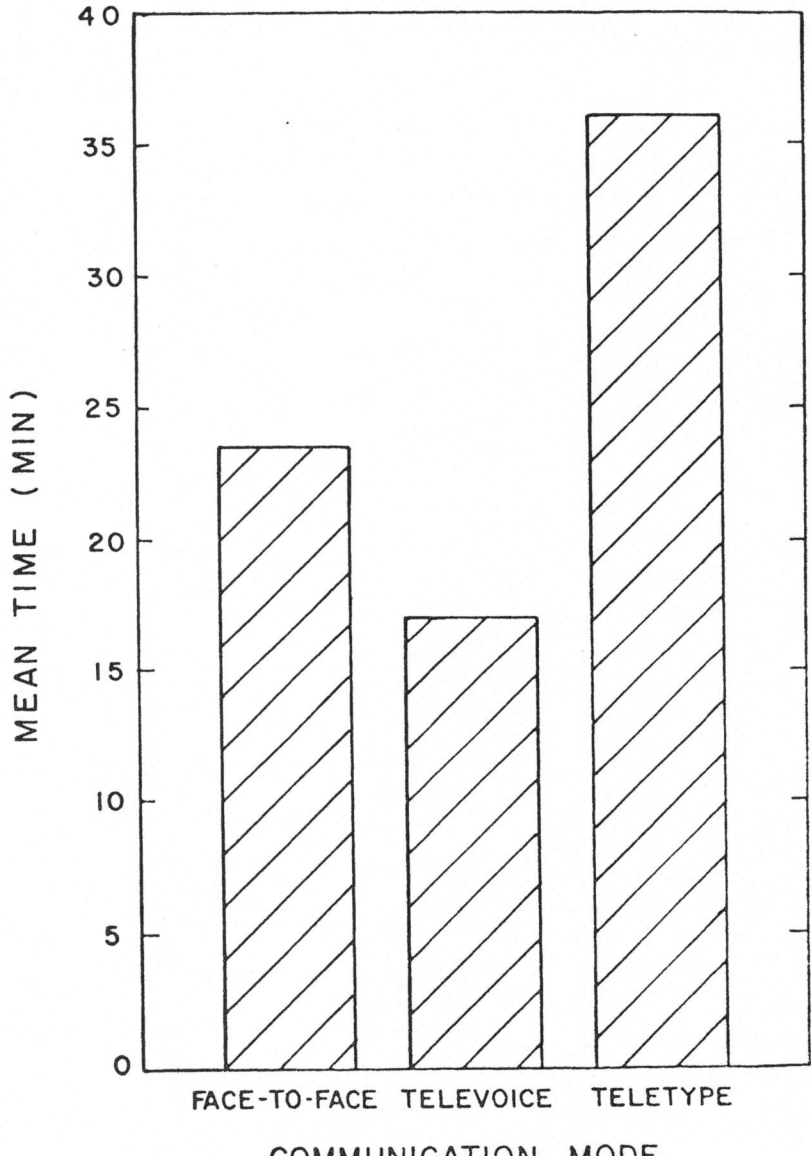

FIGURE 9. Mean times to arrive at consensus agreements in three
communication modes. Each bar is an average for three
groups, each of which worked at a different task on each
of three successive days. Each set of three groups was
made up of a 2-person, a 3-person, and a 4-person group.
(From Krueger, unpublished data)

Face-to-Face Versus Voice Communication

A second strong generalization is that:

2. Both co-operative and conflictive problems are solved
   about equally fast in voice-only modes of communication
   as in face-to-face communication.

This finding came as a surprise to us initially but we have found
it in no less than five different experiments (Chapanis et al.,
1972; Hoecker, unpublished data; Krueger, unpublished data; Ochsman
and Chapanis, 1974; and Weeks and Chapanis, 1976). The data in
Figures 7 and 8 show that the voice-only modes of communication are
a little slower than face-to-face communication in those two experiments. In neither case, however, is the difference statistically
significant. In one very large experiment, the data came out the
reverse, that is, voice only was faster than face-to-face communication (Figure 9). Once again, however, this particular difference
is not statistically significant. Contrary to what one might expect,
being able to see the person(s) with whom one is communicating
does not appear to be of any substantial advantage in solving the
kinds of problems we have tested.

Skilled Versus Unskilled Typists

Of particular interest to man-computer interactions is that:

3. Typing skill does not appear to be a significant factor
   in the kind of communication with which we are concerned

This finding appeared in our first experiment (Figure 7) in which
we tested a group of high-school boys who had completed a one-year
course in typing and another group without any formal typing
education. As is apparent from Figure 7 the difference between
the performance of the two groups was trivial. This finding was
so unexpected that we tested it in another more elaborate experiment with a completely different set of subjects (Weeks et al., 1974).
The essential findings of that experiment are shown in Figure 10.
The skilled typists solved problems about nine minutes faster than
did the unskilled typists in the typewriting mode. However, the
skilled typists were faster than their unskilled counterparts by
very nearly that same amount in the communication-rich (face-to-
face) mode as well. So, although the skilled typists seem to
have been able to solve these problems somewhat faster, there is
no evidence whatsoever in these data that typing skill per se gave
the skilled typists any differential advantage.

84

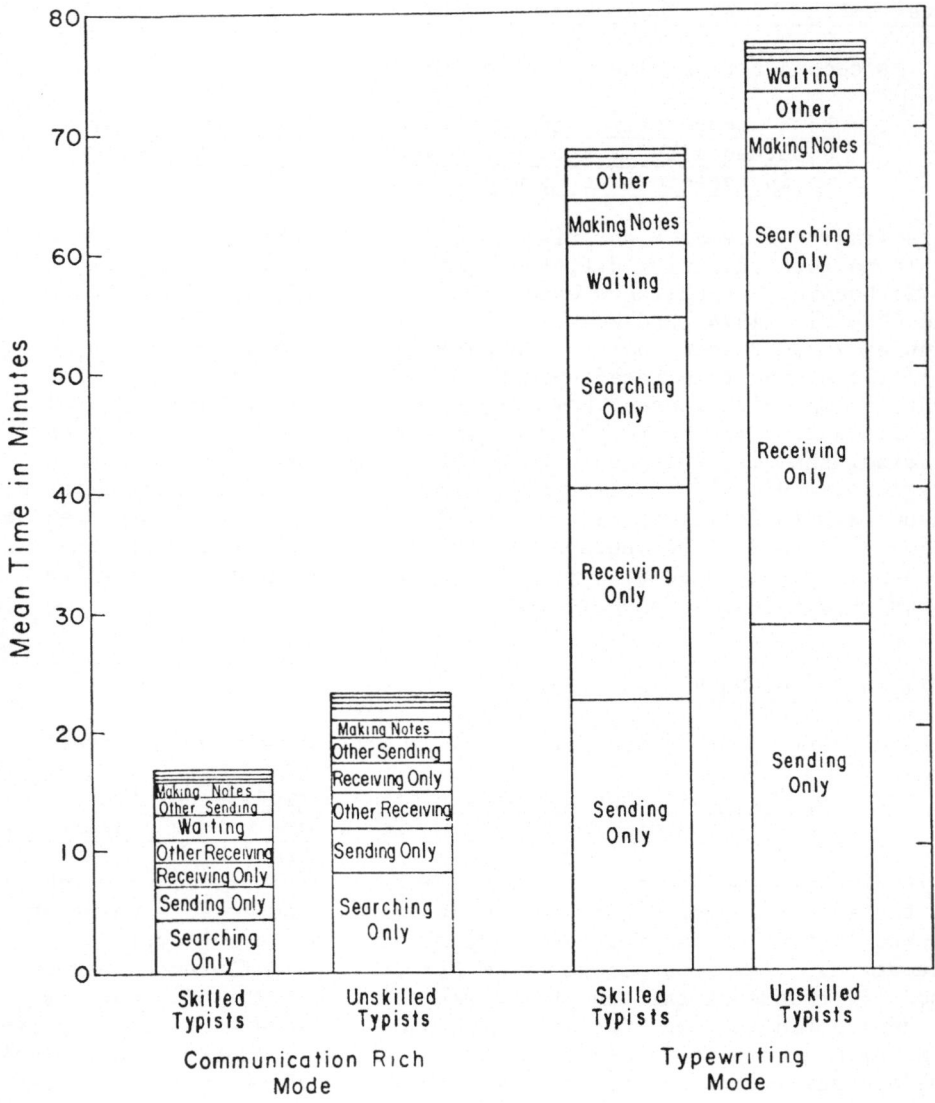

FIGURE 10. Mean times to solve problems by pairs of skilled and unskilled typists each of which solved problems in two communication modes. Each bar is an average for four groups each of which solved a different problem on each of two different days. The segments of the bars show the average amounts of time subjects spent in each of nine activities. (From Weeks, Kelly and Chapanis, 9174)

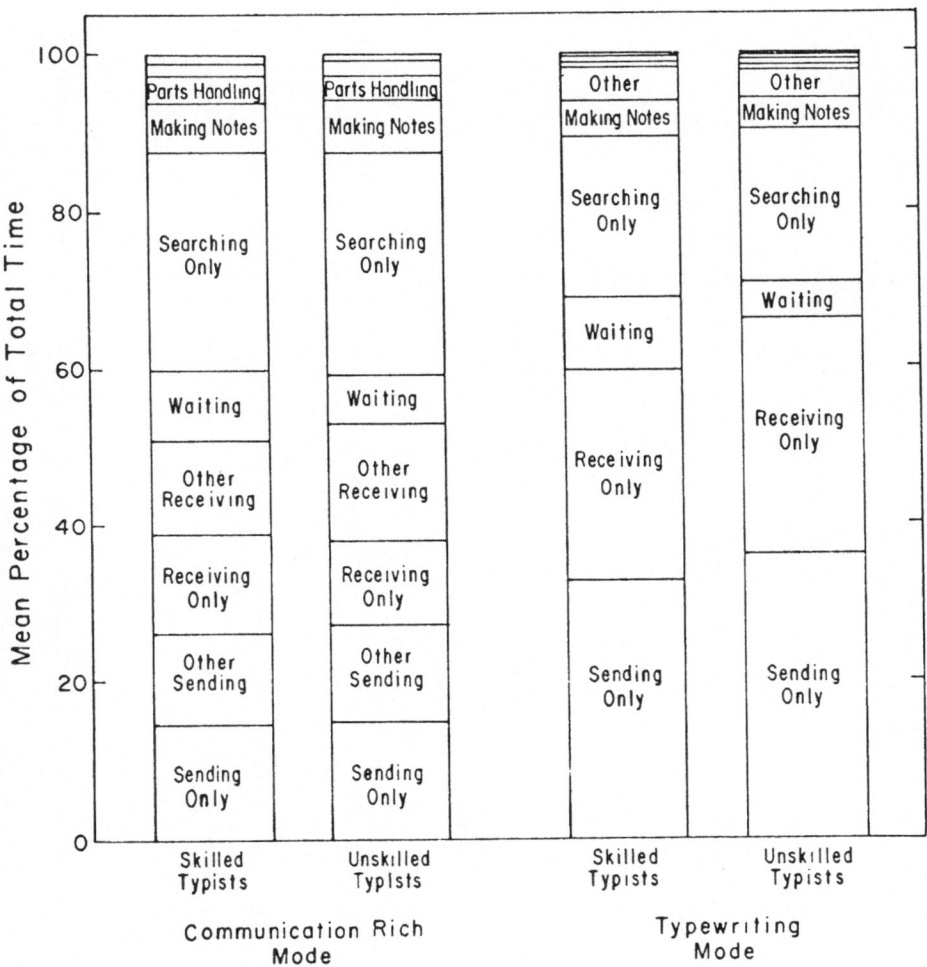

FIGURE 11. The data of Figure 10 are here replotted as percentages of the total time. (From Weeks et al., 1974)

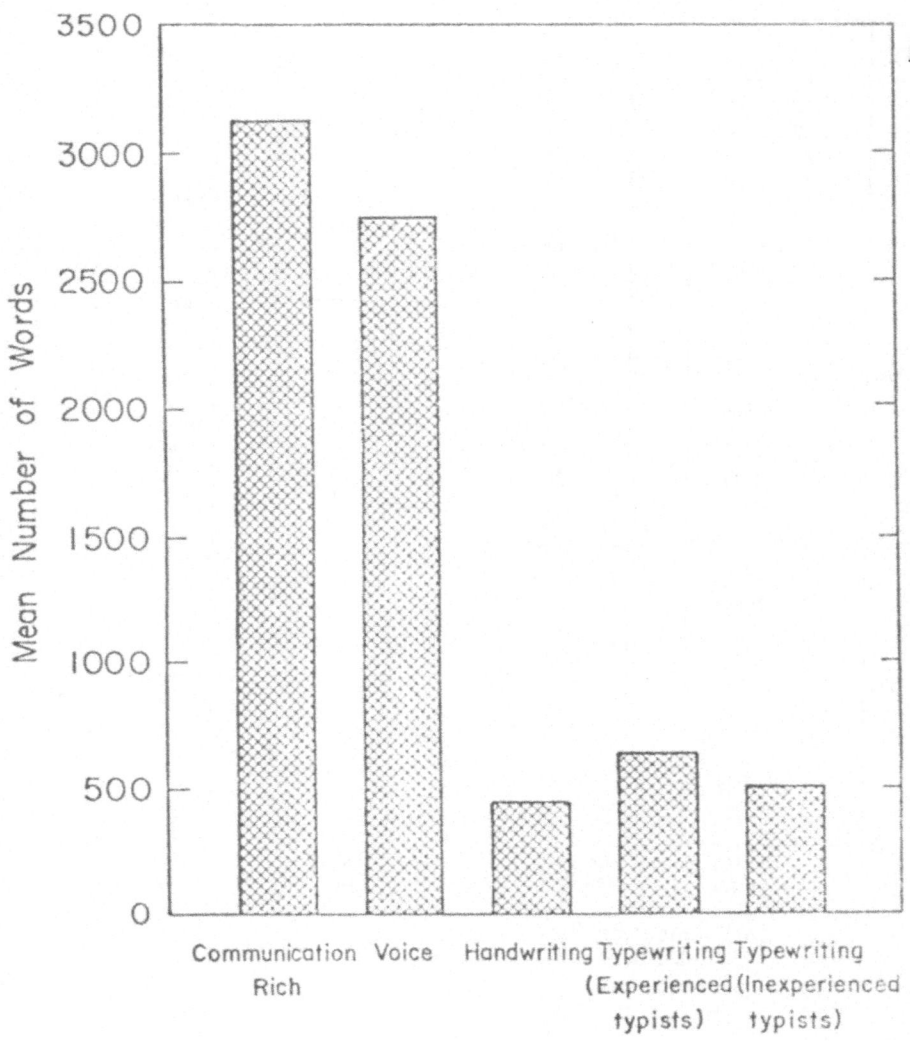

FIGURE 12. Mean number of words used in the solution of problems
in each of four communication modes. These data and
those in Figure 7 are from the same experiment.
(From Chapanis et al., 1972)

The apparently counterintuitive finding that typing skill does not significantly aid interactive communication via typewriters can be explained by two additional considerations: (a) Activity sampling data on how subjects actually spent their time (Figures 10 and 11) show that only about one-third of the total problem-solving time is spent in sending, that is, in typing. This means that any potential advantage a subject might have due to typing skill would be operating only one-third of the time. (b) Typing skill is normally measured by the speed and accuracy with which typists copy prepared text. These communication situations, by contrast, require a great deal of planning and decision-making as subjects decide what to say and then compose their messages at the typewriter. Typing skill does not have very much to do with that kind of planning and decision-making.

Verbal Output

Another strong finding from a number of our experiments is that:

4. <u>Modes of communication that have a voice channel are much wordier than those that do not have a voice channel.</u>

This generalization holds no matter how one measures wordiness, or verbal output. Figure 12 shows the number of words communicated in the four modes tested in our first experiment. These data match those in the same experiment for which Figure 7 gives times to solution. Considering that problems are solved about twice as fast in the voice modes as in the hard-copy (handwriting and type-writing) modes, the data in Figure 12 become all the more impressive (see also Figure 14). Figure 13 shows communication rates from the same experiment. These were computed by dividing the number of words used by each subject by the actual amount of time he spent communicating. If computers will ever be able to accept spoken words, communication rates will be much greater than has been the case with typewritten inputs.

Face-to-Face Communication Versus Communication by Voice Only

A small, but consistent finding that has turned up repeatedly in our work is that:

5. <u>Face-to-face communication is wordier than communication by voice only.</u>

Data for this generalization appear in Figures 12 and 13. The differences between the communication-rich and voice only data in these two figures are not statistically significant and one might be inclined, therefore, to attribute them to chance variations.

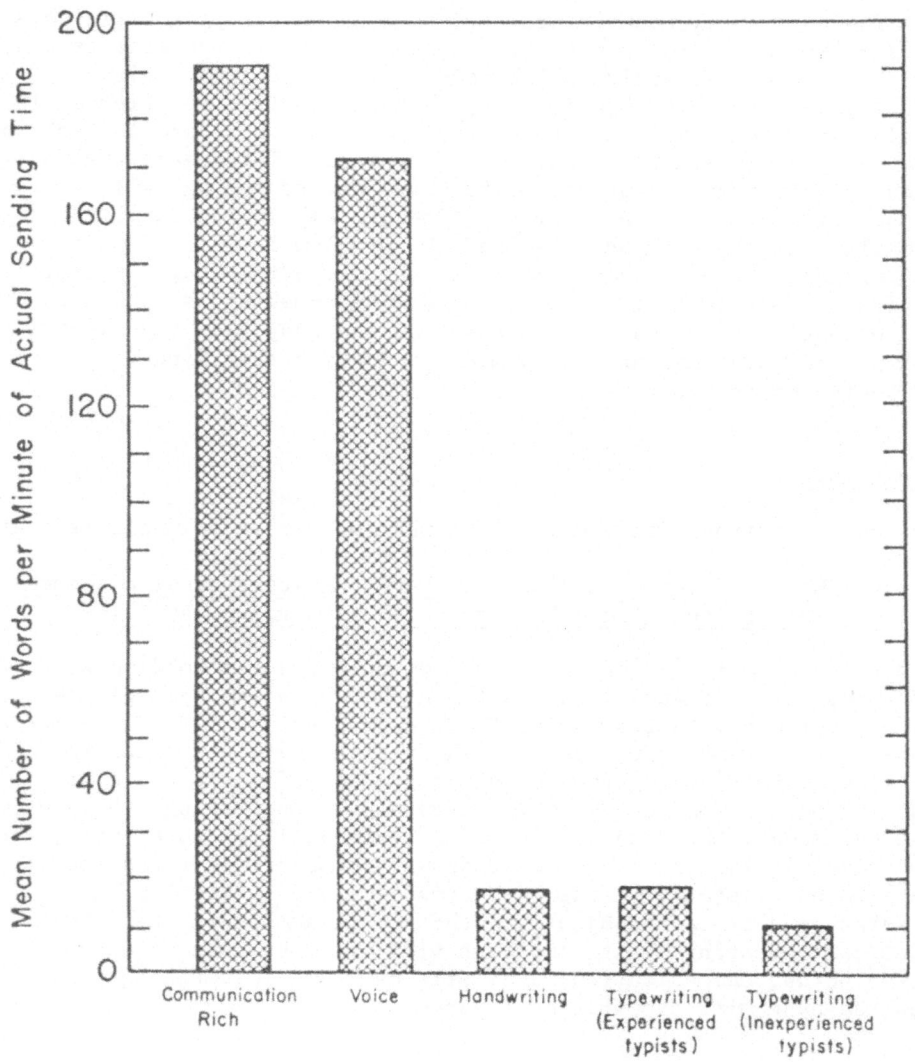

FIGURE 13.   Communication rates in the solution of problems in
             each of four communication modes.   These data and
             those in Figures 7 and 12 are from the same experiment.
             (From Chapanis et al., 1972)

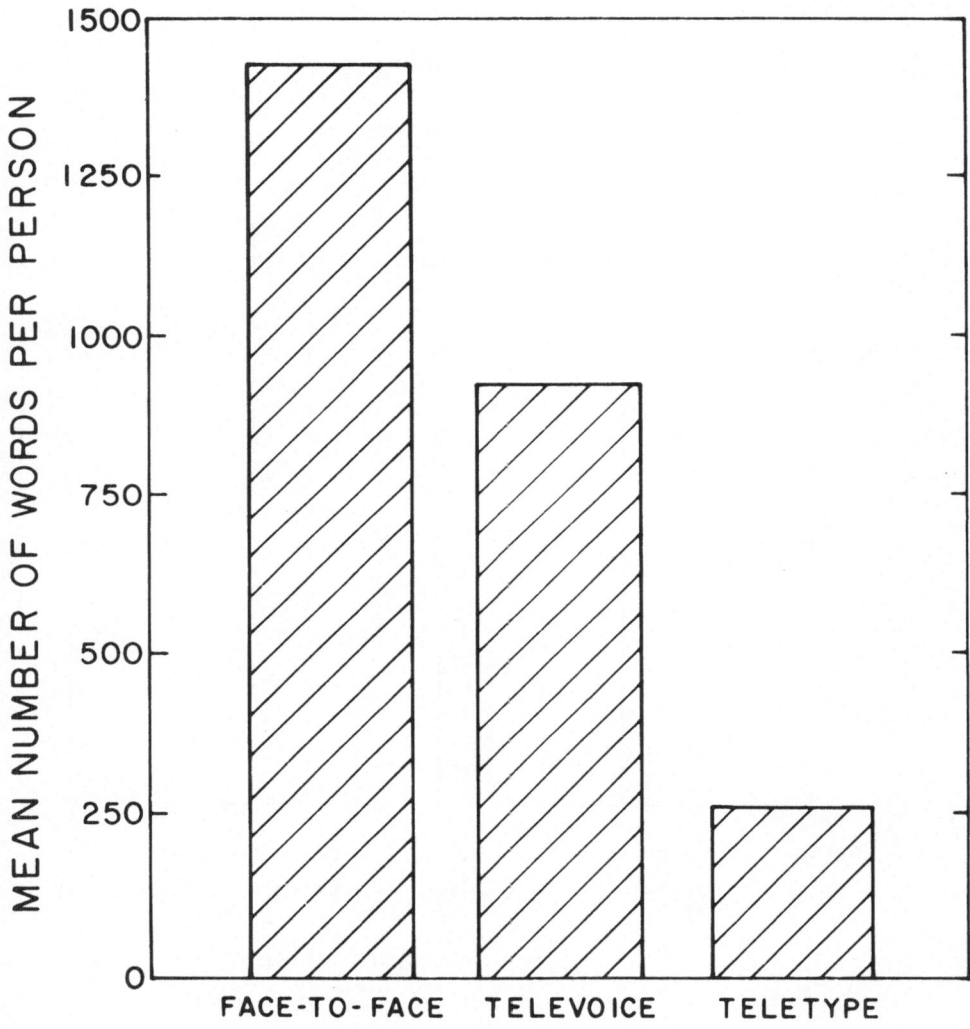

FIGURE 14.   Average number of words used in arriving at consensus
agreements in three communication modes.   These data
and those in Figure 9 are from the same experiment.
(From Krueger, unpublished data)

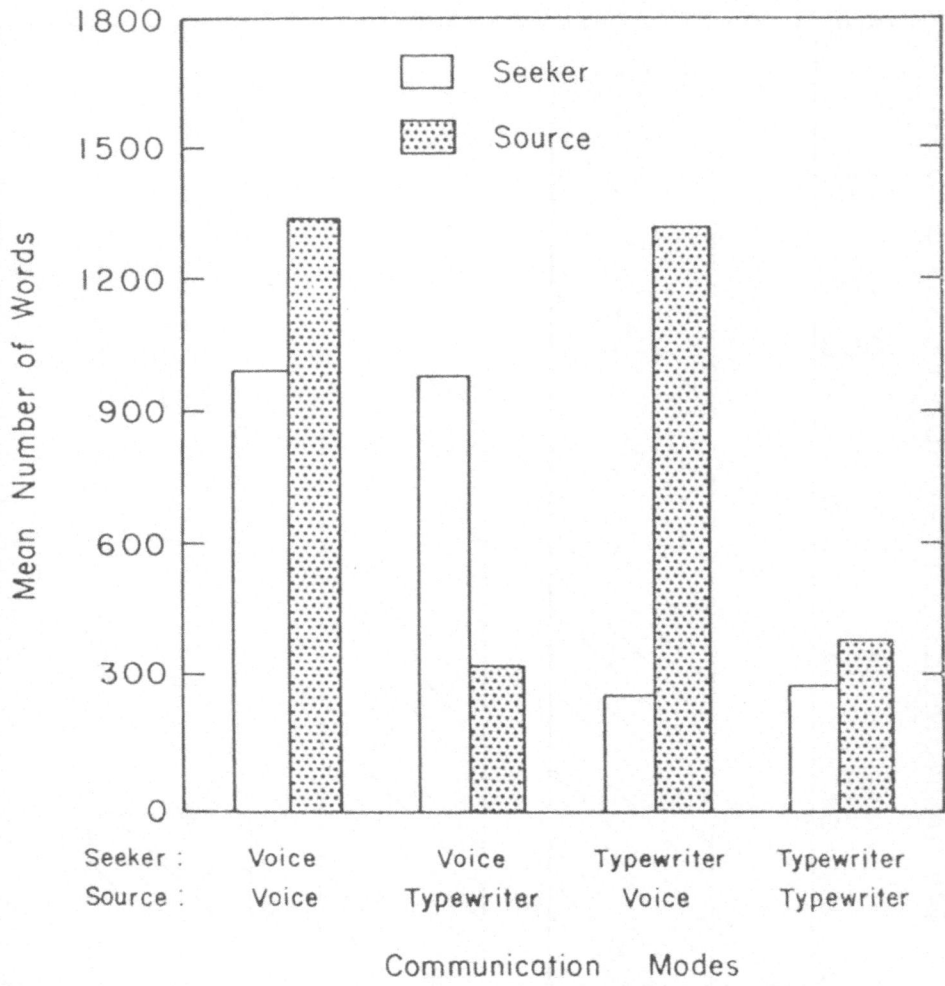

FIGURE 15. Mean number of words used by sources and seekers when
            two channels of communication were tested in all
            combinations. Each bar is the average for eight
            subjects, two each of whom solved one of four different
            problems on one of four different days. (From Chapanis
            and Overbey, 1974).

However, the finding has turned up in all four experiments in
which there has been a comparison of the verbal output in face-to-
face and voice only modes.   Figure 14, for example, shows another
and much greater difference than we found in our earlier work.
Being able to gesture and use body movements to convey information
actually seems to increase the number of words communicators use.

Verbal Output Independent of Mode of Communication

An interesting finding that has turned up in our experiments
bears on the stability of the verbal output in the several modes.
It is:

6. The number of words used by a communicator is a function
    of the communication channel and that number is not
    influenced by the channel available to his partner.

Data supporting this statement are shown in Figure 15.   The left-
most pair of bars gives data for a situation in which both the seeker
and source had a voice channel.   The second pair of bars is for a
condition in which the seeker had a voice channel, but the source
could communicate only by typewriter.   The third pair of bars is
for the reverse situation: the seeker could communicate only by
typewriter, while the source had a voice channel.   The right-most
pair of bars is for the condition in which both persons could
communicate only by typewriter.

When both communicators had a voice channel (left-most pair of
bars), the seeker used more words than did the source (see the
filled bar).   When the seeker had a voice channel and the source
a typewriter channel (third pair of bars), the average number of
words used by the seeker was almost identical to the number used
by seekers in the voice-voice condition.   Similarly, the numbers
of words used by sources was almost identical when they communicated
by voice, irrespective of whether the seeker had a voice channel
or a typewriter channel (compare the open bars in the first and
second pairs).   Similar findings apply to the data for the typewriter channels.   To sum up, the number of words used by a
communicator is a function of the channel available to him and is
not influenced by the channel available to his partner.

Interrupt Capability

In one experiment we tested the effects of giving communicators
the freedom to interrupt their partners.   The findings of that
study support the conclusion that:

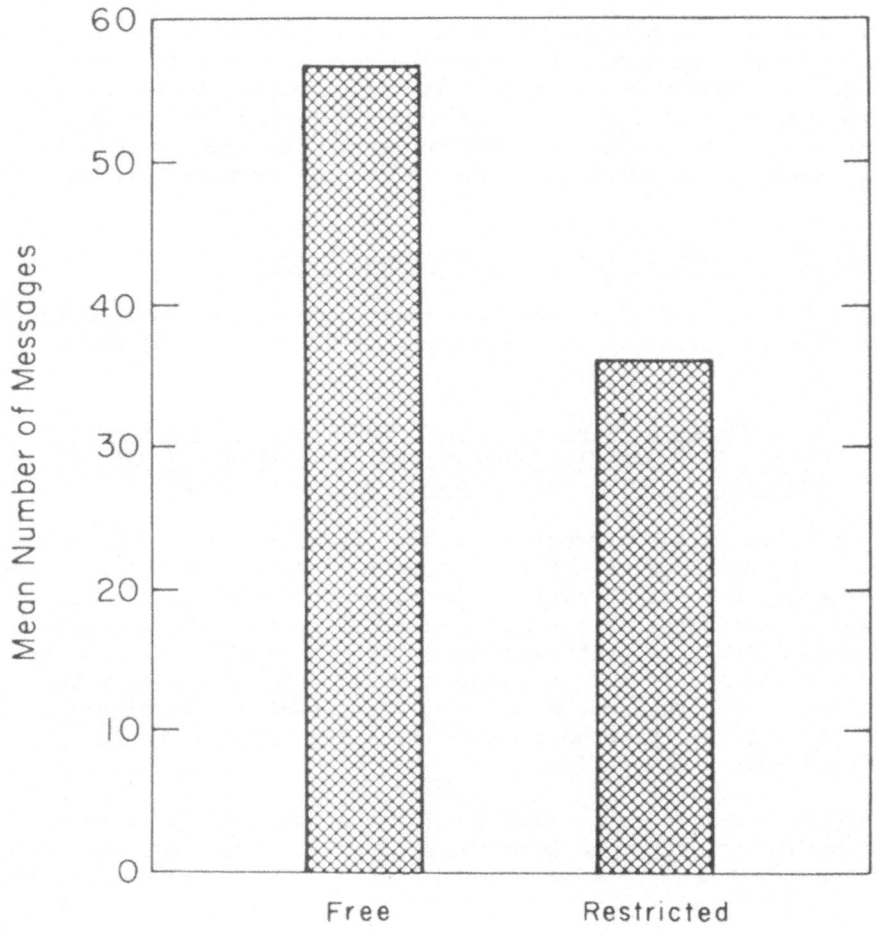

FIGURE 16. Mean numbers of messages exchanged under conditions of free and restricted interchange. Each bar is an average of 64 observations. Eight two-person teams each solved four different problems on four different days using each of the channel combinations illustrated in Figure 15. (Chapanis and Overbey, 1974)

7. Giving communicators the freedom to interrupt has no
    effect on problem solution time or on the number of
    words used.   Words are, however, 'packaged' differently.
    When communicators have the freedom to interrupt, they
    use more messages and messages are shorter.   When com-
    municators do not have the freedom to interrupt, they
    use fewer messages and messages are longer.

Data supporting these conclusions are given in Figures 16 and 17.
In the free interchange conditions, a communicator could interrupt
his partner at any time and take control of a voice channel, or a
typewriter channel.   In the restricted interchange condition, a
communicator had to wait until his partner had finished talking,
or typing, and had released the channel to him.   The data in the
two figures are almost mirror images of one another   When the
two sets of data are multiplied together, they yield essentially
equal numbers of words.

Control Over Communication Channels

In one experiment we gave subjects two buttons.   When a
subject pressed one button, he relinquished control of the communication system to his partner.   When a subject pushed the other
button, he took control away from his partner, even if the partner
was in the process of communicating.   The findings of this experiment suggest that:

8. Communicators are much more likely to take control
    of a communication system (that is, to interrupt) if
    the system has a voice channel.   Subjects voluntarily
    relinquish control of a system about as often as they
    take control if the system has only hard-copy channels
    of communication.

Data supporting this finding appear in Figure 18.   Note that in
every one of the five pairs of bars on the left, subjects took
control of the communication system much more often than they
relinquished control.   All five of those communication systems
have a voice channel.   By contrast, the five pairs of bars on the
right are about equally high.   Those five pairs of bars are for
communication modes that do not have a voice channel.

Time Spent in Various Activities

In seven of our experiments (Chapanis et al., 1972; Chapanis
and Overbey, 1974; Kelly, 1976; Ochsman and Chapanis, 1974; Parrish,
1974; Weeks and Chapanis, 1976; Weeks et al., 1974) we used activity
sampling procedures to record what subjects were actually doing in
the problem solving sessions.   The findings of those experiments
lead us to conclude that:

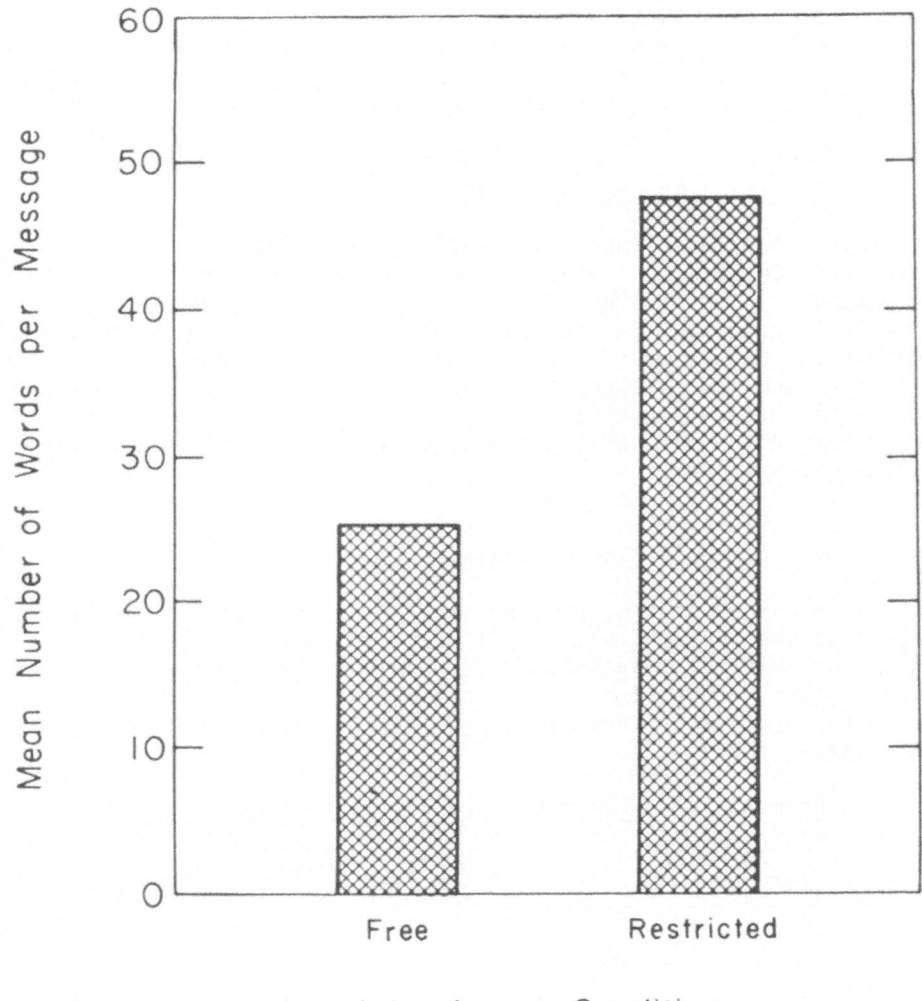

FIGURE 17.   Mean message lengths for the same data as are shown
in Figure 16.   (From Chapanis and Overbey, 1974)

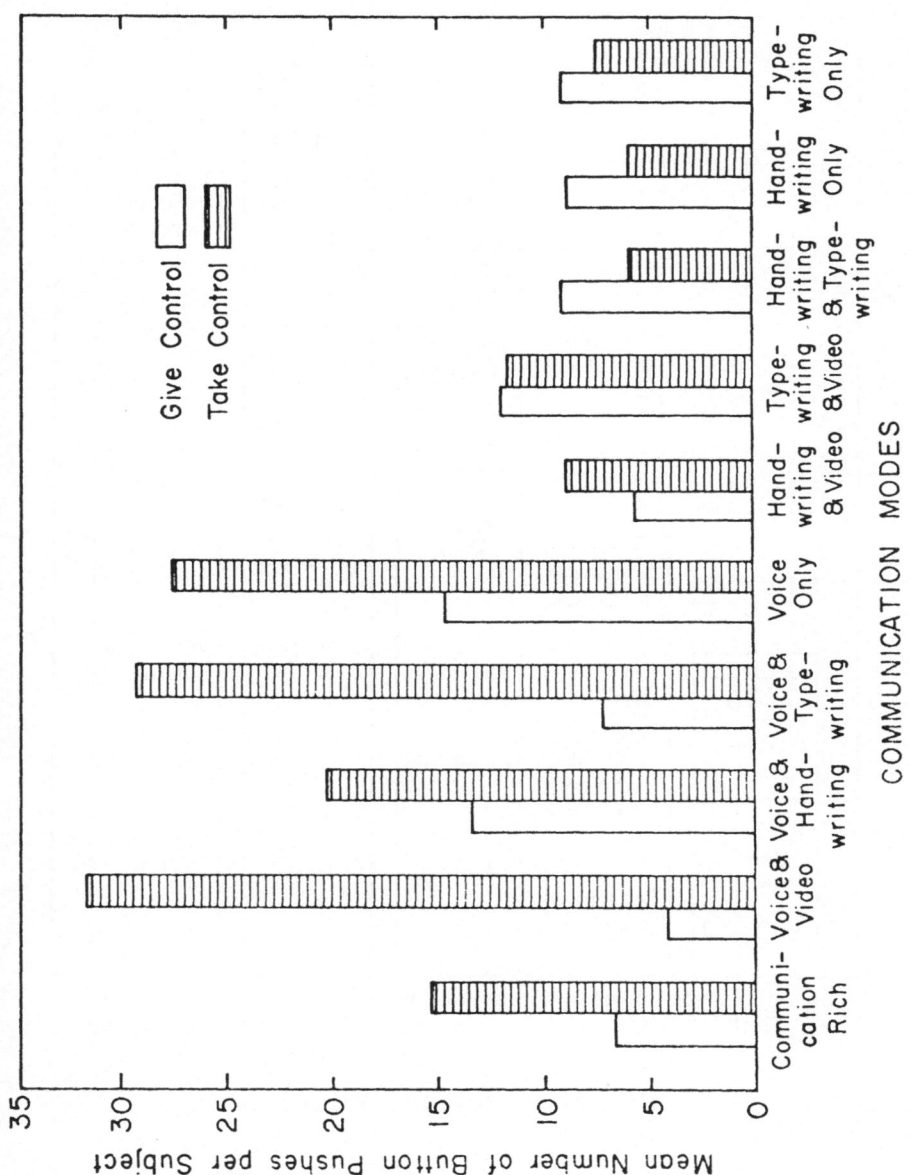

FIGURE 18.   The mean number of times subjects gave and took control
of communication channels.   These data and those in
Figure 8 are from the same experiment.   Each bar here
is based on 12 observations.   (From Ochsman and Chapanis,
1974)

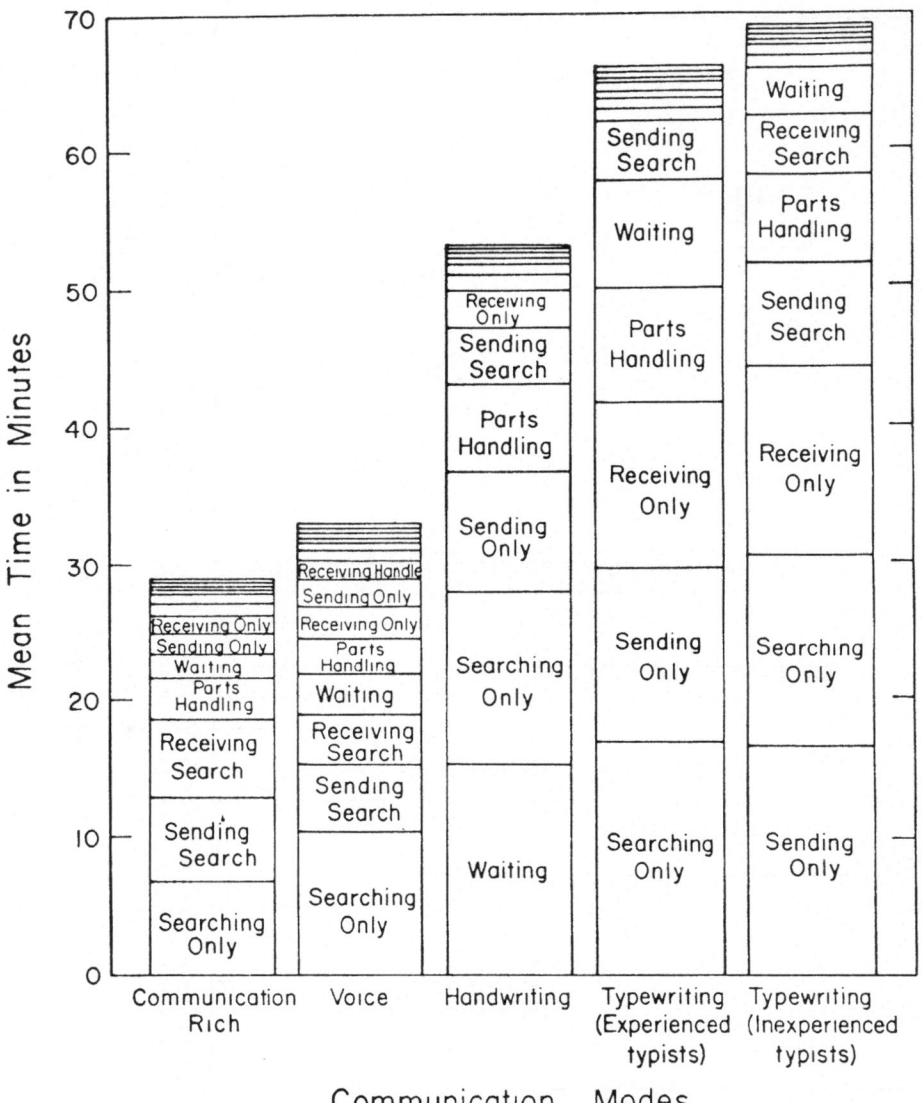

FIGURE 19. The data of Figure 7 are segmented here to show the amounts of time subjects spent in each of 15 different activities during problem-solving sessions. (From Chapanis et al., 1972)

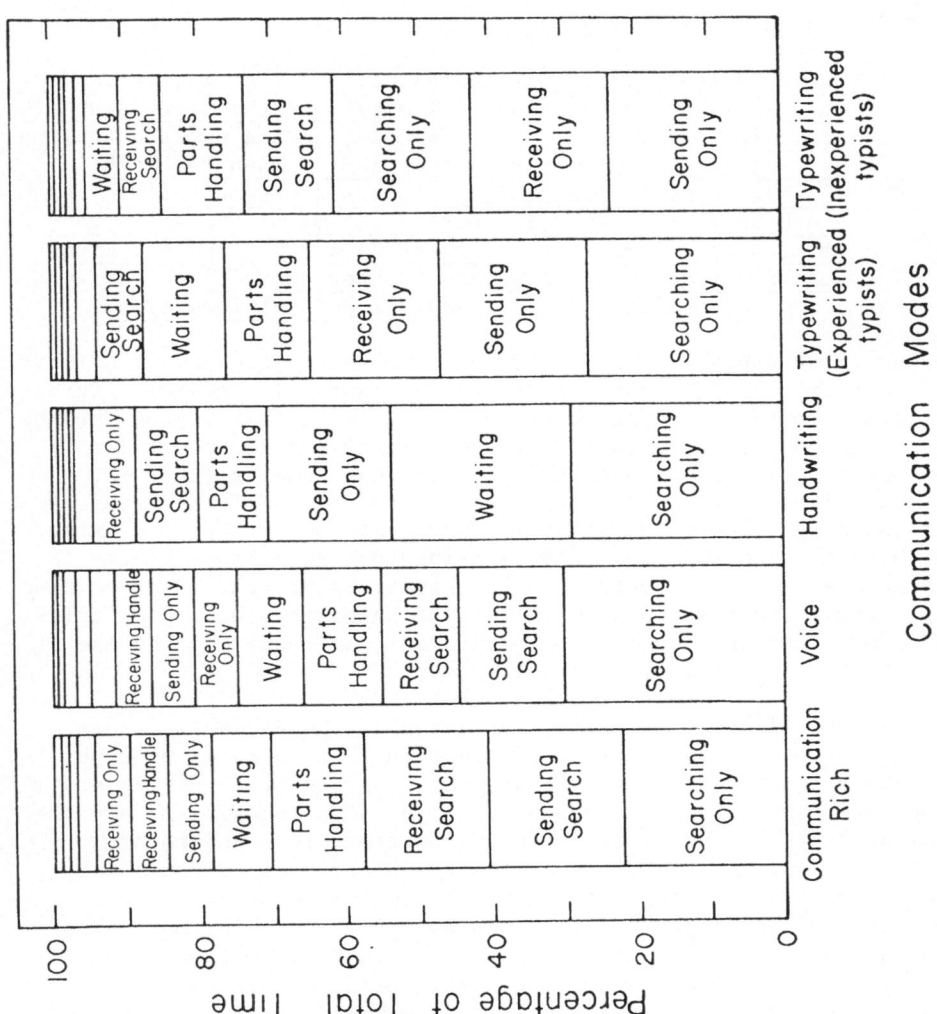

FIGURE 20. The data of Figure 19 are replotted here as percentages.
(From Chapanis et al., 1972)

9. <u>In tasks requiring the exchange of factual information to solve problems, only about half a communicator's time is spent in actual communication, that is, in sending or receiving information. The rest of the time is spent in doing other things, for example, making notes, handling parts, or searching for information. When the task involves the exchange of opinions and argumentation, as much as 75 per cent of a person's time may be spent communicating. However, at least 25 per cent of a communicator's time is still spent in other activities, for example, making notes and searching for information.</u>

In our first experiment, we recorded behavior in each of 15 different categories. The data are shown in Figures 19 and 20. Perhaps the most impressive thing about both figures is that in four of the five bars the behavior consuming the largest single amount (or percentage) of time was something other than sending (that is, communicating). Only in the case of the inexperienced typists did sending take up the greatest amount, or percentage, of time. In this experiment, one problem solving task required subjects to assemble a trash can toter (rubbish bin trolley), the other to find a particular address on a street map of Washington D.C. from telephone directory information. These are tasks requiring the use of pieces of equipment, or pieces of paper.

Our conflictive problems, for example, the national issue-ranking problem, are quite different in that there is no supplementary material required to arrive at agreement. Pieces of paper are typically used, however, to jot down notes. Mainly the communicators are required to voice their opinions and to argue the merits of their respective positions. Under these circumstances, the proportion of time spent communicating increases and it has gone as high as 75 per cent. Even so, 25 per cent or more of a typical communicator's time is spent in other activities, for example, making notes, searching for information, or waiting. Data to support these findings are not given here, but may be found in Weeks and Chapanis (1976).

Level of Sophistication of the Communicators

We have completed two experiments in which the level of sophistication of the communicators was systematically varied. At the time of this writing, the data from one of those experiments have still not been completely analyzed. Hence, the following two generalizations are based on the results of only one experiment (Parrish, 1974). Those findings show that:

10. <u>The greater the level of sophistication of the communicators, the more quickly they are able to solve problems.</u>

Data supporting this generalization appear in Figure 21.   The
teams here were made up of various combinations of high school and
college students who served as seekers (SK) and sources (SO).
College teams arrived at solutions fastest; high school teams
slowest.   When teams were mixed, it was better to have a college
student as the source rather than as the seeker.

These findings can be explained by the greater facility
college students have in using language.   In our problems, the
source was given the bulk of the library-like, or stored information.
It was he who gave directions or instructions to the seeker about
how to complete the problem at hand.   This accounts for the faster
performance of the mixed teams in which a college student served
as source.

Even more interesting, perhaps, is the finding that:

11. In these communication tasks, college students and
     high school students do about the same kinds of things,
     and in the same proportions.   However, college students
     do everything faster.

Data in support of this conclusion are given in Figure 22.   The
four bars in Figure 22 are so nearly alike that they seem to be
traced from the same pattern!

Impersonality of the Communication Modes

It has been claimed that teletype or computer conferencing is
more egalitarian and impersonal than face-to-face communication.
We have some evidence for that claim from one of our experiments.
The findings of that experiment suggest that:

12. Communicators in teletype modes of communication are
     much more likely to share equally in the exchange of
     information than are communicators in face-to-face
     or voice only modes of communication.

Data for that generalization are given in Figure 23.   The mean
relative variability (MRV) is based on a statistical measure called
the co-efficient of variation, $MRV = CV = 100 \frac{SD}{M}$.   In essence,
this measure is an expression of the amount of variability (SD)
among the various communicators in the numbers of messages they
exchanged, when that variability has been compensated for the
average number of messages (M).   Larger numbers indicate greater
disparity in the numbers of messages produced by the several
communicators.   Smaller numbers indicate that the several communicators shared more nearly equally in the production of messages.

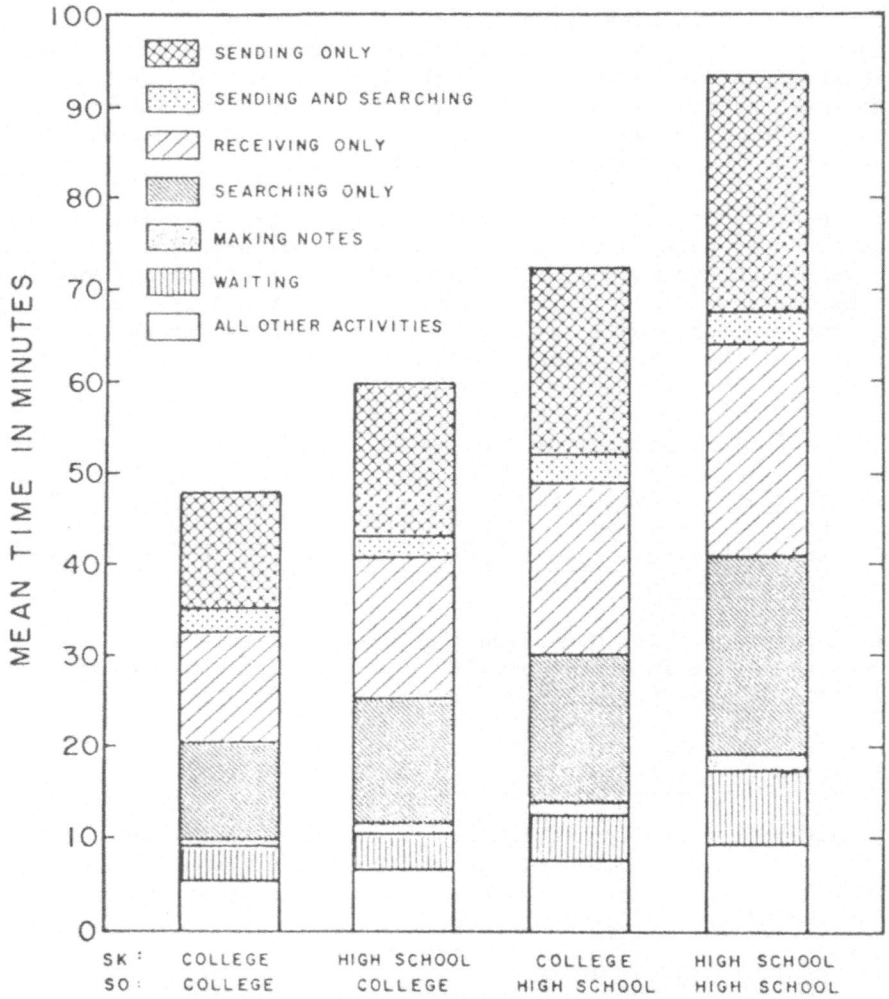

FIGURE 21. Times to solve problems by combinations of high school
            and college students. Segments of the bars show the
            amounts of time spent in each of seven different
            activities. (From Parrish, 1974)

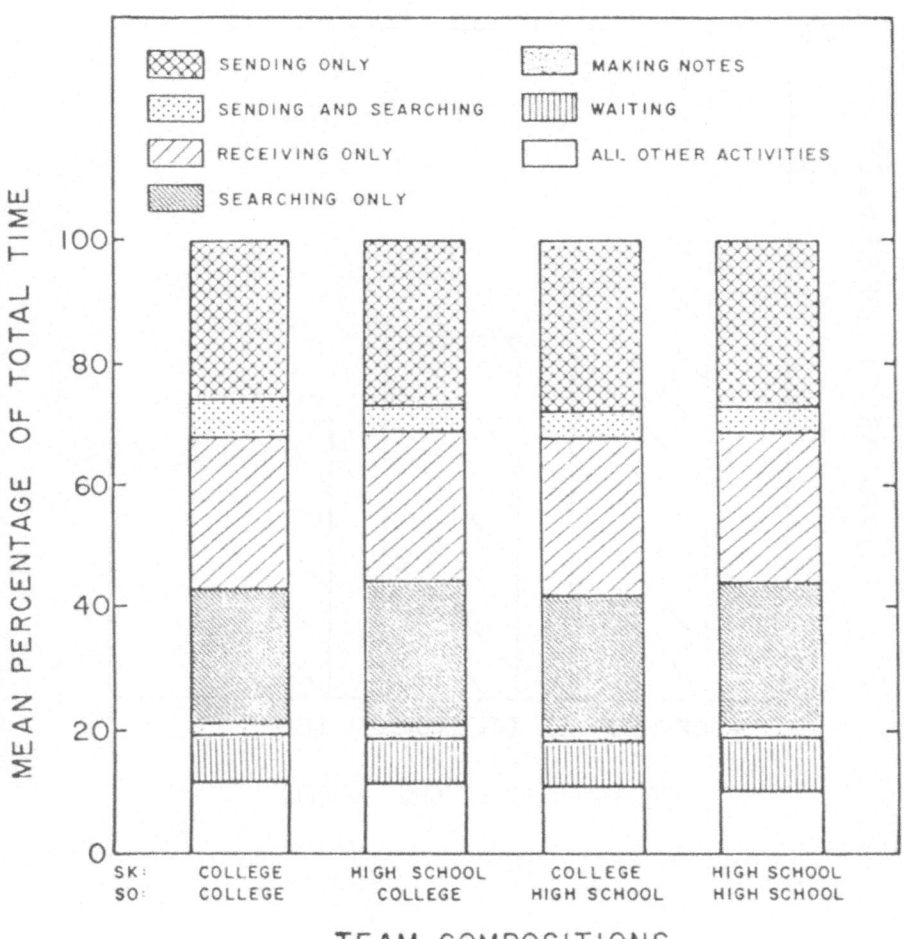

FIGURE 22. The data of Figure 21 are here represented as percentages. (From Parrish, 1974)

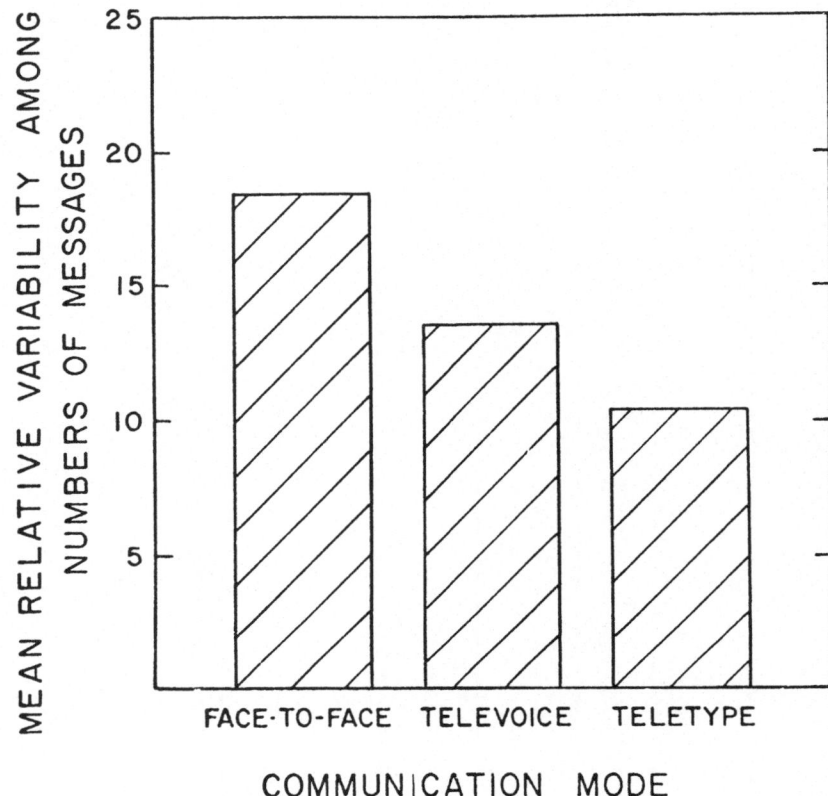

FIGURE 23.   Mean relative variabilities among the numbers of
             messages produced by communicators in three modes.
             Each bar is the average of 54 data points.   Data
             are averaged for three sizes of conference group,
             each of which arrived at solutions to three different
             problems on each of three successive days.
             (From Krueger, unpublished data)

The figure shows that communicators in the teletype mode produced much more nearly equal numbers of messages than did communicators in either of the voice modes. Conversely, in the voice modes, some communicators tended to produce a disproportionately large number of messages, while others tended to be less communicative than would be expected. These data, incidentally, are averages for 2-person, 3-person, and 4-person conferences. Since there was no significant interaction between size of group and communication mode, the data in Figure 23 hold for all three sizes of group.

Linguistic Categories in the Several Modes of Communication

The striking differences in verbal output among the several modes of communication (Refer to Figures 12, 13, 14, and 15, for example) have led us to examine more closely the kind of language and words that are used in the various modes of communication. Here I shall only give two generalizations that seem to emerge from our studies.

13. We have not been able to find any outstanding differences in the various kinds of words people use in the several modes of communication.

Figure 24 shows the average numbers of words in each of six linguistic categories based on a modification of the Fries (1952) classification system. These data and those in Figure 12 are from the same experiment. About the only thing one can conclude from Figure 24 is that the differences among the several modes revealed by total word counts appear to hold for words in every linguistic category. Indeed, when the data of Figure 24 are converted to percentages (Figure 25), the prevailing impression one gets is that there are no striking differences among the various kinds of words in the several modes of communication. That impression is confirmed by appropriate statistical tests of the data.

The foregoing notwithstanding, additional studies lead us to conclude that:

14. Oral communication is highly redundant and most communication can be carried on effectively with a small, carefully selected set of words.

Because of the nature of natural language communications, redundancy cannot be measured in the ordinary mechanical ways that have been developed from Shannon's theory of information. However, using some plausible assumptions, we have been able to estimate that oral modes of communication use about 12 to 14 times as many words as are necessary and about 4 times as many different words as are necessary (Chapanis, Parrish, Ochsman, and Weeks, 1977).

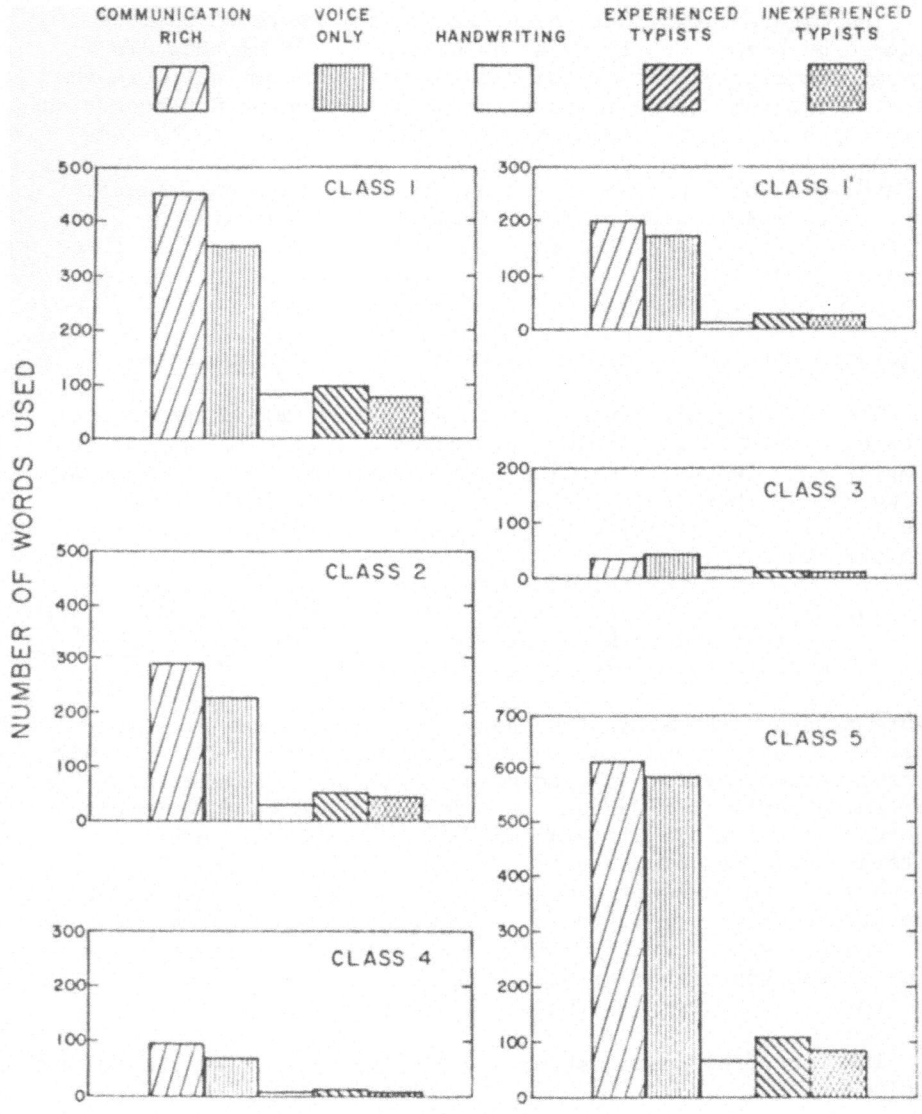

FIGURE 24. Average numbers of words in each of six linguistic categories by subjects in each of four modes of communication. (From Stoll et al., 1976)

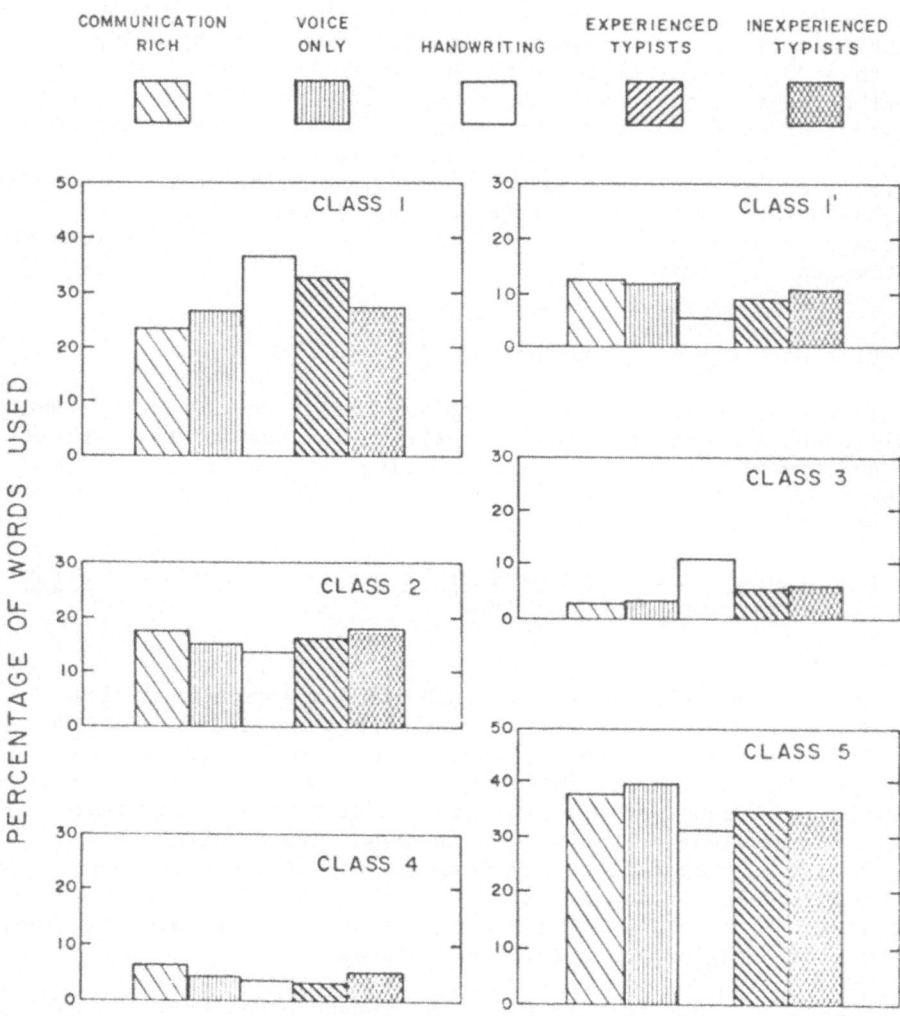

FIGURE 25. The data in Figure 24 have been here converted to percentages (From Stoll et al., 1976)

One heartening thing for purposes of man-computer communication
is that people can carry out our communication tasks by using no
more than 300 words (Kelly, 1976) and can do the tasks just about
as effectively as they can with no vocabulary restrictions.   Let
me assert at once, however, that this is a specially selected subset of 300 words.   Not any set of 300 would do.   Additional
studies (Ford, unpublished data; Michaelis and Chapanis, in progress)
are looking at still more restricted sets of language and their
effects on communication.   It is still too early to say what these
experiments will show.

The Chaos of Ordinary Communication

In the preceding sections of this paper, I have spoken rather
glibly about numbers of words and numbers of messages as though it
were no trouble at all to count such linguistic units.   Let me
disabuse you of that impression with my next generalization and
with some illustrations:

15. <u>Natural human communication is extremely unruly and often
    seems to follow few grammatical, syntactic, or semantic
    rules.</u>

Most psycholinguistic experiments and most man-computer dialogs
are done with what I have called "immaculate prose".   Words are
formed into perfect sentences, with nouns, verbs, adverbs, and
other parts of speech all in their correct order.   Natural human
communication is not at all like that.   Most people know that
ordinary communication tends to be somewhat disorganized, but
few of us really appreciate how disorganized it can be.   Many
of our protocols contain not a single grammatically correct
sentence.   Moreover, we find every rule of spelling, abbreviation,
punctuation, and format repeatedly violated.

Figure 26 shows the start of some interchanges between two
persons who communicated via teletypewriter to solve a faculty
selection problem.   Figure 27 shows the start of the interchanges
between two persons who communicated by voice to solve the problem
illustrated in Figures 5 and 6.   Figures 28 and 29 are segments
of two protocols from persons who communicated by telepen to
solve the wiring problem illustrated in Figures 3 and 4.   The
protocols in Figures 26, 27 and 28 are typical of what one can
get in these various modes.   Figure 29 is an extreme example
to show how bad protocols can get.

Perhaps the most impressive thing about these samples of protocol is their extreme unruliness.   It is even difficult to know
what to count as a word, a sentence, or a message.   I think we
have made a good start on this problem and a recent paper (Chapanis,
Parrish, Ochsman, and Weeks, 1977) describes some empirical rules
we have developed for dealing with some of these natural language
protocols.   That same study leads us to conclude that:

SK: Need information . Use form of a list for clarity. Present info on all candidates in the area of research each has done..

   end my typing go.

SO: A: The Eskimo as a Minority Worker in Alaska
       Sikudaruty (Ignore)   Solidarity Fornation Between Blue and
   White Collar Workers in Adverse

SK: wait/////////////   ignore info about topics ... Can you give
   data of 1. quantity of research done as manifested in # of publications
   etc. If not, move on to (past experience in teaching) present in same
   fashion..... Please give SYNOPSIS of material for efficiency/////±±±±±±

SO: A: 3 publications
   B:none
   C: 3 pub.
   D: 4 publ.
   E. Dissertation research: The Existance of a Pecking Order in Penal Cloonies

SK: Information on AWARDS RECEIVED BY ANY OF CANDIDATES OR HINT OF QUALITY
   OF RESEARCH ?   Then move on to teaching

SO: A: Best Paper, honor graduation, member of 2 Honor Societies
   B:Phi Beta Kappa, most promissing grad, cited for contribution to science
   C:Top 5%of class, Phi B K
   D:

SK: from what institutions   ?   TYPE FASTER TURKEY   go

SO: First change above A¢ A, B, C to B, C, D Sorry

SK: ok   go

SO: B: Grad from Duke Unev.
   C: Harvard and Oxford
   D:Univ. of Montana, Cornell
   E:U. of Calif at Berkeley , UCla

FIGURE 26.   Start of the interchanges between two persons who
            communicated in the teletypewriter mode to solve a
            faculty selection problem.   On the original protocol
            the seeker's messages (SK) were in black type, the
            source's in red.   The vertical spacing has been
            adjusted here to make it more regular than on the
            original.   The horizontal spacing duplicates that
            on the original protocol.

So: Well, it's, it's a clip now, right?

Sk: Yeah, it's a clip.

So: How how wide is the clip?

Sk: It's ah, a little bit wider than than the socket.

So: How does it fit now, does it fit...Is it go on the bottom of it or it's it's definitely parallel to it?

Sk: Right.

So: It's definitely parallel

So; to it?

Sk: It's

Sk; parallel so that when you clip it...

So: Okay I got you, but it's wider than it right?

Sk: Yeah, a little bit wider.

So: A little bit wider.....Okay wait a second.   Uh how wide is the socket is it, you know the socket itself

So; is it/

Sk: Okay

So; wide or thin cause I have uh two two just about like that, what you described

Sk: Okay now, uh there's a socket and then there's a clip...

So: I have the clip on and everything I've got that.

Sk: Right. Okay now perpendicular to the socket there are two flanges...

FIGURE 27.   Start of the interchanges between two persons who communicated by voice to solve the object identification problem. So refers to the source; Sk to the seeker. Braces on the left identify instances in which both source and seeker were talking at the same time. A semicolon indicates a message that continues without interruption with material above it.

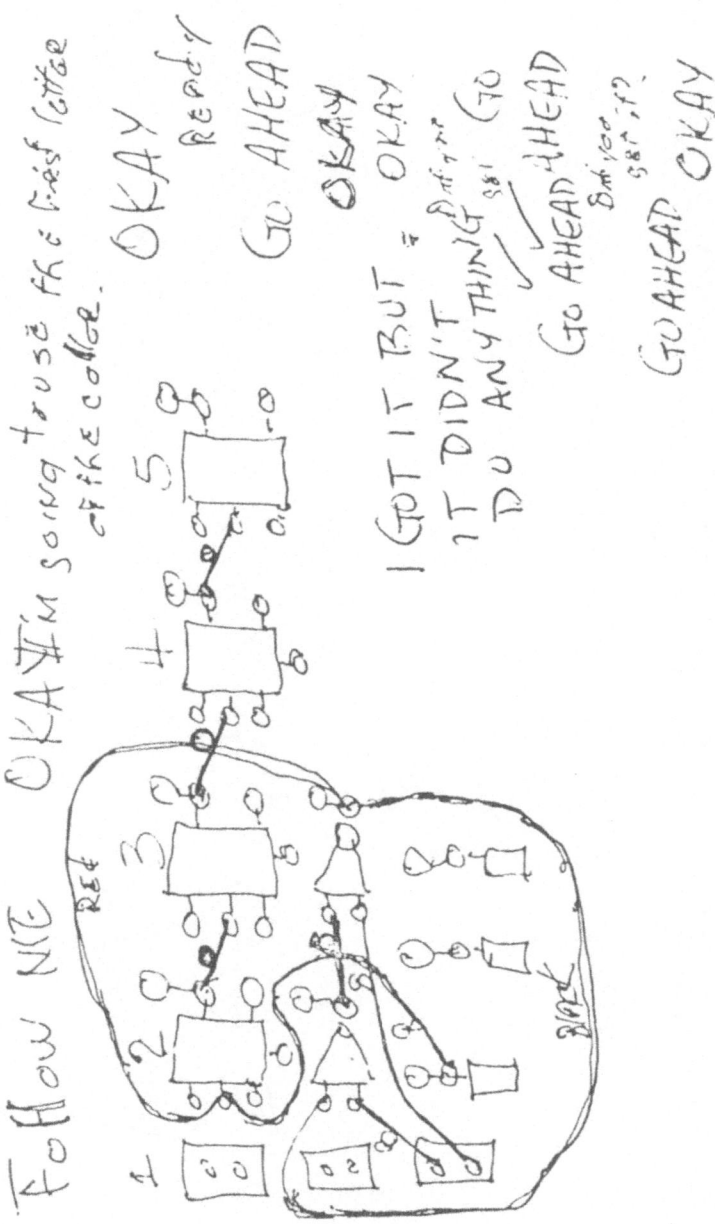

FIGURE 28.   One segment of a telepen protocol made by two persons
who solved the wiring task illustrated if Figs. 3 and 4.
This black-and-white illustration does not show that
messages by one person were in blue ink, by the other
in red ink.   Careful study will reveal, however, that
there are 14 separate messages here with each communicator in turn adding to earlier messages.
(From Hoecker, unpublished data)

110

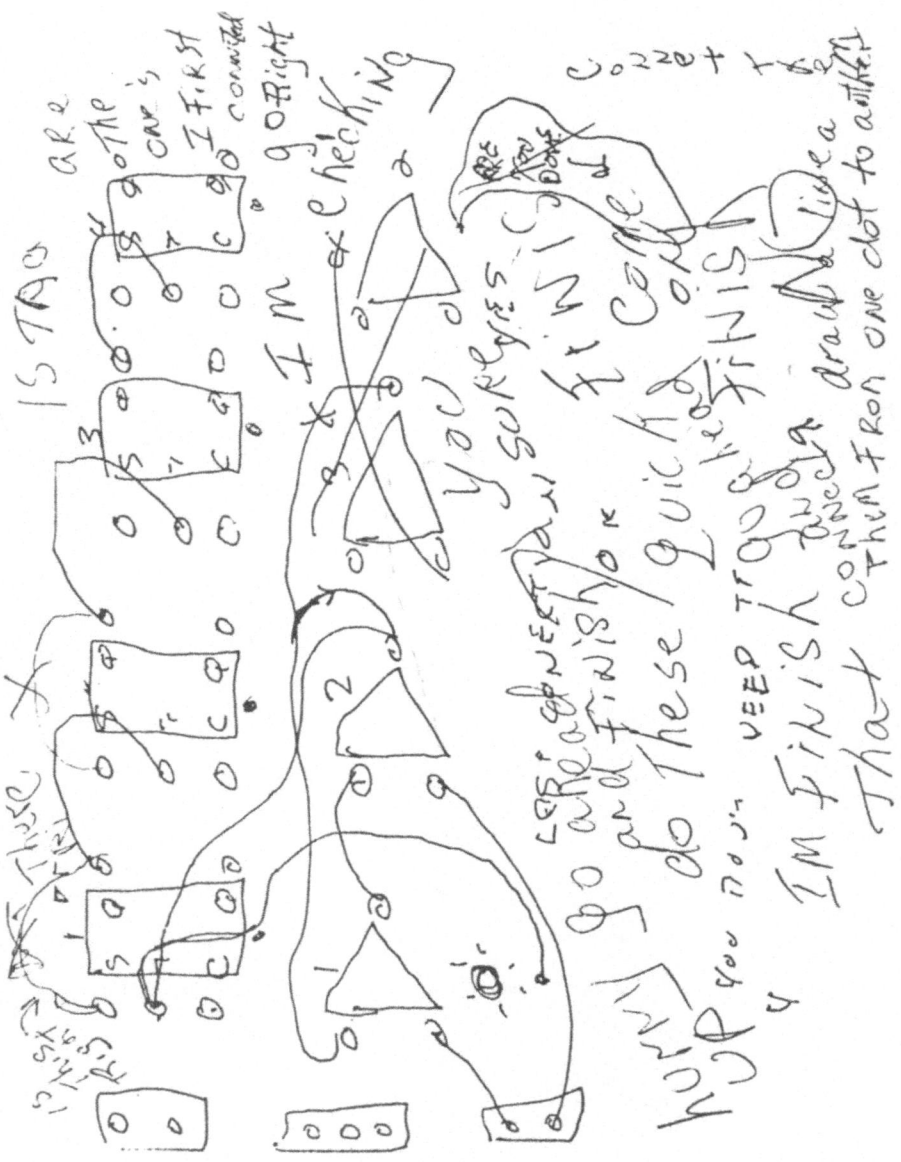

FIGURE 29.   A segment of an extremely disorganised protocol from
the same experiment that produced the protocol in
Figure 28.   (From Hoecker, unpublished data)

16. Natural language communications may be described by a surprisingly short list of perhaps no more than seven linguistic measures.

In our study we defined and examined some 182 measures of linguistic performance, most of which turned out to be redundant and some of which were useless or meaningless. In the end we came up with the following list of linguistic measures that we think are meaningful for this kind of research:

1. The number of messages used by a subject, and, a measure highly correlated with that one, the number of sentences used. The former, however, is much easier to score than the latter.

2. The number of words per message, and, a measure highly correlated with that one, the number of words per sentence. The former measure, however, is much easier to score than the latter.

3. The percentage of messages that were interrupted.

4. The total number of words used by a subject.

5. The total number of unique words used by a subject.

6. The type-token ration, that is, the ratio of 5 to 4 above.

7. Communication rate, that is, the number of words communicated per minute of time spent communicating.

In one sense, our findings are disappointing: there appears to be very little to show for so much effort. In another sense, however, they are gratifying: the linguistic performance of people who communicate naturally can be distilled to a rather small number of quantitative measures. In any case, our experience in trying to grapple with these problems will hopefully be useful to others who may try to carry on this kind of research.

CONCLUSION

I said that our work is a start and I meant precisely that. I have no illusions about what our researchers have told us. It is difficult to find the rules that underlie natural human communication and we are just beginning to get an inkling of what those rules must be. There clearly must be rules, because problems get solved and get solved rather expeditiously at that. If we are ever to have computers that can interact with their human counterparts in natural English, by typewriter, by voice, or by handwriting, we will somehow have to discover at least some of the rules that apply to natural, unconstrained communication. Discovering those rules is, in my opinion, one of the most fascinating and challenging problems facing both basic and applied scientists in this area of man-computer interaction.

ACKNOWLEDGEMENTS

The research reported in this paper was supported at various
times during the past seven years by the following agencies:
National Aeronautics and Space Administration under Research Grant
NGR-21-001-073; National Science Foundation, Office of Science
Information Service, under Research Grants GN-890 and GN-35023;
Office of Naval Research under Research Contract Number N00014-75-
C-0131; and National Science Foundation, Division of Advanced
Productivity Research and Technology, under Research Grant Number
APR-7518622.   I am indebted to each of these agencies for the
support that made my research program possible.

REFERENCES

Berkeley, E.C.   1949   Giant brains or machines that think.
                                New York, Wiley.

Bush, V.   1945   As we may think.
                                Atlantic Monthly, 176, 101-108.

Chapanis, A.   1971   Prelude to 2001: Explorations in human
                                   communication.
                                American Psychologist, 26, 949-961.

Chapanis, A.   1973   The communication of factual information
                                   through various channels.
                                Information Storage and Retrieval, 9,
                                   215-231.

Chapanis, A.   1975   Interactive human communication.
                                Scientific American, 232(3), 36-42.

Chapanis, A.,   1972   Studies in interactive communication:
Ochsman, R.B.,   I. The effects of four communication
Parrish, R.N. &   modes on the behavior of teams during
Weeks, G.D.   co-operative problem-solving.
                                Human Factors, 14, 487-509.

Chapanis, A. &   1974   Studies in interactive communication:
Overbey, C.M.   III. Effects of similar and dissimilar
                                   communication channels and two inter-
                                   change options on team problem solving.
                                Perceptual and Motor Skills, 38, 343-374,
                                   (Monograph Supplement 2-V38)

Chapanis, A.,   1977   Studies in interactive communication:
 Parrish, R.N.,   II. The effects of four communication
 Ochsman, R.B. &   modes on the linguistic performance
 Weeks, G.D.   of teams during co-operative problem
                             solving.
                             Human Factors, 19.2, 101.126.

Fries, C.C.   1952   The structure of English.
                             New York: Harcourt, Brace.

Kelly, M.J.   1976   Studies in interactive communication:
                             Limited vocabulary natural language
                             dialogue.
                             (Doctoral dissertation, the Johns
                             Hopkins University, 1975).
                             Dissertation Abstracts International,
                             36, 3647B. (University Microfilms
                             No. 76-1518).

Licklider, J.C.R.   1960   Man-computer symbiosis.
                             IRE Transactions on Human Factors in
                             Electronics, HFE-1, 4-11.

Licklider, J.C.R.   1965   Libraries of the future.
                             Cambridge, Mass., The M.I.T. Press.

Ochsman, R.B. &   1974   The effects of 10 communication modes
 Chapanis, A.   on the behavior of teams during
                             co-operative problem-solving.
                             International Journal of Man-Machine
                             Studies, 6, 579-619.

Parrish, R.N.   1974   Interactive communication in team
                             problem-solving as a function of two
                             educational levels and two communic-
                             ation modes.
                             (Doctoral dissertation, The Johns Hopkins
                             University, 1973).
                             Dissertation Abstracts International,
                             34, 5721B. (University Microfilms
                             No. 74-10, 440).

Stoll, F.C.,   1976   The effects of four communication modes
 Hoecker, D.G.   on the structure of language used
 Krueger, G.P. &   during co-operative problem-solving.
 Chapanis, A.   Journal of Psychology, 94, 13-26.

Turing, A.M.   1950   Computing machinery and intelligence.
                             Mind, 59, 433-460.

Turoff, M.   1975   The future of computer conferencing:
                                        An interview with Murray Turoff.
                                    The Futurist, 9, 182–190 & 195.

Weeks, G.D. &   1976   Co-operative versus conflictive problem
Chapanis, A.   solving in three telecommunication modes.
                                    Perceptual and Motor Skills, 42, 879–917.

Weeks, G.D.,   1974   Studies in interactive communication:
Kelly, M.J. &   V. Co-operative problem solving by
Chapanis, A.   skilled and unskilled typists in a
                                        teletypewriter mode.
                                    Journal of Applied Psychology, 59,
                                        665–674.

Weizenbaum, J.   1970   Contextual understanding by computers.
                                    In Z.W. Pylyshyn (Ed.), Perspectives
                                        on the computer revolution.
                                    Englewood Cliffs, Prentice-Hall.

PART 3   —   ASPECTS OF THE HARDWARE INTERFACE

PREVIEW

What the user must input to the computer, and what the user
sees in return, is the user's interface to the machine.   The
interface comprises not only the obvious hardware elements used
by an operator but also such aspects as the organisation and
layout of the communication messages and the documentation to
help users and maintainers.   So the interface can usefully be
differentiated into hardware and software aspects.

However, the close-coupled interactive form which MCI should
take causes any such subdivisions of the whole user-task-computer
triad to be neither comprehensive nor entirely satisfactory.   This
hardware-software subdivision of the interface may become less
clear with the growing ambiguity between facilities provided by
hardware and software, and is perhaps less useful because it makes
no distinction between structure and meaning.   Nevertheless,
while the designers of hardware and software are still usually
different people, with different backgrounds in engineering and
programming, the hardware-software differentiation may continue
to be of some value.

In recent years there has been some improvement in interface
design, for example quieter teletype and similar printers, cheaper
video display units with better editing facilities, etc.   But
the mismatch between machines and man is still very evident,
especially with regard to many detailed ergonomics aspects such
as legibility on video display units, complexity of command
structures for computer-naive users in applications packages
(such as for word processing), and physical size and workspace
design of display units, desks and consoles in relation to such
aspects as comfort and eyestrain.

We are not attempting to provide detailed prescriptions, in
this book, for the specific design of various hardware devices.
General ergonomics textbooks and handbooks are available (for
instance E.J. McCormick 'Human Factors Engineering', McGraw-Hill,
B. Shackel 'Applied Ergonomics Handbook', IPC Science & Technology
Press).   Moreover, specific texts and manuals are now becoming
available with data and methods directly oriented towards the
design of computer interfaces.   Amongst these can be suggested
those by D. Grover 'Visual Display Units and their Applications',
IPC Science & Technology Press 1976, and by A. Cakir, D.J. Hart
and T.F.M. Stewart 'The VDT Manual', IFRA 1979, understood to be
published soon as 'Visual Display Terminals', Wiley 1980.

The papers here by Ostberg and Ivergard deal with and usefully draw attention to two major aspects of the hardware interface, as well as quite a number of smaller issues. Aspects of desk design and workstation layout are considered by both Ostberg and Ivergård; visual and ophthalmic issues of terminal design are discussed in some detail by Ostberg, and various aspects of interaction in public systems are discussed by Ivergård.

Ostberg summarises the bases and the facts of the new Swedish working environment law and especially its consequences for office automation. He then outlines recent Swedish work leading to improved desk designs for computer terminals, including a brief summary of the design process. Finally, he presents a very useful general review of the visual and ophthalmic issues involved in terminal and workstation design.

Ivergård briefly discusses aspects of terminal and interaction procedure design. He then presents two major case study examples, concerned with telephone system customer information and service records and with the checkout stations at supermarkets. From these he draws some conclusions and suggestions for the future.

OFFICE COMPUTERISATION IN SWEDEN: WORKER PARTICIPATION,
WORKPLACE DESIGN CONSIDERATIONS, AND THE REDUCTION OF VISUAL STRAIN

Olov Östberg

Department of Human Work Sciences,
University of Luleå, S-95187 Luleå, Sweden.

INTRODUCTION

In Sweden, as in most industrialised countries, a very rapid
computerisation of office work has taken place during the last
decade, and the number of CRT computer terminals is still increasing
progressively.   To this should be added a great number of less
spectacular computer linked machines, such as teletypes, mechanic
and magnetic key punch machines, and microfilm reading apparatus
(for Computer Output on Microfilm - COM).   It is especially in
systems dealing with transport and financial administration, and
in the society's health and welfare administration, that the typical
office worker is likely to be using one of these machines during
a substantial part of the working day.   This trend has not escaped
the notice of politicians, business management, and the trade unions.
The topics raised at the socio-economic 'macro level' can be grouped
into four main issues:
- Fear of diminished individual privacy: What can be done to
  prevent the abuse of the commercial and governmental data banks?
  (Aner, 1974)
- Fear of diminished business management power: What can be done
  to prevent the traditional business managers from being puppets
  on the computer specialists' strings? (Hedberg, 1974)
- Fear of diminished trade union power: What can be done to
  prevent the computer resources from being used against the
  workers in the same way as with the traditional production
  resources? (Nygaard and Bergo, 1974).
- Fear of diminished face-to-face communication: What can be done
  to prevent humans from becoming psychologically and physically
  separated from each other through the intervention of computers
  and a too abstract and synthetic computer language? (Palme, 1975)

The present paper, however, is concerned with the problems at the 'micro level', ie. the workplace. Despite their abundance, workplace problems arising from office computerisation, have received only a scanty examination (Ostberg, 1975). Bearing in mind that the proportion of white-collar workers in technologically advanced countries amounts to up to 50% of the total work-force, Udris and Barth (1976) quite rightly demanded that more ergonomics research effort should be directed to this area. Man-computer interactions have certainly been dealt with in the ergonomics literature, but mainly as a design support tool for sophisticated systems in for example weaponry and space projects (Van Cott and Kinkade, 1972). Although some of these ergonomics findings are generally applicable (Shackel and Shipley, 1970), they are, by and large, either of limited relevance or otherwise not applicable to the CRT tasks of the office worker.

THE FRAMEWORK OF WORKER PARTICIPATION IN THE PLANNING OF THE WORKING ENVIRONMENT

The office workers in Sweden have gradually become more and more conscious of the need to unite against the trend towards 'office factories'. Computers are generally blamed for creating the same type of alienation among office workers as was previously experienced by factory workers (Shepard, 1971). As a result, the Swedish Central Organization of Salaried Employees has launched an attack against the deterioration experienced by its members of their mental and physical working conditions, and the Federation of Swedish Trade Unions has actually appointed an ombudsman of computer affairs.

In parallel with this, the Working Environment Commission (SOU, 1976) outlined in its final report how these negative phenomena should be dealt with through a partial reform of the occupational safety legislation. In keeping with the current, broader view, the Workers' Protection Act now becomes the Working Environment Act. The basic principle of the Act is that working conditions must be adapted to human needs and aptitudes, both physical and mental, so as to overcome problems which exist, caused by monotony, stress, social isolation, etc. Furthermore, in order to provide the essential elements of job satisfaction, the work must be organized in such a way as to enable the employee to play an active part in the design of his own workplace and job routines. Extensive co-operation between employers and employees has long been the established practice in the sphere of occupational safety negotiations in Sweden, and legislation now exists making this co-operation mandatory. Prior to this legislation reform, the employer federation and trade unions in 1976 signed an agreement which, in effect, commissions the local unions to take the responsibility for the creation of sound working conditions. The local working environment committee with its employee majority is therefore made in effect the supervisor of the medical officers and safety engineers.

At each specific work place, with five or more workers, at least one worker shall be elected to act as their safety delegate (safety ombudsman), and in practice there are on average one senior safety delegate and one more safety delegate per 20-50 workers; in mid-1976 there were all together more than 100,000 safety delegates registered in Sweden. Previously the safety delegates had the right to suspend work in hazardous situations. They were also supposed to help generally in the enforcement of the occupational safety legislation and to look out for the more serious negative aspects regarding safety and health in the working environment. In the new Working Environment Act however, the very important part played by safety delegates in establishing a positive working environment is underlined. Not only will they be given wider powers to suspend hazardous and unhealthy working situations, but now the employer must also notify the safety delegate of any changes which can have a significant bearing on the working conditions within the delegate's area of responsibility.

To support and enable the delegates to carry out their duties they have had to take part in a local study circle 'Better Working Environment' (1974). The minimum study time is 3 days (paid working time), but quite frequently 3 weeks are allocated, especially for the senior delegates many of whom are employed full time as safety delegate. Each safety delegate also obtains the monthly journal 'Working Environment' (Arbetsmiljö).

OFFICE COMPUTERISATION AND WORKER PARTICIPATION

As indicated above the trade unions' demands for better working conditions have resulted in the establishing of both a broadened and a deepened framework for worker participation. Regarding office computerisation, this has in turn rapidly brought pressure to bear on the National Board of Occupational Safety and Health (the 'Board'), and the Agency for Administrative Development (the 'Agency'). The latter is responsible for virtually any kind of office computerisation within the vast government-controlled administrative systems, and the former has the duty of working out appropriate 'musts' and 'must-nots', and of supplying the co-operating/negotiating parties with objective support (eg. such as factual reports).

Figure 1 may serve to illustrate a typical situation concerning worker participation, and the roles played by the Board and the Agency in office computerisation. The picture, showing a female safety delegate and a male purchase engineer, comes from the safety delegate study circle 'Better Working Environment'. When the safety delegates, of a governmental office block for example, heard that the management had asked the Agency to look into the possibilities of computerising some of the administrative routines, the

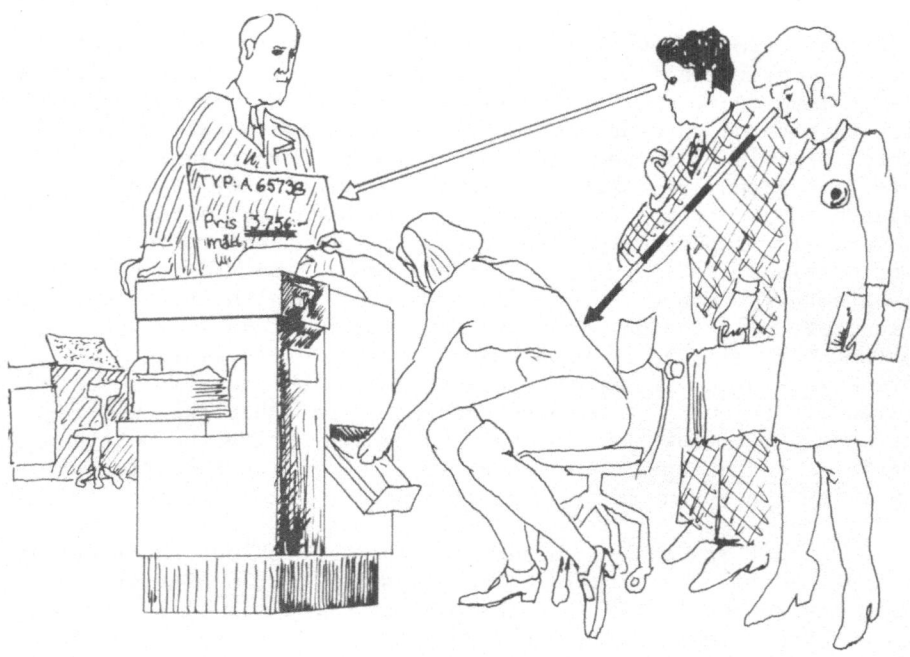

FIGURE 1. Swedish safety delegates are taught: "Demand ergonomics facts when new equipment is being considered to be introduced, and compare these with your own demands." (After Better Working Environment, 1974).

FIGURE 2. Travestying figure 1, it takes more than a three-day study circle before a meaningful worker participation can be exercised in the hocus-pocus realms of computer system specialists.

concerned delegates demanded that they should take the matter up
with the local working environment committee before any decisions
were taken.   To prepare themselves, the senior delegate phoned
the Board to check whether there were any 'musts' or 'must-nots'
regarding this, and to ask for relevant ergonomics information.
As a result of this, the delegates later decided not to accept
the CRT terminal suggested by the computer specialists of the
Agency – the suggested terminal did not have a keyboard that could
be separated from the display unit, and the delegates rightly
considered this to be a serious drawback.

Eventually the Agency asked the Board to produce a once-and-
for-all ergonomics checklist, in order that the suggested equipment
could be pre-screened so as to eliminate the risk of it being
rejected when brought to the attention of the safety delegates.
The Board commissioned a comprehensive survey of the literature
(Stewert et   al., 1974), but instead of producing a traditional
static checklist, that could at best be of limited value (compare
Siegel and Fischl, 1971), the outcome was a terminal users' handbook (Ostberg, 1976a).   The aim of the handbook is to point out
to safety delegates, management and system designers, that there
is more to the design of acceptable computer terminal workplaces
than merely buying ergonomically sound terminals and putting them
on to ordinary office desks.   Another point made in the handbook
is illustrated in figure 2: It is virtually impossible to have
effective worker participation in abstract and complex situations
unless the safety delegates or some other employee representatives
are thoroughly taught the secrets of the system designers' hocus
pocus.

Safety delegates have refused even to accept computerisation
before the Board had firmly declared that working at a computer
terminal

1.   does not increase the total exposure of ionizing or ultra-
     violet radiation,
2.   does not provoke epileptic seizures,
3.   does not destroy colour perception,
4.   does not speed up the ageing of the eyes.

In order to give an objective account of some of these worries,
an article reviewing negative findings was published in the
safety delegates' monthly journal 'Working Environment' (Ostberg,
1976b)

122

FIGURE 3. Typical working postures of terminal operators:
raised arms, stretched neck, raised line of vision,
and twisted back.

WORKPLACE DESIGN CONSIDERATIONS

During the preparation of the terminal users' handbook
(Ostberg, 1976a), the picture group in figure 3 was drawn.   These
situations were selected as showing operators' typical working
postures, and the more extreme operator-terminal mismatches have
deliberately been left out.   The working postures shown in the
figure do not at first sight seem to be too bad, but a closer
examination shows them to have the following negative features:
- raised arms due to high mounted keyboard
- raised neck and gaze due to high mounted display screen
- faulty posture due to requirements imposed by the handling of
  the documents
- faulty posture due to requirements imposed by the handling of
  the terminal.

Obviously, the operators' working postures are far from good.
In fact, in some computerised offices the operators have had so
much muscle and eye strain (and felt so bored) that they have
refused to do certain terminal jobs for longer periods than two
hours in the morning and two hours in the afternoon, ie. they have
demanded (and obtained) job rotation.   In other computerised
offices, a physiotherapist regularly comes to help the operators
'soften up' strained muscles and joints by means of organised
group gymnastics.

These problems are a result of the failure to recognise that
the introduction of CRT computer terminals radically alters the
physical and mental activities of the office worker.   Management
seems to consider terminals as 'job aids' that can simply be introduced into conventional workplaces.   On the other hand, the
terminal manufacturer is concerned with producing a cheap apparatus
that can be used almost universally, and therefore is not concerned
with producing integrated workplaces for particular situations.
Irrespective of who is to blame, the fact remains: today's
terminals are often full-time workplaces but as often look like
infrequently used job aids.

Elsewhere (Ostberg, 1975) it has been pointed out that unless
closer attention is paid to operator discomfort caused by the lack
of ergonomics consideration in the design of terminal workplaces,
the discomfort will sooner or later become manifested as specific
occupational diseases (see also Onishi et al., 1973).   Unfortunately,
Carlsöö (1976) very soon showed this to be an accomplished fact.
He reported that office computerisation is accompanied by an
increased frequency of upper back ailments, which have been shown
by EMG studies to be caused by the working postures imposed by
the keying and the visual tasks.   Concerning EMG studies of neck
muscles in relation to visual taks, reference should also be made
to the early paper by Simons et al. (1942).

124

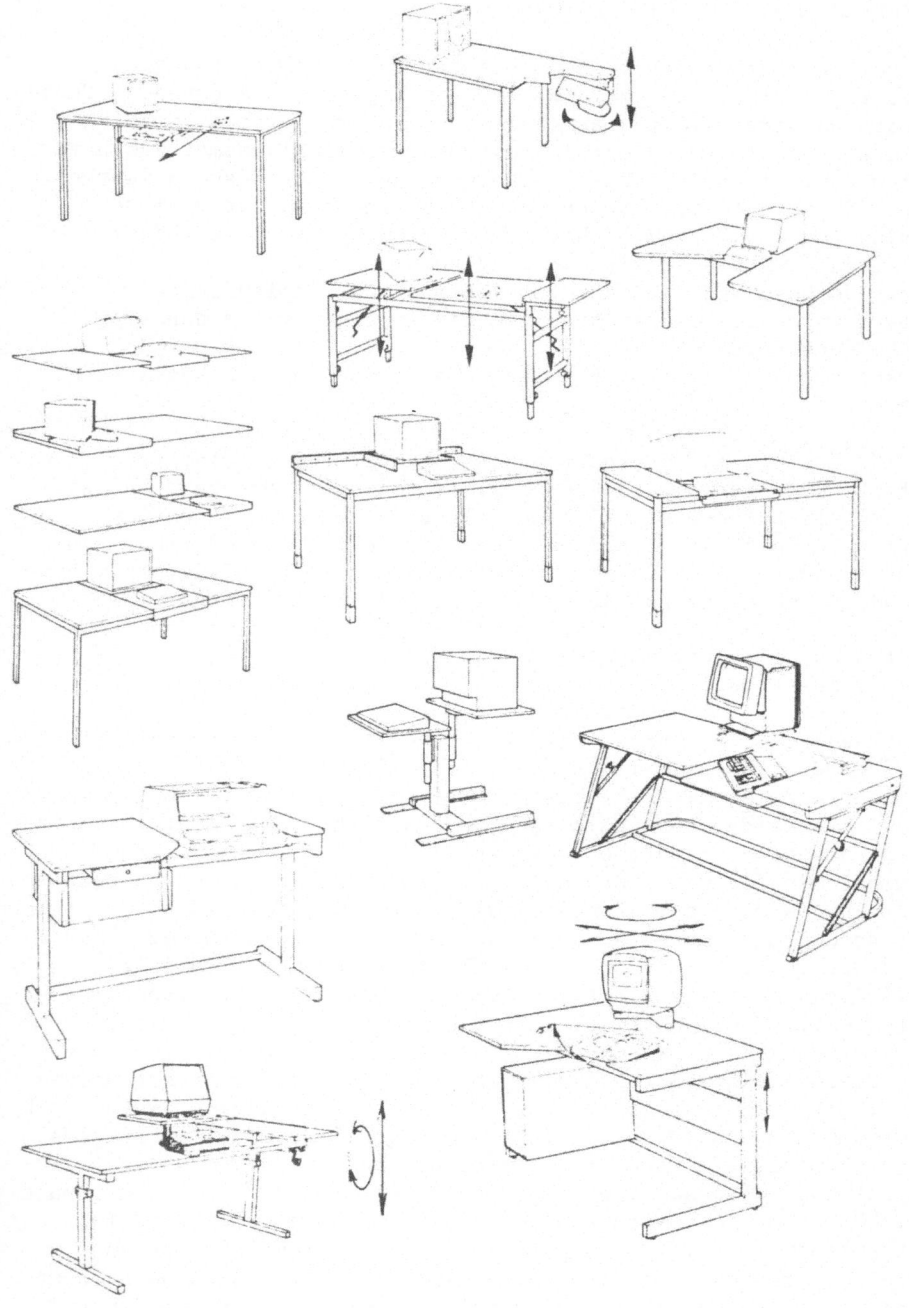

FIGURE 4.   Examples of purpose-designed "terminal desks" now on
the market in Sweden.   (After Ostberg et al., 1976)

In co-operation with a couple of government institutions just about to be computerised, the Board made extensive attempts to stimulate manufacturers of office equipment to start producing office desks suited for the building-up of integrated terminal workplaces. To set an example, such a desk was actually designed at the Board. The response has generally been favourable, and figure 4 shows some of the desks which have now been marketed. The Board's desk talent-scouts also came across an impressive number of attempts by terminal users to modify traditional office desks to suit the placing of a particular terminal in a particular application. As virtually none of these users had heard of any other similar desk-modifying attempts, the Board decided to publish an illustrated book called 'Desks for CRT computer terminals' (Ostberg, et al., 1976). In the terminal users' handbook (Ostberg, 1976a), it is stressed at the same time that it is seldom sufficient merely to select a 'good' desk. The recommended steps in the design process were as follows:

Job analysis specifications. Different terminal applications may need totally different workplace layouts. If the terminal operator is involved in serving customers, the terminal must be within easy reach, yet not obstructing operator-customer communication. If the operator has to move about near the terminal, the chair may be equipped with wheels, but frequently used job aids, such as manuals and charts, should normally be close to the operator. Associated equipment (hard copy printers, microfilm readers, etc.) should be integrated with the workplace and not just put there. Free table space should be reserved for the handling of documents, especially when hand writing is necessary. Document holders and a telephone head-set may be useful.

Anthropometric specifications. Chairs and desks must fit the body dimensions of the specific operator population. When more than one operator is using the workplace, arrangements must be made to allow for quick seat height adjustment, etc. The height of the table top and the keyboard should comply with current ergonomics standards for paper handling tasks and keying tasks respectively. The positioning of the display screen should be such that the operator normally looks slightly downwards. Screen and keyboard should be separate.

Design specifications. The table must be large enough to accommodate papers, source documents, and other equipment. The keyboard must not be too spacious, and should not therefore have a separate set of numerical keys if there is no need for them. A recessed keyboard might be a way of obtaining both a suitable keyboard height and a suitable table top height, although the keyboard position should not be fixed.

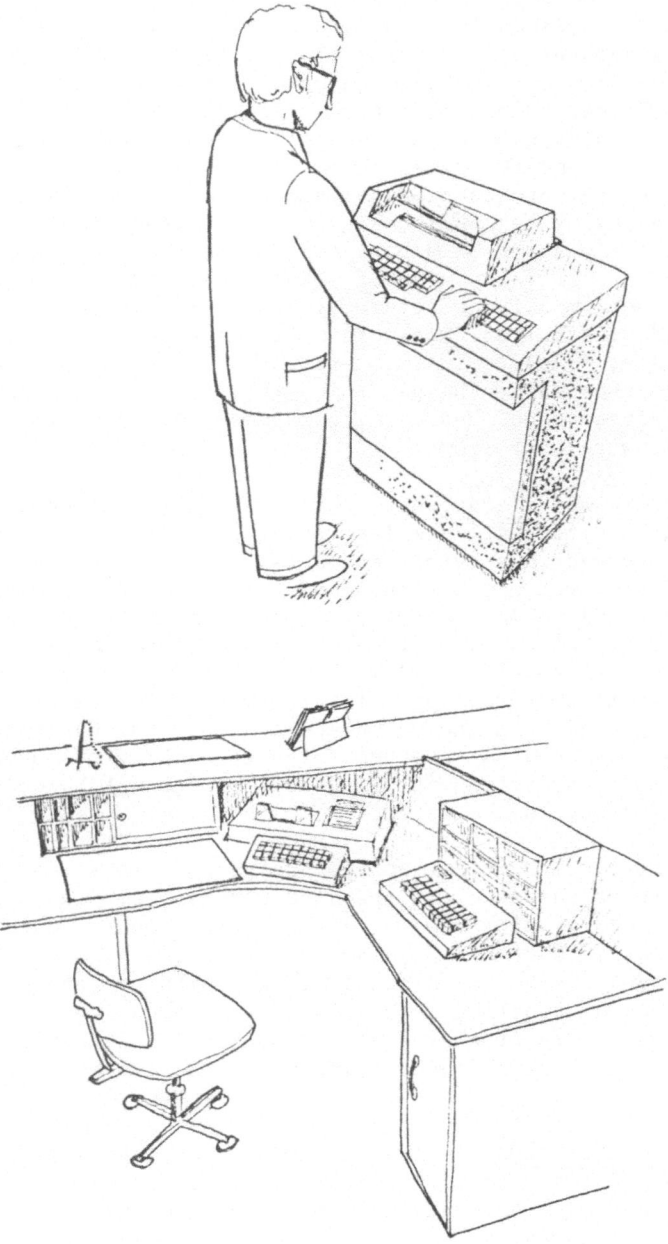

FIGURE 5. The terminal (above) had to be completely dismantled
and rearranged to create an acceptable terminal workplace (below).

Environmental specifications.   Some terminal printers are
noisy and some display units constantly produce a very high-pitched
tone which some operators are not willing to tolerate.   The fan
removing excess heat can also produce an irritating humming and an
unpleasant air stream.   Such environmental factors must not be
neglected.   Most important, however, are the environmental factors
that affect the ease of seeing, eg. the lighting conditions, which
in turn influence the operator's working posture.   Good lighting
for the reading of printed information (500 lux, perhaps) is not
the same   as good lighting for the reading of CRT pictures (150 lux,
perhaps), but these aspects are dealt with further in the next
sections.

Most of the workplace requirements listed above can be taken
into consideration only if the terminal itself fulfills certain
requirements.   For example, the display screen and the keyboard
must be separate to allow for individual positioning according to
the job and operator demands.   This is not always the case, and
figure 5 nicely demonstrates the enormous effort a bank had to put
in to create a satisfactory workplace out of the original equipment.
The terminal virtually had to be completely dismantled and
rearranged.

DELINEATION OF THE VISUAL PROBLEMS

The need for 'terminal spectacles' has proved to be a debated
issue within many computerised systems in Sweden.   To some extent
the discussion concerns the provision of free working spectacles
in general.   Apart from the severely visually handicapped, the
purchase of spectacles is in no way subsidised by the National
Health Service.   On the other hand, it is stated in the Workers'
Protection Act that the employer   shall supply the employee with
proper eye protection devices and any necessary visual aids which
the employee would not normally have.   It remains therefore to
analyse to what extent the demands made on the eyesight of the
terminal operator call for the provision of specially designed
spectacles.   Later it will be shown that in some cases this
provision is necessary, but first an account will be given of the
scope of these visual problems and the possibilities of solving
these without prescribing 'terminal spectacles'.

Devos-Petiprez (1973) investigated the working conditions of
a large company's 245 female computer terminal operators (mean age
23 years).   The visual problems were easily the largest source of
operator discomfort.   Every third operator wore spectacles and,
due to the visual strain that had been experienced, most of these
had had to see an ophthalmologist after having taken up the work
with the terminal.   The spectacles were in some instances tinted
in an   attempt to alleviate the discomfort caused by glare and high

128

FIGURE 6. Visual problems are commonplace in computerised offices:
long viewing distances, accommodation difficulties due
to blurred characters, reflections, glare, adverse
luminance ratios, etc.

contrasts. The operators had themselves switched off parts of the installed electric lighting, and achieved approximately 200 lux of general lighting, but still they had not been able to prevent veiling reflections on the CRT screens, specular reflections on the keyboards and discomfort glare from the luminaires and windows. Devos-Petiprez believed that the 'defocalisation' effects of these visual disturbances could in the long run create myopia, but her thorough examinations of the vision of all operators did not lend support to this hypothesis.

Such a situation, as the one described by Devos-Petiprez, is rather more universal than unique (Hultgren and Knave, 1974; Peters, 1975), and similar conditions are found also in the use of microfilm readers (Ostberg, 1976c). One of the main difficulties in further discussion of visual problems is that visual fatigue by its very definition overlaps with general fatigue to a considerable degree: "A weariness resulting from bodily and mental exertion of seeing" (Weston, 1954). Obviously, however, visual fatigue could most conveniently be said to originate from one or more of the following sources: (1) the eyes, (2) the light reaching the eyes, and (3) the visual task. The present paper does not deal with the 'technical' aspects of the task, such as character legibility, flicker, and phosphor chromaticity (dealt with by Stewart et al., 1974), or the design of the man-computer dialogue (dealt with by Martin, 1973), but rather with the visual problems related to workplace design in typical computerised offices. Figure 6 illustrates such typical problems, of which some are listed below.

Long viewing distances. Due to the difficulties in arranging an efficient, over-all workplace layout (screen, keyboard, documents, etc.), the operators frequently have the display screen located at a viewing distance of 50-100 cm. This should be compared with the viewing distances normally found in office tasks (ie. paper handling), which, according to Crouch and Buttolph (1973), is approximately 33 cm. Ophthalmologists' prescriptions for spectacles are likewise based on a hypothetical viewing distance of 33 cm., which is not therefore, ideal for terminal jobs. It must also be remembered that the operator must be capable of clearly seeing the source documents, the CRT display, and visiting colleagues and customers.

Accommodation difficulties. Unfavourable viewing distances are not the sole cause of accommodation difficulties. Contributing factors also include blurred characters, jerky lines, veiling reflections on the screen, and non-fused elements (dots) making up the generated characters. All these factors make it difficult for the eyes to get a clear retinal picture.

FIGURE 7. Attempts made by terminal operators to alleviate the
visual strain may include: adjustment of the general
lighting, bringing together the visual work, wearing
tinted spectacles, building a terminal booth, using
only a table lamp, and modifying the display unit.

Reflections and glare. Light falling upon a matt CRT screen produces a contrast reducing veil, whilst upon a non-matt screen produces reflections.   These problems are seldom satisfactorily solved, and the operators constantly have to tolerate patches of unwanted light on the screen.   Windows and luminaires also produce direct discomfort glare, partly because the otherwise acceptable glare level for office tasks is made ineffective by the requirement of a raised line of view during CRT viewing.   The more difficult the task is, the more sensitive the operator is to glare exposure, and vice versa (Ostberg et al., 1975).

Adverse luminances. The display screen is fairly dark but, because of its comparatively bright surroundings (in a well lit office), the operator's eyes are not adapted to it; besides decreased visual performance, this may cause eye strain ('astenopic symptoms').   This is especially true where the terminal has been placed near a window.   It should also be noted that for his total viewing field to be well balanced from a luminance point of view the operator may prefer to push away the dark screen (and thereby increase the reading distance).

Unsuitable spectacles. Terminal operators seldom can watch the CRT screen with lowered eyes, and accordingly bifocal lenses of standard type are not suitable for display work, however suitable they may be for ordinary office tasks.   Normally-ground, ordinary spectacles sometimes are also not suited for terminal work, at least not for elderly operators.

REDUCTIONS IN VISUAL STRAIN IMPLEMENTED BY OPERATORS

Many terminal operators are simply not aware of the visual problems they are actually exposed to.   It is for instance, not uncommon that operators wearing ordinary bifocals have never realised that they sit all day long with backward bent necks when reading the displayed pictures on the CRT screen.   Others sit facing a screen in front of a bright window where the Venetian blinds are never used.   However, quite a few operators are painfully aware of the visual problems and try in various ways to improve these conditions.   The drawings shown in figure 7 seek to illustrate some of these attempts.   As a rule, the achieved improvements have been initiated by the employees and they have only had little support from the employer.   Some of the frequent ways of improvements are listed below.

Tilting the display unit. In order that the light from luminaires and windows shall not be reflected by, or otherwise reach the display screen, the back of the display unit may be raised by means of 'hind legs'.   A punched-card box makes very nice hind legs.

Fitting a hood on the screen.   Almost every microfilm reading apparatus is equipped with a hood to shut out unwanted light, but almost no CRT display terminal has such a hood – not even as an option for those who are willing to accept this extra cost.   Home made cardboard hoods are, of course, easy to tape on to the terminal – it takes some operator initiative though.

Building a terminal booth.   This can be an efficient way of controlling the lighting environment at the terminal.   A completely built-in terminal, using high shielding screens, might be useful from an illumination point of view.   However, then there are no distant points within the ordinary visual field, and the operator would not get any periods of eye strain relief and relaxation by letting the gaze wander away from time to time.

Adjusting the general lighting.   In some large general office rooms the terminal operators have had the maintenance depart- ment remove two fluorescent tubes out of three in the luminaires closest to the terminals.   In some cases they have also managed to get the rest of the luminaires equipped with glare-free louvres. In special terminal rooms, solely inhabited by terminal operators, it is not uncommon totally to switch off the general lighting, and rely only on table lamps.   Unfortunately, some companies with office landscapes have adopted policies that make such initiative impossible: there must not be any table lamps or any shielding screens.

Bringing together the visual work.   Sometimes an operator is willing to sacrifice a good working posture in order that the display screen, source documents, and keyboard may be brought together. The positive effect is that all visual objects now appear at approximately the same viewing distance and angle.

Wearing special spectacles.   A great many terminal operators strongly believe that the eyesight is gradually deteriorated by the daily eye strain associated with the work.   Some operators have asked an ophthalmologist for "stronger glasses" than they would otherwise need; some have had a minor astigmatism corrected for, even though the ophthalmologist said that normally it was unnecessary; others have asked for tinted glasses.

OPHTHALMIC CONSIDERATIONS

The visual demands on an operator of a CRT display terminal are great, and even minor defects in the operator's visual functions might be of significant importance.   The present author is not an ophthalmologist; the ophthalmic issues raised here should be looked upon as discussion points.   More research is definitely needed before any recommendations can be made.

It is noteworthy that, based on ophthalmic investigations, the Austrian Central Organization of Salaried Employees has demanded that "after every hour of intense CRT viewing, there shall be at least one hour of eye rest" (Höller et al., 1975). It is therefore also noteworthy that, from an ophthalmic point of view, the human visual system is not normally without defects. For example, in a normal population of office workers, some 80% are heterophoric, some 80% hyperopic, and every one over 40 years of age presbyopic. Before continuing with the ophthalmic aspects of computer terminal work, reference will be made to figure 8.

Ideally, one should match the visual demands of the work to the capacity of the operator's eyes, but unfortunately not very many degrees of freedom for matching are left over in the typical situation shown in figure 8. The distance from the eyes to the display screen usually has to be at least 50cm (due to the given physical dimensions of operators, office furniture, and computer equipment), whereas 33 cm is the normal reading distance used in the judgement of the need for spectacles. The display screen, because of 'hardware limitations', also cannot be placed to give the same viewing angle as the paper documents on the table top. As mentioned above some of the 'hardware limitations' can be overcome (eg. by tilting the screen), but other limitations, for instance the size of the screen, cannot usually be alleviated so easily. Eventually, the terminal manufacturers will have to improve their products. There is much room here for product development.

The use of bifocal spectacles can be taken as an example of a situation in which the operator's ordinary spectacles are not ideal for terminal work. When the operator repetitively reads the upper lines of the picture on the display screen through the lower part of the bifocal spectacles for near sight, the result may be a type of pain in the neck and arm usually referred to as the cervical syndrome (Jackson, 1966; Johnson and Wolfe, 1972). Before further discussing the ophthalmic consequences directed towards properly corrected eyesight with terminal work, it should be pointed out that although this visual task usually is of great significance in the determination of the working posture (Fourcade et al., 1975), it does not necessarily mean that terminal work is always a difficult visual task. In fact, the terminal may be used merely as a one-way data entry machine, where the operator only glances now and then at the screen to check for keying errors. This last point is sometimes not accepted by the operators, who might claim that, as they are working at a CRT terminal, they must have free spectacles and regular ophthalmic check-ups.

Even under optimal conditions, the reading of a CRT picture is not as easy as the reading of its equivalent on paper. It has been shown repeatedly, however, that CRT viewing often has to be performed under far from optimal conditions. This means that if the terminal work implies intense CRT viewing, the operator will have a considerably more difficult visual task than in a traditional office job, and hence it may be important to check the operator's eyesight and to remedy and correct even minor insufficiencies. The most common insufficiencies are listed below:

Hyperopia; the optical condition in which the refractive power of the eye is 'too weak' (better: the eye is too short). Up to the age of 35, people with a mild degree of hyperopia (up to about + 2.5 D insufficiency - D = diopter strength) can sometimes carry out CRT reading tasks without spectacles. People who are older or with a higher degree of hyperopia should use glasses for terminal work.

Myopia; the optical condition in which the refractive power of the eye is 'too strong' (the eye is too long). Up to the age of 55, people with a mild degree of myopia (down to about - 1.0 D) may carry out CRT reading tasks without spectacles. A myopia condition of more than - 1.5 D usually has to be corrected for in terminal operators.

Astigmatism; the optical condition in which the refractive power of the eye is not uniform in all meridians, and cylindrical rather than spherical correction lenses are needed. Terminal operators with astigmatism of more than about 0.5 D should always wear correction lenses. However, after the correction for higher degrees of astigmatism (more than about 2 D), some retinal blur may still persist and such persons are probably not suited for terminal work. Younger people on average have zero astigmatism, whereas older people on average have 0.5 D astigmatism (which should be corrected for). The retinal blur in an astigmatic eye increases with increased pupil diameter, and accordingly, a dark screen is more difficult to read than a light paper document.

Convergence insufficiency; the muscular condition in which the two eyes cannot simultaneously be directed towards near objects. To most people, an object as close as the tip of one's nose is extremely difficult to focus on for more than a few seconds. As computer terminals do not usually call for real close-up work, a moderate convergence insufficiency probably does not hinder a terminal operator.

Heterophoria; the muscular condition in which there is a latent tendency of the eyes to deviate, which is prevented by fusion. This is a very common condition, and moderate heterophoria is probably also a factor which may accelerate the onset of (visual) fatigue in terminal operators, especially when there is an exophoric (diverging) tendency.

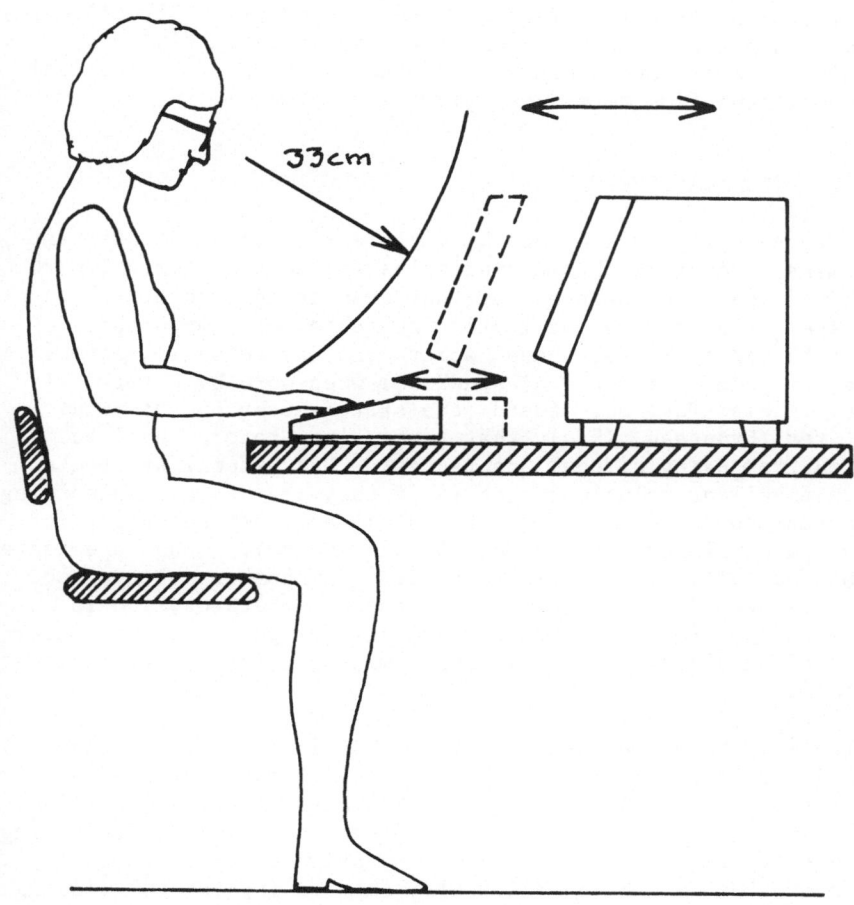

FIGURE 8.   Spectacles are normally designed for a reading distance
            of approximately 33 cm.   Due to the constraints imposed
            by the task, and the given physical dimensions of the
            operator, office furniture, and equipment, the eye-screen
            distance typically often amounts to 50-100 cm.

Presbyopia;   the optical condition in which there is a
diminished power of accommodation, arising from impaired elasticity
of the ageing eye lens.   By the age of 40, presbyopia usually
becomes noticeable through difficulties in seeing near objects
clearly (accommodation insufficiency), and at 60 virtually all
accommodation power is lost.   Therefore, it is essential that
presbyopic terminal operators use spectacles which fit the actual
visual conditions (in terms of viewing distance).

A CASE FOR 'TERMINAL SPECTACLES'

Merely adhering to good ophthalmic practice does not warrant
that terminal operators obtain spectacles suited for terminal work.
Previously it has been pointed out that even though ordinary
bifocal spectacles may be perfectly suitable for a hyperopic
person of 55 years of age, these spectacles may actually provoke
neck and arm pain (the cervical syndrome) when worn by a terminal
operator.   This fact has caused the statement by one terminal
manufacturer (Stansaab, 1976), that terminal operators shall be
prohibited from using bifocal spectacles.   But bifocal spectacles
can be an excellent solution, that is if they are designed according
to the actual conditions (eg. 33 and 70 cm) and not according to
the usual ophthalmic practice (eg. 33 and 200 cm).   Such spectacles
could then be called 'terminal spectacles'.   Another solution to
this problem would be to equip the presbyopic operator, who is
privately using bifocals, with non-bifocals designed for some intermediate reading distance, that is again with a pair of 'terminal
spectacles'.

Following the normal practice for prescribing presbyopic's
spectacles, it would mean that the range of distance of easy
reading for persons of 45, 50, 55, and 60 years of age, on average,
would be 22-100, 23-50, 25-40, and 28-33 cm respectively.   Referring
to figure 8, this in turn can be seen approximately to mean that
persons above 50 would have difficulty in carrying out CRT viewing
tasks when equipped with ordinary spectacles.   From an ergonomics
point of view, great care must be taken to ensure that no employer
ever uses these facts as selection criteria, and it is not acceptable to allow the exclusion of persons over 50-55 years from this
type of work, as was suggested by Kryzhanovskaya and Navakatikayan
(1970).   Even when no direct selection takes place, the trend now
recognisable is that older office workers gradually become unable
to continue their work after the office has been computerised.
This trend must be stopped, but not by equipping operators with
ingenious 'terminal spectacles'.   The terminal equipment first
of all should instead be more carefully designed, proper terminal
workplaces built up, the illumination matched to the visual tasks,
and the psycho-motor, mental, and visual aspects of the actual
information handling more carefully thought out.

SUBSEQUENT LEGISLATION ON READING DISPLAY SCREENS

Since this paper was prepared for publication, the Swedish
National Board of Occupational Safety has published Directive No.136
on 'Reading of Display Screens' which gives the following rules
for operation.

1. Ambient lighting must be suitably adapted. Special importance
    must be attached to lighting conditions at work places where
    reading of display screens occurs regularly. Generally the
    illuminance required is lower than in ordinary office work.
    In work places where work is continuously conducted at display
    screens, an illumination of between 200 and 300 lux may be
    suitable.

    Note: Lower illumination levels may be appropriate in certain
    working environments of a special nature (eg. monitoring and
    traffic control).

2. When ambient lighting is subdued as per point 1, supplementary
    lighting must be provided for other working areas near the
    display screen. Supplementary lighting must be adjustable
    and fitted with glare control arrangements.

3. Excessive differences of luminance in the field of vision
    produce what is termed contrast glare. The work place should
    therefore be organized in such a way that the background of the
    display screen is of suitable luminance and the employee's field
    of vision does not include a window or any other glaring
    luminances. Bright reflections in the display screen are to
    be avoided.

4. The visual distance to the display screen and the angle of
    inclination of the display screen should be individually
    adjustable with due regard being paid to other ergonomics
    requirements. In the case of employees who wear spectacles,
    it is important that the optical correction is well adapted
    to the visual distance, and vice versa.

    Note: Ordinary spectacles for private use are often unadapted
    to the visual distance occurring in display screen work.
    Traditional bifocal lenses are unsuitable in many cases, because
    they often entail a strenuous work posture when used for display
    screen reading.

5. If an employee has a refractive error and incurs visual
    discomfort in connection with display screen work when using
    spectacles intended for normal purposes, the display screen
    must be moved to a position where the discomfort is eliminated.
    If this is not possible, the employer is to provide the employee
    with special spectacles which have been tested for display
    screen work.

6. If eye fatigue or visual discomfort tends to develop, the work must be organized in such a way that the employee can intermittently be given periods of rest or work involving more conventional visual requirements.

CONCLUSION

This paper has set out the developing situation in Sweden, with a detailed summary of approaches to improve the design of workplaces and reduce visual strain. It is hoped that this review of Swedish experience may be helpful to others with similar problems.

ACKNOWLEDGEMENT

This work was supported by a grant from the Swedish Fund for Technical Development (STU LÖp dnr 75-4511). The author would like to thank Berit Calissendorff, Dag Holmgren, Howell Istance, and Ingeborg Lomaeus for their help in the preparation of this paper.

REFERENCES

Aner, K.   1974   Attack is the best defence.
                             Proceedings of the ALTORG Conference on
                             'The Impact of Computers and Automation on
                             Management, Structure and Work Design'.
                             Berlin Int. Institute of Management.

Anon   1974   Better working environment. Study Circle I.
                                (In Swedish)
                             Stockholm, Brevskolan.

Carlsöö, S.   1976   People with a stiff back should not perform
                             keying tasks. (In Swedish)
                             Arbetsmiljo, 7, 23-25 (And personal commun-
                                ication).

Crouch, C.L. & 1973   Visual relationships in office tasks.
   Buttolph, L.J.   Lighting Design and Application, May, 23-25.

Devos-   1973   A propose des facteurs d'ambiance au poste
   Petiprez, C.   de terminal d'ordinateur.
                             Dissertation, Department of Occupational
                             Medicine, Lille.

Fourcade, J.   1975   Attention visuelle posture.
  Martin, J.P. &   Le Travail Humain, 38, 119-132.
  Defayolle, M.

Hedberg, B.   1974   The system designer - decision maker
                                or puppet on a string?
                                Proceedings of the ALTORG Conference
                                on 'The Impact of Computers and
                                Automation on Management, Structure,
                                and Work Design'. Berlin, Int.
                                Institute of Management.

Holler, H.   1975   Arbeitsbeanspruchung und Augenbelastung
  Kundi, M.   an Bildschirmgeräten.
  Schmid, H.   Wien; Automationsausschuss der
  Stidl, H.G.   Gewerkschaft der Privatengestellten
  Thaler, A. &   (Verlag des ÖGB).
  Winter, N.

Hultgen, G.V. &   1974   Discomfort glare and disturbances from
  Knave, B.   light reflections in an office land-
                                scape with CRT displays.
                                Applied Ergonomics, 5, 2-8.

Jackson, R.   1966   The cervical syndrome.
                                Springfield, C.C. Thomas (3rd ed.)

Johnson, E.W. &   1972   Bifocal spectacles in the etiology of
  Wolfe, C.V.   cervical radiculopathy.
                                Archives of Physical Medicine and
                                Rehabilitation, 53, 201-205.

Kryzhanovskaya, V.V. 1970   Changes of information parameters of
  Navakatikayan, A.O.   the visual analyser in persons
                                engaged in intellectual work depending
                                upon their age. (In Russian; English
                                summary).
                                Gigena Truda i Profesional 'nye
                                Zabolevanija, 7, 28-32.

Martin, J.   1973   Design of man-computer dialogues.
                                Englewood Cliffs N.J., Prentice-Hall.

Nygaard, K. &   1974   The trade unions - new users of research.
  Bergo, O.T.   Proceedings of the ALTORG Conference
                                on 'The Impact of Computers and
                                Automation on Management, Structure,
                                and Work Design'. Berlin, Int.
                                Institute of Mangement.

Onishi, N. 1973   Fatigue and strength of upper limb
  Nomura, H. &   muscles of flight reservation
  Sakai, K.   operators.
                    Journal of Human Ergology, 2, 133-141.

Ostberg, O. 1975   CRTs pose health problems for operators.
                    Int. J. Occup. Health & Safety,
                      Nov./Dece. 24-26, 46, 50, 52
                      (reprints available from author).

Ostberg, O. 1976a Designing CRT workplaces. A handbook.
                      (In Swedish).
                    Stockholm, Statskontoret.

Ostberg, O. 1976b Terminals are not dangerous.(In Swedish)
                    Arbetsmiljö, 1, 24-26.

Ostberg, O. 1976c Review of visual strain, with special
                      reference to microimage reading.
                    Proceedings of the International
                      Micrographics Congress, Stockholm.

Ostberg, O., 1975 Free magnitude estimation of discomfort
  Stone, P.T. &   glare and working task difficulty.
  Benson, R.A.   Goteborg Psychological Reports, 5, No.15.

Ostberg, O. 1976   Desks for CRT computer terminals -
  Holmgren, D. &   a review. (In Swedish).
  Gunnarsson, E.   Stockholm, Arbetarskyddsstyrelsen
                      (AMMF 101/76).

Palme, J. 1975   Interactive software for humans.
                    FOA 1 Report. (Stockholm, Swedish
                      National Defense Research
                      Institute C10029-M3(E5)).

Peters, T. 1975   Datenterminalarbetsplatze aus arbeits-
                      medizinischergonomischer Sicht.
                    Arbeitsmedizin - Sozialmedizin -
                      Praventivmedizin, 10, 193-196.

Shackel, B. & 1970 Man-computer interaction. A review of
  Shipley, P.   the ergonomics literature and related
                      research.
                    Report DMP 3472, EMI Electronics Ltd.,
                      Feltham, Middlesex.

Shepard, J.M. 1971 Automation and alienation: A study
                      of office and factory workers.
                    Cambridge Mass., MIT Press.

Siegel, A.I. &   1971   Dimensions of visual information
  Fischl, M.A.   displays.
                            Journal of Applied Psychology, 55,
                              470-476.

Simons, D.J.   1942   Experimental studies of headache:
  Day, E.   Muscles of the scalp and neck as
  Goodell, H. &   sources of pain.
  Wolff, H.G.   Research Publications of the Association
                              for Research in Nervous and Mental
                              Disease, 23, 228-244.

Stansaab.   1976   Work stations with data terminals.
                            Stockholm, Stansaab Elektronik AB.

Stewart, T.F.M.   1974   Computer terminal ergonomics.   A
  Ostberg, O. &   review of recent human factors
  Mackay, C.J.   literature.
                            Stockholm, Statskontoret (2nd ed.
                              Dnr 170/72-5).

                   1976   SOU 1976:1. Working Environment Act.
                              (In Swedish; English summary).
                            Stockholm, Arbetsmarknadsdepartementet.

Udris, I. &   1976   Mental load in clerical work.
  Barth, H.   Proceedings of the 6th Congress of
                              the International Ergonomics
                              Association, 192-197.
                            Human Factors Society, P.O. Box 1369,
                              Santa Monica, California 90406.

Van Cott, H.P. &   1972   Human engineering guide to equipment
  Kinkade, R.G.   design.
                            Washington D.C., US Governmental
                              Printing Office.

Weston, H.C.   1954   Visual fatigue.
                            Illuminating Engineering, 49, 63-76.

MAN-COMPUTER INTERACTION IN PUBLIC SYSTEMS

Toni B.K. Ivergård

Ergolab AB., Stockholm, Sweden.

1.   INTRODUCTION

In this lecture I shall first give some definitions, and then some examples of systems which I want to call 'public systems'. Two projects which can be called 'public' will then be presented in more detail, and the final discussion will include a look at the future, with the emphasis on the impact and effects of computer systems on society and the individuals in it.   Some examples of points of conflict between the interested parties will also be given.

When man-computer interaction is discussed by ergonomists, what is meant is normally the different forms of on-line and time-sharing computer systems, with terminals, display screens and such-like.   There are people of different grades who are employed to work in the system. Only rarely does one realise and/or consider that there is another user group, less well definable, which is the general public, who are also affected by and interact with the system more or less directly.   The public will be referred to for brevity as the 'consumer' in the rest of this paper, whether or not a proper producer-consumer relationship exists in practice.

In Sweden, and other countries, the press and news media have taken up the questions of security and privacy of the public in connection with the building-up of large computer systems and data banks.   People are afraid, for example, that personal details which are stored in computer systems could be misused and become a threat against personal integrity.   This type of problem is very important, but will not be dealt with in this paper as it falls largely out-side the frame of what is normally meant by the ergonomic aspects of man-computer interaction.   This paper will instead deal directly with man-computer interactions with special reference to the wide range of ergonomic problems for the ordinary consumer.

2. SOME SUGGESTIONS FOR A TAXONOMY

Before being able to discuss the different forms of man-computer interaction more closely, it is necessary to define what is meant by 'man-computer interaction'. This term will not be used here in any limited or constricting way, in the sense that only time-sharing, on-line or computer terminal systems would be dealt with. Instead, the wider definition suggested by Shackel (1969) will be used, because computer systems affect so many other people than just the operators:

"Therefore, while accepting the phrase 'man-computer interaction' as a useful shorthand to refer to the multi-access , on-line, method for providing immediate computer service, this term should by no means be restricted to that aspect. A more appropriate, and also widely used, meaning of the term man-computer interaction is in the sense of very direct, close-coupled computer usage, and this inter-pretation seems much more useful and acceptable. However, for this survey of the field, the term will be used in its widest sense and all significant ways in which man may interact with computers will be included, with the aim of emphasizing those aspects and variables which are dominant for the human side of the man-computer equation."

In this talk in relation to this definition I shall stress that it is not only the operators and employees who must be considered, but also other forms of users, such as customers.

What is meant by 'public' man-computer systems as opposed to other forms? A public system is defined here as one of which the users (direct or indirect) include people who are not employed or paid to use the system. The most common condition is that these forms of non-employed users are consumers in the parent system of which the computer system is a part. The computer system used in new supermarkets have the supermarket itself as the parent system. The consumer of the supermarket's services is the customer, who will use the new shop-computer system without receiving any direct or indirect financial reward. Similar types of system are to be found in, for example, banks, post offices, chemists and to some extent in telegraph offices. Other systems with often less direct contact for the consumer are found in, for example, insurance companies, advertisement-ordering offices and telephone companies, where the consumer contacts the terminal operator by telephone.

Most if not all computer systems will have some kind of impact on the public as such, but only those where the public is direct user of the system will be included in this paper. Figure 1 shows some examples of the interaction of the consumer with the man-computer system.

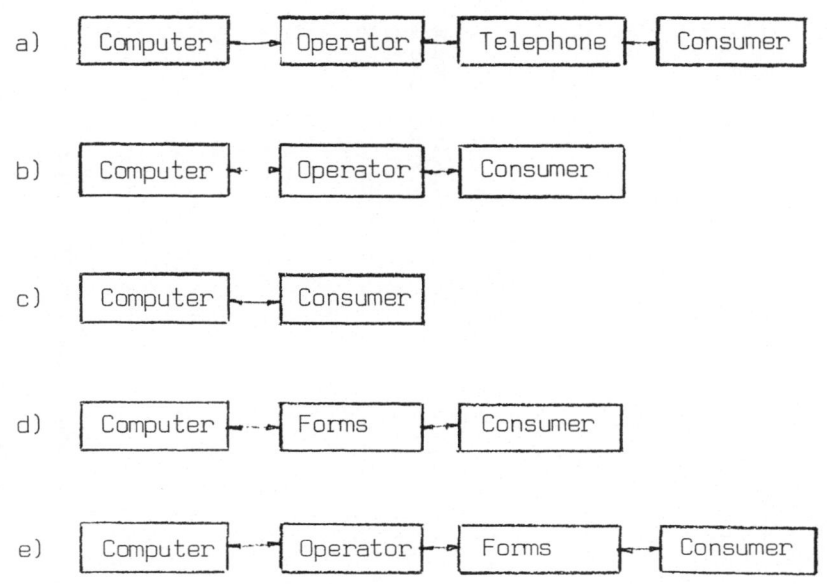

FIGURE 1.   Some examples of consumer interaction in man-computer
            systems.

        The consumer can in some cases be a direct user of the computer
system, as in example (c) (for example by means of a special terminal
system as in some new types of banking system where money can be
collected directly).   This happens also in certain shop computer
systems, where the consumer himself places the goods, which have
optically-read coded price tickets, directly into the computer
terminal.

        Of the systems existing today, (a) and (b) are much more common.
Consumers in (b) are in direct contact with an operator who acts as
the link for transfering data to the central computer (eg. in the
supermarket computer system).   In other cases, the customer's
contact with this linking operator takes place by telephone (a),
eg. in the ordering of advertisements in a newspaper.   Another
common method by which the consumer interacts with the computer is
where forms have to be filled in which can be read in directly by
means of different computer peripherals (d).   This is an important
form of consumer-computer interaction.   However, the computer's
lack of flexibility and perceptual ability often leads to the forms
being designed purely to suit the computer, and not the consumer,
which in the best case can give trouble and irritation and in the
worst case cause more serious misunderstandings.   In practice this
system often will be as in (e), because an operator is needed to
interpret the forms the customer has filled in.

146

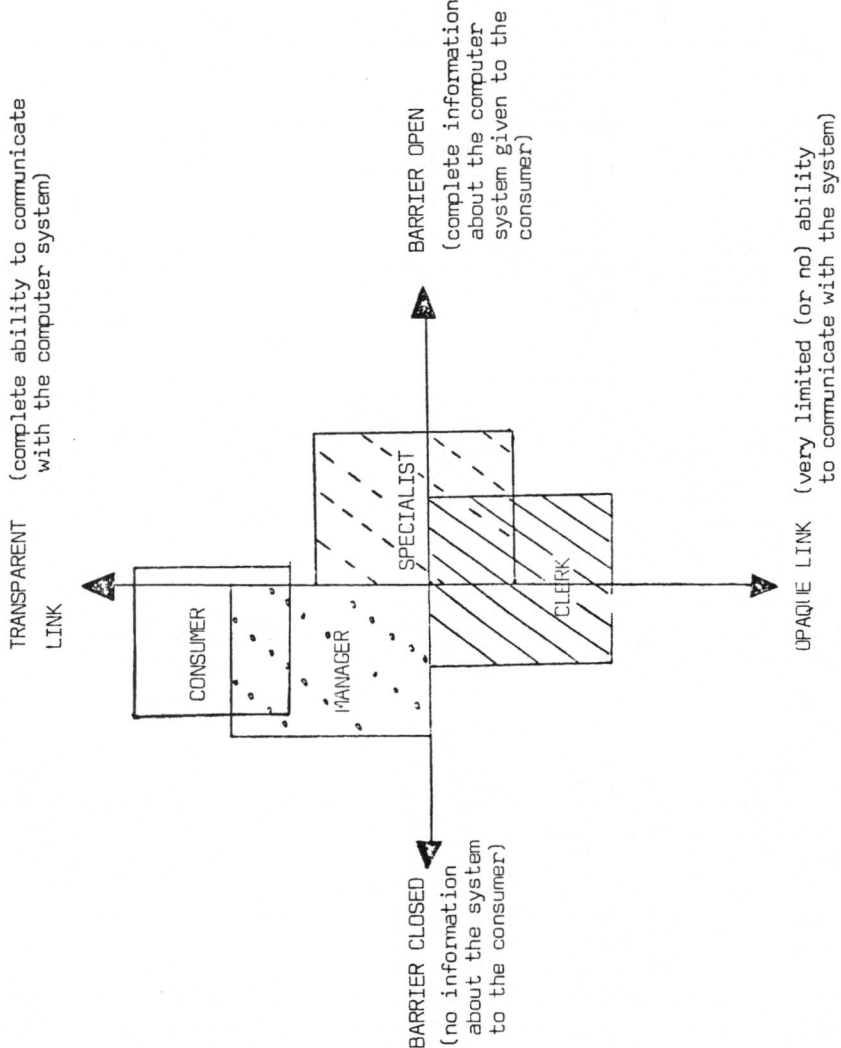

FIGURE 2. Some examples of consumer interaction in man-computer
systems.

Stewart (1974) has shown the different demands the different types
of user make upon the design of the computer system. Different
types of users have different interface requirements, even when
using the same system. Stewart defines three groups of users:
Managers, Specialists and Clerks. Stewart points out that these
three groups have different requirements as to how easy and understandable the use of the system should be. He defines this as

the amount of transparent links between the user and the system.
He also states that for some users it would be valuable if there
were a barrier to how much information about the system was presented
to the users.   In Figure 2 the requirements of different user
groups are presented.   In the figure, I have also introduced the
fourth user group, the consumer, which is not mentioned by Stewart
and his colleagues.

It is stated by Stewart and his colleagues that the manager
requires a highly flexible, adaptable information service.   The
rather complex information must be relevant to his changing needs.
On the other hand, he is unlikely to be prepared to spend time or
effort in learning how to use the system.   The manager's links to
the computer system would apparently be almost completely transparent,
so that he can communicate easily and fully with the machine.   This
is also to some extent important for the other user groups, but the
specialist should find the links sufficiently transparent to allow
him to tackle his problems without too much modification or constraint.
He would be prepared to learn to use a system to a certain extent,
and will modify his own methods and expertise to improve man-machine
communication.   The clerk can cope to some extent with a fairly
'opaque' link.   In fact, although he needs a transparent link at
the beginning of his training, even relatively lowly clerks will
learn all kinds of code routines, etc., and may in fact actually
want an opaque link.   If there is a need for a manager to have a
very transparent link, the need from the consumer in this respect
is even greater.   The consumers are not at all prepared to learn
or to be forced to learn how to use the system.   If the link between
the computer and the consumer is not transparent enough it will come
into conflict with the primary aim of the parent system (ie. it will
upset the consumer).

The manager may need some barriers in order to be protected by
the interface from some aspects of the system or processing which
are unnecessarily complex or are not required for his current task.
This could be, for example, due to the time pressure under which
most managers work.   The specialist, on the other hand, is more
concerned with understanding the full potential of the computer and
the system.   He therefore requires the interface to allow him far
enough into the computer system to exploit this potential and not
to be limited by a barrier.   The clerk is probably somewhere in
between.   It would be useful for the clerk to know a bit more about
the computer than is strictly necessary for his job, so that he can
then, with his experience and knowledge of the system, try out new
ways of using the computer which the designer could not have anticipated.   For most consumer-oriented systems, the consumer's needs
in this respect are about the same as for managers.   One could
perhaps think of systems of which the consumers are frequent users,
and who would therefore need about the same amount of barrier as
the clerk.

3. EXAMPLE 1

The Swedish Telephone system (Televerket) has up to now used a manual card system for details of subscribers, etc. If a consumer wished to change the address of his phone, for example, he would ring Televerket, or visit their office. The customer's card is then fetched, with the help of a comprehensive register; the necessary alterations are made, and instructions for the work to be done, etc., are typed out for the engineers. A computer based system is in the process of being introduced, where all the details about the subscriber's telephone are stored in the computer's memory. The operator will work directly with the computer via a terminal with a display screen. The service time for each customer will be considerably shortened by avoiding the need for the manual search for his card. Other considerable savings are expected in placing orders, registrations and so on.

ERGOLAB was given the job of designing the working places for computer terminal operators (Berns and Soderberg, 1974). This project was limited to the physical layout of the workplaces, and had nothing to do with the design of the computer program outputs or inputs as a whole; it touched only briefly on the layout of information presented on the terminal display. Televerket was, however, conscious that perhaps the most important ergonomic aspects were already decided upon at the stage of the general design of the system. A more long-sighted development programme was initiated by Televerket to be undertaken at Linköping University of Technology (Bertil Andersson and Bengt Johnsson). In connection with this development programme, ERGOLAB was asked to carry out a pilot study (Istance, 1974), and also to provide suitable customers for the evaluations included in this project.

Because the first ERGOLAB project for the Swedish Televerket was limited mainly to workplace design, the customer aspects were only taken into account in certain parts. As regards telephone contact between customer and operator, only the operator's side of the conversation was of interest because of the dividing up of the project. On the other hand, face-to-face contact with the customer, when he visited the office, was naturally taken into account in the relevant part of the project; for example, should the customer sit or stand? Discussions with the operators, together with detailed interviews, showed that a seated customer relaxed better, giving better contact and an easier flow of information between him and the operator. Eye-contact was better, and this also helped to speed the information flow.

It was also necessary to design a suitable barrier between the customer and the system. One restriction from Televerket was, for example, that the customer should not be able to see the display directly (it is possible that when going through the data, certain

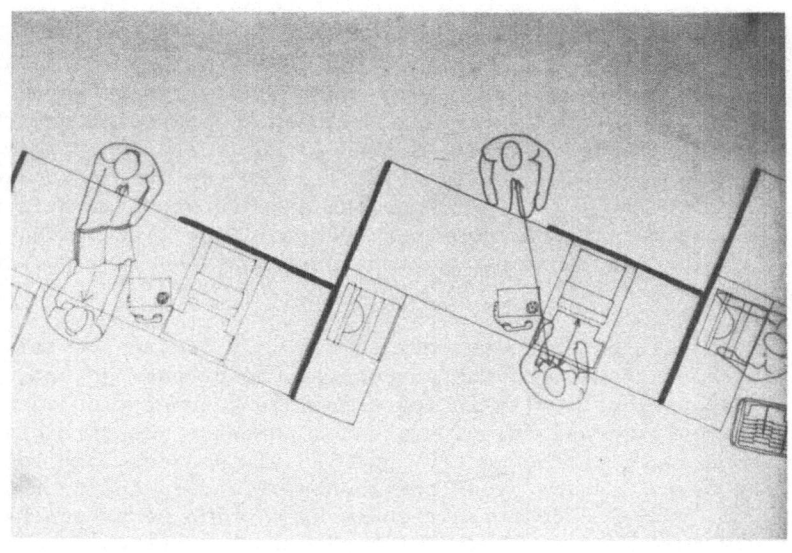

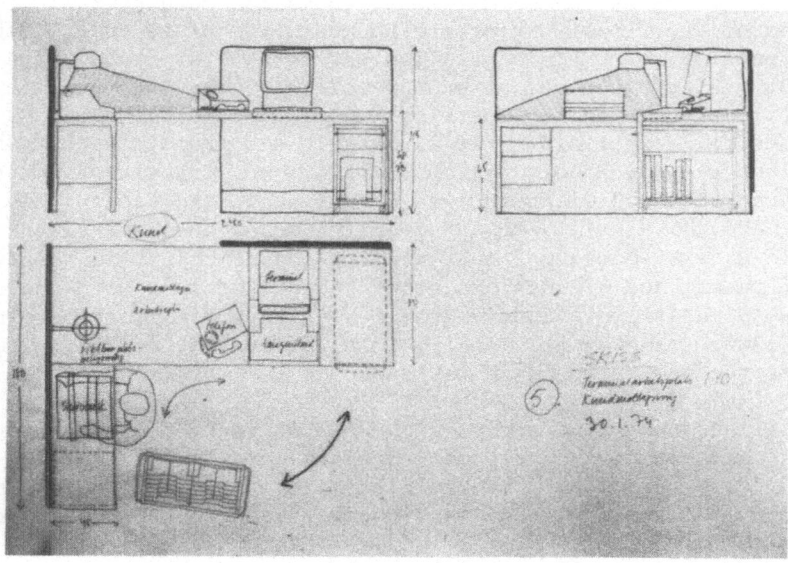

FIGURE 3. Some possible workstation layouts considered for customer interview positions for the Swedish Telephone system.

information comes onto the screen which it is not desirable that
other people see).   Other information and objects (eg. the
operator's personal effects, etc.) are only relevant to the
operator and not the customer.   Some examples of layouts considered
are given in Fig. 3.   The interface between the customer and the
operator had also to be designed so that it was suitably screened
from the rest of the room, while still allowing the operators free
access to each other.   In the system there is an operator acting
between the consumer and the computer system.   The link could
therefore be expected to be enough transparent as the operator could
act as an interpreter.

The project in general was carried out in close co-operation
with the users.   Because of the preconceptions of the project, the
operators were systematically included in this co-operation, and
the customers only occasionally.   Great importance was attached to
creating a meaningful exchange of views in this project, and to
this end the users must be given the chance of understanding the
background material and research results upon which we asked them
to give their judgements.   A good example was our method of
presenting drawings.   Ordinary plan drawings are very difficult
to understand for those who are neither engineers nor architects,
and even for these it can be difficult to gain a good overall
impression of the final working environment from plans only.   Other
forms of models, for example parallel perspective drawings, were
developed.   Figure 4 gives an example of this, showing the plan
drawing (a) and the parallel-perspective drawing (b) of the same
environment for comparison.   It is easy to see from this that the
latter gives a considerably better basis for constructive discussion
of the advantages and disadvantages of the suggested design.   In
order to make the finally suggested design more concrete, simple
full-scale models (mock-ups) were constructed of chipboard sheets
and metal tubes, and discussions around these together with the
operators and users were most valuable.   Afterwards, more permanent
prototypes were made professionally to allow evaluation over a longer
period before the final design was decided.

The aim of the pilot study which ERGOLAB carried out in connection with the long-term development project was also to test and
choose suitable criteria to be included in the final project.   One
side-effect of the pilot study was that we realised the importance
of having realistic customers for experiments of this kind.   In
order to simulate a realistic dialogue between customer and operator
of the type expected in the proposed system, a realistic simulation
using customers is required.   Simulation of customer/operator
situations can also be used for experimental purposes and evaluation
purposes.   In the pilot study Istance (1974) used people who
phoned operators and ordered the telephone equipment that they
already had in their homes.   This provided a very realistic simulation but was not possible in the main study as the number of

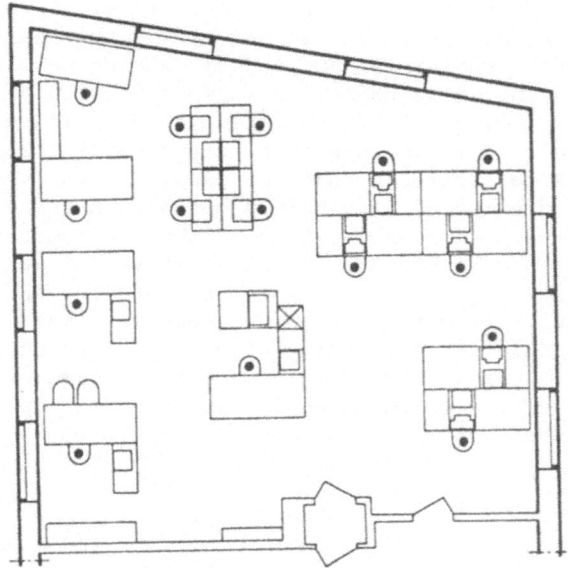

Normal drawing of an office plan

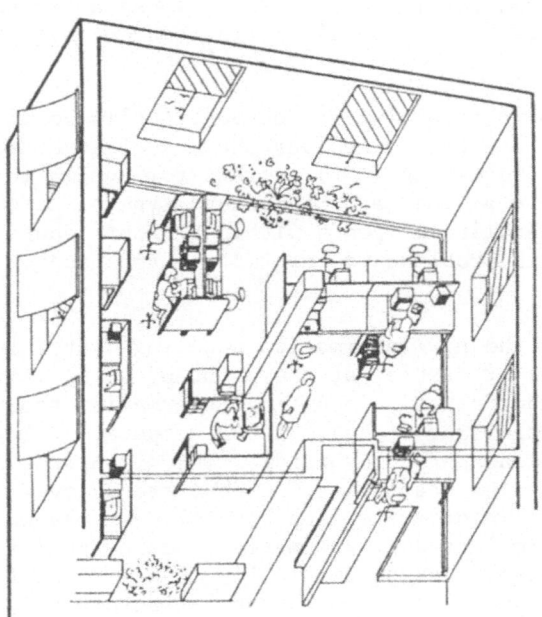

Parallel perspective drawing of the office plan

FIGURE 4.   Different ways of presenting proposals to assist discussion of alternatives with users during the design process.

required enquiries was far too large.   Therefore, it was decided
that ERGOLAB's consumer panel should be used in this case.   This
consumer test panel consists of 40 randomly chosen people from the
Stockholm area.   They have undergone various physiological,
anatomical and psychological tests, including body measurement,
strength and intelligence measurements, etc.   By these means it
has been possible to ascertain that the people on the test panel
are truly representative of Stockholm's population in terms of the
parameters measured.   The variability of these parameters can
moreover be used as a co-variable in the statistical analysis of
certain experiments (eg. in analyses of variance).   There are as
yet no final results from the main experiment mentioned above, but
purely from the administrative point of view the use of this
consumer panel has worked very well.   There are however some
indications that a free dialogue would give a better open link
relationship than a restricted dialogue.

4.   EXAMPLE 2

4.1 Introduction

In the 1970's there is going on a substantial technological
development in new retailing systems.   These new automatic and
mechanised systems will probably be introduced in a large scale in
the 1980's.

Automation in retailing can conventionally be discussed under
two headings.   The first involves the use of keyboards and associated
automatic data processing (ADP) systems for automatic handling of
information in retailing, and the second type of automation involves
the automatic handling of goods within and into shops.   This paper
deals mainly with problems of information and goods handling at the
points-of-sale.

Basically, the new information handling system in retailing
involves a clerk or cashier at the point of sale, (eg. the check-out-
point in the supermarket), inputting information about goods sold,
(eg. type, quantity and price), into a computer.   Information input
is achieved by means of a keyboard.   The aim of the system will be
(a) to provide sales statistics, so that trends over time can be
rapidly obtained in order to keep control over the whole credit
situation, (b) to introduce automatic ordering and/or recording of
goods, (c) to keep track automatically of how many of each type of
goods are in stock, so that an instant inventory of goods is available (these last two factors make it possible to order more accurately
the goods needed to replace those already sold).   By these means
the quantity of goods in store, and hence the required storage area,
in supermarkets and other retail outlets can be decreased.   Other
aims of the new electronic systems are (d) that the clerk cannot

make inadvertent or purposeful errors, as such errors will be
immediately recognised by the computer, (e) that the customer
cannot cheat the firm by altering coding (if present) on goods which
are inputted into the computer, and (f) that the sales clerk or
cashier is not subject to lapses of memory concerning prices, taxes,
etc., as code numbers are available on all goods.

When I started this project it was not possible to find any
reports in the literature of objective evaluations of this kind of
system in terms of the implications for man appearing in the role
of supervisor, cashier, labourer or customer.   When the advantages
and disadvantages of this kind of sytem are discussed, the discussion
is mainly centred upon theoretical calculations.   Furthermore, it
is mainly the retailer's or wholesaler's point of view which is
considered.   Greater assurance that goods will not be stolen by
customers and personnel is often claimed to be a great advantage of
this new system (Unger, 1970, Boutet, 1967).   Petersen (1971), for
example, in discussing an electronic point-of-sale system called
"Trader", describes how through the Trader system a woman who had
an overdrawn credit was discovered: "The woman ran as fast as her
legs would carry her for the nearest exit".   This is surely a very
inhuman point of view when reviewing the merits of such a system.

4.2   The Aim of the Project

In my Ph.D. thesis (Ivergård, 1972), a comprehensive evaluation
of ergonomic problems in automated check-out systems in self-service
shops is described.   The project includes observation and questionnaire studies, and interviews with customers and operators, among
other things.   Some of the more important results and conclusions
for the customer will now be discussed, together with the consequences
of automation of shops in general and its effect on society as a
whole.

The main parts of the check-out system studied is presented
in Fig. 5.   All goods in the shop are code marked, and the customer
collects the goods in the supermarket and brings them to the cashier
at the cash desk.   The cashier reads the code and keys it into the
cash register, which, via a communication network, asks a mini-computer
what price is connected to the code.   The mini-computer takes out
the price from the price memory and sends it back to the cash register,
where it is printed on a receipt and presented on a display.   Sales
statistics etc. are recorded in a magnetic tape memory.   Changes
of price could, for example, be carried out by means of a typewriter
connected to the mini-computer.

154

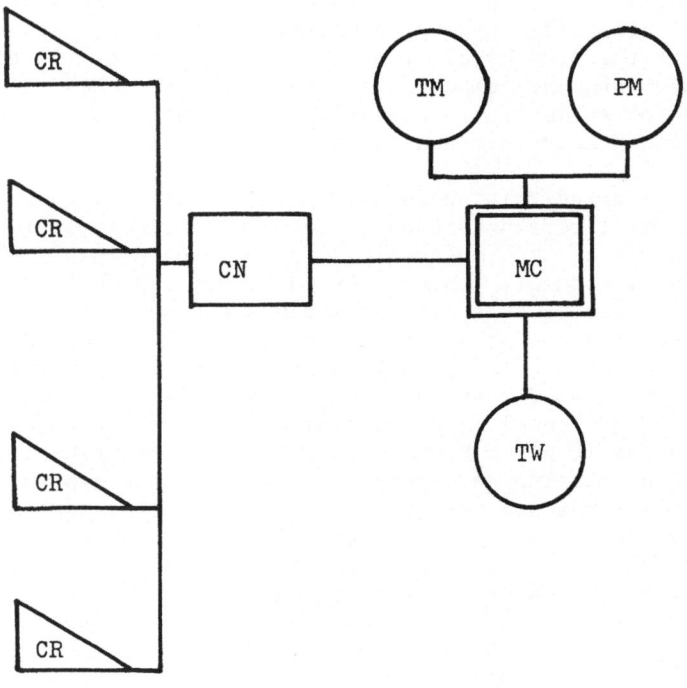

CR = Cash registers

CN = Communication network

MC = Mini-computer

PM = Price memory

TM = Magnetic tape memory

TW = Typewriter

FIGURE 5. The main feature of the new planned system for the
           Swedish Co-operative shops.

4.3 Some Results of the Study

Part 4 of the project comprised four different studies:

1. An open interview with cashiers
2. A questionnaire study with cashiers
3. A structured interview with customers
4. An observation study of check-out systems.

The aim of the interview, questionnaire and observation studies was to compare the function of a new cash desk (included in the cash computer system) in relation to the old cash desk, in order to obtain information on the different technical problems associated with cash desks, so that future cash desks could be designed better. A further aim of Part 4 was to study the general working conditions for the cashiers.

The secondary aim of Part 4 (ie. the study of general working conditions for cashiers) was examined only in the cashier questionnaire study (2). The other studies dealt with the problems which could affect both cashiers and customers. The first study was substantially the basis on which the following studies were grounded. Questionnaire, formalized interviews and observation forms were designed to collect information which was seen to be significant in terms of the results obtained from the open interviews with cashiers.

In brief, the results from the four studies indicated that a number of malfunctions associated with technical problems occurred in the use of the new cash desk. Although most of the malfunctions occurred relatively infrequently, some of them were very troublesome for both customers and cashiers.

The cashiers generally liked their job. However, their working conditions could be improved if a number of points were taken into account. Some examples will be mentioned. The present working hours are viewed with disfavour by the cashiers, and one alternative is to change these hours so that they are more convenient. Unfortunately, this is likely to mean that customers would suffer, because cashiers would prefer not to work late in the evening and at the weekends. One alternative is to recognize the inconvenience caused by working in the evenings and at the weekends by the provision of financial incentives to compensate the cashiers. Another unpleasant feature of the working situation was that the cashiers were unable to get breaks in their work sufficiently frequently and of long enough duration. Clearly, if attention was paid to this problem a solution could be found which was acceptable both to the cashiers and to management. The cashiers also clearly disliked the task of checking the customers in various ways. If the checking function was removed from the cashier's duty it would undoubtedly make her task less unpleasant and arduous.

TABLE 1. Disadvantags and advantages for different groups of people involved in the new computer system from features of the new system.

Neutral (0), disadvantages (-) and advantages (+)

Features which will be changed in the new system	Wholesaler	Retailer	Customer	Cashier
Slow work in cash desk (codes price keying)	-	-	-	-
Fast work in cash desk (only codes keying)	+	+	-	0
All goods price-marked	-	-	+	+
Large investment cost in the computer	-	-	-	0
Turnover of goods per storage area increases as retailer's storage area decreases	-	+	0	0
No loss in sales due to shortage of goods in storage	0	+	0	+
Less loss for the shop due to keying errors	0	+	0	0
Better checking of customer	0	+	-	-
Better checking of personnel	0	+	0	-
Less manual inventories	0	+	0	+
Less investment in shop storage space	0	+	0	0
More impulse buying	+	+	-	0
Promote the use of credit cards	+	+	-	+

Turning now to the check-out system situation from the point of view of the customer, it is quite clear that she is not so bothered about the actions or tasks as such which she has to perform as by the stress induced by the rapidity with which the tasks have to be carried out when there are many other customers near or in the system. Recommendations to alleviate this problem have been given in the project report. From work carried out in the project it has not been possible to make any definite predictions about the advantages customers would obtain from the introduction of the new system of which the new electronic check-out is a part. From the general features of this type of new automatic computer system, it is possible to hypothesise several advantages and disadvantages associated with this kind of system for the different interested parties. These advantages and disadvantages as regards the different groups of people involved are further amplified in Table 1. From this table it may be seen that most of the advantages accrue to the wholesaler, the retailer and the cashier. The customer benefits least. Also, one of the advantages from the customer's point of view (ie. that all goods are price-marked) may not be strictly relevant to the proposed system as the goods will mainly be code-marked and only very infrequently price-marked.

It will, perhaps, be the manufacturers of these cash-computer systems who will get the largest benefits of a general introduction of this kind of system.

5. SOME GENERAL CONSIDERATIONS

In the design of a specific system such as a cash computer system, it is necessary to look not only at the system directly under study, but also at the way in which it interacts with other systems related to it. When a check-out system connected to electronic computer systems and retailing systems is studied, it is important to examine potential or actual effects, not only in the shops themselves, but also on society as a whole. This, of course, is a very difficult problem as there will also be other important factors which affect the socio-economic and socio-geographical situation.

For the cash computer system which was studied, it seems reasonable to suppose that the large investments involved in the introduction of the system will result in still larger supermarkets in order to get profitability out of the system. Because of land costs these larger supermarkets are likely to be located more remotely from the city and town centres, perhaps serving several cities or towns where population density is high. This has already occurred on a small scale in the United States and Sweden. Very remote location of supermarkets for the customer may be unwanted from his or her point of view. In some cases, not only may travelling be unwanted, but it may also be impossible for particular sections of the population such as the elderly, physically disabled and the poor to get there at all.   Unfortunately, these kinds of predictions cannot be made with any high degree of precision.   In spite of this, it is possible at the system design stage to try to anticipate deleterious effects on the population so that provision can be made to avoid them in the final design of the system.

An alternative development of the information system and related electronic equipment can for example go in the direction of the 'electronic mail order' system.   In small corner-shops, which can only keep a limited number of different types of goods in store, the assortment can be extended considerably by the introduction of computer terminals consisting of a video-display (in colour) and a keyboard.   Goods which the customer is unable to get in the shop can be displayed on the video screen and ordered through the keyboard.   The system can also be connected to the telephone network, which would make it possible for people who are severely disabled or temporarily ill in bed to do their shopping from their homes.

Automation regarding both the automatic handling of information and of goods holds great possibilities for the future.   However, considerable risks are attached to its use if it is going to be developed without systematic consideration of human needs and requirements.   For example, the new cash computer system considered in this paper may result in all prices of goods in the shops disappearing and the goods being marked only with code numbers.   The main argument in favour of this possibility is that price marking of goods is very expensive and it is advantageous from several points of view for the shop not to have the goods price-marked.   It is, for example, easier to change the prices of the goods if they are not price-marked, as changes need only be made in the computer memory.   It is sometimes claimed that the customer is not interested in the price, and if she is interested in the prices she will be given access to a computer terminal in the shop by means of which she could find out the prices of different goods.   In this way legal requirements relating to price information could be met.

In a system like this it is extremely difficult for the customer to establish the relative cost of the same goods being provided by competitors, and the seller could, to a certain extent, vary prices more or less at will in a semi-concealed manner.   At the same time special prices and special reductions can be offered on some goods and displayed outside the shops, without extensive inconvenience, in order to get the customer into the shop and at the same time do other types of shopping.

Another possible development in the future is that all the buying and ordering of goods could be done at home, by means of the new pushbutton telephone.   This kind of system could, however,

create social and psychological isolation, giving rise to severe
problems to a large number of people.   Such a system may prove to
be economically profitable both for the wholesaler, the retailer
and perhaps also for society as a whole.   It will almost certainly
not be advantageous to society in other ways.

The lines which the development of automatic information and
goods handling systems follow in the near future will not merely
be of marginal interest for individuals or for the society at large.
It is of vital importance that the consumers' social, psychological
and other needs and requirements are considered in the design of new
shopping and, indeed, other systems.   Up to now, in the development
of the main criteria for a system of this kind, generally speaking
only economical and technical aspects are considered.   The Swedish
government has, for example, recently formed a parliamentary
committee to study the distribution of goods in the society of
tomorrow.   The delegates in this group represent mainly retailing
and wholesaling business interests and not consumers' or workers'
interests.   The committee in its work has not so far considered
the consumers' interest in a systematic and fundamental way.   In
the future it is to be hoped that systematic design methods, including ergonomic considerations and direct influences from the consumers,
will be used both in high level planning in society and in smaller
independent design projects, to the advantage of man, not against him,

To summarise, two types of system have been discussed here,
supermarket and telecommunication systems.   In both these systems
it is clear that one needs a very transparent link indeed.   This
is especially true for the check-out system in supermarkets.   Other
studies strongly indicate that the customer really feels bothered
and disturbed if he or she does not understand how to use the system.
A system which is difficult to understand may result in the customer
choosing to shop elsewhere.   Side-effects of the cash-computer
system, as for example no price-marking on goods, may also have the
same effect.   Even in systems such as the telecommunication system,
however, it is clear that the consumer would like a transparent link.
Therefore, it is good if the dialogue between the consumer and the
operator is as free as possible.   The customer may feel disturbed
and get upset if he or she is obliged to ask questions in a theoristic
way.

The need for a barrier is not so clear.   A certain type of
barrier is required for the telecommunication system.   However,
this is not so that the customer should not understand the system,
but that the customers not be allowed to get hold of private information (for example other customers' telephone numbers, addresses,
etc.).

Findings similar to those here have come from studies of computer terminals systems in banks and air-ticket booking systems. However, another type of interaction with the public is found with computer-terminal systems for editing newspapers. It is here very difficult to judge what kind of impact this type of system will have on the type and forms of editing quality, etc.

6. A GLANCE AT THE FUTURE

In the Journal of the Society of Information Display (SID), Ulbrich (1972) stated that we are standing at the beginning of an important new technological development stage. The last decade has seen enormous steps forward in the fields of electronic communications, which in turn has made possible an enormous increase in the amount of information available to the private individual. At the same time the field of computer technology has, as is well known, developed incredibly quickly. The next development, according to Ulbrich and others, is a coupling of computers and telecommunications. One result of this is the so-called 'demand-information' system, which will be further discussed below. One of the higher directors of the Swedish Post Office and Telephone company (Televerket) has revealed some long-term plans in Sweden for TV-telephones and has reviewed the potential possibilities of this system, including the coupling-in of computers in for example shops, banks and schools.

These 'demand information systems' are presented more and more often in popular science literature, technical TV and radio programmes, in very enthusiastic terms and as an important new development stage. But very few people ask the basic question: for whom are these systems of value, and what consequences will the systems have for society and the private individual?

Up to now, communications technology has been mainly directed towards the broadcasting of information, ie. one-way traffic. Examples of this are radio, newspapers, books and TV (the telephone is the exception). The amount of information to which the individual has been exposed in these ways has increased rapidly during this century, and he has today little chance of making use of more than a very small part of the total amount of this information (see Figure 6). The figure is adapted largely from Ulbrich (1972), and it suggests that we are approaching an asymptote; increase of information in the future will probably be very small.

We are thus exposed to a large amount of information, of which we can only make use of a small part. Much of the information transferred can therefore be thought of as redundant, but in many of the more common computer terminal systems the situation is very different. By asking different questions the operator can obtain information via the terminal, and this information is usually, it is hoped, all relevant to the job in hand. A similar technique could thus also be used for general information transfer in the society at large (eg. as regards the news, information about entertainments - films, theatre and suchlike - educational information, etc). In every household, the television set could be connected to a special keyboard, which in turn could be coupled to computers via the telephone network. By means of this terminal system, the user himself could call up the type of information which he wants. This 'free' choice of information would thereby increase, and this would minimise the 'risk' of being exposed to information which is not wanted. The effectiveness of information retrieval and usage would probably increase by the introduction of these types of system.

In a modern society, a demand-information system of this type would certainly have many advantages. However, there are also, of course, many important questions, points of view and prejudices against this type of system to be taken into account. A society in which we have a continuous personal choice as to what information we wish to receive runs the risk of becoming very conservative - perhaps conserving the whole society and the existing way in which it runs; this information system would also obviously have a conservative effect on the individuals' personal development. The wide and many-facetted information offered and broadcast in a real free society means that we must always think and take our own

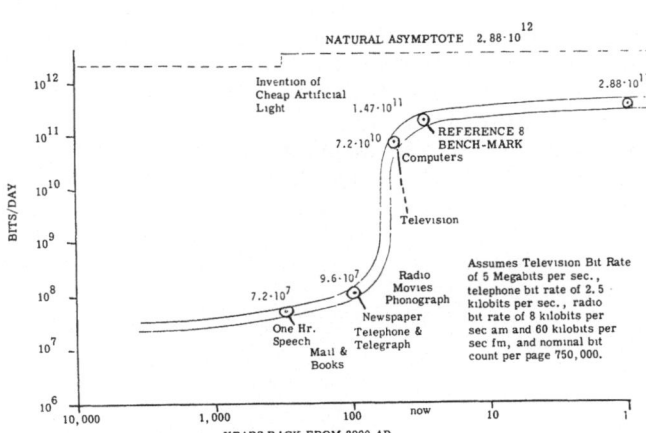

FIGURE 6. Household use of artificial information.
(Ulbrich, 1972)

personal standpoints towards it.   We are influenced in different
directions and get new ideas and stimulation.   If we ourselves
have the possibility of deciding which information we want to obtain,
this choice will be made from the starting point of our own personal
frame of reference, which in turn is based on earlier experiences,
especially those of childhood and youth.

Another related risk of demand-information systems is that the
answers to the questions are given in a way adapted to the system
controller.   This will mean the State in communist countries and
Big Business in the typical Western countries.

Interactive man-computer systems of this kind could have
very considerable implications for the general public and for our
present social order.   The ergonomist is often involved in the
development of this new type of system, by providing the basic data
on how the keyboard can be made easily and effectively used, how
the information presentation on the screens should be designed to
make it easily assimilated, etc.   From the public's point of view,
the ergonomist helps to design the system so that it will be easy
and comfortable to use, and so that it does not lead to difficulties
which could unintentionally scare off potential users.   We, as
ergonomists, will in other words make it easy to manipulate man and
make it easy for man to be manipulated.

It is only rarely that we ergonomists are called in to tackle
the more embracing overall problems of evaluating the implications
and consequences of this type of system.   The evaluation of these
overall implications would, however, be of very great value in
creating a broader understanding, and thus also in helping the
general public opinion to decide for or against such a system.
Such evaluations would also give politicians the possibility of
taking an informed standpoint, in order to be able to influence and
control the development in a direction which is a positive benefit
to individuals and to society as a whole.

REFERENCES

Berns, T. &   1974   Utformning av dataterminalarbetsplatser.
Söderberg, I.   (In Swedish).
                            In: Proceedings of the conference
                            "Människor & Datorer", Nordic
                            Ergonomics Society, Stockholm, 1974.

Boutet, M.   1967   L'electronique au service de la question
                            des supermarchés.
                            Libre Service Actualité, no. 211.

Istance, H.   1974   A pilot study for a man computer
                            dialogue project.
                            In: Proceedings of the conference
                            "Människor & Datorer", Nordic
                            Ergonomics Society, Stockholm, 1974.

Ivergård, T.B.K.   1972   An ergonomics study of the check-out
                            system for self-service shops in Sweden.
                            Ph.D. Thesis, Loughborough University
                            of Technology, England.

Petersen, R.M.   1971   TRADAR: Death of a retailer's dream.
                            Datamation, June, 34-37.

Shackel, B.   1969   Man-computer interaction - the contrib-
                            ution of the human sciences.
                            Ergonomics, 12.4, 485-499.

Stewart, T.F.M.   1974   The software interface and displays.
                            In: Proceedings of the conference
                            "Människor & Datorer", Nordic
                            Ergonomics Society, Stockholm, 1974.

Ulbrich, E.A.   1972   The social implications of demand
                            information systems.
                            SID Journal, 1.3, 5-29.

Unger, H.G.   1970   Electronics may bring relief to check
                            out lines.
                            Self-Service and Supermarket, Jan.
                            no. 1, 36.

PART 4   —   ASPECTS OF THE SOFTWARE INTERFACE

PREVIEW

The software interface comprises those parts of the man-
computer communication medium which are not hardware, are often
more transitory and are usually variable by program control: for
example, the logical structure of content and procedures, and the
format, layout, verbosity, etc. of sequences of man-machine
messages.   By definition we are not concerned with the system
aspects of the programming language in use.   The subject here is
the grammar, syntax and other language aspects of the communication
process between man and machine during the actual running of
programs.

However, as noted in the preview to Part 3, the distinction
between hardware and software interfaces is only of partial value.
The medium, the message and the meaning are all interwoven during
successful MCI; the whole must be viewed as an integrated entity
and subdivisions are only suitable for convenience of exposition.

Again, we are not aiming to be comprehensive or prescriptive.
Those seeking specific advice with regard to dialogue design should
start by referring to J. Martin 'Design of Man-Computer Dialogues',
Prentice-Hall 1973.   Those concerned with format design will
receive much help by referring to J. Hartley 'Designing Instructional
Text', Kogan Page 1978.

This part begins with an excellent review by Palme on many
aspects of designing interactive software for people, demonstrates
with Sime's example the type of detailed experiment needed to study
software interface aspects of computer languages, and concludes
with Fitter's example of how users could be assisted to develop
empirically the organisation and interface features of an interactive computer aid for decision making.

In his first sections, Palme suggests some of the basic human
needs for good interaction and then discusses how computer systems
at present do not meet these needs.   He shows how the process of
computerisation at present leads to computer experts defining the
problems and solutions in their own terms to suit the computer's
capability rather than to match human needs.   It is noteworthy

how Palme draws many of the same conclusions, from his viewpoint
as a sensitive computer specialist, as are emphasised for example
by Nickerson and others.   Then, in an extensive and valuable
section, he offers advice and prescriptions to system designers
on technical requirements to meet human needs and on ways of
improving the design of computer systems to provide good MCI.

After first discussing whether natural English is needed for
MCI and whether MCI languages should be more or less 'natural',
Sime presents the results of a programme of experiments on how to
make syntactic constructions easier to use.   These 'cognitive
ergonomics' studies, as he calls them, probe the various ways in
which conditional (if ..... then) constructions could be arranged
for easier interpretation.   The research studied the performance
of both naive and experienced programmers.   The results suggest
that this type of approach, if extended to tackle many of the
major issues, could be of considerable value especially in relation
to the design of procedural languages.

Fitter describes an experimental exploratory system to study
the ways in which users could develop rules and constraints by
which computers could help them with the scheduling decisions
typical of an engineering job-shop.   He then discusses design
principles and potentially desirable features for systems to aid
people in doing this task interactively.

INTERACTIVE SOFTWARE FOR HUMANS

Jacob Palme

Swedish National Defense Research Institute,
S-104 50 Stockholm 80, Sweden.

ABSTRACT

Which are the human needs that are affected by the use of
computers? How will computers affect the humans using them? What
kinds of communications between humans will the computers cause?
How can computer systems be designed better to satisfy human needs?
What design principles should be used for such systems? What kinds
of human-machine interaction will better satisfy human needs?

This paper discusses these problems and presents various methods.
Computer-driven, command-driven and natural-language interaction is
discussed.

HOW THE TEXT OF THIS REPORT WAS PREPARED

The text of this report has been extended and modified many times.
A number of people have read it and commented on it (Lars Enderin,
Arne Grip, Hans Karlgren, Ulla Ljung, Kalle Mäkilä, Mats Ohlin,
Brian Shackel, Per Svensson, Jan Wirstad). Thank you!

In spite of this, no typist has had to retype the text several
times. Instead, the text was stored in a computer, and automatic
text editors and page formatters were used to make changes and
additions and still producing a nice copy.

This is an example of how a computer can abolish dull and tedious
work (retyping almost the same text many times). That is how
computers should be used!

168

CONTENTS

1. INTRODUCTION

The price/performance ratio of computers is rapidly going down.
The lower prices mean that people are finding the use of computers
feasible for more and more applications. More and more people are
becoming involved with computers.

Are we moving towards a "computer age" in which computers have
taken over much of the communication now handled by other means? A
"computer age" in which most humans will spend a large portion of
their time communicating with computers? Or will the trends stop?

The future is not shaped by chance, it is shaped to a large extent
by human actions. Will humans want or accept more computers?
Should they?

The purpose of this paper is to present certain problems which
occur when humans interact with computers. I will then present
techniques for human-machine interaction, and discuss if they can
solve these problems.

2. HUMAN NEEDS

Computers are for the good of humans, not humans for the good of
computers. A good starting point in discussing human-machine
interaction is therefore the human. Which are those human needs,
whose fulfillment is influenced by computers? Here is an
incomplete list of them:

> ACCEPTANCE: Humans need to be accepted by their peers. Other
  people should have time to listen to them, when they have something
  to say. Other people should show respect for them as individuals.
  (See Harris 1969.)

> TWO-SIDED CONFLICT-SOLVING: When a problem occurs, people should
  try to find a solution which reasonably well satisfies the needs of
  all people involved. One person or one side should not impose its
  solution on the other side. An important initial phase of
  two-sided problem-solving is that both sides listen to each other
  and try to understand the other persons needs and ideas. (See
  Gordon 1970 and Gordon 1974.)

> PERSONAL DEVELOPMENT: Humans should have the right and the
  opportunity of developing themself, of learning more, of improving
  their skills.

> ABILITY TO MODIFY THE ENVIRONMENT: Humans should have the means of
changing their environment, of improving the environment when it is
bad for them. A recent study has shown that a feeling of
helplessness, that is, a feeling of not being able to solve
problems by influencing one's environment, is an important cause of
human depressions. (See Seligman 1975.)

Sociologists talk about AUTHORITARIAN and DEMOCRATIC social
systems. The authoritarian system is based on rigid lines of
commands, people are expected to do what they are told and not ask
questions. In the democratic system, communication is more
two-way: There is no boss who dictates his/her wishes without
listening to and being influenced by the people. The democratic
system will easier give solutions which are satisfactory to more
people, and it will better satisfy the human needs listed above.

3. THERE IS A HUMAN BEHIND THE COMPUTER

(This chapter is largely influenced by Grip 1974.)

Compare two systems for doing the same job, one with and one
without computers. Humans play an important part in both systems.
But in the computer system certain functions are handled by
computer programs.

3.1 THE PROCESS OF COMPUTERIZING A JOB

To understand the effects of this one must look at the process of
computerizing a job. This process begins with the recognition that
computers might be advantageous. Special experts are given the job
of finding out if computers should be used, and if so how.

These experts usually have a technical education. They have been
taught about computers and systems analysis, but not so much about
humans and human relations.

This alone means that there is a large risk that they will design a
system solution which does not satisfy human needs.

The experts will analyze how the job is done without computers.
They will make a detailed plan of how the job should be done with
the help of computers. This plan often means certain changes in
the previous procedures to make them more suitable for computers.

Such a plan will include a detailed chart of the flow of
information in the system: Which information is necessary as input
to certain subtasks, and which information is produced by the
subtask. Which tasks should be performed by humans, and which
tasks can better be handled by a computer program?

The goal of the plan is to do the job cheaply, efficiently and well. Often, the specification of the job will be changed to include extra benefits, like more statistics, which at little extra cost can be produced when the job is computerized.

The plan is then presented to the management, which has to judge if the plan will agree with their long-range goals. They will check the plan against goals such as profit, product quality, public image, and sometimes also the well-being of their employees. Naturally, the management tends to check the system especially against their own needs. Among these are the needs of the management to control the flow of information and the lines of control.

When the plan has been approved, the experts take over again. A group of people begin to implement the plan, that is buying the computer, writing the programs, teaching the employees their new tasks in the computerized system, etc.

This implementation process often takes a long time. Especially, computer programming is often time-consuming and expensive.

Finally comes the day, often years later, when the new system is started. There are troubles in changing over, and sometimes the system will never work as intended. In such cases the system may be scrapped, or people will do the computerized subtasks manually beside the computer.

The reason for such doubling of the work may be conservatism among the employees, but may also be the fact that the computerized system does not do the work as well as needed. The computerized system may not provide certain information needed, or may be too slow in getting certain things done. Since the development of the computer system has taken several years, it may be partly or wholly obsolete.

People will easier accept and be satisfied with computer systems if they find that the system is of benefit to them. If they only have disadvantages from the system, but do not get anything back which they find valuable, then they will probably not be satisfied with it. It is therefore important not to design systems with the only goal of providing information for the top people in an organisation. The needs of the people at lower levels must also be taken into account. If each person who has contact with the computer system also can see direct personal benefits from the system, then he/she will better accept the system and it will work better.

If the system is successfully implemented and people do begin to use it, there are still problems. People will always complain about deficiences in the computer system. It does not provide certain needed information in a certain form, or certain common tasks are too difficult to do with the computers, or the computer system is error-prone in certain ways, etc. etc.

This means that there must be people who change the computer programs. For large systems, there is a large group of computer programmers continually doing nothing except updating the system to satisfy new user requirements.

But this is a time-consuming process, and a change needed by a user may take months or years to realize, depending on its priority.

3.2 THE COMPUTER WILL DO WHAT IT IS PROGRAMMED TO DO

Those tasks of the new system which depend on the computer will only work in the way the computer is programmed. The previous system was probably a manual system, where humans performed directly many tasks now delegated to computer programs. In this manual system, there were ways of bypassing the normal routines. Questions could be answered, orders processed, short-cuts devised for special tasks, new ways devised for new problems.

The manual system could continually adjust itself to new situations or changes in the task. These adjustments were often made in a quick and flexible manner. They did not require months of work of highly trained computer specialists, they could be done in a few minutes by just a human talking to another human.

Note, however, that if the system before the computer was partially automized using less powerful machines than computers, e.g. ledger-poster-machines, then the computer may give more flexibility than the previous machines.

Why then does the computer system not provide the same flexibility as manual systems? The excuse always given by the computer people is:

"This was not foreseen from the beginning. If we had only known that you wanted to do this and this and this, then we could have made such a system. But you never said this when we asked you what the system was to do. And you accepted our plan of the new system. And now it is very difficult to put your changes in afterwards."

The basic fault seems thus to be that everything was not foreseen from the beginning. But no one can foresee all future needs from the beginning. It is usually not even possible to make a complete inventory of the needs today, or of all the functions provided by the manual system which is to be computerized.

The fault is rather in the whole design process. The typical design process, as described above, involves studying the existing system and creating an ideal plan of how the system should work. Very often this ideal plan is imperfect in itself, especially if the future users of the system did not take part in the design process. Example: it may only optimize technical efficiency without taking human needs into consideration. Even if the plan is good, it still gives some people a static picture of the system at just one time.

The best design process is one which produces systems that will satisfy even those requirements which were not explicit when the system was specified. This is possible if the system is so designed that the users themselves can modify the system to do new or different things.

Most systems do not give the users that facility. The computer only works in the way it has been programmed. Everyone (systems designers, programmers, office workers) are forced by the computer to work according to the original plan. The short-cuts and flexible solutions in the previous manual system are often no longer possible.

One can view this as a communication process. The computer is a means of communicating the plan to the employees. By designing and writing the computer program in a certain way, the experts are communicating to the employees their view on how things should be done.

This communication process is characterized by two things:

The communication is delayed. The computer was often programmed a long time before the employee receives the message.

The communication is authoritarian. The employee usually has to do as the computer people say, since otherwise the computer will not work.

It is obvious that often such a communication process will not satisfy the human needs specified in section 2. above.

Example: The National Agricultural Board wanted all forest surveyors to use one way of estimating the value of forests. They then developed a computer program to be used for forest value estimates. This program could only handle estimates made in the way preferred by the National Board. There was a lot of grumbling among the surveyors, but everyone was forced to do the estimation in one way. Thus, the computer was used, by the National Board, as a method of imposing their will upon the surveyors.

Example II: In Stockholm, there was for many years a marked shortage of apartments. A public body was set up to distribute the available apartments to those who had the largest need and had been queuing for the longest time.

In 1975, the situation were the opposite. There was too many apartments, and the task of this public body was changed into helping people find the best apartment among those available. However, the computer program used to distribute apartments did not fit this new task. The program stored a lot of information about income, number of children, time in the queue etc., which was needed for the previous task of distributing apartments to those with the greatest need. The program stored little information about personal requirements on the apartment, since little choice had been available.

This example shows how a computer program can make it difficult to adjust a system to new needs in a changing environment.

If one computer is doing the task of hundreds of people, then a centralized decision to change this task can be made just by changing the computer program. Such a centralized decision might often be more difficult to enforce in a manual system. A computer will therefore sometimes create a system where centralized decisions of changes are simpler to implement, but where local changes without centralized approval are more difficult to make.

3.3 THE COMPUTER AS THE LONG ARM OF THE CENSOR

One can understand this by comparing with a famous section in
George Orwell's novel "1984". That novel depicts a future society
in which a totalitarian state watches everything people are doing
to check that nothing forbidden is done or said.

A section of the book contains a discussion of how to stop people
thinking illegal thoughts. It is observed that our thoughts are
governed by the language we use. Orwell suggests the invention of
a new language, such that illegal thoughts cannot be formulated in
that language:

> "The purpose of Newspeak was not only to provide a medium of
> expression for the world-view and mental habits proper to the
> devotees of Ingsac, but to make all other modes of thought
> impossible."

The computer has, in fact, already provided an instrument for
partly realizing Orwell's prophecies. A computer can talk about
nothing but the topics it has been programmed to handle. Program
designers can thus decide what kind of messages should be allowed
or disallowed. The computer gives them power to enforce their
decisions on the people using the computer.

The more we let computers take over human communication processes,
the more these processes can be closely guarded and censored by the
program, which acts as the long arm of the program designer.

Some examples:

> Some of the input to the computer has to be phrased in a complex
specialized language which only a few people know. In that way the
computer can be used to decide who is allowed to use the computer.
Ordinary people are not accepted.

> The management would find it embarrassing if certain facts were
known. The computer is programmed so that those questions cannot
be asked.

> The output from the computer is phrased in such a way that certain
things are very difficult to read. I have for example a wage slip
from an employer (not my own) who perhaps did not want his
employees to find out how the wages had been calculated. The
various sub-fields are tagged by integer codes, explained in small
print on the back, so that it becomes very difficult for someone
who is not an expert to read and interpret it. It is not very
surprising that one thing is very easy to read from the wage slip.
That is the net amount of money being paid out.

An interesting fact is that even when there seems to be no premeditated intention of the systems to satisfy the people responsible for the computer rather than the ordinary users, the systems still tend to come out that way.

In this way the designer of a computer system can make it easy to get information which he/she wants people to have easy access to, but can make it difficult or impossible to get information which he/she does not want people to have easy access to.

This is in some ways similar to the special languages which professionals (lawyers, medical doctors, clergymen etc.) of all times have used (See Hoare 1975). But the computer is a more powerful tool for enforcing a mode of communication. This mode of communication is also often much more restricted.

3.4 YOU ARE ALWAYS COMMUNICATING WITH A HUMAN

Every communication between a human and a computer is in reality a communication between humans:

> The computer system is constructed by humans.

> The computer programs were written by humans. They laid down the rules for how the computer should answer questions from a human user.

> When a human stores information in a computer, which is later transmitted to other humans using the system, this is also a delayed human-to-human communication process.

However, the human-to-human communication through computers is different in several ways from direct, face-to-face human conversations:

> In a human-to-human face-to-face conversation, the participants can through an iterative process come to an understanding of the problem and each other´s views, and then find a solution based on this mutual understanding.

> In a human-to-human face-to-face conversation, natural built-in human factors protect us from inhuman decisions. It has been said that it is easier to kill millions of humans by pushing a button than to kill one human face-to-face. The same principle applies also to less severe acts than killing.

> In a human-to-human face-to-face conversation, the facts about the people present are taken directly from each person directly. Mistakes and misunderstandings will then be less common. With a computer, facts are instead often taken from data bases which may be faulty or misleading through incompleteness.

Constructed example: An employer is going to select someone for a task requring a reliable person. The employer uses data from a computerized data base. Two people are equally merited, but one of them was on sick leave four weeks last year. (The computer does not contain the cause of the sick leave: an accident in the workshop.) The other person gets the job. And the next time someone is to be chosen for a difficult task, he/she will have had more experience with such tasks. This example shows that incomplete information from a computer can hit a person unjustly.

> In a human-to-human conversation, the listener is continuosly informing the speaker if he/she understands and agrees, so that the speaker can adjust the language to the reactions of the listener.

See further Chapanis 1975. ou

Communication between humans through a computer has some similarities with written communication through letters, forms or other documents. However, the computer can be made to govern the communication, e.g. by selecting what to tell whom. This ability of the computer is felt beneficial by those who can tell the computer how to govern the communication, but may be felt less acceptable by those who cannot modify the workings of the computer according to their needs.

Another difference between communication through computers and through written documents is the speed with which the user gets a response. If the response can be generated from the programs and data already in the computer, the user can get an immediate response from the computer just like in a vocal human-to-human communication.

3.5 SOME HUMANS PREFER COMPUTERS TO PEOPLE

Many people will sometimes find face-to-face communication with other people troublesome. They find certain communication situations emotionally trying or stressful. People might then prefer to communicate with other people through a computer.

Example I: An extreme example of people who do not accept normal, vocal communication with others are certain children who do not speak at all. Such children also often have violent seizures of temper. The cause of this is believed to be that these children have been frightened off human communication because of psychological problems with such communication, which the children could not solve.

In an experiment, described in Kent 1975, such children have been treated by letting them interact with a computer programmed to be very patient and very responsive to the wishes of the children. The machine does not, for example, mind at all if the child asks it, a hundred times in succession, to show a running fire engine on the screen, together with suitable sound effects from a loudspeaker.

The computer treatment was applied to twenty-five children, on whom all previous treatments (with human therapists) had failed. In a large majority of cases, the children improved much in their ability to communicate with humans after having taken the first steps together with a computer.

The probable reason for this result is that the computer presented a communication situation which did not have the frightening aspects which human communication had for these children.

Example II: Many people find it difficult to speak up in a group of other people. When communicating through a computer, such people are often found to have valuable contributions to make which were previously unheard because they dared not express their opinion. The computer gave them the possibility to phrase their contribution carefully in a situation which was less stressful to them than a meeting with a group of other people.

Example III: Certain people with emotional contact problems find it difficult to establish working contacts with other humans. At the computer, they find solace in a machine which responds to them in a way they can understand and master. (One can compare with people who prefer pornographic magazines to the real thing, for similar reasons.)

Example IV: A human who wants to or has to hurt another human may prefer to deliver the message through a computer. The computer is a machine which can be used to manipulate others, with the manipulator protected from certain unpleasant consequences which would occur in face-to-face encounters.

The use of computers has obviously both advantages and disadvantages from this viewpoint. The advantage is that certain people will at certain times prefer, and perform better in, the protected environment provided by the computer. The disadvantage is that they may sometimes flee to the computer when direct face-to-face communication would have been better.

Example V: A person prefers to get a regular financial report from the computer because it gives the same report format computed in the same way reliably every time. Note however, that if the computer prepares its report from data which humans have given it, these data may have hidden subjectivity, and the objectivity of the computer report may be misleading and therefore dangerous.

A commonly stated view is the fear of private personal information in computers. However, computers can be designed to protect private personal information better than manual systems, e.g. so that no one is ever allowed to take out the private data except the person himself. Others would only get statistical tables of means etc., where single persons are not identifiable. In this case, people may prefer computers just because they protect data better than manual systems.

One might claim that some people, who prefer computers, would in the long run be better helped by psychotherapeutic treatment to overcome their contact problems, rather than with a machine which makes hiding even easier. However, such treatment is not always very effective, and the computer may be a more workable solution (Changing the environment rather than changing the people).

The wish to use a computer to avoid certain stressful human communication situations can sometimes also be viewed as a natural and responsible way of reacting to certain situations.

3.6 COMPARING COMPUTERS AND MASS COMMUNICATION

The increasing use of computers for human communications has thus obvious dangers compared to human face-to-face conversation. However, sometimes computers replace human communications which were previously transmitted by one-directional, written media like letters, pamphlets or mass communication (radio, TV, newspapers etc.).

One of the differences between human-to-human communications through mass communication and computers is that the computers increase the possibility to decide selectively who is to receive or not receive a certain message.

This can be done in two ways:

> By programming the computer to check information about the individuals (their occupation, their interests etc.) to decide if they are to receive a certain message.

> By letting the human who wants information get it by asking questions to a computer system.

In both these cases, the computer can give different information to different users. Mass communication media are much more crude. The computer is better at selectively distributing information to those who need it, or to whom the sender needs to transmit it.

If a computer system answers the questions which the user wants from it, then the user will often be much more satisfied with the computer than with mass media.

If a computer system distributes information automatically, using selection criteria set by the receivers of the messages, then the receivers will also be more satisfied.

However, the computer system is often governed more by the sender of the messages than by the receivers. The sender decides what to store and who should be selected to get certain messages (e.g. advertising material), the sender decides which questions the computer should answer and not answer.

If a sender decides not to send information to some people needing it, those people may feel neglected and may not be able to assert their rights.

If many senders send too much information to someone, that person
may feel overburdened with information he/she does not need and did
not ask for.

In most cases, a sender-driven system for distributing information
through computers is dangerous, while a receiver-driven system is
beneficial.

Systems which are basically sender-driven can be improved by giving
the receivers some right to ask for information not sent to them,
and some right to stop information they do not want.

Some people have claimed that such receiver-driven computerized
communication systems will be used by people to restrict their new
impressions to a limited area of interest. Since different people
do this in different ways, they will have less knowledge in common
and therefore find it more difficult to communicate. Society will
be more divided into groups with their own interests and ideas.

I personally feel that variation in society is beneficial, a
powerful driving force towards testing and trying new ideas and new
approaches.

It might also be possible to design computer systems which help
people get away from confinement into restricted areas of interest.
Note that conventional communication restricts an individual to
rather coarse interest groups: the readers of a specialist
magazine or the members of a specialized society. In
non-computerized systems, the movement to another interest may be a
large step. With computerized systems, a person could change
his/her interest profile in a number of small steps, slowly and
carefully moving towards new interest areas.

3.7 THE HUMANS INVOLVED WITH COMPUTERS

Different groups of people are involved with computer systems:

> Experts (System designers, programmers, repairers etc.), a group
  whose size increases rapidly with computerization,
> Managers, who hope to get better efficiency with computers,
> Employees, whose tasks are changed or taken over by computers,
> Outsiders, that is people outside the place where the computer is
  used, who are influenced in various ways by it.

The e x p e r t s are a group which generally has high status and
a rather varied, creative work. Because everyone who uses a
computer system has to use it the way it is programmed, these
experts also get power. For all these reasons they usually get
good work satisfaction from computers. If the use of computers
mean more people with this kind of "expert" work and fewer people
with boring routine work, then the average work satisfaction may

increase.

This does not of course mean that all computer experts are always
satisfied with their jobs. The computer system may be so badly
designed that not even the experts can get it to do what they want
in reasonable ways. Sometimes, the managerial organization makes
them less satisfied. For example, the organization may be such
that the experts at a lower level are not able to see the meaning
of their work, perhaps, but not necessarily, because the work
really is meaningless or detrimental. In such a situation, the
experts tend to try to find satisfaction in the intellectual
challenge presented by their tasks. But do we want such experts?

The m a n a g e r s will sometimes find that they are restricted
by the rigidness of computer systems, even though they have
themselves approved of the specifications. The tasks are changing,
and an old, large computer system may be a hindrance to changing
the organization in accordance with a new situation.

In some places, the process of computerization has moved much power
within a place of work from the ordinary lines of management to the
computer system developers. This has caused conflicts with the
ordinary management, who feel bypassed by the computer people.

Groups who may be in trouble are the ordinary e m p l o y e e s
and the o u t s i d e r s.

Some ordinary e m p l o y e e s lose their jobs. In many cases,
it is difficult to find new jobs for them, because the new skills
are so different or because they have to move. Example: In
newspaper production, manuscripts are more and more often stored in
computers, and the type-setting is done automatically by the
computer. This takes away some of the work of the type-setters.
The type-setters will then require that they get the new jobs of
handling the computer and putting data into it. However, in many
cases it is natural that a journalist or an advertisement receiver
inputs the data directly, and then the old type-setters cannot take
over that job unless they become journalists or advertisment
receivers.

A computer is a very good machine for doing simple, routine tasks
automatically, guided by its program. One would therefore expect
that the computer would remove boring routine jobs and let people
do jobs more suitable to humans. To some extent this is also true.
But often the result is different. Because the computer systems
are designed to do the task in just one way, the ordinary employees
have less freedom than before. Also, if the computer takes over
many steps in a manual process and leaves only one step for a
human, this means that the job for this human will have less
variation.

When jobs become too simple because of automation, a common way of treating this problem is to change the work plan so that each person handles a series of tasks. Instead of having separate people just keypunching data into the computer, the person who receives the data (e.g. customer orders) could both talk to the customer and input the data into the computer. In other cases, it is possible to let the data go automatically into the computer without any human intermediary. For example, a balance might transfer weight information directly into the computer.

The computer systems can be programmed to monitor everything that is going through them. They can monitor the speed and efficiency of every employee, and they are often programmed to do this. This continuous supervision is a closer control of the employees than that of a human supervisor who sometimes goes away.

Example: At the Viking Askim rubber company in Norway, the workers discovered that their tools were connected to a computer, which received a signal for every operation made on the tool. A strike resulted, and the strike was resolved by an agreement that the company should not use the data from the tools to do any kind of individual performance measurement on the employees.

When ordinary people in the street (the o u t s i d e r s) are asked their opinion about computers, they often express feelings of unease. They regard the computers as instruments for increasing centralized power, because computers have been used very much in this way. The computer has become a symbol of centralized power in a way which means that people transfer their negative feelings about centralized power to negative feelings about computers. Can this public feeling towards computers be changed into a more positive feeling, if computer systems are developed and used in ways which people conceive as beneficial and useful?

3.8 EMPLOYEE PARTICIPATION IN THE DESIGN PROCESS

In Norway, experiments have been made with employee representatives in the design process. The Norwegian Trade Union Federation was very early aware of the risks to the employees with the introduction of computers. They felt that computers, if governed solely by the management, could mean more power and control in the hands of the management and less influence for the employees. They started experiments with employee participation, contracted computer consultants of their own and they have today arrived at a written agreement with the Employer's Association Federation about the use of computers.

The agreement says that not only technical and economic, but also
social aspects shall be taken into consideration in the design of
computer systems. The employers must, at a very early stage in the
design process, tell the representatives of the employees about
their plans. Those employees who are directly concerned by the
computer systems should also take part in the design work. The
agreement specially states that information should be given to the
employees in a language which they can understand.

The employees can, if they so want, appoint a special
representative for computer problems. This representative shall
have access to all documents about the computer system and take
regular part in the design work. The representative shall, at the
employer´s cost, get the necessary education about computers.

A local agreement must be reached about all use of computerized
personnel files. If an agreement cannot be reached, the conflict
should be moved to the national associations.

Such employee participation has many advantages:

> The employees learn enough about the computers to be able to put
force behind their requirements.

> The designers are forced to listen to the employees, and this is an
important way of teaching computer system designers more about how
to design better systems.

The problems with employee participation are:

> The employees do not always know enough to be able to talk back to
experts who say: "This is not possible."

> The employees may be led to compromise and hence to accept systems
which in practice are found to be bad. The designer can then say:
Well, you accepted our specifications! In fact, many philosophies
about customer participation, as stated by system designers, seem
more to aim at binding customers to a specification so that future
trouble can be blamed on the customers instead of on on the
designers.

I personally believe that employee participation is very important.
But I also think that it would be dangerous to believe that this
will solve all or most of the problems.

There is an obvious risk of designing too much user control and
restrictions into a system even if the system is designed by a
well-meaning group with representation for all involved groups of
people. This risk occurs because even a system which is designed
with only the best intentions may still turn out to be too
restrictive when put into practical use. It is very easy for a

design group to specify, with the best of intentions, too many
principles and rules into a system. In fact, the situation of
computer system design seems in some not yet understood way to be
"alluring" towards such an overdesigned system specification.
Employee participation gives no guarantee against this risk.

An ideal computer system may not be one which satisfies all the
requirements put by the users during the design process, but rather
a system which is flexible enough to be able to adjust itself to
the needs of the users on a day-to-day basis.

3.9 COMPUTERS AND HUMAN NEEDS

If we look at the human needs listed in section 2. above, we thus
find:

> ACCEPTANCE: Computers will often give people a feeling of
insecurity. The computer system poses rigid requirements on its
users, but the person who designed the system and invented these
requirements is far away. The typical attitude of the designer of
the system is that of an expert talking to laymen. The designer is
transferring this attitude to the computer system, so that the
typical attitude shown by the computer to its users is: I´m OK,
you´re not OK. (See Harris 1969.)

Even when the computer is not OK, when the user knows much better,
it still transmits this attitude which it has been given by its
designers. The continuing supervision of its users performed by
some computer systems for their managers also adds to this
situation. Thus, the computer will often cause situations where
the human need for ACCEPTANCE is badly satisfied.

Sometimes, computer system designers give people the feeling that
their job is something a machine will take over in the near future.
This may make the people feel unaccepted, if there is no other
better job they can do instead.

> TWO-SIDED CONFLICT-SOLVING: A computer is often a tool for one
side, the designer and his/her principal, to impose their view of
how things should be done. Such a computer will badly satisfy this
human need.

> PERSONAL DEVELOPMENT: In a manual system, humans usually have the
ability to modify their way of handling things to do them better.
With the computer, this ability is often circumscribed by experts
difficult to reach.

> ABILITY TO MODIFY THE ENVIRONMENT: Since the ordinary user usually does not have the right or ability to change the programs of the computer, this human need is circumscribed. Computer programmers, however, often feel that computers are good just because the computers give them this ability of modifying the environment.

3.10 CAN WE DESIGN BETTER COMPUTER SYSTEMS?

Can computer systems be designed in such a way that they will better satisfy human needs? I believe so. Here are some of the things we could do:

> Postpone the decision about computer or no computer until the evidence is strong enough to make such a decision.

> Teach the designers of computer systems much more about human needs and about how systems should be designed to satisfy them better.

> Let the employees and the outsiders take part in the design process, not only the designers and the managers.

> Teach ordinary people more about what computer systems can do, so that they ask for more and do not accept bad systems.

> Always remember that the goal is to use the computers to help people. Each computer task should be questioned from the viewpoint: Which people are helped by this and how? Do they feel so themselves? Are other people negatively affected, and if so how?

> Create good computer systems, publicly available, so that people are shown what can be done. They will then not as easily accept other less good systems. An example of such a good public system would be a system with data bases containing information people often need, and with terminals at public libraries where anyone can use them.

> The way to design good systems is not to design them so that they can only do things the way the designer plans. Instead, the users of the system should have the possibility of making the system do things the way they want. The user should be in command of the system, not the system in command of the user. This will be discussed further in the next section of this paper.

4. FROM HUMAN NEEDS TO TECHNICAL REQUIREMENTS

This chapter will discuss various ways of arranging the
human-machine interface.

The main conclusion of the previous chapter was that a computer
system will be more acceptable to humans if the system gives power
to the humans who are working with it. If the humans who are
working with a computer have power over the system, can get the
system to do what they want, if the system and the computer is a
useful tool helping them, then they will find the computer system
acceptable.

If, on the other hand, they are guided through the computer in an
authoritarian way, restricting their freedom and their possibility
to solve their problems in a simple, natural and flexible way, then
the computer system will be an obstacle to them.

How then can we design computer systems to provide power and
freedom to the people who get involved with them?

4.1 ALL DATA EASILY AVAILABLE

The people which are using the computer should have available to
them all the information which they need, and which is stored in
the computer. The important thing here is what their needs are
regarded to be. Often, the system designer has an "ideal" model of
the tasks performed by the people using the computer, and each of
them is then given access only to the data needed to perform this
"ideal" task.

However, this does not take into account the fact that in special
circumstances the users very often want to do something different
from the "ideal" task. The users should then have the facilities
to get the information they need. The best way to give the users
this freedom is to:

> Store all data in a general-purpose data base handling system,

> Let every user have access to a general-purpose enquiry language
which can get all the information in the data base handling system.

To avoid misunderstanding, I do not mean that all data base
accesses always must go through user queries in the general-purpose
enquiry language. But this facility should be available when
needed.

A conflict may arise with secrecy requirements for certain data, e.g. military secrets or personal data.

An important political question in the future will be what information should be available to whom. Is it necessary with so much commercial secrets, or do they hinder progress? Will computers be used to make more facts available to more people, or will they be used to protect information and only make it available to a small elite?

A computer can be a very powerful tool for protecting information. But a general-purpose enquiry handler will be less useful and meaningful if the main goals are protection rather than openness.

Very important is that people designing data base systems are aware of this conflict. It is so easy to use the secrecy requirements as a pretext for designing a system which forces all users to work as the system designer wants them to and for disregarding the human needs of the people who are going to use the system.

A common complaint against computers is that they produce too much information. A human mind does not have the capacity to grasp and handle large amounts of information. A human therefore wants to have only the most important data presented. He/she wants data ready-treated for their needs.

If, for example, the user asks for the number of accounts larger than 2000, the user does not want to get a list of all the accounts, but only a number. It is important that the query language is flexible enough to allow the user to select exactly what he wants.

With a conversational system, it is especially important that the user does not have to wait for long printouts of things he does not want. Every message to the user should be short. With a display terminal, the message should be small enough to fit into one screen. This requires a flexible query language to allow the user to state exactly what is wanted. If a user asks a question which requires a lengthy output, he/she should be told so and asked what to do about it before the long answer is output. This is just the kind of power over the computer which is good for the human.

4.2 THE COMPUTER SHOULD ADJUST ITSELF TO THE USER

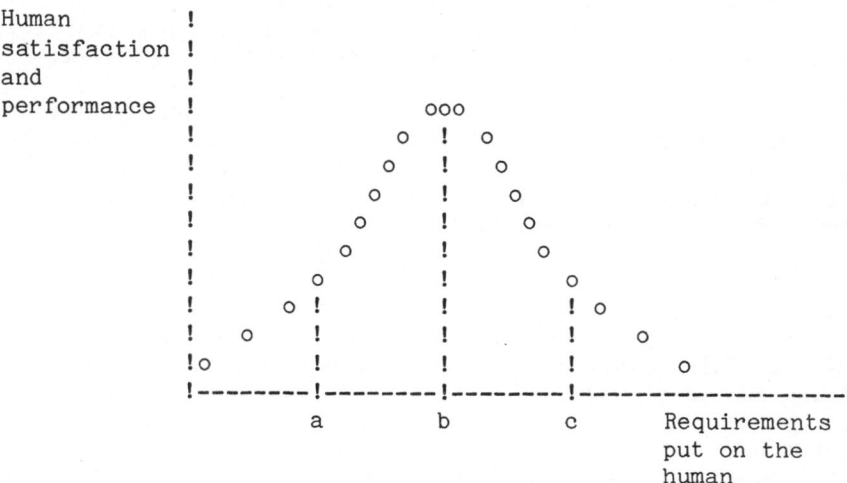

The curve above illustrates how the satisfaction and performance of
humans varies with the requirements put on them. If too much is
demanded of them (point c on the curve) then they will be
overstressed, and their satisfaction and performance will be
lowered.

If, on the other hand, too little is demanded from them (point a on
the curve), then they will find their task dull and tedious. They
will find it difficult to concentrate on their job, and their
satisfaction and performance will again be lowered.

They will be most satisfied and perform at their best if the
requirements on them are well adjusted to their abilities and
ambitions (point b on the curve).

Since people are different, the first conclusion from this is that
the same mode of interaction is not the best for every user.

For example, an inexperienced user may prefer a computer which
guides the user along with explanations and explanatory questions.
A very experienced user may on the other hand prefer a very
powerful and concise command language, in which much can be said to
the computer with few keystrokes.

But even for one single person, his/her requirements vary with
time. His/her requirements are different when he/she begins to use
a computer and when he/she has much experience with it. And
changes in his/her tasks will also influence what computer
behaviour is best.

For example, a special work situation one week may require the person to input an almost identical series of inputs to the computer a large number of times. He/she then needs a facility to shorten this special series of inputs just during that week.

The repetition of the same trivial series of commands many times can become tedious and dull for a human. Therefore the computer should take over such repetitions when needed by the user. The ability to turn such repetitive work over to the computer is a computer facility which should be made easily available to its users.

Because a computer can be programmed, the computer can be made to adjust itself to different user needs much easier than many other machines. This advantage of the computer compared to other hardware should be used.

When two humans talk to each other, they will automatically adjust their language so that the other understands. (One of many cases where humans are more automatic than machines!) A computer can be programmed to have at least some of this ability.

4.3 PEOPLE HAVE THE RIGHT TO CHANGE THEIR MINDS

Linguists sometimes make transcripts of spoken human language. These transcripts are very interesting to read. They contain a large number of linguistic errors. The speaker stops in the middle of a sentence, restarts something else, leaves out important parts of his/her phrases, makes a large number of trivial errors which he/she immediately corrects. Obviously, this way of talking is natural for a human. People listening are usually not irritated either, they have the ability to understand such incomplete and corrected language.

Since this is a natural mode of using language for a human, a good computer should also be programmed to allow it. Thus, humans at computer terminals should have the ability to correct things they have previously put into the computer.

Ideally, the users should be allowed to go back as far as they want in the conversation, correct only what they want to change, and then continue where they stopped. They should not be forced to input again a number of already correctly input data just because they want to change one previously input item.

Certain computer programs work in such a way that the users are led through a program-defined path of questions and stages of execution, with very restricted or no possibilities for the users to change their mind about previous answers to the questions. Such systems are not good.

Even when data have already been stored in a data base, there is still often a need to correct them. Example: A customer may call to change or cancel a previous order.

The problem here is that there may be other data dependent on the corrected item. Example: First a person got too much pay. Then this was corrected, but too much tax was deducted, based on the previous faulty wages, so that he/she now got too little money.

4.4 HUMANS AND MACHINES MAKE ERRORS

To be able to work at all, a lot of time in every large computer system is spent on errorchecking at different interfaces: User - machine, program - language system, language system - operating system etc.

If an error anyway has to be corrected, it is much better to correct it as early as possible.

It is important that the error is explained to the users in a language relating to their terms of reference. If by mistake a user tells the computer that the name of someone is "45" then the computer should answer "I do not understand numerical names". The computer should not answer, e.g., "Illegal memory reference" or "Pushdown list overflow" or "Array bounds error".

The computer should answer politely, especially in cases where the computer may be in error rather than the user. If the computer expects a number and gets the input "twenty", then it should not be programmed to answer "ERROR: Input was not number".

The person who writes a computer program tries to envisage what kinds of correct and incorrect answers a program will receive. But no person is ever able to envisage all kinds of correct and incorrect answers people will actually give to the program in field use.

A good way of finding out is to write the program in such a way that it saves all answers received in a file. In my experience, when the program has been tested by more than fifty different human users, then this file will contain enough data to predict almost all kinds of answers which people will try to give to the computer.

Only when the program has been corrected on the basis of the data in such a file can it be called acceptably responsive to human behaviour.

If the error checking in the computer system is bad, then a small mistake by a human at a terminal can cause much trouble. Obviously this risk puts stress on the human. Therefore, good, early and immediate error checking by the computer will reduce stress.

Example: Cashiers in post offices in Sweden have a responsible task. They are also personally responsible for losses, which by mistake they may cause the post office. A lost receipt can cost the cashier thousands of kronor. This risk makes the work of the cashiers stressing. In the last year, the post offices have begun using cashier computer terminals. Inger Evenfelt, who has been a postal clark since 1948, says "This is the best that has happened in 25 years." She thinks of the error and validity checks in the computer program, which helps her avoid her own mistakes. This is an example of a property of a computer program which often makes people like using it.

In direct human-to-human communications, the people involved will adjust their error checking to the special needs of a special day and to the special characteristics of the other people involved.

Example I: When inputting data about individual persons, other checks may be appropriate than when inputting data about enterprises.

Example II: A certain person may have a tendency to mis-spell certain words. He/she may then want the computer to help with just the mis-spellings which are a problem to that person.

In both cases, there is a need for the human to be able to modify the error checks in the computer according to the specific needs of a special work situation or a special human user of the computer. As before, the human using the computer needs power to influence the way the computer operates.

Certain error checks will detect obvious logical errors (like negative mass). Others will find things which are probably errors (like a wage decrease). The latter tests are often very useful, but they will depend on the circumstances more than the logical tests, since a piece of data which is highly unlikely one day may be much more plausible another day.

When an error occurs or is recognized, the human is aided if the consequences are not unnecessarily grave. A machine-malfunction should mean the loss of a few seconds of human work, rather than many minutes or hours of work.

For trivial errors, the consequences should be trivial, for serious errors, the consequences may have to be more troublesome. Thus, there should be several levels of errors. All errors should not immediately abort the program or the computer system.

When the execution of a program enters a stage where especially severe errors may occur, extensive error checking is advised before entering that stage.

Example: If people type in commands which would delete much information, then the computer might ask them again if they really are sure that this is what they intend to do.

Humans generally put rather high requirements on the reliability and repeatability of computers. They regard computers as technical systems, just like telephones or typewriters or railway trains or the distribution of electrical power. They expect the same kind of reliability from computers as from other technical systems. People also would like a computer system to give some kind of response even when the system is partially faulty. In the worst case, this response may just be a message about the error and the probable time of correction.

On the other hand, computer systems which help a human in troublesome and problematic situations are often liked by people. people are asked why they like and are satisfied with good computer systems, they often say that the aid in avoiding and coping with errors is important. However, often the code to cope with errors and difficulties will be much larger than the code to handle normal, troublefree operation (See Duncansen 1971 and Hockenberry 1971).

For more information about how to respond softly to errors, see Randell 1975.

4.5 RESPONSIBILITY FOR ERRORS IN DATA

In computerized data bases it is often impossible to find out who is responsible for individual pieces of data. This means that humans who are hurt by erroneous data in computers find it difficult to defend themselves.

A solution to this would be to tag every individual piece of data with an indication of who is responsible for it. If such tagging is built into the data base handling system, it is not difficult to use. If an item of data is created by a computer program, then it should be tagged by both the person creating the input data and the person responsible for the program.

Such tags might require more secondary storage memory, so this is a case where cost and efficiency requirements may come into conflict with reliability requirements. Sometimes, the information about who is responsible is stored in logs on cheaper media like magnetic tape. But this means that a question about who input what will be difficult and very costly to get an answer to.

A problem with such tagging is that it may increase the stress on the people inputting the data. Example: In a key-to-disk operation, the computer monitored every single mispunch made by the operators, and provided error statistics for the manager. This created a very difficult stress situation for the operators.

But this is an example of misuse of computer monitoring of who is responsible. The information about who input what should be there, but it should be used properly.

4.6 FITTING THE VARIATIONS OF REALITY INTO COMPUTERIZED MOULDS

A very common reason for humans to be frustrated with computers is that the computer program does not allow them to input or handle reasonably accurate descriptions of reality.

Everyone who has filled in a form knows that it is sometimes difficult to fit the things you want to say into the mould given by the form. There may not be a space for the thing to say, or every alternative answer may be misleading, or an answer may be misleading if it is not explained further, but there is no space for further explanations.

If the form was produced by a person or institution with certain values, then the form may mislead the answers according to the ideas of its producer.

Example I: A woman named "Alexandria" had too long a name to fit into the mould for "given name" in the system used by a hospital. Her name was shortened to "Alex", which meant that her sex was later mistakenly changed to "Male" which meant that her records disappeared.

Example II: A file may contain information that a certain individual at a certain time did not pay a certain bill properly. But if there is no space to store the fact that the cause of this was a faulty delivery, then the information may give a very misleading impression of this person.

A nice partial solution to this problem would be if the computer allowed the user to affix an explanatory message to each individual piece of data in the data base. Other people might be allowed to add further explanatory tags. It is important that these tags do not disappear during the processing of the data. If certain data are created by computation from other data, then it would be best if any tags on the input data were also noted on the output data. But there is a problem when one output item is computed from many input items, like a mean value. The tags may be too many to list individually, but some kind of processing of them might at least be possible.

Time restrictions on the validity of data could also be added in similar ways, so that data items are not used at times when they are no longer valid.

4.7 ORGANIZATION OF DATA BASES FOR COMMUNICATION

The increasing use of computer networks means that computers are more and more used as a communication tool between remotely located humans. Data base systems are sometimes used as such a communication tool, with many people having access to the same data base. But the increasing understanding that this is a communication task, and not only a data base handling task, has led to development of new ways of organizing such data bases.

Information in computers is more and more often stored through data base handling systems. This is intended to give more general-purpose systems, where more kinds of different information can be stored without difficult reprogramming every time you want to store new kinds of information in the data base.

There are two basic kinds of data base systems, fixed field bases and text-oriented data bases. A common kind of fixed field data bases are relational data base systems. They look at data as logical relations. The disadvantage with many relational data base systems is that they require data of a very fixed structure and thus do not give very much freedom for saying things which do not fit into this structure.

Text-oriented data base systems regard the data basically as text. Sometimes, a record in the data base can contain several text items with different labels, like an "author" field, a number of "keyword" fields and a "message" field. In the text-oriented system, users cannot always get direct answers to factual questions. They can instead get an indication that some text items in the data base might provide them with the information he wants.

There are also systems which try to combine certain ideas from both relational and text-oriented data base systems.

Some such systems are based on the idea of teleconferencing, like the EMISARI system designed by Murray Turoff and described in Renner 1973 and Turoff 1975. There are other systems based on similar ideas.

These systems regard computerized data bases as primarily a medium for exchange of information between humans. Data are structured into a number of "activities" where each activity consists of a number of text items. Examples of "activities" are "conferences", "personal mail", "news items", "policy decisions", "enquiries", "expense accounts", "payments" etc. A number of humans and/or programs have access to the text items in an activity. Some of the systems also allow the handling of tables and other more formalized items.

A piece of text in the system can contain a command which means that parts of other text items are inserted into the text when it is typed out, so that e.g. the text "Weekly report" may print out different material every week even though the basic text of the notice "weekly report" is the same.

In EMISARI, the users store messages which are of interest to others in the organization. They can also send messages personally to just one receiver.

When users log onto the system, they first get any pending messages to themself (if they want them) and is then allowed to store information, or search for information. Search is done by author, by date limits, or by keywords. One can for example search for any news item on insurance within the last week.

Groups of people with interest in a common subject can have computerized discussions going on in the system.

An important property is that any user of the system can store and retrieve information. Every user will thus have immediate benefits from the system. This means that the users like the system much better than systems where they just have to feed in information but seldom get anything they need back from the computer.

Another important property is that every item, even every single figure in a table, can have a tag with an explanatory message or a comment. Other people can add further messages, so that a long series of messages can in theory develop out of a single controversial item in a table.

Computerized teleconferencing systems are especially useful in
large companies or institutions, especially if they are spread over
several geographic locations. The systems make people in the
institution more aware of what is going on in other parts, and make
it easier for them to get necessary information about what is
happening.

The EMISARI system was used at the USA "Office of Emergency
Preparedness" which had to cope with adminstrating a wage-price
freeze across the USA. Administrative people without computer
experience could very easily master the system and use it at short
notice for a new crisis type problem. The system provided a means
for interchange of information between employees all over USA.
Bell Telephone in Canada has also used a similar system very
successfully to exchange information between its employees spread
all over Canada. Hiltz 1976 contains a very interesting discussion
on how such systems may change the communication within
organizations of the future.

Computer teleconferencing systems are more and more widely used to
allow remote groups of people to communicate in a communication
process going on over several weeks or months, without any need for
the involved people to travel or even to use the system at the same
moment of time. Each user can connect to the computer at times
suitable for that person, and will then get new items and input
his/her own items into the data bases.

I personally believe that we will in the future get systems which
combine within one system the facilities of both relational and
text-oriented systems. A text can for example be used to explain a
certain item in a relational data base. Palme 1978 discusses in
more detailed how such a system might be designed.

There is a growing trend of going over from large, centralized
computers to local minicomputers. Apart from the technical reasons
for this trend, an important reason is often that this is a way of
distributing power over the computers. A local group can manage
its own computer and the power of the centralized computer
department decreases.

One most however not forget that an important goal of most computer
applications is the communication of information between humans,
and this communication is easier if the computer system is
organized so that all the communicating humans perceive the system
as one single system, where everyone can reach everyone else. Such
a system will also create a feeling of unity in the organization,
while a policy of "each his own minicomputer" may cause
isolationism and loss of cooperation.

A way of combining the advantages of local minicomputers with those of large united centralized systems is to design systems consisting of local minicomputers connected to central "data base computers". The local minicomputers can provide the fast direct user interaction needed by the users, while the central data base computers provide the communication tool for exchange of information between large groups of people.

Many people believe that these local minicomputers will be single-user systems. I instead believe that they will be shared within groups of 10-20 users. Such a computer could be called a "corridor" computer, since it serves the people working in one office corridor. Note that many such local "corridor" computers will in the future be equivalent in power to rather large time-shared computers of today.

5. HUMAN-MACHINE INTERACTIVE TECHNIQUES

Chapter 4 showed how human needs affect the design of computer systems. Chapter 5 will discuss various human-machine interactive techniques to realize these design principles.

5.1 COMPUTER GUIDED INTERACTION

Perhaps the most common kind of interaction is that which is guided by some form of questions from the computer.

        (1)
Example:
DO YOU WANT TO STOP NOW? no

The question from the computer can also be some kind of text describing what kind of input is expected.

Example:
INPUT THE TEMPERATURE,
 FOLLOWED BY "F" FOR FAHRENHEIT OR "C" FOR CELSIUS:
23 c

A common kind of question is one in which the user is given a list of alternatives to choose between. Often the user only has to answer with the number or the first letter of the chosen alternative:

----
1) In the examples I will use upper case for what the computer writes, lower case for what the human answers.

Example:
```
  DO YOU WANT TO
  RETRIEVE INFORMATION FROM:
1 PERSONNEL FILE
2 ARTICLE FILE
3 NEWS FILE
4 POLICY DECISION FILE
  OR
5 UPDATE A FILE, OR
6 STOP.
```

This kind of selection between given alternatives is often called a "menu" conversation.

The advantage with computer guided interaction is that the language can be natural or almost natural human language, thus easy to understand for a human, and that the inputs from the human to the computer are still easy to interpret with a simple computer program.

The main disadvantage is that people have rather limited freedom in how to perform their task, since they must follow the order of questions determined by the computer program.

In many cases, this restriction is a serious drawback, causing much dissatisfaction among humans using the program, but careful programming can give the user more freedom within the framework of computer guided interaction.

The methods of increasing the power of the user within the framework of computer guided interaction are:

> To design the sequence of questions carefully so that the users have the choices they need to do things in different ways at different times.

> To include escape facilities, e.g. a special key to push to leave the normal sequence and go into a mode where commonly needed deviations from the normal sequence are available (e.g. to return to a previous question in the sequence).

One problem with the computer guided interaction is that the questions from the computer have to be rather verbose to be understandable by a user who has little experience with this program. But an experienced user may be thoroughly bored by the verbose explanations.

One solution to this is to have several modes of interaction, with different verbosity, which the user can choose between.

Another solution (often combined with the previous one) is the HELP facility described in the next section.

5.2 PUTTING THE MANUAL INTO THE PROGRAM

Sometimes, when people use a program, they need further explanations about what they can do with the computer at that point in the execution of the program. For this purpose, many programs are equipped with a so-called "HELP" facility.

The idea of the HELP facility is to have a special escape key or escape command, often "?", which allows a user at any time to get a more complete explanation of what to input. A HELP facility is very useful also in conjunction with other modes of interaction than the computer-guided.

The HELP facility can also choose between different explanations depending on the experience of the user.

If the available HELP information is larger than fits into the display screen, then it can be divided into screen-size chunks, and the users can be given a menu to choose what kind of help they want.

The HELP facility should be designed together with the explanatory messages given when the computer does not understand what the user writes to it, and both are acceptable only when the program has been tested on many people, and the questions asked and comments given by these people have been collected in a file and processed by the system designers.

A carefully planned HELP facility, combined with good validity-testing and good explanatory messages for input not acceptable to the program, can mean that a program is usable with almost no prior instruction and that an inexperienced user always gets the help he/she needs, but still that the experienced user is not burdened with explanations which he/she does not need.

Since the computer will give the user the explations needed, the user does not have to consult a program manual as often. One can therefore regard this as a method of putting the manual into the program itself. (See Oskarsson 1975.)

Oskarsson says that it is important that an inexperienced user does not get into an input loop. Such a loop can happen if what the user inputs is swallowed by the computer without explanations about what is happening, or when all input is rejected with insufficient explanations about why.

Example I: The computer waits for a special final character, and swallows all input until this final character comes. Even the help-requiring "?" command may be swallowed. If the user does not know that the computer waits for this special final character, he/she cannot get out of the loop.

Example II: A user tries many possible commands, but they are all rejected by the computer without sufficient explanation. An ideal system should in such a situation automatically turn to simpler and more complete explanations.

Ohlin 1975 describes a program package designed to simplify the writing of a computer guided interaction with help facility and a simple restoration facility.

5.3 FORM FILLING

With form filling, which is most common on display terminals, users are presented with "forms" with blank fields on the screen of the terminal, and they are asked to fill in the fields.

Example:

```
SUBJECT = ORDER
ITEM TYPE        = pen
NUMBER  = 200
LAST DELIVERY    = 1975-06-16
CUSTOMER NAME    = johnson & co
CUSTOMER ADDRESS         = big street 5, smalltown

SPECIAL NOTES:
:               :
:               :
:               :

NEXT FORM WANTED        : order
```

Form filling is really only a special case of computer guided interaction, but the fact that many questions are presented to the users at the same time gives them a better overview of the situation. They often also have certain freedom to move within a form.

Certain computer systems are designed in such a way that the computer processing of even the simplest input from the user is delayed several seconds. With such systems, form filling is often used. In such a case, the filling in of the form is handled entirely at the terminal, so that an interaction with the slow computer only occurs when a form is full.

However, this means that the power of the computer is only available to the user when the form is fully filled in. Error checking of the input data is for example not performed immediately, and special functions like escape and help functions are only available when the form is ready or in some systems by temporarily leaving the form. A better way would be to design the computer to be able to respond immediately to simple inputs from the user.

Users tend to be frustrated with computers which take a long time to do simple things, but they accept long delays for actions which they understand are complex to do. People are especially frustrated with computers whose response time varies in an unpredictable way.

Another disadvantage with form-filling without computer contact except at the end of a form is that other ways in which the computer can aid a user will be more difficult, like for example having the computer automatically fill in parts of the answers, depending on what was input previously.

A problem with form filling is that forms are often designed in such a way that the space for data is sometimes insufficient. Also, the user is often not provided with enough possibilities of inserting explanations and comments in cases where there is no straightforward answer to a certain subquestion in the form.

5.4 COMMAND-DRIVEN INTERACTION

Another very common interaction mode is that in which the computer is driven by commands from the user.

Examples:

set speed to 300 m/s

display order summary

search newsfile for insurance and (europe or america)

display number of sales employees for each department

A typical command begins with the name of the command. After that
follows further information on how the command is to be performed.
This further information can be binary choices, parameter values or
formulas in some kind of formula notation.

Often, the amount of possible information is very large. Since it
is difficult for a human to formulate complex commands, default
values are assumed for certain information if that information is
not given by the user.

In natural human language, defaults play a very important part. We
do not say "Every human being on board the ship was seasick on the
first of August 1975", we just say "Everyone was sick", and this
statement, taken in context, transfers the same message to the
listener.

However, the disambiguation of defaults requires a mental process
which is sometimes difficult to put into a computer.

If defaulted information is misunderstood by the computer, then
errors may occur. Because of the limited facilities for
disambiguation in most computer programs, they can accept less
defaults than humans can in natural language conversations.

The defaults will often vary from user to user and from time to
time. A system which allows the user to influence the process of
defaulting may therefore be more satisfactory to the users than a
static defaulting algorithm.

A good command interpreter should, if the user omits certain
compulsory information, ask for that in a series of questions after
the command.

The same information to the computer could thus be given within the
same system in one of the three following ways:

search newsfile for insurance after 1975-06-01

search newsfile after 1975-06-01
FOR WHAT? insurance

search
WHICH FILE? newsfile
FOR WHAT? insurance
ANY TIME RESTRICTION? after 1975-06-01

The command-driven interaction can give the users more power, since they can choose between a number of commands and they can themself choose the order in which the commands are given to the computer.

However, the command-driven interaction requires that the users are very familiar with those commands they need to use, and is thus best for experienced users.

With command driven interaction, it is much easier to provide the users with facilities for going back or changing their mind. They simply use the same command again or a special resetting command to change previously given data.

The program should be designed as much as possible so that the different commands can be given in random order by the user. One should, as much as possible, avoid letting the program go through several "stages" with different sets of commands at each stage, except where the user is free to move back and forward between the stages.

5.5 THE PROGRAMMABLE INTERFACE

A command-driven interface give users a selection of commands to perform the tasks at the computer. But very often users want more powerful commands because of their special needs.

Example I: Users very often need to give the same series of commands in succession, and they do not want to have to repeat them all every time.

Example II: A user wants default values different from the usual ones for parameters to a certain system command.

Example III: A user wants special error checks added to the interpretation of certain of his/her commands, e.g. checks that he/she did not omit certain information which normally is defaulted, or checks on the allowed values of certain command parameters.

Example IV: A user wants the computer to remember certain previously entered data, and use them automatically again for part of a new command.

Example V: A user wants an extra command to be given automatically to the computer every tenth time he/she gives another command.

It should be possible to put as much as possible of such special user's requirements be able to be put into the computer without any special programming.

If a user wants to add new types of data to the data base, then this should for example not require any explicit programming. The ideal system would just accept the new data and establish the necessary structures.

If a user wants to get data from the data base reported in a new way, then this should not require any programming in the ordinary sense. A nice partial solution to this is used in the EMISARI system (See Renner 1973). A document in that system can contain within it special commands to include, at that point in the document, information taken from other documents.

Sometimes, however, programming is necessary to satisfy special user needs. Since this programming is very dependent on invidual user's requirements, and sometimes varies from day to day, the person doing the programming should be easily available to the user, sometimes maybe be the user himself.

It is n o t acceptable to input the user requirements to a central systems group which may take a long time before they can honor the request.

The additional programming should be simple to make for someone who is not an expert on the inner workings of the system, and the additional programming should not endanger the safety of the system.

The solution to this may be to include in the command language of the computer system a special programming language for writing such simple additional user commands.

This language should have available certain simple programming tools plus all commands which the user is allowed to make directly.

Since programs in this language can do nothing except make ordinary user commands, they will not endanger the safety of the system in the way which ordinary programming in the system does.

The additional language should be recursive, so that programs written in it can use commands previously defined in the same language.

When the users themselves, or people close to them, have evolved very useful new commands in such a language, the systems people should add these commands to the central part of the system. In this way the user language can serve as a communication link between users and systems people.

Hans Karlgren has pointed out that this is analogous to what happens in ordinary natural language. One person invents a new construct and begins to use it. If other people find it useful, the new construct may be adopted by more people, and some such new constructs become a permanent new part of the language.

Such a user language will very much increase the power of the users over the system. But it requires that one person close to each user group is trained in writing programs in the user language.

Experience with computer systems has shown that so-called "local experts" play an important role. Local experts are local people, close to the users, who because of interest and ability have learned more than other users about the system. The programmable interface is a tool to help these local experts, so that they can better help themselves and other people who are using their abilities.

Because the user language increases the power of the users, it will better satisfy their human needs.

Inexperienced users can use the basic commands and user language commands written by someone else for them, and more experienced users can learn to use the user language himself. Thus, a user language allows the users to expand their own skills and to use their new skills to adjust the environment to their own needs.

These kinds of user languages are common in applications, where users work with sets of data, on which they need to perform various operations. They may want to fit their data to a certain shape, or experiment with difficult variations of the data etc. Examples:

1) A writer wants to test variations of a text.

2) A designer wants to test various designs.

3) A statistician wants to test various treatments of statistical data.

4) A budget maker wants to compare variants of a budget.

5) A planner wants to test different variants of a plan.

For this kind of application data is kept in a workspace. Single commands, or series of commands in small routines, are executed by the user at the terminal. The commands operate on the data. This is very different from the activity of a programmer who wants to develop large program products. The routines are instead often written for once-only use, and a large task is divided into several small routines prepared one-at-a-time by the user.

This way of working at a terminal has become very popular, because the user has close control all the way of what is happening. This is an important reason for the popularity of the well-known programming systems APL, LISP and TECO.

Programmable user interfaces are discussed further in Palme 1975.

5.6 SAVE-RESTORE FACILITY

If a human has been sitting for a long time in front of a computer terminal, then that human will naturally not be happy if he/she has to re-do everything he/she has been doing during the terminal session.

However, re-doing everything may be necessary if he/she has made an error previously during the session, if the only way out of the error is to restart from the beginning and make the computer forget everything that has been input.

Two ways of solving this problem are the save-restore facility and the back-up conversation file.

With the save-restore facility, information about the status of the computer is saved at regular intervals, either automatically by the program or by commands from the user.

The user is then allowed to back-up the computer to the status at any of the previous check-points.

With the back-up conversation file, all conversation between the human and the computer is saved in a special back-up file.

Users can then, if they so want, restart the program but with input from the back-up file instead of from the users directly. By using only part of the back-up file, or by editing the back-up file before restart, they can correct the error without having to repeat the whole conversation.

Fully covering save-restore systems are very difficult or impossible to make, especially if several people have been using the computer system simultaneously and only one of them wants to recover. But even imperfect systems can be a great help.

If the computer or program is not fully fool-proof, but has a tendency to go down, then the programs have to be designed in such a way that as little as possible is lost. If data are stored in secondary storage, and if primary storage is lost when the system goes down, then the programs can be designed in such a way that all information is moved into secondary storage and the secondary storage files are closed before every interaction with the user at the terminal. Then, only one interaction will be lost at the system failure.

5.7 NATURAL LANGUAGE INTERACTION

Some advantages of natural human languages are:

> No special training in a specialized command language is necessary.

> The range of what can be said in the language is very large.

However, there are also difficulties with natural human language:

> Compared with well designed artificial languages, natural languages require longer texts to say the same thing. This is important if a user has to say almost the same thing hundreds of times a day to the computer.

> Natural language statements are often vague or ambiguous. This is often an advantage in talking with humans, but may be a disadvantage with computers because of the risk of misunderstandings.

> Programming a computer to understand natural language is a very difficult task.

Natural language is not at all always a superior language for human-computer interaction. In situations where the users have much training in the use of the computer, a more compact language can be better for them.

However, specialized languages, difficult to use, will restrict access to the computers to those who have this special training, and to those who have access to assistants with the special training. People will be divided into classes, those who have access to the computer and those who have not. And this kind of class division can be dangerous.

The class division furthers centralization of power, since access
to information is so central to power. People who are affected by
the computer, but who are denied access to it, may often not be
happy with it.

Sometimes one gets the impression that computer systems are
intentionally written so that their language is difficult to
interpret, just because the designers want to restrict
understanding to a small group of people.

A well designed computer-guided interaction can easily use natural
or almost natural language, since the messages from the computer
are in natural language, and since the user answers are short words
which are easy to make the computer interpret.

A smooth, natural-language-like user interface to a program can
mislead the human into believing that the program is more
intelligent than it is. Many people believe computers to be more
clever than they are, and it is important to avoid enforcing this
untrue belief.

Certain computer programs take input in an artificial language
which is carefully chosen so that programs written in it look like
natural language. Examples of such languages are Cobol and
Simscript II. The advantage is that it is easier for non-experts
to read such texts. However, it is not necessarily easier for
non-experts to produce the texts, since they may easily be mislead
into believing that the computer actually accepts natural language,
and not just a restricted artificial language which looks like
natural language.

With command-driven interaction, natural language becomes more
difficult to use. No one has yet succeeded in writing a computer
program which can understand natural language nearly as well as a
human.

It has been proved that such a program must have not only
linguistic capabilities but also knowledge about the world and
reasoning capabilities. Only by using such capabilities can a
computer correctly interpret even the simple word "they" in the
following texts:

The soldiers shot at the women. They fell down.

The soldiers shot at the women. They used machine guns.

> The city councillors stopped the demonstrators, because they feared violence.
>
> The city councillors stopped the demonstrators, because they were going to burn an american flag.

Programs to understand natural human languages have thus been much more successful if they are only designed to accept phrases about a restricted subject area, like a time table, or a street plan of a city.

Here is an excerpt of a conversation with such a program:

> where is the nearest restaurant?
>
> THE DISTANCE TO BALDAKINEN AT DRAGARBRUNNSGATAN BETWEEN S:T-PERSGATAN AND VAKSALAGATAN IS ONLY 500 METERS.
>
> how can you go to the galejan with a car?
>
> FOLLOW KUNGSGATAN IN THE NORTH-WEST DIRECTION. TURN TO THE LEFT AT S:T-OLOFSGATAN.
> etc.

The way such programs are usually written nowadays is that they recognize certain key words in the sentence, and that they have some kind of semantic data base to which they try to relate the concepts in the given sentence.

In a conversation between humans, each speaker adjusts his/her language to the others abilities, and questions are asked when the listener does not understand.

The same is to some extent possible in a conversational program, where the human users can adjust themselves to the rather limited capabilities of the natural language understanding program, and where the program can ask questions when it does not understand.

However, there are not many computer programs which can adjust their language to the capabilities of the human except in rather simple cases. But even such rather simple adjustment can be a large improvement compared to no such ability at all.

A way of avoiding misunderstandings is to let the computer rephrase what it was told in other words. The human will then easily see if the computer has misunderstood something.

Natural language is therefore much easier to use in a conversational environment than in an application where the computer is expected to read pages of natural language text.

For further information about natural language understanding, see Palme 1973 which also contains a bibliography of relevant material.

In summary, even if a system does not use full natural language, a human is greatly aided if the language is reasonably close to natural language. Certain computer system designers seem to love numerical codes for things easier said with normal words, even though a computer can as easily be programmed to read words as numbers. However, there may be larger risks for misunderstandings with a computer understanding a limited natural language than with a computer understanding a more strict artificial language, especially because the human may be led to believe that the computer understands more than it does, and because the computer program may have to make uncertain guesses.

6. CONCLUSION

This paper has showed that many serious problems for the humans involved often occur when computer systems are introduced. An understanding of these problems and their causes when designing and using the systems is important. There is also a growing knowledge of techniques which can be used to alleviate the problems. However, the reader is warned not to believe that all the problems are easily avoided just by using some of the techniques discussed in the paper.

7. BIBLIOGRAPHY

Chapanis, Alphonse 1975: Interactive human communication. Scientific
            American, Vol. 232, No. 3, March-April 1975, pp
            36-42.

Duncansen, L. A. et al 1971: Interfaces with the Process Control
            Computer. In "Interfaces with the Process Control
            Computer", published by the Instrument Society of
            America.

Gordon, Thomas 1970: P. E. T. - Parent Effectiveness Training.
            Wyden, New York 1970.

Gordon, Thomas 1974: T. E. T. - Teacher Effectiveness Training.
            Wyden, New York 1974.

Grip, Arne 1974: ADB-system och kommunikation.
            Hermods-Studentlitteratur, S-221 01 Lund 1, Sweden,
            1974.

Hiltz, Starr Roxanne et al 1976: Potential Impacts of Computer
            Conferencing Upon Managerial and Organizational Styles.
            (New Jersey Institute of Technology research report.)

Harris, Thomas A. 1969: I´m OK - You´re OK. Harper & Row, New York
            1969.

Hoare, C. A. R., 1975: Software design: a Parable. In Software
            World, vol. 5, Numbers 9 & 10.

Hockenberry, Jack et al 1971: The Human Environment Misfit Factor
            Concept. In "Interfaces with the Process Control
            Computer", published by the Instrument Society of
            America.

Kent, Jan 1975: Datamaskinassistert undervisning for ikke snakkende
            barn. Presentation at NordDATA-75.

Marguiles, Fred 1976: Not for the people, but with the people. Data
            no. 10, 1976 pp 17-19.

Ohlin, Mats 1975: SAFEIO - system for safe and fast conversational
            SIMULA programming. FOA 142, July 1975.

Oskarsson, Östen 1975: About design of conversation interfaces for
            non-expert users. Datalogilaboratoriet, Sturegatan 1,
            S-752 23 Uppsala, Sweden, January 1975.

Palme, Jacob 1973: The SQAP data base for natural language
          information. FOA P Report C8376.

Palme, Jacob 1974: The General Public Democratic Information System.
          Data, Copenhagen no. 3, 1974 pp 22-24.

Palme, Jacob 1975: REAL TIME - easing the user task. In Software
          World, Vol. 5, No. 8, pp 9-11. (Also published as FOA
          HE 1 report C10001, July 1974, under the title "A
          method of increasing user influence on computer
          systems".)

Palme, Jacob 1977A: A Human Computer Interface Encouraging User
          Growth, FOA 1 Report C 10073, September 1977.

Palme, Jacob 1977B: Conversational Computer Terminals. FOA 1 Report
          C 10074, December 1977.

Palme, Jacob 1978: Teleconference-based Management Information
          Systems. FOA 1 Report, October 1978.

Randell, B. 1975: System Structure for Software Fault Tolerance. In
          proceedings of the 1975 International Conference on
          Reliable Software, pp 437-449.

Renner, Rod L 1973: EMISARI - A Management Information System
          Designed to Aid and Involve People. In Proceedings at
          the Fourth International Symposium on Computers and
          Information Science (COINS-72), Miami Beach, Florida,
          December 1972, also available from the Office of
          Emergency Preparedness, White House, Washington D.C.

Shackel, Brian 1969: Man-computer interaction - the contribution of
          the human sciences. Ergonomics, 12:4 (July 1969) pp.
          485-499.

Seligman, Martin E. P. 1975: Helplessness. On Depression,
          Development & Death. W.H. Freeman, San Francisco,
          1975.

Turoff, Murray 1975: The Future of Computer Conferencing. The
          Futurist, Vol. IX, NO. 4, August 1975, pp 182-195.

THE EMPIRICAL STUDY OF COMPUTER LANGUAGE

"So I said in the most natural way _if_ x=0 _then_ _begin_ ...."

M.E. Sime

MRC Social and Applied Psychology Unit,
Department of Psychology, The University, Sheffield.

INTRODUCTION - THE NEED FOR COGNITIVE ERGONOMICS

The need for good physical design in accordance with the anatomical characteristics of the human body is obvious, and the methodological route to achieving such design is well trodden. Less easy to negotiate has been the route to designing controll-able control systems. Methodology has emerged however for the evaluation of instrumentation and control characteristics in accordance with man's perceptual/motor characteristics. Many of these characteristics, discrimination thresholds, movement ranges, response latencies, perception/motor output compatibilities etc. have been well mapped.

In recent years however the digital computer has changed things. Dealing with computers instead of motor-cars is like playing chess instead of tennis. Although the computer presents many problems which fall naturally within the scope of traditional ergonomics, it also represents a point of departure. The emphasis changes from the perceptual/motor to the conceptual/perceptual; from moving a lever to cancel an error signal to offering an algorithm to meet a contingency. I believe this conceptual interaction to be the most exciting challenge now to be met by the discipline of ergonomics. The need is to develop an applied science of 'cognitive ergonomics' closely integrated with the whole field of cognitive psychology.

That ergonomic principles should be ignored in the design of a motor car or an aircraft would nowadays be considered a culpable omission. But this was not always so and there was a time when heavy reliance was placed on the man in the system to adapt to

what he was given.   The high cost of such a procedure in human
terms of safety, stress, fatigue and general efficiency was of
course the forcing agent for the development of ergonomic principles.
In the world of computers the need for good cognitive ergonomic
design is once more obscured by man's adaptability.   The case is
even worse here, for man can bend his mind in more directions than
he can bend his arm, and can adjust his cognitive behaviour to cope
with the most perverse of systems.   Nor is the cost of asking him
to do so apparent, as we seldom know the savings which would be
achieved by making such systems less perverse.

But what is perverse and what is congenial in cognitive systems?
It is tempting for the designer, if unversed in ergonomics or
behavioural science, to think the answers will be obvious, just a
matter of self-knowledge, intuition, or asking the opinions of
operators who have used similar systems.   The limitations of such
an approach are however legion.   The operator, even the very expert
operator, has a learning history that could have been different and
has therefore no yardstick to compare his current performance with
his potential performance.   Nor is the operator versed in two
systems a reliable witness to their relative efficiency, for a
primacy effect, or the reverse, can well prove dominant.   The
praises of various computer languages are often sung differently
depending on the learning history of the singer.   The reliability
of intuition, even with the very expert, is also made suspect by
the frequency of controversy between experts.   Some of our own
research which I will be describing arose out of such well-published
controversy on the matter of GOTO statements.

SOME LANGUAGE PROBLEMS

Despite the astonishing developments in computing science and
practice over the last two decades, it is probable that computers
are in their infancy.   In the general areas of data processing,
communication and automation there have been marked successes;
let the space program be witness.   In other areas where expectations
have been high there has been comparative disappointment.   Looking
back twelve years we find the following prediction from Sir Leon
Bagrit's Reith Lectures (Bagrit, 1966, p.15):

"Without automation, the manager is compelled to spend his
    time making a series of decisions on the basis of very
    limited information and a great deal of 'hunch' or
    experience.   The computer-aided manager is in a completely
    different position.   Before he gets it, and even before he
    needs it, the information is processed or digested, all
    action which can be decided by the machine already taken,
    giving him the essential facts not as a rag-bag, but in a
    clear-cut form, so that he may sometimes be faced with two

or three basic choices, but he knows what the choices are
and he is aware of the consequences of his choice in advance,
because the computer allows him to test them.   Before he
makes his final decision he is very likely to ask the
computer a question: 'If I decide to do this instead of that,
what will the consequences be?'   And he may then find, from
the answer the computer gives him, that he has to refer the
problem to his superior for a decision of a final nature.
One welcome result would be that committee meetings and
conferences could be made much briefer, and much more
business-like and in many instances abolished altogether".

Regrettably few managers today see the computer as providing
the congenial scenario outlined by Sir Leon.   But surely his
expectations were reasonable;   and haven't many of them largely
been met in functional terms?   Information is often much richer
and better digested with computer systems.   Predictions   are
possible with simulation techniques and are used for many purposes,
including the evaluation of putative actions.   It is the expected
fluency of interaction, the symbiotic relationship, the congenial
manager-to-computer conversation, without the screen of expert
computer staff between manager and machine, that is chiefly missing.

Was then the popular image of man-machine interaction at fault?
Is our popular image of computer conversation unduly anthropomorphic,
as the ancient image of aircraft with flapping wings was unduly
ornithomorphic?   Can the functional requirements of man-computer
interaction (M.C.I.) be better met by something less like human
conversation?   Certainly existing computer language is quite unlike
natural language in all but superficial respects.   Should it be
like natural language?   Is it a shortcoming that it is not?   I
ask these questions not to attempt to answer them, but to point out
that they are live questions.   Wrong answers could result in our
research and development taking a wrong direction.

IS NATURAL ENGLISH NEEDED FOR M.C.I.?

First let us take a look at the popular image of M.C.I. from
Science Fiction.   In Arthur C. Clarke's (1968) novel '2001 - A
Space Odyssey' - Hal the congenial sounding, if later troublesome,
computer says:

"Sorry to interrupt the festivities," ..., "but we have a problem."
"What is it?" Bowman and Poole asked simultaneously.
"I am having difficulty in maintaining contact with Earth.   The
   trouble is in the AE 35 unit.   My fault prediction centre
   reports that it may fail within seventy-two hours."
"We'll take care of it." Bowman replied.

and later on Bowman reports that same fact to Earth:

"Mission control, this is X-Ray-Delta-One.   At two-zero-four-
five, on-board fault prediction centre in our nine-triple-zero
computer showed Alpha Echo three five unit as possible failure
within seventy-two hours.   Request you check telemetry monitoring and suggest you review unit in your ship system simulator.
Also confirm your approval our plan to go EVA and replace Alpha
Echo three five unit prior to failure.   Mission control, this
is X-Ray-Delta-One, two-one-zero-three transmission concluded."

Notice how Hal is made to use free natural language, whilst Bowman
in a man-to-man communication uses 'technish' jargon.   It is only
fiction, but the point is reflected that for specialised purposes,
eg. transmission over a potentially noisy channel, a formalised
natural language is in fact often adopted.   Formalised language
allows a better comparison with the receiver's expectations than
would be achieved with free language.   To carry the point further;
I.D. Hill (1972) has argued that rather than attempt to make computers
handle natural English, there are many purposes in man-man communication for which we would be better employed teaching people to
handle a formalised computer-like language.   In the following quote
Hill is referring to Jean Sammet's book Programming Languages:

"Looking to the future, in Miss Sammet's Utopia we shall be
able to talk to computers in English just as we do to people.
In my own Utopia however, we shall be able to write instructions
for people in programming languages, just as we do for computers."

His point is of course on of ambiguity reduction.   I commend his
paper to the reader, both for the insight he shows and for his
extremely amusing treatment of the topic.

Hill is not just arguing that to develop computer systems
which communicate in ordinary English is difficult or impossible,
but that for many purposes it is undesirable.   His argument is that
ordinary language is a most unsatisfactory medium for communicating
with precision.

A major type of communication that we address to present day
computers is the specification of a procedure, or 'algorithm', that
we want the computer to follow.   Hill shows that English is not
very good for this purpose.   One problem is that instructions in
English often presume a lot of common-sense and knowledge, although
they may look quite innocent.   Compare the statement "Crash helmets
must be worn" applying to motor-cyclists, with the statement "Dogs
must be carried", seen on the underground; what is the penalty for
not having a dog?   How do you parse "I don't know nothing", or
"I don't suppose you don't know nobody who hasn't got no pigs they
don't want to sell, do you?"   Not the Queen's English, but such

language is used. Even with conventional grammar and avoiding the
abuse of negatives, Hill shows that there are a host of problems of
ambiguity arising from the way that words like 'if', 'again',
'repeat' etc. function in ordinary language. These and many other
difficulties lead him to argue that ordinary language is unsuitable
not only for computers but for many other applications where
ambiguity cannot be tolerated. He draws examples from errors of
parliamentary draftsmen who certainly aim to be, and are in general
very expert at being precise but are often foiled by the difficulties imposed by the language they use. Here is another of his
compelling examples!

> "For the purpose of the pool betting duty, any payment which
> entitles a person to make a bet by way of pool betting shall
> if he makes the bet, be treated as stake money on the bet, and
> this subsection shall apply to any payment entitling a person
> to take part in a transaction which is, on his part, only not
> a bet made by way of pool betting by reason of his not in fact
> making any stake as if the transaction were such a bet, and
> the transaction shall accordingly be treated as a bet for the
> purpose of the pool betting duty."

Lord Brabazon is said to have remarked "Whoever drafted that must
have had something in his mind - God knows what." English seems
to be spectacularly unsuitable for that kind of precision.

But let us suppose that these objections have been met, that
the computer knows what it needs to know and that all terms are well-
defined. Now we come to strictly psychological questions about
the design of the language. The importance of good language
design is apparent in the history of mathematics, which is largely
the emergence of better designs for stating certain types of
procedures. Contemporary algorithmic language such as school
algebra are so well designed that we tend to take them for granted.
But consider the following comparison between plain English and an
algebraic language. A leading scholar of his day gives an algorithm
for finding the area of a triangle:

> For example: a triangle with unequal sides and acute angles,
> 15 from one side, 14 from the other side and 13 from the third
> side. Whoever wants to measure, let him seize the three of
> them together, they amount to 42: let him take the half of it
> and see how much greater it is than the first side, and let
> him multiply the half upon the differences, this is 21 into 6,
> which gives 126, and put it on the side; let him again for
> the second time take the half and see how much greater it is
> than the second side, and let him multiply the difference,
> which is 7, into the first 126, which amount to 882, and put
> it on the side; let him again, for the third time take the
> half, and see how much greater it is than the third side,

and let him multiply the difference, which is 8, into the last 882, and this amounts to 7056 and its root is 84, and this is the measure of the area.

R. Nehemiah, c. 150 AD; from Midonick, 1968.

Today a school boy would write

$$A = \left[s(s-a)(s-b)(s-c) \right]^{\frac{1}{2}}$$

where s = $\frac{1}{2}$(a+b+c) and a, b, c, are the sides of the triangle.

Why is school algebra so much better? One reason is that the formula can easily be manipulated. Furthermore, with a little training it is very easy to understand. As a medium of communication it is far better, the notation of school algebra being a highly evolved compromise between conciseness and simplicity.

Hoare (1973, p.16) has cited the notation of elementary algebra as a prime example of a notation that is good for its purpose. He states some principles of 'structuring' which are all achieved by the notation:

"transparency of meaning and purpose, independence of part, recursive application, narrow interfaces and manifestness of structure".

So far, then, we have advanced the argument that even when it is technically possible to make computers understand English, people may still prefer to use some other style of communication for many purposes. This is particularly so for the precise specification of procedures, rather than for, say, asking questions of fact, for which English may be more suitable. At present specifications of procedures are a major type of communication, and until that situation changes there seem to be very strong reasons for attempting to improve the design of existing programming languages, hoping that ultimately they will become as well-fitted to their task as is school algebra.

HOW 'NATURAL' CAN A PROGRAMMING LANGUAGE BE?

Many well-known programming languages, such as Fortran and Algol, are in fact founded on algebraic notation. Algebra on its own however is not sufficient, since one must tell the computer what to do with the results, what to do if the data are unsuitable, how many times to perform the calculation, and so on. As algebra does not provide for statements of this kind various linguistic devices have been introduced into programming languages to cope with the extra requirements. If today's computers are not as congenial as they might be, one reason is undoubtedly that these linguistic devices are not as easily learned and as natural to use as we would wish. Presumably the ideal programming language would combine the precision, conciseness and freedom from ambiguity of algebraic notation, with the effortless congeniality of man's everyday speech. For the present, however, there is much to be done in trying to make today's programming languages more natural to use than they are, leaving the ideal for another day.

The problem is knowing what is natural. Perhaps 'natural' here means something like 'compatible' does in the case of control-display relationships. As the hand might move more naturally in one direction than another in response to the properties of a given stimulus, so perhaps problem situations can be characterised where the mind naturally takes one turn rather than another. Or if that is too fanciful perhaps we can characterise the qualities a situation must have to possess various desirable properties such as being easily understood, not subject to confusion and forgetting, not prone to this or that type of error, easily manipulated and so on.

To put the matter in more concrete terms consider the problem of choosing between the four programming languages shown in Example 1. One of the cognitive ergonomist's problems is to discover a methodology by which he may evaluate them in terms of their naturalness.

All of the programs in Example 1 do the same thing; they read a set of numbers, find their arithmetic mean, and print this out. Were we giving these instructions to a man we would say something like:

'Add together the numbers in that list and divide your answer by the number of numbers that you added together. Write down the answer.'

The first program shown is part of a COBOL program to do this. The missing part, which is for this program about the same length as the procedure division shown, is mainly concerned with defining the structure of the data.

As can be seen, the COBOL program is verbose in comparison with the others. This is partly because COBOL is intended to be readable by non-programmers, or at any rate by people with a minimum of training in programming. For this purpose an English-like syntax is adopted and few abbreviations are used. Another reason for this verbosity is that COBOL is a language in which every action to be taken must be explicitly specified, particularly for input and output.

222

COBOL

```
PROCEDURE DIVISION.
        OPEN INPUT CARDS-IN.
        OPEN OUTPUT PRINT-OUT.
        READ CARDS-IN AT END GO TO NO-INPUT.
        IF ITEM-COUNT NOT NUMERIC OR CONTROL-FILL NOT EQUAL SPACES
                THEN GO TO BAD-CONTROL.
        MOVE ITEM-COUNT TO ITEMS.
        PERFORM READ-IN UNTIL J EQUALS ITEMS.
        MOVE SPACES TO PL.
        COMPUTE AVERAGE ROUNDED = TOTAL / ITEMS.
        WRITE PL.
        CLOSE CARDS-IN PRINT-OUT.
        STOP RUN.
READ-IN.
        READ CARDS-IN AT END GO TO UNEXPECTED-END.
        PERFORM ACCUMULATE VARYING I FROM 1 BY 1
                UNTIL I GREATER 20 OR J = ITEMS.
ACCUMULATE.
        IF NUMBER (I) NOT NUMERIC THEN GO TO BAD-DATA.
        ADD NUMBER (I) TO TOTAL.
        ADD 1 TO J.
NO-INPUT.
        STOP '**** ERROR **** NO CARD INPUT'
UNEXPECTED-END.
        COMPUTE TEMP = 1 + (19+ITEMS) / 20.
        DISPLAY '**** ERROR **** EXPECTING ' TEMP ' CARDS INPUT.'
        STOP 'PLEASE CHECK CONTROL CARD AND NUMBER OF ITEMS.'
BAD-CONTROL.
        STOP '**** ERROR **** INVALID CONTROL CARD.'
BAD-DATA.
        DISPLAY '**** ERROR **** NON-NUMERIC DATA ITEM NUMBER ' J '.'
        STOP 'PLEASE CORRECT AND RE-INPUT'.
```

FORTRAN

```
        DIMENSION X(1000)
        READ(2,6) N,(X(I)I=1,N)
6       FORMAT(I5,(E15.5))
        S=0.0
        DO 4 J=1,N
4       S=S+X(J)
        AVG=S/N
        WRITE(3,5) AVG
5       FORMAT (E15.2)
        END
```

PL/I

```
AVERAGE:PROC OPTIONS (MAIN);
        DCL ARRAY(N) DEC FLOAT (6) CTL;
        GET LIST(N);
        ALLOCATE N;
        GET LIST(ARRAY);
        PUT LIST ((SUM(ARRAY)) / N);
        END;
```

APL

```
+/X     X
```

EXAMPLE 1. Programs from a paper presented to the Institute of
            Civil Engineers by D.N. Saunders of Sharp Associates Ltd.

The PL/1 and Fortran programs are each about the same size. Fortran makes use of default attributes for variables, and the structure of the data is specified in part by FORMAT statements, so that a data division is unnecessary. The input and output statements have been compressed to one line specifying the action to be taken (read or write) and one line specifying the format of the data, though this latter does not look very natural. Four lines are used for the computation, which again must be specified as a series of steps, but which uses a more concise representation than the COBOL program.

The PL/1 program makes use of abbreviations (PROC for PROCEDURE, DCL for DECLARE, etc.) and provides higher level functions for input and output. Apart from the two lines specifying the structure of the data, this program is possibly the most understandable of the four by the non-expert. The computation is done at a higher level than in the previous programs, using the function SUM.

The last program is in APL. Here conciseness has been taken to the limit by providing very general input and output formatting and by using a very rich set of operators which means that many more of the commonly used computations may be expressed easily. However, this last program is not easily understandable to the non-expert, though it is claimed that APL is easily learned and reasonably natural to use.

WHAT CONTRIBUTION CAN THE HUMAN SCIENTIST OFFER?

The very marked differences between these languages indicate the range of choice open to a designer in specifying a language. His choice will depend upon many factors relating to the use and the users for which the language is being designed. He will most certainly be concerned with human factors and will draw upon his own experience and that of the computing community to achieve a syntax and structure which is as well fitted to the user population as he can make it. It is needless to say that professional computer scientists have a perfectly good knowledge of how to do their job. They arrive at this knowledge by observing themselves and their colleagues and by discussing their observations. The question is whether anything can be added to the rapidly growing expertise of computer science by introducing the formal apparatus of behavioural science and ergonomics - the controlled experiment, the test of significance, the null hypothesis and the rest?

Together with my colleagues at Sheffield I believe the answer to be yes; if, that is, methodology can be developed to tackle so complex a task. The intuitions of experts cannot be replaced by experiment but in many cases they can be evaluated and verified and the route to the evolution of good language made more sure.

There is little to be gained from a wholesale comparison of existing
fullscale languages, as a rule; the points of difference are too
numerous. Except for the special purpose of choosing between
competing, pre-existent systems, the experimenter should always aim
for a generalisable result.

The target of behavioural experiments on programming, as we
see it, is to help the designers of future languages and the teachers
of present ones. To do this we must certainly aim, at the very
least, for a working knowledge of which language features are good
and which bad, for novices as for experts, and the role of empirical
assessment in attaining such knowledge is fairly clear. If possible
it would be nice to know why some features are good - that would
be explanation at the highest level of generality.

Two experimental paradigms are popular at the moment. The
first, which might be called the observational paradigm, is based
on the argument that to help a programmer you must first understand
what he or she is trying to do, and so your language design should
be the outcome of an intensive study of a few people's programming.
A good example comes from a study by Lance Miller (1974), in which
subjects with no previous computing experience were asked to write
programs to sort cards using a miniature language of the BASIC
family. Miller was able to locate certain sources of difficulty
that were effectively universal in his sample, these difficulties
being mainly to do with conditionals which included disjunction
and negation. Anothr interesting example is a study by Thomas &
Gould (1974) of a technique called 'Query by Example'. From work
of this type one can draw conclusions about where the design effort
can most usefully be applied to produce a language in which fewer
errors are made.

In our own work we have tended to use the comparative paradigm.
In its simplest form one linguistic choice can be compared to an
alternative by having one group of subjects try each, and comparing
the results. But as we have already said, working with full-scale
language is unnecessarily laborious because of the many differences
between any two. A better way to meet these aims of rigorous and
generalisable results is to invent languages that are reduced to
the bare minimum. To quote from a paper by Ledgard (1971): "In
teaching programming languages, one immediate problem is that most
languages are so complex that any attempt to isolate their important
features requires a good deal of study. There is clearly a need
for small, digestible examples to illustrate critical issues and
make them a simple object of study" (p.116). One can design one
language in which the requirements of say, loop control are met in
one way, and another language where they are met in another way -
but with no differences between the languages except in the single
feature of interest. Programmers are then asked to write programs
in the languages, or to answer questions about existing programs,

and the number of mistakes made in the two languages are compared - or the time taken to write programs or to answer questions, or the efficiency of the programs produced, or whatever other yardstick the experimenter chooses, as long as he and the programmers are all trying to meet the same criterion.

I want to stress the generality of this approach, because we shall be looking at very particular types of language and at very particular syntactic constructions. Nevertheless any result obtained will apply (if correctly interpreted!) to other syntactic constructions, other programming languages, and other programming levels such as job control languages or interactive systems. In fact the results ought to apply to procedural instructions of every sort. All kinds of instructions which specify a procedure or sequence of actions, including computer programs, give information about the actual actions - "break an egg", "check the brakes", "take the square root" - and information about the sequencing of actions and the conditions under which actions are to be performed: "first, do this", "if such-and-such, do this", "if such-and-such, do that", etc., information which controls how we work through the procedure. The control information is conveyed by grammatical constructions which are applicable to all sorts of cases, whereas the actual actions are usually restricted to certain types of task. Knowing how to design good control statements is therefore the most important step forward in improving programs.

THE FOCUS OF OUR PRESENT CONTRIBUTION

One particular control statement will be discussed, the conditional statement "if .... then ...". This one was chosen for three reasons:

(i) It is the simplest non-trivial control instruction.

(ii) There are two important styles in common use. Each of these two styles is favoured about equally (sometimes acrimoniously) by the designers of the leading programming languages. These are the nesting style in which one conditional may be nested inside another, and the jumping style which sends you on to a labelled point in the program (rather like Snakes and Ladders). Here is what to do when the light goes out in the room in which you are sitting at home, taken from Green (1977).

Example 2 (nesting style)

if all your other lights are also out then
        if next door's lights are still on then mend your fuse
        else go to the pub till the power cut is over
else change the bulb.

Example 3 (jumping style)

```
1:  if all your other lights are also out then goto step 3
2:  change the bulb
3:  if next door's lights are on then goto step 5
4:  go to the pub till the power cut is over
5:  mend your fuse.
```

(iii) The choice of style is a small but crucial part of the controversy between the 'structured programming' school and their
critics.   The structured programmers maintain that a program
should have a simple correspondence between the spatial structure of the program text and the dynamic course of the program's
performance.   In psychological terms, the spatial layout
provides (by indenting and other means) a redundant recoding
of the program's behaviour.   Their critics point out that
there is no proof that any such correspondence makes it easier
to understand the program.   The lengthy arguments will not
be rehearsed: enough that the nested conditional is one
example of structuring (and the goto of un-structuring), and
it is vital to the case of the structured programmers that it
should be easier to comprehend.

Experiment 1

     Our first studies were directed at the sort of person who
might become a non-specialist computer user - young people with a
good education but no previous experience of programming.   We
quickly discovered that it is not so easy to get non-programmers
to come and write programs, but we solved a lot of problems by
building the Hungry Hare.   This animal, a primitive card-sorter,
feeds on 'vegetables' (edge-punched cards), discovering how to cook
them by obeying a short program and lighting lamps in its ears to
show how the cooking was performed, and then sorting the cards into
piles of correctly-cooked and wrongly-cooked.   Our subjects were
asked to write the cookery programs; everything was done on-line
to our computer, so the subject could prepare his program on the
VDU, by pointing to items in a dictionary, press a 'check' button
to make sure that the program was grammatical, and then press a
'go' button and start to feed the cards into the Hungry Hare.

     One problem with using naive subjects is that they must learn
to use the micro-languages, and this poses a methodological difficulty.
Normally if we were to write instructional materials we would
evaluate their efficiency in terms of the performance achieved by
the students who had read them (Kay, Dodd and Sime, 1968).   In
this case, however, we wish to evaluate the performance, under the
assumption that the instructional material is equally good for
each micro-language.   There is no certain answer to this problem.
The approach we took was to balance the teaching of the concepts
for each language very rigorously.

Statement of problem

Fry:	everything which is juicy but not hard
Boil:	everything which is hard
Chop and roast:	everything which is neither hard nor juicy

Solutions in three different micro-languages

(a) *Jump*
   if hard *goto* L1
   if juicy *goto* L2
   chop roast stop
L2 fry stop
L1 boil stop

(c) *Nest-BE*
if hard *then*
   begin boil *end*
else
   begin
   if juicy *then*
      begin fry *end*
   else
      begin chop roast *end*
   end

(b) *Nest-INE*
if hard : boil
not hard :
   if juicy : fry
   not juicy : chop roast
   end juicy
end hard

FIGURE 1. A cookery problem for the Hungry Hare's diet, together
with solutions in each of three miniature languages.

Of the several studies we have performed using the Hungry
Hare scenario, one of the most informative has been the comparison
of the three miniature languages illustrated in Figure 1. Two of
these languages use the nesting style of conditional, (cf. Example 2)
while the other one uses the jump-to-label style (cf. Example 3).
The two nesting styles are structurally quite identical, but of
course that doesn't mean that they are equally easy to use. Nest-BE
is based on Algol 60. Nest-INE has not been put to real use, so
far as we know, but was specially devised for our purposes, having
repetitions of the predicate 'green' etc. which were logically
unnecessary but potentially helpful for people. Jump is related
to Basic.

Problems were presented in the format illustrated by the
example at the top of figure 1. Each subject did five problems
graded in difficulty from the very easy to realistically hard.
The one shown is from the middle range. Fifteen subjects tackled
the problems in each language.

Four measure of performance were taken. These were (i) the number of problems successfully completed. (ii) The number of syntax errors made. (iii) The number of semantic errors made; semantic errors are those cases where a program, which was syntactically correct, did the wrong thing. (iv) The number of attempts needed to correct an error when it occurred; we have called this "the error lifetime".

The results showed an overall superiority for the Nest-INE language. It came equal first on the first three measures and a clear first on the error lifetime measure. (See Table 1 for medians, ranges and significance figures.) Overall one would say that Nest-INE was better than Jump on semantic errors; better than Nest-BE on syntax errors; and better than either for debugging.

The three languages differ in a number of respects. In the Nest languages there is an imposed structure, and transfer of control within its program is implicit in the syntax. The Jump language imposes little structure and transfer of control is explicit. Nest-INE contains additional redundancy, compared to Nest-BE, in requiring a restatement of the predicates. Why then is Nest-INE so much better, and does knowing that it is allow us to make any design recommendations?

TABLE 1. (See also figure 4a)

Experiment 1:   Three Microlanguages Compared

Comparisons of error frequencies and lifetimes

| | GROUP | | | |
	Nest–INE	Nest–BE	Jump	Sig.
Semantic errors per problem	0.04 (0.08)	0.07 (0.27)	0.40 (0.22)	1%
Syntactic errors per problem	0.13 (0.17)	0.85 (0.75)	0.20 (0.25)	5%
Error-free problems/subject	2.33 (1.31)	1.15 (0.38)	2.60 (1.05)	5%
Error lifetimes	0.09 (0.50)	1.60 (0.78)	1.06 (0.87)	2%

Entries are medians, with semi-interquartile range in brackets. The Kruskal-Wallis test was used.

Let us begin with the syntax errors.   Although these errors
should never reach run-time, they can waste huge amounts of time
for both the programmer and the system.   Why are they so much
more frequent in Nest-BE than either Nest-INE or Jump?   A closer
analysis of the syntax errors made by the Nest-BE subjects revealed
that the bulk were due to the omission of ENDs.   Our impression
is that our subjects hold up bits of program to their mind's eye
and try to copy them down; but the trouble is that BEGIN and END
are not part of the structure of the program, just fillers to show
how far the scope of the conditional extends.   In consequence
when a program is typed out from a mental representation of its
structure there is no obvious reminder to put the ENDs in. Another
way to put it is that these are careless mistakes.

Semantic errors were most frequent in the Jump language.
Our impression is that these arise in two ways: careless omissions,
which in Nest-BE would cause syntax errors, will cause semantic
errors in Jump - because of the lack of syntactic structure imposed
on the program; while the problem of discovering the meaning of
a program, when the programmer wants to check his work, is more
acute in Jump than in the nesting styles.

This problem of discovering the meaning of a program comes
to the fore when debugging (although it is also present during
writing, of course).   A possible explanation for the quick debugging of Nest-INE is that Nest-BE and Jump obscure information which
is necessary when trying to discover what a program does - in short,
they are hard to understand.   Possible reasons why will be discussed
below.

In brief, this study (which is fully reported by Sime, Green
and Guest, 1977) suggests that Nest-INE is a good language for
unskilled programmers, and it poses two further questions, one
relating to careless mistakes and the other to the comprehensibility
of programs in the three languages.

Experiments 2 and 3

Our next move was to investigate a way of reducing careless
syntax errors in writing Nest-BE.   One way to reduce the frequency
of careless syntax mistakes is to make them impossible, by having
the subject write his programs not a word at a time but a whole
construction at a time.   In the earlier study, subjects wrote
"IF juicy THEN BEGIN .." by selecting 'IF' with a light pointer,
then selecting 'juicy', etc.   In Experiment 2 we arranged a
condition known as 'Automatic' in which the dictionary units were
whole constructions, such as the string "IF juicy THEN BEGIN xx
END ELSE BEGIN xx END".   This string was displayed to the subject
simple as 'juicy', but the effect of selecting that one word with
the light pointer was to write the whole string.   At a later stage

the string might have been "IF juicy THEN BEGIN oo chop oo END
ELSE BEGIN xx END". The effect of selecting the one word "chop"
from the dictionary displayed on the screen was to replace "xx"
with "oo chop oo". The symbols "xx" and "oo" were markers indicating the only points in the text where further statements may be
inserted. "xx" had always to be replaced, but replacing "oo" was
optional. In this system the subject had no way to leave out an
END. Although automated syntax is no doubt a long way ahead for
conventional programming, its effects on programming performance
are important to our discussion on error reduction. It could turn
out that non-programmers find the language Nest-BE difficult to
understand in some non-specific way; the result of which would
probably be that they made a large number of random errors, showing
up as syntactic errors in the earlier studies but as semantic errors
in the Automatic condition. The purpose of this condition was to
determine whether an overall reduction in errors could really be
achieved by the means proposed, or whether the argument above was
mistaken.

Should the Automatic condition succeed in reducing the number
of overall errors, then one would expect to ask whether it was
possible to do the same by simpler means. Removing careless
mistakes can be considered as a training problem. It is customary
to teach the structure of programming languages, showing how statements are built up from elements, and that is how the instructions
in our earlier experiments were phrased; this approach leaves it
to the individual to create a procedure for writing programs, based
on what he has learnt about the language's structure. But an alternative is to prescribe a fixed procedure which subjects are to
follow, and this we did in one of our groups known as the Procedural
condition. The procedure was to write a basic statement, which
would eventually be the outermost conditional of the program, and
then to insert further statements into it; in fact, subjects were
unwittingly simulating the Automatic condition. The procedure that
is implicit in the usual structural teaching of programming is
considerably different, in that the whole structure is held in the
mind and is then copied out onto paper, or some other medium. That
method obviously invites one to forget closing ENDs of long statements, whereas the procedure we devised was not only made explicit,
in itself perhaps an advantage, but also made it much harder to
forget ENDs.

Finally, a third condition replicated exactly the way in which
the Nest-BE language was learnt in the first experiment, and this
will be called the Plain condition. Replication is statistically
desirable in such situations, rather than re-using the previous
data, because otherwise one freak sample can generate a chain of
spurious findings.

Once more the Hungry Hare scenario was used.

TABLE 2.   (See also figure 4b)

Experiment 2:   Nest-BE Plain, Procedural and Automatic

Comparisons of error frequencies and lifetimes

	GROUP			
	Plain	Procedural	Automatic	Sig.
Semantic errors per problem	0.07 (0.04)	0.05 (0.03)	0.15 (0.07)	5%
Syntactic errors per problem	1.10 (1.87)	0.10 (0.30)	n.a.	$2\frac{1}{2}$%
Error-free problems per subject	1.10 (0.73)	3.00 (1.50)	4.10 (1.25)	2%
Error lifetimes	2.10 (3.10)	0.75 (0.62)	0.75 (0.57)	>30%

Entries are medians, with semi-interquartile range
in brackets.   The Kruskal-Wallis and Mann-Whitney
tests were used.   Every solved problem is included.

The results shown in Table 2 show us that significantly more
problems were solved first time in the Automatic condition than in
the Plain condition, and the Procedural condition was likewise
better than the Plain; but there were no corresponding improvements
in debugging, as measured by error lifetimes.   The first result
from our Automatic condition gives some estimate of what improvement
in performance could be achieved if nobody ever made syntax errors -
but the Automatic condition is not one that could easily be put into
everyday use.   The result from the Procedural condition gives some
estimate of what might perhaps be achieved by practical means.   A
simple procedure, explicitly prescribed, brought the number of errors
down by a large factor for a minimal price - a couple of dozen extra
lines in the experimental instructions.   So we have here a possible
way of reducing the number of careless mistakes in programs.   (For
a full report see Sime, Arblaster and Green, 1977).

```
        if soft then goto L2;
        if flat then goto L1;
        jump;
L1:  walk;
L2:  if poor then goto L6;
        if blue then goto L4;
        if round then goto L3;
        run;
L3:  drive;
L4:  if cheap then goto L5;
        swim;
L5:  ride;
L6:  fly;
```

IS	IS NOT
soft	flat
blue	poor
cheap	round

jump	walk	run	drive	swim	ride	fly
●	●	●	●	●	●	●

FIGURE 2.   Experiment 4:   Program and response delay

The subject's task is to report the first action
performed by the program, given the truth-values
displayed in the columns IS and IS NOT.   In this
example the correct response is 'ride'

In experiment 4 where the task was to discover the action
performed, given the truth values of the predicates, a significant
but not very large improvement in performance was observed with
the Nested languages compared to Jump (Table 3).   The two Nested
languages were not significantly different from each other.   With
the other task however (Exp. 5), in which a subject had to determine
the set of truth values which would result in a given action, the
differences were much more marked.   Again the Nested languages
were better than the Jump language and this time Nest-INE gave
significantly better results than Nest-BE (Table 4).

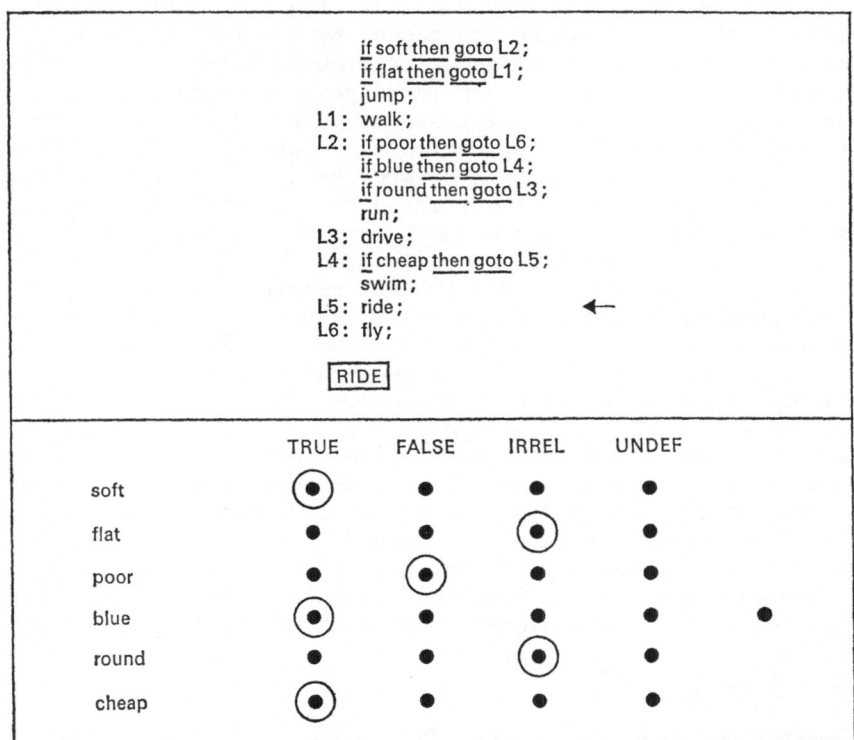

FIGURE 3. Experiment 5: Program display (upper panel) and
response display (lower panel)

The subject's task is to report the predicate
conditions causing the designated action 'ride'
to be the first action performed. The full
response has been set up; touching the right-
hand spot will complete it.

A similar argument can be applied to the high incidence of semantic errors in the Jump language - if, that is, these errors are caused in the way we suggested above, by careless mistakes, creating semantic rather than syntactic trouble because of the lack of syntactic structure in the Jump language. Working to a specified procedure should cut out many of these mistakes and thereby reduce semantic errors. A second suggestion above was that Jump programs were less comprehensible. Since working to a specified procedure can encourage programmers to adopt structures resembling those of the nested language, which may be more comprehensible, both our postulated causes of semantic errors in Jump should simultaneously be cured by this treatment. Preliminary results from a pilot experiment show the expected effect - programming in accordance with procedural instruction in Jump produced significantly fewer errors than was the case when only structural teaching was used. (Sime, Arblaster & Green, in preparation).

We have then some results from naive users. But to be really useful the findings should be equally valid for novice and maestro alike. We therefore turned to professional computer programmers, to get a second view. Because they could already program we could adopt the rather simpler approach of just showing them programs, asking them questions, and timing the response. This we did with quite complex conditionals expressed in each of the three languages.

Experiment 4 and 5

Two further experiments were done (Green, 1977) using two different comprehension tasks. The first task, Exp. 4 was to trace the actions of the program given the truth-values of the predicates (see Figure 2). The second task in Exp. 5, using identical programs, was to discover what truth-value would cause a given action to be performed (see Figure 3).

The stimuli were shown on a visual display; responses were made by touching conductive spots on a transparent screen. Twelve highly experienced programmers (mostly professionals from the University Computing Services and Computing Science Departments) took part in each experiment, each contributing 132 responses (plus warmup) on each of three consecutive days. They were asked to respond as quickly as they could but to aim at making less than 5 per cent errors. They all managed to stay within this error rate and, as there were no significant differences in error frequencies between the conditions, the response times can be taken as a true measure of the difficulty of the task.

SUMMARY OF RESULTS

To summarise these five experiments:

(1)   The nested micro languages resulted in a much lower incidence
of semantic errors than did the Jump languages. (Exp. 1,
Table 1).

(2)   Where syntax errors were concerned there was nothing to choose
between Nest-INE and Jump, but Nest-BE was very poor by
comparison producing a large number of these errors. (Exp. 1,
Table 1).

(3)   The removal of syntax errors from Nest-BE by providing an
automatic entry method resulted in a small but significant
increase in semantic errors. (Exp. 2, Table 2).

(4)   Encouraging the subjects to adopt a fixed writing procedure
for Nest-BE statements resulted in a reduction in the troublesome syntax errors by an order of magnitude.   This was
achieved with no apparent increase in tendency to make semantic
errors.   (Exp. 2, Table 2).

(5)   Our pilot experiment indicates that a writing procedure
encouraging the use of a fixed structure when writing in the
Jump language can reduce the semantic errors found to be
troublesome in this language.

(6)   Error correction was found to be very much better in Nest-INE
than in either Nest-BE or Jump.   (Exp. 1, Table 1).

All the above results (see also Figure 4) applied to subjects with
no previous experience of writing computer programs.   Turning to
professional programmers (see also Figure 5) and the task of program
comprehension we find:

(7)   When the task is to trace an outcome given the truth values
of a set of predicates, the nested languages result in rather
faster performance than the Jump language with no significant
difference between the two nested languages. (Exp. 4, Table 3).

(8)   When however the task is to determine the relevant predicates
and the truth values that they must have to result in a given
outcome, the two nested languages differ from each other.
Not only are they both significanly better than Jump but
Nest-INE is for this task significantly better than Nest-BE.
(Exp. 5, Table 4).

TABLE 3.   (see also Figure 5)

Experiment 4 - tracing a program

Mean response speeds and summary statistical comparisons

	GROUP		
	Jump	Nest-BE	Nest-INE
Mean RT (seconds)	6.20	5.84	6.06

Planned comparisons:
1) Jump vs. both Nest styles: $F = 5.27$, df $= 1,22$, $p = 0.032$
   Saving of Nest over Jump $= 4\%$

2) Nest-BE vs. Nest-INE: $F = 3.26$. df $= 1,22$, N.S.

TABLE 4.   (see also Figure 5)

Experiment 5 - extracting taxon information

Mean response speeds and summary statistical comparisons

	GROUP		
	Jump	Nest-BE	Nest-INE
Mean RT (seconds)	8.06	7.50	7.04

Planned comparisons:
1) Jump vs. both Nest styles: $F = 29.84$, df $= 1,22$, $p = 0.00002$
   Saving of Nest over Jump $= 10\%$

2) Nest-BE to Nest-INE: $F = 7.62$, df $= 1,22$, $p = 0.011$
   Saving of Nest-INE over Nest-BE $= 6\%$

     *'Taxon' should be read as 'The relevant set of predicates
     and the truth values that they must have to define a given
     outcome'.

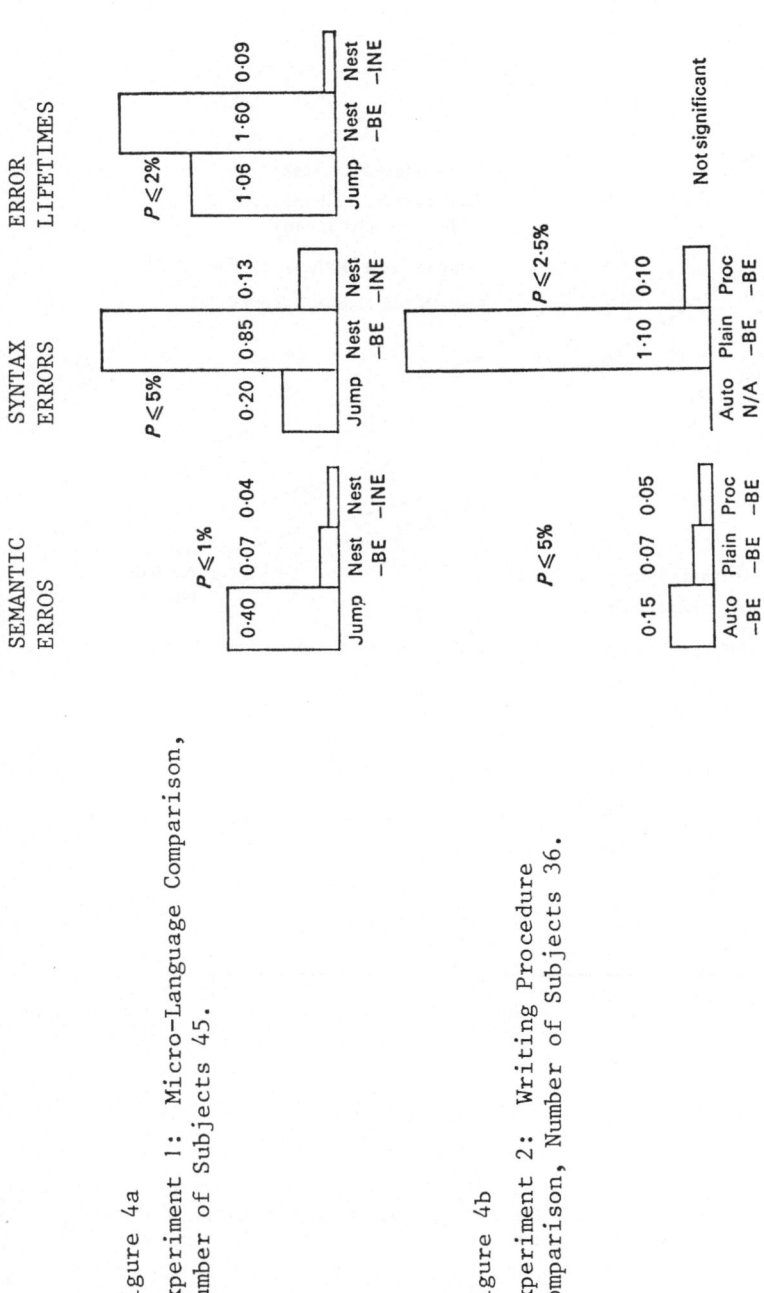

FIGURE 4. Comparison of findings from Experiments 1 and 2 (See Tables 1 and 2)

238

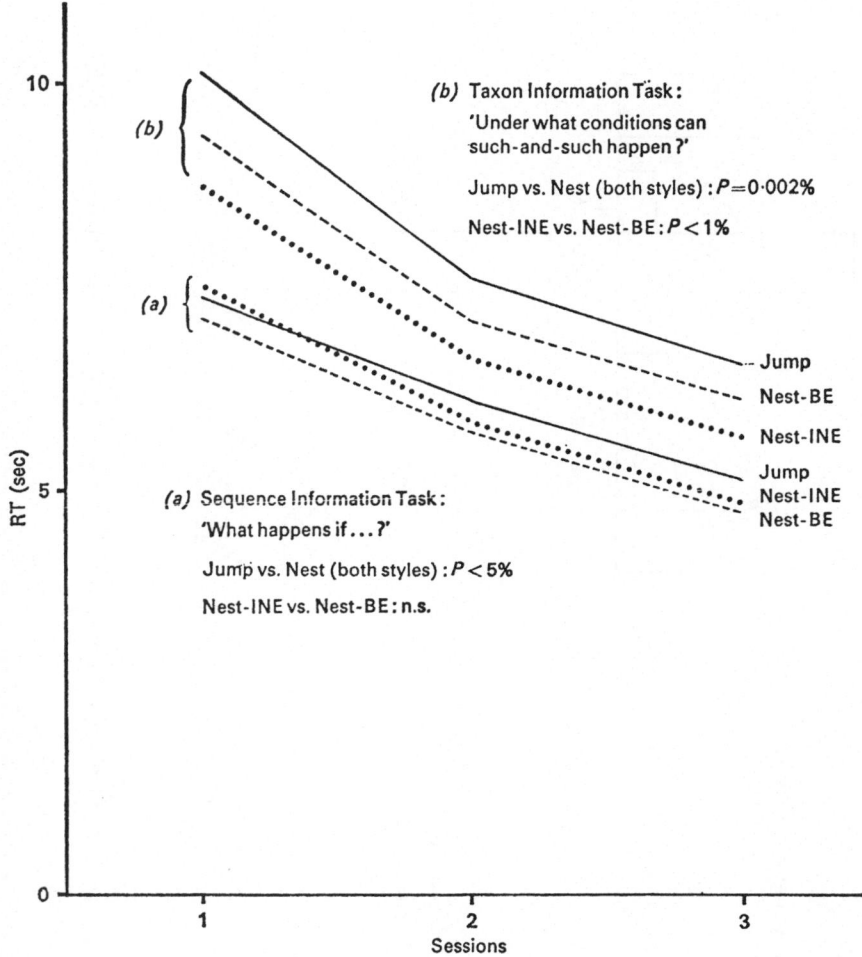

The figure shows a plot with RT (sec) on the vertical axis and Sessions (1, 2, 3) on the horizontal axis.

(b) Taxon Information Task:
'Under what conditions can such-and-such happen?'

Jump vs. Nest (both styles): $P = 0.002\%$

Nest-INE vs. Nest-BE: $P < 1\%$

— — Jump
- - - Nest-BE
······ Nest-INE
——— Jump
······ Nest-INE
- - - Nest-BE

(a) Sequence Information Task:
'What happens if ... ?'

Jump vs. Nest (both styles): $P < 5\%$

Nest-INE vs. Nest-BE: n.s.

FIGURE 5. Response times of professional programmers. (See Tables 3 and 4)

In overall terms then we must conclude that, whether considering non-programmers or professionals, the nested languages result in better performance than the Jump language, and furthermore the Nest-INE language is better than the Nest-BE language. All this of course within the limits of the tasks set. How far we might safely generalise from these results is another matter. To do so we require at the very least, an explanation of why they were obtained.

DISCUSSION

Why do the nested languages result in fewer semantic errors? Is it because they are more natural, in the sense that they read more like English than does the Jump language? Certainly a basic statement from Nested language might look like English: if, that is, we omit the Begins and Ends.

"If next door's lights are still on then mend your fuse else go to the pub till the power cut is over". This certainly is acceptable English, but when the statements are combined they look no more like English than does the Jump language (see Figure 1). In fact we have found that the superficial resemblance to normal English of the basic Nest statement can be troublesome to the non-programmer subjects. In a recent experiment we compared the following two types of nested syntax.

Example 4

(i) if green then
   begin chop fry end
  else
   begin roast end

(ii) if green then chop fry
   else roast
  end

We expected (ii) to be the easiest to use as it is not cluttered up with begins and ends. We were astonished to find that practically all the subjects using the language (ii) simply folded up at the first problem which required nesting. We assumed our instructions to be faulty so we rewrote them and tried again - with practically the same result. We are still not certain what was happening but a clue is given by their frequent complaint when shown the solution, "But that's not English!" The subjects who were given syntax (i) on the other hand had no such problem; they would see quite readily that the language was not English, from the

presence of the begins and ends, so they were forced to read the
instructions we gave them with full attention.   The subjects
learning syntax (ii) however seemed to decide that it was so like
English that they need only skim through the instructions.   They
then came promptly to grief when they met a problem requiring the
very un-English construction.

> if green then
>> if juicy then ...

This artefact, which as a matter of fact ruined our experiment
so far as our intended purpose was concerned, indicates that being
like English can be a mixed blessing where non-programmers are
concerned.   It is probably worth observing in passing that deeply
embedded structures in English, eg. "The vase that the maid that
the agency hired dropped broke on the floor" have been shown to be
rather difficult to understand (Miller and Isard, 1964; Stolz, 1967)
whereas our findings are that the problem is less acute in programming language.

As to the question of whether the English-like look of the
basic nest statements account for the low incidence of semantic
errors, I would suggest from the above arguments that the answer
is most likely to be no.

Another, and I believe more likely, explanation is that the
severe constraints imposed by the structure inherent in the nested
languages demand that the programmer thinks very seriously about
the form his program will take before he starts writing.   It
really matters in this language which predicate is tested first for
the solution of a given program.   The need to take such care is
much less obvious when writing in the free environment of the Jump
syntax.   This view gains credibility when we consider finding
(5) in the summary above, viz. that the imposition of structural
constraints on the Jump language, by adopting a fixed writing
procedure, was found to reduce semantic errors.   The idea that
these errors are due to insufficient pre-planning of the program
structure receives further support from finding (3) above.   Although
there is no less structure in the nested syntax when implemented
by our automatic entry method, there is an obvious temptation,
from the ease with which entries can be made, to indulge in trial
and error, or at any rate to relax rigour of thought.   A consequent
increase in semantic error is observed.

A general principle then might be to impose structure on the
task, either by teaching fixed writing procedures, or by designing
syntax in such a way that the programmer's degrees of freedom are
adequate for the task but that an excessive number of options are
not available to him.

The matter of the excessive tendency to make syntax errors in the Nest-BE language need not be pursued here at length. They can be reduced by teaching a writing procedure. A better approach however would be to <u>design syntax which is not cluttered by syntactic devices which have no obvious relevance to the main concept structure of the program</u>.

Possibly the most interesting finding in the above experiments is the superior error correction performance of subjects writing in Nest-INE when compared with those writing in either Nest-BE or Jump (Finding 6). This to be understood must be related to finding (8) ie. that the professional programmers identified relevant predicates and their required truth values more quickly in Nest-INE than in the other languages.

It is worth commenting here that finding (8) counters any thought that 'familiarity' and 'naturalness' can be equated. The professional programmer subjects were all very familiar with Algol 60. Both the Nest-BE and the Jump programs they saw were realised as legal Algol 60 sequences; the Nest-INE programs were however in a language which was novel to them.

Despite this disadvantage, superior performance was achieved with Nest-INE. Nest-INE seems then to be better fitted for this task in some more fundamental way. Our suggestion is that it is easier to trace the flow of control in the nested languages than in the Jump language and that Nest-INE is superior to Nest-BE when tracing backwards through the program. Why tracing backwards? A study of the texts shown in Figure 1 should allow the reader to evaluate the following observation.

Jump is harder because, no doubt, it takes time to pick one's way from one fragment of text to the next. Working forwards, in program tracing, the difficulty is in finding the label associated with a <u>goto</u> command. Working backwards from a given outcome up to the start of the program, as one must in taxon* extraction, the task has two difficult components: going from a label backwards, one must sweep through the program looking for a matching <u>goto</u>; and going through a conditional <u>goto</u> which was not obeyed, one must register the negation of the predicate tested by the conditional and use it in forming the taxon. The Nest styles avoid the matching <u>goto</u> problem by imposing a spatial structure, so both Nest styles make the taxon extraction task easier to that extent; Nest-BE still requires the subject to register the negated predicate when leaving an <u>else</u> branch, but Nest-INE with its redundant repetition avoids that problem as well.

---

* 'Taxon' should be read as 'The relevant set of predicates and the truth values that they must have to define a given outcome

It is, we would suggest, the increased clarity of the information required to trace back through the programs, resulting from the redundant restatement of the predicates after <u>not</u> and <u>end</u>, which accounts also for the efficient correction of errors by the inexperienced programmers when using Nest-INE.

The lesson to be learned is therefore that <u>the syntax and spatial structure of program text should be designed to allow two-way tracing of the control structure. This means that the information required for such tracing should be overt and obvious and not demand undue visual search.</u>

Even within the narrow confines of the experiments discussed above many residual issues remain to be cleared up. The interactions of these phenomena with the many other problems that arise in life-size programs need to be studied and a more exhaustive treatment involving a wide range of problem types would give greater assurance of a truly generalisable result. For example, most languages allow boolean operators ('and', 'or', etc.) which were excluded from our microlanguage: how would their availability affect the findings? Again, the problems we have studied have been 'hierarchical' in that the problem space is partitioned disjointly by each test on a predicate - to put it another way, these are decision <u>trees</u>, not decision <u>graphs</u> in which the twigs are allowed to meet. The problems raised by both points are illustrated when one tries to say "<u>if</u> A or B, but not both, <u>then</u> ..." in a nested syntax without using the boolean operator 'or'. Besides the conditional, there are other structures equally deserving of attention: loops, data declarations, parameter passing and even something as simple as where to put a space, are all problems on which every programmer has stubbed his toes at one time or another. Every time a new programming language is designed a host of such detailed syntactic decisions is called for.

CONCLUSION

Apart from the detailed examination of particular constructs the cognitive ergonomist will also, sooner or later, have to ask more profound questions. Might it prove possible to characterise some of the underlying forms of grammatical rules that are convenient for the human - and if so, might these forms not turn out to resemble that well-evolved structure, natural language, after all? Not a resemblance at the surface level, in which constructions are copied directly from English into the programming language (we have remarked on this above), but a resemblance at the deeper level of the <u>type of grammatical rule</u> frequently found in natural language. For example, repetitive phenomena are very frequent in all languages. Plural subjects take plural verbs; a single tense is used consistently throughout a passage; many other examples can be found. These repetitive properties were also present in the most ergonomic of our conditional structures; the Nest-INE construction <u>if</u> p ... <u>not</u> p ... <u>end</u> p. Coincidence or re-invention?

In the world of computers, 'what is possible' expands by the day. The explosive energy of computer science offers a continuing stream of inventions and through a process like natural selection some are found to be well fitted, and so survive. Perhaps cognitive ergonomics can accelerate this process.

ACKNOWLEDGEMENT

I wish to thank our C.T.L. Modular One for its help, without which much of our data could not have been obtained.

REFERENCES

Bagrit, Sir L.	1966	The age of automation. Harmondsworth: Penguin Books.
Clarke, A.C.	1968	2001 - A space oddyssey. London: Arrow Books.
Green, T.R.G.	1977	Conditional program statements and their comprehensibility to professional programmers. J. Occup. Psychol. 50.2, 93-109.
Hill, I.D.	1972	Wouldn't it be nice if we could write programs in ordinary English - or would it? Computer Bulletin, 16, 306-312.
Hoare, C.A.R.	1973	Hints for programming language design. Computer Science Report STAN-CS-73-403, Stanford University.

Kay, H.
  Dodd, B. &
  Sime, M.E.
	1968	Teaching machines and programmed instruction.
		Harmondsworth: Penguin Books.

Ledgard, H.F.	1971	Ten mini-languages: a study of topical issues in programming languages. Computing Surveys, 3, 115-146.
Miller, G.A. & Isard, S.	1964	Free recall of self-embedded sentences. Information and Control, 7, 292-303.
Miller, L.A.	1974	Programming by non-programmers. Int. J. of Man-Machine Studies, 6, 237-260.
Midonick, H.	1968	The Treasury of Mathematics. Harmondsworth: Penguin Books.

244

Sime, M.E.   1977   Reducing programming errors in nested
  Arblaster, A.T. &   conditionals by prescribing a
  Green, T.R.G.   writing procedure.
                            Int.J. Man-Machine Studies, 9.1, 119–126.

Sime, M.E.   1977   Scope marking in computer conditionals –
  Green, T.R.G. &   a psychological evaluation.
  Guest, D.J.   Int.J. Man-Machine Studies, 9.1, 107–118.

Stolz, W.S.   1967   A study of the ability to decode
                            grammatically novel sentences.
                            Journal of Verbal Learning and Verbal
                            Behaviour, 6, 867–873.

Thomas, J.C. &   1974   A psychological study of query by
  Gould, J.D.   example.
                            IBM Research Report RC5124,
                            Yorktown Heights, New York.

TOWARDS A DESIGN FOR AN ON-LINE SCHEDULING AID

M.J. Fitter

MRC Social & Applied Psychology Unit,
University of Sheffield, Sheffield S10 2TN.

INTRODUCTION

For many years computers have been used to forecast the requirements and expected output of production plants. For the purpose of medium to long term forecasting, algorithms have been developed which determine the output capacity of a plant given the resources available. However such models do not necessarily inform the scheduler <u>how</u> to achieve the output, only of what <u>should</u> be possible.

Our own research has been concerned with the problems of short term forecasting in which the actual sequence of activities in a job-shop must be decided. It is true that algorithmic/mathematical solutions can and have been used to produce such schedules, but there are disadvantages to using mathematical methods.

There is no known method which guarantees an optimal solution to the general job-shop problem and there are usually too many alternatives to evaluate all possible solutions exhaustively, even using a high-speed computer. Thus heuristics (rules which guide the planning process towards a satisfactory if not optimal solution) must be used to narrow down the number of possible solutions by eliminating the less likely ones from consideration. These heuristics are often 'opaque' to the scheduler, so that he may not understand how a solution was derived and therefore finds difficulty in questioning it. Often a number of alternative computer-generated schedules are offered to the scheduler, who must pick the best one, and then if he is not completely satisfied with it, he must change it himself. Then, when he finds that the schedule cannot be implemented anyhow, because a machine has broken down or some material needs further treatment before it is within tolerance, he must ask for a revised schedule or try to patch the original one himself. A serious problem with using a computer generated revision is that it may look completely different from the original one. A small change in the circumstances may cause a large change in the solution that the computer considers to be best. This can be unacceptable to the scheduler and to the shop floor who will quite reasonably not wish to make major changes to their plans for relatively minor reasons.

We, therefore, advocate an interactive computer aid where the user and computer share the task of producing schedules, the user being able to decide how much of the planning he does, and how much the computer does. To illustrate and evaluate our ideas we have developed a Scheduling Heuristic Evaluation Device (SHED), a computer system which evolves as we learn more about the desirable properties of scheduling aids.

This paper highlights some design principles underlying such interactive computer aids and the language of communication they require.

PRINCIPLES OF SHED

1.   Prediction Simulation

We wish to simulate the environment and provide a model which will allow future states to be predicted.   This necessitates:-

(a)   specifying the contraints of the environment, eg. number of machines available, the route from machine to machine that each job must follow.
(b)   providing rules (or heuristics) to generate possible future states, eg. when several jobs are queuing for a machine give priority to the job that has been waiting longest.

Thus a schedule can be produced by applying the rules iteratively within the constraints of the environment, but this alone is not enough.   We want the user to be actively involved in the planning and so we introduce the concept of:-

2.   Progressive Automation

The user must be able progressively to tutor the computer in ways of scheduling and then hand over controls to the computer, but also be able to recover control when he wants to.   This can be achieved by:-

(a)   The user providing the rules by which schedules are produced.   These rules can be elaborated, changed or deleted as the user discovers more about scheduling. We must also encourage the user to evaluate his rules by

(b) providing good feedback on the effect of rules to allow
     them to be improved, and by

(c) allowing the user to pre-empt manually or override the
     rules if he thinks they are inadequate.

DESIGN OF SHED

The main features of the initial system that we built are
illustrated in figure 1.   The system was experimented with and
used by ourselves and four 'naive' subjects whose actions and
impressions were recorded.   Some parts were shown to be quite useful
as aids to the scheduling process, whilst others were either little
used or positively frustrating to use.   A brief outline and evaluation
of this original system follows, but a fuller discussion is given
in Fitter (1976).

1.   Display of Current State

A graphical representation of the data base was displayed on
a VDU.   The information given in the display included the jobs
currently being processed, jobs waiting to be processed, the routes
that jobs had to follow through the shop and the number of jobs
finished.   That is, the contraints of the system were contained in
the data base and were reflected in the display.   This display
was the principal means by which subjects knew what was happening
in the system.   It seemed fairly easy to comprehend but, because
it showed the current state of the job-shop at a stationary point
in time, it was difficult to integrate changes that occurred over
time.   Subjects found it difficult to form a mental picture of
the progress of a particular job as the simulation moved on.

2.   Touchboard

The touchboard was the input device used to interrogate and
control the system.   It consisted of brass studs placed in a large
rectangular surface and a stylus for selecting the studs.   The
names of the studs were printed beneath each one, except for a subset which could be named and defined by the user.   The layout of
the touchboard is shown in figure 2, the device itself being fully
described in Fitter and Daly (1975).

The touchboard provides an easy method of input requiring no
mechanical skills and also allowing the structure of the communication language to be partially represented explicitly by the layout
of the studs.   However, with such a large number of studs subjects
were sometimes in doubt as to which ones were syntactically allow-
able at a particular time even though they had been functionally
grouped.   So, more recently, we have inserted a light (L.E.D.)
into the centre of each stud to illuminate the inputs which are
grammatically acceptable at the current moment.

248

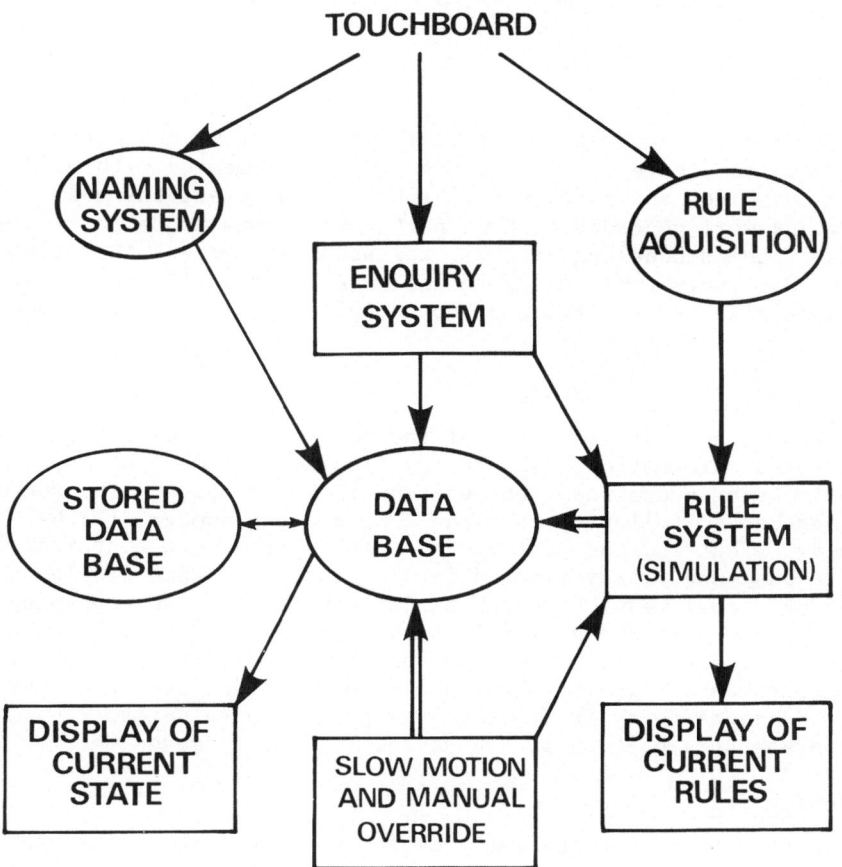

FIGURE 1.   SHED Overview

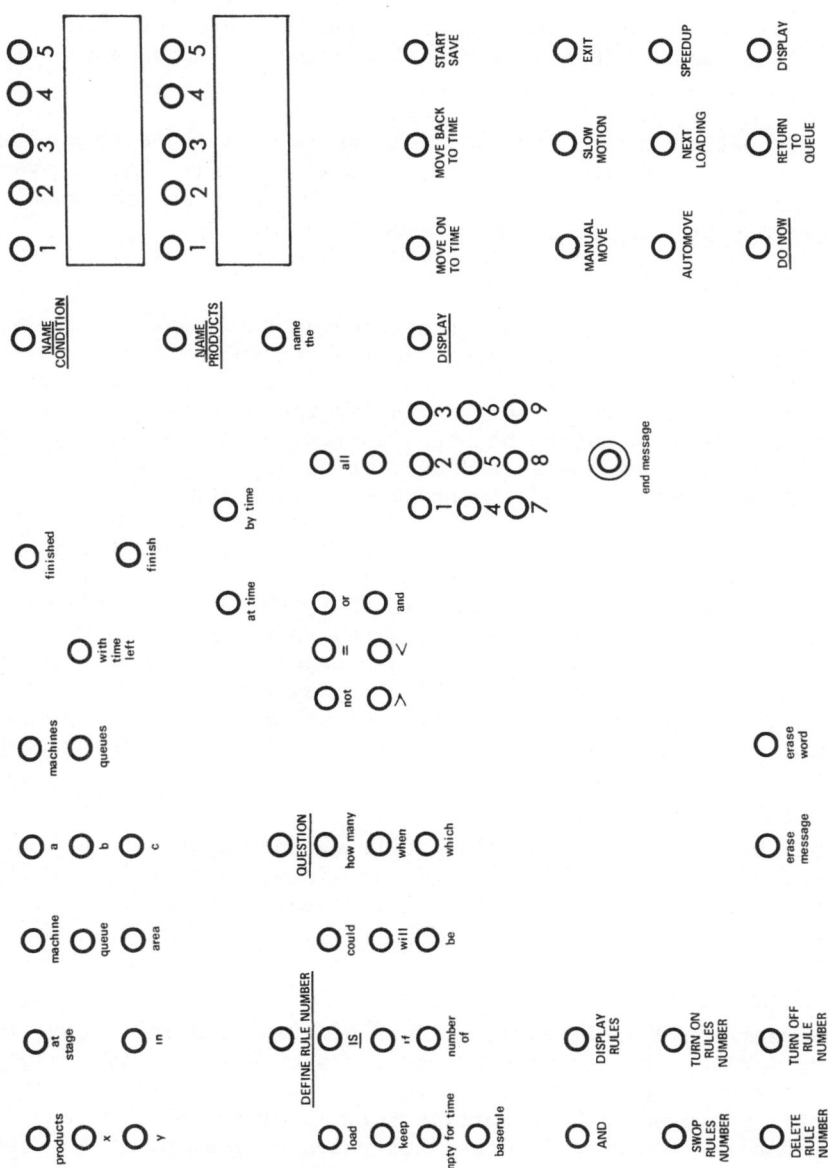

FIGURE 2.   The Touchboard

Considerable effort was made to make the communication language appear natural ie. English-like. A paired-grammar translator (Green, 1975) was used to translate the user's sentences into 'machine language'. This same translator could also be used for translation in the reverse direction.

We now believe that there are dangers in making the communication language too English-like. Subjects tended to assume that it was English and that they did not need to read the instruction manual very carefully because it seemed all very obvious.

3. Rule System

The rule system is the part that created the possible future states of the job-shop by applying the loading <u>rules</u> to the <u>constraints</u> of the data base. It was possible to move forwards or backwards in simulated time and display the ensuing state, forward moves being made by obeying the rules currently in the rule system and backward moves being effected by tracing back through a trail of the changes that were made to produce a given state.

The rules were expressed in the form of productions for a production system (see Davis and King, 1975, for a description of production systems), and could be defined by the user himself in an English-like language. Figure 3 gives an example of some rules. There are several advantages and disadvantages of using production systems to specify control instructions. We now believe that the disadvantages outweigh the advantages for job-shop scheduling, but the issues are complex and will be discussed in a forthcoming paper.

4. Display of Current Rules

Since the user is continually revising the rules he can call up the current rules on the VDU. If he wishes to suspend a rule but leave it in the rule system for later use, then the rule can be 'turned off'.

5. Slow Motion and Manual Override

The user could observe the effects of his rules in 'slowmotion' by asking for the jobs to move around the shop one at a time, so that he could see which rule was responsible for a particular action. This facility proved to be a particularly important part of the system, enabling the user to debug his rules by examining the trace of the program.

If the user found that the rules were doing something undesirable, he could override them manually and see if his manual interaction produced a more satisfactory future state by running the forecaster on. If it did he could amend the rules to incorporate the effects of the manual override.

```
1          LOAD Y AT STAGE 2

ON


2          IF NUMBER OF Y IN MACHINE C = 2 AND

ON         NUMBER OF Y   6 LOAD Y AT STAGE 1


3          LOAD X AT STAGE 2

ON


4          LOAD Y AT STAGE 3 OR LOAD X AT STAGE 3 OR LOAD

ON         Y AT STAGE 4 OR LOAD X AT STAGE 4


5          BASERULE

OFF
```

FIGURE 3. Example rules

6. Naming System

Users could give selected jobs names of their own choice if
they wanted to follow their progress through the job-shop. They
could also give a name to the condition under which certain rules
were to be applied so that they could define the rule in terms of
the special name.

For example   TOO MANY :=   NUMBER OF PRODUCTS in QUEUE C $>$ 8
and then a rule could be defined as:-

           IF TOO MANY LOAD Y IN MACHINE C

These naming and macro facilities were little used by subjects.

		1	2	3	4	5	6	7	8	time (hrs)
jobs	1	L	L	B	B	G	B	B	-	
	2	-	-	L	B	B	B	G	G	
	3	G	-	-	L	-	G	B	B	
	4	B	B	B	G	-	-	-	-	

(a) 'job' Gantt chart

		1	2	3	4	5	6	7	8
	L	1	1	2	3	-	-	-	-
	G	3	-	-	4	1	3	2	2
machines	B	-	-	1	1	-	1	1	-
	B	4	4	4	2	2	2	3	3

(b) 'machine' Gantt chart

FIGURE 5.   An example of 'job' and 'machine' Gantt charts.
There are four jobs (1, 2, 3, 4) scheduled over eight
hours in four machines of three different types; a
lathe (L), a grinder (G), and two boring machines (B).
The two charts represent equivalent information.
(Dashes in the job chart indicate that a job is waiting
and dashes in the machine chart indicate that a machine
is idle).

WHEN WILL 3 PRODUCTS AT STAGE 2 WITH TIME LEFT 1 FINISH?

WHEN COULD ALL PRODUCTS IN MACHINE NOT B FINISH?

WHICH X NOT AT STAGE 4 WILL FINISH BY TIME 8?

WHICH PRODUCTS WILL FINISH AT TIME 12?

WHICH PRODUCTS IN AREA B COULD FINISH BY TIME 6?

WHICH Y AT STAGE 1 WILL BE IN MACHINE C AT TIME 15?

HOW MANY X AT STAGE 2 AT TIME 4?

HOW MANY Y FINISHED AT TIME 14?

FIGURE 4. Example questions

7. Enquiry System

In addition to observing the graphical representation of the current state, users could ask questions about what would or could happen in the job-shop under the currently active rules.   These questions were phrased in an English-like language and some examples are given in figure 4.

Subjects made virtually no use of this interrogation facility. They commented that the questions gained them little information that could not be obtained from the display.   Rather than discovering what would or could happen they wanted to know the process by which it would occur.

TOWARDS A BETTER SYSTEM

Time Integration

As was mentioned, users had considerable difficulty in integrating their schedules over time because the display only presented the state of the job-shop at a given instant.   One subject in fact kept a paper record of the progress of jobs through the various machines.   An obvious solution is to display a Gantt chart or timetable of planned activity.   A Gantt chart (Clark, 1952) can either represent jobs or machines against time (see figure 5).   With such a chart the user can follow the progress of a job and see how long it is spending queuing for machines or readily see how often a machine is standing idle.   There is of course a disadvantage to using this representation.   Much more information needs to be presented on the display which is therefore likely to have inadequate

capacity for a realistic job-shop.   Another way must be found
to break the representation into sub-units.   The most appropriate
way will depend on the nature of the job-shop being simulated but
we now believe that a display should be integrated over time.

Time-Transcending Schedules

Techniques for scheduling by rule, including the one described
in the first half of this paper, start at the beginning of the chart
and allocate jobs to machines as time progresses until a complete
schedule has been built up.   Then if the schedule is unsatisfactory
part or all of it is 'unwound' and a new one is woven.   The process
follows the natural one of making the immediately necessary decisions
as time progresses, and can be thought of as simply a problem of
queue sequencing.   However, with a Gantt chart it is possible to
make a schedule by timetabling the events for tomorrow before
deciding on the sequence of events for today.   It becomes possible
to develop time-transcending schedules, a concept discussed by
Gere (1966), who states,"We conclude, without experimental validation,
that a time-progression program with a look-ahead feature is as
effective as a time-transcending program and a much easier program
for the computer".   With the exception of a study by Jones et al
(1969), time-transcending computer aids do not appear to have been
developed although we think they offer considerable promise including
the possibility of time-transcending rules.

Manual Scheduling

To discover what features might be useful for a computer aid
to scheduling on a Gantt chart, we carried out a paper and pencil
experiment in which four subjects spent up to ten hours each solving
job-shop scheduling problems based on exercises from the Harvard
Business School.   All subjects solved five problems and tape
recorded protocols during their problem solving activities.   They
were given the choice of using either a 'job' or 'machine' Gantt
chart (or using both simultaneously) to devise their solutions.
After experimenting with both, all subjects chose to use the machine
chart.   From study of the subjects' protocols and their errors
(Fitter and Sime, 1976), a prescription for a computer aided system
was derived.   In passing, it is interesting to note that (with the
exception of the first problem given) all subjects produced better
solutions than the best computer solution, which for each problem
was chosen from six solutions based on conventional priority
allocation heuristics.

Techniques of Chart Manipulation

There are two principal methods by which Gantt charts can be manipulated:-

(1) By maintaining constraints

This technique allows jobs to be inserted and slid around provided, at all times, the constraints of the number of machines available, job routes, etc., are not broken. Thus, at all times, the schedule is feasible but the task is to find a better one.

(2) By progressively imposing constraints

This technique initially inserts all jobs into the most compact space without regard for the number of machines available, etc. Conflicts are then resolved one by one until eventually a feasible schedule is produced which does not break any constraints. The technique, as applied to single track railway scheduling, has been described by Cherniavsky (1972), who also provides an algorithm for producing solutions. Laios & Gibson, of Loughborough University, have developed a mechanical analogue of the technique, which they call a scheduler's abacus (see Laios and Gibson, 1977).

The techniques of (1) maintaining and (2) progressively imposing constraints can both be applied to either (a) job or (b) machine charts.

Underlying Processors

Techniques (1) and (2) rather obviously imply different manipulation processes. For (1), when a job is slid along the chart it is necessary for it to 'push' other jobs with it, so as not to break any constraints. For (2), this is not necessary. Rather less obviously, although the job and machine charts are merely different representations of the same data-base each requires a different method of manipulation whether technique(1) or (2) is being used. Thus there are four (2 x 2) basic methods of manipulating Gantt charts.

Each of the four methods implies (or can be described by) a different Underlying Processor (UP), which is a dynamic (rather than static) description of the task. The description is not in machine or user language but in an abstract task language.

In his paper on programming language design, Sime (this volume) describes three micro languages - a JUMP style and two nest styles, NEST-BE and NEST-INE. The NEST and JUMP styles have different UPs, JUMP being more general and powerful than NEST which is more specific but also more suitable for the problems set to the subjects. However, NEST-BE and NEST-INE have identical UPs, and they differ only in their 'perceptual properties' ie. they use different user languages.

User Language

Although we have said that the UP is an abstract task description it must of course be represented in both computer language (which will impose constraints on the user) and in user language (so that the user can control the computer). The computer language is of little psychological interest here, being a matter of implementation technique. The user language is all important since it determines how the user perceives the system.

The two types of Gantt chart are different representations in user languages and they will influence how the user produces schedules even though they represent the same data-base. It has been stated that the job and machine charts require different UPs when using technique (1). In principle, it would be possible to use the same UP for both charts (the program would run), but the way in which the entities moved around the screen would not appear 'natural' to the users. The UP must be represented to the user as transparently and naturally as possible, so that he can understand the internal activity when he hands over control to the computer.

Moreover, each representation highlights different features which may or may not be essential to the task. For example, the job chart highlights job route and job waiting times whereas the machine chart highlights machine usage and the sequence of jobs through a machine. Which representation is better will depend on the precise goals of the user.

The three micro languages described by Sime (this volume) each have their own representation in user language, perceptual aids such as indenting being used to make the NEST structure more transparent.

Naturalness

We have talked of processes being natural, but actually to define what we mean by natural would be much too difficult. We offer a few pointes towards this illusive naturalness however.

It is not to be achieved by providing the user with a general purpose, flexible, simple language, nor even with an English-like language.

It is necessary to choose an underlying processor structured to the task requirements - this means the degree of specificity and complexity required by the task.

It is necessary to provide a user language which makes the underlying processor as transparent as possible (not obscuring it by apparently easy style), and which highlights the features essential to the task as directly as possible.

A Revised Design of SHED

Our original version of SHED allowed the user to build up a control program in a production system; he thus had very few constraints on how to produce schedules (except that they should be time-progressing – which we now believe to be unnecessarily restrictive). We now argue that the user should be more constrained, but in the right way. Possibly problem solving can be aided more by the constraints of a computer than by its flexibility. Rather than providing the user with the basic bricks and mortar of a production system, we should give him the prefabricated slabs representing characteristic functions of the assumed Underlying Processor (or a choice of several) which is made as transparent as possible by providing clear plans of the rules and constraints operating. The difficulty is, of course, finding out what are the right constraints.

We also spoke of Progressive Automation in the introduction. How is this affected by larger building blocks? The emphasis has changed. Rather than the user building up a controlling program from scratch, he now selects techniques, and can hand over control to the computer on specific matters. The essence of the system is still interaction and the sharing of control between man and machine. To conclude we offer a list of the ways that control can be shared in the SHED system using Gantt charts.

Things user can do:-	Things computer can do:-
allocate jobs to machines	check on legality of an allocation
slide jobs along or swop job positions	update necessary consequences of a change
fix reservations in chart – prohibit a job being scheduled at a specified position in chart	keep check on reservations and prohibitions – use rules to fill in rest of chart
Ask for a job to be scheduled "if it will finish in time"	check in job chart to see if any reservations or prohibitions prevent it from finishing on time
change his mind about a decision	backtrack to previous states
decide when a solution is satisfactory	highlight conflicts still to be resolved

ACKNOWLEDGEMENT

Many of the ideas underlying the research described in this paper are due to Max Sime, who has led the project.

REFERENCES

Cherniavsky, A.L.   1972   A program for timetable compilation
                                 by a look-ahead method.
                                 Artificial Intelligence, 3, 61-76.

Clark, W.   1952   The Gantt Chart.
                                 Pitman, London.

Davis, R. &   1975   An overview of production systems.
  King, J.   Stanford Artificial Intelligence
                                 Laboratory, Memo AIM-271.

Fitter, M.J.   1976   Computers as aids to forecasting and
                                 control.
                                 MRC Social & Applied Psychology Unit,
                                 Memo 117.

Fitter, M.J. &   1975   An extensible touchboard for on-line
  Daly, C.   experiments.
                                 Quarterly Journal of Experimental
                                 Psychology, 27, 673-676.

Fitter, M.J. &   1976   An empirical study of job-shop
  Sime, M.E.   scheduling by Gantt Chart.
                                 MRC Social & Applied Psychology Unit,
                                 Memo 136.

Gere, W.S.   1966   Heuristics in job-shop scheduling.
                                 Management Science, 13, 167-190.

Green, T.R.G.   1975   Computer translation with paired grammars.
                                 Behaviour Research Methods and Instrum-
                                 entation, 7, 557-562.

Jones, C.H.,   1969   A comparative study of computer-aided
  Hughes, J.L. &   decision making from display and
  Engvold, K.J.   typewriter terminals.
                                 IBM Poughkeepsie Lab. Technical Report,
                                 T.R. O.D.1891.

Laios, L. &   1977   The design of interactive planning
  Gibson, R.   displays for scheduling.
                                 In 'Human Operators and Simulation',
                                 Proceedings of International Symposium.
                                 London: Institute of Measurement and
                                 Control, 20 Peel Street, London W. 8.

Sime, M.E.   1979   "So I said in the most natural way, if
                                 x = o then begin ..": The empirical
                                 study of computer language to appear
                                 in Shackel, B. (ed). Proc. NATO ASI
                                 On Man-Computer Interaction (this volume).

PART 5 — TRAINING AND EDUCATION

PREVIEW

Training is an easily neglected area, in the design and
implementation of a computer system, and yet its importance cannot
be over emphasised.   Both with a new system and when changes are
made, and however good the system and equipment design has been
for MCI, there will still be a need for training as one particular
form of user support.   The general process of user support involves
any procedures needed to achieve an evolving man—computer relationship; unless the given system can continue to develop and match
the demands for change as they arise, it will gradually fail and
lose its value.   The crucial mediators who transform the potential
power of the computer system into an actual resource are the human
users, and it is they who must therefore be supported with training, manuals, 'help' facilities, local experts, etc.

Damodaran discusses user support as a major need, which was
revealed by the Eason, Damodaran and Stewart survey in 1974 as
seldom adequately provided.   She then reviews the various user
support mechanisms which may be needed and outlines various
solutions.   She argues that only by the provision of good user
support can the potential power of computer systems be achieved
in reality through successful MCI.

The whole area of education, computer—aided instruction (CAI)
and computer—aided learning (CAL) is a separate major field.   However, this volume on man—computer interaction would be incomplete
without some consideration of these topics.   Annett does not
attempt to review the progress in this area, but provides references
to some substantive reviews.   Rather, he distils from past work
and from his extensive experience the problems and issues upon
which concentration is essential if good MCI is to be achieved,
whether in training or in educational settings.

THE ROLE OF USER SUPPORT

L. Damodaran

Department of Human Sciences,
University of Technology, Loughborough, U.K.

INTRODUCTION

Man-computer interaction transforms the potential power of a computer system into reality.   The first essential condition for interaction is a physical means of achieving communication between the computer and the man, using the hardware of the former (computer terminals, data preparation forms, print-out, etc.) and the sense modalities of the latter.   The next requirement is a shared, symbolic coding system which allows the meaning of the communication to be understood by man and by computer.   Both these pre-requisites for interaction then require active support of a human user to achieve the transformation into a viable system. The primary focus of this paper is the support given both by the user and to the user in the interaction process.   The contents of the paper are based mainly upon findings of the MICA Survey (A Survey of Man-Computer Interaction in Commercial Applications, Eason et al., 1974) of over 250 people who are not computer professionals but who make use of computer systems in their work roles.   It is important to note that before this survey the role of user support as a significant variable in determining the effectiveness of man-computer interaction had not been recognised. For that reason it was not examined in a systematic way using structured questions.   In consequence the findings discussed here are of a mainly qualitative nature and should be regarded as a basis for quantification in future investigations.

THE SUPPORT FUNCTION: COMPENSATORY OR EVOLUTIONARY?

The minimal user support required to sustain man-computer interaction is that which ensures (i) that system input requirements are met by users and (ii) that system output is received and understood in the way intended.   The need to equip users to conduct these tasks was recognised as a necessity in all of the 26 organisations surveyed.

In order for any prospective computer user to become an active user he is required (i) to understand the system facility available to him, (ii) to conduct the operating procedures as prescribed, and (iii) to assimilate input and/or output activity in a work role. Fulfilment of these requirements represents the minimal user support necessary for the system to survive and to offer the prescribed service.   The role of the user is often clearly defined by the system's characteristics.   His behaviour vis-a-vis the system is determined by availability of the system, knowledge of the operating procedures, understanding of available output and acceptance of the rules and constraints of computer usage (limitations of data fields, demands for unambiguous messages, and careful precision).

The design of most computer systems takes for granted that people will conform to such demands.   This expectation reflects the assumption that the computer system offers an unquestionably superior approach to effective achievement of the organisation's goals and that users will therefore adjust their behaviour to meet the demands of the system.   The main rationale for the assumed superiority of the computer system is that it is designed on the basis of how the organisation should operate in order to optimise its performance.

When a system designed on such an idealised basis is put into operation, considerable accommodation to the constraints and pressures of the real situation are often encountered.   In the idealised situation users would be numerate, conversant with the rigid limitations of computing and familiar with codes and abbreviations. There is an inevitable short-fall between ideal and actual user characteristics and between the service provided by the computer and that needed by the user.   This requires considerable compensatory activity on the part of the user.   He has to learn to initiate interaction, to terminate it or to change direction.   He must be able to interpret system messages, to understand output, to cope with system malfunctions and even system breakdown.   He has, in other words, to compensate for his own lack of expertise and also for the inadequacies of the system.   Thus one role of user support is compensatory.   In recognition of this need, training is generally provided in operating procedures and in all routine aspects of system usage.

A compensatory support function can be appropriate where the system offers easy-to-use facilities and involves only input or output modes of interaction. Where a computer system offers a more substantial service, for example, to enable the user to interrogate a data base, to manipulate his data using statistical packages or by running 'models' a different support function is required. The more complex facilities carry with them the penalty of being much harder to understand and to put into effect. The relationship between modes of interaction and complexity of usage is shown in Figure 1. The conclusion to be drawn from this relationship is that substantial changes must occur in the user if he is to make use of the more complex and potentially more valuable modes of interaction. To exploit computing power in a sophisticated way the user needs to evolve with the system developing his interaction to suit his task needs. The existence of a continuum in the support role from compensatory to <u>evolutionary</u> is therefore postulated.

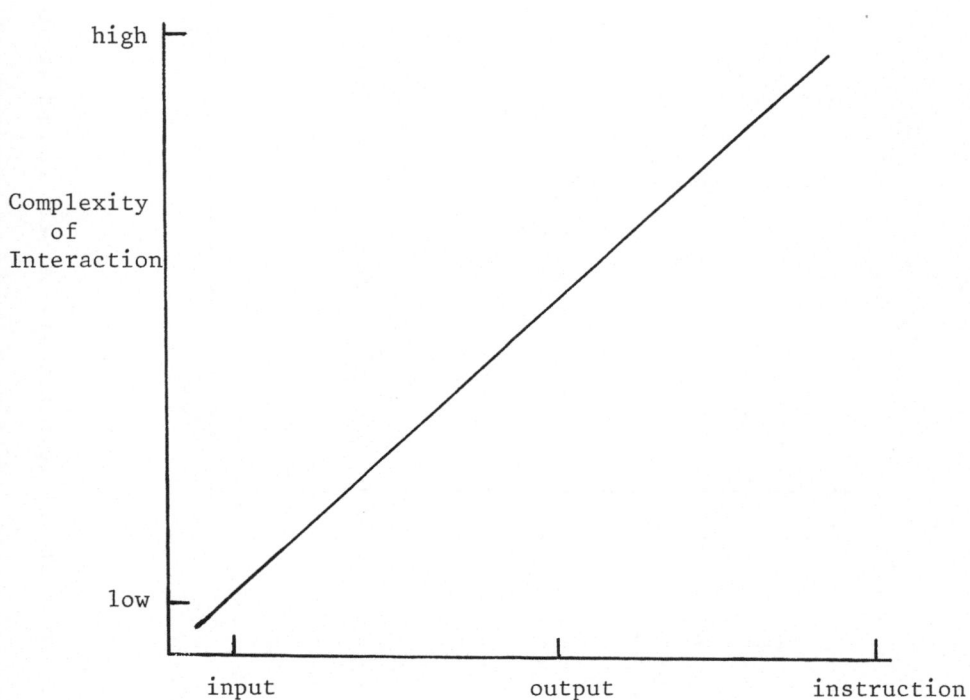

FIGURE 1. The relationship between modes of interaction and complexity of interaction.

264

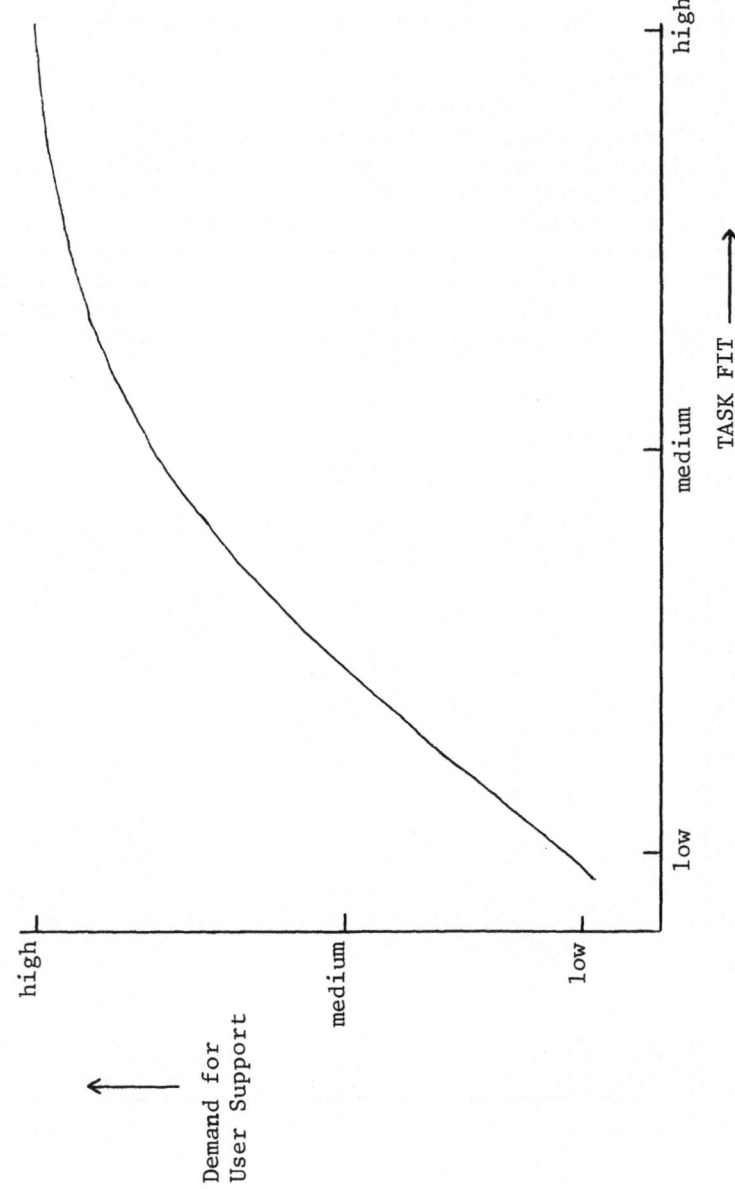

FIGURE 2. Hypothetical relationship between demand for user support and task fit.

Some evidence that the user support role is more than compensatory is gained from consideration of the relationship between 'Task Fit' and demand for User Support. 'Task Fit' is a composite measure made up of questions relating to the relevance, completeness, accuracy and timeliness etc., of the service they receive and is therefore a measure of the match between task needs and information service. If the user support function was purely compensatory we would expect demands for user support to be very low or non-existent where 'Task Fit' was high. In practice, the only computer applications where user support was not required were those where the system had fallen into disuse or very limited use (see Figure 2). Where users report a high Task Fit it appears that, since computer use has proved to be a rewarding experience for them, they want to increase their use of it and therefore have greater rather than lesser demands for user support – particularly of an evolutionary nature. They want to know more of the system's potential contribution to their work role and to realise more of that potential.

TYPES OF USER SUPPORT

The survey showed that all of the 26 computer applications studied had two kinds of support mechanism, documentary and human support mechanisms, as listed below:

Documentary

1. Instruction manuals
2. Within system aids
3. Circulars

Human Support

1. Formal training instructors)
2. Computer advisory personnel) system-centred
3. Dedicated programmer   )

4. Local experts   )
5. Human interface   ) user-centred
6. Organisational representatives)

Each of these support mechanisms fulfils a different kind of need and each has its limitations and problems (Damodaran, 1976). For our present purposes it will suffice to note that the documentary support mechanisms fulfil a largely compensatory function, as shown in Figure 3. Although they facilitate user development through learning, the range of facilities is finite and therefore prohibits user-system evolution. The same limitations

	Compensatory Function	Evolutionary Function
DOCUMENTARY SUPPORT		
Instruction manuals	*	
Within system aids	*	
Circulars	*	
HUMAN SUPPORT		
Formal training instructors	*	
Computer advisory personnel	*	
Dedicated programmers	*	*
Local experts	*	*
Human interfaces	*	
Organisational Representatives	*	

FIGURE 3.   The functions of User Support Mechanisms

exist for formal trainers, for most, but not all, computer advisory services, for human interfaces and for organisational representatives. These facilities all help the user, with varying degrees of effect-iveness, to reach a state of knowledge recognised by the system designers to be necessary to use the system successfully (see Figure 4).   There are also users who deviate from this desired norm either by wanting more information than was planned for them or by evading the pressures to learn the required amount.   User support mechanisms are rarely designed to meet these difficulties but a pattern of user response is beginning to emerge.   In the case of the task determined need for more technical information it is generally the specialist user who is involved.   As his knowledge of the system increases so the pressure he places on computer advisory staff increases and he may 'overtake' them in knowledge of the system.

It is almost exclusively managers who resist learning the basic essentials for interaction, and for them the most common solution is to provide a human interface who operates the system on their behalf, thus freeing them from the constraints of operating procedures.

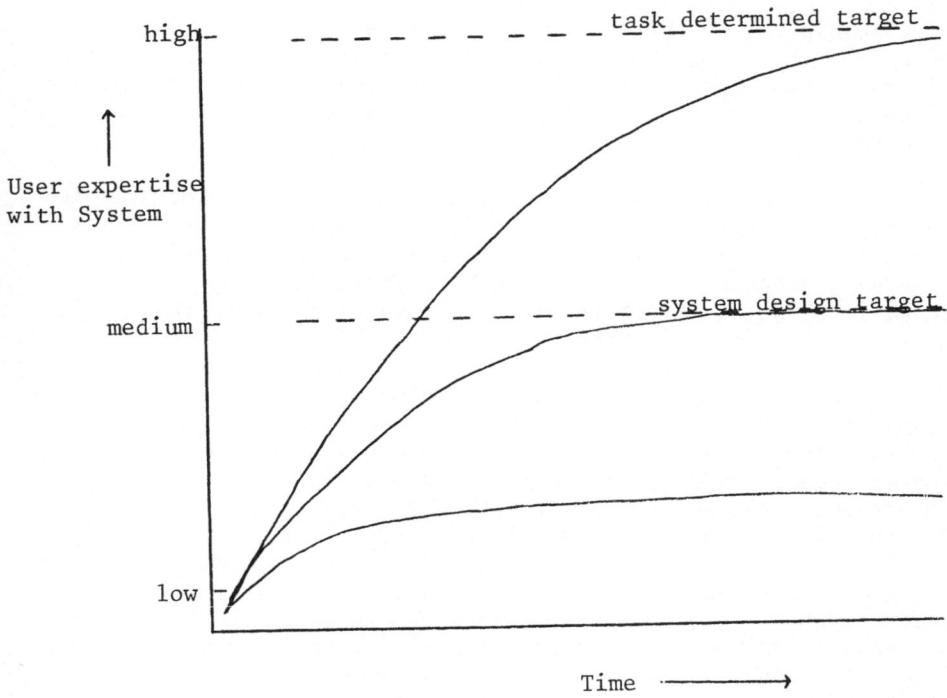

FIGURE 4. Actual versus expected user expertise in system design.

USERS' NEEDS AND VARIOUS SOLUTIONS

That there is a need for an evolutionary support role is
manifested by the behaviour of certain users.   Users in two
different task roles exhibit powerful motivation to know more
about the system than the support mechanisms generally recognise.
One situation arises where a specialist (designer, engineer,
psychologist etc.) with a complex task requires sophisticated data
processing and modelling techniques to manipulate his data.   In
such cases there are task-determined needs for high levels of user
support.   The second case involves clerks whose work role is
virtually synonymous with system operation and who are less 'users'
than 'servants' of the system.   Their case presents the dichotomy
of prescribed need and actual need.   Since their jobs are concerned
with routine data input or data handling they are making extremely
limited use of the computing power potentially available and
through repetition they are very familiar with the necessary
operating procedures.   From a strict definition of their work role
there is little need for user support in the day-to-day performance
of their tasks.   However, since they identify strongly with the

computer system, in the absence of any other way of understanding
their job, they search for meaning and context in their activities.
This means that certain clerks are interested in the wider context
of the system for their own psycho-social needs, not for task
performance.

In the case of the specialist needing extensive computer aid,
the computer department can solve this by designating one of its
programmers to work only for the specialist user's department.
While a 'dedicated' programmer can be a great advantage to a user
group, in reducing effort required to develop software for itself,
there are also disadvantages.

For example, the individual programmer has the task of gaining
an understanding of the subject area in which the specialists
operate before he can develop appropriate software.   Since the
problems under study by the specialists are usually complex, the
demands upon the programmer attempting to understand them are
correspondingly great.   This need to learn about the specialist
area is difficult enough but the difficulty is compounded when the
programmer is based at the computer centre, identifying with the
other computer personnel, responsible to the Data Processing
Manager and aspiring to a career path within the computer department.   In such circumstances, the programmer's reference group
will continue to comprise the staff at the computer centre and he
will tend to operate in such a way as to further his own career
and to maintain good relationships with these other computer
personnel.   In consequence, he may be more concerned to develop
software which is technically impressive or to minimise cpu time,
for example, than to develop the most effective and appropriate
tool for the specialist.   Thus, he is likely to want to modify
the definition of the specialist problem or the methodology to
develop software in a way that will enable him to meet his
personal objectives.   Clearly his objectives will not be completely
congruent with those of the specialist user whom he is supposed to
assist.   Where a programmer is committed to the goals of the user
he offers evolutionary user support but organisational problems
frequently prohibit this development.

In the absence of organisational solutions to these difficulties
many specialists have tended to develop their own computing
expertise.   There is some evidence to suggest that this trend may
have adverse effects upon their problem-solving performance because
their repertoire of solutions becomes constrained by the available
software (Stewart, 1974).   In any event, support mechanisms for
the specialist user appear far from adequate.

The clerks seeking information to provide some satisfaction
in their work fare even worse.   In most cases their attempts to
learn more about the system were discouraged.   It is "not done"

for clerks to question the purpose of the system, or to ask about
its performance or to seek an understanding of its role in the
parent organisation.   In other words, none of the support mechanisms recognised their "need to know" as legitimate or important.

THE LOCAL EXPERT - A SPECIFIC SOLUTION

The survey provided evidence that one type of support mechanism
has the capability of promoting evolution of the user and the system:
this was the "local expert" role.   Local experts often change
spontaneously from being an 'ordinary' user by asking questions,
experimenting with the system and developing more knowledge about
it than other users.   Characteristically, early exploratory
behaviour of the potentially 'expert' user gives him a superior
level of knowledge which is subsequently in demand from other users
when they face problems in routine or non-routine aspects of system
usage.   A source of local experts is generally required once system
staff have absented themselves from the user department following
successful implementation of the system, and the more knowledgable
users step in to meet the need.   Although development of computing
expertise is a deliberate process on the part of some prospective
local experts, who recognise it as a path to promotion, for others
it is a role they acquire because they happen to know more about
the system than anyone else in the user department.   The spontaneous
development of a local expert is almost certainly fostered by the
absence of alternative sources of computing expertise within the
department.   Despite its considerable value to user departments
the role of local expert was recognised in a formal way in only
two of the organisations surveyed although in all but three
applications users could readily point out a local expert.

The main problems of being a local expert without formal
responsibility for a support function are the increase in workload
and potential disruption of task performance.   Giving advice or
solving problems for other users can be a time-consuming process
for local experts when these activities are additional to an existing workload.   For clerical users this may not be very serious as
the role was often welcomed as a source of prestige and status.
Some specialists, however, resented the role as an unwelcome intrusion
into their 'real' work, and, with varying degrees of subtlety,
discouraged users from consulting them.   This may mean that users
make less than optimum use of the computer facilities unless
another source of assistance at an appropriate level is available.

The above discussion relates mainly to local experts who arise
spontaneously.   Occasionally organisations recognise prior to
implementation that there will be a need for explanations, guidance
and assistance for new users, and therefore select a prospective
user to train as a local expert, perhaps as supervisor over the

other users.   A local expert with a formally recognised role
faces less severe problems, since he is given the support he
requires and some of his other duties may be taken away to allow
him to meet users' needs for assistance.

EVOLUTION OF AND CRITERIA FOR SOLUTIONS

     To compensate for the shortcomings of each kind of support
mechanism the survey provided evidence that a network of mechanisms
evolves.   In most cases this network had developed in response
to user needs rather than as a designed feature.   The network
generally comprised a related series of human intermediaries
who facilitated use of documentary support mechanisms and who formed
a chain of contacts to bridge the gap in focus, language and concepts
which exists between computer users and the computer.   In some cases
there was a chain of three or four human intermediaries between
programmers or other systems personnel and the users.   It may be
that this kind of network offers a paradigm for future design of
support mechanisms since it provides choice in the level of help
a user can seek.

     In attempting to establish further criteria for the design of
support mechanisms it is important to include the requirement for
on-going support.   When a user's early needs for learning how to
operate the system have been met, it is tempting to consider that
user support has been completed.   The evolutionary support role
can, by definition, never be regarded as "complete" because the
human capacity for learning means that however ignorant of a system
the user appears at the outset, he soon changes.   With experience
of using the system he will begin to want to know more about it,
typically he will begin to ask whether it could perform a wider
range of functions for him or whether existing procedures could be
improved.   The fact that a user learns means that he soon needs
more knowledge than any initial instruction could appropriately
apply.   This dilemma cannot be resolved simply by telling him
more about the system at the outset.   At the early stages further
information would not be assimilated and could not cover future
changes.   This therefore argues for a continuing process of user
support rather than a one-off training course.

     A design consideration, implicit in the problems of one-way
transmission of information through most of the documentary
support mechanisms, concerns the user's need for unstructured
exploration of the potential capability of the machine as well as
his need for reassurance and encouragement.   In both of these
needs the support requirement is for two-way communication.

     A further requirement is that assistance should be available
to users on demand.   Task performance may suffer if help is
delayed; serious morale problems and alienation are other potential
dangers when help is not readily forthcoming.   A check list of the
criteria to be met in order to provide effective user support
mechanisms is presented below (see Figure 5).

CONCLUSION

In conclusion, man-computer interaction offers a potential
power to its users that is greatly under utilised. This paper
suggests that one serious impediment to greater exploitation of
the computer is the lack of user support and the preoccupation
of available support with a compensatory rather than an evolutionary function. The design solutions require organisational changes
to legitimise the support function, to promote the effectiveness
of user support and to design a reward system for support staff.

---

1. Formal recognition of user support role.

2. Adequate resources (a range of levels of expertise).

3. Recognition of a heterogeneous user population.

4. Evolutionary.

5. Available on demand.

6. Available at point-of-need.

7. Career opportunities for support personnel.

8. Congruence of system staff goals with user goals.

FIGURE 5.   Criteria for Effective User Support

REFERENCES

K.D. Eason,   1974   A Survey of Man-Computer Interaction
L. Damodaran &   in Commercial Applications.
T.F.M. Stewart   LUTERG Report No. 144, Department of
                                 Human Sciences, University of Technology,
                                 Loughborough, U.K.

T.F.M. Stewart   1974   The Software Interface and Displays.
                                 HUSAT Memo No. 95, Department of Human
                                 Sciences, University of Technology,
                                 Loughborough, U.K.

L. Damodaran   1975   Support Facilities for Computer Users. HUSAT Memo No. 97, Department of Human Sciences, University of Technology, Loughborough, U.K.

PROBLEMS OF MAN-COMPUTER INTERACTION IN EDUCATION & TRAINING

John Annett

Department of Psychology, University of Warwick, Coventry.

INTRODUCTION

Computers have been used in instructional and educational settings for something like 15 years. In the early 1960's a number of developments conspired to make a Computer Aided Instruction (CAI) a practical possibility. The first mini-computers became available and together with high level programming languages found their uses in the psychological laboratory. Some psychologists had already been involved in the development of computer controlled simulators and extension of the new technology into the classroom soon followed. As with many new developments the effect was first and foremost on thinking about teaching and learning, for CAI still has to make its impact on practical teaching. In the early 1960's teaching machines had introduced the idea of 'programmed' instruction and their initial success had been tinged with some misgivings about the adequacy of Skinnerian 'learning theory' to cope with the complexities of instruction in real-life skill and in areas of academic knowledge. At the same time the world-wide demand for training in sophisticated technologies and for educational opportunity as a basic human right was increasing rapidly, and mechanisation seemed one possible answer to the foreseen explosion in demand.

I shall not attempt to review all the developments during the past 15 years in this paper but rather to concentrate on a limited number of problems essential to man-machine interaction in the training or educational setting. The reader who would like a more detailed review of developments in the U.K. is referred to Hooper (1975), Hooper & Toye (1975) and Annett (1976a & b).

274

BRIEF SUMMARY OF THE CURRENT STATE OF THE ART

The classic example of full-blooded CAI is the PLATO project
of the University of Illinois (Meller 1974). The essential
features of the system are its size, up to 4,000 terminals operating simultaneously, and the fact that it attempts to carry out
most varieties of educational task, that is, it is a potential
teacher substitute. The system is based on a CDC Cyber 73-24
with two Central Processing Units (CPU's) and 65,000 words of
central memory controlling extended core store, a number of discs
and other forms of auxiliary stores. The student terminals of
which there will be 4,000 are, however, the most interesting
technical development. Don Bitzer, the originator of PLATO
recognised that standard teletype terminals are noisy and limited
in the rate and variety of visual output and that Video Display
Units (VDU's) whilst silent are still limited in the kind of
information they can present and are, moreover, very expensive.
In a system of PLATO's size the terminal, the actual man-machine
interface, could constitute a major cost so Bitzer developed a
plasma panel display. This is a sandwich of plasma gases between
sheets of glass and contains a grid of 512 x 512 fine wires.
Voltages applied to pairs of wires cause the plasma to glow at
their intersections. The panel is a storage device and so there
is no need for the computer to refresh the display. It can also
function as a back-projection screen so that locally stored film
or microfiche material can be presented and the screen can also
be arranged to be touch-sensitive so that more direct responses
than typewriting can be accepted.

The software system includes a high level language, TUTOR,
in which teachers can prepare, edit and test their material using
any of the terminals. On my latest information, now almost
certainly out of date, some 4,000 hours of teaching material
ranging from basic reading through aspects of veterinary medicine
had been produced. But PLATO does more than just present pre-
programmed lessons. It can provide monitored drill and practice
in basic skills or an environment for problem solving of the kind
pioneered by Papert (1971a & b) or laboratory simulation facilities
(Hyatt et al, 1972).

It is as much an economic as an educational question whether
the way ahead lies with large general purpose systems like PLATO
or with the development of smaller more specialised systems based
on much cheaper mini-computers or perhaps even microprocessors.
CAI is not by any means a uniform technique but, like human teaching, a battery of tools which can be used selectively according
to the objectives, the student population and the practical
resource situation in which the teaching is to take place.

Examples of a variety of techniques can be found in recent British work. One of the least glamorous uses of the computer is as an <u>exerciser</u>. Following on the work of Atkinson (1976) and others at Stanford, Hartley and his group at Leeds (Hartley, 1975) have developed successful 'drill and practice' programs in arithmetic. These have proved of value in coping with mixed ability classes on entry to junior high school. The simple but effective instruction provided on a couple of terminals has reduced individual differences in basic skills, enabling the teacher to proceed with the new syllabus rather earlier than would otherwise have been the case. Experiments by the Leeds team clearly demonstrate that the immediate feedback automatically provided on the terminals is largely responsible for the success of the drill and practice method. The Leeds project has also developed the use of computer simulations as a partial substitute for practical work in University level chemistry.

Time and materials can be saved if the aim of the practical is to demonstrate a dynamic process which could be represented and manipulated numerically. A project jointly managed between University College and Chelsea College, London and the University of Surrey has developed a number of simulation packages (Annett 1976b) in physics, chemistry, biology and statistics. Programs are written in FORTRAN or BASIC for ease of transfer between institutions. An example in physics is a simulation of the relationship between speed and launching angle on the orbit of a satellite. The student can experiment by entering different values of the essential variables and noting the effect on the orbit represented on a VDU. A more dramatic demonstration comes from the Glasgow project on medical education (Taylor, 1975). An emergency case is simulated. Information including the answers to questions is provided on a VDU and the student's task is to make a correct diagnosis and apply emergency treatment under time pressure. The vital signs, respiration, pulse and blood pressure are displayed and all respond to the 'state' of the simulated patient and to remedial actions by the student such as giving pain killers or plasma. the patient either stops 'bleeding' and begins to recover or 'dies'. Two points are of particular interest in this example. The first is that dynamic simulation is not in this case a substitute for more 'realistic' training since the sort of experience provided is just not found in the current medical curriculum. The second is that this kind of simulation depends on a knowledge base, a store of information about the simulated patient which must be assessed in real time in response to questions put in as natural a manner as possible.

A computer may, however, be used educationally without necessarily working from a base of stored information. Most teachers of programming agree that "hands-on experience" is an essential tool in learning to develop programs. Papert (1971a & b) has gone further in using a programming language called LOGO, developed by

W. Feuerzeig, for educational purposes. LOGO is an easy to understand language which can be used to make terminal devices such as
a graphics display or a moving trolley (know as a 'turtle') to carry
out various procedures. For example, the 'turtle' can be made to
trace out a square on the floor by making a short journey, turning
through 90 degrees, making another journey of the same length,
turning again and so on. The educational philosophy behind this
is that much of what is taught in schools could be described as
procedures for finding solutions. In the geometrical example just
given 'square' is defined in terms of the procedures which will
produce a square. When a child is unsuccessful in solving a
problem the reason for the failure is not always clear unless all
the steps can be recalled and individually checked just as a
programmer 'debugs' a program which has not worked quite as expected
on the first trial. Papert argues in general that constructing
a program to produce something in such a way that the procedure
can be debugged if it does not work first time, should give the
child a more insightful and more encouraging way of learning mathematics. LOGO laboratories have been set up at MIT and the Department of Artificial Intelligence at Edinburgh for experimental work
on the analysis of children's thinking (Howe et al., 1975, Annett,
1976a).

   In the examples I have described so far the computer, or at
least a terminal, makes a direct connection with the learner. It
could be argued that there is a great need for data-processing in
education without necessarily interfacing directly with the individual learner. The rationale for computer managed instruction (CMI)
is essentially economic. In Britain for example the computer plays
an essential part in the Open University system. Whereas an assignment marked by a human tutor costs something of the order of £2.00
each computer marked assignments cost only a few pence. The computer
also keeps track of the 50,000 or so registered students, the courses
they are doing or have passed, the number expected to take examinations, attend summer schools in different regions, and so on. The
computer as a manager of learning is an attractive proposition at
all levels. Experiments in the London Borough of Havering (Broderick 1975) have successfully managed a course in Biology and in
Hertfordshire (Annett, 1976b) a large bank of mathematics items is
kept and pupils' performance on them automatically scored. At the
New University of Ulster (Annett, 1976b) trainee teachers have
recently had the opportunity to follow a course in curriculum development under computer management. It was essentially a multi-media
resource-based course and students were offered study 'prescriptions'
based on the results of computer-marked tests. Interestingly the
first results suggest that students who chose to follow the computer's
prescriptions did rather better not just in tests of factual information but also in creative curriculum project work.

Space has permitted only the briefest summary of some of the
work currently in progress in Britain, much of it sponsored by the
National CAL Development Programme and the Social Science Research
Council.   Many of these projects are subject to both educational
and financial evaluation studies which are still in progress and
are expected to appear towards the end of 1977.   Accumulated
experience is however beginning to reveal some of the problems which
will have to be solved.

THE PRINCIPAL ISSUES AND PROBLEMS

Table 1 follows Paul Fitts's famous list comparing the attributes of humans and machines but in this case specifically comparing
human teachers and CAI or CMI according to the current state of the
art.   The first column lists teaching functions.   My list is
fairly comprehensive, at least in my personal 'theory' of teaching.
I see the most important function of a teacher as the analysis and
specification of learning objectives.   This is perhaps the most
creative of those functions subsumed under the teacher's art, but
perhaps only a few teachers do more than follow conventionally
agreed objectives.   It is certainly not the kind of function
performed by any computer at present, although it might be argued
that the very process of programming and mechanisation of instruction forces the human teacher to analyse his objectives much more
thoroughly than he would normally care to do.

The next teacher function, acting as an information resource,
implies storage and retrieval of information and the generation of
examples.   Human teachers are above all else expected to 'know'
their subject matter, that is they are some kind of information
store.   There is little doubt that just about anything a human can
keep in memory can also be stored in a computer and much of it, of
course, can be stored in books or other coded forms such as tapes
and slides and a variety of other physical forms.   The problem,
however, is not storage as such but retrieving information when it
is suited to a particular occasion drawn from a knowledge base in
the subject being taught.   We shall return to this rather important
problem a little later.

Having selected appropriate information the teacher must display
it to the students.   The unaided teacher is rather limited in this
respect unless he is also a good artist and mime or can arrange
demonstrations.   The sort of aids which the teacher often uses,
such as pictures, can equally well be presented by computer either
directly through a VDU or indirectly by the control of peripheral
devices.   In practice it is often the case that the only display
available is a teletype which is adequate for short alpha-numeric
messages but very limited for anything else.   The Bitzer terminal
is certainly an improvement, but surprisingly little development

work seems to have been done on producing an easy to read, modestly
priced VDU with audio facilities.   On the whole film loops still
constitute the best current solution for many visual display purposes, except where dynamic interaction with the student is essential.

When we turn to the functions of receiving and interpreting
information from students we hit some fairly severe problems.   A
number of British investigators have discovered that, by and large,
students are very inexperienced typists.   A major barrier between
men and machines is therefore at this, the simplest ergonomic level
in designing interface equipment suitable for the mass market of
inexperienced operators.   Even with a much improved keyboard there
are still considerable problems to be faced.   The computer must
receive all its data in the form of a simple digital code.   This
is a limitation even with relatively straightforward verbal messages
where the alternatives are essentially a form of multiple choice
or, as with PLATO, a system of keyword matching which is only
moderately effective.   To take an imaginery example; in answer to
the question "Who discovered America?" a relatively simple system
could distinguish between and even identify "Columbus" and "Eric
the Red" even if they were misspelled.   But a system which simply
relies on identifying key words may be misled by a more sophisticated
answer such as "It can't have been St. Columba".

A major limitation on computers as teachers is that they just
do not understand natural language.   The human teacher is often
interested in why a particular response should occur at all and
the analysis of errors becomes very important.   In trying to probe
the student's understanding of the subject matter the teacher may
sometimes rely on superficially trivial cues such as the use of a
word in an unusual context.   In short the teacher can be thought
of as entertaining and testing hypotheses about the state of the
student's understanding of the subject matter and, from his own
knowledge of the subject matter, inventing strategies for correct-
ing misunderstandings.   Interpreting information from the student
is closely related to the 'knowledge' functions I referred to
earlier.   A computer program which 'understands' the subject matter
in its store will probably also be able to interpret students'
questions about the subject matter and also interpret both right
and wrong answers.   That such programs are in principle possible
has been demonstrated by Winograd (1972) in the PLANNER program
which 'understands' a miniature world consisting of a table top
with variously shaped and coloured objects which can be moved
around, or, more generally, can stand in varying relationships to
each other.   PLANNER not only follows instructions, in English,
but can also answer questions about current and past states of the
miniature world and give reasons for particular sequences of actions.
In this way it is taken by some as a prototype of a knowledge-based
system which can answer unanticipated questions and could, perhaps,
generate example material.

TABLE 1.   A "Fitts' List" of Teaching Functions Comparing Generalised Human and Computer Teachers.

FUNCTION	HUMAN	COMPUTER
Analysing & Specifying teaching objectives	The theoretically primary function, often "fudged".	At present incapable.
Knowledge store		
1. Size	Almost unlimited.	Limited by cost.
2. Accessibility	Usually good over very wide range of items.	Good only for closely specified items.
3. Generating examples	Almost unlimited.	Good only in limited areas.
Information display	Good for verbally coded materials, otherwise severe limitations.	Can display anything which can be coded in electrical signals. In practice limited by terminal.
Receiving information	Can receive all kinds of signals, e.g. answers, distress, pleasure.	Range severely limited by terminal.
Interpreting information from student	Can interpret almost any response, given one student at a time.	Severe limitations, understands formal language but not natural language.
	Poor at collating data over large numbers of students.	Can deal with large numbers.
Supervision and control of learning	Wide range of strategies but applies these inconsistently.	Very limited range of strategies but consistently applied.
Cost	Fairly expensive to train and maintain and getting more expensive.	High capital cost on both hardware and software but hardware getting cheaper fast. Inexpensive for simple functions where student population is large.

280

A series of experimental teaching programs from a group at
Bolt, Beranek and Newman (Collins et al. 1974) represents a more
pragmatic approach than PLANNER which was not designed as a teacher.
These are STUDENT developed by Carbonnel, and its successor SCHOLAR
further developed by Collins and others and SOPHIE by J.S. Brown
(Brown & Burton, 1975). This family of programs is knowledge-based
and characterised by the ability to shift the initiative between
the teacher and learner. The structure of the knowledge base has
features in common with the semantic network now familiar to
psychologists in the work of the LNR group (Norman et al. 1976) in
which concepts are represented as directed labelled graphs.
Figure 1 shows an example of a semantic network concerned with
"Luigi's tavern". The items in the boxes and the relationships
represented by the lines joining the boxes can of course be much
more abstract. The value of a semantic network, as opposed to a
stored set of 'facts' is that meanings and events can be reconstructed
by operating on the network. SCHOLAR, for example has a data base
in South American geography in which 'facts' about places or natural
features and even relationships between them can be reconstructed.

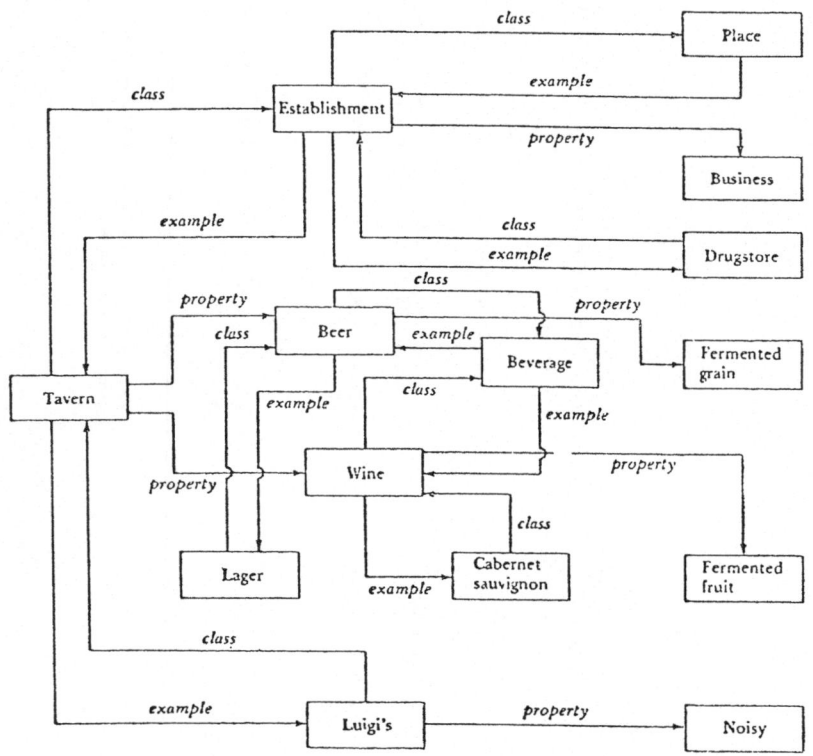

FIGURE 1. A simple semantic network. From Lindsay & Norman (1972)

THE CITIES IN BRAZIL ARE ------.

RIO DE JANEIRO, BUENOS AIRES, AND TITICACA

"RIO DE JANEIRO" IS FINE.
I DON'T THINK BUENOS AIRES AND TITICACA ARE CORRECT.

YOU COULD ALSO MENTION SAO PAULO, BRASILIA, PORTO ALEGRE,
SALVADOR, RECIFE, SANTOS, MANAOS, AND BELEM.

BUENOS AIRES IS NOT IN BRAZIL BUT IN ARGENTINA.

TITICACA IS NOT A CITY BUT A LAKE IN SOUTH AMERICA.

WHERE IS BRASILIA

    BRASILIA IS IN CENTRAL BRAZIL.
    IT IS IN THE BRAZILIAN HIGHLANDS.

WHAT IS THE MOST IMPORTANT DIFFERENCE BETWEEN BRASILIA AND RIO

THE PRIMARY DIFFERENCE IS:

    BRASILIA IS IN CENTRAL BRAZIL.
BUT   RIO DE JANEIRO IS IN EASTERN BRAZIL.

SELECT AN ALTERNATIVE FROM THE LIST:

ASIA
NORTH AMERICA
AFRICA
SOUTH AMERICA

TO COMPLETE THE SENTENCE:

BRAZIL IS LOCATED IN ------.

BRAZIL IS IN SOUTH AMERICA

THAT'S RIGHT.

TELL ME ABOUT THE AMAZON

    THE AMAZON IS NAVIGABLE.
        IT IS A RIVER.
        IT IS IN BRAZIL AND PERU.
        THE LENGTH IS 4,000 MILES.   Fig. 2 cont...

PLEASE TELL ME MORE ABOUT THE AMAZON

    THE MOUTH IS IN THE ATLANTIC.
    THE TRIBUTARIES ARE IN THE MARANON, THE RIO NEGRO,
    THE JURA, THE PURUS, THE TAPAJOZ, THE MADEIRA,
    AND THE TOCANTINS.

IS SAO PAULO A CITY IN BRAZIL?

I THINK I HAVE ALREADY TOLD YOU ABOUT IT.

YES.

FIGURE 2.   Illustrative dialogue between SCHOLAR and a student.
                Student inputs are between asterisks.
                From Collins et al. (1974)

A small sample of dialogues between SCHOLAR and a student illustrates some of the resultant properties (Fig. 2). One of the more interesting properties is that the program is able to produce a reasonable answer to a question about differences between two cities based on a search through their relational properties. SOPHIE is, as its name suggests, probably one of the most sophisticated of the knowledge-based systems available at present. Its semantic network describes electronic circuits and its purpose is to teach fault-finding. Like SCHOLAR, SOPHIE does more than represent knowledge and answer questions. It can take teaching initiatives and uses a variety of heuristic strategies for manipulating the student's interaction with the knowledge-base, that is the exercise of fault-finding skills.

This brings me to the last of the main teacher functions in my list, the function of control. It is assumed that the teacher not only formulates knowledge goals, himself possesses and is able to transmit the requisite knowledge, but that in various ways he controls the interaction between the student and what is to be learned. Techniques of control can be crude or subtle. Crudely the teacher can demand that a set of facts or a specified sub-skill be mastered to a given criterion, even by a particular time. More subtly he can stimulate the student's curiosity by presenting a limited amount of material in a way which encourages the student to want to know more. Examples and tasks can be matched to the student's pre-existing knowledge and interests or even ability and personality characteristics. In SCHOLAR control is exerted by asking questions about relatively neglected aspects of the subject matter. In the Leeds arithmetic program control can be exercised by selecting levels of difficulty which are empirically optimal.

In several computer-managed systems control is exerted by varying the teaching prescription as a function of test results. Questions of the kind and degree of control have been with us for quite a long time (eg. Swets, 1962) and quite recently Atkinson (1976) has provided some results in learning German language vocabulary indicating once again that control strategies can be found which do better, on average, than students' self-selected strategy. The same kind of result emerged from preliminary experiments in the CAMOL project (Annett, 1976b), but as these investigators pointed out an important aim of education is to make students better able to learn for themselves. A high degree of control may in the long term be counter-productive. Any student wishing to control a computer teacher has, of course, only to pull out the plug, or walk away from the terminal, yet such is the awe in which computers are held that one never hears of this reaction from any of the many thousands of students who have received CAI. Some have remarked that the unflappable, untiring image presented by the CAI terminal gives the impression of a hard task-master, a teacher without human weaknesses. Those educational researchers who, like myself, have become interested in CAI have, on the whole, prided themselves on their hard-headed analytical approach to problems of teaching and learning. They have had to master a complex technology and to cut through some of the many ambiguities which surround the mysteries of education. They may, therefore, be less sensitive to the social and even moral significance of CAI and to be too dismissive of the attitudinal problems which arise because control appears to be vested in a machine rather than a human agent.

It seems a pity that the last word must be on cost. There is little doubt that our technical ability to devise effective instructional and educational systems, computerised or non-computerised, exceeds society's willingness to meet the cost. The capital cost of a system like PLATO IV runs into many millions of dollars. This might not be so bad if it were not, in effect, an add-on cost. A system big enough to take over substantial responsibility from the conventional teaching system has not yet been devised. However, the comparative cost of CAI is far from being a simple story. The cost of providing a computerised tutorial system which will, for example, carry on an intelligent dialogue on the interpretation of Shakespeare's sonnets would probably be enormous and certainly much more expensive than very adequate human teachers. At the other extreme the cost of a computer-controlled simulator, although often high, compares very favourably with the cost of more realistic training on real aeroplanes. Most education and training problems lie somewhere in between these extremes.

284

CONCLUSION

Almost every subject matter, even at University level, has
its basics which must be mastered and its classical problems, all
well-worn paths which succeeding generations of students must tread
and which only a degree of intelligence, perhaps not very great,
is needed to teach. We appear to be in the middle of a technological revolution in computing hardware with the recent advent of
microprocessors and this is reducing the cost of CPU (as opposed
to peripheral) hardware at an estimated 30% per annum. This is,
of course, happening at a time when the cost of teachers' salaries
has increased by a similar amount over the same period in the U.K.
Given that processing capacity is becoming rapidly cheaper and
given that some progress is made in developing a cheap terminal,
it seems very probable that the present relatively small foothold
of CAI will be extended to a bridgehead and that during the last
quarter of a century computers will become as familiar in schools
as the blackboard.

REFERENCES

Annett, J.   1976a   Computer assisted learning 1969/75.
                                London: Social Science Research
                                    Council, (Temple Avenue, London EC4).

Annett, J.   1976b   Report on a research seminar on
                                    computers in education, at the
                                    University of Warwick, 14-16 July 1976.
                                Available from author.

Atkinson, R.C.   1976   Adaptive instructional systems: some
                                    attempts to optimise the learning
                                    process.
                                In Klahr (1976).

Broderick, W.R.   1975   The Havering computer managed learning
                                    system.
                                In Hooper & Toye (1975).

Brown, J.S. &   1975   Multiple representations of knowledge
    Burton, R.R.   for tutorial reasoning.
                                In: Bobrow & Collins (Eds),
                                    Representation & Understanding.
                                New York: Academic Press.

Collins, A.   1974   Analysis and synthesis of internal
    Warnock, E.H. &   dialogues.
    Passafiume, J.J.   Bolt, Beranek & Newman, Report No.2789,
                                    50 Moulton Street, Cambridge,
                                    Mass. 02138, USA.

Hartley, J.R.   1975   Some experiences with individualised
                               teaching systems.
                               In Hooper & Toye (1975).

Hooper, R.   1975   Two years on: the National Development
                               Programme in Computer Assisted Learning.
                               London: Councils and Educational Press
                               Ltd., 10 Queen Anne Street, London W1.

Hooper, R. &   1975   Computer assisted learning in the
   Toye, I.   United Kingdom: some case studies.

                               London: Councils and Educational Press
                               Ltd., 10 Queen Anne Street, London W1.

Howe, J.A.M.,   1975   Artificial intelligence and the
   Knapman, J.   representation of knowledge.
   Noble, H.M.   Dept. of Artificial Intelligence
   Weir, S. &   Research Report No. 5, Edinburgh
   Young, R.M.   University.

Hyatt, G.W.   1972   Computer-based education in Biology.
   Eades, D.C. &   BioScience, 22, 401-409.
   Tenczar, P.

Klahr, D. (Ed.)   1976   Cognition and Instruction.
                               New York: Wiley.

Lindsay, P.H. &   1972   Human information processing.
   Norman, D.A.   New York: Academic Press.

Meller, D.V.   1974   Using PLATO IV.
                               Report from Computer-Based Education
                               Research Laboratory, University of
                               Illinois, Urbana, Ill. 61801, USA.

Norman, D.A.   1976   Comments on learning schemata and
   Gentner, D.R. &   memory representation.
   Stevens, A.L.   In Klahr (1976).

Papert, S.   1971a   A computer laboratory for elementary
                               schools.
                               AI Memo 246, Artificial Intelligence
                               Laboratory, M.I.T., Cambridge,
                               Mass. 02139, U.S.A.

Papert, S.   1971b   Teaching children thinking.
                               AI Memo 247, Artificial Intelligence
                               Laboratory, M.I.T., Cambridge,
                               Mass. 02139, U.S.A.

Swets, J.   1962   Learning to identify nonverbal sounds:
                               an application of a computer as a
                               teaching machine.
                               U.S. Naval Training Device Centre,
                               Tech. Rep. No. 789-1.

Taylor, T.R.   1975   Computer assisted learning in classical
decision making.
In Hooper & Toye (1975).

Winograd, T.   1972   A program for understanding natural
language.
Cognitive Psychology, 3, 1-191.

PART 6   -   MANAGER AND ORGANISATION

PREVIEW

The growth of computing with regard to managers and organisations has inevitably gone through a number of fashions and
selling themes in the market place.   The first major marketing
phase was the concept of the data processing system to replace
clerks;   this gave a big sales bonanza until business and local
government learned the hard way that there were few clerks less
in the end and therefore cost effectiveness was questionable.
So the marketing concept moved on to Management Information
Systems;   the big scheme with a total data base management system
was supposed to yield a big bonus - until managers found they were
buried in paper but starved of information (eg. Eason, Damodaran
and Stewart survey of 1974).   In recent years the industry has
moved on to more cautious and realistic approaches as managers and
organisations have required better evidence of potential success.

With regard to decision making by managers, rather little
knowledge is available as yet about the cognitive ergonomics
aspects, despite all the computer industry activity on management
information systems.   The best evidence of inadequate design for
MCI by managers and directors is the very small number of cases
where they work directly with the computer, and the very large
number of cases where they work through a 'human intermediary'
(eg. a secretary, personal assistant, statistical analyst, financial
planner, etc.).   Inadequate design for MCI is not the only reason
why managers mostly adopt this strategy, but it is probably the
main reason.   We need to understand much more about the rich
variety of cognitive behaviour involved in the very wide range of
tasks typical of managers' jobs, before a reasonably adequate
prescription can be written to define their MCI needs.   The same
remarks apply 'mutatis mutandis' to organisations.

The papers in this part all relate to various aspects of such
issues as how to define the needs of managers or organisations,
how to implement applications, what are the results for organisations
of the major changes involved, and how can knowledge and methods
from the human sciences be transferred to improve MCI for managers
and organisations.

In order to explain the critical comments made by managers about computer-based management information systems, Eason presents a task-tool analysis which highlights the problems of trying to serve the manager's information requirements.   The responses of the manager to a task-tool mismatch are examined and two (partial use and distant use) are discussed in some detail. From the analysis he deduces consequences and shows how these relate to the all too common experiences of managers.   He concludes that the manager is a particularly difficult customer for the computer, and that achieving effective manager-computer interaction is a major challenge for research in MCI.

Based upon a thorough review of the relevant literature, Vanlommel et al. offer a very interesting set of conceptual propositions.   They describe their empirical investigations to test these and report that few of the propositions could be fully confirmed and indeed some are contradicted;   however, most are not so much denied as not proven.   This paper shows the complexity of running valid studies in this important area of the organisational effects of introducing computers.

Bair first describes the facilities provided by the general purpose communication and information handling system developed by the Augmentation Research Center at Stanford Research Institute. He then outlines the proposed sequence of procedures to help client organisations to adopt the system and then adapt to it and also adapt it to help themselves; the types and procedures of application are described in considerable detail.   Finally, he discussed the principles and procedures they use to help clients achieve the 'technology transfer' involved in adopting this computer-based type of communication inside the organisation.   He concludes by emphasising that the process is not as simple as might appear from a straightforward description; there are of course many difficulties along the path, and the system and whole process is essentially evolutionary.

As a computer scientist Martin points out, now that some of the major constraints of equipment technology have been overcome, that we are recognising the real issues to be what people need, find useful and can use.   So the emphasis must be moved onto the end user's needs.   He discusses various examples and aspects of the process of 'needs assessment'.   Finally, he draws attention to the problem of the potential conflict between the individual needs of each user, related to his own particular tasks, and the designer's need to make his system saleable by being more or less suitable for the needs of many users even though an exact match for none.

A TASK-TOOL ANALYSIS OF MANAGER-COMPUTER INTERACTION*

K.D. Eason

Department of Human Sciences,
University of Technology, Loughborough, U.K.

1. INTRODUCTION

The prevailing theme of human science analyses of the impact of computers upon management is that of information ownership and access. Information is valuable and the creation of a data base may well change the distribution of information in an organisation. It may, for example, mean that the chief executive can examine in detail the activities of his subordinates. It may also mean that a department gains access to information previously under the control of another department which may well influence relations between them.

It is interesting to note that this is not the dominant theme of the computer literature on management information systems. Here the issue is well summarized by Ackoff (1968) in his article 'management mis-information systems'. He suggests that the anticipated benefits of computers for management have largely been lost in bulky printouts which are often irrelevant, out-of-date and inaccurate.

---

* The survey reported in this paper was partly sponsored by the Social Science Research Council.

The 'information ownership' approach contributes little to our understanding of the situation Ackoff describes and it appears that we need an approach which will provide an explanation. This approach should provide an understanding of the manager's task and the way he performs it. As a result it should demonstrate the kind of information service the computer should give if it is to be successful. This analysis should also highlight the deficiencies of the present day systems which have been the subject of so much criticism.

It is the purpose of this paper to conduct an analysis of manager-computer interaction in these terms. This may be called a task-tool analysis in which the focus is upon the ability of the computer (the tool) to meet the needs of the management task.

2. ELEMENTS OF A TASK-TOOL ANALYSIS

The elements in this analysis are presented in Figure 1. The central proposition is that, to be successful, the tool must support the user's interpretation of his task. It is not sufficient for the tool to serve the system designer's view of the task because the user's interpretation may be very different. The consequence of a mis-match between these elements may affect the use of the tool, the interpretation and execution of the task and the experiences and attitudes of the user. The consequences of a mis-match for the management user are explored later. The first stage of the analysis is to explore the characteristics of the management task and user and by this means to highlight the demands they are likely to make of a computer system.

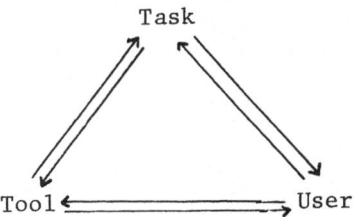

FIGURE 1. Elements of a task tool analysis

2.1 The Task

The term 'manager' is used to cover a wide range of jobs and to attempt a precise definition would probably be unproductive.   Suffice it to say that a manager directs and controls a work system comprising men, machines and materials, in the pursuit of its objectives.   His functions include policy formulation, the establishment of goals, planning, monitoring the execution of plans and 'trouble shooting' when there is a difference between desired and actual progress.

From the perspective of a computer system designer there are two characteristics of the manager's task which are of importance :-

(1) The manager needs information.   To take appropriate decisions relating to the work system he controls, the manager needs information about its current state, its predicted future state and desired future states.   He may also need information about external forces (markets, competitors, suppliers etc.) which may influence the behaviour of the work system.   The computer can serve as a tool to collect, summarise and present this information in a form suitable for the manager's needs, and this has been its principle role in management.   There is another function which can be served which is to model alternative future states of the work system in order that the manager can ask 'what happens if?' of many alternatives before taking his decision.   This function has to date played a secondary role to that of information dissemination.

(2) The variability and unpredictability of the task. Almost by definition the manager's task is variable and unpredictable.   One of his functions is to resolve the unexpected dilemmas which beset the work system, to handle novelty and ambiguity, and to determine action in circumstances where the organisation has no established procedure to fall back on.   It is possible therefore to specify that one of the manager's tasks is to 'trouble shoot', but the form this activity will take will vary considerably from one occasion to the next.   So also will the information the manager will require to perform the task. This is not to say that a manager's life is not without its regularities.   The manager may well make a regular practice of monitoring key indices and he may well take part in regular planning exercises, e.g. budget preparation.   However, for most managers these are islands of routine in a sea of the non-routine.

Nor can the fact that they are routine be used by the systems designers to provide a standard service throughout the organisation. Manager's have considerable discretion over the interpretation of their task, and even where there is predictability of task there may well be variability of interpretation between managers, even perhaps between successive holders of the same position.

To summarize, the management task is one that requires an information service and perhaps an information processing service, but it is also one in which there will be considerable variability in the specific information required from one occasion to the next.

2.2 The Manager

The computer user in this particular instance is a person of relatively high status and considerable discretion. If the manager does not feel he is getting an adequate service from a computer system, it is unlikely that he can be forced to use it; he may well, for example, develop his own manual systems to compensate for the weaknesses in the computerised system.

He is also likely to be a difficult customer to please. Using a computer system is likely to be a very small element in the totality of the job and one which will be low in the manager's priority order. If he is a busy man he is unlikely to wish to spend a lot of time and effort on matters peripheral to the important components of his job. This means that the 'ease of use' of a computer system may be a vital issue for the manager. His tolerance for a system that provides a service which involves him in a lot of personal effort is likely to be low. This may mean that a lot of systems become dis-used, not because they lack the potential to provide a valuable service but because they do so in a way which is unacceptable to the user. In essence this argument suggests that a user's response to a system is defined by a cost/benefit analysis where cost is measured in terms of personal time and effort. It also argues that managers expect higher benefits per unit cost than other types of user.

2.3 The Tool

From the above we can develop a prescription for the form a computer system should take if it is to be acceptable to a manager. This prescription covers three issues:-

(1) The system should supply information (or information processing facilities) commensurate with the specific tasks of the manager.

(2) The system should be capable of covering the breadth of service that will be required as the manager's demands vary with time. The manager represents a 'moving target' upon which the system must seek to score a high number of 'hits'.

(3) The provision of this service should involve an amount of time and effort from the manager commensurate with his valuation of the service provided.

3. AN EVALUATION OF DIFFERENT TYPES OF COMPUTER SYSTEM

With the critical demands a manager will make of a computer system in mind, it is possible to examine the different kinds of system currently in use and to evaluate how well they meet these demands. In making this evaluation use will be made of the results of a survey of different kinds of non-specialist ('naive') computer users. This survey covered many kinds of users, e.g. clerks, designers, economists etc., and included 82 manager users who employed between them 17 different systems. This survey is reported in detail elsewhere (Eason, et al. 1974; Eason, et al. 1975). Only a summary of the results for management users will be presented here.

The survey revealed a number of different types of computer systems used by managers and, for the purposes of this analysis, the diversity of systems will be classified under three headings:

(1) The Batch Processed (Standard Output) Management Information System.

(2) Data Base Systems with Retrieval Facilities.

(3) Computer Models for Decision Evaluation.

3.1 The Batch Processed (Standard Output) Management Information System

The most common way by which a computer is used to provide management information is the production of standard outputs by batch processing. In this approach the computer generates a set of printouts on a regular basis which may range from daily to annually. The service is often provided for a large number of managers, the same basic formats for printouts being used for all, although the information content of printouts varies from manager to manager.

In the survey 50% of the managers interviewed (n = 41) employed systems of this kind. These users were asked a variety of 'task fit' questions, i.e. questions relating to the degree to which the information received is accurate, timely, reliable, relevant and comprehensive with respect to the task that is to be undertaken. The average 'task fit' index for these users was 57% compared with an average of 63% for the total sample of 254 users. The main problems experienced were high levels of irrelevant information combined, paradoxically, with a lack of comprehensiveness. There were also problems of timeliness and accuracy. On 'ease of use' issues these managers complained of the difficulty of locating relevant information in bulky print-outs and of having to re-cast the information given to get it into a useful form.

The majority of the literature on management reactions to management information systems is concerned with this kind of system and these results reflect the general conclusions of this literature. The picture that emerges is of a manager surrounded by printouts which tell him everything that he does not want to know and little of what he does want to know.

The task-tool analysis presented earlier can be used to explain this situation. The assumptions behind this kind of system are that each manager in the organisation needs a similar kind of service and that he can be supplied with this service on a regular basis. However, the analysis suggests that management tasks vary with time and so, therefore, do information requirements. Furthermore, tasks may be fundamentally different from one manager to another, and the amount of discretion each manager has, to determine for himself how he wishes to interpret his task, may mean that superficially similar tasks are treated in very different ways.

It would appear that this kind of system is inherently too rigid to supply the kind of service required. It may be a good way of meeting the routine demands of the manager, e.g. to enable him to regularly monitor important performance indices, but it is inadequate when used to provide a comprehensive information service. Trying to meet the user's requirements within the constraints of this kind of system can lead to a particular dilemma for the system's designer. The designer is faced with a system which needs a complete specification of the information it will hold and distribute and a user population which can specify its future requirements in only the most global terms. How can he respond? Typically there are two responses. First, the designer can assume there is order where there is chaos and can decide for himself which information is critical and arrange for it to be provided. Since he has no way of forcing the user to agree with his interpretations, the designer will probably find that the outputs are regarded as irrelevant and lacking in comprehensiveness. The second strategy is to try to encompass every item of information. This strategy tends to result in large printouts which are difficult to use. These outputs may contain relevant information but the manager may never locate it and his 'task fit' views of the system may remain poor.

3.2 Data Base Systems with Retrieval Facilities

The problems listed above have not gone unnoticed by computer specialists and a new kind of system is emerging which has the potential to overcome many of them. The concept is that data will be collected and will be held in a data base. Rather than automatically disseminating it to the user population, each user will be given facilities whereby he can search the data base and retrieve selected pieces of information. This approach has the advantage that users can seek information when they want it rather than receiving it according to a fixed timetable, and by selecting information themselves they can avoid irrelevance. Some of these systems are terminal based which means that, in theory, the manager can request and receive information in a matter of seconds. Some systems of this kind, however, operate in a batch processing mode which retains the flexibility of the approach but lengthens the time before the request is answered.

There is a rather limited literature on managerial reactions to this kind of system although two major studies have been reported by Morton (1967) and by Hedberg (1970). In both of these studies favourable management attitudes to the system were reported which stand in stark contrast to the widespread negative attitudes engendered by the standard output systems. There are two possible explanations for this difference. It could be, as hypothesised in this paper, that the greater flexibility of the data base concept enables these systems to provide a better service. It could also be that the experimental nature of these systems gave the investigators more opportunity than is usual to control the management tasks being served and hence to ensure they were providing a relevant service.

In the survey 15 managers used a total of 6 systems of this kind, 5 of the managers employing a terminal to interact with the system. These managers were interviewed in the same way as other managers and a score of 66% was obtained on the task fit index, a considerable improvement on the 57% obtained for users of standard output systems. This was a significant improvement but was not perhaps as great an improvement as might be expected given that the user is now able to define his own service. An examination of the individual questions revealed that the most significant gain was in relevance; only 7% of this sample complained of substantial amounts of irrelevance as compared with 39% of the users of standard outputs. A puzzling feature of the results was that complaints that the service was insufficiently comprehensive remained high (59%). One

explanation for this might have been that the data base did not
include the required information but explorations after interviews
made it clear this was often not the case.   The problem was that
the system contained the information but users were unable to
extract it because they found the retrieval facilities they were
given difficult to use.

This raises the general question of 'ease of use'.   In the
standard output type of system 'ease of use' relates to problems
of searching and assimilating the information in a printout.
When a data base system with retrieval facilities is used there
is still the potential for this kind of problem but, because the
user has some degree of control over the output, it is much less
significant.   Unfortunately there are now other 'ease of use'
issues which may be much more significant.   The standard output
system is automatic in the sense that users do not have to do
anything to receive the service.   The data base system demands
that the user operates retrieval facilities to obtain an output.
The problem of utilizing these facilities, whether manually or by
using a computer system, was of considerable importance to this
group of managers;   36% of them reported difficulty in using the
procedures that were provided.   This compares with an average of
26% for the total sample which includes many users, e.g.
engineers, scientists, who made use of much more complex operating
procedures.   It appears that managers complain much more readily
than other users about 'ease of use' difficulties.   This lends
support to the hypothesis that in making a cost/benefit evaluation
they make more stringent demands for high benefits at low
personal cost than other users.

In the terms of the task-tool analysis the current status
of these systems appears to be as follows.   They offer the
flexibility required to meet the variability of the task demands.
However, in offering this flexibility, the system makes demands
upon the user and, in the case of the manager, these demands are
often evaluated as excessive causing him to use the system in a
less than optimal manner.

3.3 Computer Models for Decision Evaluation

The systems discussed above permit the manager to receive
information from a computer system but do not permit him to
process information.   The manager may well wish to explore what
will happen to company turnover, profits, sales, labour etc., if
a certain policy is implemented, and this involves processing
information according to a set of rules which simulate the dynamic
nature of company operations.   There are now many computer systems
which enable managers to ask these 'what happens if?' questions
and thereby evaluate the advantages and disadvantages of decisions

they might take. These systems range from relatively simple ones, which mirror the profit and loss entries of the balance sheet, to complex systems which embody operations research techniques such as network analysis and linear programming. They are systems which are often operated in a batch processed mode but the user is able to explore alternatives more quickly if he employs an interactive terminal.

The literature on the use of these systems offers many examples of wonderful systems but, where user reactions are given, it is often in terms of resistance or inability to use them effectively. Bluck and Taylor (1968) report the case of a resource scheduling system which is symptomatic of the problems of this kind of system. Starting as a very sophisticated tool employing many operations research techniques, this sytem was progressively simplified until it was relatively trivial in the eyes of the management scientists. It was only at this stage that it became acceptable to its management user.

The survey included 24 managers who made use of 6 systems of this kind. Eight of the managers used terminals to interact with the system. Despite the fact that these systems provide managers with more sophisticated information handling facilities than any others used by managers in the sample, the task fit score was 52%, i.e. well below the score achieved by the other systems serving managers. The two major reasons for this low score were the number of complaints about accuracy (42%) and relevance (38%). Since most of the data used in these systems originated from the user this seemed rather surprising, and a closer analysis revealed that the major complaint was about the validity of the operations performed upon the data and hence the conclusions drawn. For example, in a stock control system the re-order levels were set for times of plenty, and in times of scarcity the recommendations of the system were totally misleading. For the manager, the problems of using this kind of tool are first to understand what assumptions it makes and secondly to find ways of modifying them to fit the current situation. Often these systems were acceptable at the time of design but were not sufficiently flexible to take account of changing situations.

Another problem accentuated by this kind of system is that of 'ease of use'. Not only does the user have to operate this system but he has to understand what it is doing. In the preceeding section it was noted that 36% of users reported difficulty in using the retrieval facilities of data base systems; 69% of users reported difficulty in using the procedures necessary to operate these computer models. Once again it is easy to find other types of user with systems of comparable complexity who do not feel the procedures are difficult to use, and this adds further support to the cost/benefit inter-pretation of 'ease of use'.

4. THE CONSEQUENCES OF A TASK-TOOL MISMATCH

The assumption that underlies this task-tool analysis is
that the user seeks a good 'fit' between the task and the tool.
If he finds it presumably the task will be undertaken
effectively and the user will be more inclined to use the tool
next time he identifies a similar task.   Of greater interest
is the question of the user's reaction if the 'fit' is poor.
The preceeding analysis demonstrates that, for most managers,
the computer systems they employ are not at present providing
them with a good 'task fit'.   Where there is the potential for
a good 'fit', it is usually accomplished by use of a set of
complex procedures which may be unacceptable to the management
user.   As a result the potential is not realised and the result
is a poor 'task fit'.   What then is the response of the
management user?   In Figure 2 a summary is presented of the
range of options open to any user in this situation.   The purpose
of this section is to examine which of these options are most
likely to be adopted by the manager.

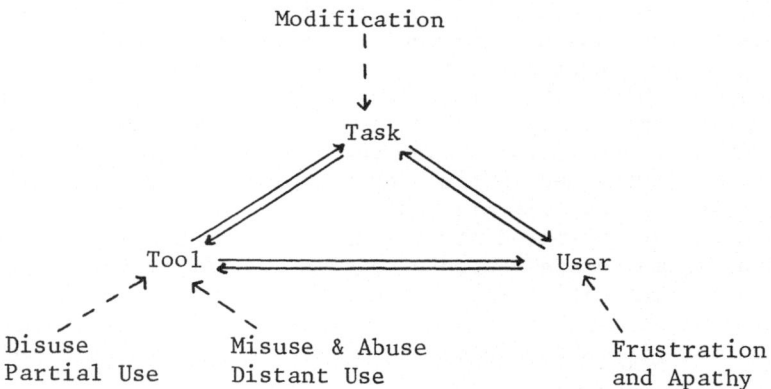

Figure 2: Possible Consequences of a Task-Tool Mismatch

The view adopted here is that, finding himself in a mismatch situation, the user will seek a way of reducing the effects
of the mismatch and therefore of completing his task.   He may do
this by:-

(1) Changing his use of the computer system or changing
    the system itself so that it is a more acceptable
    'tool'.
(2) Changing the nature of the task, i.e. if the tool does
    not 'fit' the task, the task may be modified to 'fit'
    the limitations imposed by the tool.
(3) Engaging in compensatory activity whereby he accepts
    the extra work necessary to make task and tool 'fit'.
    As Figure 2 suggests, frustration and apathy can result
    if a user finds that he has to engage in these activities
    on a regular basis.

Which of these options is the most likely for a management
user?   It is appropriate to consider them in reverse order:-

4.1 Compensatory Activity by the User

This is an option used when no others are available.   It is
probably most appropriate for users of low discretion such as
clerks, who are faced with well defined tasks and tools they have
to use.   Managers have too many other options available to them
to find this a necessary option.

4.2 Modification of the Task

This option is most commonly found in circumstances where
the user has little choice but to use a tool or alternatives to
its use have grave disadvantages.   For example, as Stewart (1974)
has indicated, specialist users of the computer (engineers,
designers, etc.) have a vested interest in using software packages
designed for them because alternative approaches may involve
weeks of tedious calculations.   In these circumstances it is
easier for the specialist to modify his task to fit the software
package he has available.

It is unlikely that a manager would find himself in this
position because there are always likely to be alternative sources
of information.   However, in the survey, there were examples of
minor ways in which computer systems had begun to influence the
nature of the management task.   In the use of standard output
systems, for example, information tends to become available on
certain dates and many managers commented that the decision-
making cycle of the organisation had shifted to fit the timetable
set by the computer system.   There were also many instances where
the particular ways in which the computer system formalised
information dissemmination also tended to formalise the decision-
making process.   For example, systems may adopt particular rules
of thumb in presenting information, e.g. that there are 240

working days in a year and all calculations of man-years work are based on this rule. There will be a tendency for managers to accept these rules even if they do not adequately reflect their own tasks or reflect the traditions of their department, because to employ an alternative rule means not using the system or engaging in extra work to convert the data.

It would seem that these pressures for task modification are more pervasive in standard output systems than they are in data base retrieval systems because the flexibility of the latter leaves control in the hands of the user. We have elsewhere (Damodaran, et al. 1974) described the latter as 'passive coupling' of man and computer because the computer leaves control in the hands of the user. The relationship between man and computer in systems generating standard outputs we have termed 'active coupling' because some of the control has been lost to the computer. The same paper also gives examples of 'dominant coupling' where control is firmly within the computer system, an arrangement to be found in some clerical computer systems.

In summary, it is unlikely that task modification will be a major reaction of the manager to task-tool mismatch. A cautionary note should however perhaps be added. The manager's task is subject to interpretation by the manager; it has little 'objective definition'. In these circumstances it is difficult to say how the task would have been interpreted were the computer system not present. The nature of available tools may have a variety of insidious effects upon the way a task is interpreted.

4.3 Use of the System

If the user has the discretion to vary the extent to which he uses the system then the most obvious way of resolving a task-tool mismatch is to modify system usage. Of all user types, managers probably have the most discretion in this respect and it may be anticipated that they will make considerable use of this strategy. The variety of available responses may be classified as follows:-

(1) Dis-use. If the manager perceives a mismatch between his task and the service offered by a computer system, he may simply cease to use the system. However, it is probably not the absolute degree of mismatch that influences this decision but the availability of an adequate substitute. In management environments it is quite likely that adequate information service substitutes can be found and, although it is difficult to measure, dis-use may be quite common. There are many stories of managers maintaining, or even creating, small scale manual information systems which duplicate the function of computerised systems but

are under the personal control of the manager and presumably offer him a better service.

(2) <u>Mis-use and Abuse</u>. A phenomenon well known to those who study human use of technological systems is the way operators 'bend the rules' of the system to accommodate their own particular needs. The same phenomenon is to be seen in the use of computer systems; for example, if a user seeks the same kind of information from a system on many occasions, and each time he has to go through a series of, to him, entirely redundant choice points, he is likely to seek ways of short-cutting this process. If he is successful he will save himself time and energy but, because his actions are not strictly in accord with the procedures of the system, they may have adverse effects upon the integrity of the system. Although this kind of response is common amongst full-time users of computer systems, it is less appropriate for intermittent users. It is therefore unlikely to be common amongst management users.

(3) <u>Partial Use</u>. Many systems have a variety of functions and hence can be regarded as a collection of 'tools' rather than a single entity. This is particularly true of flexible information systems of the data base variety. In using these systems the user is not simply making a use/non-use decision but is able to make comparative decisions amongst the different options provided by the system. On a rational basis it would be anticipated that the option chosen would be the one which most nearly meets the particular requirements of the task. It is, however, widely reported by systems designers that, where a system offers choice to the management user, some options become very popular whilst many others are rarely used. It could be argued that the distribution of usage fits the demands of tasks but the evidence suggests this explanation accounts for only a small part of the response. The reasons for this kind of behaviour will be explored in more detail below.

(4) <u>Distant Use</u>. If a system provides a valuable service but to obtain the service requires an unacceptable amount of time and effort from the user, he can resolve his difficulty by getting someone else to obtain the service for him. This option is only available to those with the status and discretion to deploy resources in this way and many managers are in a position to do this. As a result one finds that managers who enjoy having interactive systems in their office when a system is implemented, often have them removed after a few months or ask members of their staff to operate them on their behalf. This was the fate of an IBM Management Information System whose history has been documented by Martin (1973). In this system terminals were removed from manager's offices and a central information room developed to which managers could send their

information queries. The system described by Eason and
Corney (1970) was eventually used by the manager's subordinate
rather than the manager himself. In the survey managers who
were, at that time, using a terminal were almost universal in
foreseeing a future in which it would be used by someone else on
their behalf. The common nature of this phenomenon raises many
questions and these are considered below.

5. THE FUTURE OF MANAGER-COMPUTER INTERACTION

The foregoing analysis of the consequences of a task-tool
mismatch for managers leads to a number of conclusions. First,
the main casualties are likely to be the acceptability and degree
of use of the system. There may be effects upon the user's task
and on the user himself but, if it is a question of which is to
suffer, the manager has the power to ensure it is the system that
suffers first. Secondly, it is not simply a matter of use or
dis-use of the system because there are a number of more subtle
patterns of response available to the management user. Two of
these, partial use and distant use, appear to be quite common.
In an effort to understand more fully why this is so and to
explore the long term consequences for manager-computer interaction, these two patterns of response are explored more
thoroughly below.

5.1 Partial Use

If a manager has a choice between a number of options within
a computer system, why does he not always choose the one best
fitted to his task needs? In order to try to answer this
question a study was undertaken of a system which offers staff of
a service organisation, both clerks and managers, 28 different
methods of accessing the information about a customer's account
held on a data base. Computer logs of the use of this system
showed that three of these methods accounted for 77% of system
usage. These were the methods which were designed for the needs
of frequent, routine, tasks and hence were expected to be highly
utilized. Usage was not however, expected to be as high as the
figure obtained and it was not anticipated that methods
specifically included for known tasks, albeit less frequent,
would be virtually ignored.

An analysis of the variety of tasks for which the system
could be used revealed that, for most of them, a number of
different methods would give the required information with more or
less precision and with more or less irrelevant information
included in the output. For example, one of the most
frequently used methods gave the last 16 items on the account.

This method could be used for a wide variety of tasks and could easily be used in place of a method which gave the specific piece of information required.

In order to investigate the dynamics of user behaviour with this system, a series of typical tasks were constructed and users were asked to specify how they would go about getting the information necessary to complete the task. They were permitted to nominate a specific method or to select a search method, e.g. look in the manual, if they were not sure. The results showed that in 53% of instances users selected the methods which designers felt were the most appropriate, in 26% of instances they selected other methods that would have been effective, and in 9% of instances they selected methods that would not have been effective. In only 3% of instances did users opt for a search strategy. A significant feature of these results was that in only 13% of the instances in which a wrong but acceptable strategy was employed was the best strategy listed as a known alternative. This indicates that we are not dealing with a conscious process in which the best alternative is considered and rejected as, for example, too costly in terms of personal effort. We are apparently dealing with a situation in which the first acceptable alternative is selected and no effort is made to locate the best possible alternative. This process is reminiscent of the decision-making process Simon (1960) has called 'satisficing' in which the decision-maker selects the first alternative to meet the minimum requirements of his goals. In this case, the well known alternatives are the general purpose ones used for routine tasks. A striking feature about these solutions is that they probably involve more time and effort to use than do the correct solutions because relevant data has to be sifted from irrelevant data and it often has to be transcribed into a more appropriate form. An explanation based on an 'ease of use' assessment of alternatives by the user is therefore inadequate.

A more plausible explanation is that the user is avoiding having to think about the process of gathering information. He is concentrating his attention upon the task in hand and thinking about which method to use would be a source of distraction. He is therefore likely to use a known alternative even if it is less efficient to save himself engaging in a conscious search (perhaps unproductive) for a better alternative.

It will be noted that this explanation means that users will learn very slowly about the system they employ; they will only learn when they encounter tasks for which known methods simply will not work. The likely outcome of this process is that some methods will rarely be used although a good case can be made for their existence. Designers may be tempted to remove these methods from the system on the basis that they serve no

useful purpose.   Earlier we noted the need for a flexible
service to managers.   Now we see that offering choice is not
sufficient because there are psychological forces which make it
difficult for the user to accept the opportunity to choose.

5.2 Distant Use

The second strategy found amongst managers is to ask
someone else to operate a computer system on their behalf.   Once
again this appears to be a reaction not to the irrelevance of the
system but to the demands its operating procedures make upon the
user both in terms of actual operation and of learning to operate
it.   There is a considerable attraction in getting the benefits
of computer aid without any personal costs by stating your
requirements to another human being rather than translating them
into a form the computer can understand.   The arguments for this
approach are so appealing to the busy manager that it may be that
this is the best way to serve his needs and all efforts to
encourage and sustain direct manager-computer interaction should
cease.   However, it is possible to argue that this approach has
disadvantages which may be listed as follows:-

(1) Manager-man-computer interaction will inevitably be a
more time consuming process than direct manager-computer interaction and the extra steps involved may be vital to the success
of the interaction.   If the theoretical considerations of
Miller (1968) and the empirical work of Yntema et al. (1969) are
correct,the response speed of a system is critical if man-
computer 'symbiosis' is to be achieved.   Any extra functions
that have to be performed which prevent the computer's answer
reaching the manager before his thoughts have turned to other
matters would seem likely to degrade the quality of the interaction.

(2) There is some evidence to suggest that the role of
'human interface' in these systems is difficult to fulfil.   To
be successful the individual must understand the system and its
data base; he will, therefore,be a highly knowledgeable person
with no clear promotional ladder before him.   In some instances
these people have become important power centres in organisations
not so much serving management as guiding and advising them.
This role is sometimes encouraged,by managers who feel that,
once operation of the system has been handed over, they no longer
need to concern themselves with it and can get on with the real job.
In this situation the interface can find his advice going unheeded,
with the effect that a cleavage has been created between the
manager and the system which may mean the system plays no part in
the decision-making of the organisation.

If there is any truth in either or both of these admittedly hypothetical considerations, there is some reason to continue striving to create acceptable direct forms of manager-computer interaction.

6. CONCLUSIONS

Approaching manager-computer interaction as an exercise in task-tool analysis reveals that the computer has an important part to play in the service of managers but that its performance to date is far from perfect. The difficulties stem from the fact that the unstructured nature of the management task makes it difficult to serve the manager adequately unless the service is flexible. Unfortunately, at present, a flexible service means the manager experiences the problem of operating the system. The designers of technical systems have traditionally relied upon the operator to adapt his behaviour to suit the constraints of the system. In the manager's case there is little indication that he is prepared to adapt his behaviour to the computer.

The consequence is that, at present, the computer is well established as a tool for the manager to use but the grand vision of 'man-computer symbiosis' provided by Licklider (1960) are far from being achieved. As soon as the opportunities for direct interaction of reasonable sophistication are offered, the manager retreats to a safe distance, accepting only that service which is possible with the limited amount of personal effort he is prepared to offer. The manager, perhaps more than any other type of user, represents a challenge for designers who seek to create effective man-computer interaction. Christensen (1976) quotes George Bernard Shaw as saying that progress depends on the unreasonable man. The manager is surely the unreasonable man of man-computer interaction. If we are able to create a form of man-computer symbiosis acceptable to managers we will also learn how to serve many less demanding users.

REFERENCES

Ackoff, R.L.	1968	Management Mis-information Systems. Management Decision, 2.1, 4-8.
Bluck, P.M. & Taylor, D.R.	1968	An Interactive Computer Based Production Planning System. Proceedings of the Annual Conference, Operational Research Society of U.K.
Christensen, J.M.	1976	Ergonomics; Where have we been and where are we going II. Ergonomics, 19.3, 287-300.

306

Damodaran, L.   1974   Socio-technical Ramifications of
    Stewart, T.F.M. &   Forms of Man-Computer Interaction.
    Eason, K.D.   Paper to ALTORG Conference, Gothenburg.
                                Department of Human Sciences
                                HUSAT Memo No. 78, available from
                                the author.

Eason, K.D. &   1970   The Evaluation of a Small Interactive,
    Corney, G.M.   Management Information System.
                                IEE Conference on 'Man-Computer
                                    Interaction' held at the National
                                    Physical Laboratory, Conf. Public-
                                    ation No. 68, 113-120, from IEE
                                    Savoy Place, London W.C. 2.

Eason, K.D.,   1974   A Survey of Man-Computer Interaction
    Damodaran, L. &   in Commercial Applications.
    Stewart, T.F.M.   Report to the Social Science Research
                                    Council (Grant No. HR 1844/1), 270pp.,
                                    Department of Human Sciences Report
                                    LUTERG No. 144, available from the
                                    author.

Eason, K.D.,   1975   Interface Problems in Man-Computer
    Stewart, T.F.M. &   Interaction.
    Damodaran, L.   In: E. Mumford and H. Sackman,
                                    Human Choice and Computers,
                                North-Holland, Amsterdam.

Hedberg, B.   1970   On Man-Computer Interaction in
                                    Organisational Decision-Making;
                                    A Behavioural Approach.
                                Gothenburg University Press.

Licklider, J.C.R.   1960   Man-Computer Symbiosis.
                                IRE Transactions of Human Factors
                                    in Electronics, Vol. HFE-1, 4-11.

Martin, J.   1973   Design of Man-Computer Dialogues.
                                Prentice-Hall, Englewood Cliffs, N.J.

Miller, R.B.   1968   Response Time in Man-Computer
                                    Conversational Transactions.
                                Proceedings of the Fall Joint Computer
                                    Conference, AFIPS Conf. Proc.
                                    33 Pt. 1, 267-277.

Morton, M.S.S.   1967   Computer-Driven Visual Display Devices:
                                    Their Impact on the Management
                                    Decision-Making Process
                                Doctoral Dissertation, Graduate School
                                    of Business Administration,
                                    Harvard University.

Simon, H.A.   1960   The New Science of Management
                                        Decision.
                                     Harper, New York.

Stewart, T.F.M.   1974   Ergonomics Aspects of Man-Computer
                                        Problem Solving.
                                     Applied Ergonomics, $\underline{5}$.4, 209-212.

Yntema, D.B.,   1969   Effects of Response Delay on
   Morfield, M.A.,   On-line Problem Solving.
   Weisen R.A. &   Paper to the International Symposium
   Grossberg, M.   on Man-Machine Systems, Cambridge
                                        U.K.; M.I.T. Lincoln Laboratory
                                        Report No. MS-2519.

THE IMPACT OF COMPUTER-USE ON ORGANIZATION STRUCTURE*

B. De Brabander[‡], E. Vanlommel[‡], D. Deschoolmeester[‡],
R. Leyder[‡]

Rijksuniversitair Centrum, 2020 - Antwerpen, Belgium.

* This research was supported by a grant from the Council for
Scientific Policy to the Belgian Productivity Agency which en-
trusted the research to the Çenter for Productivity Study and
Research at Ghent University.   For their aid at various stages
of this research, we want to thank F. BRACKE, J. MAGHERMAN,
M. SELS and J. VANHOORDE.   Special thanks are due to Prof.
Thomas L. WHISLER, who acted as a consultant to the research
team.   The study to be reported on in the second part of the
article is part of a major research project on computer use in
business firms in Belgium.

Three major topics have been investigated:

1. The relationship between several task-characteristics of
   industrial firms and the degree and kind of computer-use
   (Computer-applications).
2. The relationship between the organization of EDP-activities
   and several aspects of the success of computer-use.
3. Organizational consequences of computer-use.

This article describes the findings with respect to the third
topic.   Several times mention will be made of the survey which was
done in order to obtain the data relevant for the first topic.   A
detailed description of the survey and its results can be found
in an article in the January 1972 issue of the Journal of Business,
entitled: "The effect of task-volume and complexity upon computer-
use".

‡ Research assistants at the Center for Productivity Study and
Research, Ghent University.   DE BRABANDER is presently assistant
to the chair of management (Prof. Dr. E. VANLOMMEL) at the faculty
of applied Economics, University of Antwerp; R. LEYDER is
presently with Intermarco-Publicem, Brussels.
‡ Professor of Management, Universities of Ghent and Antwerp,
Project Co-ordinator.

PART ONE: REVIEW OF THE LITERATURE

Since LEAVITT and WHISLER's thought-provoking article about the future of management in the computer-era[1], a number of students or organizations have directed their attention towards the study of the impact of electronic data processing on the functioning and structure of complex organizations.

In many respects the content of these publications is disappointing.   In the first place, a number of these writings are highly speculative in nature.   In the few cases where research-results are reported, the limited number of (sometimes very unsystematic and subjective) observations do not engender conclusive evidence.   In the second place the conclusions themselves are often vaguely formulated, unduly generalizing and at times even contradictory.   With a few exceptions[2,3] the underlying hypotheses do not seem to stem from a coherent theoretical framework.

Given the state of the art, an exhaustive review of the relevant literature is not an easy task.   We have therefore limited the discussion to those dimensions of the organization which seem to have attracted the bulk of the interest of researchers.

At the same time we consider them as being crucial characteristics of the structure and functioning of complex organizations:

1.   the members of the organization;
2.   jobs;
3.   decision-making;
4.   communications;
5.   authority.

A.   SUBSTITUTION EFFECTS

High-speed electronic computers have proven to be able to perform a wide range of clerical and administrative tasks.   Since the introduction of computers in business one has therefore raised the question whether this has in fact resulted in a substitution of employees at various levels of the organization.

It appears to be extremely difficult to give a straight-forward and unequivocal answer to this query, because of the following reasons:

1) Other technological and other socio-economic developments do influence the growth rate of the firm.   The effect of information technology is hard to isolate.   For, in order to do so one should be able to assess the hypothetical growth in number of employees if no computer had been introduced.

This would be crystal-ball gazing instead of sound inference.
2) The introduction of computers generally implies or causes a number of organizational developments. The induced changes, rather than computer-introduction itself, can therefore be the primary determinants of changes in personnel stock.
3) Often the researcher has to resort to poor data; either too specific (data about one particular firm or a small number of firms) or too general (aggregated census data).
4) In a large number of firms computer-use is too recent to have caused any substantial changes in occupation.

Notwithstanding these constraints most researchers have concluded that substitution in effect takes place. In 1960 already the U.S. Bureau of Labor Statistics published the results of a study showing that in 20 firms, heavy users of EDP-equipment, the number of clerical personnel had been reduced by 20% and the number of administrative staff by 2%[4].

In a more recent study in 19 life-insurance companies[5] respondents were asked to estimate the number of clerical personnel, supervisors, and managers to be hired on the assumption that one could no longer use the computer. Data for 15 companies showed that an additional 60% of clerks, 9% of supervisors and 2% of managers would be required. The reliability and validity of such estimates is subject to severe doubts. Nevertheless they seem to confirm the trend observed earlier (see also WEBER[6]).

The substitution-issue has also been studied in a number of Belgian firms (170 manufacturing and distribution firms, 8 insurance companies and 10 financial institutions)[7]. The results indicate that only in those firms using the computer for more than 5 years, a lower growth-rate in the number of white-collar workers relative to the growth-rate of shipments could be observed in the subsequent period than in firms using the computer for less than 5 years or using no computer at all. Since firm-size and sector did not seem to have any systematic effect upon the ratio of both growth-rates in the sample of firms studied, the observed trend cannot be accounted for by size- or sector disparities; the hypothesized effect of computer-use therefore becomes more plausible.

B. CHANGES IN CONTENT AND IMPORTANCE OF JOBS

Changes in job-content have been studied at various levels in the organization. The WHISLER and MEYER study[8] reports that changes in content of clerical jobs have been perceived in 53.5% of the cases. In 31% the scope of the job, as indicated by responsibility and the degree of routine, has been narrowed; in the remaining 22.5% of the cases it was enlarged. With respect

Organizational Level	Percent of EDP-affected departments in which it is reported that:		Percent of reported changes in skill level (Col.A) in which skill went:	
	Skill Changes occurred (A)	No skill changes occurred (B)	Up (C)	Down (D)
Clerical	90	10	70	30
Supervisory	87	13	93	7
Middle-management	56	44	92	8
Top-management	41	49	94	6

TABLE 1: IMPACT OF COMPUTER-INTERVENTION ON SKILL-REQUIREMENTS

to middle-managers, no quantitative evaluations are available.

However, in 17 of the 19 companies studied and where changes have been reported, the most frequent observation is that their responsibilities have been broadened.

The impact of computers on middle-management-jobs has been more exhaustively investigated by SHAUL[9]. He found that middle-managers in 25 manufacturing and 28 service organizations generally spend more time on planning, staffing and guidance of personnel and less on supervision and on control after the computer.

These findings are in line with SIMON's expectations in this respect[10]. SHAUL did not find that the job-content of middle-managers becomes more structured. On the contrary, their jobs seem to become more complex: a larger range of varied activities which is in contradiction to LEAVITT and WHISLER's speculation stating that the job of middle-managers would be reduced to "straight leadership and supervision"[11].

Since job requirements may be considered to be indicative of job complexity, reported changes in job requirements may provide indications of changes in job-content. In the computerized departments studied by WHISLER and MEYER the reported changes in job requirements ran as follows:[12]

See Table 1 opposite

The increased job requirements for clerical personnel seem to be in contradiction with the assertion that job content has narrowed. The apparent contradiction may be explained by the fact that, although their jobs have become less complex in terms of responsibilities, other aspects of the job put higher requirements on the job-occupants. Among these are: a higher degree of accuracy, larger volumes of work, more rigid planning and an increased number of deadlines. This is in fact what MUMFORD and BANKS[13] have observed in a bank office in England.

With respect to the question of relative status of the jobs after computer introduction, the interest has been focussed on the middle-management level. Two contradictory hypotheses are adhered to: one, originated by LEAVITT and WHISLER, stating that their status will be reduced to the role of supervisor due to the fact that their most characteristic task, making structured decision about the planning and organization of the work flow, will be taken over by the computer. The other hypothesis, engendered by ANSHEN[14], briefly states that the middle-manager's job will become similar to the job of top-managers: they will devote more time to the definition of problems, the search for alternatives, and the evaluation of alternative courses of action, and the development of new decision procedures. To put it in SIMON's terms[15], this would amount to increased "systems thinking" and "preventive maintenance". These accrued responsibilities are likely to enhance their status.

It is striking that one and the same stimulus is thought to lead to entirely different outcomes. This is due to a difference in conception about the nature of the intervening process postulated. The basic change induced by the computer relieves middle-managers of a number of time-consuming structured decisions.

They seem to hold different assumptions though as to how middle-managers will allocate this surplus time. As a matter of fact, we strongly believe that both assumed intervening processes (more supervision versus more search) are feasible. The final outcome is rather a consequence of organisational characteristics than a consequence of computer-use. Depending on the direction of choice, the status of middle-managers is then likely to be affected in one or the other of the predicted directions.

VERGIN[16] actually investigated the status-issue in a heterogeneous group of eleven organizations in various sectors and belonging to different size-classes. He concludes that in no case was a middle manager relieved of his job or had his remuneration reduced. However the most affected managers (whose decisions had been programmed as much as feasible) reported that their functions of motivation and co-ordination had been reduced. This brought about some reduction of work, thus giving rise to the feeling of being less important.

SHAUL[17], in his more extensive study, found that most middle-managers reported an improvement in status due to the fact that they experienced their job as more complex and themselves as less replaceable.

C. IMPACT ON DECISION-MAKING

Most authors agree that decision-making will become more rational as a consequence of computer-use and the more rigorous techniques of analysis made operational by high-speed electronic data-processing.

One frequently encountered argument is that the programming of the preparatory stages of the decision-process stimulates managers to critically review their decision rules and to make the decision-criteria explicit. A common observation is the simplicity of the rules of thumb used, the intuitive character of the criteria and the limited number of factors taken into account[18].

A second argument is that, since managers are relieved of the collection of data and the computational work involved in the preparation of the decision, they can devote more time and attention to the more important stages of evaluation and search for alternatives, a fact which is likely to favor the degree of rationality of the decision-process. This is at least LEE's conclusion after depth-interviews with a number of managers in three firms of three different sectors[19].

Another consequence often predicted is the fact that the computer helps to reintegrate separate decision-areas. Without the computing and information-storage capacities of the computer the decision-makers were often faced with the problem of getting hold of all the relevant information distributed over different functional areas of the firm, so they opted for a fragmentary approach to decision-making. Integrated data-processing made feasible by the computer greatly removes this obstacle towards integrated decision-making. As a result one can observe a trend towards the consolidation of formerly separated decision-areas. The underlying desire for integration may be supposed to stem from a basic need for co-ordination of the firm's operations. Symptoms of such reintegration are that decision-areas are becoming larger in scope, that more decisions are made collectively and that organizational units responsible for formerly separated decision-areas merge. In their study of 19 life-insurance companies WHISLER and MEYER have observed that in all instances, in which changes in decision-making were reported, changes went in the expected direction. In no case did the inverse occur[20].

Partly owing to the consolidation of decisions, decision-making becomes more rigid. According to WHISLER and MEYER the cost to change large decision-systems is higher than the costs associated with modifications of small independent decisions. Consequently one does not seem inclined to implement real changes in spite of the frequent revisions. Out of 31 respondents 20 replied that the number of revisions increased after computer-introduction, but of 30 of those 31 respondents 19 asserted that actual changes occurred less frequently[21]. These findings suggest that computer-use emphasizes the need for flexibility - what else should one make these revisions for? - but that realization is becoming increasingly unfeasible.

The respondents also told why changes became unfeasible: either because too many operational difficulties were involved or because it was too expensive. In our opinion both reasons amount to the same, for, if it were not for the extra expenses, these operational difficulties would be no real obstacle since every time a change is desired an entire new system might be developed.

D. IMPACT ON COMMUNICATIONS

Communications may be supposed to depend to a great extent on
the content of the jobs involved.   Routine jobs generally require
few joint consultations because of the high degree of programming
of activities characteristic for these jobs.   On the contrary,
non-routine jobs are generally less structured and claim more
information gathering.

The above mentioned findings of WHISLER and MEYER[22] have shown
that clerical jobs become more routine after the computer.   For
supervisory and managerial jobs the reverse trend seems to occur.
Parallel to these findings, it was found that clerks communicated
less after computer introduction and supervisors and managers more.

As to the usage of communication channels HOOS[23] already
reported in 1960 that the communication flow became straight
forward, that is, decision-makers at various decision loci tended
to communicate directly with each other passing the formally
established communication channels.   The computer itself becomes
a central point to and from which the bulk of information flows.
The total communication net more and more resembles a wheel
with the computer as the axis.

As a consequence of the computer's central position, WHISLER
and MEYER expect that interpersonal communications will gradually
decrease as computer-based informations systems will increasingly
pervade the firms' total information system[24].

According to GILMAN[25] one can doubt whether this will happen.
He believes namely that managerial time saved by computer-use is
likely to be spent on consultation with peers and subordinates.
He strongly believes that managers are in favour of frequent
interpersonal contacts as theory Y of McGREGOR claims, but that
up to now they have not had time to put this desideratum into
practice.

A second reason why WHISLER and MEYER's proposition seems
doubtful will become apparent in the theoretical framework of the
study below.

E. IMPACT ON AUTHORITY STRUCTURE

A central theme with regard to the authority structure is the
question whether authority will be centered to the top of the
hierarchy as a consequence of computer-use, or not.

Three lines of thought can be distinguished:

The first, put forward by LEAVITT and WHISLER[26], expects that the computer will allow top-management to assume more decision-making power, owing to the consolidation of decisions caused by computer-use and a reduced necessity to control routine-tasks. Behavior and results at the operational level will become more visible for them. Also the perception of the firm as a whole will become more feasible. Besides, computer-based information systems can economically produce short-cut reports on activities and outcomes sufficient for the important decisions to be made by higher levels of management. All this permits top-management to reassume a number of responsibilities they formerly delegated. This proposition presupposes of course that top-management is willing to do so.

The second line of thought is engendered by ANSHEN[27]. He claims that the computer will only slow down and eventually reverse the ongoing decentralization-movement. Some decisions, to which THOMPSON[28] refers as institutional decisions, will always have to be made by top-management. Some however were delegated by top-management because of their complexity which required expert knowledge. ANSHEN sees no reason why these decisions, which cannot be programmed altogether, would be reassumed by top-management. So only a number of fairly simple and structured decisions which eventually were delegated might be recentralized at the top.

The third line of thought is defended by DEARDEN[29]. He suggests that the computer does not affect the authority structure at all. He believes that top-management is motivated to delegate decisions because they rely upon the specialists' expertise rather than upon their own judgement which necessarily is less valid because they do not dispose of the specialists' knowledge and experience. According to him, computer-use cannot provide this, so there is no apparent reason to cease to delegate.

Most of the evidence reinforces the first line of thought. WHISLER himself has been able to demonstrate, both in a military organization and in the life insurance sector that higher centralization is the rule after computer-introduction using as an indication the degree of concentration of compensation[30].

HOOS[31], VERGIN[32] and LEE[33], inferring from interview material, came to the same conclusion.

ADAMS[34] on the other hand, was able to observe in a large oil refinery a tendency to delegate several decisions to lower echelons due to computer-use.

Finally, SHAUL[35] did not find that middle-managers, at whose expense increased centralization normally is established, possessed less decision-making responsibilities and authority after the introduction of the computer.

A recent study by KLATZKY[36] in 50 U.S. labor offices sheds some new light on the issue. Contrary to her expectations she finds that the degree of computer-use (as indicated by the complexity of the hardware) is inversely related to the degree of centralization of the organizations' most important decisions. She explains this finding by means of what she calls a "cascade effect": in contrast with the general belief that top-management is essentially in favor of centralization, she infers from her research data that top-management in fact wants to decentralize and the more so to the extent to which the organization becomes larger and more complex.

Since the computer mainly takes over a number of routine-tasks at the lowest echelon of the hierarchy, first-line supervisors are partly relieved of daily routine duties. This allows middle managers to delegate a number of responsibilities, of which they want to be freed, in order to assume new responsibilities shifted on to them by top-management. Top-managers in turn are then able to devote more time to activities particularly belonging to their sphere (the institutional sphere recognized by PARSONS and THOMPSON)[37] such as long-range planning and maintaining contacts with the environment.

KLATZKY's data also show that the cascade process is initiated by top-management.

These findings show that one cannot speculate about the effect of computer-use without considering the larger organizational context, especially the strategic choices of the organizations' chief decision-makers. One such choice, implicitly assumed in the theoretical propositions which guide the research endeavour to be exposed now, is that decision-makers in the organizations studied aim at rationality, that means that they want to make the best possible decisions at the right time.

PART TWO: AN EMPIRICAL INVESTIGATION OF SOME MANAGERIAL AND
            ORGANIZATIONAL CONSEQUENCES OF COMPUTER-USE

A.   PURPOSE OF THE STUDY

The survey of the literature has shown that the studies of
the managerial and organizational consequences of computer-use in
particular bring those changes into focus that may directly be
attributed to E.D.P. activities.   Besides, the investigators
generally seem to confine their studies to a sort of inventory of
the effects of computer-use, omitting to fit them in with a
coherent theory.   Little if any consideration has been given to
the consequences of the altered task-environment of the people in
the organization caused by the use of a computer.   It is true
investigators have tried to account for some changes in job-content
of managers by the fact that the computer has now taken over a
number of tasks, but they have omitted to explain how these changes
will affect further readjustments in jobs, communication and
decision-making.

As the direct consequences of computer-use have already been
submitted to close investigation and, on the other hand, the
indirect consequences are considerably important, we have thought
it useful to study mainly the latter.   It will be, moreover, the
authors' purpose to increase the coherence in this study by
examining just one single kind of change in the task-environment
of the firm and the effects hypothetically resulting from it.   As
will be explained in the following section, there are good reasons
to assume that the computer mainly takes over routine-tasks.   If
so, changes ensuing from it are likely to modify the managerial
jobs in such a way as to reduce the number of routine decisions
and problems, for these will be dealt with in the programs.   It is
this change our exclusive attention will be fixed on.   The
consequences studied are all considered as the consequences of
this change.

B.   CONCEPTUAL FRAMEWORK

1.   Computer-use and degree of routine of task-environment

As to MARCH and SIMON[38] the activities in an organization can
be characterized to the extent that each activity passes off automatically when the stimulus-situation occurs.

At one end of the continuum are the routine activities that
pass off fully automatically, at the other hand the activities
that cannot start without preliminary search.   They further
assume that as the stimulus situation occurs more frequently the
activities will gradually become more routine.   This means that
the stimuli will automatically evoke a well structured definition

of the situation and a number of performance programs including the procedure to choose out of these programs. In more unique circumstances the situation has first to be recognized and structured before alternative actions can be elaborated and chosen.

The information processing necessary for routine-tasks remains confined to checking the conditions under which such or such previously established performance program should be chosen and carried out. The information processing preceeding non-routine tasks requires in addition that the situation is analyzed and structured, and that alternatives are elaborated and evaluated according to a number of goal-criteria. Eventually these goals must first be made explicit and defined.

It goes without saying that the information processing implied by routine tasks is much better suited for computer-programming than the information processing of non-routine tasks, not only because of its greater simplicity but also because routine tasks are more frequently performed. The programming costs will consequently pay off more quickly.

In effect, we could observe[39] that the computer is mainly used for routine-tasks. As to the more unique and ill-structured problems only a few firms made a tentative start to use the computer. Heuristic programs which, according to SIMON[40], may offer a solution in such cases are very seldom used.

When the computer does the information-processing human errors are to a great extent avoided. The need for control is thus diminished. Also, once a task is programmed for the computer, it becomes fixed. A number of intervening decisions are consequently cancelled.

As a result managers are likely to have spare time which can be devoted to the part of their task-environment not yet programmed. If this is so, managerial jobs will become more characterized by non-routine decisions and problem-solving.

1.1 <u>Proposition</u>. The more the computer intervenes in the managers' task-environment the more they will become concerned with the non-routine decisions and problems.

2. <u>Computer-use and Reduction of Uncertainty</u>

Evidently, non-routine decisions and problems create a greater amount of uncertainty than routine decisions and problems. If prediction 1.1 is plausible managers are likely to become increasingly aware of uncertainty in their jobs and to modify gradually their behaviour in order to cope with it.

We see three important ways to reduce uncertainty:

1. Long range planning so as to anticipate future situations and possible action patterns.
2. Search so as to increase understanding of cause-effect relationships in general ("generalized uncertainty"[41] reduction) as well as the predictability of environmental reactions to organizational action ("contingency-uncertainty"[41] reduction)?
3. Systems-analysis of organizational functioning in order to reduce the uncertainty associated with the interdependence of organizational components[41].

2.1 Proposition. The more the computer intervenes in the organization's task-environment, the more persons with adequate knowledge and skills required for long range planning, research and systems-analysis will be employed. It is assumed that university graduates, especially graduates in the natural sciences and technology, are better qualified.

2.2 Proposition. The more the computer intervenes in the organization's task-environment the more likely it is that the organization will create specialized functions for coping with uncertainty such as long range planning-staff, research-staff and system-analysts (including eg. Operational Research).

2.3 Proposition. The more the computer intervenes in the organization's task-environment, the greater the fraction of the total payroll that will go to these staffs.

2.4 Proposition. The more the computer intervenes in their task-environment, the more of the managers' time that will be spent on long range planning, search and systems-analysis. This proposition is supposed to hold only when the organization does not create specialized functions for coping with uncertainty. Consequently it is conditioned by the plausibility of proposition 2.3.

3. Computer-use and Adaptability to Environmental Change

In more or less unique circumstances successful action is partly dependent upon the speed at which the organisational decision-makers can formulate their decisions. Therefore they must be able to perceive quickly the changes, they must obtain quickly the relevant information and choose as soon as possible appropriate action.

The more intense the inter-communications in the organization and the less restricted they are by the formal pattern of hier-archical relations, the easier changes will be perceived and the faster the relevant information will be obtained by the decision-maker who has to decide upon the action.

3.1 <u>Proposition</u>.   The more the computer intervenes in the task-environment, the more frequently managers will communicate with others.

3.2 <u>Proposition</u>.   The more the computer intervenes in their task-environment, the more of the managers' time will be spent on communication.

3.3 <u>Proposition</u>.   The more the computer intervenes in their task-environment the more of the managers' time will be spent on information gathering communications versus expediting, supervisory and co-ordinative communications.   Chances are high that they will spend relatively more time on communications with persons outside the organization than with superiors, subordinates and colleagues.

3.4 <u>Proposition</u>.   The more the computer intervenes in their task-environment the more managers will communicate by other channels than those established by the formal hierarchical structure.

3.5 <u>Proposition</u>.   As a consequence of the foregoing propositions, one can say that, the more the computer intervenes in their task-environment, the more likely the managers will perceive information exchange to be adequate to their needs.

Once the change has been perceived and the decision formulated, the speed of action mainly depends on the degree of autonomy of the decision-agent.   If he is completely autonomous, he will neither waste time on convincing his superiors of the adequacy of his choice nor on persuading his colleagues to accept or support his decision.

The necessity to consult fellow-managers is dependent on how widely decision-making responsibilities are spread over the management group.   The more they are concentrated on a few decision-makers the less time will probably be spent on consultation in order to achieve co-ordination.   Therefore, the speed of action may also be supposed to be related to the degree of concentration of decision-making responsibilities.

3.6 <u>Proposition</u>.   The more the computer intervenes in their task-environment the higher the decision-making autonomy of the decision-makers.

3.7 <u>Proposition</u>.   The more the computer intervenes in the organization's task-environment the greater the degree of concentration of decision-making responsibilities.

C. METHOD

1. Sample of Firms

If we had enough time available we would have preferred to do a follow-up study of a number of comparable computer-using and non-computer-using firms in order to compare the organizational changes we are interested in.

Actually we had to confine ourselves to a collection of data at one moment in time, hoping that the requested historical and prognostic data would somehow compensate.

We intended to select trios of firms of equal size and principal product-category, differing in level of computer-use: (1) using no computer at all, (2) using the computer for applications of lower managerial level (giving instructions and recording results) and (3) using the computer for applications of higher managerial level also (control and planning).

A number of firms which already co-operated in an earlier survey on computer-use were contacted (see footnote on title-page). Very few could be found to participate in this part of the research project because of the considerable amount of effort required on their side. We then extended our demand to other firms. Still a great resistance to co-operate was encountered. Therefore it was impossible for us to stick to the three levels of computer-use. In the end we obtained the co-operation of eight firms. There are four pairs of firms of the same product-category. For three pairs the sizes are more or less the same. In each pair there is one member which rents or owns a computer and another which does not. The latter kind, however, may run a few applications on the computer in service-bureau. As will appear the difference in the degree of computer-use as expressed in number of applications between the firms with and without computer remains sufficiently large. Table 2 depicts the product-category, total employment and year of introduction of the computer in the eight firms.

2. Data-Collection

The data were gathered by means of the questionnaires depicted in Appendix.

Questionnaire I aimed at obtaining information from each manager about:

- the degree to which each manager is confronted with non-routine

Pair of firms	Type of Product	Firms with computer		Firms without computer
		Total employment	Year of introduction	Total employment
A	electrical household uses	2000	1970	635
B	pharmaceuticals	731	1965	628
C	clothes	633	1967	598
D	metal construction	450	1968	594

TABLE 2: TYPE OF PRODUCT, SIZE AND YEAR OF COMPUTER INTRODUCTION IN SAMPLE

decisions and problems: the actual situation and future
changes;
- time spent on various responsibilities: idem;
- intercommunications between managers: the present situation;
- decision-making responsibilities; the present situation.

It should be underlined that the data are not factual but
perceptual data.   Owing to the short time-period granted for
this part of the research project it was impossible to resort to
direct observation.   Data about the job-content of managers are
obtained by means of the Work Analysis Forms elaborated by
Stogdill and Shartle[42].   This questionnaire was used because of
its appealing reliability and validity.   It is the result of
a considerable amount of preliminary exploratory research, and
it seemed beyond us to improve it.

Intercommunications were measured by means of a socio-metric
technique.   Instead of asking for likings between persons we
inquired about the frequency of contacts and the degree of
adequacy of information-exchange.

The list of decisions used for inquiring about the degree of
autonomy of decision-responsibilities was made up in a sort of
brain-storming session in which several researchers participated.
They were asked to elaborate a list of important decisions that
occur in all industrial firms.   This had already been done for
other purposes.

Questionnaire I was presented as a paper and pencil questionnaire.   Initially we intended to present the questionnaire to all
managers (first-line supervisors excluded) of the firm.   As we
were faced with considerable resistance of top-management to have
a large group interrogated we had to confine the group of
respondents to two (4 companies) or three (4 companies) levels
below the chief-executive.   In the paired comparisons only data
reported by managers of the same hierarchical levels were used.

As the study finally aims at investigating changes at middle
and higher levels of management the choice seems satisfactory.
We had two reasons for concentrating our attention to the middle
and higher levels of management, one being that the saturation of
non-routine decisions and problems is mainly expected to happen
there, the other reason being that the final structure of the firm
is believed to depend mainly upon their choices.

Questionnaire II asks for:

- the organization-chart in order to obtain data about the formal
  inter-relations between managers.   We also hoped to be able to
  infer from the organization chart the status of planning,
  research and systems and procedures activities in the firm (cf.

proposition 2.2).   The descriptions were so general that the desired information could not be obtained.
- the degree of concentration of wages over a number of years in order to see if different evolutions occur in computer-using and other firms.   The degree of concentration of wages is considered by Whisler[43], et al.
We hoped with these data to corroborate proposition 3.7.   Data obtained are too incomplete to be used in the analysis.
- data about the distribution of various kinds of personnel. From these data indices for the dependent variable in prediction 2.1 would be inferred.   Incompleteness of answers has forced us to leave proposition 2.1 untested.
- the relative amount of wages paid to staff personnel, the dependent variable in proposition 2.3.   Because of partial lack of data proposition 2.3 had also to be dropped.

Questionnaire II has been answered by the manager who acted as contact-person.

Questionnaire III served to measure the number of computer-applications and is answered by the EDP-manager in the firms with computer and by the person judged to be informed best in the other firms.

3.   Analytical Model

Initially we intended to test the propositions through comparisons of global values on the dependent variables of firms with and without computer of the same product-category.

This is essential in case of propositions 2.1, 2.2, 2.3 and 3.7, since there is only one answer per firm.

For the other propositions several answers are available.   In fact for each of a number of managers questioned an answer is obtained.   It makes no sense to aggregate without distinction all the answers and compute one score per firm.   The main reason is that the functional structures of firms, even within the same product-category and of the same size, may differ.   For instance only one of the firms may have an engineering department, or one of the firms may not have a sales department because it is a production branch of a larger corporation.   The hierarchical structures may also be different.   Function and hierarchical level certainly affect the degree of saturation of non-routine decisions and problems, as well as job content (i.e. time spent on various responsibilities), communications and decision-making autonomy.   In order to control for these influences one may only compare answers of managers of the same functional area and hierarchical level.   In order to do so we grouped the managers according to their hierarchical level and according to the ten functional areas which form the major headings of the list of information processing applications in questionnaire III in the appendix.

Comparisons (or differences) between firms with and without computer, only based on data of comparable groups of managers (same levels and functions), will be analyzed.

As a consequence, not all of the answers to questionnaire I could be used in the comparative analysis of the present situation for users and non-users. All of the answers were however included in the paired comparison about predicted changes in degree of saturation of non-routine-decisions and problems, job content, communications and decision-making autonomy because they are supposed to go in the same direction for all the levels and functions studied. Therefore, it did not seem necessary to in fact control for hierarchical level as well as for functional area.

Furthermore, as indicated in table 3 the overall disparities in numbers of respondents for hierarchical level and functional area are very small relative to the total number of respondents in firms with and firms without computer.

There were rather few managers who reported future changes. It therefore was necessary to include in the analysis as many answers as available. This is the more opportunistic reason why all answers were used.

4. Variables and Measures

The data were gathered by means of the questionnaires depicted in the appendix. The intensity of computer-use or degree of computer-intervention is measured by the number of computer-applications, as indicated by the answers to questionnaire III. The total number of computer applications reflects the degree of computer intervention for the firm as a whole. As was mentioned already the list of possible applications is sub-divided in ten functional areas.

Managers are grouped also according to these ten areas. The degree of computer intervention in the task environment of managers is then measured by the number of computer applications in the area they are working in.

The degree of saturation of non-routine decisions and problems is measured by the average of response-scores in section I.3 in

	Hierarchical Level				Functional Area										
	Top	Top-1	Top-2	Top-3	I	II	III	IV	V	VI	VII	VIII	IX	X	Other
pair A															
- firm with computer	0	3	4	10	0	1	1	0	0	0	14	1	0	0	0
- firm without computer	0	2	6	1	0	2	1	1	0	0	4	0	0	1	0
pair B															
- firm with computer	0	16	0	0	2	4	1	3	0	2	1	0	0	3	0
- firm without computer	0	14	1	0	1	2	1	3	0	1	4	0	0	2	0
pair C															
- firm with computer	1	5	20	0	1	2	1	5	1	3	7	2	1	1	3
- firm without computer	1	3	9	0	1	2	1	3	0	0	5	1	0	0	0
pair D															
- firm with computer	1	3	4	3	1	1	0	2	0	1	3	0	0	2	0
- firm without computer	0	3	3	4	0	0	0	2	0	1	7	0	0	1	0
total															
- firms with computer	2 (3)*	27 (36)	28 (38)	13 (18)	4 (5)	8 (11)	3 (4)	10 (14)	1 (1)	6 (8)	25 (34)	3 (4)	1 (1)	6 (8)	3 (4)
- firms without computer	1 (2)**	22 (46)	19 (40)	5 (10)	2 (4)	6 (13)	3 (6)	9 (19)	0 (0)	2 (4)	20 (42)	1 (2)	0 (0)	4 (8)	0 (0)

TABLE 3 – first part (continued on next page)

GRAND TOTAL

- firms with computer   70 + 4   (not classified)
- firms without computer   47 + 1   (not classified)

*   Percentage of grand-total 74.
**   Percentage of grand-total 48.

TABLE 3:   NUMBER OF RESPONDENTS OF DIFFERENT HIERARCHICAL LEVELS AND FUNCTIONAL AREAS IN PAIRS OF FIRMS (WITH AND WITHOUT COMPUTER)

questionnaire I for all managers in the same functional area.
The average of average scores on both questions is taken as the
degree of non-routineness of the task-environment.

Since propositions 2.2 and 2.3 cannot be checked because some
firms could not furnish the relevant data, there is no need to
elaborate measurements for the dependent variables.

The dependent variables in propositions 2.4 are:

- the relative time spent on long-range planning
- the relative time spent on research
- the relative time spent on the inspection of the organization
- the relative time spent on investigation and preparation of
  methods and procedures.

The measurements are directly derived from the answers to
questions of the Work Analysis Forms.

The dependent variable in proposition 3.1 is measured by
means of the average of the average frequency of intercommunications
between a manager and all the others studied, for all the managers
in a functional area.   Frequency scores are: 4 for daily
communications, 3 for weekly, 2 for monthly and 1 for yearly
communications.

The relative time spent on communication (proposition 3.2) is
measured by means of the average of the percentages of time spent
on communication as indicated by the answers on the Work Analysis
Forms, by the managers of the same functional area.

The dependent variables in proposition 3.3 are:

- relative time spent on communications with other persons than
  superiors, colleagues and subordinates
- relative time spent on communications with others.

The dependent variable in proposition 3.4 is measured by
means of the ratio of the average frequency of communications sent
by a manager to all other managers not directly linked to him,
according to the formal hierarchical structure to the average
frequency of communications to managers with whom he is in formal
relationship.

The degree of adequacy of information-exchange mentioned in
proposition 3.5 is measured by means of the average of scores for
judgements about the degree of completeness of information
received by a manager from other managers with whom he communicates.
The source-data are the answers given in column 6 of I.5 in
questionnaire I.   C (complete) gets score 2;   I C (incomplete)
score 1 and V I C (very incomplete) score 0.

The <u>degree of decision-autonomy</u> (proposition 3.6) is measured by means of the average score of judged autonomy for all the decisions in which a manager intervenes by making the actual choices. A score of 2 is given when the manager answers that he acts in his own right, 1 when he must first consult his colleagues and a zero-score when he needs preliminary approval of one or more superiors.

The <u>degree of concentration of decision-responsibilities</u> (proposition 3.7) is measured by the Gini-formula, computed as follows:

$$C = \frac{\displaystyle\sum_{i=1}^{n-1} (X_i - Y_i)}{\displaystyle\sum_{i=1}^{n-1} (X_i)}$$

wherein X_i = the cumulated percentage of managers making decisions in their own right up to manager I, (starting with the manager who makes the fewest number of autonomous decision-interventions).

Y_i = the cumulated percentage of autonomous decision-interventions up to manager i.

D. FINDINGS

Table 4 depicts relative differences on the variables studied between comparable groups of managers in firms with and in firms without computer.

A relative difference Dij is defined as

$$Dij = \frac{Wij - W'ij}{\text{Range of the scale}} \times 100$$

wherein
Wij = the score (or average score if more managers are involved) of the manager (or managers) of functional area i and hierarchical level j in a firm with computer
W'ij = idem, in the firm of the same product category without computer.

Average relative differences are calculated for the 4 pairs of firms, and for the 3 pairs of firms (B, C and D) wherein size-

Variable		Da**	N	Db***	N
X	Computer-intervention	<u>19.96</u>	26	<u>22.29</u>	21
Y1	Degree of non-routine of decisions	-13.81	26	-11.71	21
Y2	Degree of non-routine of problems	- 7.11	26	- 1.76	21
Y3	Degree of non-routine of task-environment	<u>-11.46</u>	27	- 8.11	22
Y4	Relative time devoted to long-range planning	- 0.60	27	- 1.26	22
Y5	Relative time devoted to study and research	- 0.60	27	0.00	22
Y6	Relative time devoted to inspection of the organisation	- 1.69	27	- 1.41	22
Y7	Relative time devoted to analysis and preparation of procedures	1.32	27	2.32	22
Y8	Average communication frequency	- 7.04	27	- 2.36	22
Y9	Relative time devoted to communication	- 2.83	27	<u>-11.13</u>	22
Y10	Relative time spent on communications with other persons other than superiors, colleagues and subordinates	- 6.55	27	- 7.45	22
Y11	Relative time devoted to communications with outsiders	- 0.06	27	- 0.34	22
Y12	Surplus communication outside the formal communication channels	- 5.00	13	- 4.56	9
Y13	Degree of adequacy of information exchange	<u>- 9.62</u>	24	<u>-11.79</u>	19
Y14	Degree of decision autonomy	-11.95	20	-19.92	15

  * Positive values reflect higher scores for firms with computer
 ** Da: Differences in four pairs of firms
*** Db: Differences in three pairs of firms
    Note: ____ Implies a statistical significance of P<.05 (two-sided t- test)
               ____ Implies a statistical significance of P<.01 (two-sided t-test)

TABLE 4: AVERAGE RELATIVE DIFFERENCES(*) WITH RESPECT TO THE VARIABLES STUDIED BETWEEN FIRMS WITH AND WITHOUT COMPUTER

differences are negligible, this is in order to exclude the
possible disturbing effect of size-disparities.

From table 4 we may conclude that:

- On the average the degree of computer-intervention is higher in
  firms with computer.   Since size (at least in three pairs of
  firms) and product-type are the same in each pair, differences
  in other variables may rather be attributed to differences in
  computer intervention than to differences in size or product as
  well as a number of characteristics associated with it.
- Proposition 1.1 seems to be contradicted since on the average
  the task-environment of managers of the same functional area and
  hierarchical level is statistically significantly more routine
  (= less non-routine) in firms with a computer and this mainly due
  to a higher degree of routine of decisions.   However, the size-
  difference of pair A seems to have played a role because when
  this pair is excluded from the analysis, the difference becomes
  statistically insignificant (= 0.05).
- Since proposition 1.1 is not confirmed there is no reason why
  the others should be because they rely on the intermediate effect
  described in proposition 1.1.   As expected propositions 2.4,
  3.1 to 3.6 are not confirmed by the data.
- Propositions 3.2 and 3.5 seem even to be contradicted.   Managers
  in firms with a computer seem to spend less time on communication
  and seem to be less satisfied about the adequacy of information
  received.

Table 5 depicts the correlations between relative differences
in computer-intervention in the task-environment of comparable
groups of managers in firms with and without computer, and relative
differences in the dependent variables, again in 4 and 3 pairs of
firms.   The correlations between differences are a more accurate
measure of association than the average differences between firms
with and without computer.   Still they lead to more or less the
same conclusions.   Now, however, only one statistically
significant finding appears: the more the computer intervenes in
their task-environment the less managers spend time on communication.

Dependent Variable	Ra*	N	Rb**	N
Y1	− 0.04	26	− 0.17	21
Y2	0.13	26	− 0.02	21
Y4	− 0.04	27	− 0.16	22
Y5	− 0.10	27	− 0.17	22
Y6	0.18	27	0.08	22
Y7	0.13	27	− 0.03	22
Y8	0.12	27	0.10	22
Y9	− 0.44	27	− 0.43	22
Y10	0.07	27	0.20	22
Y11	0.08	27	0.03	22
Y12	− 0.10	13	0.14	9
Y13	− 0.03	24	− 0.04	19
Y14	− 0.30	20	− 0.16	15

*Ra: Correlations in four pairs of firms

**Rb: Correlations in three pairs of firms

Note: _____ Implies a statistical significance of P<.01 (two-sided t-test)

TABLE 5: CORRELATIONS BETWEEN RELATIVE DIFFERENCES IN COMPUTER INTERVENTION AND RELATIVE DIFFERENCES IN DEPENDENT VARIABLES

The only proposition of the ones we were able to test, which seem to be confirmed is proposition 3.7. If one looks at the data in table 6 it appears that in 3 of the 4 pairs of firms the degree of concentration of decision-authority is higher in the firm with computer. In pair A, the reverse can be observed. However in pair A, the computer-using firm is much larger than the firm without computer. Concentration of decision-authority when measured as we did is likely to be higher with a greater number of managers (in larger firms). So the size-difference may be supposed to have obscured the effect of computer-intervention.

Pair of firms	Firms with computer	Firms without computer
A	0.52	0.55
B	0.41	0.33
C	0.52	0.51
D	0.31	0.28

TABLE 6: COEFFICIENTS OF CONCENTRATION OF DECISION
RESPONSIBILITIES IN FIRMS WITH AND WITHOUT COMPUTER

In the margin it may be observed that the coefficients of concentration differ less between firms of the same pair than between firms of different pairs. Factors associated with the type of product thus seem to bear a certain amount of influence upon the degree of concentration of decision-responsibilities.

Taken together, the findings do not support the piece of theory put forward. Does this mean that the propositions are invalid or is there another explanation?

Maybe an unknown factor has counteracted between firms with and firms without computer which was overlooked e.g. the fact that firms without a computer may have been confronted with special circumstances (reorganization, or special environmental changes) which, while impeding a computer introduction, confronted them with a great number of unique problems and decisions.

Characteristics	Firms with Computer	Firms without Computer
1a Changes with respect to the degree of non-routine of decisions:		
- average in four firms	0.55 (N=71)****	0.13 (N=46)
- average in three firms **	0.58 (N=52)	0.27 (N=37)
1b Changes with respect to the degree of non-routine of problems:		
- average in four firms	0.30 (N=73)	-0.04 (N=47)
- average in three firms **	0.28 (N=54)	-0.05 (N=38)
2. Changes with respect to relative time spent on long-range planning, search, inspection of the organization, study and preparation of procedures:		
- average in four firms	0.91 (N=67)	0.11 (N=47)
- average in three firms **	1.18 (N=50)	-0.18 (N=38)
3a Changes with respect to relative time spent on communication with outsiders, and other persons than superiors, colleagues and subordinates:		
- average in four firms	0.63 (N=73)	-1.33 (N=48)
- average in three firms **	0.07 (N=55)	-1.95 (N=38)
3b Changes with respect to total time spent on communication:		
- percentage increased ***		
- in four firms	43 (N=30)	41 (N=16)
- in three firms **	42 (N=22)	36 (N=11)
- percentage decreased ***		
- in four firms	1 (N= 1)	13 (N= 5)
- in three firms **	0 (N= 0)	16 (N= 5)
- percentage no change ***		
- in four firms	56 (N=39)	46 (N=18)
- in three firms **	58 (N=30)	48 (N=15)

  *The figures represent average differences between judgement scores about the actual and the expected situation; for items 1a and 1b on a five-point-scale, for items 2 and 3a on a percentage scale (100 points).

  **The pair of firms with size difference excluded.

  ***The percentage refers to the relative number of respondents.

****N stands for the total number of respondents.

TABLE 7: EXPECTED CHANGES* WITH RESPECT TO SOME OF THE ORGANIZATIONAL CHARACTERISTICS STUDIED

We do not think that this had happened. The selection of
the firms was too accidental for that.

Another possibility is that our measurements are of such poor
quality (unreliable and/or invalid) that no systematic differences
could be expected. However, so many significant findings have
been done with very similar measurement techniques. Why should
this study make an exception?

The most plausible explanation of the fact that the findings
in general do not confirm the propositions, is that the observations were made in the wrong kind of firms. We should have
taken firms with a longer history of computer-use. The secondary
effects implied in the propositions may be expected to occur with a
certain delay. Managers do not become immediately aware of the
changed task-environment induced by computer-intervention, and
certainly do not react immediately. It takes some time to adapt.
Also a certain degree of computer-intervention is needed before the
task-environment becomes significantly less routine.

However, only large firms in Belgium have used computers for
a longer period of time. The amount of questionning we should
have done in larger firms would have taken much more time, too
much in our case. Therefore, we could only request the co-
operation of smaller firms. Also some larger firms which initially
agreed to co-operate withdrew later on because the amount of work
involved became too great a burden.

The two significant findings (namely the fact that a higher
degree of computer intervention is associated with a reduced
amount of managerial time spent on communication and the fact that
it is associated with a higher degree of concentration of decision-
authority) may be considered as more immediate effects, i.e.
immediate consequences of the transfer of a number of clerical and
managerial tasks to the computer.

Yet, we have certain data which seem to indicate that in the
future of the firms studied our propositions might become
plausible. Table 7 depicts how managers in firms with and firms
without computer expect a number of characteristics of their task-
environment and job-content to evolve in the future. The
differences are systematically and clearly in the expected
direction.

E. CONCLUSIONS

The present study differs in several respects from other studies about organizational consequences of computer-use.

1. We have tried to elaborate a conceptual framework which highlights the inter-connectedness of changes in different characteristics. The linking concept is the expected decrease of routine in the task-environment of managers.
2. We have concentrated on secondary effects of computer-use i.e. adaptations by management to a changed "human" task-environment. This does not mean that we have studied other dimensions than those studied by other researchers. It only has led to different expectations.
3. The source data are different. Generally the researchers have based their conclusions on opinions of managers who know and who mostly were told that the study was about the impact of the computer. Also the questions are asked in such a way that the manager should express, himself, how the computer has influenced a certain characteristic, either directly ("Has the computer affected... and in which way?") or indirectly ("How was it before the computer ... and afterwards" or "What has changed since the introduction of the computer?").

In our study the respondents were not informed about the real purpose of the study. They were told the study was about organizational change in general. The questions asked of the managers do not refer to the computer either. We did so on purpose in order to avoid the pitfalls of the alternative way of questionning.

These pitfalls are:

a) that the respondents are somehow suggested that the computer "should" have an effect why else would someone start questionning about changes associated with the use of computers. Consequently some changes may be 'invented'.
b) that the opinions expressed reflect the rumors, common-sense notions and prejudices about the impact of computers in general rather than the actual changes which occurred in the environment of the respondent.

Our approach, however apparently has led to rather disappointing results. Only a few significant results could be obtained: that a higher degree of computer-intervention seems to be associated with a reduction of managerial time spent on communication and also that a higher degree of computer-intervention seems to bring about a higher degree of concentration of decision-responsibilities.

Projective perceptions of the future by the respondents seem to indicate that: the change towards a less routine task-environment of managers will effectively occur; that they will spend more time on long range planning, research and analysis of the organization and that they will communicate more with others, especially with outsiders and other organizational members than immediate superiors and subordinates or colleagues.

The complete set of findings do not strongly support nor do they contradict the propositions.

The conclusions one might draw from such findings are:

1. If the predicted effects are plausible, they will only show up in firms wherein the computer has been used for a longer time period (at least longer than was the case in our example). This is deduced from the supposition that managers adapt to changes in their task-environment (perceiving them and adjusting their behavior) with a certain amount of delay.

2. The effects seem to be rather limited in scope. This is certainly true for the immediate changes and seems likely for possible longer term changes also. The differences in projected changes in firms with and firms without computer are actually very small. There are several reasons. First, the managerial levels studied are middle and top. The impact of computer-use is generally believed to start at the bottom of the hierarchy and to end at the top. The degree of intervention in the firms studied is probably not sufficiently high to affect the higher levels profoundly. Second, even when changes in those managerial jobs and activities are studied with a mode of questionning which enhances the reporting of changes, the findings still are not very impressive as the review of the literature shows. We could not expect to find an equal or greater impact. Third, managerial and organizational structure is above all determined by the volume, complexity and technology of the organization's task.
    The use of computers has not been reported yet to have had an appreciable impact upon size, task-complexity and technology. So maybe one should not expect striking changes in managerial and organizational structure, an attitude which is also expressed in the conclusions of Simon's book "The Shape of automation for men and management".

340

REFERENCES

1. H.J. Leavitt and T.L. Whisler, Management in the 1980's.
   Harvard Business Review, November-December, 1958.
2. D. Klahr and H.J. Leavitt, Tasks, organization structures
   and computer-programs. IN: C.A. Meyers (ed.), The impact of
   computers on management. Cambridge, Mass., MIT-Press, 1967.
3. H.A. Simon, The shape of automation for men and management.
   New York, Harper and Row, 1965.
4. U.S. - Bureau of Labor Statistics: Adjustments to the installation of office automation. Bulletin nr. 1276, Washington
   D.C.., Department of Labor, May, 1960.
5. T.L. Whisler and H. Meyer, The impact of EDP on life company
   organization. Personnel Administration Report, nr.34, Life
   Office Management Association, November, 1967.
6. E.C. Weber, Changes in managerial manpower with mechanization
   of data processing. The Journal of Business, 32, pp. 155-163,
   1959.
7. B. De Brabander, D. Deschoolmeester, R. Leyder, and E.
   Vanlommel, Informatietechnologie en organisatiestructuur,
   Seminarie voor Produktiviteitsstudie en -Onderzoek,
   Rijksuniversiteit, Gent, 1970.
8. T.L. Whisler and H. Meyer, o.c., pp. 88-89.
9. D.R. Shaul, The effects of data processing on middle-managers.
   Ph. D. Dissertation. University of California, Los Angeles,
   1964.
10. H.A. Simon, p.c., pp. 42-49.
11. H.J. Leavitt and T.L. Whisler, o.c.
12. T.L. Whisler and H. Meyer, o.c., p. 95.
13. E. Mumford and O. Banks, The computer and the clerk. London,
    Routledge and Kegan, P., p. 97, 1967.
14. M. Anshen, The manager and the black box, Harvard Business
    Review, November-December, 1960.
15. H.A. Simon, o.c., pp.42-49.
16. R.C. Vergin, Computer induced organization changes. MSU
    Business Topics, Graduate School of Business Administration,
    Michigan State University, Summer, 1967.
17. D.R. Shaul, o.c.
18. R.C. Vergin, o.c.
19. H.C. Lee, Weerslag van de computer op het middenkader.
    Synopsis. Juli-Augustus, 1968.
20. T.L. Whisler and H. Meyer, o.c., pp. 44-51.
21. T.L. Whisler and H. Meyer, o.c.
22. T.L. Whisler and H. Meyer, o.c.
23. I. Hoos, The sociological impact of automation in the office.
    Management Technology, 1, pp. 10-19, 1960.
24. T.L. Whisler and H. Meyer, o.c.
25. G. Gilman, The computer revisited. Business Horizons,
    Winter, 1966.
26. H.J. Leavitt and T.L. Whisler, o.c.

27. M. Anshen, o.c.
28. J.D. Thompson, Organizations in action. N.Y. McGraw-Hill, 1967.
29. J. Dearden, Computers and profit centers. In: C.A. Meyers (ed.), The impact of computers on management. Cambridge, Mass., MIT-Press, 1967.
30. T.L. Whisler and H. Meyer, o.c.
    G.P. Schultz and T.L. Whisler (eds.), Management organization and the computer, Chicago, Glencoe, 1960.
31. I. Hoos, o.c.
32. R.C. Vergin, o.c.
33. H.C. Lee, De electronische breinen en hun weerslag op de bedrijfsstructuur. Synopsis, Juni, 1966.
34. R.S. Adams, The effect of information technology on management and organization. Ph.D. Dissertation. Louisiana State University, 1965.
35. D.R. Shaul, o.c.
36. S.R. Klatzky, Automation, Size, and the locus of decision-making: the cascade effect. Journal of Business, Vol. 43, pp. 141-151, 1970.
37. J.D. Thompson, Organizations in action, N.Y. McGraw-Hill, 1967.
38. J.G. March and H.A. Simon, Organizations, N.Y. Wiley, Chapter 6, 1958.
39. Results of the survey mentioned in the footnote of page 1.
40. H.A. Simon, The shape of automation.... o.c.
41. J.D. Thompson, o.c.
42. R.M. Stogdill and C.L. Shartle, Methods in the study of administrative leadership. Ohio Studies in Personnel, Research Monograph, No. 80, Bureau of Business Research, The Ohio State University, 1955.
43. T.L. Whisler, H. Meyer, B.H. Baum and P.F. Sorensen, Centralization of organizational control. An empirical study of its meaning and measurement. Journal of Business, 40, 10-26, 1967.

APPENDIX

Simplified version of questionnaire-items

QUESTIONNAIRE I

I.2   Identification of interview

       Date:
       Firm:
       Department:
       Section:
       Job-title:
       Number of immediate subordinates:
       Immediate superior:

I.3   Describe the typical kind of decisions you make in your
       job. (Check one of the answer-possibilities with xx).
       Do you experience a change. If so, check with x the
       answer-possibility which describes best the situation
       to which your job is evolving.

       Value: 5 (   ) 1. More or less unique decisions (the
                           choice-situation is never the same).
       Value: 1 (   ) 2. Routine-decisions (the choice situation
                           is repeatedly the same).
       Value: 4 (   ) 3. A mixture of 1 and 2 with a predominance
                           of unique decisions.
       Value: 2 (   ) 4. A mixture of 1 and 2 with a predominance
                           of routine decisions.
       Value: 3 (   ) 5. A more or less balanced mixture of 1
                           and 2.

       Describe also the typical kind of problems you are
       confronted with (check xx) and the situation towards which
       your job is evolving (check x).

       Value 1: (   ) 1. The solution of the problem consists
                           practically always of a routine-solution
                           (a standard procedure).
       Value 2: (   ) 2. The solution is routine most of the time.
       Value 4: (   ) 3. The solution is seldom routine.
       Value 5: (   ) 4. The solution is practically never routine.
       Value 3: (   ) 5. The solution is routine in more or less
                           50 percent of the cases.

I.4   A translated version of the work-analysis forms of
      STOGDILL and SHARTLE. Questions were added to ask for
      expected changes in time spent on the various items.

I.5   Below you will find a list of persons employed in this
      firm.   Besides his name, each person's job-title and
      department or section is indicated.   Please indicate the
      frequency of contacts you have on the average with each
      of them in order to exchange job-related information
      (daily, weekly, monthly, yearly or very seldomly and
      never).   Indicate also the degree to which the information
      received from each person is sufficient for your purposes.
      (Complete, incomplete, very incomplete).

I.6   Below you will find a list of important decisions.
      Please indicate for each decision.

      1. if in some way or another you are involved in the
         decision-process related to that decision.
      2. if so, whether:
         - you are involved in the preparatory stages
         - you actually make the choice
         - you are responsible for the execution.
      3. your degree of autonomy in those decisions in which
         you actually decide yourself:
         - completely on your own responsibility
         - you need the approval of one or more superiors
         - you must first consult your colleagues (of the same
           hierarchical level) in order to request their approval.

      The list of decisions presented was the following:
      Decisions
      1. Acquisition of capital goods (production equipment)
      2. Commercial investments
      3. Investment of excess-cash
      4. Pricing
      5. Determination of the volume of production
      6. Advertising budget and implementation of
          promotorial efforts
      7. Choice of sales territories and distribution channels
      8. Sales promotion decisions
      9. Decision about the opportunity of sub-contracting
          marketing research
      10. Extension of trade credit to customer
      11. Selection of suppliers
      12. Determination of order quantities
      13. Product design
      14. Long term production planning
      15. Determination of quality standards

16. Maintenance policy and maintenance planning
17. Determination of personnel requirements
18. Renumeration system
19. Training and personnel development
20. Choice of financial resources
21. Determination of productivity standards
22. Make or buy decisions for parts
23. Choice of transportation media
24. Clerical procedures
25. Planning of shipments
26. Relation with trade-unions
27. Decision concerning over-time labor
28. Assessment of delivery schedules and order-priority
29. Inventory levels.
30. Determination of inventory levels of spare-parts for service after sales
31. Safety stock and minimum level input-products
32. Safety stock and minimum levels for end-products
33. Collection procedures for accounts receivable
34. Decision about localisation of new units
35. Product-mix
36. Deciding about deviations from sales conditions
37. Deciding about dividend payments
38. Deciding about bonusses, stock-options, stock-splits, etc...
39. Acquisition, merger, other forms of co-operation
40. Selection and recruitment of personnel.

QUESTIONNAIRE II

II.1 A detailed organization chart: actual and planned changes.

II.2 What percentage of the total payroll is actually paid as
      salaries to the

      top 1% (i.e. the 1% persons receiving the highest salaries)
      top 2%
      top 5%
      top 10%
      top 20%
      top 30%

II.3-II.4
      Give the following information for each successive year
      from the date of 3 years before the computer was installed
      in the firm.   (Non computer-users for the last 10 years)
      as well as your expectations for the next 5 years:

      - number of white-collar workers
      - number of blue-collar workers
      - number of administrative personnel (staff)
      - number of administrative personnel (line)
      - number of university graduates or graduates of technical
        schools of equivalent level
      - number of university graduates of applied disciplines
      - the percentage of the payroll paid as salaries to staff-
        personnel

II.5 An open question about corporate planning in the firm.

QUESTIONNAIRE III

Below you will find a list of information-processing applications.
Please indicate for each application:

- if in some way or another it is applied in the firm
- manually, on the computer or on punched card equipment.

Then follows the lists of applications described in the article
about the survey-results in the January 1972 issue of the Journal
of Business.

The ten functional area in which the applications are grouped
together are:

I.	Long-term planning
II.	Management control and financial applications
III.	Personnel applications
IV.	Sales analysis and market research
V.	Inventory administration, control and management
VI.	Purchasing
VII.	Production, planning, dispatching and control
VIII.	Maintenance orders or expansion projects
IX.	Shipping
X.	Product design and development, engineering.

STRATEGIES FOR THE HUMAN USE OF A COMPUTER-BASED SYSTEM

James H. Bair

Augmentation Research Center
Stanford Research Institute
Menlo Park, California, USA

ABSTRACT. A comprehensive approach to the innovation transfer and application of a system for significantly improving individual and collective information activities is described. Five areas are addressed from an applied social science perspective: 1. System facilities; 2. The principles that must be followed during the development of applications; 3. The strategy for developing applications; 4. Models of user applications; 5. The strategy for transferring the innovations to potential users.

INTRODUCTION

The purpose of this paper is to describe a comprehensive approach to the transfer and application of a system for significantly improving individual and collective information activities. The prototype system has been developed by the Augmentation Research Center, Stanford Research Institute, during the past 14 years. The two major components of the system described here are the strategy for transferring the technology into a community whose members may be widely distributed geographically, and the development of application models within participant groups and organizations.

Participation in this human-computer system implies that ongoing work can be substantially shifted from conventional information-handling methods to those based upon computer support. Our goal is for this shift to enhance the productivity and effectiveness of individuals, organizations, and communities. To accomplish this we define the "system" to include the computer-based

Footnote   This paper was prepared, edited and printed for
          publication using a word-processing computer.

system, the human support and service system, and the application system (which includes user working methods, procedures, and culture). It will become apparent that realization of such a goal by system developers is fraught with both technological and human pitfalls, and that the far-reaching, global system can be realized only in an evolutionary fashion. It probably will be many years before all those who can benifit will be ready to employ this system. The evolutionary process includes flexibility and responsiveness to actual experiences. Neither the technology nor the strategy is static; they change continually, while remaining consistent with our long range philosophy.

The first section of this paper gives an extremely brief but necessary overview of the activities that are now being carried out with the system. The second section enumerates the principles that must be followed during the development of applications. Then, in the third section, the strategy for developing applications is discussed. Descriptions of model applications in the fourth section provide further insight into what the system is and what can result from its use. Finally, the strategy for transferring the innovations to potential users is discussed. The paper is written from the perspective of the technology transfer specialist, social scientist, and user, and focuses on behavioral variables and environment rather than the hardware and software facilities.

System Facilities

The presentation of a description of the technology is difficult due to the wide range of activities that it is intended to support within a complete system. It is important in the context of this discussion of the transfer and application to provide a list of the exemplary facilities that are included in the system.

(1) A highly interactive, user-oriented, computer interface with online usage assistance;

(2) Unique text editing, reading, portrayal, and graphics facilities;

(3) Document production and control facilities (including phototypesetting);

(4) Teleconferencing among distributed geographical locations;

(5) Automatic "mail" delivery, cataloging, retrieval and storage;

(6) Hierarchical information structures and user facilities for
    interlinking nodes in these structures;

(7) Personal information management (including automatic
    calendars and complete privacy);

(8) Organizational information management (including financial,
    personnel, and planning information);

(9) Special capabilities for custom-building subsystems.

The general-purpose, information processing technology that
supports these facilities is called the "Online System" or "NLS".
The software resides on a large time-sharing computer and it is
currently accessed through data communication networks by
organizations scattered across North America. Since January 1974,
the Augmentation Research Center has operated a small-scale service
to build a user community and gain experience at technology transfer
(Norton, Watson and Engelbart, 1975). The central computer facility
is operated by a commercial time-sharing company under contract to
the Center. By the Spring of 1976, the service had grown to a $1.2
million per year venture. Many government agencies and commercial
organizations are realizing direct value from the service, and the
scope of exploratory applications is continuing to expand.

APPLICATIONS OF THE GENERAL PURPOSE, HUMAN-COMPUTER SYSTEM

Applications are the results of using technology to accomplish
specific tasks according to systematic plans. The process is
analogous to that in the building trades where the tools (computer
technology and methods) are applied to materials
(knowledge/information) to construct a building (application) based
upon architecture (strategy).

In addition to the specific plans for the use of the
technology, a general strategy for building a user population is
necessary. Effective matching of the user population and the
applications also requires a set of applications principles that
have evolved from planning and experience. The strategy and the
principles will be described in the following sections. It is
important to note that feedback serves as the basis for the
continued development of applications, so that they continually
represent the optimum use of the technology in changing
environments. The system is formalized to include not only the
developers, appliers, users, and the technology itself, but also
feedback through these parts of the system.

The general strategy incorporates the elements of technology transfer into a gradual building of user expertise. Emphasis is on the development of understanding and seasoning of representative groups within the organization rather than the provision of service to the largest group as rapidly as possible. This emphasis is necessary to impart the procedures, methods, and other human aspects of the system to users so that the organization can participate fully in the development of applications (c.f. Engelbart, 1973).

Steps of the General Strategy

1. Identify Participant Organizations. The first step is the most crucial: to identify the organization that is to participate as a member of the user community. This is not a unilateral effort, it is a mutual decision heavily emphasizing the readiness of the organization to explore highly advanced technology. Important factors are a willingness to start small (6 - 15 persons) and increase the user population over a period of years; an interest in gaining experience with some deferment of financial return; a commitment to evolution rather than to a fixed system, and so on. We have developed a special mechanism, the one week technical and planning seminar, as a key way for the organization and SRI to reach the understanding necessary for a decision.

2. Select the Architect. The identification of a person within the organization to serve as "architect" or "gatekeeper" (c.f. Allen, 1970) usually occurs in parallel with the contact between the Center and the interested organization. In many cases, the architect is the technologically sophisticated person assessing the availability of innovations for his company and reporting to management. This role is somewhat analogous to Roger's concept of change agent (Rogers and Shoemaker, 1971).

In discussing the communication of innovation, Rogers points out that the change agent must understand both the innovation and the recipient of the innovation. In addition, he/she must have sufficient status in the organization to influence decisions and comprehend the far-reaching implications of the innovation for the organization's future. As noted by Keen (1976), it is also important that the transfer of the innovation be of value to the agent's success in the organization.

The role of architect, delineated by Engelbart, is that of the resident expert, planner and "pusher," analogous to the architect in the building trades (Engelbart, Watson and Norton, 1973). This role is a vital element of our shared-effort strategy. The architect, or "gatekeeper," must act as an intermediary agent between two information networks: the external network of information sources, our transfer specialists and consultants and other architects, and an internal network of users.

The architects for the using organizations are merged into a community of specialists. They collaborate across their organizational boundaries as well as with the Center to greatly facilitate the transfer. Our transfer specialists rely heavily upon architects for scheduling, support coordination, strategic planning, feedback, and input for continued development.

3. Select the Core User Group. Once a decision has been made and the architect selected, a group is identified in cooperation with the architect that will serve as the core group for the initial application. The group must be able to follow the application principles (see below), have a potential application that can be readily defined, and be close to the architect in the formal organization. Most importantly, group members must be motivated to explore alternative ways of working, and find innovations not threatening personally or to their organizational position. Our experience has been that groups of six to fifteen persons, including a wide variety of roles but with common tasks, are most likely to be successful. Selection of this core set of users is critical to the success of the strategy: they must be or have high potential for becoming visible to the rest of the organization, sympathetically managed, and technologically adept.

4. Identify the Initial Application. Selection of the initial application requires considerations not necessary with subsequent applications. A visible, immediate product that does not require extensive skill with the technology or complex procedures is crucial. Less tangible applications, such as communication support within the group, may not be as effective as the production of a document or the building of a small data base.

5. Begin Technology Transfer. In parallel with the selection of an application, the technology transfer services must begin with hardware installation, consulting, training, and delivery of documentation, as required parts of a package. This necessitates a certain scale of operation, adequate computer support, and a long enough commitment to warrant the investment on the part of both organizations (3 to 6 months as a minimum). Although the details are not necessary here, enough access to the technology in terms of time-sharing computer power must be available to support the nucleus group of six to fifteen persons. The package policy requires a corresponding amount of technology transfer service.

The service provided includes a consultant who will work closely with the architect. A trainer will also be assigned to an organization on a continuing basis. As one might expect, continuity is important in these relationships, particularly for the consultant. During this process, the consultant and her/his support staff learn about the organization, its structure and personality; this is of comparable importance to the participant organization's understanding of the system and its implications. A formal systems analysis may be done to describe the work activities within the organization and potential application areas.

6. Evolve the Applications. Application development should expand as the organization perceives system utility across a broader range of its information tasks, employing the system for more and more of its information needs. The application models discussed later are essentially the individual components of this global utility, to be incorporated in stages as growth toward complete use of the system for all information activities proceeds.

Application Principles

A set of application principles have evolved that are vital to system utilization. These illustrate the emphasis of our approach upon the environmental, social and psychological aspects of the system. Obeying these principles is not mandatory for success--we have had serendipity successes--but following them facilitates the smooth transition to new working methods while maximizing the probability of goal attainment.

1. Level of Usage. The close integration of the computer technology and methods for accomplishing most of a user's information handling work requires a high usage level. With the exception of programming applications, online time is relatively low in traditional computer applications. The realization of the full potential of our system is dependent upon more extensive online time.

In some cases, this requirement results from the broad nature of the application. For example, experience and studies have shown (Bair, 1974) that almost daily use is necessary for the system to serve interpersonal communication of the group. Unless a user participates in the system for some other application, he may not be available to receive computer-based mail. Conversely, if enough services are available through the technology, there will be sufficient attraction to the services to ensure daily use.

Also relevant is skill acquisition, which necessitates some regular experience interfacing with the technology. The technology transfer strategy emphasizes practice with the system tools as part of the graduated training. We have noted that participation tends to terminate if the threshold of usage necessary to retain skill is not maintained (Bair, 1974).

Consistent with this principle is the charging algorithm for computer service that is being maintained in spite of competitive disadvantages: charges are not based on computer access time ("connect time"). This aspect of service is provided based on a percent of the time-sharing computer. Thus cost is not a deterrent to increasing the amount of use.

2. <u>A Flexible, Workstation Oriented Environment</u>. Special attention must be given to the environment in which individuals will use the computer technology for most of the work day. The group should have the facilities which promote the incorporation of new technology and procedures into their offices. The "open office" is probably most amenable to the allocation of space for equipment, and the provision of the necessary power, lighting, sound absorbtion, and communication lines. In addition, the office landscape will more effectively support the system if there is visual and audio privacy. One approach to an ideal office environment has been specified by Herman Miller Research Corporation (Propst, 1968) with whom we have collaborated.

Heavy usage of the terminal equipment increases the importance of the human factors in office environments. Interacting through terminals for 6 to 8 hours a day could cause user fatigue and cumulative discomfort that can impair performance. Comfortable, adjustable furnishings are needed. It is readily demonstrated in human factors and ergonomics literature that display resolution, keyboard touch, the height of chairs relative to the display, lighting that could glare on a display terminal, and so on, affect the utility of the overall system. In this case, these factors can constitute negative reinforcement and result in rejection of the innovation. In general, the working environment is as important to our strategy of information-worker support as it is in factories (c.f. Shackel, 1969).

3. <u>Equipment Availability</u>. Experiences have reinforced the principle that equipment should be available to each individual participant at all times during his working day. Detailed descriptions of the problems and effects of equipment nonavailability have been presented (Bair, 1973 and 1974). Although hardware availability and function are often relegated to "shadow functions" (unperceived causal factors, Holzman, 1976), they are vital to the development of applications. Shadow functions include environmental factors which must be conducive to equipment installation and accessibility. Our system includes the display workstation, a teletypewriter (usually as an alternative), a high-speed printer, and optionally a high quality, medium-speed

printer. The terminals should be provided to users within easy reach of their office or most desirably within each individual office. It is consistent with the level-of-usage-principle that each person have his own terminal and immediate access to printing facilities. Optimal support requires a display workstation, but teletypes have been found adequate for individual offices if displays are available elsewhere.

Ultimately (20 to 30 years), the workstation configuration will probably replace the usual office furnishings as the organization evolves toward the "paperless office," a concept beginning to gain acceptance within the business community as part of the "office of the future" (c.f. Busines Week, June 30, 1975). It is not our goal to eliminate the traditional use of paper, but rather to integrate this and other conventional methods into the system.

4. System Participants: All Knowledge Workers. A fundamental application principle is that the system is being designed to include all the people who work with information, covering the widest possible range of roles. System users find it difficult to accept this concept, but it is not difficult to implement. It will become clear through the discussion of application models that participation by persons in all roles is integral to system design. Engelbart, Watson, and Norton (1973) have drawn heavily upon the concept of "knowledge worker" suggested by Peter Drucker. Drucker (1968) forecasts that within the coming decade more citizens of industrialized nations will be professionals, managers, technical specialists, clerks, and information specialists than industrial workers. He predicts that the growth of these roles will be paralleled by a growth of systems, technological and human, to support them. The scale will be analogous to the industrial revolution resulting in another "age of discontinuity" in man's socio-cultural evolution. It is all of these "knowledge workers"--managers, clerical personnel, scientists, system developers, executives, etc.--that can be integrated into our system.

However, the acquisition of the necessary skills and knowledge frequently requires the allocation of time and energy that may not be available to the executive. The system was designed to promote ease of use by the nontechnical person unfamiliar with computers. Although the technology is used effectively by such persons, failure can result from innovation rejection or a simple lack of typing skill. The problem of typing ability and its negative association with menial work can be solved using intermediaries.

Intermediaries have been successful in a number of executive applications. Typically, the executive's secretary becomes an expert at the relevant applications and delivers printed versions of the computer-based information to the executive. This arrangement tends to be less effective than direct use, owing to the secondhand nature of the interaction.

The customization of the interface to provide a subset of the command language and features is also used to extend the technology's range of users. Typically, a subset is all that is desirable when the technology is introduced and during the initial stages of learning. Provision of a simple version can enhance learnability, decrease threat, coincide with the exact material presented in the corresponding course, and so on. The author has experimented with the capability for easily creating a subset from the full repertoire of online capabilities, by building a much simplified introductory subsystem. This demonstrated that customization for varying user needs can be done by nonprogrammers. Customization can be extended readily to almost any conceivable application through the use of the Command Meta Language (Irby 1976).

5. Communication Need within the Application Community. There should be a need for users to communicate with other members of the application community. A community is defined by, among other things, a communication network resulting from common ground among the members. Common goals, tasks, management, and interests generate communication traffic. The absence of an explicit need to communicate renders it rather meaningless to participate in a system that places such emphasis upon interpersonal communication. Studies have supported the notion that the absence of a need to communicate can result in the failure of technology transfer, regardless of the other services available (Bair, 1974).

This principle is subject to the reciprocity phenomenon, where system participation generates increased communication opportunity and need, and certain needs are prerequisite to system participation. This has been observed in three situations: first, ease of communication promotes quantity of communication; second, the use of a new technology and working methods generates a need to communicate about the system itself; and third, serendipitous contacts are possible while using the technology for the purpose of communication. The last has spawned valuable contacts beyond the reach of usual communication channels. There is an increase in communication potential if a data network is used which provides links to users of other systems (e.g., ARPA Net).

6. Mission or Discipline Oriented Community Development. Applications should be developed across two kinds of communities, mission-oriented or discipline-oriented (Engelbart, 1973). A mission orientation is toward a common goal, usually one that is the raison d'etre for an organization. For example, the military forms

missions oriented around defense needs such as strategic or tactical air defense, or research and development to maintain or achieve detente. Missions can exist on many levels such as strategic defense (high level) and research and development (low level) support. Within the corporate world, similar missions exist: to develop new products or services.

In all of these cases there is a community, usually formally organized but with many informal aspects, which includes those persons employed to achieve the mission objective. Thus, a mission-oriented community participates in the system based on predetermined membership which must be taken into account in the application development. There certainly are communication channels that can be supported both horizontally and vertically within the organization, and including staff or support groups attached to the organization.

The discipline-oriented community offers a different membership based upon a common discipline that crosses organizational boundaries. Examples include worldwide sensing of seismic activity and its subsequent analysis, administration of energy resources, or medical research on a common problem such as cancer. The communities tend to be widely distributed geographically and may be part of mission-oriented communities. Special care is necessary to generate the momentum for each isolated group. Since there is a lack of shared physical space (with all its inherent opportunities for contact), a shared information "space" becomes more crucial. The payoff for applying the technology may be greater due to the availability of communication channels that are not defined by formal structures.

Application Models

The strategy for application development, guided by the set of principles, can result in unique applications for each situation. However, each of the applications appears to be a combination, in varying degrees, of one or more models--applications that could stand alone, although they rarely do. This section discusses five of the more common models based on existing software.

1. Intellectual Support. Increased intellectual effectiveness has been experienced within our user community when the system has been used in most of the participant's information activities. "Intellectual" is used here to denote a person's thought processes--the creation, condensing, filtering, reorganization, storing, etc., of language based symbols, referred to also as "human information processing" (c.f. Bair, 1971). It is imperative that the application principles are followed to the fullest extent. A

computer-based extension of memory, for example, is only as valuable as it is available.

The scenario begins with the individual at a terminal during the process of generating and composing his ideas. Essentially, the model is a communication dyad similar to that of face-to-face interpersonal transactions. Although the display presentation is passive, its highly dynamic responsiveness is attention-gaining on a sensory as well as cognitive level.

In the mode of online composition, raw ideas are entered into a selected place in the information structure. These places are defined by the computer-maintained hierarchical structure and selected by pointing to a node in that structure. Each node in the structure is a variable length text field (up to 2000 characters) that may contain very cryptic or expository information, e.g., headings or paragraphs. The hierarchy typically serves to represent the standard dimensions of information relationships: level of detail, importance, quantity, quality, etc.

The hierarchically structured information is also defined by a network for interconnecting the places ("idea nodes") regardless of their hierarchical position. "Links" are established by entering text that names the connected-to node, delimited by parentheses. For example: (bair,application-strategy,1) is the link to the heading of the introduction to this paper. The node is reached by pointing to the link. When the information at the linked-to node is presented, the hierarchical context displayed may contain additional links, and so on, to create a network of information. This network can include the information spaces of other members of the system (following a set of practical conventions).

Idea composition typically evolves into forms intended for others such as papers, publications, manuals, communications, and thinkpieces, through the insertion of ideas, text, and data into a growing hierarchy which will then be expanded into paragraphs, headings, tables, and diagrams. An author may have several "files" on different work areas that he is developing, with the added synergy of his parallel information activities.

As described in a study of a group of users from 1971 through 1973 (Bair, 1974), the intellectual facilitation provided by a highly interactive computer is more attractive than conventional pencil and paper adjuncts to thought. A person experiences freedom from the rigidity of written information--a release from the necessity of maintaining recorded ideas. Traditionally, there is negative reinforcement associated with changing written matter, even if it is only a personal working document. The flexibility gained with this system is analogous to thinking where information can be

altered in almost any way at any time. This encourages the
uninhibited entry and manipulation of ideas. Computer maintenance
of the hierarchical and network relationships enable them to be
exploited much more fully (Bair, 1974, p.34).

2. <u>Interpersonal Communication</u>. Models of interpersonal
communication support are best described employing the dichotomy
that has been in vogue since the advent of teleconferencing systems.
Asynchronous refers to those transactions where the participants are
not involved simultaneously. In synchronous communications,
individuals are interacting in real time as they would be in a
face-to-face situation. Although synchronous interaction beyond the
reach of one's voice is more generally available and accepted,
asynchronous capabilities tend to be more advantageous (see
Engelbart, 1975, for a thorough description of the system
teleconferencing features). First we will discuss synchronous
interaction, which supports distributed community collaboration.

Real-time or synchronous modes of communication are well
supported within our system (Engelbart, 1975). Real time
computer-based conferencing is receiving increased attention
elsewhere by efforts such as that of Bell-Northern Research, Canada
(the "Scribble-phone"), and others (c.f. Turoff, 1971). The need to
provide channels in addition to the audio, and more recently, video,
is being recognized. Many computerized approaches provide for
asynchronous interaction only (e.g., FORUM, Vallee, 1976).
Generally, we have experienced a greater need for asynchronous
support as described above, but in keeping with the philosophy of
full support for information activities, there is a "shared
terminal" facility.

Another application of the teleconferencing features is the use
of the display, through a number of slave monitors or a large screen
projector, for presentations to large audiences. We typically use a
video projector driven from a display terminal to demonstrate the
system. It is a very effective use of such features as the ability
to back up to any previous view, or the ability to "jump" ahead to
predefined views (analogous to viewgraphs). Of course, the full
power of the technology is available to retrieve online information
and modify it in response the immediate situation.

The facility is analogous to a "virtual" blackboard, upon which
individual, group, and public information can be edited under the
control of the remotely located participants. This visual channel
is virtual in the sense that the relevant information can be
retrieved, displayed, erased, rewritten, reordered, viewed at
various levels in the hierarchy, and so on. It is a means by which
a common intellectual space (as described above under intellectual
support) may be developed for the group. Important adjuncts to the

shared control of the display (also serviceable on a teletypewriter) are the windows for comments (a parallel phone connection is not imperative), and the split screen feature which allows several views of the same or different files simultaneously. Thus, one participant can present his visual-textual ideas alongside others for direct comparison or as source material.

The flexibility of shared-screen teleconferencing is limited by two factors: current screen size and one's imagination. However, real-time conferences can include groups of individuals at distributed locations clustered around displays with a "scribe" entering and modifying the agenda, idea scratch pad, etc. The result is immediately available for printing, distribution, editing into other forms, and so on. In one-to-one situations, assistance can be delivered by displaying the text, program code, or process for both the teacher and the user.

These briefly outlined models of applications to interpersonal communication have the obvious potential for changing organizations into what can be called "online organizations." If we accept Conrath's notion of an organization as being the sum of its communication behaviors, then this provision of a dramatically different medium has far-reaching impact (Conrath, 1972). Little has been done to investigate this kind of impact, not from lack of interest but from lack of funding. There are only rare opportunities to examine organizational behavior change where complete facilities for the communication needs of an organization have been implemented. Organizations participating in the SRI system may offer the only such opportunities. A small-scale analysis of computer-mediated organizational communication has been reported (Bair and Conrath, 1974). There are many interesting changes as the number of participants within an organization approaches the total number of employees. These are significant enough to warrent a new concept: the online organization.

Management becomes more accessible, both vertically and horizontally. No longer is it necessary for shadow functions (Holzman, 1976) to interfere with communication transactions. Instead, messages are delivered for perusal at the recipient's convenience. The ease of reaching across scheduling and availability difficulties is supplemented by the ease of message retention and response. There has been some speculation that the need for middle management would diminish; however, this author believes that filtering and delegated responsibility will continue to be necessary between levels of management.

The online organization also begins to lose its boundaries as cross-organization channels open and common-interest communities develop. The richness of interpersonal networks unbounded by the

labor of traditional correspondence, freedom from the shadow
functions of busy signals and nonavailability, the immediate
retrieval of the recorded transactions for store and forward tasks,
the ease of text preparation and distribution, and so on, could
revolutionize the human organizational processes that govern so much
of modern civilization. In our system this potential is enhanced by
the support of complementary information activities, for example,
document production.

Extension of the intellectual support described above to groups
of individuals is easily done through a time-sharing computer, and
may be called "shared information space." Files containing the
hierarchically stored information are available to all participants
in the system, using a number of agreed upon options for privacy and
access. These files may be interlinked to create a shared network
of information with all the inherent flexibility of the individual
application. Geographical distances are transparent as a result of
remote computer entry through data communication facilities
(telephone and data network).

The model usually depends upon the entry of the ideas and the
elaboration of idea nodes into a narrative by each member of the
collaborating team. In the case of a single product of the team
effort (a proposal, report, study, etc.), agreements must be made to
permit access. Participants will follow some protocols; for
example, only one writer can modify the shared file at a time (a
logical necessity). The result of the model as each person
manipulates, adds to, and studies the common information, is similar
to that of passing around a draft for comments. Differences are
that there is no retyping phase, the material constantly reflects
the latest modifications (not only a savings in time to distribute
the draft, but in the menial aspect of retyping the draft).

The collaboration on a common product extends to "public"
sources of information that may be studied and perused by
individuals where appropriate agreements have been made, or where
the data bases themselves are public. Public data bases resemble
libraries, containing, for example, information about the operation
of the technology or containing online publications.

Expanded, shared spaces require some retrieval support which
can take many forms. For this model, the use of an online table of
contents is the most pertinent. The table of contents for public
files (or private subsets) consists of lists of titles and names of
files, abstract-like descriptions, and links to desired nodes in
each file. In addition to the interlinking as described above, the
table of contents ("locator") is hierarchically organized permitting
categorical relationships and viewing which facilitate the easy
searching of the locator.

Once information is located (there are a host of fast searching mechanisms), it is available for direct citation through the editing capabilities. Although plagiarism is a conceivable concern, the free availability of information to facilitate cooperation and collaborative synergy is the goal and the result to date. Records are maintained on individual authorship for each file or node in the file indicating last writer, date, and time, but these are to promote coordination, not guarantee author credit. Ideally, the facility to make all information available to all participants would be employed for mutual benefit.

In addition to shared information space, most time-sharing systems provide some sort of interpersonal message handling that is simple and fast. As a component of our overall system, this message facility becomes most useful. The application is as broad as the need of any person or persons to communicate within the system environment, usually as an alternative to face-to-face or telephone interaction (Bair and Conrath, 1974). Its exceptional utility may be due to the regular, extensive use of the technology which permits frequent access to message facilities. The inability to reach an individual due to temporary nonavailability has long been a hidden cause of lost resources. Here the individual is notified that he has new "mail" whenever a connection to the computer is made. He then may view the message (including authors, title, distribution, date/time), act upon it (with automatic distribution of responses) and store it for later reference if he wishes.

This quick, easy communication is the fabric of online communities, particularly where there is frequent need to coordinate access to shared files and collaborate across geographical separation.

Dialogue support, in our sense of the application, requires facilities in addition to those for quick messages. Dialogue implies a longitudinal series of transactions that are interrelated to varying degrees. To fully support task oriented dialogue, a history of the dialogue must be accessible through reasonable retrieval mechanisms. The history should provide a chronicle of transactions, a diary or "journal" of the business of a group or organization. A substantive part of our work has been the development of software to support this application, as initiated by Engelbart in 1966 and described by him in some detail (Engelbart, 1975).

This model incorporates natural extensions of individual and interpersonal communication support. Having created an online record of thoughts and ideas, the authors may distribute it to a larger group, in many cases a public audience. The author identifies the completed information structure, which can range from a file of hundreds of pages to a one sentence message.

Distribution is aided by the ability to identify a predefined group of recipients using a single name, or to specify individuals by a unique set of initials that are maintained in a separate identification data base with a person´s address and "mailing information." Having specified the distribution, source information, and additional authors if any, the author adds a title. If comments (analogous to a preface) are desired, a paragraph may be appended to a collection of the foregoing fields. Other fields are added automatically, such as date and time. There are many less frequently used fields which provide the computer basis for fairly complete handling of this unit of dialogue.

An author essentially creates, with online guidance, a citation for the designated block of information that will be entered into library-like, computer-based catalogs and "delivered" to each recipient. The citation is automatically formatted, containing title, author, and so forth, but usually not containing the dialogue itself. The item is stored in a central location and is linked to by the citation. Automatically generated links appear with the citation which uses an accession number assigned during the submission process.

The central storage of dialogue entries (each with a permanent accession number) becomes a record, including replies, links to references, and essentially a network of interrelated submissions. The technology offers central storage for the same reason as any library--it is too costly for every individual to maintain his own collection. Another factor is the maintenance of the collection, which would be prohibitive for each individual. General access to the data base is through catalogs that are indexed by author, number and title word. Searches through the catalogued citations may also incorporate the information-retrieval facilities discussed below, such as a free text search on the citations.

Subcollections for groups or organizations can be optionally maintained that are essentially the organizations´ management information, a record of its internal and external business. Typically, proposals, executive actions, contracts, plans, and the like, are interlinked in the subcollection, replacing the vast arrays of file cabinets. More importantly, they are generated as part of the daily working processes within the organization and do not require extra effort for recording. The computer based dialogue record renders the geographical dispersion of the organization unimportant.

It has been argued that dialogue support coupled with the fast message facility would eliminate the need for face-to-face transactions, a conceivable outcome with the imaginative amplification of these application models. However, we do not yet understand the implications of substituting computer-mediated communication for more human contact, particularly on organizational attitudes or morale. Although there is a need for much more research in this area, it is probable in most application environments that there would be enhanced effectiveness. The relationship between the two models of interpersonal communication support suggests this metaphor: if the message-memo facility is the fabric of community collaboration, dialogue support is the thread.

3. Document Production. The technology includes the basis for creating, modifying, disseminating, and controlling documentation. The capabilities discussed above have particular advantages for the easy modification of master copies, large-scale modification and reorganization of documents either as initial drafts or revisions after publication, facile detailed editing, and a variety of printed output, including line drawings. It has been applied for over 6 years to produce reports, users´ guides, proposals, and other technical documents in the range of thousands of pages (van Nouhuys, 1975).

Input, as with the other applications, is through typing directly online at a display terminal or teletypewriter, offline onto a magnetic medium that is later read into the computer, or through copying online files from other computer systems.

Input to magnetic tape is available which can operate through several terminals and digital cassette recorders. It is possible to record limited editing during input to this "batch" medium.

In this model, hierarchical structure facilitates draft development by providing the analogue of an outline form. Commands are used to rearrange and reorder the outline more rapidly and flexibly than is the case with paper copy or online systems that address text line by line. This facility is particularly useful during the initial stages of creating a document. Similar commands can transfer or copy files or parts of files according to their outline position or content.

Editing through copying, transfer, and replacement commands that operate on small units of text can greatly increase productivity. Automatic editing facilities are available to support larger editing tasks. For example, there are facilities to generate a table of contents, generate an index, correct the number of spaces between sentences, and automatically format a file.

Illustration facilities allow users to draw and edit simple

illustrations that are part of system files, e.g., organization or flow charts. Text and graphics are fully integrated. Users with displays of sufficient resolution may view and edit drawings and print them through appropriate devices.

Output facilities allow printing text in a simple draft form or a format with headers, footers, control of top and side margins, etc. A monospace font may be used on a local printer or terminal, or output may be via microfilm and offset plates with a variety of type sizes, fonts, and columns per page. Coded directives, visible online but not printed, control format through an output processor. Such directives are most often inserted automatically, but may also be inserted by users with special training.

Document control is provided by the automatic numbering and indexing services described above under asynchronous communication--recorded dialogue. This same facility serves as a medium for freezing, cataloging, identifying documents, and recording their standing with respect to updates.

This application offers new freedom to the publications process. Procedures that have in the past been forced by the medium, for example limited distribution of drafts, become matters of option (van Nouhuys, 1975).

4. Personal Information Management. The foregoing models introduce many facilities and methods which are applicable to other models as well, such as the individual's management of his day-to-day personal information. This value is particularly dependent upon the application principle of relatively high usage level, where access to a user's information space is made regularly, preferably daily. The user then receives reminders, views agendas, marks calendars, keeps notes, makes things-to-do lists, and the like, all structured as he prefers. When these are coordinated with message and mail transactions, an individual's business may be completely handled technologically. Other personal services can include phone number and address lists, reference lists, and financial records. Our practice usually includes these easy applications of the technology.

5. Organizational Information Management. The online organization can be fully supported through interpersonal communication and dialogue facilities, but there are also needs for more structured approaches often referred to as management information systems. The emphasis in the models discussed above is on free textual information where the structural nodes are paragraphs, headings, citations, and names, and addresses, that may be retrieved by scanning text "pages" showing different levels in the hierarchy, or by searching for strings of text. Also available

is a special way of designating a text string to be the address of the node, supplementing the numbers that are available. The storage of specially identified text is analogous to an inverted index for fast, efficient retrieval using the text as a "keyword." This retrieval facility forms the basis of simple data base search, or can be amplified into full-scale management information service using the programming capabilities.

A simple management data base is built by following the rules for identifying text to be the keyword. Keywords can be part of the information in each field or can be invisible. Fields, the common element of data management, are interrelated in the same manner as nodes used for any other purpose. The hierarchy serves to identify records, each containing fields that may be filled by personnel names, addresses, phone numbers, job data, etc. The hierarchy is used to organize records into higher-level records. For example, top-level nodes would be identified by the keyword of a company name, with the second level based on the names of personnel. The data base retains a clean appearance in this model because the keywords are unique for each field, can be part of the field, and do not require any visible delimiters. The same text-searching facilities are available in any application. There are no further inversion or inclusion capabilities in this model, but it has the advantage of being immediately available to every participant.

The full-scale approach, although currently limited in size by our file structure, employs programmed additions to the foregoing model. Complex data base structures can be defined where fields may be retrieved by the type of field in addition to the keyword. For example, a retrieval could be done of all fields of a common type (i.e., the "values" of these fields would be retrieved), such as position in an organization, or date. Retrieved "hits" would identify records, such as the name of each person with a certain position. Application subsystems have been built by us and other participants for financial data management, marketing data bases, and personnel data bases, to name a few. These subsystems have their own command set, provisions for automatically formatted reports, consistency checking and control, and arithmetic modeling.

The user interface is consistent with the rest of the technology including all the features described above. With the simpler programs, little new code is necessary because the existing code may be copied or referenced and modified. More complex designs have drawn upon the full extent of "software engineering" support extending to dynamic modeling programs for plotting the relative location of moving vehicles. This indicates the range of application models when programming is done. It must be emphasized that our intent is to make it very easy to extend the software

capability, but that the system already contains programs that serv
the majority of applications.

A HUMAN-CENTERED TECHNOLOGY TRANSFER STRATEGY

The goal of the strategy is to introduce technological and
non-technological innovations into organizations. This should
enable these organizations to participate in a comprehensive syste
for most of their information needs. We refer to the process as
technology transfer following Gruber's definition: we are bringin
about the utilization of an existing technique in an instance wher
it has not been previously used (Gruber, 1969, p. 256).

The strategy has six elements emphasizing the human factor:
training, courseware, application documentation, a feedback
mechanism, community development and representation, and consultin
support. These are aimed at joint implementation with the user
community.

Our experience has reinforced our assumption that it is
necessary to overcome inappropriate fears, prejudices and
expectations, and general resistance to any innovation. The
strategy must include continual effort to evolve skills and
knowledge toward increased effectiveness, rather than providing
one-shot training and consultation. There is also a need to crea
the circumstances to motivate participation by subtly concentrati
effort on reward-reinforcement as suggested by Gruber (1969). Fc
example, management may note the use of the technology in personr
evaluations.

The importance of technology transfer is often underestimat
Many system failures result from the lack of a systematic transf
strategy and constant attention to the transfer process. The
strategy becomes even more important when the the system is larg
and general purpose.

Elements of a Comprehensive Technology Transfer Strategy

1. <u>Face-to-face instruction</u>. Face-to-face instruction wit
supporting courseware and documentation is the primary technique
our technology transfer. Formal training programs are the most
obvious strategy employed and the most abundantly described in t
technology transfer literature (c.f. Murdock, 1974). They offer
most flexibility and dependability, and are the most desirable
during early stages of the general acceptance of a single-system
approach to information activities. Krubeck (1975) and Jones (

corroborate our selection of this approach. There are specific
factors surrounding this choice.

The more complex or rich the interface appears to the user, the
more opportunity there is for problems to result from unpredicted
interactions; these problems often result in "frustration states"
with beginning users (c.f. Melnyk,1972). For example, situations
arise where the user's repertoire of commands or functions does not
apply (e.g., an error condition), or where he desires to accomplish
some task for which his operative skill and knowledge is inadequate.
Frustration which can greatly impair the progress of transfer can
be minimized if most of the situations occur with a trainer present.

Greater complexity usually means a longer learning curve and
the necessity to have cumulative learning, where later facilities or
capabilities depend upon prior mastery of more basic functions. A
controlled progression through the material has been found to be
most easily and flexibly provided by face-to-face contact.

Technology stability is a vital consideration in any technology
transfer, particularly when the underlying philosophy emphasizes
evolution. If there is any development work paralleling system
implementation which alters the technology, training provides the
flexibility to initiate users to the new developments and minimize
the effort required to transfer the change to the user population.
Since our system represents a commitment to evolution, there is
periodic change resulting from continuous refinement.

Special characteristics have been identified for transfer
specialists. The most successful transfer specialists are those who
do not psychologically threaten prospective users either by being
too aggressive (like the stereotypical salesman) or by displaying
superior qualifications and knowledge too obviously. Our experience
has been that a low-key approach is imperative, because of the
potentially high threat associated with a new technology. There is
a great potential for arousing anxiety in persons who have not been
exposed to new technologies; the potential can be minimized by a
trainer who is younger and keeps a low profile.

The target student population should be clearly identified and
understood prior to training. This may seem obvious, but assessing
the experience and background of prospective students has been
difficult. Jones (1972) suggests that an assessment of performance
be the basis for determining the extent of the training required. A
pretest is strongly advocated by Smith (1972) to determine the level
of prospective in-house programmers, a situation more
straightforward than ours. Our trainees have such a broad variety
of roles and backgrounds that it is virtually impossible to have a
class homogeneous enough for meaningful test results. We have not

directly addressed the problem of the resistance and threat
associated with any kind of testing, including posttesting.
However, face-to-face training in small classes should provide ample
opportunity for real-time adjustment to each trainee's peculiar
level, role, and personality.

In addition to the usual visual aids, we have found that it is
extremely valuable to provide training while the user is at a
terminal, particularly for introductory levels. This limits the
size of the class to the number of terminals available.
Demonstrations in lieu of direct experience at a terminal have not
been found to be adequate.

Other transfer techniques based on a variety of media are
possible, including instructional documentation, computer-based
assistance, linked or shared computer terminals, and video tapes.
However, when a complex system is periodically changed more
resources are required for alternative transfer techniques. We have
experimented with some alternative techniques such as video and
programmed instruction and found that they require an excessive
commitment to stability and retard system development. In addition,
computer-based techniques require computer power that detracts from
that available for work.

Future developments in computer-based instruction may alleviate
the current high demand for computer resources. Although present
computerized instruction may not be humane, rapid development is
being made (Bair, 1975a). The opportunity for each student to move
at his own pace is a significant advantage if the other problems are
solved. This opportunity might help when training heterogeneous
classes where the target students are difficult to define. Some
pioneering work in computer-based instruction has been done for our
system as reported by Grignetti et al. (1975).

2. Courseware. Training requires the development of a
curriculum based on an analysis of the behavioral objectives, a
process that is described in some detail by Jones (1972).
Generally, this results in specific behaviors (skills and knowledge)
and a detailed curriculum to obtain the desired results. We have
developed our curriculum in the form of outlines for each level or
"graduation" of the training. These outlines are important enough
to be a separate element of our transfer strategy, and receive
significant resources for their updating and maintenance. They
provide for gradual slopes in the learning curve during which the
user develops skills and confidence while having enough capability
to accomplish some meaningful work.

The courseware was designed with a great deal of attention to
the selection of the commands, functions, and concepts that are

included at each level. The criteria for the selection include: the difficulty of comprehension and usage of a particular command, concept, etc.; the relationship to the conceptual organization of the system; and whether or not command alternatives are useful but not necessary at lesser levels of expertise. The levels also serve as the basis for dialogue about proficiency, permitting reference to relative user capability and training experience.

Course length was influenced by considerations such as the minimum disruption of work schedules, as well as psychological and system factors. The courses are designed to be covered in a 2-day period of fairly intense interaction (4 to 6 hours per day). Since it is extremely important for users to have the opportunity to gain hands-on experience before receiving additional instruction, an attempt is made to include enough material to provide the impetus and capability to explore the technology.

The system is divided conceptually into ten categories for the purposes of training. This organization is important (and consistent with learning theory) to establish some high-level relationship between task areas familiar to the user and those defined by the technology, for example, "typing text in." The categories are reasonably straightforward: getting to and from the computer, printing, editing, communicating, troubleshooting and help, formatting, programs, and customization of the system. This paradigm has been followed at lower levels of organization as well, and we find it more successful than typical approaches to computers (e.g., "partitioning memory blocks", "file dump and saving core images", and so on). The commands in each category can be used to perform the general task denoted by the category heading; the complete syntax is provided for each command phrase including feedback and field names.

In addition to the graduated courses, a comprehensive week-long seminar is offered. It covers the body of system philosophy, methodology, and practical operation that is necessary to impart an understanding of the overall system to individuals uninitiated to its specialized aspects. The seminar is oriented toward technologically fluent attendees who understand the information environment at their organization. As a result of the seminar, persons who are not experts in our system may be able to assess the appropriateness of the system to their organizations.

3. Application Documentation. Documentation may appear in a range of forms, from cue cards to reference manuals and complete userguides. The heterogeneity of system participants requires a variety ranging from the step-by-step, cookbook approach to quick-reference listing of commands and syntax. We have developed two specialized forms of documentation (in addition to userguides).

The first, "procedural tutorials," document the step-by-step alternatives and pitfalls to avoid. The second, "application tutorials," present higher level methods and procedures for accomplishing clusters of related tasks. These are an important kind of documentation, necessary where a general purpose technology is being mapped onto a specific set of information tasks.

4. Feedback Channel. Although the best documentation and assistance may be available and frequent courses given, a continually available channel of communication with the transfer support staff is necessary to technology transfer. Feedback is a vehicle for users to ask questions at any time and receive a relatively fast response from an expert (24 hours is our outside figure) and submit design suggestions which may eventually be included as part of the system. This channel also serves as an information distribution service. We have prepared the system mechanism and staff specialists to provide answers to all questions, forward reports of malfunctions for appropriate action, and maintain a data base of transactions serving as potential guidance material for further development.

5. Inside Coordinator--The Architect. The role of "architect," as discussed earlier, was delineated by Engelbart as that of the resident expert, planner and "pusher." This role of a special individual acting as a transfer facilitator is a vital element of our shared-effort transfer strategy. Our transfer specialists, whether training or involved in other activity, rely heavily upon architects for scheduling, support coordination, planning, feedback, and input for continued development.

6. Application Consulting. Training, in spite of all the elements in its favor and the attention we give to its support, is not adequate to maintain the continued long-term growth of applications. It is necessary and fundamental to begin with a structured, formal approach, but later learning and application development must be highly flexible, responsive, and personalized. This kind of attention can only be provided by persons with the explicit responsibility for an organization or group, a role analogous to counselor.

The counselor role includes that of advisor, which was deemed crucial by Jones (1972). But persistent attention, coupled with residence at the users' site, expands the role. In our scheme, the consultant does not do the training, but is responsible for its coordination as well as for providing direct assistance. The psychology of responsibility is intentional in this approach, not only for the consultant but through the clear provision of a personal contact for the participants.

There is wide latitude in the amount of support delivered through the consultant, ranging from full-time residence to occasional visits. Residence involves the consultant in the daily work of the organization, where he contributes directly to the tasks as an unofficial member of the organization. It is difficult to predict the support level beforehand, but there is a direct relationship with the architect's execution of his role. Occasionally, consulting is expanded to include custom programming and similar highly technical support.

CONCLUSION

Problems

We have offered strategies based on a humanistic perspective, but have given little attention to the problems that abound within our system, and any other for that matter. There are clearly two problem areas, the technical and the human, but closer examination reveals the platitude that all the problems are human (a theme recurring in the work of Sackman, Weinberg, Shackel, Martin, and others including this author). The issue can become one of problem definition: do the boundaries of overtly technical problems exclude the behavioral dimension? Is this not in essence what Weizenbaum portrays in his vivid image of the computer "hackers" who have defined the boundaries of their world in terms of machines? (Weizenbaum, 1976)

This paper is offered as a description of the strategies of transfer and application as an ideal rather than an actuality--a deliberate result of minimizing discussion of problems. This is because I believe that the problems can and should be addressed in a systematic, thorough, analytical way--a pragmatic empiricism. There are bugs in the technology, capabilities not yet provided, recalcitrant users, reluctant managers, computer crashes, and other evidences of fallibility. The common thread (across technical and strategic areas) is individual difference and social context. I question that our goal of system consistency and coherence might be counter to the human predilection for difference. In my empirical studies, individual differences were as often as not the significant causal factor where problems were isolated.

One probable conclusion forthcoming from a discussion of problems is that there are two needs: one, for increased attention to the principles and strategies presented here, and, two, for increased commitment by the information-using society. One of Dr. Engelbart's stated objectives for the Augmentation Research Center is to make three aspects of our work clear: our long term objectives, the potential value of the system, and the strategy for realizing that value. This paper primarily addresses the last aspect, in the hope that explicit strategies will better generate strong commitment (Engelbart, Watson, and Norton, 1973).

Evaluation and Analysis

More arguments for the evaluation of technology implementation through investigations of user behavior are being heard. It is probably true that there is not a sufficient body of theory upon which to base a user science (Martin, 1973). However, there are methodologies that have been espoused (Bair, 1975b) which could reveal the psychological and sociological causality of success, failure, and shades in between. Numerous reports of such investigations are beginning to make an impact, particularly within management science. There remains, however, a practical need for funding further research, particularly on the scale required for our system.

Comments on The Future

The future is filled with exciting developments in information-handling technology: microprocessors, increased central processor and memory speed, memory capacity increases, high resolution displays, high-speed and wide-band networks with widespread availability, and more, all at tremendously decreased costs. Microprocessors alone may revolutionize the application of computers. Every person will be able to have his own computer, connected through networks to powerful computer mainframes with vast memories. Techniques for managing these vast resources are also developing, for example, under the aegis of the National Software Works (White, 1976). We are contributing to the development of future technology through such means as splitting the software part of the system to run on local mini- and microcomputers as well as distributed, time-sharing mainframes. We are continually exploring new interfaces and new capabilities as part of our commitment to evolution.

It may appear that the future belongs to technology, but as stated earlier, there is increased awareness of the human basis of the success of technology. In fact, the value of any development is dependent upon humane concern for the user in the design, transfer, and application processes.

REFERENCES

Anon   1975   The office of the future.
Business Week, June 30, 82-58.

Allen, T.J.   1970   Technology transfer to developing
   Piepmeier, J.M. &   countries: the international
   Cooney, D.   technological gatekeeper.
ASIS Proceedings, entitle "The Inform-
ation Conscious Society", Jeanne B.
North (Ed.), Washington D.C.:
ASIS, 7, 205-209.

Bair, J.H.   1974   Evaluation and analysis of an augmented
knowledge workshop.
Final Report for Phase I, Rome Air
Development Center, RADC-TR-74-79.

Bair, J.H.   1973   Experiences with an augmented human
intellect system: Computer Mediated
Communication.
Proceedings of the Society for Information Display, 14.2 Second Quarter,
42-51.

Bair, J.H.   1971   Human information processing in man-
computer systems.
Presented at the Annual Conference of
the International Communication Ass.
Phoenix, Arizona.

Bair, J.H.   1975a   Technology in instruction and education.
In: Technology Transfer: A State of
the Art Survey, Tom Anyos and Kenneth
Hirschberg (Eds.), Menlo Park, Calif.
Stanford Research Institute, Final
Report, 103-110.

Bair, J.H.   1975b   Sociometric measures of computer systems
impact in non-programming applications.
Presentation to the Workshop on Psychological Research on User Online Interaction, American Society for Information Science Annual Conference,
Boston.

Bair, J.H. &   1974   The computer as an interpersonal
  Conrath, D.W.   communication device: a study of
                             augmentation technology and its
                             apparent impact on organizational
                             communication.
                             Proceedings of the Second International
                             Conference on Computer Communications,
                             Stockholm, Sweden, August 1974.

Conrath, D.W.   1972   Measuring the computer's impact on
                             organizational structure.
                             Stanley Windler (Ed.), Computer
                             Communication, First International
                             Conference on Computer Communication,
                             Washington, D.C., October 24-36, 68-73.

Drucker, P.F.   1968   The age of discontinuity: guidelines
                             to our changing society.
                             New York, Harper and Row.

Engelbart, D.C.   1973   Co-ordinated information services for
                             a discipline- or mission-oriented
                             community.
                             Proc. 2nd Ann. Computer Comms. Conf.,
                             California State University, San Jose,
                             Ca., U.S.A.

Engelbart, D.C.   1975   NLS teleconferencing features: The
                             journal, and shared-screen telephoning.
                             In: How to Make Computers Easier to Use,
                             Digest of Papers, COMPCON 75, IEEE
                             Computer Society Conference, 173-176.

Engelbart, D.C.   1973   The augmented knowledge workshop.
  Norton, J.C. &   AFIPS Conf. Proc., National Computer
  Watson, R.W.   Conference, June, 42, 9-21.

Grignetti, M.C.   1975   An 'intelligent' ouline assistant and
  Hausman, C. &   tutor - NLS SCHOLAR.
  Gould, L.   AFIPS Conf. Proc. Nat. Comp. Conf.,
                             45, 775-781.

Gruber, W.H. &   1969   Research on the human factor in the
  Marquis, D.G.   transfer of technology.
                             Factors in the Transfer of Technology,
                             Gruber and Marquis (Eds.), Cambridge,
                             Mass.: MIT Press, 255-282.

Holzman, D.   1976   Presentation at "Workshop on Evaluating
                             the Impact of Office Automation".
                             Xerox Palo Alto Research Center,
                             Calif., May.

Irby, C.H.   1976   The command meta language system.
AFIPS Conf. Proc. Nat. Comp. Conf.,
Vol. 45.

Jones, B.A.   1972   The functions and elements of a
training system.
In: AFIPS Proc., Spring Joint Computer
Conference, Montvale, New Jersey:
AFIPS Press, 42, 53-58.

Keen, P.G.W.   1975   Managing organizational change: the
role of M.I.S.
Paper to Ann. Conf. Society for Management Information Systems, New. York.

Krubeck, R.D.   1975   Training the systems information
specialist and the information user.
Journal of Systems Management, 26.8,
24-25.

Manning, G.D. (Ed.) 1974   Technology transfer: success and
failures.
San Francisco: San Francisco Press.

Marting, T.H.   1973,   The user interface in interactive systems.
In: Annual Review of Information Science
and Technology, C.A. Cuadra, A. Luke,
(Eds.), Washington, D.C.: ASIS Press,
8, 203-219.

Melnyk, V.   1972   Man-machine interface: frustration.
Journal of the American Society for
Information Sciences, 23.6, 392-401.

Murdoch, J.W.   1974   Information processes in technology
transfer.
Technology Transfer: Success and Failures,
G.K. Manning (Ed.), San Francisco:
San Francisco Press, 7-17.

Norton, J.C.   1975   Aspects of the Center's technology
Engelbart, D.C. &   transfer strategy.
Watson, R.W.   Knowledge Workshop Development, Final
Technical Report for March 1972-74,
Menlo Park, Calif.: Augmentation
Research Center, Stanford Research
Institute, 19-33.

Propst, R.   1968   The office: a facility based on change.
Zeeland, Michigan: Herman Miller, Inc.

Rogers, E.M. &   1971   Communication of innovations.
  Shoemaker, F.F.   New York: The Free Press.

Sackman, H. &   1972   Online planning: toward creative
  Citrenbaum, L.   problem-solving.
  (Eds.)   Engelwood Cliffs, New Jersey:
                                      Prentice-Hall Inc.

Shackel, B.   1969   Man-computer interaction – the
                                      contribution of the human sciences.
                                    IEEE Transactions on Man-Machine Systems,
                                      Dec., MMS-10.4, 149-163.

Smith, G.A.   1972   Computer training, present and future.
                                    AFIPS Proc., Spring Joint Comp. Conf.,
                                      Montvale, New Jersey: AFIPS Press,
                                      42, 77-101.

Turoff, M.   1971   Delphi and its potential impact on
                                      information systems.
                                    In: AFIPS Conf. Proc., Montvale,
                                      New Jersey: AFIPS Press, 39, 317-326.

Vallee, J.   1976   The FORUM project: network conferencing
                                      and its future applications.
                                    Computer Networks, New York: North-
                                      Holland Publishing Company, 1.1, 39-52.

van Nouhuys, D.H.   1975   Introduction to documentation through NLS.
                                    Augmentation Research Center Journal
                                      Publication No. 26136, Stanford
                                      Research Institute, July.

Weinberg, G.M.   1971   The Psychology of Computer Programming.
                                    New York: Van Nostrand-Reinhold Co.

Weizenbaum, J.   1976   Computer power and human reason: from
                                      judgement to calculation.
                                    San Francisco: Freeman, January.

White, J.E.   1976   A high-level framework for network-
                                      based resource sharing.
                                    AFIPS Conf. Proc., National Comp. Conf.
                                      Vol. 45.

ACKNOWLEDGEMENTS

During the 14-year life of the Augmentation Research Center many have contributed to the development of the system. There are now some 40 people - clerical, hardware, software, information specialists, social researchers, writers, and others - all contributing significantly to the goals described here. The work has been supported by the Advanced Research Projects Agency of the Department of Defense, the Rome Air Development Center of the Air Force, the Stanford Research Institute, the Office of Naval Research, and by our many subscribers. Assistance on this paper has been generously provided by Nina Zolotow (editorial review), Laura Metzger (assistance with the literature review), and Dirk van Nouhuys and James Norton (review and comments).

APPROACHES TO DETERMINING FUNCTIONAL NEEDS OF INFORMATION SYSTEM USERS

Thomas H. Martin

Annenberg School of Communications, University of
Southern California, Los Angeles, California.

INTRODUCTION

A viable information system consists of more than machines.
It involves people – whether end users, managers, vendors, or the
public-at-large.   People are the ones who decide when to begin and
when to quit using computers.   They must perceive the benefits to
be greater than the costs.   People rarely see much benefit in
giving up old work habits all at once (Rogers and Shoemaker, 1971).
The logical beauty of a new technology is not enough to guarantee
usage – people must be trained, must be supported when they encounter
difficulties, must be able to break the learning process into
graduated stages, and must be able to personalize the technology
so that it merges into the work environment.   Failure to meet
people-oriented needs has definite costs, such as resistance to
change, inefficient usage patterns, and under-utilization.

This human side of information systems has not received adequate
attention.   Until recently it was all that technologists could do
to provide reliable service at economical rates.   Now, however,
information systems technology has progressed to the point where a
vast range of services can be provided at prices many potential
users can afford.   The time has come to take the rough edges off
the technology and to focus not on what can be done but rather upon
what people find useful.   Unless emphasis shifts to the constraints
and requirements in the end user's task environment, information
systems technology is unlikely to attain its full social benefit
(Bennett 1972).

THE BACKGROUND OF NEEDS ASSESSMENT

In considering approaches to the assessment of user needs, one must consider the different environments within which systems are to function and the different stages in the needs formulation process. Initially all parties are driven by dreams, hopes, hunches, and frustrations. Occasionally a well-organized group of users will know exactly what they are looking for, but generally system designers are faced with an amorphous population of potential users. Users rarely know what they want until they have something concrete to react against. Then the pressure for change they apply is likely to be transient. Only if perceived benefits of future changes outweigh the costs of complaining will users continue to apply pressure. Designers who respond too readily to suggestions face the danger of making the system unwieldy. The user community needs mechanisms for clarifying what they really want, just as the designers need mechanisms to help the users appreciate the consequences of proposed changes. If all parties are ready, responsive and restrained, hopefully community and system evolution will clarify needs. Otherwise users are likely to drift away or learn to live with what is available and designers are likely to learn that changes in the system only lead to complaints (Martin, 1973).

Why is it that traditional market mechanisms of innovative competition are not likely to lead to clarified user needs? Information systems such as storage and retrieval services or computer-assisted learning gain most of their value from spreading costs over a large user population. In order to keep training, maintenance, and consulting costs low, the number of users in any particular location has to be large. The system typically comes as a total package and it is hard for most users to distinguish between the communications network, the terminal, the operating system, the command language, and the data base or courseware. There is little room for competition and the disgruntled person's only choice is often between usage or non-usage. Of course, in situations where competition is still active, much can be learned about user needs from marketplace behavior.

In this paper a number of studies are discussed that have probed user needs at various stages in the evolutionary cycle of information systems. Some of the studies have approached the problem from the user's perspective while others have approached it from the designer's perspective, but all share an interest in approaches to determining functional needs. It is method rather than actual findings that is of greatest concern in this paper, although some of the findings are mentioned. It should be made clear that methods for assessing needs do not automatically translate into system design. Needs assessment can help the designer know the limits within which he is to work or has been working; it cannot tell him how the system should look. It can tell him what the most important or most frequently used functions are or will be; it cannot tell him what to do in all conceivable circumstances. If needs assessments are carried out over time (eg. evaluation before, during, and after the load on the system has stabilized) they can tell the designer whether he has succeeded; they cannot tell him how he did it. It should also be mentioned that needs assessments are not recommended for everybody. Early adopters of new technologies tend to be different from late adopters (Rogers and Shoemaker, 1971). The former tend to be more concerned about evaluating their early experiences before getting totally committed to the new technology. Late adopters are less likely to go through this probing or bargaining stage. Because the innovative ones probe, they can often request modifications. Needs assessment is recommended for those user groups who are in a position to bargain and for those system designers who have incorporated enough flexibility into their systems so that room for bargaining exists.

NEEDS ASSESSMENT DURING SYSTEM DESIGN

Needs assessment often occurs at the very earliest stage of system design. If the users are organised, it is possible to study how they behave in their organised setting. Traditionally this has meant systems analysis. Charts are made of the task elements and flows. A weakness of systems analysis as typically practised is that it elicits information about what is formally or rationally known. Yet students of organisational communication are aware that informal and apparently irrational modes of communication are often as essential to organisational health as are the formal channels (Farace and Danowski, 1973). For example, many system analysts studying hospital communications might overlook the need for methods for doctors to make golfing dates. Yet time after time designers have noted that the esprit de corps of a group has evaporated after an automated system has been installed. In order to avoid wreaking havoc on the informal channels for communication, it is important to consider them in the needs assessment. Holzman and Rosenberg (1976) point out the importance of what they call "shadow functions". These are all of those functions people never mention unless they are forced to discuss them. They include needs like going to the bathroom, going around a superior in order to get something done, taking a break while appearing to be busy, and trying to figure out how to make simple things work (eg. calling someone long-distance who is not in his office). Holzman and Rosenberg are alerted to these "shadow functions" when accounted-for time and actual time do not match up, or when results of management interviews do not correspond to results of employee interviews. The intention is not to abolish the shadow functions but rather to make sure there is provision for them in the automated system.

Carlisle (1976) takes the approach that the needs assessor should be unobtrusive rather than active. He should gather "structured data" that allows him to model the critical events in task and/or communication sequences. This approach requires a high degree of co-operation between the researcher and the organisation, but in exchange it can incorporate far more of the actual events and environmental variables than can be garnered from interviews or questionnaires. Such a high level of trust can be obtained only if the members of the organisation feel they are not being manipulated and that the automated system is intended to respond to their actual needs rather than their presumed needs.

Often it is necessary to figure out what users who are not organised or who have no common organisational affiliation will need. For example, in a study by Martin et al. (1975) an attempt was made to determine the functions needed in terminals for computer-assisted and computer-managed instruction by 1985. In this case, representatives of a variety of different computer-assisted learning roles participated on a panel. They represented instructional researchers, coursewriters, software designers, managers of existing computer-assisted learning projects, and a few terminal designers. Actual learners were not included because it was felt that they were too diverse to be represented and that few actual users had enough experience to comprehend the variety of options open to them. The study was not an iterative questionnaire in the traditional delphi sense. The panelists had so little in common that it was more important to build up shared meaning than to attempt quantitative refinements of assumed shared meaning. Panelists were presented questions like "do you think an investment in the development of new terminals will have a significant payoff?", "are mainstream terminal vendors likely to be responsive to CAI/CMI user needs, and, if not, what needs are likely to go unmet?", and "in what other areas might an investment lead to more significant payoffs?" It became clear that at least three areas other than investments in terminals looked significant, so users were asked to prioritize the four areas. Investments in terminals fell below investments in courseware and in intelligent software. Panelists also were asked to suggest terminal features to rate and then rated each of twenty-four features in terms of how definitely they felt terminals should provide for the feature. By moving the panelists from an open format to a structured one it was possible to elicit fairly meaningful needs statements from them.

NEEDS ASSESSMENT FROM SYSTEM USAGE

Turning from presystem studies to those done after the introduction of a system, research can either be done on single systems
or on groups of systems. Vallee et al. (1974, 1975) at the Institute
for the Future carried out a number of studies of computer conferencing using their FORUM system. A variety of methodologies were
employed ranging from experiments to interviews to questionnaires
to analyses of monitor logs. Hypotheses were formulated about the
characteristics and requirements of computer conferencing and the
various pieces of data were analysed in terms of the hypotheses.
During the studies the conferencing system underwent considerable
evolution.

From personal experience in designing a large information
retrieval system, the author (Martin and Parker, 1971) has found
that monitor logs capturing actual user input are extremely valuable
in system evolution. Without actual transcripts showing usage
patterns, programmers are likely to be so blinded by their assumptions
that they cannot foresee user oversights and misinterpretations.
When monitoring is done, it should be with the informed consent of
users and with due regard to their privacy. As Vallee et al.
point out, using a variety of data gathering techniques leads to
more robust results than using a single technique. Interviews,
for example, can clarify why some people did not use certain
features or how they supplemented computerised interaction with
face-to-face or telephonic interaction. Questionnaires can
indicate general trends that are not apparent when considering
isolated experiences.

A technique that differs from all of these was used by Martin
(1974) in synthesizing experience in the information retrieval
market. During 1973 and 1974 interactive information retrieval
caught on in the United States. Most systems that competed for
the market had been undergoing evolution in their design for at
least five years, and many potential competitors had ceased to
exist. Most of the systems had been designed independently of
the others. The assessment technique that was used was to analyse
the various functions of eleven different systems, and then bring
the designers together to compare their design decisions on a
function-by-function basis. What proved fascinating was that
functionally the various systems were quite similar while syntactically the various command languages were quite different. A
frequent comment made by the designers was that they had had to
revise features or add new ones in order to satisfy users. For
example, one of the features all systems had and which the designers
rated as essential was live help - a telephone number to call if
desperate or a command for requesting help from an on-line human
consultant. Many designers admitted having learned of the need
for this feature only through experience. A feature that many

systems include is on-line documentation but this was not felt to be an essential feature by the designers. They commented that users rarely looked at advice or explanations. Perhaps this was a function of cost or a result of poorly worded messages, but what is interesting is that most designers had learned through experience that on-line documentation was not as critical as once thought.

A feature that differed on systems was access to the searchable vocabulary. Designers who did not provide access were aware of user frustrations in trying to think up words. Designers who once had not provided access but now did, commented that access to the vocabulary and its frequency of use in documents improved searching and satisfied users. Search vocabulary display was one of the features the designers concluded was essential. Social scientists will recognise that this feature made it possible for users to rely on recognition rather than recall vocabulary. Other psychological principles emerged from the discussions. One of them was the advantage of numbering fragments of search logic that later could be referred to by number. This made it possible for users to break the problem down into manageable pieces and then to combine the pieces. It also made it possible for users to display a list of the search fragments and thereby get an overview of their progress.

A weakness of looking at system features and talking to designers is that it does not give an explicit voice to actual users. An independent follow-up study was done by Wanger et al. (1976) of the opinions of actual searchers and managers. Questionnaires were sent out to as close to all of the regular users of interactive retrieval systems as was possible. Follow-up in-depth interviews were conducted to cross-validate the questionnaire results. The user survey took many of the features from the feature analysis and asked users to rank them. For example, in a list of ten on-line aid features, users ranked access to the searchable vocabulary as third in importance while access to command explanations was ranked seventh in importance. Unfortunately, the feature lists in the two studies were different, so there can be no direct comparison between designer perceptions and user perceptions. For example, live help was not included in the rankings, but instead two separate questions probed how important users considered telephone consultation with the vendor to be and how important they considered on-line consultation with the vendor to be. About 70% of the respondents considered telephone contact to be essential and another 25% felt it to be important. Only about 20% of the respondents considered on-line consultation to be essential and another 50% considered it to be important.

One of the significant findings of the Wanger et al. (1976) user survey was that 76% of the searchers were paid intermediaries (eg. information specialists or librarians). In the early days of information retrieval system design it had been expected that end users would do their own searching. As in so many other histories of the application of computers, the final set of inter- active searchers were those who were paid to use the system. This most likely results from a number of different factors: (1) that effective searching requires training, (2) that it is probably more cost-effective to have trained specialists search regularly than to have untrained end users search infrequently, and (3) terminals for searching are typically located in or near the library or information center. While questions were asked about training, ranking was not used to compare methods of learning with preferred methods of learning. At least 52% of the respondents learned how to use their first system by attending formal training from vendors, with another 33% learning from users' manuals or from trained colleagues.

One of the strengths and weaknesses of both the feature analysis and user impact studies was that the researchers were very involved with information retrieval systems. In the first study the researcher was a designer and in the second study the researchers were affiliated with one of the vendors. This was a strength in that researchers in both studies knew which questions to ask. It was a weakness in that the subject matter of the study took priority over methodological rigor.

At some time in the evolution of a system there is value in forgetting about the system and in using a reliable technique for focussing on user priorities directly. Stabell (1975) conducted such a study of portfolio managers who had been using an interactive decision support system for assisting in portfolio management. His major concern was to map out the constructs or decision factors used by portfolio managers. He then attempted to relate the constructs to features available in the decision support system and to features used by the managers. He found that the system and managers differed considerably and that the features used tended to be those that matched manager constructs. Managers tended to view client relations as very important and structured decisions around the client. The system was intended to facilitate comparisons across portfolios, but was not used heavily in this way.

CONCLUSION

In summary, there is a dynamic tension between needs from the user's perspective and needs from the designer's (or information system's) perspective. The need begins with the user and ultimately remains his responsibility. The designer to some extent must learn about the need and to some extent must force it into his own criteria. The user is likely to center around his task and view the system as only one component. The designer is likely to center around the system and see the user as only one person from a very diverse community of potential users. Analysis can focus on users - their constructs, patterns of behaviour and priorities; or upon systems - their usage, features, and user reactions. Both approaches are necessary for the clarification of the functional needs of information system users.

REFERENCES

Bennett, J.L.　　　1972　　The User Interface in Interactive Systems
In: Annual Review of Information Science and Technology, $\underline{7}$, 159-196.
American Society for Information Science, Washington, D.C.

Carlisle, J.H.　　　1976　　Evaluating the Impact of Office Automation on Top Management Communication.
In: Proceedings of the 1976 National Computer Conference, pp. 611-616.
AFIPS Press, Montvale, New Jersey.

Farace, R.V. &　　　1973　　Analysing Human Communication Networks
Danowski, J.A.　　　　　　　in Organisations: Applications to Management Problems.
Paper to Annual Meeting of the International Communication Association, Montreal, Quebec.

Holzman, D.L. &　　　1976　　Understanding Shadow Functions: the
Rosenberg, V.　　　　　　　Key to System Design and Evaluation.
Paper to the Workshop on Evaluating the Impact of Office Automation
(XEROX Palo Alto Research Center, Palo Alto, California, May 1976).

Martin, T.H.   1973   The User Interface in Interactive Systems.
                               In: Annual Review of Information Science
                               and Technology, 8, 203-220.
                               American Society for Information Science,
                               Washington D.C.

Martin, T.H.   1974   A Feature Analysis of Interactive
                               Retrieval Systems.
                               Report PB 235952/AS from Institute for
                               Communication Research, Stanford,
                               California.

Martin, T.H. &   1971   Designing for User Acceptance of an
  Parker, E.B.   Interactive Bibliographic Search
                               Facility.
                               In: Walker, Donald E. ed. Interactive
                               Bibliographic Search: the User/Computer
                               Interface, pp.45-52.
                               AFIPS Press, Montvale, New Jersey.

Martin, T.H.   1975   A Policy Assessment of Priorities and
  Stanford, M.C.,   Functional Needs for the Military
  Carlson, F.R. &   Computer Assisted Instruction Terminal.
  Mann, W.C.   Report for ARPA Order No. 2930 NR 154374,
                               from Information Sciences Institute,
                               Marina Del Rey, California.

Rogers, E.M. &   1971   Communication of Innovations.
  Shoemaker, F.F.   New York: Free Press.

Stabell, C.B.   1975   Individual Differences in Managerial
                               Decision Making Processes: A Study
                               of Conversational Computer System Usage.
                               Ph.D. Dissertation, Sloan School of
                               Management, M.I.T., Cambridge, Mass.

Vallee, J.   1974   Group Communication Through Computers,
  Johansen, R.,   Volume 2.
  Randolph, R.H. &   Report R-33, from Institute for the Future,
  Hastings, A.C.   Menlo Park, California.

Vallee, J.   1975   Group Communication Through Computers,
  Johansen, R.,   Volume 3.
  Lipinski, H.,   Report R-35, from Institute for the Future,
  Spangler, K.,   Menlo Park, California.
  Wilson, T. &
  Hardy, A.

388

Wanger, J.,   1976   Impact of On-line Retrieval Services:
  Cuadra, C.A. &   A Survey of Users, 1974-5.
  Fishburn, M.   Report from System Development Corporation,
                   Santa Monica, California.

PART 7 - MODELLING AND PROBLEM SOLVING

PREVIEW

There is already an extensive research literature on human
problem solving, for example W. Lee 'Decision Theory and Human
Behaviour' Wiley 1971, A. Newell and H. Simon 'Human Problem
Solving' Prentice-Hall 1972, and A. Rapoport & T.S. Wallsten in
the Annual Review of Psychology 1972, 23, 131-176.   But there
has been very little focussing from this research onto the question
of computer-aided problem solving.   Moreover, we still know far
too little about how people solve practical problems and make
decisions in practical situations despite the extensive basic
research.

However, a considerable amount of empirical knowledge is
being acquired both from practical usage of systems and from
experiments about various types of decision aid - both manual and
computer based - in control situations.   For example, the usage
of computer systems to aid in the control of public utilities
(eg. electricity and gas grids), in process control (eg. oil
refineries) and in air traffic control, is growing considerably.
The most advanced developments at present are in process control.
Two very good texts are available on man-computer aspects by
E. Edwards and F.P. Lees 'Man and Computer in Process Control'
Institution of Chemical Engineers, London, 1972 and 'The Human
Operator in Process Control' Taylor and Francis 1974.

Another aspect of the theoretical understanding of human
behaviour and performance in MCI is to be able to model the human
activity either mathematically or at least in some form of
simulation.

The two papers here are important contributions to this
general problem area of the modelling of human performance and
the theory of human problem solving in MCI situations.

Baker begins by pointing out that modelling the user, in the
setting of an interactive man-computer system, has seldom been
done even in military work;   therefore he is giving his personal
view of the question from the viewpoint of militaty information
and command systems which in general are similar to equivalent
systems in non-military areas.   He then describes in detail a
man-model developed to study and then to simulate a tactical

operations system, and reviews its usage for presenting learning
situations to staff officers.   This detailed description shows
the complexity of such modelling and the degree of detail required
to be acceptable.   Baker does not claim that his examples
necessarily give many answers about how to model the user, but he
suggests that they at least show the complexity of the problem
and some of the gaps in the ergonomics knowledge needed to be able
to develop such models.

After discussing how many authors have pointed out the need
for better taxonomies and theoretical frameworks for MCI, Sackman
introduces his aim to provide a conceptual framework to lead
towards an integrated theory of man-computer problem solving.
Following a review of descriptions of the envisaged stages of
problem solving, and other related research, he proposes a
9-stage model for 'real world' problem solving.   In the second
part of his paper he then sets out the aims and benefits of a
comprehensive theory and describes in outline the six major aspects
of the general theory which he is developing.   He ends with a
brief review of seven of the more noteable issues raised at the
Institute during the extensive discussion of his paper.

MODELING THE USER

James D. Baker

U.S. Army Research Institute,
Alexandria, Virginia 22333, U.S.A.

1. INTRODUCTION

I have been asked, as my contribution to this NATO Advanced
Study Institute on Man-Computer Interaction, to address the topic
of "modeling the user." I should like to use the findings from a
study by Shubick and Brewer (1972) as my point of departure. They
recently reported the results of a detailed survey of 132 Models,
Simulations and Games (MSG)* used in the U.S. Department of Defense
(DOD). Among the findings, they discovered that only ten per cent
of the MSG's dealt with man-machine or manual system problems.
Additionally, they found that approximately seventy-five per cent
of the MSG's employed in the DOD are large and deal primarily with
machine simulations or force structure, ie. they are mainly machine
(or weapons system) evaluation tools. They also found that most
of the MSG's being used were not very scientific and, consequently,
were rarely used as research tools.

---

*Shubick and Brewer found that these three words were used so inter-
changeably by the practitioners that they surveyed that they found
it more meaningful to simply cluster the terms into a single designator
- MSG's. I believe it would help however, if definitions were
provided at the outset pertinent to the present context. According
to Chapanis (1961), a scientific model is a representation, or likeness,
of certain aspects of complex events, structures or systems, made by
using symbols or objects which in some way resemble the thing being
modeled. For purposes of this paper, simulation refers to the
construction and use of the model for purposes of prediction through
testing various design considerations. In the colorful words of
Hamilton and Nance (1969): "One 'wiggles' each part in order to see
what will happen when all parts are taken into account." To a
considerable extent, the generality of research findings depends on
the fidelity of the model that is made of the real world.

As evident from the above, to date few scientific principles concerned with modeling the man in a military system have been derived.   Therefore, the end-product of this paper will not be a 'cookbook' on how to model the user; rather, I shall simply unveil one man's viewpoint concerning the art of modeling the human factor in information systems.   It is hoped that the pragmatic approach to be described will enable the many and diverse scientists in attendance to select those aspects of the process which can contribute toward solutions to problems which they may face.

Because this is one man's view of the world, I believe you are entitled to know my biases.   My approach is considerably influenced by my long experience in the design and development of automated military information systems.   Shannon and Weaver (1949) define information as "that which removes or reduces uncertainty." Kennedy (1962) defines a system, specifically a man-machine system, as "an organization whose components are men and machines working together to achieve a common goal and tied together by a communication network."   An automated information system, therefore, may be defined as an organization whose goal is the reduction of uncertainty through man-computer interaction.

To provide a more specific setting for this discussion, the evolving U.S. Army automated military information system know as the TOS (Tactical Operations System) will serve as the point of focus.   Detailed descriptions of TOS have been presented elsewhere (Baker, 1968, 1972, 1973); suffice to say that it is a mobile automatic data processing (ADP) system which is intended to assist commanders and their staffs in the conduct of tactical operations by collecting, processing and summarizing information required for command decisions and staff actions, with emphasis on the intelligence and operations functions.   The TOS concept has gone through several implementation phases to date, starting with the SATOS (Seventh Army TOS - focusing on automation of the Army, Corps and Division level and using commercial, off-the-shelf equipment); to the DEVTOS (the Developmental TOS which used the SATOS equipment but focused upon automation of the Division and Brigade level), and has since evolved into the TOS2 phase (the TOS on the operable segment, ie. essentially a militarized hardware version of TOS).

The TOS is really a 'tool' for assisting in the conduct of Tactical Operations Center (TOC) operations.   The TOS user is a member of a military unit and has assigned to him a specific job concerned with the operations of that unit's TOC.   Three logically separable classes of TOS user can be identified: (1) the routine, clerical interface user (ie. the unit input/output device operator), (2) the supervisory level person (ie. the various staff element action officers and non-commissioned officers) and (3) the commander and his senior staff.   Of course, other personnel are involved in the TOS operation (such as the computer facility operators and mainten- ance personnel) but they are integral to the system operations whereas our concern here is with the users of the system output.

The point of focus, then, for the presentation to follow will
be on these several levels of <u>user</u> as they go about the conduct
of their day-to-day TOC activities when they have a computer at
their disposal.   It will include a discussion of the techniques
employed (and the attendant problems uncovered) and the attempts
presently underway to model this user in his milieu.

2.   OVERVIEW

An interesting aspect of TOC operations is that it can be
conceptualized as a 'world apart'.   The basic contact with the
outside world is via messages from the units it has under its
command, some lateral information (again via messages) from adjacent
units at the same echelon, and directive and query messages it
receives from above.   Its whole world revolves around the <u>message</u>,
ie. a collection of symbols sent as a meaningful statement.   Normally,
the message arrives at the TOC in one of two forms: either as a
radio/telephone transmission or as a teletype input (TWX).   Once
the message flow starts (Figure 1), the TOC operations swing into
high gear and the man, now interfaced with this communication system,
begins to perform those functions typically allocated to the 'man'
portion of military information command and control systems.

Ringel (1966) in laying out a program of research aimed at
resolving man-machine problems in the military information system
area, delineated at least five critical functional areas requiring
human factors attention: In his words:

"An automated TOS will receive vast amounts of information
of many and varied sources.   The information will vary
widely in content, form, and degree of completeness ...
The raw data will require a great deal of handling and
processing by man and equipment ... Looking at the system
as a whole, there appear to be five critical operations
that man and equipment will have to perform: <u>Screen</u>
incoming data for pertinence, credibility, impact, priority,
and routing;   <u>Transform</u> the raw data for input into storage
devices;   <u>Input</u> the transformed data into storage devices
for subsequent computation and display;   <u>Assimilate</u> data
displayed, and <u>Decide</u> on courses of action based on information
displayed and information from other sources."

The flow of these operations is diagrammed in Figure 2 and it
will serve as a general framework for my presentation.

394

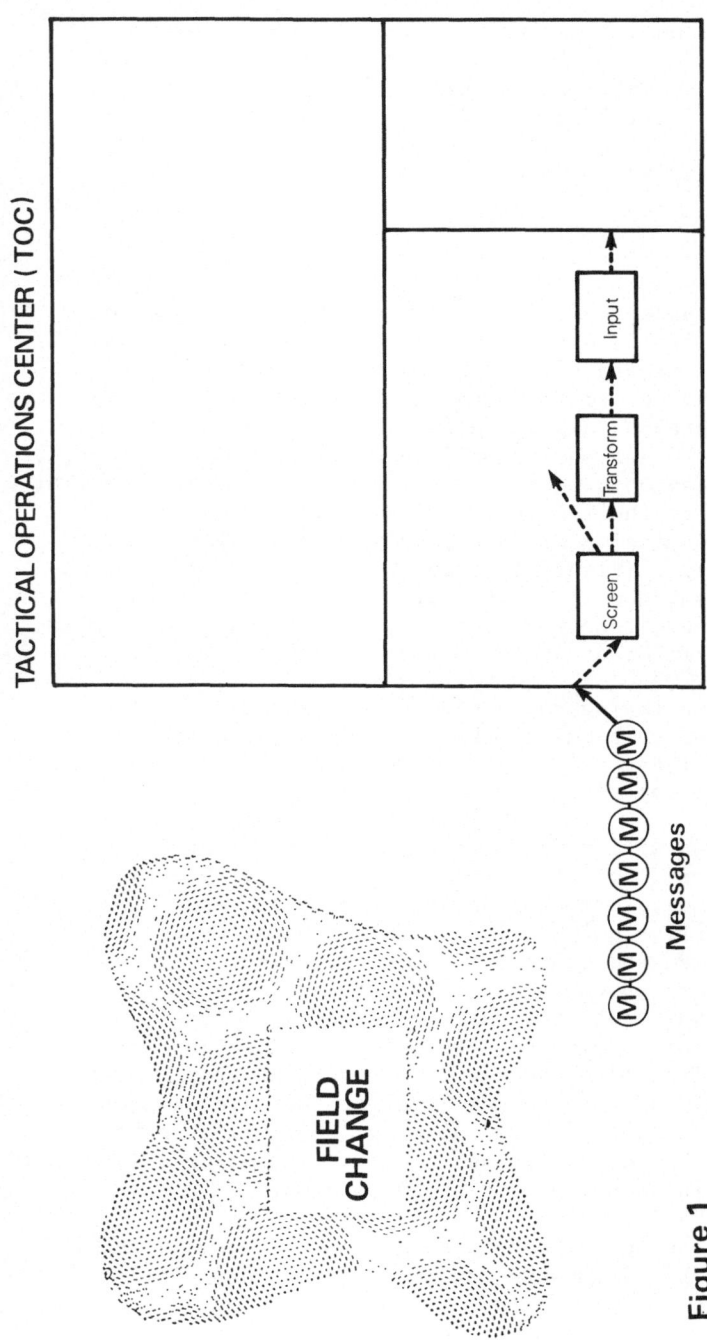

Figure 1

Schematic representation of 'outside world' and the TOC, linked together by message flow.

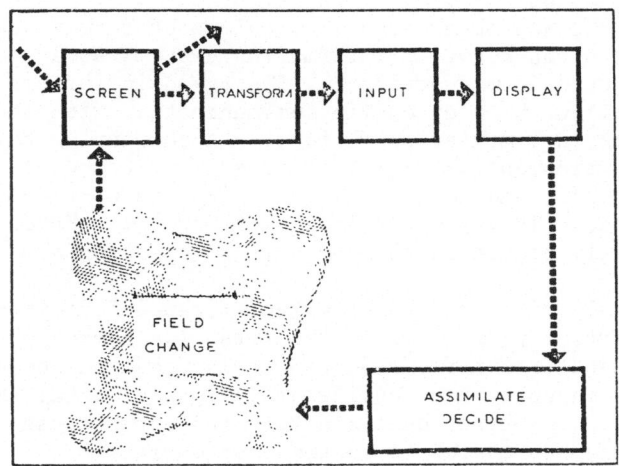

FIGURE 2. Schematic representation of operations and information
flow in an automated TOS. (Taken from Ringel, 1966)

3. MANMODEL

3.1 Basic Dimensions of Human Information Processing

As part of the TOS development, a TOS simulation model (called
MANMODEL because the emphasis is on modeling the man in the system,
rather than modeling the system itself) was developed.   The model,
among other things, was seen as a valuable tool in the conduct of
the required Cost-Effectiveness Analyses for TOS (CEATOS effort).
It focussed on the messages as they came into the TOC (Fig. 1),
tracked them through the front-end of the system (the screen,
transform and input areas) and proceeded to model the human processes
involved in the conduct of these functions.   The effort has been
described in detail elsewhere (Baker, 1970), but portions of that
description will be included verbatim here.   The necessary logic,
structure and software has been developed to produce a TOS simulation
model - MANMODEL - which combines the effects of such variables as
message queuing, detailed message processing procedures, error rates
and personnel characteristics (along with stochastic variations)
to yield predictions of system performance.   The details of this
simulation model are documented in great detail elsewhere (Siegel
et al., 1973a, b; Leahy et al., 1976a, b), so these details will
not be discussed at length here.   Rather, the emphasis will be on
the process which leads to the development of MANMODEL.

Returning to the measures of the front-end of the system (the screen, transform, and input areas), problems of format and format selection quite often occur in information systems as an adjunct to the screen and transform functions. The trend in information systems is to allow the user on-line communication with the computer and intervention in computer operations. Accompanying this trend has been the development of rigidly defined user/computer languages. These languages are, and within the current state-of-the-art must be, most precise. They are intolerant of errors. Errors, even if slight, usually result in the computer's rejecting a message.

This typical inflexibility of computerized information systems accounts, in part, for problems in the first two human performance areas – screen and transform. Screening is required because most systems are not capable of accepting every iota of data. Redundant, irrelevant, and unimportant data are filtered out because the software is typically unprepared to respond appropriately. Transformation generally involves formatting and translating. Formatting is necessary because of input hardware restrictions and the fact that computers read character positions or fields, not words or sentences. A further restriction is that software frequently assigns differential meanings to positions and fields. Thus, a '2' in column one is not necessarily equal to a '2' in column ten. This restriction leads to translation requirements. Because the user/computer language typically requires exact syntactic structure, abbreviations, and terminology in order for the message to be accepted by the computer, the typical free text that characterizes military messages in nonautomated systems must be transformed into a rigidly defined format before the user can interact with the computer.

With this general framework in mind, let us now turn to the model itself. The model has been developed along three basic dimensions which are reflected in figure 3. The first, that of Data Flow and the processing it requires, constitutes one dimension of importance. Hence, it is critical to 'flow chart' the sequence of events or operations that constitute the logic of the system under examination. A basic consideration in identifying each event is that the sequence must be structured in terms of an observable start and stop point before it can be quantified in terms of time measures.

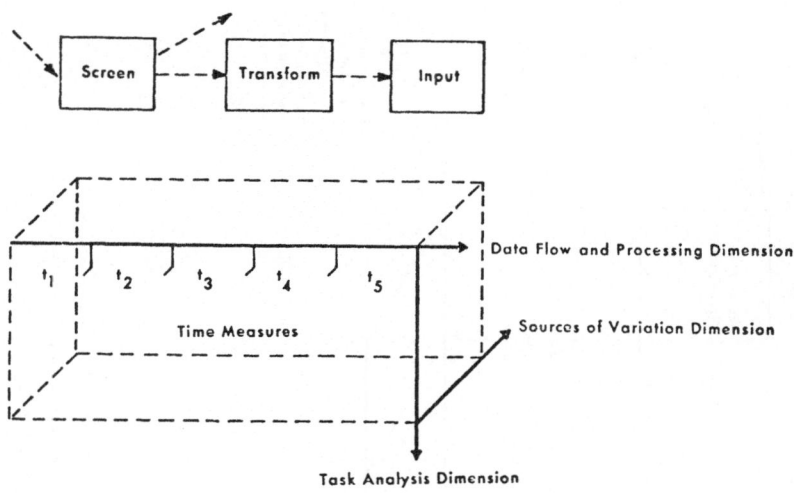

FIGURE 3. Basic dimensions of the MANMODEL.

For the second dimension, Task Analysis, each event in the data flow sequence is examined with respect to the task-equipment interactions that constitutes that portion of the operator's job. An example would be to do a task analysis of the input operator's activities during Time Interval t_5. Essentially, a task analysis consists of the enumeration of the discriminations, decisions, and action responses which are necessary and sufficient to operate each component of the system.

The third dimension refers to outside Sources of Variation which are normally considered external to the man-computer system, for example, the impact on system performance when level of training is varied or when group structure or operations change over extended periods of time.

398

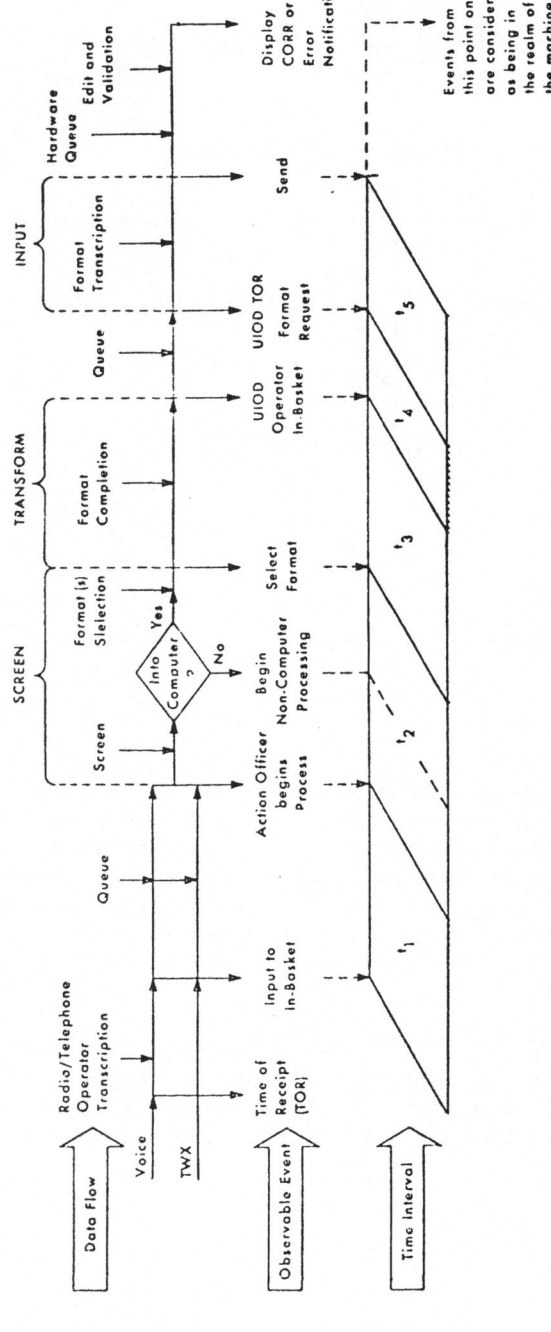

FIGURE 4. Data flow, observable events and time interval aspects of MANMODEL as they relate to the human performance functional areas of screen, transform and input. (Taken from Baker, 1970)

3.2 Data Flow and Processing Dimension

How do we go about applying these concepts to a specific information system?   We begin with the assumption that a conceptual configuration of our information system has been spelled out in a set of design specifications, and we wish to examine and relate the effects of a variety of human performance measures on this sytem. To establish the horizontal dimension which directs the basic flow of data, we use a time-line analysis approach.   A time-line analysis is essentially an analytic technique which provides a time base for the functional and temporal relationships among tasks.

Figure 4 illustrates this procedure in a military information system.   The data flow, observable events, and the time interval aspects of the system have been mapped out in terms of their relationship to the human performance functional areas of screen, transform, and input.   The input data to be acted upon have been delineated, for purposes of illustration, as military communications arriving at the message branch of an operations center by means of voice or teletype (TWX) channels.   Because our basic concern is with the human functions associated with the 'newly introduced' automation of the operation center activities, we have initiated our user performance measure at the event "IN-basket" the first point of contact between the automated system and the center operations.

In our illustration, the first time interval (t_1) begins with the insertion of a message into the action officer's IN-basket and ends when he pulls it out of the basket to begin processing it. If we were simulating this flow of events, the start time for t_1 would begin with the time prescribed by our simulation message insertion script.   The end time, however, is free to vary;   therefore, this measure would require an observer to record the interval manually.   Interval t_5, on the other hand, could be machine recorded if the simulation were run in conjunction with a computer.   The point being made here is that even though this is a man-computer system a comprehensive time base for data throughput cannot always be automatically acquired.   Rather, the summation of manually recorded as well as computer recorded measures is sometimes required in order to determine the time involved in throughputting system data when human information processing is involved.   For example, in the illustrative system (Figure 4) it takes t_k (an inserted constant for message transcription time) plus the manually measured time intervals t_1, t_2, t_3, and t_4 - as well as the computer recorded time interval t_5 - to throughput data from message receipt to arrival in the data base when the human information processing functional areas of screen, transform and input are involved.

Interval t_1 serves to illustrate another advantage accrued in performing a time-line analysis. Considered alone, t_1 provides data on queue length and time per item in queue; but by pinpointing nodes which are identified as being associated with a human information processing task, meaningful research may be undertaken in an attempt to optimize system performance by uncovering those factors which will improve human performance. For example, one could measure the impact on a queue of introducing two action officers at node t_1 during simulation to determine if system data throughput improved as a result.

Setting up the time-line dimension is not without certain difficulties. Time interval t_2, screen and format selection, is a case in point. This time interval is admittedly a weak, but important measure. Its weakness lies in the fact that it is difficult, if not impossible, to separate the screen task from the format selection task since the two may overlap and the end of one and the beginning of the other task is not always observable. At the time the action officer picks the message out of the IN-basket, he presumably scans it to determine if the information is applicable to the system's data base; or, if it is a request for information, whether the system can provide it. The outcome of the processing by this individual will be based in part upon his determination as to whether a format exists to handle the data contained in the message. To this extent he has engaged in format selection at the same time he is screening it. Measure t_2 is further complicated by the fact that complex messages may require the selection of several different formats in order to accommodate all the data included in a single incoming message.

Hence, t_2 measurement starts when the action officer selects a message and ends when he picks out a format worksheet and begins to complete it. But 'clean' format selection time can be obtained only for messages requiring a single format. For multiple format messages, the appropriate measure is t_2 through t_3, the combined selection and completion tasks.

Shifting to a molar or macroscopic level to describe certain man-machine interactions is frequently necessary in working through this time-line dimension. For example, a related situation has been reported by Scherr (1965). In his study no fine grain partitioning of activities was attempted at the input function which would distinguish the time the user spends inputting data and the time he spends thinking. 'Thinking time' was necessarily equated with the console part of the interaction in Scherr's analysis. From these, and other examples, it becomes evident that it is sometimes impossible to deal with these processes at any level other than that of a 'black box' operation.

More could be said about the specifics depicted in Figure 4, but my aim has been to describe only the general considerations involved in structuring this dimension of the model and to relate human performance to the system's data flow. To review, modeling begins with a time-line analysis which provides a time base for the functional relationships among the tasks. A comprehensive picture of the processing involved in throughputting the data is required in order to ensure that no critical man-machine interaction nodes are overlooked. A complete data flow representation is necessary if one intends to quantify human performance by employing system measures. Even in computer-based systems, some manual recording is required since processing can occur in front of, parallel to, or outside the direct man-machine interfaces. This time-line dimension helps to dramatize queue nodes where high payoff human information processing research could be conducted. Necessity may require us to 'shift gears and go to a molar level' in describing certain tasks.

3.3 Task Analysis Dimension

Given the horizontal dimension (data flow, observable events and the time interval aspects of the system), we can undertake to develop the vertical dimension for each observable event or task. Whereas time-line analysis was the tool for developing the horizontal dimension, task analysis is the technique which lends itself best to developing the vertical.

Task analysis, according to Miller (1962), is a process which provides data about human functions – data useful in determining the characteristics of job aids, training programs, and the assessment of performance of the system and its components. The total task analysis for a given system provides specific statements of all the interactions of man with machine and of man with the system environment.

Human tasks must be described within the context of the major categories of functions associated with the expected operation of the system. There are, of course, various levels at which the description of the total operations of a man-computer system may be stated. Miller (1967) suggests that, before a task analysis is undertaken, a subsystem level in the system description must be reached at which the individuals involved are performing some distinguishable portion of the system's purposes.

402

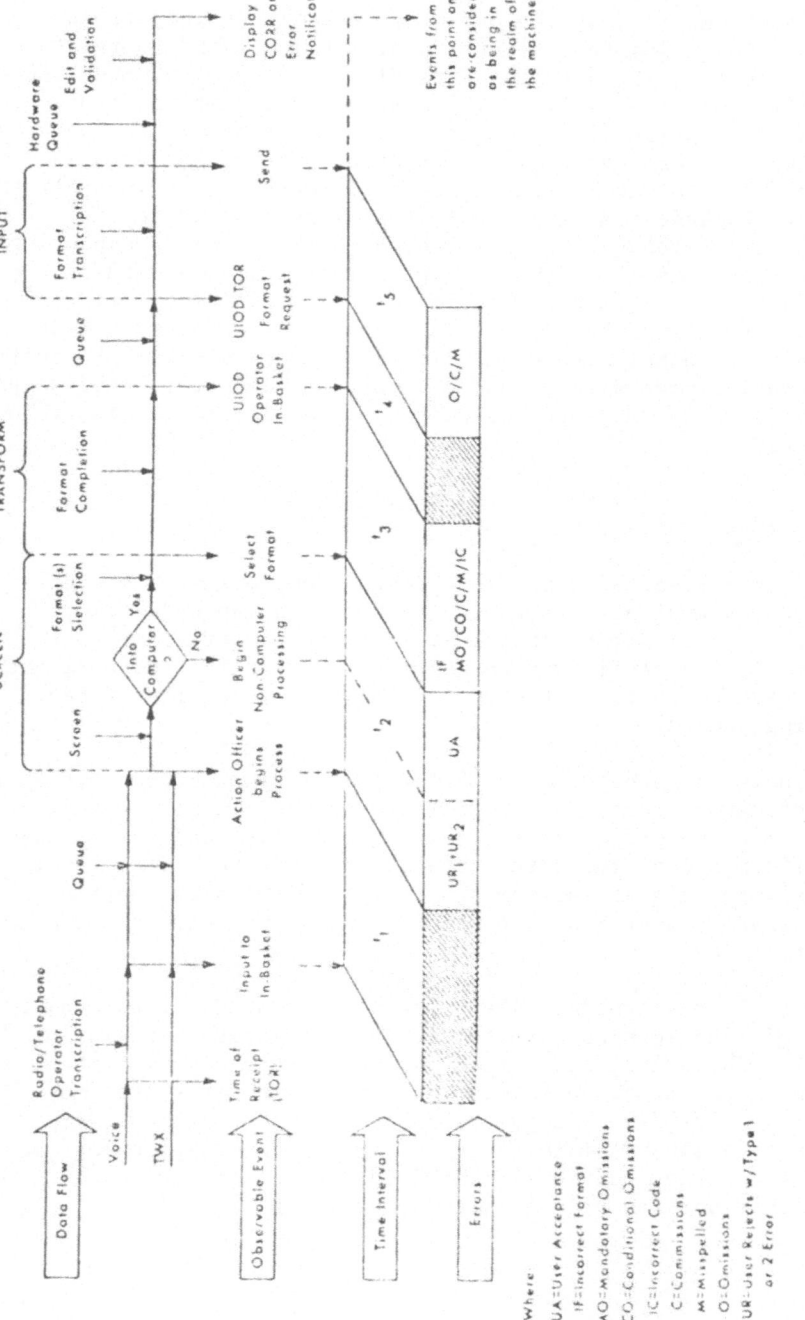

FIGURE 5. Diagram TOS-type system, as reflected in MANMODEL, showing data flow intervals and the critical errors which can occur at these intervals. (Taken from Baker, 1970)

The horizontal dimension consisting of data flow, observable events, and time interval aspects of the system can be used as a vehicle for arriving at this level. Figure 5 shows how the various levels of operational description are applied in the model paradigm. At the grossest level, level 1, we distinguish the broad categories of functions necessary to ensure that the system will fulfil the purposes for which it was designed. These are the human functions of screen, transform, and input, and the parallel (but not shown) machine functions of shunt, pre-process, queue, digital code, edit and validate that taken together constitute the data flow. So far, the functions described apply to almost any information system regardless of purpose. The next level of specificity brings us to the particular activities associated with the military information system chosen as our example - action officer selects military communication from message IN-basket. If we now consider a particular function such as completion of a format requesting the status of a friendly unit, it is evident that the progression has been from the transform function level (level 1), to the format completion level (level 2) and on to a level 3 where the specifics of transforming a particular class of message to a specific format may be delineated. It is at this level that a detailed task analysis may be undertaken.

Many techniques exist for implementing the task analysis (Miller, 1967). For purposes of illustration, an extremely simplified example is given of one such technique, taking the task group as the basic unit. A task group is the required complete sequence of responses by an operator, performed as a result of an external stimulus, or indicator action. This indicator action may be as simple as placing a transcribed message in the IN-basket or as complex as the generation of an attention device on the display surface. The indicator action is always initiated by a source external to the operator position being described. Responses to serial stimuli resulting from an individual's own actions are called feedback to distinguish them from indicator actions described above. In any event, a task group always begins with an indicator action and continues to an end event.

A truncated worksheet for analyzing the action officer's task concerned with completing a specific format in our illustrative system is shown in Figure 6. The worksheet selected is based upon a particular approach used by Warburton, Lawrence and Marks (1960). The columns in Figure 6 have meaning as follows:

Item. Number used to designate an entry.

Response Required. Response required in terms of product or result rather than method.

Action. Specific act or acts which must be taken to implement the response required.

TASK ANALYSIS

VI. Format Completion

INDICATOR: Format selected for message.   SOURCE: SOP and Handbooks.

Item	Response Required	Action	Who	Feedback	Recipient	Remarks
	Our action officer has just screened a message taken from the IN-basket and selected a Unit Status					
1.	Query message to complete		AO			
2.	Select precedence for message	Place an " I " for immediate in precedence field.	AO			
3.	Need hardcopy for own files	Place " Y " in hardcopy field of worksheet				
. . .						
Nth	Correct errors uncovered by computer	Determine if error was a mandatory field ommission	AO	Error Display on CRT	UIOD operator	Correct Worksheet and replace in UIOD operators IN-basket
. . .						
N+1	Action officer returns to screen process					

FIGURE 6.   Truncated task analysis worksheet describing responses required by an individual completing a specific format in our illustrative system.
(Based upon an approach used by Warburton et al., 1960)

Who. The person taking the action

Feedback. State resulting from an action which indicates the adequacy with which the response required has been performed; it may serve as a stimulus for serial actions.

Recipient. Person or workplace component to whom the person designated in the who column transmits information.

Remarks. Minor elaboration of content of item or cross reference.

Fall-out from the task analysis effort result in at least two products important to this model. First, subsets of time intervals concerned with each response required by each task can be identified to determine which aspects of the task are contributing most to our horizontal dimension time interval measures (t_1, t_2, etc.). Those task response times which seem likely to become inflated are prime candidates for experimental attack when one sets out to improve man's performance in order to optimize system performance. As a second valuable product, the Task Analysis helps to identify the sources and types of critical human errors that can be introduced into the system.

In Figure 5, a number of critical errors associated with the illustrative system are shown in conjunction with the data flow time interval at which they could occur. Such a list is a product of the task analysis. In our illustrative system, a 'mandatory omission' refers to the omission of certain information which causes the system to reject the message when the user attempts to input it. The result could be that the data base must wait for, or could be deprived of, the final datum required to resolve an important and puzzling problem. For example, our illustrative task analysis of time interval t_3, the Nth item (Figure 6) noted that a mandatory field omission could occur during format completion.

More could be said about the specific errors shown in Figure 5, but these are meaningful primarily in the context of the illustrative system. Each system could have its own rigidly defined, human introduced errors which should surface in the process of conducting the task analyses for that system. (Hopefully, a taxonomy of general human information processing tasks will evolve from the large amount of ergonomics and human factors research currently being conducted, to which specific types of errors may be related).

In summary, the intention of this segment of the discussion has been, primarily, to show how the data flow and processing dimension depicted in Figures 3 and 4 can be used as a jumping-off point for working down to the sub-system level at which a detailed task analysis can be undertaken. Many techniques exist for conducting task analysis, but basically, they boil down to an enumeration of the discriminations, decisions and action responses

which are necessary and sufficient to operate each component of
the system.   The Task Analysis can serve as a source of a number
of rich human factors discoveries – among them the identification
of critical subsets of human performance time data which are
operating to interrupt system data flow at designated intervals
in the system.   Also, the development of this dimension is responsible for the enumeration of errors which may impact on the total
system performance.

3.4 Sources of Variation Dimension

It was noted earlier that human performance in an information
system may be influenced by sources of variation which are normally
considered external to the man–computer system.   Among the sources
of variation particular to the military system illustrated (Fig. 7)
are staff element and echelon.   But many general things (eg. level
of training) impact on a man's job in an information system.   To
define the term job in an information system we need to return to
our preceding discussion on the task analysis dimension of the
model.   It was noted that a task analysis essentially consists of
a delineation of the response required at each step in a task
sequence.   The cluster that constitutes task sequence is a task
group.   The cluster of task groups for a given person in the system
constitutes his job.

What are some of the factors which affect the performance of
a job in an information system?   Two factors which immediately
come to mind are training and how well the equipment has been
engineered.   Training adapts a person to a job, human engineering
adapts the job to the person.   Individuals vary in intellectual
capacity, also in the capacity for adjusting to new situations and
in physiological capacities for perception.   The system may not
function optimally because a key individual does not have the
aptitude required for the performance of the job.   He may not have
the capacity to remember relevant facts or to integrate facts into
decisions.   Lack of aptitude is, by definition, irremediable.
However, if an individual has the aptitude required for a job, he
can be trained in the skills and knowledge necessary for adequate
performance.   Training is used broadly to include formal courses,
on-the-job training, and relevant experience.   The value of
appropriate selection techniques, therefore, cannot be minimized.

A man may be unable to do a task because he is too tired or
too sick, although he has the necessary aptitude and training.   So
the system may perform less than optimally because a key individual
is temporarily in a physical state which precludes adequate performance.   This situation was reflected in our illustrative system by
the inclusion of 'Time During Exercise' as a variable external to
the system (see Figure 7).

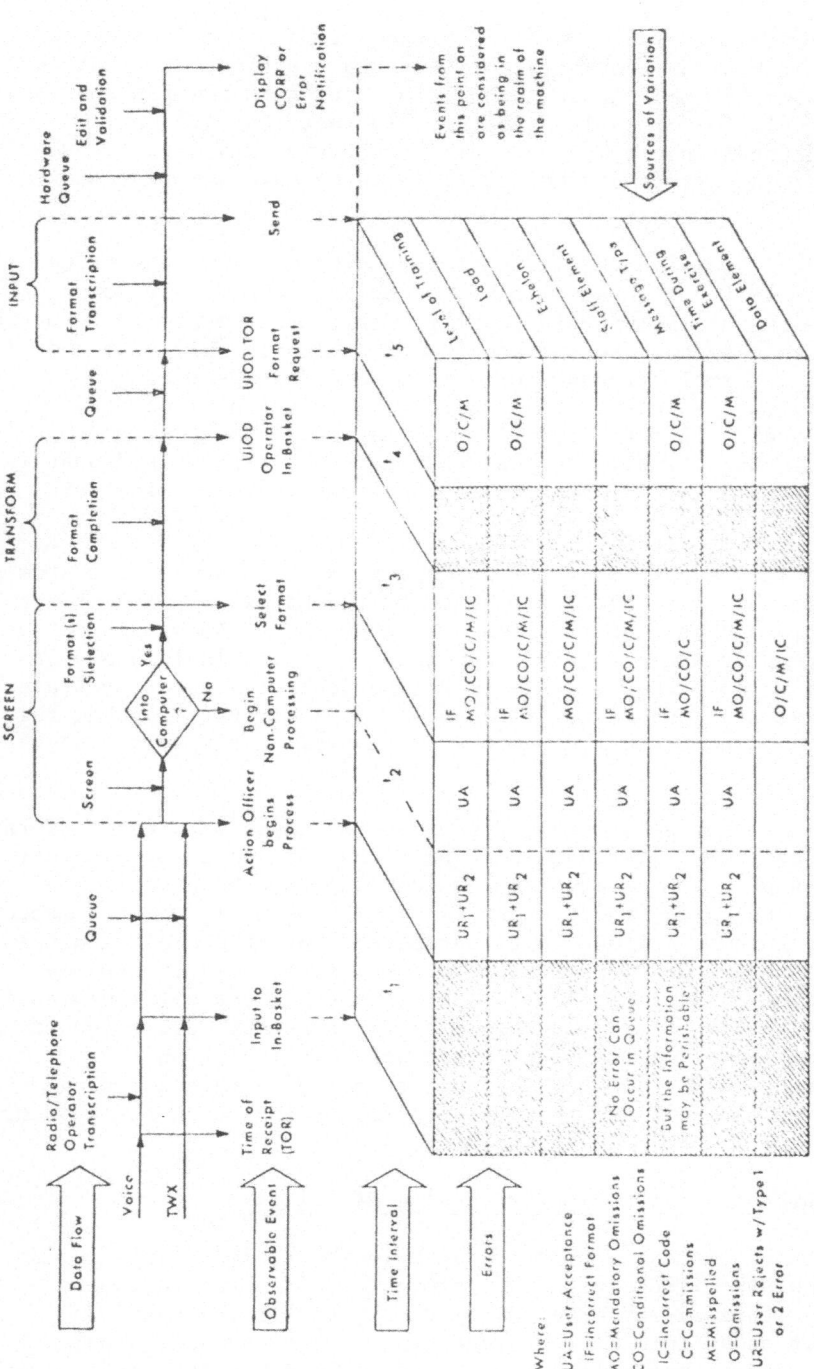

FIGURE 7. Sources of variation, normally considered external to the system, as they relate to data flow time intervals and critical errors. (Taken from Baker, 1970)

Assume that an individual is assigned to a humanly possible job, that he has the necessary aptitude and training, and that he is in reasonably good physical condition. In other words, he is able to do his job properly; whether, in fact, he will do it properly depends on his motivation. The system may operate sub-optimally if a particular individual is inadequately motivated to do his job.

However, individuals also work in groups and when the group is supposed to function as a team (and this is almost always characteristic of individuals working within man-computer information systems) group factors become pertinent. Closely allied to the formal and informal structure of a team, and dependent on these structures, is the interactions which takes place between team members, usually in the form of communication. Thus, a system may operate sub-optimally because team members perform inadequately. For example, crucial information may be transmitted too late or not at all.

The point is that many things impact on an information system's performance that are beyond the scope of the hardware and software considerations that went into the system design. Among these factors are poor human engineering of the system; individuals in the system without the aptitude to do the job; inadequately trained individuals; fatigue in key personnel; poor motivation among the operators, and poor group structure to accomplish the system's goals.

Within the present model, the impact of these external factors can be assessed by first obtaining baseline data on these elements. The effects of given external variations may then be experimentally introduced and their impact quantified. These revised performance values can then be introduced as parameters into the model and the impact of these degrading factors on total system performance can be determined. For example, the performance values for individuals at various levels of training could be introduced to determine if some optimal level of training exists which is less than that prescribed by curriculum but sufficient to insure that training beyond this level will not have a significant impact on the system.

3.5 Measures of Information Processing Efficiency

Typically, human factors research in the realm of information systems concerns itself with the effects of different variables operating within and/or external to the system on the speed and accuracy of human information processing. For example, a human factors study may manipulate input load while a man retrieves data from some analog of a storage point in the system (as in display research), or processes it (eg. in transform studies), or inputs it (ie. in keyboard studies). Meanwhile, the human factors researcher is measuring how long it took the man to do this and how many errors he made in the process. The results of the study then are presented to a system designer or research and development manager in the hope that these findings will be related, in some philosophic or logical way, to system performance. This integrating activity is required (although it frequently does not occur) because the measures themselves were not made in terms of impact on the system output but usually as speed and accuracy measures of the human performance alone.

Baker and Goldstein (1966) recognized the problem this modus operandi can create in information system display research when they observed:

"Common to all of these studies...(ie. the display studies cited in their paper)... is the fact that retrieval of data from a display serves as the subject's response and terminates the task. The retrieved data are not subsequently used by the subject. In information system operations, on the other hand, data are generally retrieved from a display surface as inputs to other complex activities. The question is raised whether the same conclusions obtain where a display-operation task is extended to include use of the retrieved data."

The same general question is faced by the system designer and research and development manager on a daily basis. Are the real, but small, differences presented to them from a human factors study, and the recommended changes based upon these findings, worth the cost of implementing them in a total system context? A statistically significant difference based upon milli-second variance measures may be swallowed up in the total system variance when queue length, for example, is being measured in terms of fractions of an hour. Thus, the designer and manager must concern themselves with operational or practical significance, as well as with statistically significant differences. Generally, however, there is considerable arbitrariness about what constitutes practical significance and this arbitrariness makes even more difficult the problem of relating statistical significance to practical significance.

The present model does not pretend to resolve this dilemma, but it does take the situation into account. While the classic human factors measures of human performance are incorporated in the present model, the impact on the total system is also considered. For example, operator performance measures in terms of error rate and speed in inputting data are obtained but they also can be examined with regard to their impact on efficiency of the system.

INFORMATION PROCESSING FUNCTION	SYSTEM PERFORMANCE MEASURES		INFORMATION QUALITY MEASURES	
	THOROUGHNESS	RESPONSIVENESS	COMPLETENESS	ACCURACY
DISSEMINATION	Percentage of messages which arrive at the proper destination.	Speed of message preparation, processing, and routing.	Resistance to information losses during dissemination.	Correctness of disseminated information.
COMPUTATION		Speed with which computational reports are requested and prepared.	Completeness of computational reports.	Correctness of computational reports.
COMPILATION		Speed with which summary reports are compiled.	Completeness of compiled summary reports.	Correctness of compiled summary reports.
RETRIEVAL		Speed with which queries yield responses.	Completeness of responses to queries.	Correctness of responses to queries.

FIGURE 8. System measures for evaluating message processing performance and information quality.

To obtain measures necessary to test for this impact upon the system, the methodology and techniques developed by Krumm (1967) are effective tools. Basic to the measurement of information processing efficiency is the concept of the message which carries information clusters, ie. associated data items that together yield a complete description of one aspect of an event. A configuration which expedites the transport of messages through the system is more efficient than one that does not. However, expedited message flow is of little merit if the quality of information in the messages is degraded. Consequently, second facet of information processing efficiency is information quality. In brief, assessment of information processing efficiency requires the measurement both of the processing of messages and of the quality of information the messages contain. Summarized in Figure 8 is a set of measures which could be used to reflect the relative 'goodness' or 'badness' of different man-computer system configurations in terms of overall system information processing efficiency.

One of the most apparent and important characteristics of an information system is the rapidity with which information is relayed from a source to a user. This can include the rapidity of the system in responding to a given query, or the special case where the system must compute or compile certain information. A measure of primary importance, therefore, is that of the elapsed time from the moment information is made available to the system until the message containing that information is made available to a user.

Earlier in this presentation we spoke of the system performance measure of dissemination responsiveness, but we did not label it as such at that time. You may recall that the measurement of the time required to complete the data flow throughput (depicted in Fig. 4) required summing over t_k (an inserted constant for message transcription time) plus the manually measured time intervals t_1 through t_4, as well as the computer recorded time interval t_5. If we add to this the machine processing time, t_m, required to shunt the message to the appropriate user station, we have a <u>dissemination responsiveness measure for the system with an exact weighing of the human's contribution included.</u>

This, of course, is a simplified case where we are concerned with a single message intended for a single user. We are also assuming that the system design specifications make explicit who should receive this particular message. Also, we are assuming that we have reliable "machine data" to plug into our metric. Additionally, we are ignoring for the moment the quality of the message at the output end. But from this simplified illustration it can be seen that this model permits one to relate human factors measures in a rather straightforward fashion to operational measures.

We will not concern ourselves in this presentation with a detailed discussion of each of the row and column intersects in Figure 8, but one aspect - information quality measures - does warrant further mention.

When a message is received by a user, four characteristics of its content are of immediate concern: relevance, timeliness, completeness and accuracy. The first concern is that at least a portion of the information be relevant to his job. If the system provides much irrelevant information, the user may be unable to cope with the bulk of the data, and the quality of his performance is subsequently degraded. Given relevant information, he may be concerned with the timeliness of the information. In a military information system, the user wants to know the time the event under consideration occurred relative to the current time. In discussing Figure 7, it was noted that errors cannot occur in queue, but to this it should be added now that the information may be perishable. Lacking other knowledge of the situation, the user must assume that he has been provided with all the information currently available (dissemination completeness) and that the provided information is accurate.

Dissemination completeness can be defined as the percentage of data items present in a message as a function of those available and relevant. Its measurement presently requires considerable subjective judgement; thus, its general use as a measure of information quality for all messages cannot be recommended. One problem encountered when using this measure is the difficulty of determining reliably what constitutes a critical item of information or information element. Consider, for example, an error of omission of the type shown in Figure 7. A message that "an enemy tank division has been sighted" may have been sent as "an enemy division has been sighted", with the word "tank" omitted. Thus, the output message is incomplete, but the lack of completeness is not measurable in the same sense as if the word "division" had been dropped (yielding "an enemy tank has been sighted"). Therefore, completeness scores for the two hypothetical messages, one of which drops "tank" and one of which drops "division", cannot be considered equivalent in terms of impact on the system, even though the completeness scores may be numerically equivalent.

In talking about what constitutes an error, therefore, one can become entangled in the issue of whether the error 'makes a difference'. But some error measures, such as accuracy in the keyboard input of messages, can be objectively measured and be directly related to system performance. We discussed earlier the transformation process intrinsic in man-computer systems. We noted that it is not generally practical to program a system to 'recognize' possible but acceptable inaccuracies. Messages containing only slight inaccuracies, therefore, will be rejected by the computer.

For example, the reader may not have noted that in each figure
presented so far which depicted the horizontal data flow dimension
the word "selection" has appeared as "slelection".   Such an error
would have been immediately sensed by the computer and, if it
appeared this way in a message, the message would probably be
rejected thereby inflating the dissemination responsiveness measure.
Thus, the primary standard of accuracy in evaluating from the system
standpoint is the original message introduced into the system.   The
system output (whether as errors in messages at the input station
or as errors in the output message which were undetected by the
computer) is therefore scored in terms of data items which correspond to the input standard.   Compilation and queries must be
evaluated against the stored items as the standard.   For output
messages which contain results of computations, acceptable limits
must be established to score in terms of the calculated values.

3.6 MANMODEL Summary

In summary, MANMODEL represents only a simplified version of
human information processing in series (ie. it is not representative
of parallel, multioperator, independent team interactions).   Yet
it is sufficiently complex to require a substantial computer system
to run it.   At the outset it was noted that the man in the system
would be considered a sub-system; not an independent component.
The end-result of this approach is key to a very important consideration: When viewed this way, the man in the system is the independent variable (I.V.) and the system measures the dependent variable
(D.V.) - see Figure 9.   But in the context of a TOC, or other
command and control system, even these measures of system information
processing efficiency (often erroneously called information processing effectiveness) are not sufficient in terms of predicting how
well the system will perform its primary mission - success in combat.
It is assumed that a TOC which has rapidly and accurately processed
data will perform better than one which does not have this advantage.
But the information processing variance may be swallowed up in the
total system variance unless one seeks to measure, and subsequently
improve, the decision-making behavior of the 'rule-makers' who
utilize these data.   The next section of the paper will address
that problem.

414

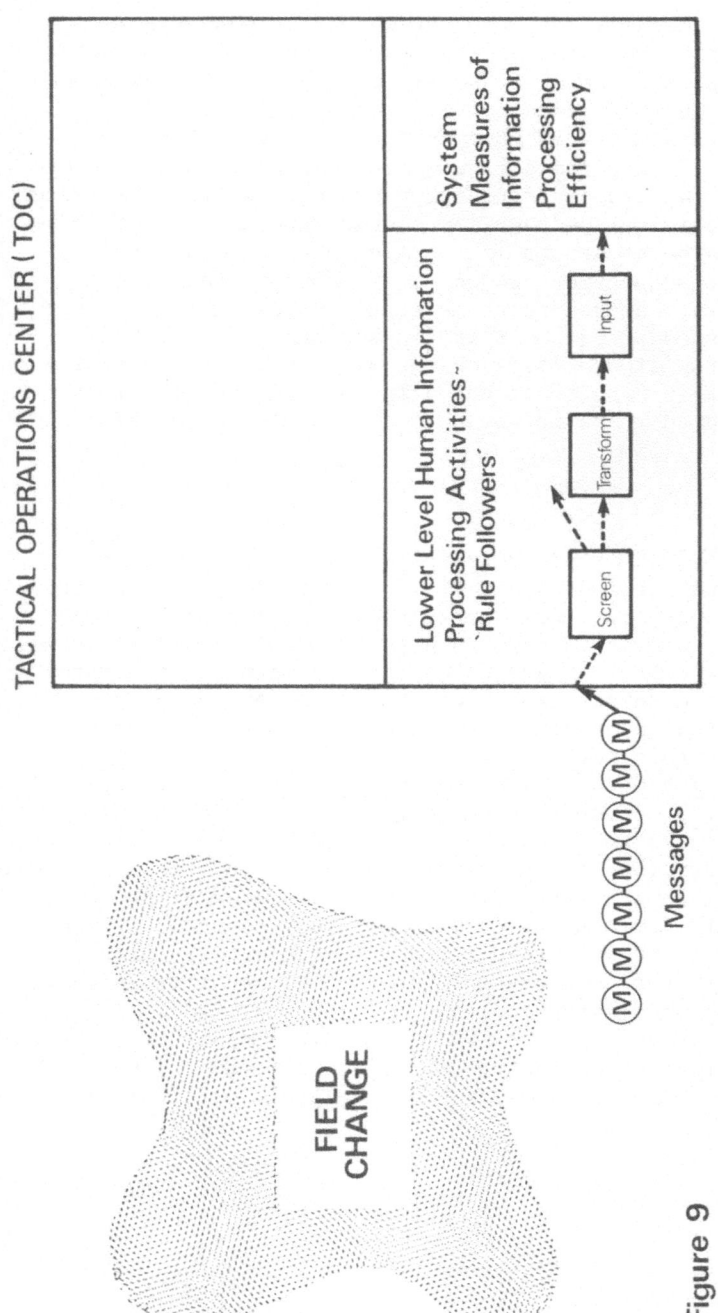

Figure 9

Illustrative diagram of flow of messages linking the 'outside world' to the TOC, the human information processing steps required to process the messages and the system performance measures used to assess the efficiency of this processing.

4.   SIMTOS

The MANMODEL just described is essentially a <u>computer simulation</u> of the lower level, human information processing activities involved in TOS operations.   In contrast, another simulation tool exists for examining human performance in the setting of military information systems, <u>viz</u>., SIMTOS (simulated tactical operations system).   The SIMTOS has been described in great detail elsewhere (Baker, 1975), sections of which will be included here.

4.1 SIMTOS Overview

SIMTOS, in essence, simulates staff assistants and other sources of data input to a decision maker, all of whom are assumed to have direct access to some form of automated information system.   The rationale here is that if it simulates the individual's staff assistants, then it simulates the sorts of data processing they would normally accomplish.   This means that the information presented to the SIMTOS subject can be expected to resemble in content and substance the sorts of information the real world decision maker would receive.   This 'pre-processed' data approach was taken because a SIMTOS subject alone could not be expected to handle and process the high volume of incoming messages that one normally finds in a TOC (tactical operations center).   Likewise, SIMTOS simulates sources of data other than those of the decision maker's staff.   It can present the sorts of processed data which the decision maker would normally receive from these other sources and avoids having the subject undertake tasks which he is not equipped to perform. Finally, SIMTOS simulates a staff which would normally communicate through an automated system so it permits the experimenter 'realis- tically' to improve or degrade data inputs, eg. in terms of time- liness, accuracy and completeness.   Aspects such as these can then become independent variables in experiments concerning inform- ation flow and data usage.

A distinction should also be made between SIMTOS as a simulator and the scenarios which are employed in exercising the simulator. The simulator software is designed to portray combat events and to provide access to the bulk data base.   The bulk data base consists of stored information which is organized in a hierarchical manner. The rationale for the bulk data base is that it is intended to be a convenient substitution for the staff which would normally provide data to the decision maker.   The structure of this data base permits analyses of the scope and level of detail of information used by decision makers in completing specified decision tasks.   Scenario software, on the other hand, is concerned with content and timing of messages and the other features unique to a specific experiment.

416

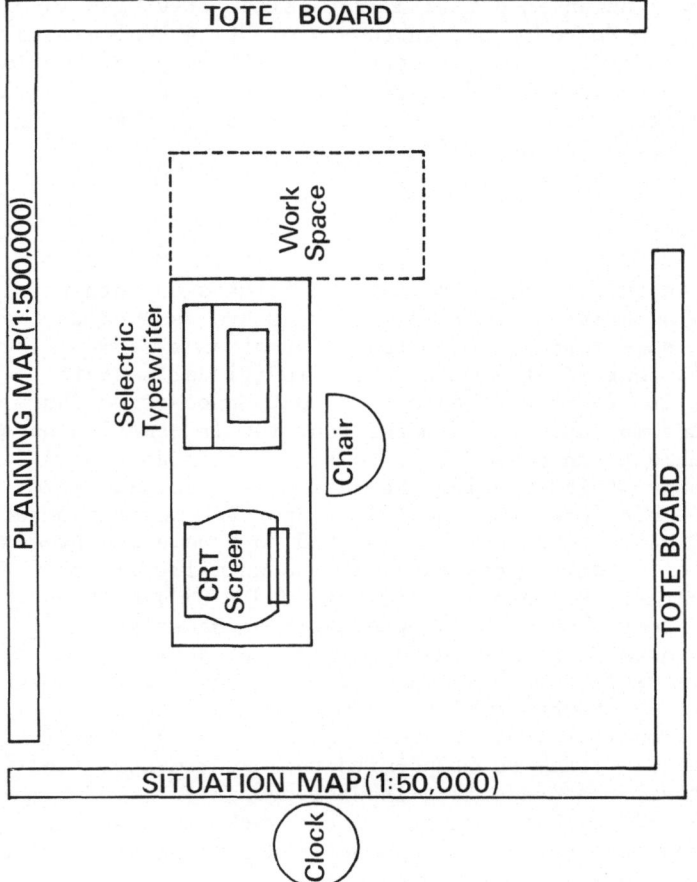

Figure 10 Schematic illustration of SIMTOS subject station

In the main, the data-base and the scenario presently being
used in SIMTOS were structured from a lesson plan and associated
test materials developed by the U.S. Army Command and General Staff
College (CGSC) at Fort Leavenworth, Kansas.   In adapting the CGSC
materials for laboratory research, it was evident that at least
some of the information necessary to support certain decisions was
not included in the lesson plans but was apparently provided during
classroom discussions at CGSC.   Thus it became necessary to generate
additional data to supplement the scenario (Ryan, 1969).   The
products from this effort were two scenarios (an offensive and a
defensive one), each of which has two phases (a planning and a combat
portion).   Additionally, the bulk data-base necessary to support
these scenarios was developed.

Conceptually, then, SIMTOS may be described as a general purpose
simulator which portrays the results of staff activities in processing information relevant to military planning and to the fulfilment
of designated staff responsibilities during combat.   It provides
a combat setting within which particular scenarios can be employed.
The scenarios constitute the experimental designs for studies of
how information flow, data display formats, co-ordination, etc.,
influence human decision making.

4.2   Subject Station

The layout of a typical SIMTOS subject station is shown in
Figure 10.   Information required to accomplish assigned tasks
resides in the computer's data base.   The participants query the
data-base by means of the computer-driver CRT displays and receive
output information via the CRT, slide projector, or typewriter -
all under computer control.   The media for the output depends on
the type of information being provided.   Situation and planning
maps, with a supply of 'stick-on' symbols, and 'tote boards and
grease pencils' are available to the subject.   A three-times real
time clock, against which the subject may compare 'present time'
to 'as of time' also makes up part of the subject station.   Normally,
the scenarios cover twenty-four hours of operations by the events
are simulated at three times real time.   Thus, the officer can
actually accomplish the mission in eight hours of actual playing
time.   Finally, a telephone intercom is available which connects
to the experimenter's station.   This allows the experimenter to
play the role of 'other-staff' in the event that data requested
are not in the computer data-base, as well as serving as a communication link between subject and experimenter for handling unfore-
seen circumstances.

In terms of the subject's interactions with the system, the
CRT and its keyboard provide him the means for accessing the information housed in the data-base.   Operation of the device is straightforward, since a split screen technique is used.   An index of the

items available appears in the upper area of the screen and
procedural instructions appear in the lower area.   To retrieve an
item of information, the subject simply enters the appropriate letter
or digit on the CRT keyboard and presses the SEND button.   The
keyboard is nearly identical to that of a standard typewriter, but
it also has special function keys such as the SEND button.

Perhaps a simplified illustrative sequence from the planning
phase of an operation may service to clarify how the subject would
interact with the system while, at the same time, conveying the
essence of the tree structure of the data-base with its successive
levels of detail.   As mentioned earlier, the SIMTOS keeps track of
retrieval sequences on the part of the subject and permits the
analysis of the scope and level of detail of information used by
the decision maker in completing specified tasks.

The sequence begins with a general "menu" display as follows:

---

(1)	G1	PERSONNEL	(6)	FIRE SUPPORT (FSCE)
(2)	G2	INTELLIGENCE	(7)	CHEMICAL (CBRE)
(3)	G3	OPERATIONS	(8)	SIGNAL
(4)	G4	LOGISTICS	(9)	TRANSPORTATION
(5)	G5	CIVIL AFFAIRS	(0)	ENGINEER

( )   ENTER NUMBER OF ABOVE CATEGORY DESIRED, AND
      PRESS SEND BUTTON

If information on G2 Intelligence was desired, the subject
would simply press the '2' key on the CRT typewriter-like keyboard
and then press the 'Send' button.

The following display would appear:

G-2 REPORTING SIR.   G-2 INFORMATION IS ORGANIZED AS FOLLOWS:

(1)   GENERAL ENEMY SITUATION
(2)   ENEMY   ORDER OF BATTLE
(3)   WEATHER FORECASTS
(4)   TERRAIN ANALYSIS
(5)   STANDARD 16 CAA MECH DIV EQUIP ALLOWANCES
(6)   AGGRESSOR MOVEMENT TIMES TO BORDER
(7)   ENEMY CAPABILITIES
(8)   ENEMY TACTICS

( )   ENTER NUMBER OF ABOVE CATEGORY DESIRED, OR ENTER LETTER OF
      ONE OF FOLLOWING OPTIONS, AND PRESS SEND BUTTON

      A.   RETURN ME TO ORIGINAL DISPLAY
      B.   RETURN ME TO PREVIOUS DISPLAY

In this particular display, if the subject selected either A or B the result would be a return to the first 'menu' display. On the other hand, if more information was desired about enemy order of battle, the subject would press the '2' key, and then the 'Send' button, and the following display would appear:

ENEMY ORDER OF BATTLE 16 CAA

(1)   550 MIXED ARTY BDE
(2)   68 AAA REGT
(3)   207 RL REGT
(4)   1st F MECH DIV
(5)   34 MECH DIV
(6)   35 MECH DIV

( )   ENTER NUMBER OF ABOVE CATEGORY DESIRED, OR ENTER LETTER
       OF ONE OF FOLLOWING OPTIONS, AND PRESS SEND BUTTON.

       A.   RETURN ME TO   E.   PERSONNEL STATUS
            ORIGINAL DISPLAY

       B.   RETURN ME TO   F.   WEAPONS STATUS
            PREVIOUS DISPLAY

       C.   ABOVE UNIT   G.   ELECTRONIC EQUIPMENT
            LOCATION   STATUS

       D.   CURRENT ACTIVITY   H.   MOBILITY EQUIPMENT
                                           STATUS

If the subject desired more information about the 207 RL Regt., he would depress key '3' and then the 'Send' button to call up the following display:

TASK ORGANIZATION 207 RL REGT

HQ BTY

1-207 RL REGT
2-207 RL REGT
3-207 RL REGT

NO FURTHER DATA AVAILABLE IN ABOVE CATEGORY, SIR.

( )   ENTER LETTER OF ONE OF FOLLOWING OPTIONS, AND PRESS 'SEND'
      BUTTON

      A.   RETURN ME TO ORIGINAL DISPLAY
      B.   RETURN ME TO PREVIOUS DISPLAY

It can be seen from the preceding displays that information is provided to the subject in greater detail as he continues to phase through his retrieval process.

It is also possible for the subject to make errors as he manipulates the CRT keyboard:

1. He might press the SEND button without having made a letter or number entry.

2. He might press the SEND button after having entered an invalid number or letter key. For example, in the above set of retrieval instructions, any number or letter other than A or B would be considered invalid.

If the subject made any of these errors, the following ERROR message would appear on the CRT screen:

ERROR MESSAGE

YOU HAVE MADE AN ERROR SIR. PRESS SEND BUTTON TO

RECALL LAST DISPLAY

ERROR MESSAGE

If the subject realized that he had made an error before he pressed the SEND button, he could correct the error simply by pressing the BKSP (backspace) key which places the cursor in proper position, then pressing the key for the proper entry and then the SEND button.

Thus, data accessed from the bulk data base are displayed on the CRT.   In other instances, eg. an evaluation of various methods of displaying information (ie. alpha-numeric vs. graphic large screen display), certain of the output was back-projected on a large translucent screen to simulate a computer generated big-board display (Nawrocki, 1973).   Messages from subordinate units, on the other hand, arrive from time to time (the times are scenario dependent and the outputs are under the control of the scenario software) and serve to drive the situation in keeping with the scenario.

Up to four of these subject stations, in any combination of offensive or defensive/planning or combat phase scenarios, can be run simultaneously in SIMTOS.

4.3 Conducting SIMTOS Experiments

The preceding sections provide a basis for a SIMTOS definition. SIMTOS may be defined as a physical simulation, ie. it is essentially a controlled exercise environment, with a goal to examine data handling by high level decision making personnel.   Within this SIMTOS environment, experiments are conducted in the setting of simulations of tactical operations systems.   SIMTOS, therefore, is not in itself an experiment - rather, it is a vehicle for conducting experiments.

With the SIMTOS, we can (and have) directly involved the user in research directed toward the design of future military information systems. Alternative approaches, for example, to displaying information to a commander and his staff, can be tested in a controlled, measureable laboratory environment which is also an environment closely akin to the setting for which the devices are intended. Further, the data used for these design decisions are generated by the actual, ultimate users themselves.

Selection as an officer participant requires that the man has graduated from CGSC and has had command experience at Battalion or above (eg. Bn CO, Bde S3, Div G3). If the officer is participating in an experiment using the offensive planning scenario, he is instructed to assume the role of a combined arms army operations officer and to plan an attack to seize the Hof Gap in Germany. Using the defensive scenario, he assumes the role of a division operations officer to plan a defense in a sector which is expecting an attack by two mechanized infantry divisions of a combined arms army. In the latter for example, the officer participant may be asked to develop a plan for the defense of a U.S. Mechanized Infantry Division sector against an attack by an Aggressor task force of two divisions and specific decision tasks are assigned. These may include recommendation of a form of defense, maneuver concept, task organization and mission directives to subordinate Brigades. The tactical planning situation incorporated into the scenario is, as was previously mentioned, based on CGSC lesson plan materials. The techniques for evaluating decision responses in SIMTOS have been jointly developed with CGSC military personnel using standards that they have evolved over the past fifteen years.

To date, nearly 200 field grade officers have participated in SIMTOS experimentation runs, mostly in the planning phase. Experimental objectives have included: the testing of several hypotheses concerning quantified predictors of decision performance (Krumm et al., 1973; Robins et al., 1974); an examination of alternative man-computer input techniques (Strub, 1971); identification of minimum essential information requirements for offensive and defensive tactical operations planning (McKendry et al., 1973; Baker and Mace, 1976; Strub, 1974, 1976); evaluation of various methods of displaying information (ie. alpha-numeric vs. graphic large screen display) under computer control (Nawrocki, 1973); an assessment of decision style and its relationship to the concept of adaptive, computer embedded decision aids (Strub and Levit, 1974); and an empirical basis for design decisions concerning the development of situation map background specifications for computer generated tactical displays (Granda, 1976).

As earlier noted, the bulk of the research to date has been conducted using the planning phase of the scenarios. But presently we are deeply involved in the conduct of research related to the combat phase of both scenarios. Our initial efforts toward a transition from the planning to the combat phase uncovered a particular problem – the static nature of the software did not lend itself to a realistic portrayal of combat operations. For example, if the subject reorganized a task force structure, the change would not be reflected during subsequent querying of the data-base. Likewise, outgoing or incoming artillery fire would not be reflected in attrition of either friendly or opponent forces. To correct the deficiency, considerable software development was undertaken to provide a dynamic simulation capability.

The effort culminated in the production of a number of combat algorithms for use in the SIMTOS. For determining unit location, a grid square x-axis, y-axis technique, both measured in meters, was developed. Unit locations are related to this grid square orientation. This unit location algorithm also includes a radius of operations component. Personnel and equipment factors are reflected in terms of number of personnel, weapons, basic loads, electronics, and mobility items – all of which can be attrited as the game is played. A hardness factor was also developed for use in conjunction with an artillery algorithm to realistically produce casualty figures. A rate of movement software package was developed which reflected two differing speeds, one for the attack mode and the other for the move mode. Also, a closest point of approach algorithm was developed to keep track of unit spatial relationships and of its possible impact on range and kill capability during weapons employment. In addition, tactical air algorithms, artillery firing algorithms, unopposed unit movement algorithms and opposed unit movement and attrition algorithms were developed. The latter includes a determination of units in contact; calculation of relative combat power, opposing troop movements, and opposing troop attrition algorithm. Finally, a unit situation algorithm was developed. The end result has been that a sophisticated and complex environment has emerged for simulating a combat setting. It has also produced two problems which presently are being tackled.

First, a Division G3 typically would not be expected to perform some of the tasks that our present officer participants are asked to do, eg. task such as calling in artillery fires and air strikes to support maneuver units. However, we need to know _when_ such support would be given and _how much_ would normally be allocated. Based on responses given by the present subjects we shall be able to program the computer to handle the fire support and tac air requirements in a realistic manner. Thus, future subjects can proceed with their normal decision tasks without this added requirement. Currently, subjects are told that "the computer will not _know_ when and how to use the simulated fire power unless we tell it. We prefer that such judgments be based on data provided by experienced military subjects such as yourself."

The second problem encountered is that which Christensen (1958) has tagged the "omnipresent criterion problem." In the planning phase we were able to use an ad hoc 'school solution' (CGSC) but ready made solutions for free floating combat operations are in short supply. Our approach to finding a solution has been to compare subject performance with performance obtained during 'base line' runs (ie. completely automated computer runs made without subject intervention). The base line runs involve no programmed artillery or air strikes by, for example, attacking forces. There-fore, in the offensive mode, if the subject uses resources judiciously, he should be able to move his forces further and with lower attrition than occurred during the base line run.

Several measures of effectiveness can then be compared. One of these is a territory measure. In a defensive operation, the measure is territory lost; in the offensive, it is distance penet-rated. In general, territory can be lost, gained or controlled - depending on the mission. Another measure is friendly attrition, ie. the number of personnel, equipment and supplies lost during the tactical engagement. Also, there is the inverse of this - enemy attrition. An additional, obtainable measure of effectiveness is resources expended. This takes into account, for example, the expenditure or artillery volleys or air sorties. Finally, there is a force readiness level, ie. the remaining combat effectiveness of the units after completion of their mission. It is also possible to weight any of these measures, based upon expert military opinion. This implies, however, that these measures have been converted to standard scores. Hence, if CGSC instructors point out that the subject's main task is to control territory, it is possible to weight territory as twice that of resources expended.

5. CONCLUDING REMARKS

Even the simplistic, serial processing, simulation models of the functions performed by 'rule followers' and 'rule makers' in a military command and control information system are extremely complex when one gets down to the nitty-gritty of modeling all of these interactive functions (see, for example, Figure 11). But the effort is worth it. It has given me whole new notions with regard to what constitutes critical problems as well as an apprec-iation of the numbers of things we, as human factors scientists and psychologists, do not know. I urge you to join in on the modeling and discover some of these things yourself.

It is probably evident by now that such endeavors constitute a potpourri of personal artistic touches and ad hoc principles, and to try to explore the whole domain in one presentation is impossible. Rather, the intent here has been to present you with a sample of what it is like to grope and cope with the problem of trying to model the user in the setting of an interactive man-computer system.

424

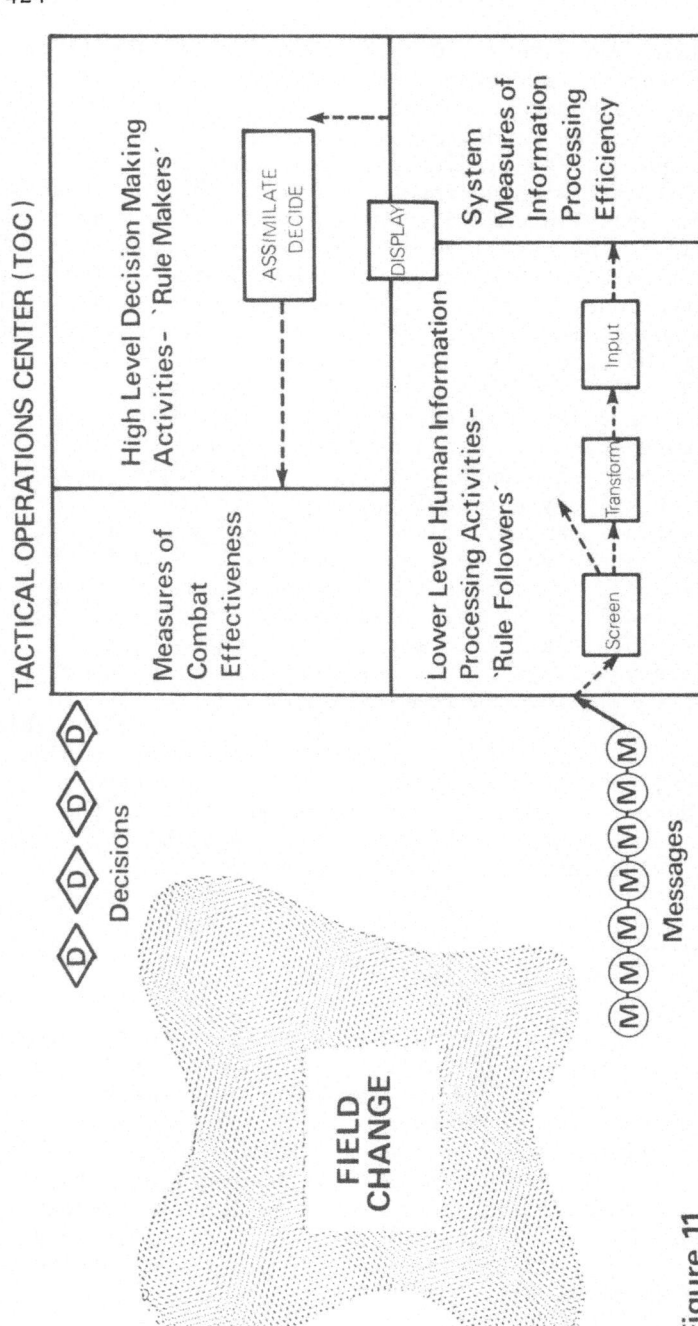

Figure 11

Composite diagram of overall TOC operations which constitute the factors one must take into consideration in order to 'model the user' effectively in an interactive, man-computer military information system.

REFERENCES

Baker, J.D.   1968 Human Factors experimentation within a
                             tactical operations system (TOS)
                             environment.
                             BESRL Research Study 68-4.

Baker, J.D.   1970 Quantitative modeling of human performance
                             in information systems.
                             Ergonomics, 13.6, 645-664.

Baker, J.D.   1972 Acorns in flower pots/psychologists in
                             the field.
                             JSAS Catalog of Selected Documents in
                             Psychology, 2, 88.

Baker, J.D.   1973 Human performance research in military
                             information systems: Quo fuimus et
                             quo vadimus?
                             Proceedings: NATO Defense Research Group
                             Seminar on Man-Machine Relations.

Baker, J.D.   1975 SIMTOS: A man-in-the-loop interactive
                             simulation of tactical operations system.
                             In: Military Strategy and Tactics,
                               R.K. Huber, L.F. Jones & E. Reine (Eds.)
                             New York; Plenum Publishing Corp.

Baker, J.D. &   1966 Batch versus sequential displays: Effects
  Goldstein, I.   on human problem solving.
                             Human Factors, 3, 225-235.

Baker, J.D. &   1976 Information requirements in a field army.
  Mace, D.J.   U.S. Army Research Institute Technical
                             Paper.

Chapanis, A.   1961 Men, machines and models.
                             American Psychologist, 3, 113-131.

Christensen, J.M.   1958 Trends in human factors.
                             Human Factors, 1, 2-7.

Granda, T.M.   1976 A comparison between a standard map and
                             a reduced detail map within a simulated
                             tactical operations system (SIMTOS).
                             U.S. Army Research Institute Technical
                             Paper 274.

Hamilton, W.F. &   1969 Systems analysis of urban transportation.
  Nance, D.K.   Scientific American, 221, 19-27.

Kennedy, J.L.   1962 Psychology and system development.
                             In: R.M. Gagne (Ed.), Psychological
                               Principles in System Development.
                             New York; Holt, Rinehart and Winston.

Krumm, R.L.   1967 Measurement of tactical military
                                   information flow.
                                   Proceedings: Thirteenth Annual Human
                                   Factors Research and Development
                                   Conference, Ft. Monmouth, New Jersey,
                                   103-114.

Krumm, R.L.   1973 Research on tactical military decision
  Robins, J.E. &   making: III. Predictor variables and
  Ryan, T.G.   criterion measures.
                                   BESRL Technical Research Note 229,
                                   (AD 765 457).

Leahy, W.R.   1974 A digital simulation model of message
  Lautman, M.R.   handling in the tactical operations
  Bearde, J.L. &   system: III. Further extensions of
  Siegel, A.I.   the model for increased interaction.
                                   U.S. Army Research Institute Memorandum
                                   74-11.

Leahy, W.R.   1976a A digital simulation model of message
  Siegel, A.I. &   handling in the tactical operations
  Wolf, J.J.   system: IV. Model integration with
                                   CASE and SAMTOS.
                                   U.S. Army Research Institute Memorandum.

Leahy, W.R.   1976b A digital simulation model of message
  Siegel, A.J. &   handling in the tactical operations
  Wolf, J.J.   system: V. Appendix: User's guide
                                   to the integrated MANMODEL/CASE/SAMTOS
                                   computer simulation.
                                   U.S. Army Research Institute Memorandu

McKendry, J.M.   1973 Application of a method for determinatio
  Wilson, R.C.   information requirements in a field ar
  Mace, D.J. &   U.S. Army Research Institute Technical
  Baker, J.D.   Paper 247.

Miller, R.B.   1962 Task, description and analysis.
                                   In: Psychological Principles in System
                                   Development, R.M. Gagne (Ed.);
                                   New York: Holt, Rinehart and Winston

Miller, R.B.   1967 Task taxonomy: Science or technology?
                                   Ergonomics, 10, 167-176.

Nawrocki, L.H.   1973 Graphic versus tote display of informati
                                   in a simulated tactical operations sys
                                   U.S. Army Research Institute Technical
                                   Paper 243, (AD 766 217).

Ringel, S.   1966 Command information processing systems -
                                   A human factors research program.
                                   Behavior and Systems Research Laboratory
                                   Washington, D.C. Technical Research
                                   Report 1148 (AD 697 716).

Robins, J.E.   1974 Research on tactical military decision
  Buffardi, L. &   making: Applications of a decision
  Ryan, T.G.   prediction concept in a SIMTOS environ-
                           ment.
                     U.S. Army Research Institute Technical
                           Paper 246.

Ryan, T.G.   1969 Studies of tactical military decision
                           making: II. An information network
                           aid to scenario development.
                     BESRL Research Study 69-11.

Scherr, A.L.   1965 An analysis of time-shared computer systems.
                     Ph.D. thesis, Massachusetts Institute of
                           Technology, Cambridge, Mass. MAC-TR-18.

Shannon, C.E. &   1949 The mathematical theory of communication.
  Weaver, W.   Urbana; University of Illinois Press.

Shubik, M. &   1972 Models, simulations and games - A survey.
  Brewer, G.S.   Santa Monica, The RAND Corporation Report
                           R-1060-ARPA/RC.

Siegel, A.I.   1973a A digital simulation model of message
  Wolf, J.J. &   handling in the tactical operations
  Leahy, W.R.   system: I. The model, its sensitivity,
                           and user's manual.
                     U.S. Army Research Institute Memorandum
                           73.5.

Siegel, A.E.   1973a A digital simulation model of message
  Wolf, J.J.   handling in the tactical operations
  Leahy, W.R. &   system: II. Extensions of the model
  Bearde, J.L.   for interactivity with subjects and
                           experimenters.
                     U.S. Army Research Institute Memorandum
                           73-6.

Strub, M.H.   1971 Evaluation of man-computer input techniques
                           for military information systems.
                     BESRL Technical Research Note 226,
                           (AD 730 315).

Strub, M.H.   1974 Tactical planning (offensive and defensive)
                           minimum essential information require-
                           ments.
                     U.S. Army Research Institute Memorandum
                           74-7.

Strub, M.H. &   1974 Computer compatibility with decision style:
  Levit, R.A.   Eddies in a bit stream.
                     Proceedings of the Eighteenth Annual
                           Meeting of the Human Factors Society.

428

Strub, M.H.   1976   Tactical planning (offensive and
                                   defensive) information requirements:
                                   Comparison of survey questionnaire
                                   and laboratory exercise data.
                                   U.S. Army Research Institute Paper.

Warburton, G.B.,   1960   SAGE task equipment analysis: Intercept
   Jr. Lawrence, K.A. &   director/intercept technician.
   Marks, M.R.   Air Force Cambridge Research Center,
                                   Bedford, Mass. Technical Research
                                   Note AFCRC-TN-59-76.

OUTLOOK FOR MAN-COMPUTER SYMBIOSIS: TOWARD A GENERAL THEORY OF
MAN-COMPUTER PROBLEM SOLVING

Harold Sackman

Information Systems Department, California State
Polytechnic University, Pomona, California 91768, U.S.A.

PROLOGUE

Licklider (1960) introduced and popularized the notion of
"Man-Computer Symbiosis" 15 years ago in his article of the same
title.   He likened man-computer symbiosis to the pollination of
the fig tree by the insect "blastophaga grossorum," where each is
dependent on the other for well-being and survival.   The symbology
of the tree alludes to human knowledge as in the biblical Tree of
Knowledge, and the repetitive, instinctually programed behavior of
insects symbolizes computers.   It is not my intent to argue the
metaphysical quintessence of man-computer symbiosis.   It is my
intent to inquire into the real-world interaction between people
and computers at this point 15 years after Licklider's challenging
article, to take stock of progress toward the symbiotic metaphor.
To accomplish this, I believe it is necessary to work toward a
general theory of man-computer problem solving.   Such a theory
would provide a more fruitful framework to evaluate progress and
prospects toward man-computer symbiosis.   Accordingly, the basic
task of this paper is to sketch the rudiments of a general theory
of man-computer problem solving.

1.   THEORETICAL LAG IN MAN-COMPUTER PROBLEM SOLVING

A sustained tradition of theoretical and applied experimental
work in man-computer problem solving does not exist in computer
science, information science, or behavioral science.   Computers
were originally employed for highly specialized users such as
mathematicians, engineers, and physical scientists, employing
cumbersome machine languages.   Narrow technical considerations
and immediate cost constraints dominated computer technology and

still dominate it today, in large part at the expense of problem requirements, human needs, and social effectiveness. Computer system professionals were not trained nor inclined to test human performance and problem solution effectiveness in computer-aided systems. A classical cultural lag arose between computer technology and verified knowledge of user behavior and mission performance.

Time-sharing systems and other forms of on-line computer services have inherited user problems over the last decade, and these problems are being transmitted to emerging public information utilities (eg. Stetten and Volk, 1973), and computer networks (eg. Greenberger et al., 1973) that will characterize the 1980's. For a great variety of historical, technical and cultural reasons beyond the scope of this discussion, the user remains the forgotten man, and the general public stands to suffer in the long run from the pervasive scientific and humanistic lag in computer-aided information services.

The experimental literature on man-computer problem solving is fundamentally fragmented, isolated, and disconnected, containing many gaps in crucial areas,with virtually no integrative concepts or theories. While it is beyond the scope of this exposition to enter into substantive details, a thumbnail characterization of this literature will help to illustrate this allegation.

Two broad research areas may be discerned in this literature - man-machine system experimentation and varieties of online/offline problem solving. The former is primarily concerned with team and organizational problem solving, as in real-time command and control systems, with a literature extending from the 1950's to the present. The online/offline category is more concerned with individual problem solving, as with time-sharing versus batch studies, and has a literature coextensive with the appearance of pioneering time-sharing systems in the 1960's up to the present. Each area is briefly characterized below.

Parsons (1972) has performed a monumental service in bringing together, in one book, some 200 experiments in 40 major programs from some 600 references concerned with man-machine system experimentation since World War II. His integrative review traces the development of computer-aided methodology in experiments concerned with man-machine system performance in organizational settings including tactical systems, logistics, air defense systems, police dispatching, air traffic control, and other applications. The pattern drawn by Parsons is one of rapid methodological growth as in gaming, simulation, and system training exercises, with much practical experience in conceiving and implementing man-machine system research, but as noted earlier, with no significant integrative theory spanning the work of the various laboratories and application areas.

In the area of online/offline problem solving, a similar pattern is observed. One subclass of these studies is concerned with descriptive statistics of user performance characteristics (eg. Scherr, 1967, and Raynaud, 1967, at MIT using the Compatible Time-Sharing System; Totschek, 1966, and McIsaac, 1966, with the SDC Time-Sharing System; and Shaw, 1965, and Bryan, 1967, at Rand with the JOSS system). These studies involved a combined total of hundreds of thousands of online user requests in diverse time-sharing systems, and provide a useful descriptive portrait of the time-sharing user. However, while methodological advances were prominent in such areas as simulation, modeling, and recording, no theory of user performance effectiveness arose from these studies.

Sackman, (1970a) has reviewed the comparative online/offline literature. While the results of some 10 experimental studies point to useful leads and many areas of needed research, here again no integrative theory emerged from any of the investigators in this area. The research motivation was oriented more toward applied problems, such as design choices between batch and time-sharing, rather than toward insight into man-computer problem solving as an area of inquiry in its own right.

Only fragmentary work has been performed in other scattered areas in the online/offline category, as in computer language comparisons (AFADA, 1963, and Rubey, 1968); comparison of user terminals (Pollock and Gildner, 1963; Barmack and Sinaiko, 1966; Swets et al., 1966; Morrill et al., 1968; and Dolotta, 1970); and system response time in man-computer problem solving (Raynaud, 1967; Parsons, 1970; Seven et al., 1971). These studies raise more questions than answers, are typically non-comparable in terms of subjects, tasks and systems, and except for some speculative commentary, have not contributed to a theory of man-computer problem solving.

A growing number of observers and critics have pointed up recurrent system requirements for computer users, leading parameters in the man-machine interface, and the need for integrative theory in man-computer problem solving (eg. Barmack and Sinaiko, 1966; Blackwell, 1972; Carbonnel, 1969; Miller, 1969; Nickerson, 1969; Parsons, 1972; Sackman, 1970b; Shackel, 1969; and Weinberg, 1971). The work of Weinberg is particularly notable in demonstrating the value and versatility of the application of psychological concepts to a behavioral analysis of computer programing. Weinberg dismisses most of the traditional psychological work in human problem solving as largely inapplicable to the analysis of computer programing on the grounds that the laboratory 'problems' and 'solutions' in the psychological literature are not comparable to the open-end, relatively unstructured problems that confront programmers.

TABLE 1. Generalised stages of problem solving.

HELMHOLTZ (1896)   WALLAS (1926)

- Preparation   - Preparation
- Incubation   - Incubation
- Illumination   - Illumination
                                          - Verification

ROSSMAN (1931)

- Observation of a need or difficulty
- Analysis of the need
- Survey of the available information
- Critical analysis of the proposed solutions for
    advantages and disadvantages
- Birth of the new idea, the invention
- Experimentation to test out the most promising
    solution; perfection of the final embodiment
    by repeating some or all of the previous steps

DEWEY (1938)

- Disturbed equilibrium, initiation of inquiry
- Problem formulation
- Hypothesis formulation
- Experimental testing
- Settled outcome, termination of inquiry

YOUNG (1940)   HUTCHINSON (1949)

- Assembly of material   - Preparation
- Assimilation of material   - Frustration
- Incubation   - Insight
- Birth of the idea   - Verification
- Development to usefulness

OSBORN (1957)

- Orientation: pointing up the problem
- Preparation: gathering pertinent data
- Analysis: breaking down the relevant material
- Hypothesis: piling up alternatives by way of
                   ideas
- Incubation: letting up, to invite illumination
- Synthesis: putting the pieces together
- Verification: judging the resultant ideas

The man-computer problem-solving literature mentioned above has not yet been integrated with the more traditional areas of the behavioral literature on human problem solving including: group versus individual (eg. DeGreene, 1970), gestalt versus behavioristic (eg. Skinner, 1969), stages of problem solving (eg. Haefele, 1962), planning and expectation theory (eg. Steiner, 1969), human information processing theories (eg. Newell and Simon, 1972), and selected studies from relevant learning theory (eg. Hilgard and Bower, 1966), cognitive theory (eg. Harper et al. 1964), thinking (Mandler and Mandler, 1964), intelligence (eg. Guilford, 1967), and work on creativity (eg. Dellas and Gaier, 1970). Various approaches to generalized stages of problem solving in the psychological literature are shown in Table 1. The cross-fertilization between the experimental literature in man-computer problem solving and the mainstream of behavioral literature on problem solving is long overdue.

2.   PRESENT RESEARCH

The above portrait of scattered studies with little cohesion and many gaps provides the backdrop for the current National Science Foundation (NSF) project on 'Psychological Studies in Man-Computer Problem Solving' (Sackman, 1973, 1974; Sackman and Blackwell, 1974). Rather than perform an additional study along lines previously explored, as indicated above, we chose to define and explore the field of man-computer problem solving from a broader viewpoint that would lead to theoretical formulation. In agreement with Weinberg's previously cited position, we felt that the available experimental studies were not representative of real-world problems. Consequently, we set up as a basic objective the investigation of "real-world" man-computer problem solving, as opposed to the traditional emphasis on laboratory problems. Real-world problems were basically limited to the occupational domain, and defined as projects essential for the individual's job or position, perceived as major tasks by the respondent, and requiring some originality in approach and execution. (A more detailed operational definition, as used in current studies, is described shortly).

Another vital evaluative area missing from the prior literature was the division of labor between people and computers. To gain better insight into this controversial area we decided to compare systematically computer-aided problem solving with non-computer problem solving in an experimental design where each individual serves as his own control. The similarities and differences in these areas would enable us to explicate, in a more precise manner, the contribution of computers to human problem solving, including disadvantages and pitfalls as well as benefits.

The third objective was to provide an initial conceptual framework in response to the lack of integrative theory in man-computer problem solving. A nine-stage model of problem solving was developed, building upon the extensive psychological literature on stages of problem solving, and updating such leads with current developments in systems and planning theory where computer systems have made a major impact.

This model consists of nine steps, with a very brief rationale for each, in parentheses, as outlined below:

1. Emergence of Problem: developments leading up to definitive recognition of the problem and initial assessment of problem goals. (This stage marks the initiation of the new problem and its links with related problems - often neglected in classical stages).

2. Competing Problem Approaches: competing exploratory alter-natives in early formulation and gross solution of the problem before any significant commitment of resources is made. (This stage permits an early test of originality in conception and approach to distinguish between 'authentic' problems and routine tasks).

3. Proposed Problem Plan: provisional statement of the problem and general approach to solution in the framework of a proposed working plan, including estimates of required time and resources (This stage highlights the integrative and evaluative functions of planning in early problem solving).

4. Consensus and Commitment: review and modification of problem proposal (with peers, management, funding agency, etc.) leading to acceptance of negotiated plan with commitment of resources and/or personal commitment of time and effort. (This stage distinguishes between potential related problems that are dropped and selected problems that are pursued).

5. Development of Problem Methods: detailed exploration, specifi-cation, and working definition of the problem including design and development of detailed methodology to solve the problem. (This corresponds to classical stages incorporating a working or operational definition and methodology for the problem).

6. Solution Testing: application of selected methodology with iterative test and evaluation leading to solutions that are accepted. (This corresponds to classical stages concerned with discovery of acceptable solutions).

7. Consolidation and Refinement: final revisions, elaboration, and rationalization of accepted solution. (This corresponds to classical 'verification' stages).

8.   Communication of Results: demonstrations, written and verbal reports to others on problem findings.   (This stage points up the extensive follow-on communication activities typically omitted from classical stages).

9.   Feedback and Evaluation: impact on others in the problem community, including feedback on dissemination, acceptance and controversy.   (This stage stresses social reaction and evaluation of the problem outcome and the link to new problems).

The above model builds upon classical problem-solving stages and reflects current trends toward more directed, formal planning in early stages of problem solving, toward increased participatory planning prior to commitment of resources, toward wider dissemination of results, and more extensive feedback on solutions from the problem community.   The increasing use of computers in problem solving and the competition for limited computer-related resources have presumably quickened the above trends.

Table 2 lists comparative problem solving in the proposed model against basic stages of problem solving in scientific method, system, development, and in planning theory.   The list runs from earliest stages at the top to latest stages at the bottom.   Comparable stages are roughly at equivalent points in each column.   The entries are hopefully self-explanatory;   no claims are made for their rigor or purity;   their purpose is suggestive and heuristic. Whether or not the reader agrees with them, the analogy reveals some of the bias and background of the proposed conceptualization of problem solving.

Thus, the three key objectives of the current NSF research are:

1.   the study of real-world problem solving,
2.   comparison of problem solving with and without computers, and
3.   testing the effectiveness of the proposed model and incipient theory of man-computer problem solving.

A pilot study and a follow-on investigation were conducted under the current NSF grant, with method and findings briefly summarized as follows.

The testing tool was a self-administered questionnaire incorporating descriptive problem characteristics, and proposed stages of problem solving, and evaluative rating scales on the problem-solving process.   The subjects consisted primarily of Rand professionals, and other professionals working mostly in research and industry.   Each subject served as his own control by reporting his experience on the questionnaire for a computer and non-computer problem.   The total sample for the pilot and main studies involved approximately 60 subjects with 120 reported problems.   Data were

TABLE 2. Analogy between the proposed model and basic stages of problem solving in scientific method, system development, and planning theory.

	Proposed Problem Stages	Stages in Scientific Method	System Development Stages	Stages in Planning Theory
1.	Emergence of Problem	Research Values and Needs	System Values and Needs	Normative Planning
2.	Competing Problem Approaches	Review of Literature	System Requirements	
3.	Proposed Problem Plan	Problem Definition	Proposed System Design	Strategic Planning
4.	Consensus and Commitment		System Authorization	
5.	Development of Problem Methods	Experimental Design	System Production	Tactical Planning
6.	Solution Testing	Experimental Testing	System Installation	
7.	Consolidation and Refinement	Analysis of Data	Operational System Testing	Operational Planning
8.	Communication of Results	Publication of Results	System Evolution	
9.	Feedback and Evaluation	Peer Feedback and Evaluation	System Obsolescence	

subjected to extensive quantitative and qualitative analyses, within and between individuals for approximately 400 objective and open-end measures collected from the questionnaire.

In selecting their real-world problems, subjects were asked to try to meet these 10 guidelines as closely as possible.

1. A project or assignment required for your work or position.
2. A major or significant problem.
3. A completed project or assignment.
4. A relatively recent problem for which you have adequate information to answer most items.
5. A problem involving at least one month of elapsed time from start to finish.
6. Not a splinter or fragment of a problem – a complete problem in its own right.
7. A problem involving significant difficulties and obstacles, requiring non-routine solution.
8. A first-hand problem where you played a substantive role, had an overview of all stages, and personal contact with other members of the team.
9. A problem requiring some form of documentation accounting for results.
10. Work problems preferred over school problems.

Note that there are no restrictions as to whether an individual or team problem is selected. Nor are there any restrictions on part-time versus full-time, except for the requirement for significant contact with the problem as a whole.

The major findings, subject to further verification by larger and more definitive problem and subject samples, are as follows.

o Computer Versus Non-Computer Problem Solving: Computer-aided and non-computer problem solving show generally similar stages and dynamics of problem solving, for the measures and conditions of these studies. Computer problems, however, have special behavioral characteristics that are uniquely associated with computer services that are not found in non-computer problems, as indicated below.

o Primacy of the Individual: The individual was consistently rated as the most important resource in getting work done and in meeting problem objectives throughout virtually all stages of problem solving, for group as well as individual problems, and for computer as well as non-computer problems. The individual was rated as more important than the team, management, others, and more important than documentation and machine resources. Reported major problem insight was primarily an individual phenomenon. Ratings of problem-solving success correlated highest with perceived importance of the individual for computer and non-computer problems.

o <u>Successful Man-Computer Problem Solving</u>: Factor analysis of 80 variables, describing the problem solver, characteristics of reported computer problems, and the problem solving process, resulted in a complementary two-factor structure directly concerned with successful solutions for computer-related problems. The first factor describes overall problem success and the second relates to that portion concerned with a good computer solution. Overall problem success is associated with relatively older individuals, who tend to be project leaders, have extensive computer experience, who work on projects where the importance of the individual is enhanced, who tend to focus their creative effort on the early stages of problem solving concerned with defining the problem and exploring competing alternative solutions, and who tend to achieve major problem insight alone, as opposed to group insight.

o <u>Good Computer Solutions</u>: The second factor, concerned with effective computer solutions, tends to be associated with more junior individuals who work on teams and are not project leaders, who have highly flexible computer skills from very extensive mathematics and computer science courses, who focus their most creative efforts on the later stages of computer solution testing and refinement of results (eg. program testing and de-bugging), and who prefer to work alone with computers.

o <u>Ideal Man-Computer Problem-Solving Team</u>: This two-factor pattern suggests a differentiation between personal creative optimization on the problem as a whole as opposed to personal creative optimization on the computer solution; sustained creative output for this research-oriented sample occurs rarely for both types of optimization at the same time. According to this evidence, the 'ideal' basic team for man-computer problem solving (for the present state-of-the-art) would seem to be a compatible division of labor between a problem or mission-oriented leader, secure in the importance of his role, who is computer-knowledgeable, coupled with a well-trained, computer-oriented specialist, with both free to do much or most of their work alone.

o <u>Role of Computers</u>: For computer-related problems, computers were rated as more important than the team, management, others, and more important than documentation and other resources. Computer services were second in importance only to the impact of the individual for reported problems. Computers were reported as generally essential for problem solutions, even though hardware and software were often inadequate for satisfactory solutions. This led to deeply ambivalent attitudes of dependency and frustration toward computer services for all levels of computer professionals and computer users. Respondents

typically used computers because problems could not be handled
manually - they had no other choice even though good computer
solutions were rarely available for most reported problems.

o Procrustean Computer Problem Solving: In many cases, virtually
  total dependence of the problem solver on the computer system
  and its software led to marginal or unsatisfactory problem
  solutions, with procrustean consequences. Dissatisfaction
  with computer solutions was the rule, not the exception. A
  hypothesized long-term psychological effect is computer tunnel
  vision, where human solution space is progressively narrowed
  into the block universe of available hardware and software.

o Push-Pull Insight: Initial evidence was obtained for a
  preliminary 'push-pull' theory of insight. Most reported
  insight occurred either during active, deliberate exploration
  and testing of data (pushing the problem), or as a reaction
  to a problem anomaly (eg. errors or difficulties) that had to
  be resolved (being pulled by the problem). Pushing is planned
  and expected, whereas pulling is disruptive and unexpected, and
  is particularly prominent with computer system feedback.

o Pattern of Computer Usage: Computer assistance is virtually
  nonexistent in early problem-finding and problem-planning
  stages, appears most frequently in later solution-testing
  stages, and contributes substantively to major problem insight.

o Proselytizing Impact of Computers: Application of computers
  to real-world problems in the job setting apparently leads to
  progressively more favorable attitudes toward computers,
  despite procrustean computer systems, resulting in a net
  proselytizing effect with increasing use.

o New Class of Problems: Computer-related problems tend to
  represent a new class of manually 'unthinkable' problems
  (quantitatively and qualitatively).

o Problem Structure: Larger problems (longer, more people, more
  resources) show greater formal structure, more problem-solving
  stages, and more specialized division of labor than 'smaller'
  problems.

o Nine-Stage Model: Response to the nine-stage model of problem
  solving was favorable - most reported problems were rated 'good'
  or better in fitting the proposed model, with team problems
  providing a better fit than individual problems. The proposed
  nine-stage model fit reported problems significantly better
  than alternative two-, four-, and seven-stage models drawn
  from the literature. The nine stages exhibited consistently
  significant statistical reliability against a great variety
  of behavioral measures in the problem questionnaire.

Subsequent to the publication and dissemination of the pilot study, a presentation by Garvey at the August 1973 NATO Institute of Information Science at Aberystwyth, Wales, indicated similar stages of problem solving for scientific research. Garvey performed an extensive series of studies for NSF from 1966 to 1971 (see Garvey et al. 1972a,b,c,d) on the information-exchange activities of over 12,000 scientists and engineers. He developed an 11 stage model of scientific problem solving from his data that matches fairly closely to the nine-stage model investigated in our study.

3. OBJECTIVES AND EXPECTED BENEFITS

The aims and expected contribution of our research programme may be listed as follows.

1. Develop a theory of man-computer problem solving based on the conception of problem solving as a special type of real-time information system proceeding through characteristic behavioral stages that converge toward system solution.

2. Develop, test, and extend the methodology associated with the theory to incorporate direct real-world experimentation in natural man-machine problem solving in research settings.

3. Contribute to the basic behavioral literature on human problem solving in four key areas: (a) real-world problems, (b) computer-aided problem solving, (c) problem solving as a manifestation of directed real-time information systems, and (d) real-world experimentation.

4. Use the theoretical framework to generate leading hypotheses and point up key research areas for more responsive and more effective man-computer problem solving.

5. The long-term benefits of a successful theory could lead to improved computer systems, more selective computer reinforcement of creative individual behaviors, a closer match between definitive stages of problem solving and associated software, optimization of individual roles in man-computer problem teams, more responsive computer programming for unexpected changes in problem requirements, a closer fit between computer services and personal job incentives, and more effective computer-aided problem solving through enhanced computer readiness for larger segments of the general population.

4. PRELIMINARY THEORETICAL CONCEPTS

The intent of this section is to provide a very brief orientation of the proposed work toward a theory of man-computer problem solving. Since the theory is still embryonic, this sketch is highly tentative. Precursors of the proposed theory may be found in the author's books on computers and society (Sackman, 1967), man-computer problem-solving (Sackman, 1970), and online planning (Sackman and Citrenbaum, eds., 1972).

By way of initial definitions provided by the above and current work, the concepts of 'real-time', 'problem', and 'problem-solving system' are defined.

Real time refers to (1) the chronological sequence, duration, conditions and dynamics of system events, and (2) in solving a problem, a speed sufficient to arrive at a solution, within the constraints of available time and resources. This emphasis on a real-time approach is based, in part, on the belief that time is a crucial resource in problem solving, often drastically shaping the range of real and feasible options available to the problem solver, a resource that has often been underplayed and neglected in the problem solving literature.

The heart of the theory starts with a fresh look at the definition and concept of a problem. Skinner (1969) points out that all behavior is to some extent problematic, and that the definition of problems should avoid the fallacy of being coextensive with behavior broadly considered. A traditional definition of problem is provided by Newell and Simon (1972): "A person is confronted with a problem when he wants something and does not know immediately what series of actions he can perform to get it" (p. 72).

Somewhat later, in the same text, they develop a more precise definition for what they call a "well-defined problem" which is described as follows: "... if a test exists, performable by the system, that will determine whether an object proposed as a solution is in fact a solution" (p. 73). This definition moves closer to the proposed theory in presupposing a systems setting and in specifying a system performance criterion. This improved definition, however, falls short of present theoretical objectives – principally in not tying testing to a real-time system setting, and in not being amenable to ill-structured problems characteristic of real-world situations where solutions are partial and open-ended.

The tentative definition of a problem for the proposed theory is as follows:

> A problem refers to the existence of an initial real-time system state where the attainment of a specified system goal, defined as a desired system state, is not quickly or easily achievable through routine or habitual system procedures.

The notion of a real-world problem refers to operational definitions of working problems in the natural, real-time environment of the problem-solver. In the current project, where the focus is primarily on research problems, we refer to the 10 operational guidelines listed earlier, serving as instructions for subjects in selecting problems to be reported on their questionnaires. Other studies, for different classes of problems, and for different objectives, would require correspondingly different operational guidelines.

A problem that is engaged by a problem solver is viewed as a problem-solving system, which is an evolving real-time information system consisting of two components: (1) the problem-solver who acts upon and tests changes in (2) the problem environment, for convergence through demonstrable problem stages toward a solution, or desired system state. The problem-solving system includes the people, hardware, software, communications, facilities, and other resources organised to achieve the desired solution for the target problem. The problem environment refers to the field in which problem-solving events take place.

The concept of man-computer problem solving as a manifestation of real-time man-machine systems has great integrative power for the proposed theory in the following respects:

1. Men and computers may be treated as information processors.

2. The division of labour between man and machine and between differential human roles in real time information systems applies with equal force to individual problem solving as opposed to group problem solving, and to small problems as well as to large problems, permitting broad generalizing power.

3. Real-time information systems incorporate the basic decision-making and problem-solving paradigm of: early warning, detection, identification, and control of anomalous events with respect to desired system objectives - a paradigm that is fundamentally consistent with analogous stages of problem solving.

Further elaboration is found in the last section outlining the scope of the theory.

5.   TOWARD AN INTEGRATIVE THEORY OF MAN-COMPUTER PROBLEM SOLVING

The proposed theory of man-computer problem solving is intended as a general theory. As such, it will attempt to provide a synthesis of research on man-computer problem solving that the author has performed in a continuing succession of studies over a period of 20 years. Included are methodology and findings of the Rand Systems Research Laboratory in 1953-54, studies in man-computer communication with the SAGE air defense system, online versus off-line problem solving studies with various time-sharing systems, together with the current NSF research. The methodology in theoretical formulation will incorporate highly sophisticated, automated instrumentation such as regenerative recording of real-time man-machine system performance as used in SAGE and in time-sharing systems, semi-automated procedures such as interactive time-sharing protocols with special manual insertions and overrides, and manual techniques such as problem-solving protocols. The synthesis of theoretical findings, as distinguished from methodology, will cover the spectrum of human problem solving in highly computerized real-time systems, (eg. military operators at online CRT consoles), through various forms of online and offline computer utilities, through indirect forms of computer support as with specialized service bureau operations. The initial theory will attempt to span the various classes of users, problems, systems, and problem-solving behaviors, drawing freely from cumulative work over two decades of research in man-computer problem solving.

The current work, with emphasis on real-world problems, with stages of problem solving for macro-theory, and on real-time information systems for micro-theory, represents the cumulative evolutionary framework of the author's thinking in which the proposed theory will be couched. While it would be rash to expect a comprehensive theory in the initial formulation, it is not unreasonable to expect a theory that is sufficiently well-defined for behavioral scientists and computer/information scientists to develop informed opinions about its potential value.

The development of the proposed theory is envisioned to encompass six areas:

1. Philosophical framework.
2. Terms, concepts, and bounds of inquiry.
3. Micro-theory.
4. Macro-theory.
5. Social implications of computers in problem solving.
6. Recommended program of research and application.

Each is briefly described.

1. The philosophical framework will describe basic values and
    assumptions. It will stress historical roots in American
    Pragmatism (eg. Pierce, James and Dewey) with its insistence
    on testing the utility of propositions by their consequences
    in practice. This is the nub of a real-time approach to
    analyses of human and machine behaviors in problem environments.

2. Some of the terms and concepts have been outlined earlier in the discussion of theoretical concepts. Key concepts will be described within qualifying bounds of inquiry. The distinctions between computer-aided and non-computer problem solving, and the focus on real-world problem solving will receive special attention. This segment will also be concerned with experimental methodology and requirements for empirical validation, including techniques used in these studies and promising procedures gleaned from the literature with emphasis on computerized instrumentation in research settings.

3. Micro-theory is concerned with on-the-spot transactional problem-solving programs and procedures of men and/or machines. An example is the interactive man-computer protocol in an online session at a typewriter or CRT console where the protocol consists of messages to and from the computer, systematic introspective comments and evaluations from the user, audio and video recording of human behavior, and any additional manual or computerized 'step-by-step' data recording of man-machine and system environment behaviors. Such micro-theory attempts to organize and explain behavior in terms of a variety of eclectic concepts: problem-solving objectives, man and machine information-processing programs, genesis of human errors, theory of insight and reinforcement, massed versus spaced timing, whole versus part problem solving, real-time testing procedures, etc. The primary empirical datum for this 'micro-theory' consists of problem-solving protocols and automated instrumentation of computer-aided problem solving.

A particularly powerful technique for automated instrumentation in real-time systems is singled out to illustrate briefly its potential for micro-theory. This is regenerative recording, mentioned earlier, originally developed in the SAGE system. With this technique it became possible to record all digital events in the man-computer interaction and to play these events back in real time for unlimited experimental exploration and manipulation at the leisure of the experimentor.

Figure 1 summarizes the basic operation of regenerative recording and introduces the notion of regenerative mutations. The first row shows the basic digital system flow of inputs-program-outputs. The second row illustrates SAGE examples of a realtime computer run. The third row illustrates direct playback of the referent real-time computer run. The fourth row shows that experimental modifications of inputs or changes in the program system, or both, result in system-atically controlled mutations of the original program outputs. Technical details of regenerative recordings for realtime systems are discussed by Sackman (1967), with extensions of the concept to planning and problem-solving in time-shared systems in Karush (1972).

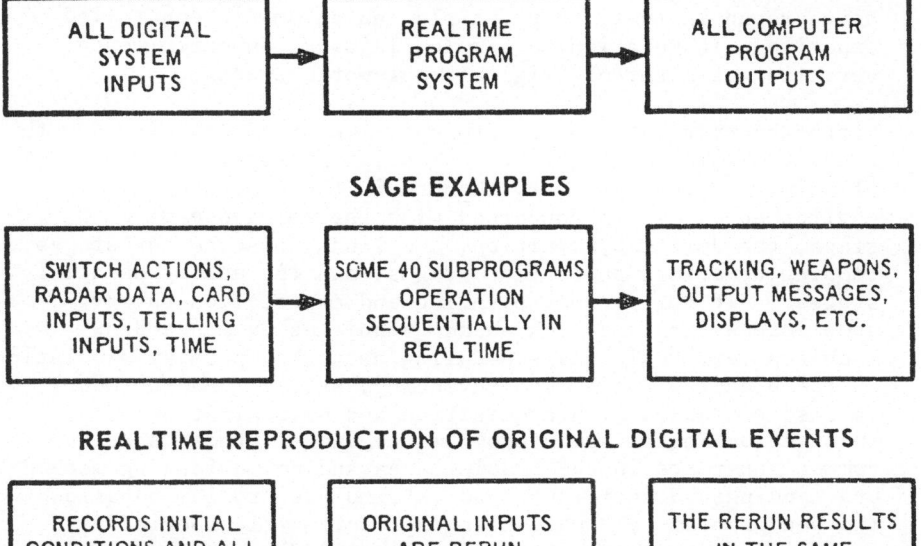

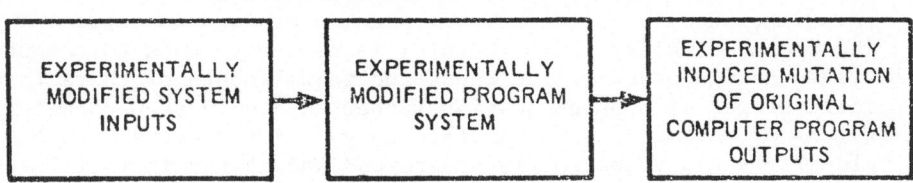

FIGURE 1.   Regenerative Recording

A powerful property of the generalized regenerative mutation
illustrated in Fig. 1 is that it represents a paradigm of
controlled digital experiment.   Program outputs from direct
playback comprise an objective, rigorous standard against
which the experimental changes may be measured.   The modified
inputs or revised portions of the computer program are the
experimental changes, the two main sources of independent
variables.   The unchanged portions of the input and the
unchanged programs are the experimental controls in the
mutation rerun.   The change in outputs is the dependent

variable, or the experimental results of the mutation rerun.
Simple regenerative reruns are direct experimental replications
of real-time digital events. Any modification of a regenerative rerun is thus, in principle, an automatic controlled
experiment in relation to simple playback, an experimental
variation of a set of original real-world events.

4. Macro-theory refers to the broader time sweep associated with
   characteristic stages of problem solving, total problem
   planning, and evolutionary changes in the embedding problem
   environment. It is concerned with the emergence of each
   stage, the duration, fruition, and links to successor stages,
   looping behaviors to earlier stages, and the use of parallel
   stages. It builds upon planning and expectation theory,
   upon forecasting and look-ahead techniques by man and/or
   machines (eg. PERT-like scheduling networks, problem simulations,
   online planning and teleconferencing, etc.). Macro-theory
   is also concerned with acquisition and dissemination of
   information in the human problem community - those sharing
   common interests in the problem area and communicating method
   and findings to anticipate and reformulate problem mutations
   and new problem-solving cycles (eg. scientific speciality
   communities studies by Garvey et al., 1972). Macro-theory
   is not elaborated in further detail here since an extended
   example has been described in the earlier discussion of
   current NSF research on stages of problem solving.

5. Social implications of a real-world theory of man-computer
   problem solving cover a broad domain, but are not intended
   to be amorphously coextensive with computers and society.
   The proposed theory may be helpful in new approaches to computer
   system design based on the needs and requirements of characteristic stages of problem solving rather than on narrow considerations of hardware/software efficiency. For example, problem
   planning seems to be poorly understood and is rarely facilitated
   by computers, according to current data. The early planning
   stages may present a fertile area for new kinds of computer
   assistance.

   The theory may also provide guidelines for tested evolutionary
   computerization of organizational procedures. For example,
   current results have indicated less resistance and more
   favourable attitudes toward computer services when such
   services are applied in the occupational setting, where they
   enhance the importance of the individual and reinforce individual
   job incentives. By the same token, the extension of computer
   services needs to be concerned with negative social effects
   associated with poorly planned computer usage. Force-fitting
   problems into available 'procrustean' software, and the
   abdication of management responsibility to computer technicians,
   are two notable examples uncovered in the current study. Leads
   for more malleable software and for more computer-responsive
   managers may be forthcoming.

The theory should prove helpful in casting some light on the role of computer services in facilitating problem insight and creativity. The timing and patterns of man and machine errors and the types of positive and negative reinforcements provided by computer feedback in problem solving are still largely unknown. The real-time division of labor between man and machine, and the impact of various classes of computer services on the effectiveness of human communication are also largely unknown. Increased computerization may lead to problem-solving behaviors characterized by increasing privatization and a reinforcement of introversive tendencies. Our findings indicate greater introversive tendencies in job behaviors of computer professionals, including lower activity levels in communicating results. The potential social impacts of the proposed theory range from more humanistic software engineering, to new forms of man-to-man and man-computer communication, and to potential long-term individual and group effects.

6. The recommended program of research and application of the proposed theory has been partially anticipated from the above discussion on social implications. The various implicit social hypotheses would need to be made more explicit and experimentally tested in the natural social setting.

The proposed theory will help facilitate real-world experimentation. With the new experience gained from protocol testing, certain key concepts and some new principles of man-computer problem solving would warrant further hypothesis testing. Similarly, new methodological issues arising from these studies might warrant further exploration and development.

It is difficult at this point to discern how the various competing research programs and hypotheses would mesh toward a concluding set of research priorities. It is believed, however, that the theoretical gap in man-computer problem solving would be at least partially bridged; that improved methodologies would be available to study real-world problem solving more effectively via longitudinal and cross-sectional techniques; that an integrated set of research hypotheses would be available concerning positive and negative effects of computer services on problem solving.

EPILOGUE: CONFERENCE FEEDBACK

The presentation of this paper at the conference drew forth extensive commentary from the participants. Seven of the more notable issues have been selected to demonstrate the type of feedback that took place, to note some of the objections raised to this approach to a theory, and fill in some of the gaps in the original version of this paper.

1. Does Human Factors Research have a Significant Impact?
The participants debated whether human factors research has significantly influenced the way computer systems are designed and implemented. Opinions ranged from relatively modest impact to none at all. If human factors work has negligible impact, why bother with a theory of man-computer problem solving? The more optimistic view was that a theory of man-computer problem solving should be a major challenge that could lead to very substantial impact on computer system design and usage. If man-computer interaction professionals do not try to meet such a challenge, perhaps they should give up this field and work in other areas where their work is more acceptable.

2. Is a Special Theory of Man-Computer Problem Solving Needed?
Here the concern is that computer aided problem solving is not really that much different from problem solving without computers. Therefore, why bother with a special theory concerned with computers? The author argued that the evidence is growing that man-computer problem solving is quantitatively and qualitatively different from non-computer problem-solving, and that the differences will become even more pronounced with the advent of mass information utilities and the continuing computerization of society. Refer back, for example, to the unique characteristics of computer problem solving emerging from the National Science Foundation research cited in this paper.

3. Difficulties in Developing a Taxonomy of Problems:
A recurrent obstacle to a generalizable theory of problem solving is the difficulty encountered in developing a useful taxonomy of problems. The difficulty is that what might be experimentally demonstrated for some problems may not hold at all for most other types of problems. With an empirically reliable problem taxonomy, however, the potential for theoretical generalization would be better understood and more systematically explored. Everyone seemed to believe that a credible and definitive taxonomy of problems is a central task facing the development of a theory of man-computer problem solving.

4. Need for Competing Theories: Participants generally concurred that no integrative theory of man-computer problem solving has yet been developed, and that, ideally, not just one, but multiple theories are needed to sharpen the issues and promote more vigorous critical experimentation.

5.   Role of Laboratory Experimentation: The author was criticized for over-promoting 'real-world' experimentation and seemingly excluding pure research and laboratory experimentation from a theory of man-computer problem solving in his presentation. The author indicated that real-world experimentation is a very new and largely untried approach, still in its infancy, and in great need of development on all sides. It was agreed, by most participants, that both approaches are needed and have their proper role in contributing to the continuing development of a theory of man-computer problem solving.

6.   Controversy over the Role of Information and Computer Specialists: There were differences in opinion among the participants as to whether users should be directly coupled to computers or whether they should get information services (including problem solving services) from a middle-man or intermediary who handles the direct interaction with computers. The author mentioned that the NSF studies reported in this paper show a definite trend toward increased specialization in the division of problem-solving labor, with growing use of computer specialists associated with more successful problem solutions. Further discussion brought out the economy in user time and effort when the services of knowledgeable and effective middlemen are available. Although it was agreed that direct interaction between the problem solver and his computer services depended on the problem situation, there was no apparent resolution of the general issue. The main benefit of this discussion was in raising the design alternative that the user might be better off, over the long run, in minimizing direct interaction with diverse computer services for improved problem solving. This runs contrary to the prevailing traditional opinion that more man-computer interaction is inherently positively correlated with more successful problem solutions.

7.   Philosophical Directions: The presentation featured greater emphasis on philosophical issues than is the case in this paper. Generally speaking, the need to develop explicit philosophical frameworks for a theory of man-computer problem solving was positively received by the conference participants. In particular, increasing cooperation with the citizenry and their elected representatives was viewed as desirable for public computer services, in line with political preferences of the community receiving such services. The widespread use of computers in mass information utilities raises major issues for a suitable public philosophy in system objectives, management, design and implementation, with major implications for a social theory of man-computer problem solving.

450

REFERENCES

| | 1963 | AFADA programing systems evaluation. Unpublished report by Air Force Assistant for Data Automation, 11 September. |

Barmack, J.E. & Sinaiko, H.W. 1966 Human factors problems in computer-generated graphic displays. Study S-234, Institute for Defense Analyses, Arlington, Va., U.S.A.

Blackwell, F.W. 1972 The probable state of computer technology by 1980. Journal of Educational Data Processing, 9.1, 12-17.

Bryan, G.E. 1967 JOSS: 20,000 hours at a console - a statistical summary. AFIPS Conference Proceedings, Fall Joint Computer Conference, 31, 679-777.

Carbonell, J.R. 1969 On man-computer interaction: a model and some related issues. IEEE Trans. Systems Science and Cybernetics, SSC-5, 16-26.

Dellas, M. & Gaier, E.I. 1970 Identification of creativity: the individual. Psychological Bulletin, 73.1, 55-73.

DeGreene, K.B. (Ed.) 1970 Systems psychology. New York, McGraw-Hill.

Dewey, J. 1938 Logic: the theory of inquiry. New York, Holt, Reinhart, and Winston.

Dolotta, T.A. 1970 Functional specifications for typewriter-like time-sharing terminals. Computing Surveys, March, 5-29.

Garvey, W.D., Lin, N., Nelson, C.E. & Tomita, K. 1972a,b Research studies in patterns of scientific communication:
I.   General description of research programme.
II. The role of the national meeting in scientific and technical communication.
Inform. Stor. Retr. 8, 111-122 & 159-169.

Garvey, W.D.   1972c,d Research studies in patterns of
  Lin, N. &   scientific communication.
  Tomita, K.   III. Information-exchange processes
                                   associated with the production
                                   of journal articles.
                             IV. The continuity of dissemination
                                   of information by 'Productive
                                   Scientists'.
                             Inform. Stor. Retr., 8, 207-221 & 265-276.

Greenberger, M.   1973   Computer and information networks.
  Aronofsky, J.   Science, 182, 29-35.
  McKenney, J.L. &
  Massy, W.F.

Guilford, J.P.   1967   The nature of human intelligence.
                             New York, McGraw-Hill.

Haefele, J.W.   1962   Creativity and innovation.
                             New York, Reinhold Publishing Corporation.

Harper, R.J.C.   1964   The cognitive processes.
  Anderson, C.C.   Englewood Cliffs, New Jersey,
  Christensen, C.M. &   Prentice Hall.
  Hunka, S.M.

Helmholtz, H.L.F. 1896   Vorträge und Reden.
                             5th Aufl., Braunschweig F. Vieweg.
                                und Sohn, Vol. 1.

Hilgard, E.R. &   1966   Theories of learning, third edition.
  Bower, G.H.   New York, Meredith Publishing Company.

Hutchinson, E.D.   1949   How to think creatively.
                             New York, Abingdon-Cokesbury.

Karush, A.D.   1972   The capture and replay of live computer
                                system operations in online planning.
                             H. Sackman & R.L. Citrenbaum (eds.)
                                pp. 315-365.
                             New Jersey, Prentice-Hall.

Licklider, J.C.R. 1960   Man-computer symbiosis.
                             IRE Transactions on Human Factors in
                                Electronics, 2.1, 4-11.

Mandler, J.M. &   1964   Thinking: from association to Gestalt.
  Mandler, G.   New York, Wiley.

McIsaac, P.V. 1966 Job descriptions and scheduling in the SDC Q-32 time-sharing system. System Development Corporation Report TM-2996, Santa Monica, California.

Miller, R.B. 1969 Archetypes in man-computer problem-solving. Ergonomics, 12, 559-582.

Morrill, C.S. Goodwin, N.C. & Smith, S.L. 1968 User input mode and computer-aided instruction. Human Factors, 10.3, 225-232.

Newell, A. & Simon, H.A. 1972 Human problem solving. Englewood Cliffs, New Jersey, Prentice-Hall.

Nickerson, R.S. 1969 A challenge for human factors research. Ergonomics, 12, 501-518.

Osborn, A. 1957 Applied imagination. New York, Charles Scribner's Sons.

Parsons, H.M. 1972 Man-machine system experiments. Baltimore, Johns Hopkins Press.

Parsons, H.M. 1970 The scope of human factors in computer-based data processing systems. Human Factors, 12.2, 165-176

Pollock, W.T. & Gildner, G.G.G. 1963 Study of computer manual input devices. Project 9678, Task 967801, Technical Documentary Report No. ESD-TDR-63-545, L.G. Hanscom Field, Bedford, Mass.

Raynaud, T.G. 1967 Operational analysis of a computer center. Technical Report No. 32, Operations Research Center, Massachusetts Institute of Technology.

Rossman, J. 1931 The psychology of the inventor. Washington, Inventor's Publishing Co.

Rubey, R.J. 1968 A comparative evaluation of PL/1. Datamation, December, 22-25.

Sackman, H. 1967 Computers, system science, and evolving society. New York, John Wiley & Sons.

Sackman, H.   1970a   Man computer problem solving.
                                 Philadelphia, Auerbach Publishers.

Sackman, H.   1970b   Experimental analysis of man computer
                                 problem solving.
                                 Human Factors, 12.2, 186-202.

Sackman, H.   1971   Mass information utilities and social
                                 excellence.
                                 Philadelphia, Auerbach Publishers.

Sackman, H.   1973   Preliminary investigation of real-world
                                 problem solving with and without
                                 computers.
                                 Honeywell Computer Journal, 7.2, 130-135.

Sackman, H.   1974   Stages of problem solving with and
                                 without computers.
                                 Report R-1490-NSF, The Rand Corporation,
                                 Santa Monica, California.

Sackman, H. &   1974   Studies in real-world problem solving
  Blackwell, F.   with and without computers.
                                 Report R-1492-NSF, The Rand Corporation,
                                 Santa Monica, California.

Sackman, H. &   1972   Online planning.
  Citrenbaum, R.L.   Englewood Cliffs New Jersey, Prentice-
  (eds.)   Hall.

Scherr, A.L.   1967   Analysis of time-shared computer systems.
                                 Monograph No. 36, Cambridge Mass.
                                 The M.I.T. Press.

Seven, M.J.   1971   A study of user behavior in problem-
  Boehm, B.W. &   solving with an interactive computer.
  Watson, R.A.   Report R-513-NASA, The Rand Corporation,
                                 Santa Monica, California.

Shackel, B.   1969   Man-computer interaction: the contri-
                                 bution of the human sciences.
                                 Ergonomics, 12, 485-500.

Shaw, J.W.   1965   JOSS: Experience with an experimental
                                 computing service for users at remote
                                 typewrite consoles.
                                 Report P-3149, The Rand Corporation,
                                 Santa Monica, California.

454

Skinner, B.F.   1969   Contingencies of reinforcement: a
                                theoretical analysis.
                                New York, Appleton-Century-Crofts.

Steiner, G.A.   1969   Top Management Planning.
                                London, Macmillan.

Stetten, K.J. &   1973   A study of the technical and economic
  Volk, J.L.   considerations attendant on the home
                                delivery of instruction and other
                                socially related services via inter-
                                active cable TV: Vol. 1: Introduction
                                and interim summary.
                                Report M72-200, The Mitre Corporation,
                                McLean, Virginia.

Swets, J.A.   1966   Computer-aided instruction in
  Harris, J.R.   perceptual identification.
  McElroy, L.S. &   Behavioral Science, 11, 98-104.
  Rudloe, H.

Totschek, R.A.   1966   An empirical investigation into the
                                behavior of the SDC time-sharing
                                system.
                                Report SP-2191, System Development
                                Corporation, Santa Monica, California.

Wallas, G.   1926   Art of thought.
                                New York, Harcourt Brace.

Weinberg, G.M.   1971   The psychology of computer programing.
                                New York, Van Nostrand Reinhold.

Young, J.W.   1940   Technique for producing ideas.
                                Chicago, Advertising Publications Inc.

PART 8   -   SPECIALIST USERS

PREVIEW

The wide diversity of computer applications of course causes a wide range of potential users.   If the efficiency and accept-ability of MCI is to be improved, then the variability of its users and the extent (or lack) of our knowledge about them should not be misjudged.   There is considerable evidence that different types of user have different types of computer needs, and that one single system cannot easily satisfy all the requirements (eg. Eason, Damodaran & Stewart, 1974 survey).

Again, with the extensive growth of computer applications, it follows that computing professionals are rapidly becoming a minority of users, and the majority come from a wide variety of non-computing disciplines and interests.   Bennett has called them 'discretionary users' and points out the implications for MCI.

These discretionary users work with computers by choice rather than by necessity.   Such people, for example lawyers, doctors, scientists and designers, are specialists and professional in their approach to work and in the kind of work that they do.   But they are not computer professionals, and they must find computers appro-priate to their needs and useful in practice.   They must not be required to have the specialised knowledge familiar to computer professionals.

From their survey, Eason, Damodaran & Stewart similarly distinguish these different professionals as 'specialist users'. They emphasise the contrast between the specialist nature of their work as experts in their own field, and their naivety, at least in the early stages, with regard to computing.   They are likely to learn rapidly how a computer might be able to help them, and how to use it, but equally they are intolerant of difficulties or handicaps in MCI which will waste their time.

This part brings together three papers about various aspects of MCI for specialist users.   Stewart addresses the problem directly of how to improve MCI for specialists.   Bernotat considers the special issue of the skilled control of aircraft by pilots and the implications of automation for this specialist situation. While a decision was made not to include Computer-Aided Design as a specific topic, because it is already an extensive field on its own, this important area is well represented by the third paper; Spence provides an excellent insight into a number of MCI aspects of vital importance for successful computer-aided design.

Stewart explores some of the consequences of introducing computer power to aid the specialist's work. He emphasises the vital importance of both hardware and software matching very closely the needs and expectations of the specialist, eg. in such aspects as layouts of processed data on displays and methods of organising information. He draws attention to the possible risk of relying too much on the computer and so of dealing with, say, 70% of a problem which can easily be handled with computer aid and neglecting the remaining 30%. He identifies different levels of specialist involvement with computer facilities and discusses some of the problems experienced at each level. Finally he suggests methods to help improve the general fit between the computing facility and the tasks of the specialist user.

A different type of specialism is involved for those who exercise high grade sensori-motor skill in the direct control of complex processes, such as some types of on-line chemical plant control or, more familiarly, aicraft piloting. Bernotat discusses various trends and issues inherent in the current development towards automation on the aircraft flightdeck. Computer aids to navigation and autopilot control are already well developed, and the concept of computer mediated control of all flight manoeuvres, with no direct linkage remaining from pilot to aircraft control surfaces, is now being explored. The aspects of task allocation between man and computer, and the importance of an excellent match at the man-machine interface, are particularly considered by Bernotat for this specialised type of MCI.

Spence sets out the essential elements of the process of engineering design and illustrates how the computer may assist. He describes what was first an exploratory tool for studying circuit design, which has now become a very successful design tool (MINNIE). From practical experience with MINNIE, Spence suggests a number of issues that require further study and proposes the need for a major increase in joint research between designers, programmers and human factors people to understand better the MCI aspects of computer aided design.

THE SPECIALIST USER

T.F.M. Stewart

Department of/ Human Sciences,
University of Technology, Loughborough, U.K.

1. THE SPECIALIST AND HIS TASK

The increasing complexity and sophistication of commerce and industry has generated many problems which require detailed and extensive knowledge of specific techniques and disciplines for their solution. In order to solve such problems, industry now employs a wide range of different specialists from financial planners and management scientists to engineering designers and stress analysts. Although these represent a considerable range of different types of people and different types of problem there are two important attributes which characterise them as a group and distinguish them from other groups.

Firstly, specialists need to simplify, quantify and manipulate complex data in order to solve their problems. Although the degree to which quantification is appropriate or even feasible varies enormously from discipline to discipline, such quantification is a necessary part of the process of understanding phenomena and is essential in designing or manufacturing. Also the problems which specialists tackle are in themselves complex and cannot readily be understood without simplification. Thus, for example, in order to determine how much a structure will be deformed by a given loading it is necessary to simplify the structure and the loading to a series of calculations about elementary components (or finite elements). The complex situation is therefore modelled as a series of many simple components. In addition to simplifying the process however, such modelling or simulation techniques also place a considerable computational burden on the specialist. When the computations are performed manually this burden is not only lengthy, error prone and tedious but it also effectively prevents the specialist from considering alternative solutions.

There is a tendency to stick to the first solution that works rather than to explore potentially better alternatives.

Secondly, the specialist operates primarily within one particular discipline or problem area. This means that the specialist has at his disposal a body of knowledge and set of techniques which he can apply to problems referred to him. In many situations only problems which seem to fit within this problem area will be referred to the specialist. Thus problems of analysing stresses in structures are referred to stress analysts and problems of electronic circuit design are referred to circuit designers. It is therefore in the specialists' interests to invest both personally and probably financially in learning new skills and in improving and developing techniques relevant to his discipline. This obvious and apparently straightforward situation does not hold for managers, even those initially trained in similar disciplines to specialists.

The manager does not have problems 'filtered' or referred to anything like the same degree. The production manager cannot ignore his employees grievances because he is not a personnel specialist or ignore faulty equipment because he is not a maintenance engineer. There is therefore little incentive to learn or develop techniques for solving one problem when a similar problem is unlikely to occur again or when the next problem is completely different in nature.

In summary therefore, specialists, although involved in widely differing disciplines and problem areas, have in common a need to handle and manipulate large quantities of complex data and an involvement in, or commitment to, a set of skills and techniques related to one particular problem area. Both these characteristics have in the past favoured the introduction of computer technology into the specialists' job. In many ways, the computer is merely the modern equivalent of the slide rule and log tables familiar to specialists in the past. In fact there are very few specialist areas untouched by computing in some form or another. Some typical specialist computer applications are listed in Figure 1.

The main aim of this paper is to explore some of the consequences of the introduction of computing power into the specialist's job, but first it is necessary to consider what particular demands the specialist's task makes on a computer aid. It is after all the degree to which these task needs are met which determines the impact of a computer system on the way the specialist works.

---

1. Statistical model of economy used by economists for medium and long term forecasting.
2. Structural Analysis system used by design engineers to analyse deflections and stress distributions of 3-D structures subjected to various loads.
3. Mathematical model of transport operation performance used by planners to produce basic data for schedules of vehicle operations.
4. Stress analysis system used by stress engineers to ensure the integrity of new designs and predicted load conditions.
5. Statistical package used by social scientists to analyse and describe questionnaire data.

FIGURE 1. Typical Specialist Applications.

2. TASK NEEDS AND COMPUTER AIDS FOR THE SPECIALIST

The two attributes which characterise specialists as a group result in some specific and exacting task needs which a computer aid must meet or fit.   The need for manipulating quantities of complex data makes demands on the computer software and hardware for inputting, outputting and processing in particular ways. The nature of the specialist's problem area and the structure of his task not only makes demands on the software and hardware but also requires the whole computing service to be organised in particular ways for its operation and development.

2.1 Software and Hardware Needs

2.1.1 Inputting to the computer.   Many specialists use the computer as model building tool to model or simulate complex processes.   For example, a typical specialist problem involves analysing the stresses in a fabricated structure using some simplified finite element model.   Even though such a model is a simplification of the real world, or perhaps because of it, there may be an extremely large volume of data to be entered into the computer before processing can commence.   Specialists therefore require a mode or type of interaction software which allows them not only to enter such data easily but also to monitor and control the accuracy of the entered data.   In addition to entering large quantities of data for new runs of the package, program, model or whatever, specialists also frequently need to explore the effects of small amounts of new data or of changing parts of the data in some way.   Thus, whereas for a sales information system the data represent historical facts, for many specialist systems the data in the program are more often a tentative solution or a proposed

design.   In such cases of course it would be extremely tedious
if the mode of interaction required the re-entry of all data for
each run or iteration of a calculation or model.

Therefore, the specialist has two types of input requirement
- large quantities of initial data and smaller amendments,
modifications and instructions - and these affect the type of
hardware he needs.

Alphanumeric data are normally entered via coding forms and
punched cards or tape in large and small quantities, or preferably
directly on a terminal keyboard in small quantities.   Where the
data are primarily graphic as in engineering drawings they can
be transferred into alphanumeric co-ordinates and entered on
punched cards.   This however is an error prone procedure and some
of the special purpose devices are much more appropriate.   For
large volume entry a co-ordinate digitiser can be used to enter
graphic data directly, and for small volume modifications or
instructions joysticks or light pens can be most effective (see
Figure 2).   There is however still a lack of adequate software
to utilise fully the graphic communication facilities of these
devices, but there are exciting possibilities in this direction.

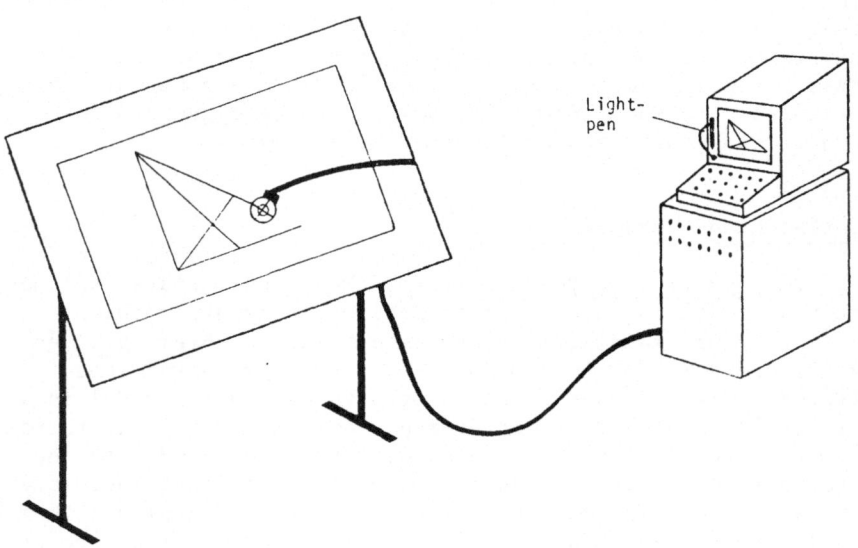

Light-
pen

FIGURE 2.   Sketch of Co-ordinate Digitiser

2.1.2 <u>Receiving output</u>.   The specialists' requirements for output fall into four categories.   Firstly, there is the need to scan the input data to ensure that they are free from errors and anomalies.   This involves presenting a fairly large quantity of data in such a way that oddities are highlighted and can be easily detected.   A good example is a line drawing output of the shape of a structure to be analysed.   A mis-placed co-ordinate is readily spotted as a 'kink' in the drawing but would be next to impossible to spot in a list or table of numerical values (see Figure 3). There is a need therefore to display the input data in a slightly processed form to aid error detection.

The second need is for displaying the results of the processing or output itself.   This may involve displaying or outputting as large or an even larger amount of data than was input or it may involve displaying some highly processed analysis, trend or representation of the data in a small space.

There is, in a sense, a conflict in the needs of the specialist for the output of a model, simulation or calculation. On the one hand he requires precision and detail and on the other hand he needs an overview of the output to provide a context in which to interpret the results.   This conflict is well illustrated in the stress analysis situation mentioned above. In this case, a line drawing produced on a graph plotter can provide a striking and convincing display of the displacement of a structure under a load.   However the stress analyst also needs to know the exact values of the displacements or stresses at particular points and these are frequently made available to him in voluminous printouts.   The integration and combination of

Plotting input X,Y Co-ordinates

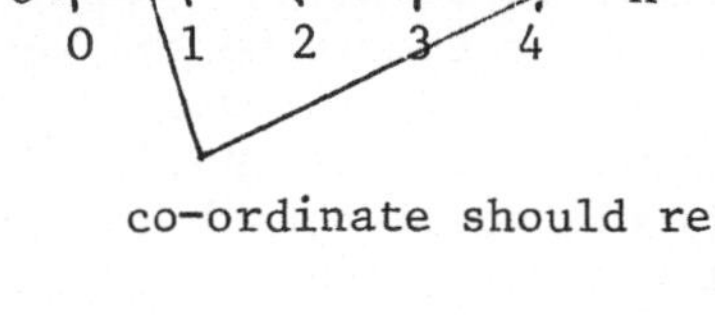

Tabulating input X,Y co-ordinates

X	Y	X	Y	X	Y
1.0	0.0	1.0	1.0	1.0	2.0
0.0	3.0	1.0	4.0	2.0	4.0
3.0	4.0	3.0	3.0	2.0	3.0
2.0	2.0	3.0	2.0	3.0	1.0
2.0	1.0	2.0	0.0	1.0	0.0

co-ordinate should read 1.0 3.0 to make shape of letter F

FIGURE 3.   Data vetting using plots and tabulations of input data.

these two forms of output is both difficult and error prone.

The third and related requirement is for the specialist to be able to scan large volumes of output quickly and easily without necessarily specifying what he is looking for.   This type of 'browsing' activity can be extremely productive and is probably an essential part of the successful problem solving process.   Having identified an area in which he requires more detail the specialist needs to be able to 'home in' on the relevant data and rapidly obtain the detail he requires.

The fourth requirement is that the specialist needs to be able to decide how the data should be presented not only at a general level but also exactly which variables should be presented together or which should be cross tabulated.   In interpreting the output of models, in many cases the most important part of the proceedings, the specialist may wish to vary the way the output is displayed.   This need not involve re-running the model itself but simply interacting with the output in order to explore fully its implications.

He therefore requires displays which allow and encourage this interaction between specialist and data through creating a dialogue between man and computer.

The specialist's task therefore requires output of four types:

1. displays for vetting input data;
2. displays of precise detail and of the general trends with easy interchange between the two;
3. displays for scanning or browsing through output with the facility for 'homing' in on specific data;
4. displays which can be manipulated to vary the way the output is presented.

The four types of output that the specialist needs to review also require different output media or hardware.

For vetting output data the graph plotter and the VDU (refreshable or storage tube) quite adequately provide hard and soft copy respectively, for checking graphical data or a graphical representation of the data.   However for combining the precision of exact values with the context provided by pictures neither these nor any other current device really meets the need. The traditional engineering drawing readily combines pictorial information with exact values and allows for extrapolation or interpolation for missing data.   At present for this and for the 'browsing' and 'homing in' type of display the specialist must use two operations.   The high resolution storage tube comes closest to filling the bill but really needs to be combined with a printer to enable the specialist to have available both precise values and pictorial or graphical information. Hard copy is frequently required in this environment and so a plotter is often needed, although high costs dictate that it has to be a central rather than a local facility.

For interacting with data and manipulating program output the VDU can be quite acceptable provided that the software encourages a true dialogue to develop. Various special input devices (light pens, touch wires) can be used in conjunction with the VDU to make such dialogues even more successful but they are better as supplements to, rather than replacements for, existing keyboards.

2.1.3 <u>Computer processing</u>. The processing required in some of the models or simulations used by specialists can range from relatively simple operations merely repeated a number of times to extremely complex matrix manipulation routines. It is essential for the specialist to know what processing is being undertaken and for him to select or even create the most appropriate processing for particular tasks. Failure to select appropriate processing can lead to invalid operations being performed or at least to sub-optimum output. It is therefore essential that the specialist interacts with the system in such a mode that he can specify the processing in this way (see Figure 4).

In order to create the models or packages to simulate some process, original or novel work needs to be done in program writing or development. Many specialists have learned programming skills themselves to enable them to develop the sophisticated programming necessary to handle their problem. There can be difficulties with this approach leading to the specialist perhaps being side-tracked from his original aim, but

Mode		Information Flow		Choice over	
		to computer	to user	Output	Proc-essing
Data Input for Pre-defined Outputs	DIPO	√	√	√	X
Instructions for Data Processing	IDP	√	√	√√	√
High Level Language Programming	HLLP	√	√	√√√	√√

FIGURE 4. Modes of interaction

this will be discussed in detail later in the paper. Otherwise
this programming mode — typically in a high level language such as
Fortran — can be an extremely powerful and flexible mode for the
specialist problem solver (it is referred to as the High Level
Language Programming mode — HLLP). Once the specialist has evolved
a suitable package or suite of programs there may be no need to
program each time the system is used. Indeed often the program
development is carried out by an advanced team of specialists
whereas the more day-to-day problem solving involves others running
existing models or programs. At this level it is still important
for the specialist to be able to decide exactly how the data are to
be processed. This mode involves the specialist in providing the
instructions for the data processing to the computer (Instructions
for Data Processing mode — IDP).

When the various processing options can be clearly established
in advance and form a set of what are effectively pre-defined
options, then it may be appropriate for the specialist to operate
in a mode where he provides data input for the pre-defined options
or outputs (Data Input for Pre-defined Outputs mode — DIPO).

Increasingly the specialist's task is itself becoming divided
into smaller specialities, and in many cases the problem solving can
become subdivided to the extent that more junior specialists merely
serve to enter the data and run packages in a DIPO mode where the
decision about the appropriateness or otherwise of the processing
has been taken by a more remote superior. This can have drastic
consequences for task performance if the trend is taken too far.

2.1.4. <u>On-line Timesharing versus Batch Processing</u>. In the
previous section various terminals were suggested for the specialist
user. This would seem to imply that on-line time-sharing systems
are preferred for the specialist although the evidence is not nearly
as clear cut as this would indicate. In computing terms, time-
sharing requires a lot of computer time and uses that time ineffic-
iently whereas batch processing requires less computer time and can
use it very efficiently, handling many jobs at once without wasting
central processing time. In users' terms however, timesharing
provides an immediate, flexible and easy to use service, using user
time efficiently, whereas batch processing is inflexible, tedious
to use and wastes user time waiting for output. Unfortunately the
issue is not as simple as these two views. Britton (1970) describes
some of the difficulties of a remote terminal service. In time-
sharing systems, infrequent users or one-off users may find it
impossible to get assistance from overloaded system staff, especially
since this type of computer usage is less easily evened out throughout the day to take advantage of 'offpeak periods'. He also considers the necessary increased expenditure and the physical location
of terminals. This can be quite a problem especially when different
departments are all likely to need to use them. In private

organisations the costing of computer time can be critical. Charging for connect time or CPU time may discourage infrequent users and so deprive them of a useful service whereas no charging may lead to undue wastage. Sackman (1968) found in a review of some studies that, for man-computer problem solving, timesharing takes less man time, roughly balanced in cost by more CPU time, and that users' attitudes favoured timesharing. Probably the most significant finding of the studies he reviewed is the enormous span of individual differences in problem solving performance.

Adams and Cohen (1969) have compared timesharing and 'instant' batch processing, with eight subjects on a programming course. Their objective measures show no advantage for either method, partly because of the large individual differences between the subjects, but they reported that the students preferred the instant batch system and continued to use it for the rest of the training period, even though both were equally available. However, the validity of and inferences from these subjective results must be viewed with caution, because of major differences in performance and facilities between the two computer systems; the timesharing one was the standard General Electric telephone service, and the batch processor was the 'in house' C.D.C. 6600 machine with an on-line plotter also available.

The most comprehensive analysis comes again from Sackman (1970) who has reviewed the area in considerable detail. He has also used a large number of students as subjects in experiments to compare batch processing and timesharing for problem solving tasks. He concludes fairly strongly that timesharing is better for problem solving tasks but that for many routine tasks batch processing can be more efficient and is certainly cheaper in computer costs. However his conclusions are based more on subject preferences than on objective performance measures.

In fact it is only part of the problem solving process for which an on-line system seems best. Clearly, for example, entering large quantities of data on-line is a gross waste of both computer and human resources. Indeed it may frustrate the user by placing more emphasis on speed than accuracy than is appropriate at this point in the process. On the other hand, the dialogue necessary between a user and the output of his model cannot be ideal unless the two parties are in direct contact with an appropriately short response delay.

It is therefore suggested that the 'best' system for man-computer problem solving probably has elements of both types of processing within it, especially since economic constraints are often real and justified. In practice the difference which does matter to the specialist is whether he can sit at a terminal and type in a few commands to modify a program and collect the output either then or after a cup of coffee, or whether the process takes up to two days and involves shuffling boxes of cards and endless feet of printout.

2.2   Task Structure Needs

It was stated earlier that one of the features which characterised specialists as a group was that they solved problems within
an area sufficiently well defined or compact to justify investing
effort and money into techniques and computer aids.   While this
may be true for individual specialists, it is an over simplification
for specialist departments or groups in an organisation or especially
in an industry.   In fact specialists' problems often change, as
for example new materials are developed or new regulations come
into effect.

2.2.1   The changing nature of the specialist's task.   The
techniques, aids and tools used are also changing and being replaced
as developments take place or as they become less relevant to the
changing task needs.   This development can be illustrated by
considering the diagram in Figure 5.   There is a period where the

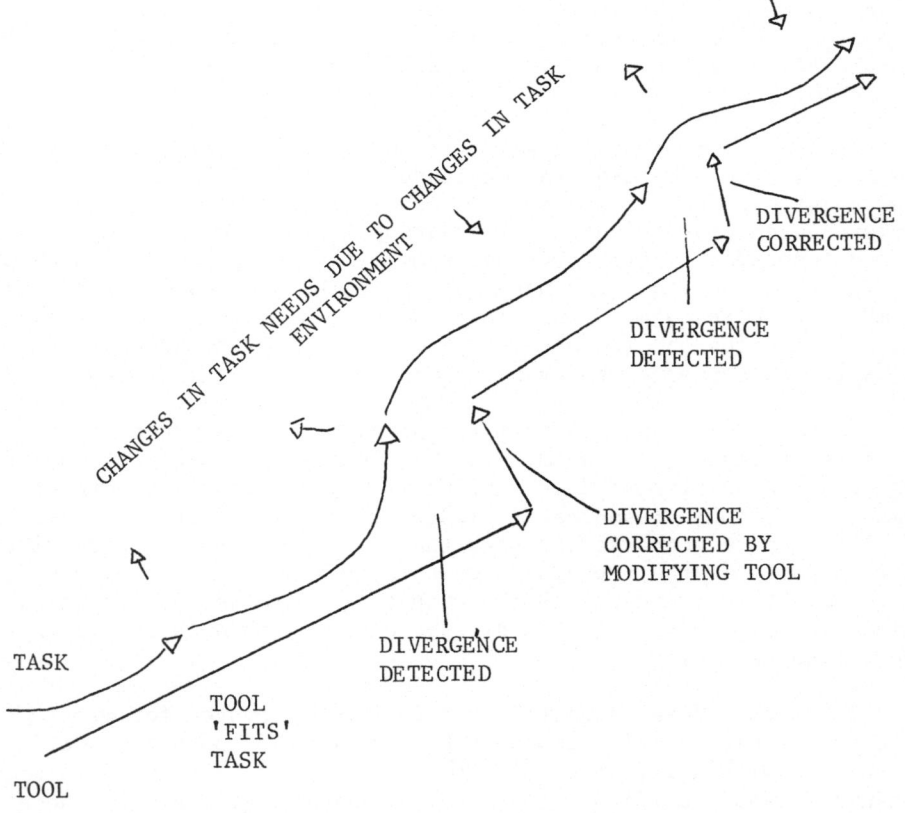

FIGURE 5.   Task Changes and Tool Changes

tool fits the task followed by a gradual change in the task (with consequent divergence between task and tool) until a critical point is reached when the tool can be modified to suit the changed task. There are a number of specific problems which can occur in this area.

People generally are poor at detecting gradual changes and specialists are no exception. There may be a sizeable delay between serious divergence developing between task and tool and this being detected and more problematically identified as such by the specialist. In fact in specialist departments where the job is highly fragmented there may be no one person in a position to detect such a divergence, and it may require a major failure or set-back to highlight the inadequacy of existing tools or techniques.

Even when a divergence is detected however there may not necessarily be an immediate change in the tool for the following four reasons.

1. Modifying tools takes time and effort and these may not be available to be spent on what may be seen by some as an unnecessary refinement.

2. Even if tool modification is approved it may not be technically feasible or possible within the limits of existing knowledge (or existing experience within the organisation) and research or other external advice or consultancy may be essential.

3. Modification may not be sufficient and so new tools may need to be redesigned or purchased which may well have considerable ramifications for other specialists or other departments not previously considered.

4. Modification may be feasible and sufficient but may require such far reaching changes for the specialists or for others that the upheaval of changing the tool is rejected until the divergence reaches some more critical point.

Even if all these hurdles are successfully overcome and a tool modification is authorised, feasible, sufficient and justified, it will still take time to develop, implement and fully de-bug the modified tool. By this time the task may have changed again and so a virtually constant process evolves with tool development as a full-time on-going activity.

Unfortunately the need for continuous development often leads to the formation of a team or sub-department solely concerned with technique or tool development and this serves to fragment the specialist's job. This can have far reaching consequences for the individual and these are discussed later in section 5.2.

The specialist therefore requires a computer aid or tool which can readily be modified to keep pace with a changing task environment. However major changes will usually be sufficiently infrequent to justify substantial development and the specialist is likely to allocate considerable effort, money and other resources to this end.

2.2.2 <u>The uniqueness of the specialist's task</u>. In addition to task variation over time, the specialist's task also varies from specialist department to department. This is due partly to the style or 'flavour' which an individual brings to his problem solving but mainly to the uniqueness of each department's or organisation's problems. Thus although stress analysts in one organisation may have much in common with their counterparts in another organisation, there are still likely to be sizeable and significant differences in their task needs. These differences mean that standard stress analysis computer program suites or packages need tailoring to individual requirements.

Special purpose software may also be necessary to extend or develop existing packages to deal with more complex task requirements or to incorporate some new theoretical advance. In fact many specialists work at the 'frontiers' of technical development and advanced thinking in their own field, and this can involve substantial software development.

Most specialists have at least a 'smattering' or more usually nowadays a working knowledge of some high level programming language such as Fortran. This is usually sufficient to understand roughly how the system works and to carry out minor modifications or enhancements themselves. When a major revision, enhancement or development is required, the specialist is faced with a choice (in theory at least although individual circumstances may dictate the outcome). On the one hand he can learn more programming and write the software himself, or on the other he can employ a full-time professional programmer to write it for him. Both these courses of action can result in sub-optimum solutions.

The specialist has little difficulty learning computer programming. The numeracy and logical thinking required in programming are second nature to most specialists and it is quite likely that they can become profficient programmers. However, since the problem was initially complex then a fairly high degree of software sophistication may be needed and this can take time. The main difficulty which can arise is that computer programming is an attractive pursuit offering fairly frequent and immediate feedback on performance. This can both seduce the specialist from his original problem area and encourage him to neglect alternative non-computer amenable approaches to his problem.

Indeed in section 3 this tendency is examined as one of the causes of the high task fit experienced by HLLP users. It is argued that the fit results from modification of the task to suit the system rather than vice versa.

If on the other hand the specialist employs a professional programmer to work on the software, then the specialist can concentrate on the task aspects and not be side tracked. However a close working relationship with free two-way communication is necessary, so that the objectives and assumptions of the programmer match those of the specialist.

This is far from easy and, in rigidly defined organisations with all computer expertise centralised in one department, may even be impossible to realise. Once the specialist is removed from a detailed knowledge of the assumptions underlying the system then he cannot use it appropriately or exploit it fully.

A compromise between these two extremes is necessary and this is discussed further in section 5.

3. THE IMPACT OF COMPUTERS ON THE SPECIALIST'S TASK

There are a number of ways in which a computer system's impact may be evaluated. It is possible, for example, to consider whether the computer provides an easy to use tool for the specialist since it is the ease of use of computers which is crucial to its success or otherwise in a number of applications. Alternatively the training requirements a system imposes may be assessed and related to the user or potential users capacity for learning or availability for training. However, with specialists it is neither of these two areas which is most important; instead it is the degree to which the computer aid fits the user's task needs which determine the successfulness of its impact. Specialists are usually prepared to devote time and effort to learning how to use a new tool provided that it offers them exactly the facilities they require. In this section of the paper, therefore some evidence of the degree to which specialists experience task fit problems will be discussed. The evidence comes primarily from a major survey of Man-Computer Interaction in Commercial Applications (MICA) by Eason, Damodaran and Stewart (1974). Approximately 70 of the 250 users who were interviewed in the survey were classified as specialists. In this survey, a task fit index was computed for each user. This measure was simply the proportion (expressed as a percentage) of task fit issues, such as the timeliness or accuracy of the information provided, which the user found satisfactory.

In general, most specialists experienced a relatively high task fit for all modes of interaction but the reasons for this differ for the different types.

3.1 Data Input for Predefined Outputs (DIPO)

DIPO specialists experienced a high fit between their task and the service provided by the computer system (task fit index = 72%). This fit could be attributed to three main factors:-

1) The DIPO job is virtually defined by the system.
2) The system designer can easily identify the task needs.
3) The DIPO specialists work hard to ensure a fit.

3.1.1 The DIPO job is virtually defined by the system.

Firstly the DUPO specialist is only really involved in part of the problem solving process. The initial decision about how to tackle the problem or even what the problem actually involves is usually taken at a more senior level and so a large part of the problem solving process – the initial formulation stage – has been solved or at least decided before reaching the DIPO specialist. In consequence the job of the DIPO specialist has frequently been prescribed by the requirements of the computer procedure used. His job is to fit the problem into the standard 'mould' and apply semi-routine techniques until the problem is solved. If necessary the DIPO job can virtually be designed to suit the system and require the human to undertake the parts of the process which the computer cannot perform itself.

3.1.2 The system designer can easily identify the task needs.

Secondly the designer of the system (either a programmer or a more senior specialist) can easily identify the task needs since the task is relatively well defined and constrained. It is therefore possible to ensure that where necessary or appropriate the system is designed to fit the user. For example, in the MICA survey, DIPO specialists were less likely to suffer from irrelevant information or unnecessary computer produced diagnostics, housekeeping or administrative output. Similarly they were less likely to need to do extra work on the computer output before they could use it and suffered fewer problems as a result of system breakdowns.

3.1.3 DIPO specialists work hard to ensure fit.

Thirdly and finally, DIPO specialists on the whole work very hard to ensure that the system fits their needs. For example, they suffer few problems due to inaccurate data but only because they devote considerable effort to its preparation and vetting. In fact, although most systems had removed a considerable amount of drudgery from the specialist's job by relieving him of repetitious and tedious calculations, many had introduced the equally repetitious tedious drudgery of data preparation. This was just as true for on-line terminal users as for the others since in most cases such data were entered on punched cards as a batch job. Where significant improvements were found, they arose because data could be directly entered into the system, feeding source documents through OMS/OCR (optical mark sensing/optical character recognition) machines or using co-ordinate digitisers.

Similarly DIPO specialists could overcome inadequacies in the
system in providing complete information by integrating and
collating graphical and alphanumeric output manually. This could
be an extraordinarily tedious job involving poring over voluminous
printouts and annotating detailed plotter drawings.

The high task fit experienced by DIPO users is therefore a
result of the way the job is defined, its relatively structured and
routine nature and sheer hard work on the part of the users. The
fit is not however so high that no problems occur.

3.1.4 <u>Problems.</u> One of the most significant task fit problems
for DIPO specialists is also present for other types of user and
therefore is discussed in a number of places in this paper. The
DIPO specialist due partly to his relatively lowly position in the
organisational hierarchy, is less likely to have been involved in
developing the system and so may not fully appreciate some of the
limitations and assumptions it embodies. Therefore in moulding
the problem to suit the system he can, unless properly supervised,
bend the problem too far. The output of the system is therefore
limited in its accuracy not just by the conscientiousness with
which the data were prepared and entered but also by the
applicability and appropriateness of that particular model of the
problem. This may best be illustrated by the example of the
student (or the professional) scientist using a statistics package
to analyse his data. He enters the data and receives predefined
outputs, namely the results of the various tests. It is quite
feasible to run such packages on totally inappropriate data and it
is by no means obvious that such a gross error has been committed
(see Figure 6). Few packages are equipped to prevent such mis-use
and in fact once nominal questionnaire items like "sex of respondent"
have been converted to numeric values, it is quite easy to obtain
such odd results as "average" or "mean" sex.

3.2 Instructions for Data Processing (IDP)

IDP specialists also experience a high task fit but for a
slightly different reason. IDP specialists were frequently
involved in the design of the system or had designed it themselves.
Once the system was designed and operational then the choice of
processing options was sufficient to enable the specialist to solve
his problems without resorting to programming. In addition IDP
specialists also have to work hard to ensure and maintain their
high task fit.

QUESTIONNAIRE ANALYSIS PROGRAMME 102

FILE: VDU USERS SURVEY
ANAL: DESCRIPTIVE STATISTICS
QUES: 04 : SEX

VAR. SEX OF RESPONDENTS

VALUE	LABEL	No.	%
1	MALE	193	47.18
2	FEMALE	216	52.81
	TOTAL	409	100%

MEAN VALUE = 1.53

FIGURE 6.   Example of failing to appreciate the assumptions behind
a computer package.

In fact the main problem for them concerned the degree of
extra work necessary to make the output from the computer fully
usable.   It may not be easy to distinguish these extra
activities from the rest of the job since the computer output
forms such an integral part of the problem solving process.
However much of this work resulted from using standard procedures
or packages for non-standard problems.   Even within a system
written by or for a particular specialist there are often cases
where some modification or adaptation is required.

On the other hand the IDP mode is in many ways the ideal
form of interaction for specialists.   It does not imply an
excessive routine content or standardisation of the work and
within it a considerable degree of flexibility is possible.
This mode is suitable both for users of on-line terminals and of
batch processing, although it may be difficult to reach a high
degree of man-machine co-ordination with the delays inherent in
most batch processing applications.

IDP mode is also the normal mode for specialists who occasionally are obliged to take up programming in order to resolve some particular difficulty or to incorporate some added refinement. Few specialists spend all their time developing the system and those that do often 'suffer the consequences' as the next section will discuss. The IDP mode therefore is usually highly satisfactory for specialists, but when problems change or do not quite fit the existing system (be it a standard package or an in-house development) then most specialists turn to high level language programming.

3.3 High Level Language Programming (HLLP)

In some ways HLLP mode represents the peak of specialist computer use. Certainly, according to the computer professionals, most users suffer from insufficient knowledge of computers and if they only could write their own program utopia would be in sight. Unfortunately the picture is not nearly as rosy as that would imply.

HLLP specialists do experience a high task fit whether they use on-line terminals or batch processing systems but the reasons for this reveal two opposing forces neither of which is especially favourable to the specialist.

1. Most HLLP specialists were or are involved in designing the system they use. Despite this (or perhaps because of it) they suffer specific task fit problems of relevance and reliability.
2. HLLP specialists may modify their tasks to fit the system.

Most HLLP specialists were or are currently involved in designing the system they use. Since they understand at least the rudiments of computing and programming they are in a good position to communicate effectively with computer professionals and make their needs understood. Being seen to have some computer competence also encourages the programmers to try ideas out on them - a particularly fruitful way of influencing a design at the early stages.

3.3.1 Problems. However, since the HLLP specialist is actually writing and running programs, it is more difficult and sometimes impossible for computer personnel to protect him from aspects of the system which do not contribute towards solving his problem. Thus although the IDP specialist can perhaps make 'crazy' input errors and merely be politely admonished, the HLLP specialist has little safety margin. It is relatively easy for him to produce errors which cause the operating system to display what may to him be unintelligable gibberish. Additionally, the HLLP specialist may use general purpose packages which have far

474

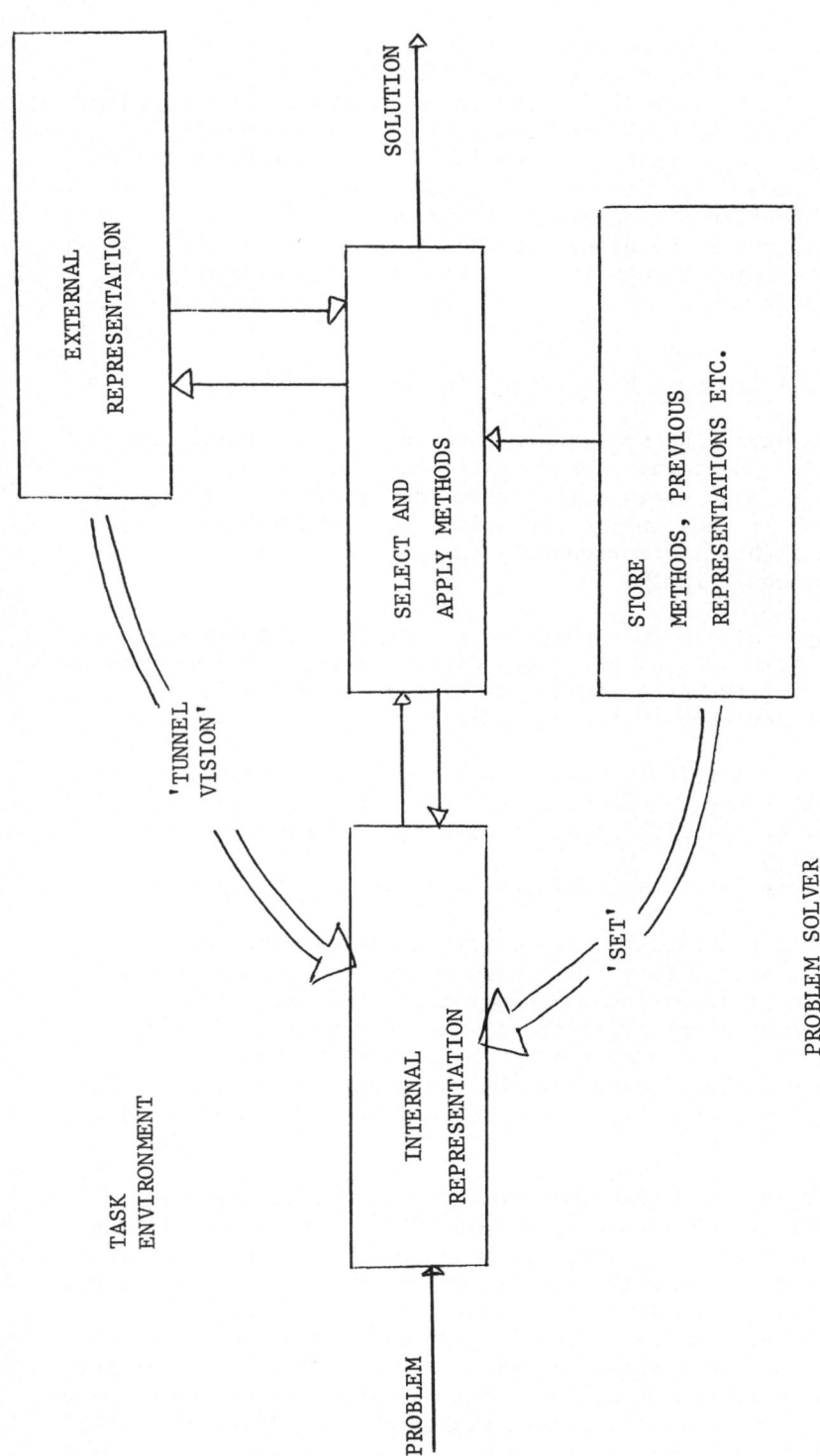

FIGURE 7. 'Blocking' in the problem solving process.

more flexibility than he needs, and so he may have to accept the redundancy which such flexibility demands.

HLLP specialists are also more likely to use computer systems directly and therefore do not have others to protect them from system administration and control information. They consequently suffer from additional irrelevant information and output. They are also more likely to suffer difficulties when breakdowns occur. This is partly due to their greater frequency of use of systems and hence they are more likely to be using a system when it malfunctions. It is also due to their greater dependence on the facilities of the computer system itself rather than on a set of output results.

3.3.2 Task modification. The second factor behind the HLLP specialist's high task fit is by far the most important and far reaching. There was some evidence from the MICA survey that HLLP specialists (and to an extent the others) tend to modify their tasks to fit the computer system.

To a degree this is both necessary and useful. It is an extremely economic form of problem solving if a new problem can be reformulated or 'bent' to allow a previous technique or solution generating method to be applied. However there is a limit and beyond this there is a real danger that the solution to the new problem will be far from optimal.

To understand how this can occur it is necessary to look at the problem solving process itself.

The problem solving process starts with the problem solver forming an internal representation of the problem (Newell and Simon, 1972). If he is to use a tool or aid he has to form what might be called an external representation of the problem or a statement of the problem in terms which are appropriate to the tools at his disposal (see Figure 7).

There are two ways in which the specialist can be blocked from forming the most appropriate representation of his problem. Firstly, the specialist may experience a psychological 'set' which leads him to see a new problem as similar to problems he has solved in the past and encourages him to try to force it into an existing 'mould'. Secondly, his commitment both personal and probably financial to the computer system he has developed can create a set which leads him to overlook and not even consider representations of the problem which may not be amenable to his system (computer tunnel vision in Sackman's terms). For example, many specialists use finite element techniques which may neither be best nor valid for their problems without ever consciously questionning this assumption.

These two forces can combine to block the ideal
representation process and can lead the specialist to at best sub
optimum and at worst inappropriate problem formulations and
solutions.

This difficulty can be magnified when, as often happens, the
specialist has a degree of choice over the problems he tackles.
In this situation he will be under considerable pressure both
conscious and unconscious to choose only to tackle problems for
which he has ready-made or nearly made tools. There is a
considerable quantity of largely anecdotal evidence that this
happens frequently, and in the long term it could have a
disastrous affect on the effectiveness of the problem solving.
For example, designing a questionnaire solely on the criterion
that it should be easy and convenient to analyse using the SPSS
package may make it wholly inappropriate for the people who have
to complete it. Once the data have been collected however, this
fact will not emerge and is likely to be concealed forever once
the analyses start to emerge from the system.

A factor which can make this process even more likely is that
programming (as mentioned earlier) is an intellectually attractive
pursuit. Many specialists admit to, and even more are betrayed
by their colleagues as, being seduced by programming and
ultimately becoming more programmer than specialist (in their
original field). With this in mind, problems and solutions
are even more likely to be selected for their computer
compatibility and the elegance of the programming they involve.

4. SOLUTIONS TO THE TASK FIT PROBLEM

4.1 Set-breaking Solutions

The task fit difficulties experienced by specialists are
quite different from those experienced by other users and the
remedies are correspondingly different. Rather than try to
encourage, say, the manager to use the computer by making its
facilities more relevant and attractive, we have to stop the
specialist from finding the computer too attractive. This is
not as straightforward as it might seem. Modifying or re-
framing a new problem to fit an existing computer-based tool is
not in itself wrong. In fact it can be a highly efficient and
successful strategy which provides a different perspective on a
problem and can facilitate its solution.

What is necessary therefore is some kind of monitor to
ensure that the problem is not 'bent' too much by the
specialist. It is relatively easy to ensure that the specialist
does not consciously distort problems inappropriately, although in

environments where the problem solving process is fragmented and
routinised this can be more difficult.   With a suitably organised
structure of supervision and management it is possible for more
senior specialists to monitor the activities of their sections
or whatever to ensure that no such distortions lead to
inappropriate problem solutions.

There are still, however, the unconscious processes of
psychological set or computer tunnel vision which can lead to
problems being tackled inappropriately, and the remedy for these
is more difficult to establish.   The literature on psychological
set tends to be more concerned with the strength of the process
rather than with ways of breaking set, but several set breaking
techniques have been proposed or described.

The majority of set-breaking techniques are concerned with
diverting the individual from his set to a known better solution
and are dependent on the characteristics of that known better
solution.   Thus, instructions at the beginning of a problem may
break set by hinting at a better way of solving the problem; an
external agency or person may intervene when the problem solver
embarks on a set solution; or the difference in effectiveness or
the quality of the set and non-set solution may be increased to
the point that the set is broken.

None of these or allied techniques are applicable to the real
life problem solving of specialist computer users where it would
be necessary to be able to break set without necessarily knowing
either what the non-set solution is or even whether it would in
fact be better.   Any set breaking technique for this application
would therefore involve analysing the individual's problem solving
process directly as it developed and then exploring potential
'set' areas.

As a first attempt at developing a set breaking technique the
author is planning a series of experiments aimed at creating
situations which encourage the problem solver to 'stop and think'
at appropriate points in the process.   There are two components
to this type of monitoring activity and both are probably critical.
The first is that the problem solver must 'stop' and the second
that he must 'think'.   This means that instead of tackling a
problem, deciding on a possible solution and then working rapidly
through testing it, the problem solver must deliberately stop
at some critical part or parts of the process and switch to a
monitoring or review mode of thinking.   This thinking should not
just follow the vertical or logical path dictated by the process
up to that point, but should attempt to be lateral or creative in
generating alternative perspectives of the problem and alternative
approaches.   There are relatively few techniques which are
successful in stimulating lateral or creative thinking in this

context, but it is hoped that a modification of the Kelly (Kelly, 1955)
Repertory Grid technique may lead to more imaginative solutions.
This would involve the problem solver in a dialogue with the
experimenter, in which the problem solver is led to analyse
systematically the problem solving process and by examining its
components in detail to generate possible alternative strategies
which he could have used.   The problem solver would then be led
to compare and contrast these alternative strategies with the
existing one and to adjust the existing approach as necessary.

The development of psychological set can of course result from
the continued use of any tool.   Computer aids are especially
interesting, not just because the greater sophistication can make
the set more complex and perhaps more disastrous but also because
the computer has the potential within it to overcome this
limitation through the virtually automatic use of some kind of set
breaking routine.   The type of dialogue envisaged between the
experimenter and the subject described above could be embodied
within the computer problem solving aid itself and provide a
powerful set breaking facility as an integral part of the package.

More complex set-breaking techniques could involve the
computer itself carrying out some of the monitoring of the task
rather than depending entirely on prompting the user himself.
Such monitoring would seem to involve more sophisticated computing
than is currently available in artificial intelligence laboratories
and certainly much more than is available in typical specialist
applications.   It is still however possible to function as a task
monitor at a relatively simple level and still influence or even
guide the user's behaviour.   The straightforward logging of user
commands, resulting in the type of dialogue shown in Fig. 8, can be
sufficient to prompt the user into exploring alternative strategies
or at least to try out new or less familiar options.

```
STATISTICS        6,7,8
IN YOUR LAST 6 RUNS YOU HAVE SPECIFIED
                SPEARMANS RHO CORRELATION
                KENDALL TAU CORRELATION
                PEARSONS PRODUCT MOMENT CORRELATION
ARE ALL 3 NECESSARY?  IF NOT YOU WILL
SAVE TIME BY ONLY SPECIFYING ONE.

ARE THERE OTHER MORE APPROPRIATE TESTS FOR YOUR DATA?

HAVE YOU CONSIDERED ......
```

FIGURE 8. Dialogue prompting user to explore more options.

Using such techniques it may be possible to break 'excessive' set in the individual user, but there are other ways in which counter-productive set may be avoided in the specialist problem solving application.

5. SET AND THE SPECIALIST'S JOB

One of the key elements in the development of a psychological set is repetition. There are other aspects and it is, of course, possible to experience set in a completely novel environment, but in most situations it is the continued repetition of a particular perspective or approach which leads to set. There are three aspects of the specialist's job which can foster this type of repetition, and it is modifying or changing these job aspects that can help to avoid counter-productive set. The three aspects will be discussed in turn below. They are the fragmentation of the problem solving process, the separation of tool use from tool development, and involvement of the specialist in computer programming.

5.1 Fragmentation of the Problem Solving Process

In many problem solving specialisms the process has been fragmented and routinised to the extent that no one individual is in a position to see the full extent of the problem or to appreciate its context. The problem may initially be accepted or identified by a relatively senior specialist, who decides on an appropriate solution or method of producing a solution and then passes it on to a junior specialist for detailed working out or feeding into a computer package. The apparent advantage of this approach is the liberation of senior specialists from the routine, tedious and intellectually relatively undemanding calculation and detailed working out of problem solutions. Ostensibly this allows them to concentrate on the more creative parts of the process but in practice it can prevent them from being exposed to the inadequacy of some of the techniques or solutions they propose. It also removes the junior specialist from the original problem and virtually re-defines his task as fitting the problem into the terms used by the computer package (or any other such aid).

This fragmentation has not been caused by the introduction of computers and in fact was probably even more extreme and dramatic in the days when large scale calculations and tabulations had to be performed manually. However, it is in this area that the computer has a potentially liberating effect which has yet to be fully realised in practice. Some of the justification for early computer aided design systems was that they would remove the tedium of manual calculation and liberate the specialist (even the junior specialist) allowing him to spend more time on the creative and fundamentally more important part of the process. Instead of tedious, boring and routine calculations, however, many specialists now have to endure tedious, boring and routine data preparation and data entry procedures. These are hardly more creative and allow the specialist little real time for creative thought other than the difficult task of determining how, for example, the co-ordinates of a complex real world structure can be entered into a computer stress analysis system.

This fragmentation also makes it difficult to see a long term career structure which allows the specialist gradually to develop the appropriate skills for creative problem solving. Indeed in many of the systems studied in the MICA survey there were specialists performing virtually clerical duties in data preparation, with little real knowledge of the technical process and with little chance of developing this knowledge from the work in which they were engaged.

Computers however have and can encourage the removal of this fragmentation in at least two ways. First, the development of new data entry hardware and software, which makes the computer do more work, makes such tasks as specifying co-ordinates, entering basic data or modifying existing data much less time consuming and arduous. It is therefore possible for more specialists to become involved in the process of working out problem solutions, and it can allow even the most junior specialists to spend at least part of their time working on the real problems.

Secondly, the use of a computer helps to make the problem solving process more explicit, and makes it easier for teams of specialists to work jointly on a problem rather than simply handling it independently or sequentially. The use of a common computer vocabulary, common data files and so on makes such team work easier and more likely to be constructive. In fact the role of computing as a medium for communication and for sharing ideas can be seen most clearly in the recent growth of inter-disciplinary research and problem solving. The fact that computing is now an integral part of most scientific university degree courses means that inter - or cross-disciplinary communication can use a common computer approach and perspective with approximately equal relevance to all. There is the danger, of course, that such computer-based communication may be more equally irrelevant to all and it can, of course, if uncontrolled create the types of set discussed in the previous section. However with the various built-in safeguards it provides a powerful platform for both inter- and intra-disciplinary communication and team problem solving.

5.2 Computer Tool Use and Tool Development

Earlier it was pointed out that the specialist's task needs were continually changing and that as a result any computer aid needed to be under constant revision and development. This often results in a special group of specialists being dedicated to developing and refining the computer programs and packages, leaving the ordinary specialist to use the existing tools. This can lead to set in two ways. First, the ordinary specialist is not encouraged to consider other ways of tackling the problem or to worry about the appropriateness of the existing tool, but only to repeat the same type of solution. Secondly, the specialist involved in development of the computer aid may find his thinking led by the possibilities of the tools rather than the problem. There must obviously be a place where new techniques in science and technology are explored mainly "because they're there" but the very fact that people are trying to explore the uses of a particular tool makes it difficult for them to judge effectively their relative worth.

An additional difficulty encountered in this situation is that, where a small group of users is intimately involved with computer personnel in developing and modifying the system, it is easy to forget that they are not typical in their knowledge of computing. Such 'super-users' can make life difficult for the ordinary user if the computer personnel believe that all users either have or should have this degree of computer knowledge and design the system accordingly. These 'super-users' do become increasingly unrepresentative of their fellow users and rapidly forget the simple, apparently trivial, problems the ordinary user can have with logging-on procedures or job control cards.

Ideally all specialists should be involved in the continued refinement and development of the computer system used. After all they are the ones most likely to experience its shortcomings directly, and their views are likely to be most useful to the system designers. Special groups which concentrate specifically on system development or on exploring the uses of some techniques, for example finite element analysis, also have an important role to play, but this should be in conjunction with the specialists involved in the on-going problem solving activity and not divorced or separated from them.

5.3 Computer Programming

Most specialists using computers at some time or other are introduced to programming. In many cases it is a passing acquaintance, but for some specialists it becomes an integral part of the job. Programming has many intellectually attractive aspects, and for the specialist dealing with extremely complex multi-

dimensional problems it can represent welcome order and structure
in a difficult and ambiguous environment.   However, as mentioned
earlier, there is a real danger that the specialist may become too
involved in programming to the detriment of the problem solving.

In order to overcome this, it is necessary for the bulk of
the necessary programming effort to be provided through full-time
programmers working to provide a service to the rest of the
specialist team.   The specialists should know enough about
programming to be realistic in their demands and to exploit it
appropriately.   The programmers over time can develop sufficient
knowledge of the specialism to ensure that they understand the
context of the problems they are helping to solve.   It can be
difficult to provide career paths for such programmers as they do
not fit neatly either into traditional programming roles or into
specialist jobs, but this can be overcome with suitable selection
and training.   What is vital is that computer programming is
essentially a service to the specialist and should in no way
become an end in itself.

6. CONCLUSION

The complex nature of the tasks which specialists undertake
means that considerable expertise is necessary.   Since the
specialist tends to a large extent to operate in one particular
problem area or even one discipline, it is worth his while investing
both financially and personally in developing tools and techniques
to help solve his particular class of problems.   This can lead to
difficulties, not because it is impossible to create computer
systems or packages which truly fit his task or which he can learn
to use but because they demand a degree of dedication.   Once the
specialist has committed himself to such a powerful computer tool
there is a number of pressures on the individual to over
value computer techniques or to overlook non-computer based
problem approaches and so modify his task to suit the tool.   This
task modification is an effective and necessary process to some
extent, but in the long term it can lead to at least sub-optimum
and at worst inappropriate problem solutions.

If on the other hand the computer aid contains within it some
type of monitor or procedures for leading the user to explore
options and try to break out of counter-productive psychological
sets, then the user's problem solving abilities can truly be
enhanced.

Excessive fragmentation and over-specialisation can limit
creativity in problem solving, but suitably harnessed computers
have enormous potential for encouraging and facilitating creative
team problem solving which will in the long term lead to better
solutions to specialists' problems.

REFERENCES

Adams, J. &   1969   Timesharing versus instant batch
Cohen, L.   processing: an experiment in
                           programmer training.
                 Computers and Automation, 18.3, 30-34.

Britton, R.   1970   A remote terminal service - the pros
                           and cons.
                 Data Processing, 338-340.

Eason, K.D.,   1974   MICA Survey, Report of a survey of
Damodaran, L &   man-computer interaction in commercial
Stewart, T.F.M.   applications.
                 SSRC Project Report on Grant No. HR 1844/1

Kelly, G.A.   1955   The psychology of personal constructs.
                           Vols. 1 and 2.
                 Norton, New York.

Newell, A. &   1972   Human problem solving.
Simon, H.   Prentice Hall, New Jersey.

Sackman, H.   1968   Time-sharing versus batch processing:
                           the experimental evidence.
                 AFIPS Conf. Proc., 32, 1-10.

Sackman, H.   1970   Man-computer problem solving.
                 Auerbach Publishers, Philadelphia, Pa.

Sackman, H.   1974   Stages of problem solving with and
                           without computers.
                 Rand Corporation, Report. No.R-1490-NSF

MAN AND COMPUTER IN FUTURE ON-BOARD
GUIDANCE AND CONTROL SYSTEMS OF AIRCRAFT

R.K. Bernotat

Forschungsinstitut für Anthropotechnik,
Konigstrasse 2, D-5307 Wachtberg-Werthoven, Germany.

1. TASK ALLOCATION BETWEEN MAN AND COMPUTER

1.1 General Rules for Task Allocation

If we look through the literature in Ergonomics, Control
Theory, Computer Sciences etc. we find a number of publications
concerning task-allocation between man and machine. Most often
there are vertical rows which list and compare the advantages and
disadvantages of man versus machine for certain functions.
Examples are the list from Fitts which was published in 1950
(cf. Shackel, 1974) and the list from Coburn (1973) which is mostly
used today. These lists are given in Appendices A and B.

In the concept phase of a new system those lists can only
provide general hints about which functions should be given to man
and which to the machine. So far there is no generally accepted
and practical method for making suitable task allocations between
man and machine (cf. McCormick, 1970) with a degree of accuracy
and rigour normally associated with science and engineering. It
is still more art than science.

Part of the reason is that the optimal task-allocation or
design decision depends not only on the characteristics of man
and the possibilities of modern technology but also is strongly
influenced by economic and other aspects. A final design decision
must be made only after consideration of such factors as system
performance, reliability, development time and cost, power consumption, maintenance and support costs, quantitative and qualitative
personnel requirements, their acquisition and support costs etc.

The cost function for a decision therefore is highly complex and has a large number of weighting factors. Furthermore, there are additional arguments based on the general social understanding of the role of the human being. Simply for this last reason, the solution of one and the same task will differ from country to country.

The methods and skills for the synthesis of complex "Ergatic Systems" has up to now been poorly developed (Müller, 1973). In the Russian language "Ergatic Systems" are defined as systems which include the human being as a control and decision element (Düring, 1976). Even if we restrict ourselves to purely technical criteria, the usual approach to the solution is mainly qualitative. "Allocating functions is often regarded as one of the least known aspects of what system designers do" (Düring, 1976). However, some efforts have already been made to develop computerised quantitative approaches (Johns and Katz, 1971; Katz, 1971).

Most of the comparisons in the Coburn list are made between man and machine in general. However, many of the statements made in the lists are also useful in making allocations between man and computer. The reason is that the performance of complex technical systems is determined more and more by the implications of modern computers. This is especially true if we talk about automation of highly complex systems.

1.2 Human Supervisory Control of Computer Controlled Systems

The level of automation which is possible to apply depends on the predictability of events and on the accompanying predictability of functions and tasks that the system will have to produce. The degree of unpredictability is called "task entropy". The relationship between task entropy and degree of automation is shown in Fig. 1 which is taken and slightly modified from Sheridan (1974).

If we assume a task entropy = 0, which means that the functional requirements are fully predictable, then it is relatively easy to automate 100% as illustrated by the clockwork example in the upper left-hand corner in the figure. If the same fully predictable tasks are allocated to a man (automation = 0) then we have the undesirable situation of a human performing "slave-like" tasks. This situation is shown in the lower left-hand corner.

Task entropy = 1 means complete unpredictability of a task and 100% automation at the same time, and would result in a "perfect robot". This type of robot which is able to cope with completely new tasks should be looked at as "critical and dangerous". Such a robot would be comparable to the human being in performance and may even be better in cases where the time duration for problem

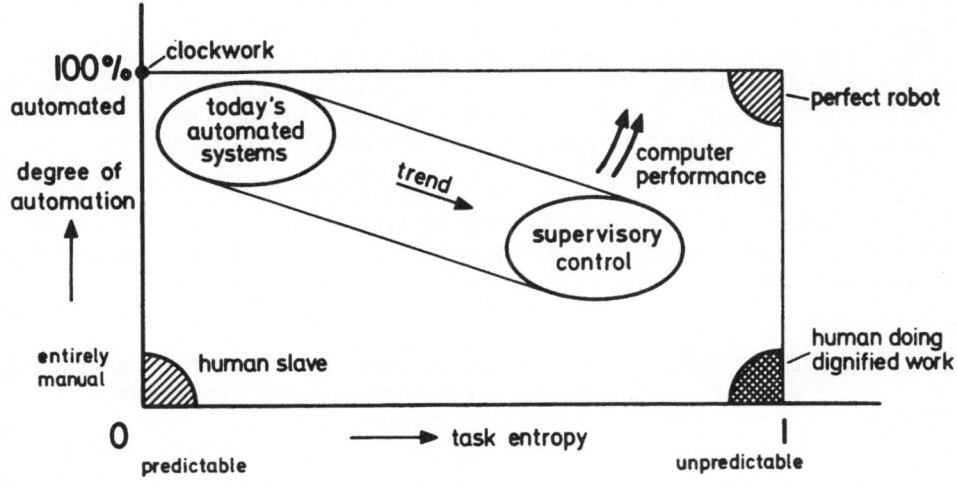

FIGURE 1.   Degree of automation as a function of task entropy
             and computer performance (modified from Sheridan, 1974)

solution is highly important.   However, this supposes the existence
of computers which excel the human brain in performance and reliability.   As far as a broad spectrum of tasks is concerned there is
a low probability that such "perfect" computers or robots will be
developed in the near future, if at all.

        If task entropy = 1, which means complete unpredictability
of task requirements and 0% automation, then we are in the lower
right-hand corner of the figure.   The flexibility, experience and
creativity of the human brain are necessary attributes to fulfil
these tasks.

        Most of our highly automated systems today can cope only with
tasks for which they are programmed and which are completely known
in advance.   The more unpredictable the task requirements the more
restricted is the possible degree of automation and man has to
take over more of the tasks.   In a well designed system these will
primarily be command or guidance functions.   He is the executive
or master who commands and supervises the machine.   Most modern
complex systems consist of various mechanical, chemical or electrical
machines which are controlled by computers.   Sheridan therefore
talks about the "human supervisor of computer controlled machines".

The exact position of the supervisory control ellipse in the figure, indicating the degree of automation of the man-machine-system for a given task entropy, depends strongly on the performance of the computer and its program. The position of the ellipse in the future will probably move up somewhat to higher degrees of automation as computer technology and application programs are improved.

But how about our basic question, the suitable task-allocation between man and computer? Based on the list previously mentioned we can postulate the following general allocation principles:

computer + machine	– All tasks which can be successfully and completely preprogrammed
	These include especially tasks which
	. often have to be repeated . are monotonous . need high reaction speed . need high accuracy . need high power
man	– Setting command values and supervising the computer in routine situations
	– For unpredictable situations he has to act as the intelligent part of the system and find a solution. This solution most times means moving away from routine programs and taking over continuous fine command of the machine.

Concerning the question of suitable man-computer or supervisor-computer interactions, quite a number of research results have been published over the last years for very specific tasks. A good survey was given recently at the symposium on "Monitoring Behaviour and Supervisory Control" in Berchtesgaden, Germany (Johannsen and Sheridan, 1976).

Let us now turn to the specific question of task-allocation and interactions of man and computer in on-board guidance and control of aircraft and spacecraft.

2. MAN-COMPUTER ALLOCATIONS IN AIRCRAFT GUIDANCE AND CONTROL
   SYSTEMS

Aircraft guidance and control system development is a suitable
example for illustrating past automation and current trends into
the near future. However, most of the discussion is applicable
to other types of system, for example, ship guidance and control
systems. Even land vehicle development programs exist which aim
at computer-assisted stability and at computer aided automatic
guidance which is adaptable to changing traffic situations.

2.1 Man and Aircraft Dynamics

An aircraft in flight must be controlled within the limits of
a number of parameters, such as attitude limits, speed limits,
time programs, fuel consumption, tolerable noise level, stall speed,
etc. The details of guidance and control loops are highly complex.
In the simplified diagram of Fig. 2 three hierarchical loops are
shown.

The lowest loop in the hierarchy is the attitude and speed
control loop which produces the signals for rudder, ailerons, flaps
and engine settings. The decision making element in the loop may
be the pilot, who compares the command data coming from the guidance
loop with the status data about current attitude and speed that he
gets from the sensors.

The guidance loop gets its command input from the navigation
loop in the form of a flight program. The pilot has to see that
the aircraft follows this program.

The navigator, or pilot in the navigator role, in the highest
loop of the hierarchy compares his current position and time with
the general mission or the flight plan of the system. In case of
deviations guidance commands are given. If deviations are very
large he may even generate a completely new flight program.

The human being usually is the decision making element in all
three loops. However, to be able to do this job he needs considerable training time to learn the dynamics of the three loops. Only
then is he able to compensate correctly for various deviations by
producing optimal command or control signals. Furthermore, he has
to practise this procedure at regular intervals in order to keep
his knowledge and skills at the necessary level. Here we have one
risk with automation. Without regular practice in manual flying
the pilot may not be able to take over from the automatic system
in case of unpredicted situations or in case of equipment failures.

The frequency and duration of task performance requirements for the human operator decrease in the higher loops of the control hierarchy. Unburdening of the pilot therefore started by automation in the lowest loop, where task loads were highest, and has moved upwards to the navigation loop today. The computer has replaced more and more of the pilot's functions in the guidance and control loop.

2.2 Status and Trend in Automation

Automation started by applying relatively simple mechanical analog computers for stabilizing aircraft attitude. The most difficult tasks of the pilot were and are take-off and landing the aircraft. On route he had to fly manually all the profiles in space if changes of altitude or course were required. Only in phases of constant attitude of the aircraft was he able to unburden himself by switching on the autopilot-computer.

Today, the trend is towards digital computers as autopilots. They still have the main task of stabilizing preset aircraft attitudes via the attitude loop. But some other tasks in the guidance loop have also been automated. Modern complex autopilots, for example, are able to follow radio beams in space or compute and follow tracks in space based on inertial or radio data. However, even the most modern autopilots have only very few programs to change over from one flight phase to another or to adapt to the local situation. That means, the computer has only a few, relatively inflexible, characteristics.

The trend in civil aircraft guidance and control automation is towards preprogramming of flight paths and close ground control. The pilot's task becomes more and more that of mode switching, supervision and take over, if still possible, in case of failure.

In the military context the situation is different. Here we require high manoeuverability and flexibility. Therefore, we find a trend to use the computer in a completely different manner. The computer is used to modify the dynamic characteristics of the aircraft in order to make the pilot's tasks easier and to increase its flyability.

Most recent developments even abandon aerodynamic stabilization normally inherent in airframe design and achieve stability by control dynamics, a task allocated completely to the computer. The resulting "control configured vehicles" most often have strongly changed dynamic behaviour and have to be flown in a different manner compared to conventional aircraft.

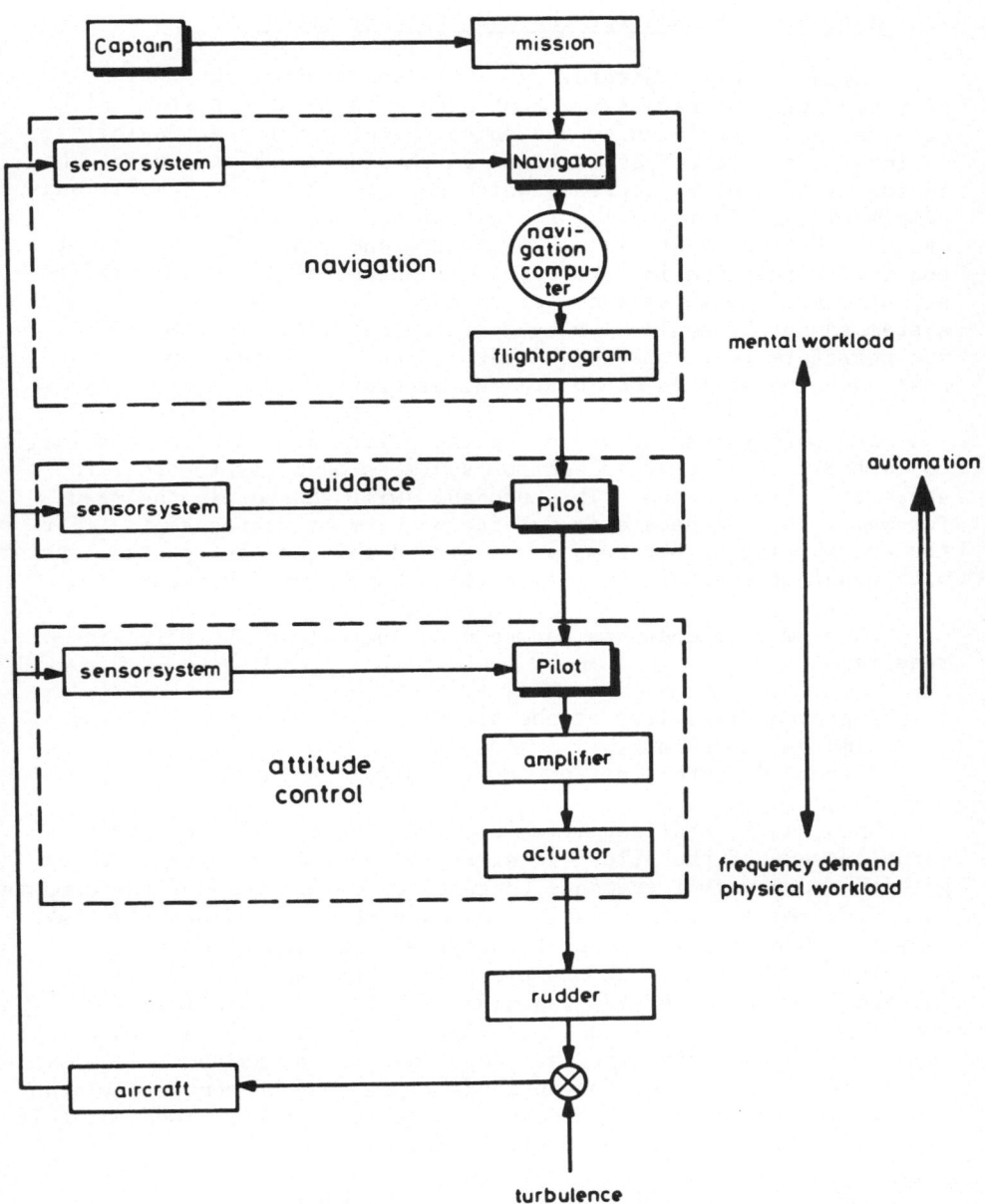

FIGURE 2. The aircraft guidance and control loops

2.3 Automation trends for the man-computer-system

Which way will aircraft guidance and control automation probably go?   We can assume that a fully automated system which requires no supervision by the human operator nor any possibility to intervene will not be realised in the foreseeable future. The reason is that only processes which can be described formally and completely, including all its constraints, can be automated (Fuchs - Kittowski et al., 1974).   The enormous multiplicity of possible situations in take-off and landing, of different traffic situations, of failures and disturbances within the guidance system, cannot be dealt with by a fully automatic system.   The man therefore remains always a part of the guidance loop.   In most cases he will be on board the aircraft.

For safety reasons up to now the pilot still has the possibility to control the aircraft's control surfaces manually in order to shape the flight path.   This probably will change in the near future.   The new generation of inexpensive microprocessors offer the possibility to get computer-assisted guidance and control systems with equal or even higher reliability than today's systems.

These microprocessors can be used to realise the following requirements:

1.   Improved flyability of the aircraft and shortened learning time of the pilot.
2.   Increased system performance.

This can be realised if we drop the requirement for direct manual access of the pilot to aircraft control surfaces.   We can get new and powerful guidance concepts if we make use of the computer to modify the aircraft dynamics in order to make the pilot's tasks easier.   Many subtasks are transferred from the pilot to the computer.   The time that the pilot needs to learn the dynamics and the interaction of the subloops as well as its influence on the flight path is shortened considerably.   Usually only knowledge about the system structure, as such, has to be gained. Acquisition of the manual skills of conventional flying may be completely aban- doned.   Furthermore, the necessity to keep a certain level of this flying ability may no longer be important.

The performance limitations in the various control subloops, which up to now have mainly resulted from the human limitations in information reception, processing and output, would therefore be eliminated.   Higher system performance of the man-machine-system can thereby be realised.

A number of ergonomic questions have to be asked at this
stage:

1. Shall we leave the pilot in the guidance loop, so that he still
    flies the aircraft manually but via the computer?   In this
    case he would give continuous command inputs to the lower loops
    in the guidance and control hierarchy.   Or shall we design
    the system in such a manner, that the pilot controls the
    aircraft discontinuously by giving data to the computer and
    calling up programs via keyboards?
2. Which dynamic characteristics should we give the computer in
    both cases?
3. It is well-known that the human being is badly 'designed'
    for monitoring.   How much of this task should be allocated
    to the computer?
4. How should displays and controls providing for communication
    with the computer be designed and arranged?
5. How should the dynamic behaviour of the back-up guidance and
    control system be designed in case of failure in the main system?

3. CONCEPT OF AN AIRCRAFT GUIDANCE SYSTEM BASED ON THE
    SUPERVISOR-COMPUTER CONTROL PRINCIPLE

Because of complexity of the cost function there are quite a
number of different possible task allocations between man and
computer, even for the same flight mission and aircraft type.   In
order to discuss the pilot supervisor concept further, an example
is given which currently is realisable because it is based on
today's technology.

3.1 The automatic mode

The first allocation decision is to have all frequently
occurring routine tasks performed automatically by the computer.
Such tasks may be maintaining altitude, speed, following radio
beams, etc.   These are tasks which are already usually performed
in today's autopilots.   Changing altitude, course or the radio
beams to be followed is done by using fixed and pre-programmed
profiles.   All the necessary subtasks during the change-over,
such as attitude change, speed change, etc., are also preprogrammed.
The autopilot follows standard stabilisation programs and standard
programs for changes.

The pilot's task is to set the command values and supervise
its fulfilment.   Adaptation of the system's behaviour (pilot-
computer-aircraft) to the changing traffic situations, to weather
conditions or to local take-off and landing procedures is optimised
by choosing and switching to the most appropriate of the different
programs.   It is essential that the automatic mode in fact be used

for routine situations only.   No attempt should be made to go
further and try to make the computer controller more self-adaptable.
The automatic system in the form discussed has only a few characteristics, all of which can easily be learned by the pilot and therefore can easily be monitored by him.   He uses the automatic mode
for unburdening himself.

3.2   The semi-automatic mode

The semi-automatic mode is to be used in situations which
are not routine, occur infrequently or are even unpredictable.
These situations require much flexibility and adaptability from the
overall system.

In the semi-automatic mode the aircraft is flown quasi-manually
by the pilot via the computer.   In contrast to the automatic mode
with its discrete setting of command values, in this mode the
command values concerning the desired flight path are given to the
computer in a continuous manner.   Essential from the ergonomic
viewpoint is that the command signal should be given by the pilot
in the usual human compatible continuous analog form.

Subvalues such as required aircraft attitude, speed, distance
to target, etc. are preprogrammed in the computer.   In some cases,
the pilot should have the possibility to choose among a number of
subvalues, for example, different pitch attitudes for the landing
approach.   The aircraft would with this allocation scheme be able
to fly any manoeuvre within its design limits.   Stability and
accuracy are gained by the system from the computer; system
flexibility is provided by the human element.   This approach is
in full agreement with allocation recommendations drawn from the
Coburn's list of advantages of man and machine.

An important question still unanswered is, which type of command
value should be given to the computer during the semi-automatic
mode in order to make the pilot's task as easy as possible?
The fact is that stabilisation for various flight regimes is
already done by the computer in the automatic mode; and the computer
in this task normally performs better than the human pilot.
Stabilisation should therefore remain a task for the computer.
Human adaptability and flexibility on the other hand is needed
to provide a full spectrum of required changeover-manoeuvres.   The
semi-automatic mode should therefore mainly be used in these
manoeuvres.   One possible way to control the changeover profile
is to command only the first derivative, for example, height change
dH/dt or course change dC/dt, etc.   The command values can be given
by the pilot to the computer using suitable analog controls such as
the usual control wheel.   The pilot in this way is able to fly the
aircraft in every profile that is within its manoeuvring scope.

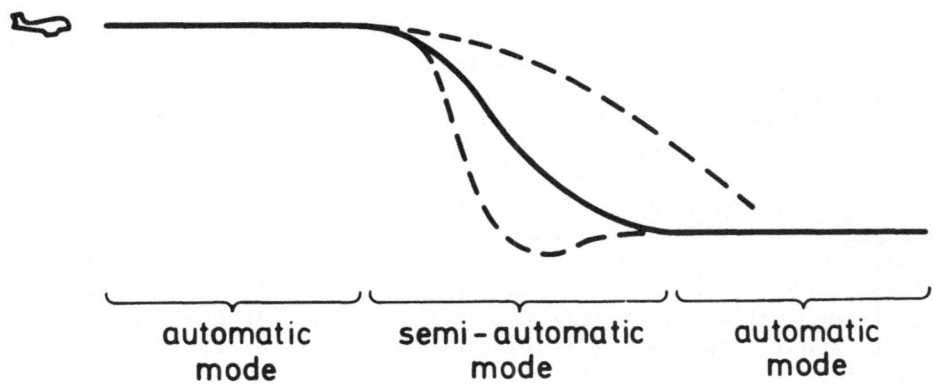

FIGURE 3. The usage of automatic and semi-automatic mode

3.3 The Back-up Guidance System

In this allocation scheme the pilot no longer learns to fly
the aircraft without computer assistance. The back-up system
therefore, which comes into use in case of guidance system
failures, should not require the use of pilot skills that differ
strongly from those required in the main system. It should be
said that a jump back to direct hydraulic rudder and aileron
control is no longer possible in the control configured vehicle.
Without aerodynamic stabilisation as in today's aircraft the pilot
would hardly be able to fly the aircraft. The future therefore
lies in improved system reliability by using redundant control
computers. The days of human direct hydraulic or mechanical
control will probably soon be over.

3.4 Displays

Human fatigue due to high mental workload has to be minimized
as much as possible. Effective pilot performance in supervising
the computerised system has to be assured. One way to reach this
goal is to design and use visual displays which are integrated in
their informational contents and which are easier to use than
conventional displays. These may take the form of integrated
pictorial displays complemented by alpha-numeric displays. Alpha-
numeric displays may be used additionally for off-line planning
of flight profiles as well as part of a two-way communication
channel between the pilot and the computer.

3.5 Controls

As already mentioned, inputs to the computer in the automatic mode are mostly discrete. Devices such as keyboards, or electronic displays with graphic or keyboard presentations over-layed with touch sensors, may be used.

For the semi-automatic mode, as previously mentioned, an appropriate multi-channel continuous analog input device such as a control wheel may be used to make manual inputs to the computer. A special device, which has become known only very recently, uses the force applied by the pilot to the control column as the input signal and the angular deflection of the column as the feed-back signal from the system to the pilot (Herzog, 1968). Merhav and Yaacov (1975) call this device the "natural feel stick" (Fig. 4). The idea behind this concept is the following: The stick or wheel represents the system which has to be controlled. A force is applied to it, the system reacts, and its reaction is fed back as the movement of the stick or wheel. In this way the human operator gets simultaneously and parallel to the display an information presentation to his kinestetic and proprieceptive channels. Experiments by the authors mentioned above as well as our own experiments at the Research Institute for Anthropotechnik have shown that this method is a very effective one. Its application can lead to higher performance of the total guidance system and reduced workload of the pilot at the same time.

Application of this special concept of a guidance system may also help to make the pilot's task easier. In the automatic mode the computer stabilises the aircraft on its prescribed flight path. The natural feel stick continuously moves by itself fully correlated with the momentary vertical speed and course changes of the aircraft.

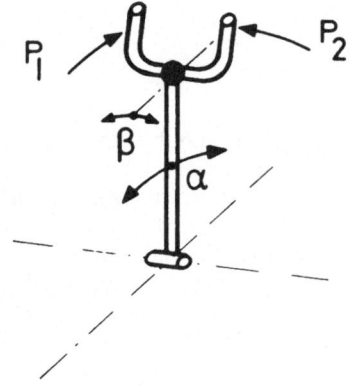

P_1 ~ vertical speed command

P_2 ~ course change command

α ~ vertical speed status

β ~ course change status

FIGURE 4. The natural feel stick

The pilot can supervise by keeping his hands on the stick and
'feeling' what the aircraft does.   If the pilot wants to change
the flight path in the semi-automatic mode he has to press a button
and to apply a force on the 'feel stick'.   The altitude and
course changes are fed back to him as deflections of the stick.
If he takes his hands off at any time, the system switches back
into the automatic mode, using the current momentary altitude and
course values as new command values.

This example further illustrates the necessity in real time
tasks for the capability for making continuous analog inputs to the
computer.

4.   CONCLUDING REMARKS

It has been shown that the computer may be used to modify and
simplify the dynamic behaviour of a system in order to make it
more controllable by the human operator.   One example of an
aircraft guidance system has been given, which describes how one
possible task allocation between man and computer would work and
what the implications might be for device selection of displays
and controls and for design layout.

REFERENCES

Coburn, R.   1973   Human engineering guide to ship
                                system development.
                              Naval Electronics Laboratory Center,
                                San Diego, California.

Döring, B.   1976   Analytical methods in man-machine
                                system development.
                              In: Kraiss, K.F. and Moraal, J. (edit.),
                                Introduction to Human Engineering,
                                pp. 293-350.
                              Koln, Verlag TUV, Rheinland.

Fuchs-Kittowski, K.   1974   Zum gegenstand der automatisierung
   Tschirschwitz, R. &   körperlicher und geistiger Tätigkeiten
   Wentzlaff, B.   Z. Messen-Steuern-Regeln, 17.8, 266-268.

Herzog, J.H.   1968   Manual control using the matched
                                manipulator control technique.
                              IEEE Trans. Man-Mach. Syst. Vol.MMS-9.3,
                                56-60.

498

Jahns, D.W. &   1971   Computer Aided Function Allocation
  Katz, R.   Evaluation System (CAFES).
                               Vol. 1. The Boeing Company, Aerospace
                               Group, Seattle, Washington, U.S.A.

Johannsen, G. &   1976   Monitoring behaviour and supervisory
  Sheridan, T.   control.
  (edit.)   Plenum Press, London.

Katz, R.   1971   Computer Aided Function Allocation
                               Evaluation System (CAFES).
                               Vol. II, The Boeing Company, Aerospace
                               Group, Seattle, Washington, U.S.A.

McCormick, E.J.   1970   Human factors engineering.
                               3rd edition, McGraw Hill, New York.

Merhav, S.J. &   1975   Control augmentation and workload
  Ben Yaacov, O.   reduction by kinestetic information
                               from the manipulator.
                               Report from the Technion-Israel Institute
                               of Technology, Haifa.

Müller, J.A.   1973   Der mensch im steuerungssystem.
                               Z. Messen-Steuern-Regeln, 16.11, 416-418.

Shackel, B. (edit.) 1974   Applied Ergonomics Handbook.
                               IPC Science & Technology Press,
                               Guildford, U.K.

Sheridan, T.   1974   The several roles of man as a supervisor
                               of robots.
                               Proceedings of the IEEE, 1974, Inter-
                               national Conference on Systems,
                               Man and Cybernetics, Dallas, U.S.A.

APPENDIX A

RELATIVE ADVANTAGES OF MEN AND MACHINES (FROM FITTS *)

	Machine	Man
Speed	Much superior.	Lag 1 second.
Power	Consistent at any level. Large, constant standard forces.	2.0hp for about 10 seconds 0.5hp for a few minutes 0.2hp for continuous work over a day.
Consistency	Ideal for: routine; repetition; precision.	Not reliable: should be monitored by machine.
Complex activities	Multi-channel.	Single-channel.
Memory	Best for literal reproduction and short term storage.	Large store, multiple access. Better for principles and strategies.
Reasoning	Good deductive.	Good inductive.
Computation	Fast, accurate. Poor at error correction.	Slow, subject to error. Good at error correction.
Input sensitivity	Some outside human senses, eg radioactivity.	Wide energy range (10^{12}) and variety of stimuli dealt with by one unit; eg eye deals with relative location, movement and colour. Good at pattern detection. Can detect signals in high noise levels.
	Can be designed to be insensitive to extraneous stimuli.	Affected by heat, cold, noise and vibration (exceeding known limits).
Overload reliability	Sudden breakdown.	"Graceful degradation".
Intelligence	None.	Can deal with unpredicted and unpredictable; can anticipate.
Manipulative abilities	Specific.	Great versatility.

500

APPENDIX B

COMPARISON OF HUMAN AND MACHINE CAPABILITIES
FOR PERFORMING VARIOUS TASKS (FROM COBURN 1973)

SENSING AND MONITORING

Man	Machine
Men are poor monitors of infrequent events or of events which occur frequently over a long period of time.	Machines can be constructed to detect reliably infrequent events and events which occur frequently over a long period of time.
Man can interpret an input signal even when subject to distraction, high noise, or message gap.	Machines perform well only in a generally clean, noise-free environment.
Man is a selecting mechanism and can adjust to sense specific inputs.	Machines are fixed sensing mechanisms, operating only on that which has been programmed for them.
Man has very low absolute thresholds for sensing (e.g., vision, audition, taction).	Machines, to have the same capability, become extremely expensive.
Expectation or cognitive set may lead an operator to "see what he expects or wants to see".	Machines do not exercise these processes.

INFORMATION PROCESSING

Man	Machine
Man complements the machine by aiding in sensing, extrapolating, decision making, goal setting, monitoring and evaluating.	Machines have no capacity for performance different from that originally designed.
Man can acquire and report information incidental to the primary mission.	Machines cannot do this.
Man can perform time contingency analyses and predict events in unusual situations.	Corresponding machines do very poorly.
Man generally requires a review or rehearsal period before making decisions based on items in memory.	Machines go directly to stored information for decision.

DYNAMIC GRAPHICAL INTERACTION IN ENGINEERING DESIGN

Robert Spence

Department of Electrical Engineering,
Imperial College, London

ENGINEERING DESIGN

Complex systems such as ships, bridges and electronic circuits take their original form in the mind of an engineering designer. The creative responsibility is his, but so also is the ensuing exploration and verification of the design.

The designer's task is at once synthetic and analytic. Synthetic in that the customer has provided a specification to be satisfied by an as-yet-unknown design, and analytic in that any proposal by the designer must be tested before manufacture or sale. It is presently the case that analysis is best enhanced by computational rather than human resources. For this reason, a substantial number of computer-aided-design (CAD) systems have been implemented whose principal function - viewed most naively - is the efficient analysis of engineering systems. The essential creativity still lies firmly within the domain of the human designer.

Since the level of visual literacy among engineering designers is extremely high, the input to and output from many of the more effective CAD systems is principally pictorial. For example, in the MINNIE system for electronic circuit design that my colleagues and I have developed at Imperial College, the designer can easily draw his circuit on a display screen (Fig. 1) by means of a light-pen, and then examine displayed graphs (Fig. 2) of predicted circuit behaviour. Moreover, much additional benefit can be gained if the interaction between the designer and the display screen can be dynamic, as we shall see later.

In this paper I shall focus attention upon the use of interactive computer graphics in view of its efficacy as a medium for the man-computer dialogue associated with engineering design, as well as its rapidly increasing acceptance by industry.

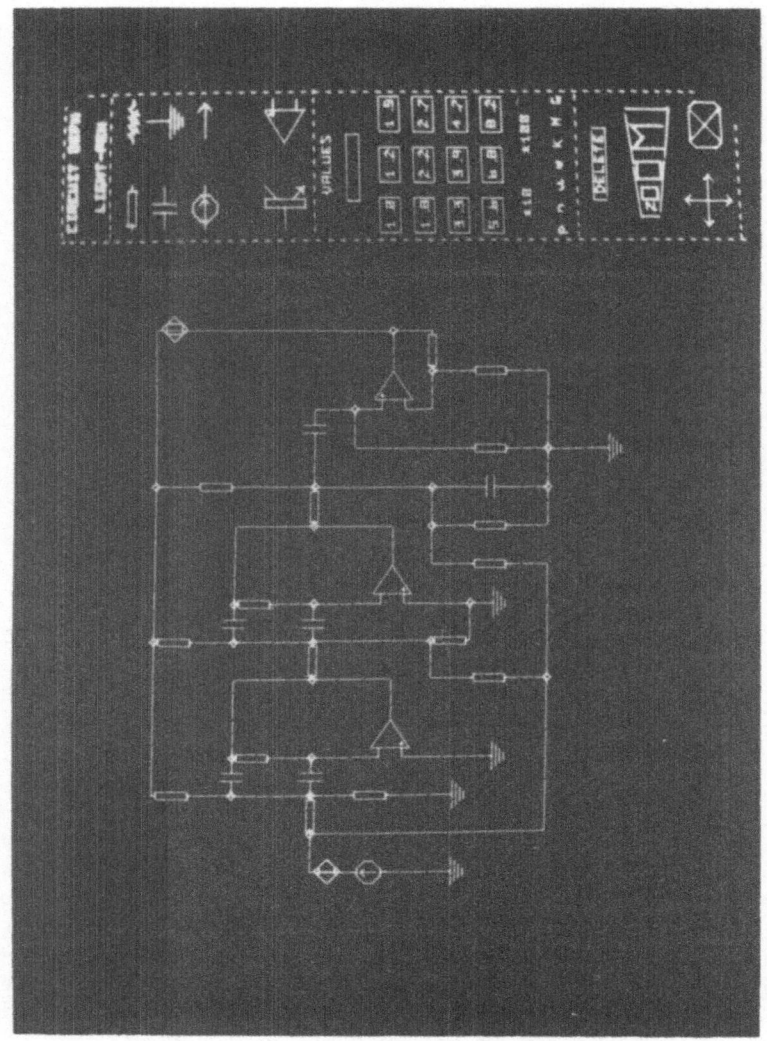

FIGURE 1. Electronic circuit diagram drawn on a computer-
refreshed display screen by means of a light-pen. A
menu of component types, component values and geometric
actions is provided on the right, and is accessed by
pointing actions with the light-pen.

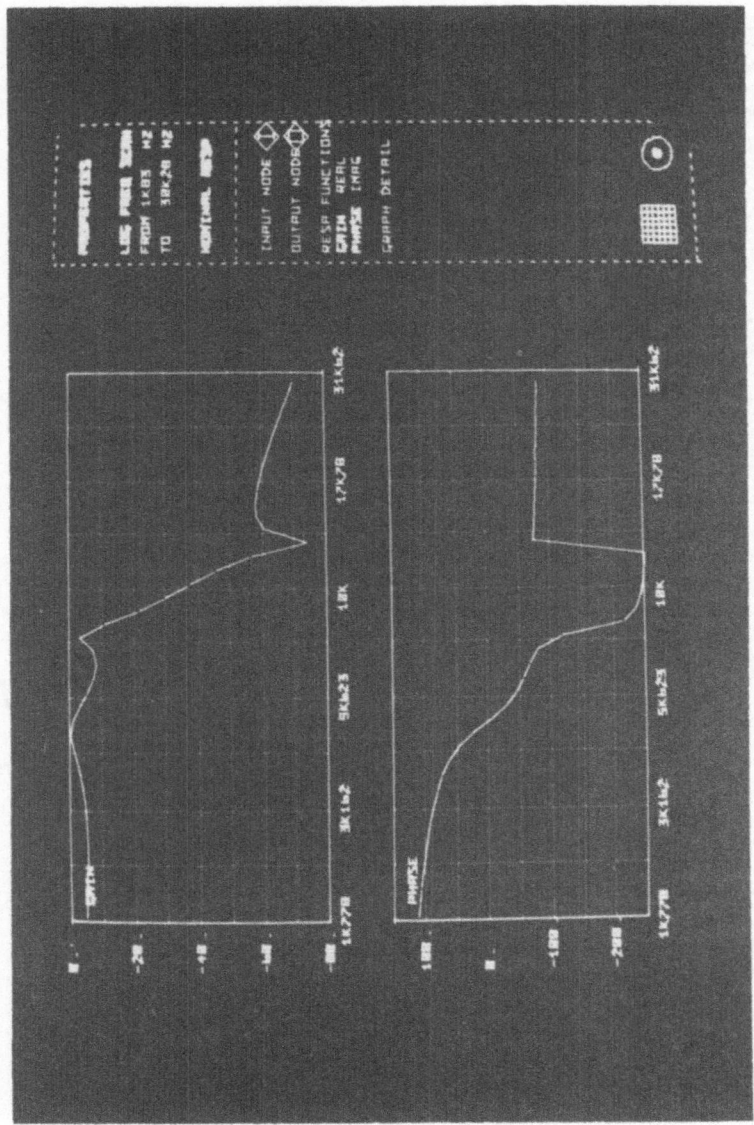

FIGURE 2. Display of the variation, with frequency, of two
circuit properties (the magnitude and phase of
voltage amplification). Menu at right allows
alternative selection of the displayed circuit
property.

504

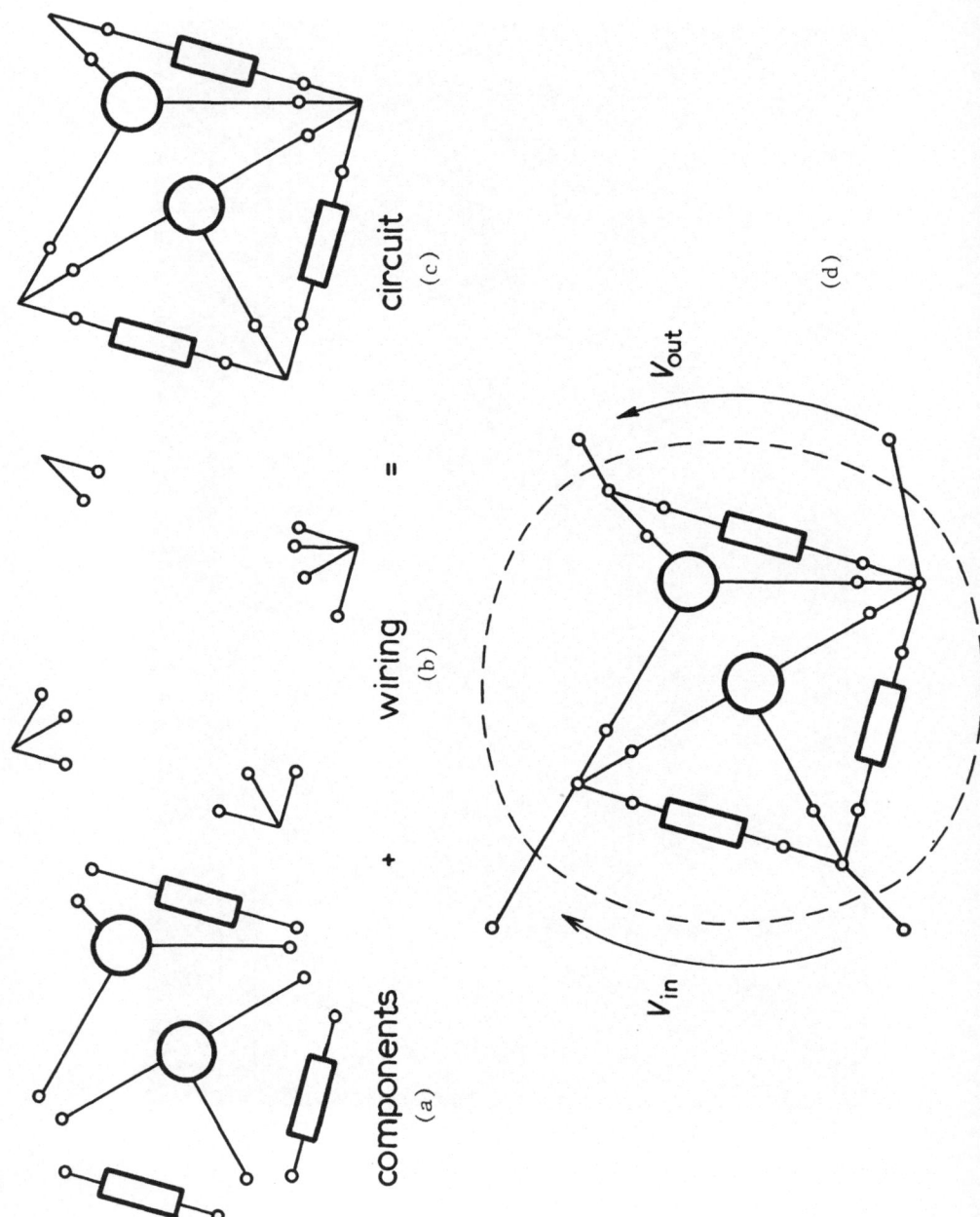

FIGURE 3. (a) selected components, (b) their interconnection,
(c) the interconnected components, (d) a circuit with
four accessible terminals.

MAN-COMPUTER INTERACTION

Other authors in this volume – Bernotat for example, have drawn attention to the violently contrasting capabilities of man and computer, and the tasks appropriate to each. It should be no surprise to find that, even if the tasks within a design process are appropriately allocated, then the man-computer interface in a CAD system is still an extremely sensitive one, requiring careful design. This view is certainly endorsed by practising industrial designers who wish to concentrate on problems to which they can bring expertise to bear, and who are irritated if expected to concern themselves with irrelevant and unsympathetic aspects of computer hardware and software.

Surprisingly, it is still commonly thought that the design of an effective man-computer dialogue is simple, straightforward, based on known principles and hardly worthy of intellectual discussion – let alone research. That it is none of these things is, of course, a personal view, and one which I now hope to justify. In doing so I shall set most of my remarks in the context of electronic circuit design, and illustrative examples will be drawn from the MINNIE system. This system was, in fact, originally developed specifically as a test-bed for innovation and experiment in human factors, but is now in use as a design tool.

THE TASK

To discuss man-computer interaction, and especially before carrying out research, we must know what the man is trying to do. In one sense the circuit designer's task is easily described – indeed deceptively so. From an available range of component types and values he must select a number of components (Fig. 3a) and wire them together (Fig. 3b) so that the resulting circuit (the dotted box of Fig. 3c) has useful properties. For example, a hi-fi amplifier would require (Fig. 3d) that the ratio A of the voltages V_{out} and V_{in} be reasonably constant over a certain range of frequency f. More generally, the permitted variation of a property like A with frequency f would be indicated by 'forbidden regions' as in Fig. 4.

But satisfying a constraint such as that described by Fig. 4 is, though necessary, only one objective of the circuit designer. The circuit must also be reliable, its cost must be minimised, its power consumption low, and its design completed by a deadline. Many other constraints exist: confidence in the final design is an important factor, but one which is virtually impossible to quantify or measure. The important consequence – especially for those doing research on man-computer interaction – is that there is no single figure of merit by which the designer can assess his design. Such

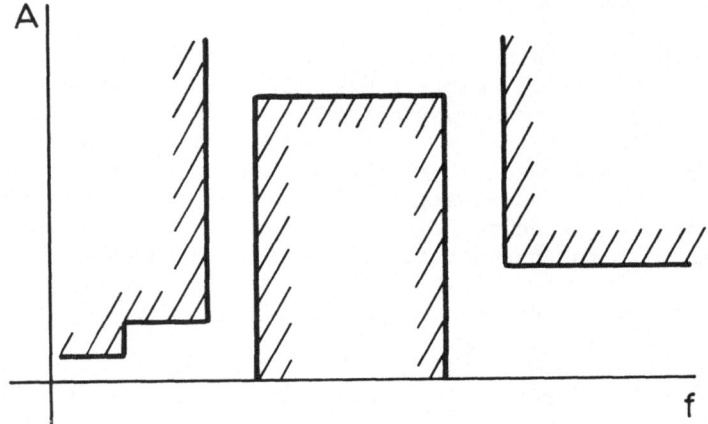

FIGURE 4. Example of the specification, by a customer, of the
desired behaviour of a circuit such as that shown in
Fig. 3d. The hatched area indicates forbidden values
of voltage amplification (A) at each frequency (f).

a figure may be formed unconsciously in the designer's mind, but
it will frequently change and rarely be made specific. Other
aspects of engineering design which complicate research into man-
computer interaction are the fact that very few designers either
can or will describe in detail the strategy and tactics adopted
during circuit design, and the fact that the approach to design
varies considerably between designers. I know of no typical
scenarios that have been proposed for the comparative evaluation
of CAD systems.

A WORKING CAD SYSTEM

The format adopted in the following glimpse of the MINNIE
system will be a factual description followed by brief comments
on associated problems on which research is required.

In the MINNIE system, a circuit or circuit modification proposed
by the designer is easily drawn by light-pen on the display screen:
wires are drawn as with pencil on paper, while a component is inserted,
and its value assigned, by pointing to its symbol and value, respectively, in a menu (Fig. 1 right, top and middle). The ease with
which a circuit is defined is clearly a function of the dialogue
design; Fig. 1 took about six minutes to complete inclusive of
values. Simple changes such as the insertion, deletion or change

in value of a single component (and this constitutes a significant part of circuit design) takes 5 seconds at most. 'Geometric' actions – magnify, move, delete, etc. – are controlled by the light buttons at the lower right of Fig. 1. All these actions are classified as <u>circuit definition</u>.

The light-pen certainly offers an excellent means for man-computer interaction, especially since it facilitates 'pointing' actions. But the 'tablet' is quickly becoming popular, and more exploration is needed of this and other input devices such as voice-recognizers, manually operated tongs, fingers, pencils, the 'mouse', etc.

In addition to circuit definition, the other principal activity within MINNIE is the examination of <u>circuit properties</u>. By extensive use of default choices and a good command dialogue – two areas where no information was readily available and innovation was necessary – the designer can easily define what effects he wishes to explore. For example, in the display shown in Fig. 5 the size of each octagon superimposed on a component indicates the effect of small changes in that component on circuit amplification (the property

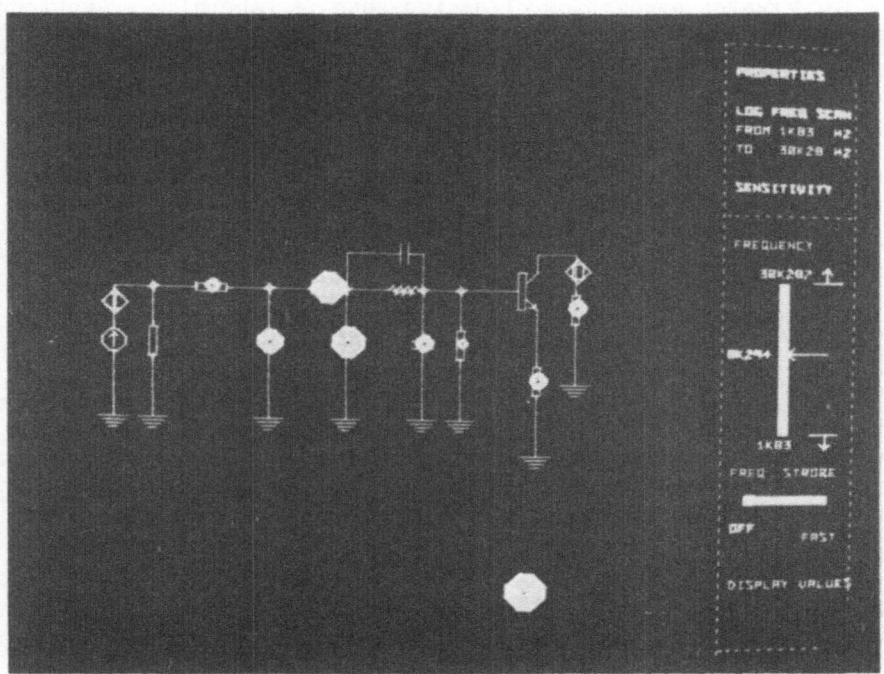

FIGURE 5. The effect of a small change in a component's value on the circuit's voltage amplification is indicated by an octagon superimposed on the component symbol: the greater the effect, the larger is the octagon.

called A in Fig. 3d). The picture changes as the frequency range associated with the light potentiometer on the right is explored automatically, or manually with the light-pen. Designers find this display useful: it provides insight into the significance of each component, it suggests which might be adjusted in order to improve the circuit, and it can give some idea of permitted component tolerances. The display acknowledges the important fact that designers frequently need qualitative rather than quantitative information. The display is an example of a symbolism which, although new and unfamiliar to designers, is accepted because it obviously has value.

The display of Fig. 5 was not, as far as I can recall, suggested by the human factors literature. Indeed, the potential offered by the appropriate embodiment of data in visual symbols - iconography - appears to have been little explored or exploited. Many approaches are possible (use of colour, flashing symbols, suppression of redundancy, stereoscopy, head-mounted displays, etc.) and much exploration and research (in that order) is needed. Information need not, of course, only be presented visually: both aural and tactile feedback should be explored.

A far greater proportion of design than is generally acknowledged is involved in speculative exploration, answering 'what-if' questions such as 'What happens if I change C9?' or 'What's the best value for R2?'. The display of Fig. 6 allows large changes in a previously identified component to be explored dynamically by movement of the light-pen along the light potentiometer. Within about half a second the new response curve is displayed (dotted). This very short response time is valuable in that it allows the designer to test ideas that he might otherwise, discard, and to effect circuit improvements quickly.

The facility shown in Fig. 6 raises the general question of the effect of computer response time on problem solving, to which we shall return later. It also illustrates a dilemma faced by designers of CAD systems which are radically different from anything currently available. There is an understandable readiness to ask the engineering designer what he wants; but there are still circuit designers who find the analysis offered by Fig. 6 a very pleasant surprise, and who would probably not have asked for such a facility in 1970 when the relevant algorithms and interaction techniques were being developed. Thus, there will always be those occasions where market research will fail, and where the CAD system designer must have the confidence to implement a scheme which can be appreciated and evaluated only when in a polished working state.

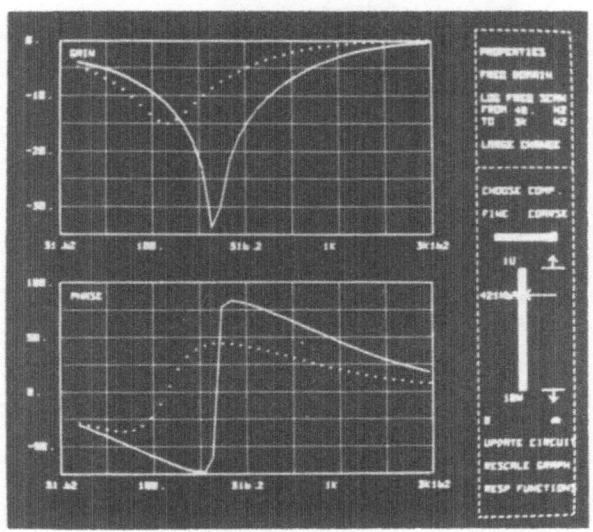

FIGURE 6. The effect of a large change in a component value is displayed by dashed curves (left) about half-a-second after the value change has been simulated by moving the light-pen along the vertical light-potentiometer (right).

Another important aspect of design which is emphasized by use of the 'large-change' analysis is the fact that the designer is often looking for the unexpected, primarily with a view to enhancing reliability of the product and confidence in the design. Thus, an apparently casual and unstructured search for the unexpected may be a very important component of the design process.

Whenever MINNIE is asked, usually by a pointing action with the light-pen, to perform some calculation (such as circuit analysis) which may occupy more than two seconds, a 'count-down clock' (Fig. 7) appears in the control section of the screen. It tells the designer (a) that something is happening, and (b) roughly how long he must wait for the result. This feature is much appreciated by designers, because a blank or static screen constitutes an exceedingly annoying response to a request for action. The count-down clock is easy to design, for each segment of its single revolution is associated with one of a fixed number of sample frequencies associated with the analysis. Interesting problems arise when the analysis requested is iterative (when the clock angle might be governed by some convergence criterion) or when data are sent to another computer for extensive processing.

510

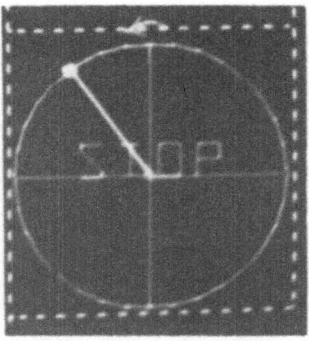

FIGURE 7. A displayed 'count-down' clock which performs one
revolution during the time required for an analysis.
It assures the designer that something useful is happening, and allows him to estimate the expected delay.

The value of the MINNIE system would have been severely
limited had it only been able to predict circuit amplification,
for many circuit properties are potentially of interest to the
designer.   The designer can, in fact, easily generate his own
personal version of MINNIE, to examine whichever property is of
interest to him, in the following way.   First, by a single
pointing action, he requests a display (Fig. 8) of the mathematical
definition of the four circuit properties available by default.
He can replace any of these properties by typing the definition of
a new one in terms of certain variables generated by MINNIE's
analysis program;   what he types appears on the display (Fig. 9).
Since the notation used is a subset of APL, the definition of the
new property is very simple and need only take a few seconds,
whereupon the name of the newly defined property appears in the
menu ready for selection.

The flexibility just described is an extremely valuable feature
of the MINNIE system, but it raises the general question of the
degree of flexibility that should be offered to the user.   I shall
return to this topic later.

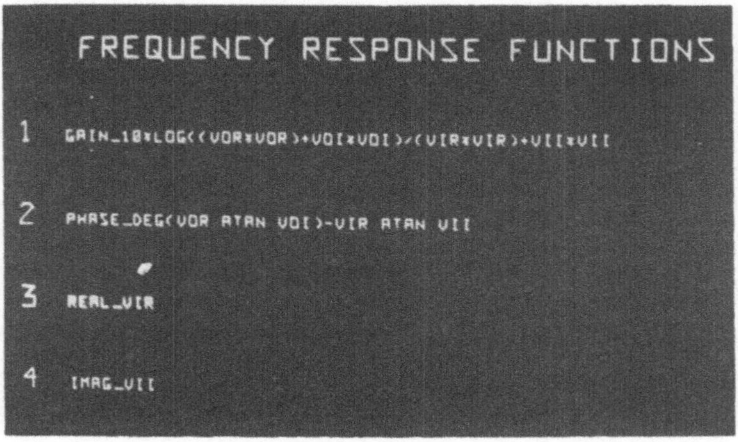

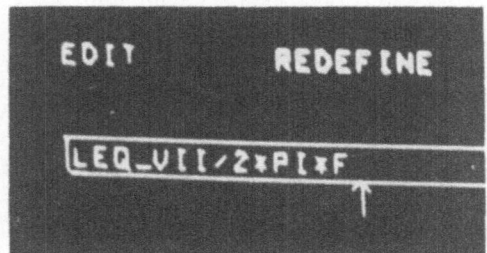

FIGURE 8. A display in which circuit properties that can be calculated are defined by mathematical expressions.

FIGURE 9. The display of the definition of a circuit property of interest, as entered via the keyboard of the designer.

PROBLEMS

Though our glimpse of MINNIE has been brief, and the reader's
experience of what is essentially a dynamic system severely limited
by the restriction to static print and picture, it is sufficient
to illustrate a number of problems which I believe require solution
if the man-computer dialogue involved in engineering design - and
with it the effectiveness of design - is to be enhanced.

1.   Response Time

Experience with MINNIE and other design systems suggests that
their effectiveness is strongly influenced by the time elapsing
between an action calling for a response and the response itself,
a period I shall refer to generally as response time.

We have isolated one aspect of problem-solving that we believe
to be common to a number of engineering design activities, and
which we suspect is highly sensitive to response time.   It is the
adjustment of a number of parameters such that a function of these
parameters exhibits desirable properties.   The parameters could,
for example, describe the components of an electronic circuit, and
the function might be the variation of amplification with frequency.

My colleague Mr. Goodman is conducting an experiment in which
the subject is seated before a cathode-ray-tube screen on which an
image such as that shown in Fig. 10 is displayed.   The subject is
asked to vary five parameters so that the dotted curve falls within
the clear region of the graph.   The parameter to be adjusted is
identified by pointing the light-pen at the appropriate numeral on
the upper right of the display;   parameter adjustment is achieved
by movemement of the light-pen along the light-potentiometer.
Between the selection of a new parameter value and the display of
the new curve a delay occurs, a delay which can be chosen by the
experimenter.   A record is kept of the total time to solution or
abandonment.   Also recorded is the entire history of the subject's
light-pen actions, so that we can examine them with a view to
clarifying the strategy adopted.   The possible influence of personality is being investigated, and we are trying to see if there is
any evidence of 'set'.

These experiments are still under way.   Later, there are many
interesting questions we would like to explore, all having relevance
to engineering design.   For example 'What is the effect of providing
an analogue indication of error?';   'Would the automatic computer
generation of random parameter combinations (on request) help the
subject to break out of set?';   'Would a display of sensitivity
(cf Fig. 5) help to reduce the time taken to achieve a solution?'

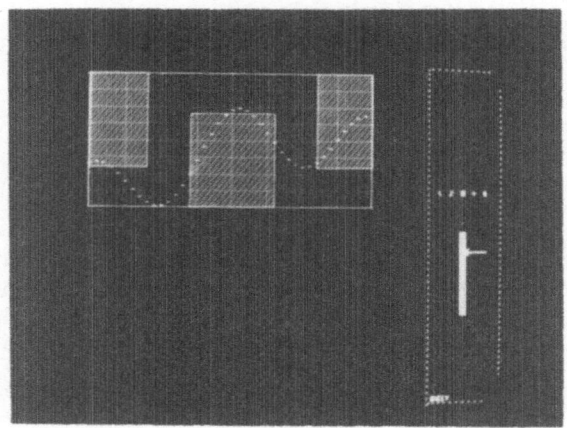

FIGURE 10. The display employed in experiments on the effect of
computer response time.   The objective is to adjust
five parameters so that the dashed curve falls only
within the clear region of the graph.

2. Trade-off Between Accuracy and Response Time

In the analysis of engineering systems it is often the case
that a system property can be predicted more accurately if a longer
time can be devoted to its calculation.   A good example in electronic circuit design is statistical circuit analysis carried out
by the Monte Carlo technique;   in a wider context we have all
observed situations in which a designer terminates a lengthy calculation because he has 'seen' a trend sufficiently accurately.

Frequently, the initial stages of design are associated with
the task of 'getting into the ball-park', while later stages are
concerned with fine adjustments to achieve an optimum design.   It
therefore seems likely that the design process may be enhanced if
the designer can choose between 'fast approximation' and 'slow
precision' as appropriate, and thereby reduce the time for design.
Our understanding of the design process could be enhanced if more
were known about the designer's decisions when faced with a choice
of this sort.

3. Iconography for Multiparameter Systems

One example of the efficient encoding of data in a visual
image (iconography) is provided by the animated sensitivity octagons
shown in Fig. 5. Many other examples can be found in a wide variety
of applications ranging from the design of reliable manufacturing
plant to a study of contraction mappings associated with transient
circuit analysis. In each case the problem is that of providing
the designer with insight into the characteristics of a multi-
parameter system. Suitable iconographic techniques do not appear
to be widely known or classified: I suspect that a great deal of
exploratory work and innovation needs to be carried out, preferably
in the context of specific applications.

4. Command Languages

A significant advantage of interactive-graphics is that the
designer can have available, for immediate consultation, a summary
of the state of the system. For example, in MINNIE, the display
in the right-hand ('control') area of the display screen describes
the properties displayed in the main screen area. The display can
also be verbalized from top to bottom. For example, I would read
from Fig. 2 that I am examining circuit <u>properties</u> in the <u>frequency
domain</u> from 10 Hz to 1 MHz: it is the <u>nominal response</u> between the
<u>input node</u> labelled ⟨I⟩ and the <u>output node</u> labelled ◈ : the
<u>response function</u> is the <u>gain</u> and <u>phase</u> of voltage amplification.

Furthermore, by making each entry in the control area of the
screen a sensitive light-button, a change of state is easily affected.
Also, by the application of simple rules for change of state, a very
<u>stable</u> command dialogue has been achieved: it is rarely that the
designer gets into a situation from which he cannot extricate himself.
Finally, very extensive use can be made of default options to
minimize the number of control actions the designer must take.

The MINNIE command dialogue was developed by trial-and-error,
since there appeared to be no readily available guidance on this
topic in spite of the key role it plays in determining a user's
satisfaction with a computer system. As the complexity of MINNIE
increases, is research needed into the design of command languages,
or will the simple innovations we have made suffice?

5. Problems: Their Classification and Representation

Dr. P. Innocent (British Ship Research Association) and
Mr. H.T. Smith (Nottingham University) have described problems of
various types which have been solved by means of a computer.
Innocent has studied the solution of the Tower of Hanoi problem

using a visual representation of the problem, and Smith has considered alternative pictorial representations of a problem in resource allocation.   I find both the problems and their embodiment in a picture of great interest, and I am led to ask if their findings are relevant to my own discipline of circuit design.   There is a clear need for a classification both of problems and their representation, so that any results obtained can, potentially, have much wider application.

6.   Irritation

As a CAD system designer, but also as a user of CAD systems designed by others, I am acutely aware that certain characteristics (eg. response time) can cause such a high degree of irritation in the user that there is a danger of the system being rejected as a possible tool for future use.   My question is, 'how can one measure parameters such as irritation and boredom which are relevant in this context?'   A satisfactory answer would allow pilot studies to be carried out prior to the implementation of a new system.

7.   People and Flexibility

Very early in our research into the potential of interactive-graphics for circuit design I saw the need to make a very clear distinction between three groups of people associated with a CAD system.   One is the user (the circuit designer in the case of MINNIE) who must be able to concentrate on design without the distraction of the irrelevancies of computer action and jargon. At the other extreme is the CAD system architect who, in addition to a good understanding of hardware and software, must appreciate the needs of the user.   (I think it is significant that the principal architects of the various versions of MINNIE, as well as its predecessor, all have a predominantly electrical engineering background). The third person involved is often called an applications programmer; with a sufficient knowledge of computers, programming and the needs of the user, he can maintain and, where necessary, modify the CAD system.   These people, their normal location and their typical 'density' are shown in Fig. 11.

In the initial development of MINNIE I kept this classification constantly in mind, since I had encountered CAD systems where the system architect clearly believed that the user would share his extensive knowledge of computers.   But it is also useful to relax the rigid classification shown in Fig. 11 to take account of differing abilities as well as general trends in education.   The question then arises as to the extent to which flexibility should be built into the system by its architect.   Opinions vary from a demand to 'let the user do anything he wants' to a call for extreme rigidity,

516

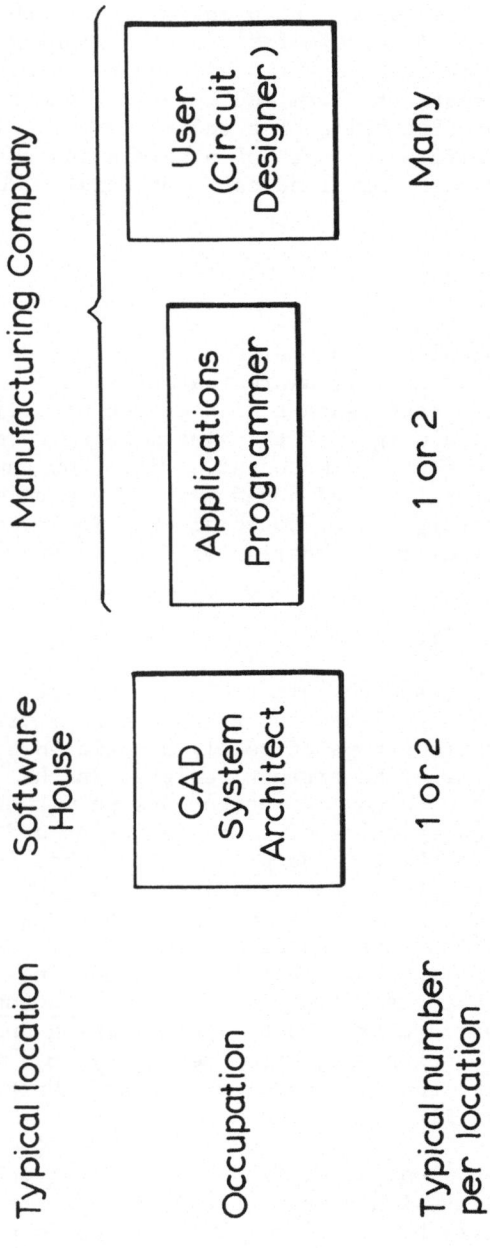

FIGURE 11. The three principal categories of people associated with a computer-aided design system.

and the answer is not clear.   I have already introduced the
flexibility illustrated in Figs. 8 and 9, particularly since the
new generation of circuit designers will find little difficulty in
using it.   I would also expect the applications programmer to be
given the freedom to introduce new device symbols and mathematical
models.   But the question remains open, and will probably only be
clarified in the long term via the success or otherwise of a variety
of CAD systems.

"After drawing the circuit diagram and
identifying M possibly redundant components,
I want to take the admittance matrix Y and
invert it to get the impedance matrix Z. $\qquad$ $Z \leftarrow \boxminus Y$

Then, I want to generate the port
impedance matrix ZP relevant to the $\qquad$ $ZP \leftarrow (\lozenge AP) + . \times Z + . \times AP$
identified components and the input and
output ports.

To test for the effect of replacing $\qquad$ $J \leftarrow \iota M$

components by short-circuits I must compute $\qquad$ $D \leftarrow DIA\ ZP$

the circuit's response deviation ΔVSC due $\qquad$ $\Delta VSC \leftarrow ZP[J;1] \times ZP[2;J] \div D$

to this change.   I then do the same thing $\qquad$ $\Delta VOC \leftarrow ZP[J;1] \times ZP[2;J] \div D - \div YB$
for replacement by open-circuits.

What I then want to do is search for $\qquad$ $\Delta VMIN \leftarrow \lfloor / |\Delta VSC, \Delta VOC$
the smallest magnitude deivation, and if it

is within the allowed error in circuit $\qquad$ $R \leftarrow (\Delta VMIN < B) \times \Delta VMIN \le |\Delta VSC, \Delta VOC$
response, identify which component removal
is possible.

This possibility of removal must then $\qquad$ $DISPLAY$ . . . .
be indicated graphically."

FIGURE 12.   On the left is a verbal description of an idea whose
viability was to be tested by implementation on a
computer.   On the right is both the mathematical
expression of the pertinent calculations and, with
very minor exceptions, the program for their execution.

8. Programming Language

Finally, I wish to describe an experience which is relevant to the ease with which potentially useful algorithms can be explored. On the left of Fig. 12 is my recollection of a conversation I had with a colleague who was being asked to write a programme for eventual inclusion within the MINNIE system. The programme was duly written, though in a time scale that one might expect from the use of FORTRAN as the programming language. Alongside, on the right of Fig. 12, I have jotted down the expressions that would be involved if the same programme were written in APL[+]; I have only cheated in assuming a complex arithmetic version of APL. (APL stands for A Programming Language; it was initially proposed as a new mathematical notation by Kenneth Iverson, and later implemented as an interactive programming language). The point I wish to make is that as well as completing the programming task in less than about one-tenth - and maybe in as little as one-fiftieth - of the time needed for the corresponding FORTRAN programme, little time and effort would have been wasted if the idea I was testing had proved to be worthless. One can make similar proposals concerning the inclusion of such an APL program within an interactive-graphic environment, and leading to simple graphical programming languages. With the rapidly decreasing cost of hardware (particularly computer memory) and increasing manpower costs, surely it would be useful for engineers and human factors specialists to propose new and simple languages, and for software specialists to look into their implementation?

CONCLUSION

From a background of engineering design I have been able to identify a number of important problems associated with man-computer interaction and whose solution could significantly enhance the efficacy of engineering design.

ACKNOWLEDGEMENTS

I gratefully acknowledge financial support from the UK Science Research Council and the UK Post Office, and the stimulating collaboration of my colleagues.

PART 9   -   EVALUATION AND THE WIDER CONTEXT

PREVIEW

When considering the question of evaluation in the wider sense
we need to ask ourselves what is MCI for?   Most if not all
people in the computing industry, or concerned with this area,
would assert that the whole activity is aimed at benefiting
people and society.   But there is something about the way in which
modern technological activities develop that seems to have a certain
inhumanity, and rapid computerisation has led to serious concern
among a growing number of people.

The successful result of more computerisation and good MCI
could be many potential benefits in terms of better working
conditions, shorter working hours, greater leisure, etc.   But one
of the major questions is how to achieve these benefits without
unacceptable costs (such as widespread disruption etc.).   Moreover, there are wider costs such as adapting to large changes in
the length and pattern of working life, which as yet have hardly
been explored.   The two biggest problems appear to be that we
need a completely new attitude to replace the traditional 'work
ethic', and we need acceptable methods of distributing the available real wealth.

As with most wider issues, it is much easier to recognise
problems than discern solutions.   We should recognise that neither
the technology nor people nor society necessarily set constraints
within this situation.   Indeed, it can reasonably be argued that
the technology enhances significantly the range of options realistically available.   The question is who will evaluate the costs
and benefits and make the necessary decisions?

The paper by Margulies considers most of these issues.   It
is concerned with evaluation, not in the more usual limited sense
of whether a system provides good MCI, but in the wider sense of
what will be the cost-benefit result for work people at all levels.
Margulies outlines the background of work in industry from the
first industrial revolution to the problems of worker alienation
today.   He then reviews the potential of computers for society
and also the problems implicit in the Tayloristic approach often
used by managers and computer designers.   He urges that the new
opportunities of computerisation must be sought through a new

approach by bringing computer people and experts and unions and work people together in a conjoint design process. An important goal to be achieved through these new opportunities, he suggests, is a major improvement in job-satisfaction for work people at all levels, as assessed against the well established job-satisfaction criteria.

Finally, turning from evaluation in a wider sense to a more limited horizon, the Epilogue briefly reviews the scope of this field of man-computer interaction and the coverage of this book. Some concluding comments are offered about the challenge for the future posed by the importance of achieving good man-computer interaction.

EVALUATING MAN-COMPUTER SYSTEMS

Fred Margulies

Austrian Federation of Trade Unions Vienna,
A-1013 Wien, Deutschmeisterplatz 2, Austria.

INTRODUCTION

The customary definition of a system states that the latter consists of a set of elements and a set of relations between these elements. Depending on the target-function of the particular system, different elements will have a different weighting of importance within this system. Turning to man-computer systems, obviously 'man' and 'computer' consistute sub-systems, each one of them consisting of a number of elements. The degree of importance attributed to man in these systems has changed over time. Today the approach is mainly based on the experience that systems will only work if man is given working conditions allowing for efficient man-computer interaction.

My point is that considering human factors solely to improve system performance is by no means sufficient. We have to answer the questions first, what this system is meant for, who is to benefit by its performance, what are (or could be) its ultimate implications. Even very efficient computer systems might have an adverse effect on man, as is shown in a rather gloomy outlook by Prof. T.B. Sheridan of MIT (Sheridan, 1976):

"The history of man has seen a gradual diminishing of man's self-image. Copernicus taught us that man is not the center of the universe. Darwin taught us that man is not different from the animals. Freud reduced man's stature still further by pointing to his irrationalities and inconsistencies. Will the computer-robot and its alienating influences be the ultimate insult to his dignity?"

Computer experts have a special responsibility to find a
better way. They will achieve this, if they develop a new
philosophy in designing their sytems, if they perceive the role
of man in a different way than Frederick W. Taylor did at the
beginning of this century, if they can find a new approach to
system design, different from if not contrary to Taylor. Social
Scientists and Trade Unions will have to play a major role in
design procedure to make this philosophy feasible, once it has
been adopted, and to help to realise it against various sources
of opposition.

THE ROLE OF MAN CHANGING OVER TIME

During the first periods of EDP-development, when labour-
saving was the declared and principal objective of manufacturers,
sellers and users alike, all emphasis in evaluating the system
was placed on computer hardware and software, on organisation and
structure, while the sub-system 'man' received little or no attention.
This neglect did not only apply to managers and computer experts,
it could be found to much the same extent with Trade Unions, then
mainly concerned about maintaining individual jobs and full employment while disregarding any other man-computer relationship.
Subconsciously, the alienation between the worker and his work
(or the product of his work), significant for the industrial
revolution and the period since, is being carried over into the
new era of the scientific and technological revolution, an era
which offers a genuine chance of overcoming alienation by means
of modern technology if applied within a new structure of society.

Since the early EDP-days things have changed considerably.
Technological development has converted the computer from a giant
toy for a few sophisticated scientists into an everyday tool for
millions of people all over the world. Thus the Unions have
become aware of the impact computers will have on the individual
as well as on society as a whole. And likewise, computer experts
have realized - much to their surprise in many cases - that computers
cannot and will not work without man. The more complex and sophisticated information systems become, the more dependent they are on
man's creativity, on his ability to think, to decide and to act
where programmes fail. The dream of the machine doing everything
on its own just cannot come true.

Our present industrial system, which started with the industrial
revolution of the 18th and 19th centuries when the material basis
of capitalism was created, has been characterized by a tremendous
development of the means of production (tools, machines, production
methods, and sources of energy) while man's development has
continuously lagged behind. In the pre-industrial age heavy
physical labour was the principal factor in production. But even
then every single production process required a mental effort in

addition to physical labour; as a rule, it was the producer himself who planned his own work, implemented and completed it.
Mental and physical labour constituted an integral whole, which
made possible a certain development of personality and required
and rendered feasible certain creative activity.

In contrast, mass factory production of the industrial era
led to increased division of labour, to a separation of mental and
physical effort.   The rising share of creative activity remained
the preserve of a relatively small group of higher employees,
whereas most of the white and blue-collar workers in production
became appendages of the machine, at best, and in extreme cases
their work was confined to the brainless and soul-destroying
repetition of unchanging tasks.

Thus the worker has lost his personality and his personal
relationship to his work.   In the working process there are no
decisions for him to make.   Every step is prescribed and the
machine to which he is subordinated is not his property.   Others
dispose of the product which he helps to create.   Very often he
does not even know what the product looks like when it leaves the
factory or what it is being used for.

In "Das Kapital" Karl Marx writes: "Even facilitating work
becomes a means of torment since the machine does not liberate the
worker from his task but rather strips work of its content."

NEW HOPES BY NEW TECHNOLOGIES

Increasingly, people resist this dehumanisation.   The elementary
need for realisation and full development of one's own personality
for purposive, gratifying and creative activity is becoming more
and more to the foreground once material want has been overcome
and the physical necessities of life are assured.   The revolt
against work on the assembly lines in the United States, Germany,
Sweden or France, and the protests against the monotony of performing
always the same manual tasks, manifest this trend, just as was the
case with the unrest at the universities or the strike of the metal
workers in the German province of Nordbaden for improved working
conditions under the slogan: "Man must get priority over productivity and profit."

The scientific and technological revolution of our age invites
the great chance of reversing the trends of the industrial system.
The new technology no longer requires the division of labour nor
does man need to continue being an appendage of the machine.
Wherever within the industrial system man became an automaton,
automata are now in a better position to perform this work quicker
and with less friction.   Man turns from a servant of the machine
into a supervisor, guide and partner.   Man finds the task adequate
to his nature in the interrelationship of the man-machine system.

MAN AND COMPUTER - ANTAGONISTIC STRUCTURES

Thus in the construction and design of this man-machine
system, the role assigned to man becomes the main problem.   Any
man-machine system, especially so a man-computer system, in
reality combines two structures of utmost antagonism (Zemanek,
1975).   The computer is a scientifically formalised machine with
stable properties;   once designed and built, it does not change
though it might fail.   Man still is, and probably always will
be natural, not formalised, never stable, changing as long as he
lives - even where he does not fail.   It would be feasible to
obtain a perfect description of any computer, enabling the user
to rebuild the original time and again with the same predictable
properties.   But in trying to describe a human being, it soon
becomes apparent that the more extensive and detailed the description, the less adequate a coverage of the real personality it
seems to be - to say nothing of the possibility of reproduction.

The computer has come nearer to human capacity than any other
machine but in that - probably more than any other machine - has
proved its dependency on the complementary functions of the human
being, ie. on the type of person who is not deprived of but who is
endowed with reason, able to make his own decisions and aware of
his power to act deliberately.   In our updated terminology we
would call this model the 'motivated man'.

OUTDATED TAYLORISM - STILL ALIVE

To bring about this motivation should really be a common aim
of unions and scientists, rather distinct from the kind of motivation
management is very often aiming at.   Their philosophy dates back
to Frederick W. Taylor, the inventor of "Scientific Management".
He perceived the worker as a person who will only render optimum
performance if his work is divided into the simplest repetitive
elementary processes, if his output is being measured with the
highest degree of accuracy and if his wage system provides incentives
for maximum effort (Taylor, 1911).

This perception basically still holds its ground with many
managers in many companies in many countries, in spite of all
warnings issued by occupational and social scientists against
these outdated views of Taylorism.   To cite just one, the German
sociologist Professor Dr. Burghardt Lutz, head of the Munich
Institute of Social Science Research, in an article (1970) touches
upon the phenomenon of neo-Taylorism in administration:

"As far as may be seen today, neo-Taylorism represents a very
efficient method for achieving short-term increases in
productivity.   There are, however, many indications that -
taking a middle - or long-range perspective - a high price
will have to be paid for such increases ......

The main advantage of neo-Taylorism – providing jobs that
may be performed by 'anybody' after brief instructions – at
the same time implies a principal disadvantage: the basic
incentive for learning that stems from the confrontation
with new problems is thus reduced to a minimum. 'Fool-proof'
jobs are jobs that bar further development of any capabilities
dwelling in the persons performing such tasks."

Would not that be an explanation why computer systems seem to
become less fool-proof, the more 'fool-proof' you are trying to
make them?

Unfortunately, system designers still seem to adhere to
Taylorism to a great extent. An international research on
"Computer Systems and Work Design" (Hedberg and Mumford, 1975)
carried out recently in several countries including Sweden and
Britain has revealed how deeply rooted Taylorism still is. The
majority of the system designers interviewed not only did not feel
responsible for the design of jobs with respect to human factors,
they did not even bother to consult systems users on more than
minor issues which would not influence the basic design factors.
Asked for their perception of the users they tend to classify them
on the line with McGregor's (1960) Theory X type (which has much
in common with Taylor's perception) as people who prefer strictly
structured work tasks where they are told exactly what to do, when
to do it and how to do it – with very little left to individual
responsibility and decision.

At the other end of the scale there is McGregor's Theory Y
type, a responsible, self-achieving individual who can take full
control of his work environment. A comparison between British
and Swedish system designers showed that the Swedish are much more
inclined to place their users into the Y type than are the British,
but in any case it looks as if the two sub-systems 'man' and
'computer' still do not receive equal treatment.

Before a new computer system is being installed, extended
investigations will be made to make sure that all requirements
are met. Experts will carry out feasibility studies, they will
check computer performance against demands and capacity against
future developments; others will design new forms for data collection, adjust the organisation if necessary, provide air conditioning
in accordance with computer specifications, and so on.

Nothing of the kind will happen with respect to the people
who have to operate the system. They will be told about the
changes in their work and in their environment on a 'take it or
leave it' basis and this attitude will be supported by the argument
that these conditions are enforced by the computer and cannot be
changed.

THE HUMANE APPROACH

'Equal treatment' requires an entirely different approach; it means putting computer demands and human needs at least on equal footing, setting out on the basis of two fundamental hypotheses:

1. Computer systems are not technologically deterministic but allow for different forms of work organisation and different job structures to meet the needs of the workers.
2. Work is not a curse but an elementary need in human life. Historically, work marks the transition from animal to man; materially, work provides the means of existence for the individual and the species; ethically, work means daily self-realisation by creativity.

Our goal, therefore, must not be to liberate man from work but to liberate work from inhuman working conditions.

This is all the more true in a society where last year 18 million people in Europe were 'liberated from work' and driven into unemployment.

What then are 'humane working conditions' and how are they to be implemented in computer systems?

It is possible to break down humanisation of work into three distinct but interconnected and interdependent levels (D.O.S.G. 1973):

1. Health and safety
2. Personal well-being
3. Chance for self-realisation and creativity.

Let us consider these levels one by one.

Health and Safety

To provide working conditions which will ensure health and safety to the employee appears to be a trivial matter. Yet, simple observation as well as sophisticated research will prove the contrary. The percentage of work places which constitute physical hazards is appallingly high and the advent of the computer has made things even worse in some respects.

Take for example air conditioning systems. They will usually be laid out according to the computer's requirements - irrespective of the operator's possible discomfort or illness; if man's requirements had been given priority, it might have caused damage to the computer and there cannot be any doubt in whose favour such a decision would be taken.

Or take the use of visual display units.   When we repeatedly received complaints from VDU operators about headaches, sore eyes, etc., at our union, we asked two institutes of Vienna University to investigate the eye-stress resulting from VDU work.   Their findings: after four hours of work at a VDU, sight was reduced by 1/4 dioptres, with recovery taking between 15 and 30 minutes. If the same measures were taken after one hour of work, sight reduction was only 1/8 dioptres or less while recovery only took 10 to 15 minutes (Haider/Slezak, 1975).

Obviously very simple and inexpensive changes in work organisation could take care of these findings without changing anything in the technology used.   Our demand that employees after one hour of intensive VDU work switch to some other task for at least one hour or else be granted a break of ten minutes after each working hour has been implemented in many instances already.

A great number of other items, risk factors to health and safety, will have to be considered when designing a computer system. Ergonomics is the science to be applied here.   It provides more or less exact figures and limits for noise and light conditions, temperature and humidity in the room, space to be allotted per person, optimum shape and design of chairs and other types of furniture, schedule of working hours and many other similar elements.

The relevant regulations are generally known or can be made available very easily (eg. Grandjean, 1963).   All that is necessary is to apply them, but no system designer will be able to settle all this or even to think of all this while he is preoccupied with problems of software packages, terminal distribution and job control. Therefore no system designer should even start his job without including a Trade Union representative, a medical doctor and an ergonomist in his team.

Personal well-being

The second level to be considered is personal well-being. "Health is more than the absence of illness", says the WHO, the World Health Organisation.   In accordance with this slogan, the second level implies going beyond health and safety provisions by offering comfortable conditions, a friendly atmosphere, flexible working hours, flexible work organisation, etc.   Here again social scientists and the people involved should have to have their say before any decision is taken.

Self-realisation and Creativity

Certainly the most rewarding but also the most demanding issue is implied on the third level: the increase of job satisfaction and the design of jobs in such a way that everybody is given a chance for self-realisation and creativity in his work.

There are many tests and studies being carried out on man's motivation in order to find out what makes him happy and content. I must admit that I am increasingly sceptical about these studies. It is not hard to find out what makes a man discontent and unhappy. Contentment and happiness, however, are made up of so many components that in most instances it is impossible even for the person himself (and less so for an outsider) to draw up a complete and integrated pattern. To me it seems the epitome of misconception to try and tell someone else how he is to become happy.

I have been told that in an American plant a group of socio-logists for the umptieth time wanted to conduct an investigation; they were received by the firm's employees with a poster stating "Do not feed the animals". If we have reached the stage when our search for man's true happiness imparts the feeling that man is to be an object of curiosity in a zoo, then we are obviously on the wrong track. We will only be able to reach our goal if we give people the chance to do their own thinking, to make their own decisions and to implement them. All those who have engaged in creative activity of some kind know from their own experience that the possibility of decision-making is the most attractive aspect of one's work.

Why should not it be possible to initiate preparations for a new computer system by informing everybody involved in its use about the qualities, possibilities and limitations of the system and then ask them to consider in small working groups what part of their work they would like to assign to a computer and what other tasks they would like to assume instead. I do not know how good the proposals of such groups will be, and I am not sure that all staff members will accept such an assignment with the same amount of enthusiasm; we must recognise the fact that desire and ability to do creative work are by no means general phenomena. Nevertheless we ought to offer a general chance to everybody to work creatively. Considering all the badly operated and incorrectly used information processing installations, the above-mentioned method should at least lead to some sort of improvement.

Another even more complicated issue concerns the work of the programmers. New programming methods such as structured program-ming, standardised programming, computer-aided programming and the like tend to convert programming from an art into a job; they spell the menace of industrialising and 'Taylorising' what for a long time was the incarnation of creative work brought about by modern technology. On the other hand, if applied in a different way, taking account of human desire for challenge and creativity in his work, these methods might very well increase the capacity, creativity and job satisfaction of the programmer, at the same time reducing time pressure, stress and overtime. A symposium

organised by our Union jointly with the Vienna University of
Technology last year dealt extensively and successfully with this
problem (Gewerkschaft et al., 1975). We are presently trying to
elaborate guidelines which will secure the 'Human Choice' when
applying new programming methods, thus making full use of their
advantages while avoiding their disadvantages.

This example might also serve to illustrate our Trade Union's
strategy with respect to technological change: while fully
approving of technological progress, we are equally striving to
have it consciously applied for human benefit in close inter-
disciplinary co-operation with scientists and experts. It is
for the human being, individually and collectively, that the
optimal operating mode must be found, and not for the computer.

ALTERNATIVE JOB STRUCTURES AND WORK ORGANIZATION

I have mentioned before that the basic hypothesis behind any
genuine attempt at 'humanisation of work' is the premise that
technology is not deterministic. The solution of any problem
allows for a choice between basically different forms of work
organization and different job structures.

Professor E. Thorsrud, until recently head of the Work Research
Institute in Oslo and one of the pioneers in this field, illustrates
his hypothesis in a paper (1974). To show what organizational
choice might mean, he looks at three basic questions and the possible
answers for them:

1. What are the standard building blocks of organizations?
    In most cases: One person and one job (or main task).
    There is a major alternative to this, namely a group of people
    and a group of tasks. These two alternatives could be used
    deliberately in a great number of combinations within each
    organization. Usually the group principle is in contrast
    to and inconsistent with the standard organizational design.

2. What is the basic pattern of information in organizations?
    The standard is: up and down the status hierarchy, and mainly
    downwards. The alternative to the vertical system of commun-
    ication and control is that it can be horizontal and functional.
    A combination of vertical, horizontal and functional systems
    of information can be used within each organization but there
    is one great limitation. If the building blocks consist of
    one person and one job, the vertical system of communication
    is encouraged by the status system that is generated as a
    consequence. To whom does the boss turn when he wants some-
    thing done? To whom does the subordinate turn when he does
    not know what to do?

3. What are the standard criteria of evaluation in organizations?
    In spite of all lip service paid to social and psychological
    criteria, the economic and technical criteria dominate in
    practical life.   The reason for this is not only that these
    two sets of criteria are still critical ones for organizations,
    but also that little is done to make other criteria practicable,
    eg. the need to provide conditions for learning, participation
    in decision-making, conditions for·co-operation and social
    support, etc.

To work out alternatives of this kind and to make them
operational, put them to discussion, disseminate all the necessary
information and give employees the chance of real participation in
the design and choice of the system.   Would that not be a major
challenge to the systems designers, organisers and all the rest
of the staff responsible for implementing a new computer system?
Would it not provide a very worthwhile enrichment of their job to
know that the system is not only technologically operable but at
the same time caters for individual, psychological and sociological
needs of the people affected?   Is it not satisfying to prove that
computer systems not only allow for but even increase the possibilities of human choice?

JOB SATISFACTION CRITERIA

Enid Mumford of Manchester Business School (1972) has compiled
a series of what she calls "contracts between management and employees".
They are meant to be implicit rather than explicit agreements,
which if implemented would both increase the job satisfaction of
the employee and help further the employees' objectives.   Five
"contracted areas" are set out as follows:

The knowledge contract
The firm needs a certain level of skill and knowledge in its
employees, if it is to function efficiently.   The employee
needs the skills and knowledge he brings with him to be used
and developed.

The psychological contract
The firm needs motivated employees.   The employee needs factors
which will motivate him eg. achievement, recognition, responsibility, status.

The efficiency contract
The firm needs to achieve set output and quality standards.
The employee needs an equitable effort-reward bargain, needs
controls, including supervisory ones, which are seen as
acceptable.

The ethical (social value) contract

The firm needs employees who will accept the firm's ethos
and values. The employee needs to work for an employer
whose values do not contravene his own.

The task structure contract

The firm needs employees who will accept any technical
constraints associated with their jobs. The employee needs
a set of tasks which meets his requirement for variety,
interest, targets, feedback, task identity and autonomy.

Mumford's hypothesis says that if an employee's needs in
these five areas are met, he will have a high job satisfaction.
Similarly, if the firm's needs are met in the five areas, they
can be expected to be satisfied with the performance and attitudes
of their employees. "A beneficial work environment for both sets
of interested parties will have been achieved."

This approach is based on the assumption that common interests
between employers and employees are the predominant feature in
industrial relations. Both theoretical consideration and practical experience show however that this need not always be so
(Mumford: "What is good for the firm is not necessarily good for
the employee"). More often than not management will object to the
kind of socio-technical approach described above as a waste of
time, money and brain power. It will do so unless the whole thing
turns out to be of considerable advantage to the firm, thus degrading
the idea of humanisation of work into what a German Trade Union
publication called "a mere lubricant for the production-and-power-
machinery to smooth the process of intensifying performance and
increasing profits".

What then can the answer be if "employer's needs" and employee's
needs" turn out to contradict each other? Which one is to be given
priority? And who is to decide on the priority scale? The computer
expert, and in particular the system designer who is aware of the
fact that fundamental changes in computer technology and application
demand equally fundamental changes in organisation and hierarchy,
might find himself between the grindstones of management and employees,
of computer and man. Obviously it would be inappropriate for the
designer to make a heroic gesture trying to fight it all out for
himself and it would be unjust to put all the responsibility upon
his shoulders. On the other hand, the computer expert by virtue
of his expert knowledge, cannot but accept a rather big share of
responsibility while looking for support.

SOLUTIONS WITH THE PEOPLE

As was shown earlier in this paper the socio-technical
approach in the design of man-computer systems is a challenge not
only to system designers but to experts of various disciplines,
such as medicine or social science. Together they will have to
work out alternative solutions, offering a genuine choice to the
employees.

The design of man-computer systems, however, is a challenge
also to our society as a whole, to make democracy work not only
in states and communities but also in plants and offices, by
offering everybody the opportunity to take his choice.

If we agree that Taylor's perception of man, if it ever was
justified, certainly does not apply today, if we want health,
human well-being and self-realisation to have priority over
economical and technological considerations, then decisions on
investments, work organisation, work structure and the like must
not be left in the hands of the employers alone. Industrial
democracy is the main prerequisite for humanisation of work and
it can only be brought about if all those really interested in
technological progress and in well-functioning man-machine systems,
if engineers, social scientists, workers and trade unions all in
their own well-founded interest, will work together. Industrial
democracy to my mind essentially means finding new solutions not
for the people, but with the people.

SCANDINIAVIAN EXPERIMENTS

Let me illustrate this by some impressions I brought home
from a ten day visit last year with an Austrian Trade Union group
to Norway, Sweden and Denmark, where we had discussions with
Trade Union and management representatives and visited one plant
in each of the three countries. You certainly know of the great
number of experiments with autonomous groups, self-controlling
groups, work structure and the like that have been carried out in
Sweden and in other Scandinavian countries. Though most of the
experiments were reported to have been successful, only one case
has come to my knowledge that has been extended to a full scale
application for the whole plant and that is the Kalmar model of
Volvo. Everywhere else apparently the experiment remained a more
or less isolated affair, either it was suspended after a while or
it is just dragging on but without any further impact on the
general structure.

My impression was that most of the experiments have been
initiated by social scientists who convinced management and unions
to participate. Only where some labour issues became real
problems (like turnover at Volvo or severe dissatisfaction with

the MTM wage system at Atlas Copco) did management or the union
or both start to look for new solutions – not so much to change
the situation fundamentally but rather to side-track the problems.
This would account for the limited objectives of most experiments
and for the limited drive to expand them once those objectives
have been achieved.

In addition to that we found many indications that the
experiments had developed their own dynamics. Workers became
more self-confident, they asked for better wage systems, for the
abolishment of incentive wages, for the extension of their autonomy
into higher levels of the hierarchy like planning, administration,
etc. Thereupon management lost interest in these experiments.

Workers also became more active in their trade union organization. Having started to taste self-government at work they
aimed at more autonomy in trade union issues as well, questioning
hierarchical and organisational structures. Consequently, some
Union officials too many have lost interest in these experiments.

In some instances workers also became selfish, they developed
some sort of group egotism, trying to expel weaker workers from
their group, etc. As a result some of the workers may have lost
their enthusiasm.

What remained were the scientists who continued to publish
papers and books on their small-scale experiments. I do not
know to what extent these rather superficial observations are
correct but I do feel that industrial democracy and humanisation
of work in Scandinavia too still remain to be realized.

WORKERS PARTICIPATION IN DECISION-MAKING

Scandinavian experiments, however, have certainly brought
about some tremendous progress in proving that alternatives to
Taylor do exist and that technology as such is not deterministic.
But these experiments have also proved that new solutions, aimed
at improving man-machine relationship, meant to bring about humanisation of work in the sense explained before, will necessarily
have an impact on the hierarchical structure of the firm, on the
pattern of distribution of power and of decision-making, and
eventually on some fundamental aspects of our society. They will
be successful only if they are accompanied by a general process
of industrial democratisation. For this reason many trade unions
concentrate on demanding participation for workers in all technological and administrative decisions (Dallinger, 1975). We want
the employers to provide full information in good time – in the
planning stage of a computer system or better still prior to
specific planning. We also want the employees to be represented

in all in-company committees dealing with planning and development
of computer systems.   This is often objected to on the pretext
that shop stewards do not have enough expert knowledge;   therefore
it would suffice to inform them once the social consequences have
become apparent - which is at a much later point in time.

I would suggest two remarks in answer to that argument.
First I would like to say that within management decision-making
power does not always go hand in glove with comprehensive knowledge.
While shop stewarts who are able to acquaint themselves at least
with the basic concepts of electronic data processing, in courses
offered by the trade unions, also have experts at their disposal
within the trade unions who may support them and give them information.   However, the second and principal argument is that the
shop steward's committee is not designed for nor does it intend
to interfere in technological and administrative details.   Its
primary task is to see that from the first moment of planning the
human problems are placed on the agenda.   The committee also has
to pass on information to those concerned and to stimulate them
to consider and formulate their own demands.   In other words, the
aim is to see that the process of humanisation of work is initiated
by the workers themselves.

If computer experts and social scientists co-operated with
employees and their representatives in order to make first-hand
acquaintance with their needs, proposals and demands, if they
would then base their design work on these criteria, they would
avoid getting between the grindstones and would succeed in developing viable man-computer systems.   On their own behalf and in the
interest of technological and social progress to which they are
dedicated, experts of all disciplines ought to become the most
fervent and determined advocates of workers' participation.

REFERENCES

Dallinger, A.   1975   Trade Unions and computers.
                               In: Proc. of the IFIP Conf. on Human
                                  Choice and Computers.
                               North-Holland Pub. Co., Amsterdam.

Dallinger, A.   1973   Menschengerechte arbeitsgestalt.
                               Deutscher Osterreichischer Schweizer
                                  Gewerkschaftsbund.
                               Kammer für Arbeiter und Angestellte
                                  für Wien.

Dallinger, A. 1975 Symposium: Neue Wege der Programmierung
und die Zukunft des Programmierers.
Gewerkschaft der Privatangestellten
und Technische Universitat Wien.
Protokoll - for further information
write to author.

Grandjean, E. 1963 Leitfaden der Ergonomie.
Ott Verlag, Thun und Munchen.

Haider/Slezak 1975 Arbeitsbeanspruchung und Augenbelastung
an Bildschirmgeräten.
Verlag des Osterr. Gewerkschaftsbundes,
Wien.

Hedberg, B. & 1975 The design of computer systems.
Mumford, E. In: Proc. of the IFIP Conf. on Human
Choice and Computers;
North-Holland Pub. Co., Amsterdam.

Lutz, B. 1970 Zu einigen problemen des technischen
fortschritts im verwaltungsbereich.
IBM-Nachrichten. August.

McGregor, D. 1960 The human side of enterprise.
McGraw Hill, New York.

Mumford, E. 1972 Job satisfaction.
Longman, London.

Sheridan, T.B. 1976 Production control task allocation to
man versus computer.
Paper to Joint Automatic Control Conf.,
Purdue University, July 27-30.
(available from author, Department of
Mechanical Engineering, M.I.T.,
Cambridge, Mass., U.S.A.)

Taylor, F.W. 1911 The principles of scientific management.
Harper & Row, London.

Thorsrud, E. 1974 Changes in work organisation and
managerial roles.
Work Research Institute, Oslo).

536

Zemanek, H.   1975   The human being and the automaton –
                              selected aspects of a philosophy
                              information processing.
                              In: Proc. of the IFIP Conf. on Human
                              Choice and Computers.
                              North Holland Pub. Co., Amsterdam.

EPILOGUE

Until the mid 1970's and even later the standard procedure
was 'computerisation'; but now one hears much more about the
'end user' and 'user-friendly systems'. Thus the computer industry
is beginning to realise the need to change from technology-oriented
criteria to criteria based upon concepts of matching the expectations, needs and satisfactions of the user. The Advanced Study
Institute upon which this book is based may have helped in some
small way to encourage that trend.

But accepting that the goal is to achieve successful and
satisfying man-computer interaction adds considerable complexity
to the process of design and application. It is not at all easy
to design for what real people really want. This is evident from
many examples. Indeed for most ordinary users and even for some
computer professionals the man-computer interface is a space
frontier and a time barrier rather than an open door to communication.

One of the most important factors adding complexity to designing for good man-computer interaction is simply the scope of 'man'
in such situations. The user is not a single entity but comprises
many different types, levels and groups of people. First there
are the directors who authorise and 'buy' computer systems (and
might use their results), then the managers who supervise them
(and may well use their results), the operators and sometimes
managers inside the system who are often the true 'end users', and
the public who may use or be affected by the system. Within such
broad groups there are many different types and levels of people
in different applications. So generalisations about 'the user'
must be made with some care.

Moreover, it follows that one human being does not represent
and cannot necessarily design at all successfully for others, just
by virtue of being a human being. Therefore, with regard to both
research about and design for MCI, it is evident that researchers
and in turn designers must first define clearly and fully each time
the exact characteristics of the people involved and the tasks which
they are doing.

This factor of the scope and complexity of human affairs,
and therefore of the field of MCI (because the computer has the
potential of becoming a useful tool or job-aid for many facets of
human affairs), is perhaps the most important feature to be

emphasised from the papers in this book.   Although this is rather an obvious truism, it can easily be overlooked and it explains the breadth of topics mentioned here: from doctor-patient inter- viewing to the theory of problem-solving and the risk of 'dehuman- ising' work.

Even so, not all the subjects are included which might have been expected.   For example, from the beginning it was decided not to include Computer Aided Instruction or Learning (CAI or CAL) or Computer Aided Design (CAD), because these are already substan- tive specific application areas.   But good MCI is clearly crucial for these applications; therefore, there are two chapters by Annett and Spence focussing specifically and to good effect upon the MCI aspects.

In general, however, it is thought that the scope of MCI has been adequately presented.   Reference to the list of major factors in MCI proposed on page 17 suggests that most areas, except for computer system performance deliberately omitted, are represented to the more detailed level, even though the extent and emphasis does of course vary between topics.   Inevitably there are some gaps in coverage.   Apart from a number of minor omissions it is believed that there are only three major gaps: privacy, speech and computer conferencing.   Privacy is as much if not more a legal and political issue and so has been bypassed.   The progress in studying and developing speech input and output is a major topic for MCI; an excellent set of review papers has been published in a special issue 'Man-machine communication by voice' Proc.IEEE, 1976, 64.4, 403-557.   Computer-based teleconferencing has similarly been well represented in publications by S.R. Hiltz & M. Turoff 'The Network Nation', Addison-Wesley 1978, and by R. Johansen, J. Vallee & K. Spangler 'Electronic Meetings', Addison-Wesley 1979.

The above references, about the areas not represented here, and the papers in this book all reflect a welcome growth in attention to the human aspects of MCI.   Such attention was relatively of little importance in the very early days when the few specialists using computers adapted their communication behaviour to the computer's rigid constraints.   But, as Eason has pointed out, "when the data processing era dawned and with it the development of computing from remote terminals, man/computer communication became an issue .because the users were the clerks and managers of business organisations.   These people did not have the professional expertise to communicate with the computer and were often unwilling and unable to develop this expertise. We are still grappling with the problems of this era but, as is often the case, technological progress has thrust us into a new era with current problems still unsolved.   With the advent of cheap microprocessors, we are now entering an era where members of the public can be the consumers of computer technology by

purchasing computers or computing power for their private interest
and amusement, or by using computers in their daily transactions
with banks, government services, shops and so on.   The widening
of the boundaries of the everyday use of computing to include
potentially the entire population brings the problems of man/computer
communication into critical focus".

Looking to the immediate future of MCI, it seems likely that
there will be considerable growth in two distinct directions.
In research and system development, the study of new possibilities
for man-computer communication will probably accelerate, in such
areas for example as speech systems, natural language systems and
storage structures using different approaches (eg. spatial data
organisation).   In application and system design, there will
probably be a marked growth of attention to formal methods of
designing for human use.   Some research will also be needed to
improve and generalise these methods, particularly the approach
of user-centred design;   but in the main the concentration needs
to be upon disseminating and applying the knowledge and techniques
already available from the human sciences.

It will be evident, from the way in which different contributions have come from widely different orientations, that the subject
of MCI is by no means yet a co-ordinated entity;   so, as a specific
field it is basically in its infancy, with much to be done and with
many interesting challenges.   For the researchers, in both computing
and human sciences, there is still much to learn about people and
the possibilities which computer technology may bring for human
development.   For the computer professional and designer, the
challenge is to learn new skills and knowledge about people, to
accept new methods and advisers, and especially to work with users.
As a result, computers in MCI partnership may gradually evolve to
a new status as useful and not mistrusted tools of society.   It
is the Editor's hope that this book may contribute to that better
usage and understanding.

B. Shackel

APPENDIX 1

CONTRIBUTORS TO THIS BOOK

Prof. J. Annett	Department of Psychology University of Warwick Coventry CV4 7AL U.K.
Dr. J.H. Bair	Manager, Behavioral Sciences Bell-Northern Research Stanford Industrial Park Palo Alto California 94304 U.S.A.
Dr. J.D. Baker	U.S. Army Research Institute 5001 Eisenhower Avenue Alexandria Virginia 22333 U.S.A.
Prof. R. Bernotat	Forschungsinstitut fur Anthropotechnik Konigstrasse 2 D-5307 Wachtberg-Werthoven Germany
Prof. A. Chapanis	Department of Psychology The Johns Hopkins University Baltimore Maryland 21218 U.S.A.
Ms. L. Damodaran	Department of Human Sciences University of Technology Loughborough Leicestershire LE11 3TU U.K.
Mr. K.D. Eason	Department of Human Sciences University of Technology Loughborough Leicestershire LE11 3TU U.K.

Dr. C.R. Evans   Division of Computer Sciences
(Died 1979)   National Physical Laboratory
                        Teddington
                        Middlesex
                        U.K.

Dr. M.J. Fitter   MRC Social & Applied Psychology Unit
                        The University
                        Sheffield
                        U.K.

Dr. T. Ivergård   Ergolab
                        Renstiernas gata 12
                        116 31 Stockholm
                        Sweden

Dipl.Ing. F. Margulies Sekretar der Gewerkschaft der
                            Privatangestellten
                        Wien, AM
                        A-1013 Wien
                        Deutschmeisterplatz 2
                        Austria

Dr. T.H. Martin   Annenberg School of Communications
                        University of Southern California
                        Los Angeles
                        California 90007
                        U.S.A.

Dr. R.S. Nickerson   Bolt Beranek & Newman Inc.
                        50 Moulton Street
                        Cambridge
                        Massachusetts 02138
                        U.S.A.

Dr. O. Östberg   Department of Work Sciences
                        University of Lulea
                        S-95187 Lulea
                        Sweden

Mr. J. Palme   Swedish National Defense Research Institute
                        FOA 1
                        S-104 50 Stockholm 80
                        Sweden

Prof. H. Sackman   Information Systems Department
                        School of Business
                        California State Polytechnic University
                        Pomona
                        California 91768
                        U.S.A.

Prof. B. Shackel

Department of Human Sciences
University of Technology
Loughborough
Leicestershire LE11 3TU
U.K.

Mr. M. Sime

MRC Social & Applied Psychology Unit
The University
Sheffield
U.K.

Dr. R. Spence

Department of Electrical Engineering
Imperial College
Exhibition Road
London SW7 2BT
U.K.

Mr. T.F.M. Stewart

Butler Cox and Partners
Morley House
26-30 Holborn Viaduct
London EC1A 2BP
U.K.

Prof. E. Vanlommel

Rijksuniversitair Centrum Antwerpen
2020 - Antwerpen
Middelheimlaan 1
Belgium

APPENDIX 2

INSTITUTE PARTICIPANTS

This appendix gives the names and addresses of all lecturers
and participants at the Advanced Study Institute on Man-Computer
Interaction.   It will be evident from their addresses and titles
that the participants reveal a very wide range of background and
expertise.   There were approximately 15 postgraduate students and
the remainder were of post-doctoral level or above including
6 full professors and one Dean of a Faculty.   In total 66
participants were accepted to attend and of these eventually
6 were unable to come to Greece for various reasons at the last
moment.   Thus the total number of 'students' was 60, together with
14 invited lecturers and 3 participants speakers, making a grand
total of 77.

The participants came from 12 different nations, with a
preponderance from the U.S.A. and U.K. as would be expected.
However, a good number of 'students' also came from the Netherlands,
Germany, France, Sweden and Greece.

Because some of the participants had already undertaken
research in the field of MCI, all were asked whether they would
wish to make a short contribution to invite comment and discussion
from the lecturers and other participants.   About half of the
participants requested to do so; these contributions were arranged
in tutorial sessions, and proved to be very interesting and relevant
in showing the wide range of research and applications already in
hand.   The detailed programme including the contributions in these
tutorial sessions is shown in Appendix 3.

NATO ASI on MCI - LECTURERS AND PARTICIPANTS

INVITED LECTURERS

Prof. J. Annett,
Department of Psychology,
University of Warwick,
Coventry CV4 7AL.
England.

Dr. J.D. Baker,
U.S. Army Research Institute,
5001 Eisenhower Avenue,
Alexandria 22333,
U.S.A.

Prof. R. Bernotat,
Forschungsinstitut fur Anthropotechnik,
Konigstrasse 2,
D-5307 Wachtberg-Werthoven,
Germany.

Prof. A. Chapanis,
Department of Psychology,
The Johns Hopkins University,
Baltimore,
Maryland 21218,
U.S.A.

Dr. C.R. Evans, (Died 1979)
Division of Computer Sciences,
National Physical Laboratory,
Teddington,
Middlesex.
England.

Dr. T. Ivergard,
Ergolab,
Renstiernas gata 12,
116 31 Stockholm,
Sweden.

Dipl.Ing. F. Margulies,
Sekretar der Gewerkschaft der
  Privatangestellten,
Wien, AM
A-1013 Wien,
Deutschmeisterplatz 2.

Dr. O. Ostberg,
Prof. of Engineering Psychology,
Department of Work Sciences,
University of Lulea,
S-95187 Lulea,
Sweden.

Prof. H. Sackman,
Information Systems Department
School of Business
California State Polytechnic
Pomona,
California 91768,
U.S.A.

Prof. B. Shackel
Department of Human Sciences
University of Technology
Loughborough
Leics. LE11 3TU
U.K.

Dr. M. Sime,
MRC Social & Applied Psychology
  Research Unit,
The University,
Sheffield,
England.

Mr. T.F.M. Stewart,
Butler Cox & Partners,
Morley House,
26-30 Holborn Viaduct,
London EC1A 2BP
U.K.

Dr. L.F. Thomas,
Department of Psychology,
Brunel University,
Uxbridge,
Middlesex.
England.

Prof. E. VanLommel,
Rijksuniversitair Centrum Antwerpen,
2020 - Antwerpen,
Middelheimlaan 1,
Belgium.

PARTICIPANT SPEAKERS

Dr. James H. Bair,
Manager, Behavioral Sciences,
Bell-Northern Research,
Stanford Industrial Park,
Palo Alto,
California 94304,
U.S.A.

Ms. L. Damodaran,
Department of Human Sciences,
University of Technology,
Loughborough,
Leics. LE11 3TU.
England.

Mr. K.D. Eason,
Department of Human Sciences,
University of Technology,
Loughborough,
Leics. LE11 3TU.
England.

PARTICIPANTS

Mr. R.G. Ashton,
R.A.R.D.E.
Fort Halstead,
Sevenoaks,
Kent,
England.

Mr. M. Ballantine,
Dept. of Occupational Psychology,
Birkbeck College,
University of London,
Malet Street,
London WC1E 7HX,
England.

Dr. H. Bergman,
Psychologisch Laboratorium,
Rijksuniversiteit Utrecht,
Varkenmarkt 2,
Utrecht 2501,
The Netherlands.

Mr. T. Berns,
Ergolab,
Renstiernas gata 12,
S-116 31 Stockholm,
Sweden.

PARTICIPANTS

Prof. J.H. Carlisle,
University of Southern California,
Annenberg School of Communications,
Information Sciences Institute,
4676 Admiralty Way,
Marina del Rey,
California 90291,
U.S.A.   (did not arrive)

Prof. J.M. Carroll,
Computer Science Department,
University of Western Ontario,
London,
Ontario,
Canada.

Mr. G. Carter,
Department of Engineering and Public Policy
Carnegie-Mellon University,
Pittsburgh,
Pennsylvania 15213,
U.S.A.

Dr. M. Cetincelik,
Association of Engineers and
    Architects in Turkey,
P.O. Box 400 - Kizilay,
Ankara,
Turkey.   (did not arrive)

Mr. D. Cheriton,
University of Waterloo,
Dept. of Computer Science,
Waterloo,
Ontario,
Canada N2L 3G1.   (did not arrive)

Mr. C. Christodoulou,
Nuclear Research Center "Demokritus",
Agia Paraskevi,
Attiki,
Greece.

Mr. A. Chrysakis,
National Technical Univ. of Athens,
Chair of Mechanics,
5, K.Zographou St.
Athens, 625
Greece.

Dr. H. David,
32 Av de la Republique,
92120 Montrouge,
France.

Ms. G. Edwards,
620 Belmont, Room 1105,
Montreal,
Quebec,
Canada.   (did not arrive)

Ms. S.M. Evans,
Research Institute,
University of Dayton,
Dayton,
Ohio 45409,
U.S.A.

Dr. C. Fields,
Defense Advanced Research
  Projects Agency,
1400 Wilson Boulevard,
Arlington,
Virginia 22209,
U.S.A.

Ms. M.K. Fishburn,
6305 Vista del Mar. Apt. 4,
Playa Del Rey,
California 90291,
U.S.A.

Dr. M.J. Fitter,
MRC Social & Applied Psychology Unit,
University of Sheffield,
Sheffield,
England.

Mr. T.J. Folkard,
MRC Institute of Hearing Research,
The Medical School,
University of Nottingham,
University Park,
Nottingham,
U.K.

Dr. G. Geiser,
Institut fuer Informationsverarbeitung
  in Technik und Biologie,
Seb.-Kneipp-Str. 12-14,
D.7500 Karlsruhe,
Germany.

Dr. P.J. Goillau,
Human Factors Section,
Optoelectronics Group (04),
R.S.R.E.
Pershore,
Worcs.
U.K.

Mr. T.J. Goodman,
Dept. of Electrical Engineering,
Imperial College,
Exhibition Road,
London SW7 2BT.
England.

Ms. E. Gunnarsson,
National Board of Occupational
  Safety and Health,
Fack,
100 26 Stockholm,
Sweden.

Prof. Y. Haitovsky,
Department of Economics,
The Hewbrew University of Jerusalem,
Jerusalem,
Israel.

Dr. M. Hatzopoulos,
University of Athens,
Unit of Applied Maths,
Panepistimiopolis,
Athens 621,
Greece.

Mr. H. Howells,
Flight Systems Department,
Royal Aircraft Establishment,
Farnborough,
Hants.
England.   (did not arrive)

Dr. P.R. Innocent,
School of Mathematics,
Leicester Polytechnic,
P.O. Box 143,
Leicester LE1 9BH
U.K.

Prof. J. Iordanidis,
Professeur Agrege a L'Universite,
Nationale Technique D'Athens,
Dom. Sarantapichou 65,
Athens,
Greece.

Mr. T.H. Johnson,
Dept. of Decision Sciences CC,
The Wharton School,
University of Pennsylvania,
Philadelphia 19174,
U.S.A.

Dr. K.F. Kraiss,
Forschungsinstitut fuer Anthropotechnik,
5309 Meckenheim,
Buschstrasse,
Germany .

Dr. L. Laios,
Systems Supervisor,
Technical Systems Department,
Hellenic Aerospace Industry,
Taragra,
Viotia,
Greece.

Dr. B. Malde,
Veranda Cottage,
3 Barrow Road,
Quorn,
Leicestershire,
U.K.

Dr. T.H. Martin,
Annenberg School of Communications,
University of Southern California,
Los Angeles,
California 90007,
U.S.A.

Prof. J.S. Minas,
Department of Philosophy,
University of Waterloo,
Waterloo,
Ontario,
Canada N2L 3G1.

Mr. T.G. Moore,
Department of Human Sciences,
University of Technology,
Loughborough,
Leics. LE11 3TU.
England.

Mr. H.F. Muller,
Institute for Perception Research,
Insulindelaan 2,
Eindhoven 4502,
The Netherlands.

Prof. L. Nauges,
11 Avenue de Segur,
75007 Paris,
France.

Mr. J.C. Newman,
60 The Village,
Ulster College,
N. Ireland Polytechnic,
Newtownabbey,
Northern Ireland BT37 0QB.

Dr. R.S. Nickerson,
Bolt Beranek and Newman Inc.,
50 Moulton Street,
Cambridge,
Mass. 02138,
U.S.A.

Dr. J.J. O'Hare,
Office of Naval Research,
800 N. Quincy Street,
Arlington,
Va. 22217,
U.S.A.

Dr. G. Olimpo,
Laboratorio Tecnologie Didattiche CNR,
Via all'Opera Pia 9B,
16145 Genova,
Italy.

Mr. D. Olivetti,
c/o Ing. C. Olivetti,
Ivrea (TO),
Italy.   (did not arrive)

Mr. J. Palme,
Swedish National Defense Research Inst.
FOA 1,
S-104 50 Stockholm 80,
Sweden.

Dr. C. Papatriontaffillou,
14 Mantinias St.
Haloudri,
Athens,
Greece.

Prof. I.A. Pappas,
Chair for Industrial Management,
National Technical University,
28is Oktovriou 42,
Athens 147,
Greece.

Dr. R.G. Parish,
Scientific Control Systems Ltd.,
Sanderson House,
49-57 Berners Street,
London W1P 4AQ.
England.

Mr. L. Pinsky,
17 rue Petit,
75019 Paris,
France.

Mr. B.R. Ryder,
Geography Department,
State University College Buffalo,
1300 Elmwood,
Buffalo,
New York 14222.
U.S.A.

Mr. G. Schwichtenberg,
Ostlandstr. 78,
5000 Koeln 40,
West Germany.

Dr. O. Selfridge,
Bolt Beranek and Newman Inc.
50 Moulton Street,
Cambridge,
Mass. 02138,
U.S.A

Dr. M. Sigala,
Greek Atomic Energy Commission,
'Demokritos' Agia Paraskevi,
Attiki,
Greece.

Dr. L. Silver,
Advanced Computer Techniques Corp.,
437 Madison Avenue,
N.Y. 10027,
U.S.A.

Dr. W. Sjouw,
Psychologisch Laboratorium der
    Rijksuniversiteit,
Psychological Laboratory,
2 Varkenmarkt,
Utrecht,
The Netherlands.

Mr. H.T. Smith,
Department of Psychology,
University of Nottingham
University Park,
Nottingham,
U.K.

Dr. R. Spence,
Dept. of Electrical Engineering,
Imperial College,
Exhibition Road,
London SW7 2BT,
England.

Dr. V. Spiliotopoulos,
236 Argyle Street,
Preston,
Cambridge,
Ontario,
Canada N3H 1P7.

Mr. R. Stamper,
London School of Economics,
Houghton Street,
London WC2A 2AE.
England.

Mr. J. Stavrakakis,
Nuclear Research Center
'Demokritos' Agia Paraskevi,
Attiki,
Greece.

Mr. R. Strong,
Applied Psychology Unit,
Admiralty Research Laboratory,
Teddington,
Middlesex.
England.

Mr. B.G.J. Thompson,
Department of Environment,
Property Services Agency
   CEDAR Project,
Room 1612, Lunar House,
40 Wellesley Road,
Croydon CR9 2EL,
England.

Ms. K. Thoresen,
Norwegian Computing Center,
Forskningsveien 1B,
Oslow 3,
Norway.

Dr. H.F. Tibbals,
Computer Unit,
Durham University,
Durham DH1 3LE,
England.

Prof. S. Treu,
Dept. of Computer Science,
University of Pittsburgh,
Pittsburgh,
Pennsylvania 15260,
U.S.A.

Ir. L. Verhagen,
Dept. of Industrial Engineering,
University of Technology Eindhoven,
Eindhoven,
The Netherlands.

Mr. M. Waygood,
Army Personnel Research Est.,
c/o Royal Aircraft Establishment,
Farnborough,
Hants,
England.

Miss Jill M. Bird,
Ergonomics Department,
Pilkington Brothers Ltd.,
Prescot Road,
St. Helens,
Lancs.
U.K.

Mr. J.E. Wood,
Royal College of Art,
Department of Design Research,
Kensington Gore,
London SW7 2EU,
England.

APPENDIX 3

INSTITUTE PROGRAMME

NATO ASI on MAN-COMPUTER INTERACTION

5 - 18 September 1976

Sunday 5 Sept.

15.00 - 18.00	Registration
20.00	Welcome and Introductions

Monday. 6 Sept.

Morning -   MCI - REALITY AND PROBLEMS   Prof. B. Shackel

-        THE WORKSTATION
Tutorial Session

S. Evans   Combiman - an interactive design
           tool for workstation engineers.

J. Wood   Case study of workstation design.

Afternoon -   THE HARDWARE INTERFACE   Dr. O. Ostberg
Tutorial Session

P. Innocent   Light pen versus keyboard
              for ship designers.

G. Schwichtenberg Hardware for solving
                   problems.

Tuesday 7 Sept.

Morning -   TRAINING AND USER SUPPORT - PART 1   Dr. L.F. Thomas
                 TRAINING AND USER SUPPORT - PART 2   Ms. L. Damodaran

Afternoon -   INTERACTION IN PUBLIC SYSTEMS - PART 1   Dr. T. Ivergard
Tutorial Session

S. Treu   On-line student debate: an
           experiment in communication
           using computer networks.

<u>Wednesday 8 Sept.</u>

Morning – INTERACTION IN PUBLIC SYSTEMS – PART 2   Dr. J.H. Bair

<u>Tutorial Session</u>

G. Carter   Increasing the human effect-
            iveness of computer based
            communications through inter-
            active graphics.

Afternoon – EVALUATING MAN–COMPUTER SYSTEMS   Dipl.Ing. F. Margulies

<u>Tutorial Session</u>

S. Treu   Methodology for interactive
            computer service measurement
            and evaluation.

R. Ashton   Evaluation of man–computer
            systems in military command
            and control.

R.G. Parish Evaluation of a military
            command and control system.

<u>Thursday 9 Sept.</u>

Rest day

<u>Friday 10 Sept.</u>

Morning –   INTERACTION WITH SPECIALIST USERS – PART 1   T.F.M. Stewart

<u>Tutorial Session</u>

R. Spence   Effects of response delays on
            problem solving.

T. Goodman Ergonomics experiments in
            computer aided electronic
            circuit design.

Afternoon – INTERACTION WITH SPECIALIST USERS – PART 2   Prof. R. Bernotat

<u>Tutorial Session</u>

L. Laios   Predictive Computer Display
            for Process Control.

L. Verhagen Computer programs for data
            management and experimental
            control of ergonomic experiments
            with a simulated process.

G. Geiser   Parallel vs serial presentation
            of information on displays for
            process control.

Saturday 11 Sept.

Morning –   Tutorial Session

H.T. Smith   Aids for process controllers.

D. Whitfield* Human factors aspects of
               computer aid for air traffic
               controllers.

*presented by Miss J.M. Bird

–   INTERACTION WITH BUSINESS USERS – PART 1   Prof. E. Van Lommel

Afternoon –   COMPUTER ASSISTED LEARNING   Prof. J. Annett

Sunday 12 Sept.

Rest day

Monday 13 Sept.

Morning –   INTERACTION WITH NAIVE USERS   Dr. C.R. Evans

Tutorial Session

T. Martin   An approach to studying
             functional needs of humans
             interacting with computers

J. Carroll   Interactive data base
             creation.

Afternoon –   INTERACTION WITH BUSINESS USERS – PART 2 Mr. K.D. Eason

Tutorial Session

L. Nauges   Impact of computers on port-
             folio managers.

T. Johnson   Interaction with business users

<u>Tuesday 14 Sept.</u>

Morning –   THE SOFTWARE INTERFACE   Dr. M. Sime

                <u>Tutorial Session</u>

                M. Fitter   User language – some design considerations.

                H.F. Tibbals The interaction between computer representation and traditional notations.

Afternoon –   <u>Tutorial Sessions</u>

                J. Palme   Giving the users more influence in computer systems.

                J.C. Newman A system for on-line experiments in cognitive ergonomics.

                V. Spiliotopolous Towards a computer interview acceptable by the naive user.

                J. O'Hare   Programmers as users.

<u>Wednesday 15 Sept.</u>

Morning –   Tutorial Sessions

Afternoon –   Rest break

<u>Thursday 16 Sept.</u>

Morning –   MODELLING THE USER   J.D. Baker

                <u>Tutorial Session</u>

                R. Nickerson Modelling for better design (?)

                H. David   Design of a simulated pilot position for a large scale ATC simulator.

Afternoon –   MAN-COMPUTER SYMBIOSIS – PART 1   Prof. A. Chapanis

                <u>Tutorial Session</u>

                O. Selfridge   ARPANET – the concept and operation

                R. Nickerson   ARPANET – human factors research programme

<u>Friday 17 Sept.</u>   <u>Tutorial Session</u>

Morning –   B. Thompson   The CEDAR Project

                R. Stamper   Aspects of the LEGOL Project

                O. Selfridge   Adaptive systems in theory and practice

      –   MAN-COMPUTER SYMBIOSIS – PART 2   Dr. H. Sackman

Afternoon –   Concluding Review Session

      –   Concluding Review Session

SUBJECT INDEX

558